THE GOSPEL OF MARK

For
Bishop Michael Russell
on his double jubilee
celebrating
sixty years as priest
and
forty years as bishop
1945-1965-2005

The Gospel of Mark

A Commentary by
Michael Mullins

the columba press

First published in 2005 by
the columba press
55A Spruce Avenue, Stillorgan Industrial Park,
Blackrock, Co Dublin

Cover by Bill Bolger
Origination by The Columba Press
Printed in Ireland by ColourBooks Ltd, Dublin

ISBN 1 85607 489 7

Acknowledgements
Scripture quotations are taken from The New Revised Standard
Version, copyright (c) 1989, by the Division of Christian Education of
the National Council of the Churches of Christ in the United States of
America. Used by permission.

Contents

Preface

As I was finishing this book on Mark's gospel during Lent and Easter 2005 I was continually struck by the appearance of the silent figure of Pope John Paul II at the windows of the Gemelli Hospital and the Apostolic Palace in Rome. The silence of his final weeks of suffering spoke volumes to the city and to the world. It proclaimed loudly the message of his life, a life which was described and interpreted in the millions of words spoken and written in the media during those weeks. I was moved by the impact of the Pope's silence to reflect on Mark's presentation of the great silence of Jesus' final hours as he stood before the Jewish and Roman courts and finally, after the excruciating agony of scourging and crucifixion, departed this life with a loud inarticulate cry. I recalled words written by my colleague Oliver Treanor in his book on the passion, *This is my Beloved Son*. He points out that to appreciate the meaning of Christ's silence at the end one needs to reflect on the speech of his life, both his words and his actions. These explain the purpose of his passion, his quiet acceptance of it, more eloquently than any comment could. To illustrate his point he quotes Ignatius of Antioch who put the message very succinctly in the second century:[1]

> It is better to keep quiet and be, than to make fluent professions and not be. No doubt it is a fine thing to instruct others, but only if the speaker practices what he preaches. One such teacher there is: 'he who spake the word and it was done', and what he achieved even by his silences was well worthy of the Father. A man who has truly mastered the utterances of Jesus will also be able to apprehend his silence, and thus reach full spiritual maturity, so that his own words have the force of actions and his silences the significance of speech. (*To the Ephesians*, §15).

The silence of Jesus' final hours moved the executioner, on seeing how he died, to proclaim that the victim was ' truly the Son of God.' This is the high point of human professions of faith in Jesus in the gospel. From that final silence Mark rolls back the film, so to speak, to the beginning of the good news, to reflect on

---

1. O.Treanor, *This is My Beloved Son: Aspects of the Passion*, London: Darton, Longman and Todd, 1997, 48

THE GOSPEL OF MARK

the speech of Jesus' life, a speech eloquent in words and powerful in actions.

I offer this commentary on St Mark's gospel at a time when
many people are taking a serious interest in the scriptures and
looking for reading material to deepen their spiritual understanding of the inspired word and broaden their knowledge of
biblical scholarship. I offer it as an aid for students of theology
and as a guide for serious readers in the hope that it will deepen
their spiritual and theological insight, and bring them to an initial
level of academic competence. I offer it also to those many
preachers who wish to underpin their preaching with serious
reading and to the many people who practise *lectio divina* and
other forms of spiritual reading. No prior technical knowledge
of biblical scholarship is assumed and I explain technical terms
and translate important Greek and Hebrew words and expressions as we meet them. Since the general reader may wish to
read the book in stages, and the student may wish to consult or
revise a particular section, there is an element of recapitulation
throughout. For the same reasons I refer to books and articles in
the notes relating to each section, in addition to the bibliography
at the end of the book. Above all I hope that this book will help
readers to appreciate the good news of Jesus Christ, Son of God.

My special indebtedness to many scholars is acknowledged
throughout the text, but there are levels of insight and understanding that cannot be easily quantified and acknowledged by
way of a footnote. In particular I wish to acknowledge the influence of my former teacher, Ignace de la Potterie SJ, at the
Pontifical Biblical Institute in Rome whose insight and approach
have continued to underpin my understanding, teaching and
writing throughout the intervening years. I owe a debt of grati-
tude to many scholars who have written on St Mark's gospel
and whose contributions greatly influenced my understanding
and approach and whose contributions will be obvious from the
quotations and notes.

My thanks are due to Bishop William Lee, my colleagues in
St Patrick's College, Maynooth, and my former colleagues in St
John's College, Waterford, for their encouragement, and to the
rector, staff and students of the Pontifical Irish College in Rome
for their generous hospitality during the writing of this book. A
special word of thanks to my colleague Dr Seamus O Connell at
Maynooth College and to Rev Sean Maher at the Pontifical Irish

College, a student of the Pontifical Biblical Institute, for their many helpful suggestions and for permission to consult their unpublished material.[2]

My thanks extend in a special way to Columba Press for their courtesy and professional competence in bringing this book to its readers.

Michael Mullins
St Patrick's College,
Maynooth
Feast of SS Peter and Paul, Apostles
29 June 2005

2. See bibliography.

Introduction to the Gospel of Mark

THE GOOD NEWS

During Holy Week 2004 a group of university students and seminarians at St Patrick's College, Maynooth, presented a continuous reading of the entire text of St Mark's gospel to an audience of staff, students and invited guests of the college. The impact of the reading, prepared throughout the weeks of Lent, was profound. Some of the audience had come because their friends were reading, some out of a sense of duty or curiosity, some as part of their penitential exercises for Lent. I watched their reactions as they entered the story world of the gospel and experienced its transforming power. Many commented afterwards that they had experienced the gospel in a whole new way and that they would never read it in the same old way again. The gospel, the good news, had worked its magic on them!

For many it was the first time they had a *transformative* rather than a merely *informative* experience because, read as a whole, the gospel draws the reader/listener into the drama of conflict, the resolution of suspense, the fulfilment of prophecies, the realisation of things foreshadowed and the uncovering of things hidden throughout the story. This experience marked a very significant change from their previously fragmented and merely informative exposure to *the good news of Jesus Christ, Son of God.* They had previously heard it read in short unrelated passages in church, or in selected readings in school textbooks. Some of the older persons present had been theology students at a time in the past when line-by-line exegesis of texts had massacred overall meaning and theology manuals had quarried the living word for lifeless proof texts. A very central consideration, the transforming power of narrative and the importance of story for both individual and community, was often completely neglected. The gospel of Mark, and indeed each of the four gospels, constitutes a unified whole whose individual parts cannot be understood separately without an understanding of the whole, and vice versa, the whole cannot be fully understood without an understanding of the parts. 'Mark has been transmitted as a book which forms such a unity that it can only be understood by someone who reads it in its entirety and tries to apprehend it as a meaningful whole.'[1] The gospel is, therefore, not a series of units loosely strung together like beads on a string, even if the sayings, stories, and other elements already existed in the oral tradition. It is a meaningful whole. The elements are arranged in an overall pattern like the panes of a stained glass window or the pieces of a mosaic which are arranged together to present a single overall picture.

The written gospels/The good news

The gospels of Matthew, Mark, Luke and John are first and foremost gospels, *euaggelia*, presentations of 'the good news' in narrative form. They contain the good news of 'the Christ event' in the literary genre which early on in the life of the church became the preferred paradigm by which to communicate the mystery of Christ.

The written gospels represent the transition from oral proclamation to written gospel, a third stage in the presentation of the good news of Jesus Christ, Son of God. They came after the ministry of Jesus and a period of oral, liturgical and epistolary transmission of the traditions about Jesus. The earliest preaching seems to have been presented around a 'two point proclamation', reflected in the sermons in the Acts of the Apostles, which could be summed up as: 'You (or they) put Jesus to death, but God raised him up.' The speeches of Peter at Pentecost, in the Portico of Solomon, to the council following the healing of the cripple, and in the house of Cornelius, are built around this two-point proclamation (Acts 2:23f; 3:13f; 4:10; 5:30f; 10:39f). So also is the speech of Paul in Antioch (13:28-30). This proclamation is the bedrock on which New Testament theology builds.

Building on the 'two point' proclamation, the language of rejection, betrayal, handing over, envy, murder, and so on, accrue to the first point ('You/they put Jesus to death') while the language of raising up, vindication, victory, glory, exaltation to the right hand of God and the establishment of the crucified one as Lord and Christ, accrue to the second ('God raised him up').

Resulting from the proclamation of the victory manifest in the Father's vindication of Jesus, the first Christians came to realise that 'in his name', that is, in the life, death and resurrec-

---

1. B. van Iersel, *Reading Mark*, T+T Clark, Edinburgh, 1989, 4.

tion of Jesus, God has given us salvation. There follows, therefore, the call to repent and to be baptised in the name of Jesus Christ for the forgiveness of sins and the reception of the Holy Spirit. Forgiveness of sins, not the destruction of the sinner, and not only the cancellation of past wrongs but the promise of new life in the Spirit, are offered to those who repent and are baptised in the name of Jesus Christ.

When Paul wrote to the Corinthians the 'two-point proclamation' which he had received as tradition and was in turn handing on, was furnished with an interpretation explaining the salvific nature of Jesus' death, 'for our sins'. It also emphasised that Jesus' death and resurrection were in accordance with the scriptures (that is, in fulfilment of God's plan). In addition, two 'apologetic' points are in evidence. He was buried, so he was truly dead. He appeared to witnesses, so he was truly risen. Paul wrote:

> For I handed on to you as of first importance what I in turn had received: that Christ died for our sins in accordance with the scriptures, and that he was buried, and that he was raised on the third day in accordance with the scriptures, and that he appeared … (1 Cor 15:3f).

For Paul and other New Testament writers the term *good news* was particularly apt for this offer of salvation revealed in the life, death and resurrection of Jesus Christ. He used the term *euaggelion*, 'good news', more than sixty times both as a proclamation and a theological synthesis of the revelation and salvation brought about through the life, death and resurrection of Jesus Christ. In the Old Testament the equivalent Hebrew term for good news, *bsr*, was used especially in the Psalms and in Deutero-Isaiah with special reference to the gracious act of God in effecting the return of the exiled or scattered people to Zion, the ending of punishment and promise of new beginnings.

Mark presents his gospel as the beginning or origin of this good news of Jesus Christ, good news that his readers or hearers may well have heard already in preaching, letters or liturgy. The gospel is a presentation of the origins of this good news in the ministry of Jesus. It presents the messenger of the good news, announces the good news, portrays Jesus as the embodiment of that good news and proclaims Jesus the Risen Lord as the vindication by God of the good news.

The nature and purpose of the gospel is very succinctly expressed by A. Stock who asserts that Mark presupposes the readers' knowledge of the events subsequent to the women's flight from the empty tomb. That means the book is intended for Christian readers who have already had the good news of Jesus' resurrection proclaimed to them and who have believed, at one time at least, if only imperfectly. The written gospel, however, points beyond itself to the living word in the church. He quotes Nils Dahl who said that 'the goal is not to awaken faith but to re-call the character of the resurrection as a mystery and wonder which could elicit fear and awe' and who further holds that 'the conclusion of the gospel suggests that the evangelist did not in-tend to write an "aid for mission work", but writes for believers and wants to clarify for them what faith and the gospel really in-volve.'[2]

The story of Jesus is told within the framework of a ' bio-graphical sketch' of the ministry, but the post-resurrection in-sights, experiences and problems of the church also play a major part in shaping the telling.

Biographical Framework
How original and how influenced by contemporary literary genres was this new approach to evangelisation, the proclam-ation and explanation of the good news in narrative form? There were many examples of biographical writing in the Greco-Roman and Jewish worlds, although they were very different from our twenty-first-century understanding of biography. How does the gospel genre relate to them?

Within the Jewish world there was the tradition of the prophetic writings, but apart from the story of Jeremiah the prophetic writings for the most part show little interest in the biographical details of the prophets. In New Testament times Philo wrote biographical sketches of the Patriarchs in which he associated each individual with a particular virtue. He wrote on Joseph as a model politician. His two books on Moses focused respectively on Moses as leader and Moses as lawgiver. In the broader world Plutarch followed a process of *synkrisis*, a com-parison and contrast between different people's lives. These lives of Pliny or Plutarch were biographies of 'ideal' or single di-mension characters. The Roman writers Sallust, Suetonius and

---

2. A.Stock, *Call to Discipleship: A literary Study of Mark's Gospel*, 61, quot-ing Nils Dahl, *Jesus in the Memory*, Minneapolis, Augsburg, 1976, 55.

Tacitus differed from this Hellenistic genre of *bios* as they focused more on complicated character descriptions and events. They could be quite critical and at times bitingly cynical of their subjects.

Rudolf Bultmann, and others following his lead, saw in the gospels an original Christian creation entirely at the service of the faith and cult, arising from and illustrating the Christian kerygma with little or no connection to such secular biography. Though there is a very clear distinctiveness about the gospels, it must be said that the gospels reflected some of the trends of the Hellenistic *bios* in so far as they endeavour to capture the essentials of the ideal character and teaching of Jesus and present it in a general 'biographical sketch' or loose overall framework of a life or *bios*.

The gospels are also very distinctive and they differ in a number of essential aspects from the Hellenistic *bios* or Roman *vita*. They are theological productions and not just interesting or entertaining accounts of great, good, interesting or wicked persons who for some reason should be remembered by future generations as heroes or villains from the past. The gospels are narratives about a person whom the writers believe to be alive and active after his execution and death.[3] They are designed to spell out in narrative genre the identity between the crucified and risen one, the identity between Jesus of Nazareth and the Christ living at the heart of the primitive Christian communities. They are narratives about someone whose words and deeds, whose life and death, whose earthly life and glorified presence are as relevant to the reader or hearer today as they were to the characters in the story being told.

A gospel is not, therefore, just an interesting story about a great person of the past. Neither is it an academic theological treatise. It is the committing to writing of a narrative of the good news, a narrative born from the faith-filled vision and theological perspective of the evangelist. The purpose of the evangelist in creating the narrative of the beginning of the good news is not just to give information but to transform the lives of the readers or listeners by engaging them in the story of Jesus and calling them to be his disciples.

---

3. C. Focant, *L'Évangile selon Marc*, Commentaire biblique: Nouveau Testament 2, Les Éditions du Cerf, Paris, 2004, 30.

II
WHO IS JESUS?

Who do you say that I am?
The call to be his disciples, in Jesus' own time, in the time of the writing of the gospel, and in the present time of the reader, is intimately bound up with the question of Jesus' identity. The reader is given privileged information about Jesus' identity in the prologue where he is described as Christ, Lord, Son of God, and Beloved Son, empowered by the Spirit. From this privileged position the reader sees the various characters in the gospel struggle with the question 'Who can this be?', 'Who do people say that I am?', 'Who do *you* say that I am?' throughout the story. However, in spite of the privileged knowledge the reader is also challenged by these same questions in the context of the unfolding, and often disturbing, events in the gospel. For the most part Jesus' identity is presented in terms of well established christological titles, adopted from Jewish and early Christian tradition and adapted for use according to Mark's theological outlook.

The New Testament affirms in different ways the uniqueness of Jesus and of the revelation of God and salvation for humanity brought about in his life, death and resurrection. The Letter to the Colossians states that: 'He is the image of the invisible God' (Col 1:15) and 'In him the fullness of God was pleased to dwell' (Col 1:19). The Johannine tradition affirms that: 'The Word became flesh and lived among us and we have gazed upon his glory' (Jn 1:14), and the Acts of the Apostles makes the point that: 'There is salvation in no one else, for there is no other name under heaven given among mortals, by which we must be saved' (Acts 4:12).

Jesus is, therefore, not just the announcer of good news, he *is* the good news. Even in his silence, Jesus is the word, the revelation of the good news. He is the embodiment of the good news which he announces. The prologue to St John's gospel sums up the situation: 'The Word became flesh and pitched tent (dwelt) among us and we have gazed upon his glory' (Jn 1:14). Paul speaks of him as 'our righteousness, consecration and redemption' and he describes the crucified Christ of his preaching as 'the power and the wisdom of God' (1 Cor 1:24). The good news, or gospel, therefore, is communicated through the impact of

Jesus' person, words, deeds, death, resurrection and glorification (his vindication by God his Father).

Mark faced the task of incorporating these insights into a narrative. He did so largely through the use of christological titles.
These titles do not function independently but help to interpret
each other and correct misunderstandings and false expectations that had grown up around the various titles. D. M.
Sweetland points this out quite clearly:

> The three principal christological titles Mark uses for Jesus
> occur close to one another at the centre of Mark's gospel.
> Peter answers Jesus' question, 'Who do you say that I am?'
> (8:29), by replying, 'You are the Messiah' (8:29). Two verses
> later Mark tells the reader that Jesus began to teach his disci-
> ples 'that the Son of Man must suffer greatly, and be rejected
> by the elders, the chief priests and the scribes, and be killed,
> and rise after three days' (8:31). Soon after this scene one
> reads about the transfiguration of Jesus in which the voice
> from heaven says, 'This is my beloved Son. Listen to him'
> (9:7) … What is often overlooked is the possibility that Mark
> expands on each title with the one that follows it. The most
> general, yet still correct, title for Jesus was Peter's: the
> Messiah (8:29). Jesus becomes more specific as he points out
> that he is the Son of Man who must suffer, die, and rise (8:31).
> This progression culminates with the use of the most import-
> ant of Marcan christological titles: 'the beloved Son.'[4]

Messiah/Christ (and Related Terms)
The title 'Messiah' (Christ) is used seven times in Mark's gospel
(Mk 1:1; 8:29; 9:41; 12:35; 13:21; 14:61; 15:32). The opening verse
of the gospel in most manuscripts combines the titles 'Christ'
and 'Son of God' (Mk 1:1), a combination made again in the
gospel on the lips of the high priest (Mk 14:61f). All manuscripts,
however, follow the introductory statement with the prologue,
which builds up to the voice from heaven declaring that Jesus is
the beloved Son. The next reference to his being Messiah is when
Peter responds to Jesus' question: 'Who do you say that I am?'
with the profession: 'You are the Messiah' (Mk 8:29). His profession is followed almost immediately by Jesus' own description
of himself as Son of Man (Mk Mk 8:31) and shortly afterwards

---

4. D. M. Sweetland, ' Mark's Portrait of Jesus and the Disciples', *The
Bible Today*, July 1996, 228-235. 228, 230.

by the voice at the transfiguration declaring him the beloved Son (Mk 9:7). On both those occasions Jesus commanded the disciples to silence. At his Jewish trial the high priest asks him: 'Are you the Christ, the Son of the Blessed One?'(Mk 14:61) in aggressive fashion and Jesus responds with a statement about his future coming as Son of Man in glory (Mk 14:62). Thus the high priest's question to Jesus, which combines the titles Messiah and Son of the Blessed, together with Jesus' response about the Son of Man (Mk 14:61f), again bring the three principal titles together. Elsewhere, the scribes' understanding of the Messiah as the son of David is 'corrected' by Jesus as he points out that the Messiah is not just 'son of David' but Lord (Mk 12:35-37). The chief priests and scribes mocked him among themselves during the crucifixion saying: 'Let the Messiah, the King of Israel, come down from the cross!' (Mk 15:31f). Of the seven uses of the title in Mark, only in the *logion* about the reward promised to those who give his followers a drink of water because they 'belong to the Christ' does the title appear to be applied by Jesus to himself without adding or following through with another title by way of explanation or clarification (Mk 9:41). These examples point clearly to the fact that for Mark 'Messiah' is a correct but inadequate title for Jesus. This is very likely because there was no unanimously agreed understanding of the identity and role of the Messiah in Jesus' time. It was a 'catch-all' term for the 'one to come' who would fulfil hopes and expectations as different from each other as the coming of one to lead a violent revolution against the Romans and the coming of a prophet like Moses who would pronounce on such matters as whether the Samaritans belonged to the chosen people and whether or not their worship was valid (Jn 4:20-26). Even among the Qumran community different sets of expectations were current, resulting in the understanding that more than one figure might appear to fulfil the roles of a priestly, a political/royal/princely, and a prophetic messiah.

The titles 'Son of David', 'King of the Jews' and 'King of Israel' are closely associated with the title Messiah. The expectation that the Messiah would be a descendant of David was common. Jesus gives it a whole new meaning in the discussion about the Messiah and the Son of David (Mk 12:35-37). He speaks of the Messiah as 'Lord', the term used as a circumlocution for 'God' in the Jewish custom of avoiding the pronounci-

ation of the Divine Name YHWH and the post-resurrection designation of Jesus as Risen Lord by the community. The expectations about the ' Son of David' and 'the coming Kingdom of our
father David' led naturally to the idea of Jesus as King. For Pilate
and the Roman soldiers who mocked Jesus, the title 'King of the
Jews' signified a political pretender to royal status (Mk 15:2, 9,
12, 18, 26). For them the use of the title was a possible act of treason against Caesar. For the chief priests and scribes the use of
the term 'King of Israel' signified a combination of religious and
political aspirations associated with the claim to be the anointed
agent of God who would free Israel from its enemies and establish the reign of God (Mk 15:31).

Son of Man
The title Son of Man occurs fourteen times in the gospel. It occurs
in very different contexts, dealing with Jesus' earthly activity, his
suffering and death and his future coming in glory. It is the most
enigmatic of the titles applied to Jesus. In fact it is the title which
he applies to himself.

In the Old Testament Ezekiel used it of a human being or of
humankind (Ezek 2:1; 3:1). Daniel used it of an apocalyptic figure 'like to a son of man' who will come 'with the clouds of
heaven' and be given power, glory and the kingdom (Dan 7:13).
In Daniel the figure is presented in representative terms (Dan
7:27), but he is also seen as an individual since he is awarded
regal status and given a kingdom. In 1 Enoch and 4 Ezra the Son
of Man appears as an eschatological judge and deliverer who
will overthrow the wicked and vindicate the righteous (1 Enoch
46-53; 4 Ezra 13). These texts are important for the understanding in the early church of the future coming of Jesus as eschatological judge and vindicator, as evident in Mark: 'You will see
the Son of Man sitting at the right hand of the Power ...' (Mk
14:62).

The first two uses of the Son of Man title in Mark deal with
the authority behind his earthly activity. They occur in the early
stage of the ministry when Jesus claims two divine prerogatives,
the power on earth to forgive sins (Mk 2:10) and lordship over
the Sabbath (Mk 2:28). By way of contrast it is used of his having
come not to be served but to serve and give his life as a ransom
for many (Mk 10:45). He is thus portrayed as a model of humility
and self renunciation. His life is exemplary and his death salvific.

Most commonly the title is used in connection with his approaching rejection, passion, death and resurrection which are in accordance with a divine necessity revealed in the scriptures (Mk 8:31; 9:9, 12, 31; 10:33f, 45; 14:21x2, 41). In accordance with the will of God, Jesus must die but will rise again from the dead. 'The Son of Man undertakes this path of suffering as the innocent, persecuted, righteous one: "For the Son of Man goes as it is written of him …" '(Mk 14:21).[5]

The Son of Man title is used also of his eschatological, apocalyptic 'coming in glory' when he will come 'in the glory of his Father with the holy angels' (Mk 8:38), 'in the clouds with great power and glory and send the angels to gather the elect from the four winds, from the ends of the world to the ends of heaven' (13:26f), and when 'he will be seated at the right hand of the Power and coming with the clouds of heaven' (14:62).

Son of God

Mark introduces his gospel as the good news of Jesus Christ (Son of God) and the prologue builds up through the ministry, witness and baptism of John, through the 'opening of the heavens' and the coming of the Spirit on Jesus to the declaration by the voice from heaven: 'This is my beloved Son.' Right at the centre of the gospel the voice from the cloud on the mountain of the transfiguration proclaims Jesus as 'my beloved Son' (Mk 9:7). The two 'interventions' of God as a character in the gospel are, therefore, for the purpose of declaring Jesus the 'beloved Son' (Mk 1:11; 9:7). It is interesting that the other declarations of his divine sonship during the ministry (prior to that of the centurion at the crucifixion) are on the part of the demons who have preternatural knowledge and feel threatened by his presence and power (Mk 1:23f; 3:11; 5:7). The charge of blasphemy brought against him by the religious authorities results from his claim to be the Son of the Blessed One, a claim made in response to the direct question put to him by the high priest: 'Are you the Messiah, the Son of the Blessed One?'(Mk 14:61f). The gospel reaches its denouement when the heavens are darkened, the veil of the temple is torn in two and in a confession on human lips re-echoing the voice from heaven at the baptism and transfiguration, and the preternatural knowledge of the demons, the cent-

5. M. Hogan, *Seeking Jesus of Nazareth: An Introduction to the Christology of the Four Gospels,* The Columba Press, Dublin, 2001, 59.

urion 'on seeing how he died' said: 'Truly this man was the Son
of God' (Mk 15:39). Because it is in the death of the crucified
Jesus that he is recognised by a human being as Son of God, the
reader can see that 'Jesus' divine sonship is is not perceived in
glory but in suffering and death.'[6]

In the Old Testament the title ' son of God' was used variously
of the angels, the prophets, the king, the people of Israel, the
righteous ones and those who received a special commission or
blessing from God. Here in Mark it is given a whole new level of
meaning in keeping with Christian belief in the unique relationship of Jesus to the Father, revealed in the ministry and vindicated
in his passion, death and resurrection.

At the eschatological sign of the rending of the heavens (Isa
63:19) and the coming of the Spirit upon him, the voice from
heaven proclaims Jesus 'My beloved Son in whom I am well
pleased' (Mk 1:11). Traditional designations of Messiah and
Servant are here combined and given a whole new meaning (Ps
2:7; Isa 42:1; 61:1). At the transfiguration the disciples are instructed: 'This is my beloved Son' and told to listen to him (Mk
9:7). The centurion, his executioner, 'on seeing how he died' proclaims him 'the Son of God' re-echoing the voice from heaven at
the beginning of the ministry (Mk 1:11; 15:39) and this will be
followed shortly by the Father's vindication of the Son through
his resurrection. The title 'Son of God', therefore, has a particularly important function at the beginning, middle and end of the
gospel.

The titles used for Jesus are pivotal in revealing his identity.
However, the titles do not function in a vacuum, they are intimately bound to Mark's unfolding narrative. M. Hogan makes
the point:

> His (Mark's) Christology can be summarised in terms of
> Messiah, Son of God, Son of Man, and yet none of these can
> be properly understood apart from his narrative. For the
> Christology is in the story, and it is through the story that we
> learn to interpret the titles.[7]

The Messianic Secret
Jesus does not reject the title Messiah but is very cautious about
its true meaning and function. He orders the disciples to tell no

6. D.M.Sweetland, *op. cit.*, 231.
7. M. Hogan, *op. cit.*, 65.

one that he is the Messiah (Mk 8:29f). Similarly he commands
the demons to refrain from proclaiming his identity as Son of
God (Mk 1:25; 3:11f). He commands the inner group of disciples
to tell no one about the Transfiguration until the Son of Man was
risen from the dead (Mk 9:1). He commands people whom he
heals and those witnessing his healings to refrain from making
his actions known (Mk 1:43f; 5:43). This 'secrecy' or 'discretion'
is very likely because of wrong expectations on the part of the
people about the role of the Messiah as a potential political agit-
ator, a military leader, a social revolutionary or an apocalyptic
style prophet who confounds his opposition with signs and
wonders. In fact Jesus warns his inner group of disciples in the
eschatological-apocalyptic discourse about the false messiahs
who will behave in some of these ways (Mk 13:5, 6, 21-23).
Instead, Jesus reinterprets his role as that of the Son of Man who
serves, gives his life as a ransom for many, suffers rejection, persecution, false judgement, execution and is finally vindicated by
God in his resurrection from the dead (Mk 8:31; 9:9, 12, 31;
10:33f, 45; 14:21x2, 41).

The early church most probably found it particularly important to speak of Jesus in terms of what has been known, since the
pioneering work of W. Wrede on this aspect of Mark's gospel,[8]
as 'the messianic secret'. In highlighting the 'messianic secret'
Mark was attempting to answer objections to Christian claims
about Jesus' identity on the grounds of his obvious refusal of, or
hesitation in claiming or accepting such titles and roles during
his public ministry, a fact compounded by the 'unmessianic'
style of his life and his shocking dishonourable death.

W. J. Harrington puts it exceptionally well:

In the long run what is incomprehensible is the rejection and
violent death of the Messiah who would reveal the Father.
The originality of Jesus flows from the contrast between his
heavenly authority and power and the humiliation of his
crucifixion. Mark's 'messianic secret' is designed to reconcile
two theological affirmations: Jesus, from the first, was indeed
Messiah; yet, he had to receive from the Father, through the
abasement of the cross, his title of Messiah … He came but he
will not impose. When it came to the test, rather than force

8. W.Wrede's work on the Messianic Secret *Das Messiasgeheimnis in den
Evangelien* was written in German in 1901 and was translated into
English by J. C. G. Greig as *The Messianic Secret*, London: Clarke, 1971.

the human heart, he humbled himself and permitted himself
to be taken and shamed and put to death.[9]

The Scandal of the Cross
While proclaiming the victory of God in the vindication of Jesus,
and the salvation offered 'in his name', the first Christians had
also to face the scandal of the cross, the shameful and agonising
death that Jesus endured and the apparent failure of his mission.
Why did the one now vindicated by God and in whose name
salvation is offered to humankind suffer such a humiliating rejection, frightful agony and shameful death? Had the divine
plan gone badly wrong? Had the forces of evil, human or demonic, frustrated God's plan for the Messiah? The traditional
view had maintained that God would empower the Messiah
and overcome his enemies. Therefore his rejection and disgrace-
ful death were 'a stumbling block' to the Jews who looked for
signs of God's power, and foolishness to the Gentiles who
looked for wisdom and the honour it brought at the end of one's
life. In response to this problem, Paul speaks of the paradoxical
nature of God's wisdom and power made manifest in the apparent disgrace and failure of the cross.

> For Jews demand signs and Greeks desire wisdom, but we
> proclaim Christ crucified, a stumbling block to Jews and fool-
> ishness to Gentiles, but to those who are called, both Jews
> and Greeks, Christ the power of God and the wisdom of God.
> For God's foolishness is wiser than human wisdom, and
> God's weakness is stronger than human strength (1 Cor 1:20-
> 25).

In thus emphasising the paradoxical nature of God's power and
wisdom Paul assures his readers that nothing had gone wrong
with God's design for the Messiah. Rejection and failure were all
part of God's wise and powerful plan. Similarly the tradition
that finds expression in the Acts emphasises the fact that Jesus'
death and resurrection were in keeping with 'the definite plan
and foreknowledge of God' (Acts 2:23).

The gospel is therefore a narrative that proclaims the good
news but does so through the telling of a story that disturbs as it
draws the reader into the fear, anomaly and uncertainty it generates both in the characters and in the reader as the initial glorious and powerful impact of Jesus' proclamation of the kingdom

---

9. W. J. Harrington, *Mark: Realistic Theologian. The Jesus of Mark*, 10.

is overshadowed and finally engulfed in the rejection, suffering and shameful execution of the agent of God. R. H. Gundry points out very clearly the task that faced Mark in presenting a narrative that did justice to both dimensions of the story:

The gospel of Mark poses a literary problem in that two disparate kinds of material make up its contents. The first kind describes the successes of Jesus which make him look like others admired in the Greco-Roman world for their divine powers of wisdom, clairvoyance, exorcism, thaumaturgy, and personal magnetism ... We may say that this material teaches a theology of glory. The second kind of material portrays quite a different Jesus, a persecuted one ... We may say that this material teaches a theology of suffering ... the basic problem in Marcan studies is how to fit together these apparently contradictory kinds of material in a way that makes sense of the book as a literary whole.'[10]

He goes on to explain:

Mark does not pit the suffering and death of Jesus against his successes ... but pits the successes against the suffering and death, and then uses the passion predictions, writes up the passion narrative, and caps his gospel with a discovery of the empty tomb in ways that cohere with the success stories, in ways that make the passion itself a success story. Thus all the materials in the gospel attain a unity of purpose. Competition ceases, and the point of the book turns christological instead of paraenetic, rather as in Peter's Pentecostal sermon ... God has made him Lord and Christ, this Jesus whom you crucified (Acts 2:22-24, 36; cf 10:34-43).[11]

This faith-filled vision which portrays the victory of God in Jesus does not, however, lessen the human experience of Jesus, of his disciples and of the readers when confronted with suffering, pain, injustice and shame. Violence and injustice not only figure as a literary theme in the gospel but in a suffering world all too familiar with bloodshed and injustice they can trigger or rekindle in the reader a personal experience that resonates with the story. D. W. Geyer points this out clearly as he reflects on Mark's gospel against the background of his own therapeutic work with people suffering from the effects of their own personal

10. R. H. Gundry, *Mark. A Commentary on His Apology for the Cross*, Eerdmans, Grand Rapids, 1993, 2.
11. R. H. Gundry, *op. cit.*, 3.

experiences of 'the anomalous, the frightening, the disgusting and the outrageously violent.'[12] He states that 'bewilderment and uncertainty are valid outcomes of reading the gospel of Mark.'[13] He goes on to say: 'We can legitimately suppose that the author of Mark intends us not to feel satisfied with our reading, but instead would seek us to feel unsettled, agitated and confused.'[14] The aptness of this comment is borne out by the reader's empathy with the fearful, confused and uncomprehending disciples who finally flee in terror from the garden or the faithful women who flee in fear from the tomb and fail to tell anyone the good news (Mk 16:8).[15] Above all it is borne out by the sense of abandonment felt by Jesus himself as he faced death alone. Mark does not portray Jesus' death in heroic, noble or stoic fashion.[16] He died praying the psalm of abandonment, his final act of trust in the God who appeared to have left him to his fate. His trust in the God who saves was all that appeared to be left of his life and work, as he gave his great inarticulate cry and breathed his last. D. W. Geyer points out that:

> Everything in Mark's gospel leads up to the cross, and the crucifixion of Jesus is the story that best correlates all other stories in Mark ... crucifixion was a horrible death, meant to fill everyone who saw it or heard about it with terror and dread. It made for an impure and anomalous death ... Such violence is surely anomalous as a central textual event. Indeed outside of the Christian gospels there is no precedent for such a composition. So why did an author create an expansive narrative around it? Crucifixion is so rarely discussed or even described in ancient narratives that we must ask why and how it could serve the gospel of Mark as a foundation for a literary presentation from which broader theses are argued. This kind of violent death was anomalous and not conducive to rhetorical aptness. Yet here it is in Mark,

---

12. Douglas W. Geyer, *Fear, Anomaly and Uncertainty in the Gospel of Mark*, xi.

13. *Ibid.*, 65.

14. *Ibid.*, 66.

15. Their flight marks the end of the original narrative. Mk 16:9-20 is a later addition to the original text.

16. See D. Rhoads, J. Dewey, D. Michie, *Mark as Story, An Introduction to the Narrative of a Gospel*, 2nd ed., 1999, 110-115, for an extended comment on Jesus' approach to death in Mark's gospel.

precisely the main event, to which every other detail in Mark is directed and around which the whole story is composed.[17] The extraordinary fact, however, is that this bewildering story of violence, fear, failure and injustice is now being written by Mark for all future generations as a proclamation of the 'beginning of the good news of Jesus Christ, Son of God.' R. H. Gundry points out that the opening verse of the gospel, the superscription identifying Jesus as Christ and Son of God 'transforms the coming crucifixion from the shameful death of a common criminal into the awe-inspiring death of a divine being who is God's appointed agent. The episode concerning the centurion at the foot of the cross will confirm this transformation (15:39)'[18] as he witnesses Jesus issuing his final great cry, and dying 'in a burst of strength', not with a whimper or following the usual lapse into unconsciousness.[19]

III
DISCIPLES AND DISCIPLESHIP

Mark's portrait of the disciples
Observing the disciples in the story, from their initial leaving all things to follow Jesus, through their experience of fear, lack of understanding, confusion and ultimate flight from Jesus, the reader is challenged through the story to monitor his/her own involvement with the unfolding events and the responses and reactions they generate. The reader is left wondering which side he/she is really on, feeling the attraction and challenge of Jesus and his message and at the same time identifying with the reactions of the disciples. D. M. Sweetland puts it very clearly:

The picture Mark paints of the disciples of Jesus is a complex one. Having both positive and negative features, they are presented by Mark sometimes in a favourable, but more often in an unfavourable, light ... What Mark does, therefore, is use the disciples to challenge his readers' understanding of the true meaning of discipleship. The Christian readers of Mark's gospel would have identified with the disciples, those who initially respond positively to Jesus. Mark anticipates and reinforces this identification by initially presenting

17. *Ibid.*, 1.
18. *Ibid.*, 4.
19. *Ibid.*, 13.

the disciples in a favourable light. As the story progresses, however, they gradually disagree with Jesus on important issues. Because their response is seen as inadequate, a real tension develops for the readers. The disciples become disastrous failures, and the readers are forced to distance themselves from the disciples. A choice must be made between Jesus, with his difficult demands, and the disciples, with whom the readers have formed a positive attachment.

Mark tells the story in this manner because he wants his readers to reflect on their own understanding of Jesus, his mission, and Christian discipleship. Mark expects this self-examination will force his readers to change their attitudes and behaviour.[20]

Throughout the story, the 'official' disciples are regularly shown up in poor light by way of contrast with 'unofficial' disciples, the 'minor characters' who display levels of faith, insight, understanding and courage which the reader would have expected to find in the 'official' disciples.

IV

INTERPRETING THE GOSPEL

Different Approaches

Study of the gospels has gone through many stages and used many different approaches throughout history. People study the gospels for different reasons and from different perspectives. Some have primarily a historical interest in Jesus as the founder of the Christian faith, the world religious leader whom they follow and/or admire and a major figure in world history. Some have an interest in the theology or spiritual message of the various evangelists as they present the story of Jesus with different insights and from different perspectives. Others approach the gospels as great religious literature and study them according to the norms of literary criticism. Others approach them with an anthropological or sociological interest to see how the gospel view and values reflect and impact on the structures and value systems of various societies. All these approaches are complementary and each has its strengths. Together they lead to a very rich understanding of the gospels. Taken in isolation each approach has its strengths and obvious limitations.

20. D. M. Sweetland, *op. cit.*, 233.

Since the early days of the church the historical approach has been in evidence in efforts to harmonise the gospels, putting the various accounts together to fill out a life of Christ. This is a noble and understandable endeavour and it helps to put together a picture of the great historical figure of Jesus. It has been the inspiration for most artistic representations of Jesus and his contemporaries. However, it tended to regard the gospels simply as straightforward biographies of Jesus and the exercise can imply that each of the gospels is a defective biography needing to be supplemented by information from the other three. This approach can easily neglect the integrity of each written gospel as a theological and literary whole. It can also take an over simplistic view of the gospels as uninterpreted chronicles. Since the Enlightenment, a corresponding approach has been taken, though in a different guise. The various *quests of the historical Jesus,* defined differently by those involved, have taken the focus off the gospels themselves in the search for the holy grail of a Jesus and his environment reconstructed from 'historical' data, rather than a Jesus seen through the eyes of faith and the integral picture presented by each of the gospels.[21] As a result of the quest, *Source Criticism* became very important as it sought the sources detectable within the gospel texts, and others sources extraneous to the canonical gospels. Much energy has been spent seeking these sources, from secular writings, archaeological findings, and religious writings, including documents the early church regarded as lacking credibility, the so-called apocryphal documents. Mark's gospel was originally regarded as the most 'historical' gospel, an eyewitness account coming from Peter through Mark,[22] until it was rightly appreciated as a very theological and subtly literary document. Though a great deal was learned about Jesus and his times from these quests no one agreed picture of the 'historical' Jesus has emerged. The *Historical-Critical Method* has given us a great deal of valuable information about Jesus and his world, preventing otherwise purely subjective or sectarian interpretations, but it can give a fragmented image of Jesus' person and mission, depending on the

21. These two dimensions are conventionally referred to as the 'Jesus of History' and 'Christ of Faith'.
22. This was an oversimplified understanding of the Papias tradition reported by Eusebius. See the essay at the end of the commentary dealing with Markan identity and authorship.

criteria and pre-suppositions of the individual scholar, and the approach taken.

Form Criticism examines the literary forms in which the gospel material was cast during the process of oral transmission and investigates the social background in which they were developed. It turns the spotlight on the communities in which the traditions were nurtured and applied to community needs and expressed in community language and thought categories. Again much was learned from *Form Criticism* about the transmission process.

Interest in the theology or theologies of the evangelists resulted in *Redaction (editorial) Criticism*. Comparison of texts for purposes of discovering editorial work further sharpened awareness of the production process, particularly in comparative studies in the synoptic gospels and between the synoptics and John. The mind of the author discovered from these comparative studies became the dominant goal of research, a process of examination often running the risk of overlooking the independence of the final text as a work in itself. *Literary Criticism* declared the 'death of the author' and redressed the balance by insisting on the integrity of the work itself irrespective of its pre-history, the world behind the text and the mind of the author, except in so far as it can be understood from the work itself. Therefore interest in the 'actual' author has given way to interest in the 'implied' author, that is, the 'author' as he/she can be deduced from the text, almost a personification of the text with its worldview, interests, agenda, body of information, literary skill etc. On the negative side, this approach can sometimes run the risk of forgetting the importance of history and tradition when dealing with a document that serves the purpose of engendering and transmitting the faith of a community ultimately rooted in a historical person and event outside the world of the individual text in question.

On the positive side, these various approaches have given great insight into the complexity of the process of transmission of the traditions and their final articulation in the literary genre of the written gospels. Perhaps the most positive result from seeing the shortcomings of various other approaches is the awareness of the importance of a return to focusing on the text itself as a theological and literary whole and an appreciation of the fact that it is a narrative, a story written to engage the reader as a person and not just in an academic context.

V
THE GOSPEL AS STORY

Story, a narrative that engages the reader, is perhaps the best and most effective form of communication, and the reawakening in recent times of an appreciation of the power and impact of story, for both the individual and the community, has brought a whole new dimension to the study and interpretation of the gospels.

In this commentary, I follow the narrative structure of the gospel, seeing it as a story, but keeping in mind that the story is set in a society, culture and time very different from our own. There are therefore many things that need explanation. The story is a vehicle for theology, christology, soteriology and eschatology and so attention has to be paid to these more theological issues. Attention must be paid also to the influence of the Old Testament in the formation and articulation of the narrative, and to the concerns of the Christian community which helped to shape it.

The story of Jesus in the gospels is really the outcome of three stories inexorably tied together. As the story of Jesus is told, the Old Testament story of God and the chosen people is re-echoed in allusion, quotation and festal celebration, and at the same time the story of the early Christian community shapes and shines through the story of Jesus as it is told from the perspective and experience of the community.

Writing a Story
Essential to any story are the narrator or storyteller, the plot, the characters, the settings and the various rhetorical techniques used to capture and maintain the interest of the reader or hearer. We look at each in turn.

The Narrator
The person who tells the story is the *narrator*. The author uses the narrator to tell the story and to tell it in a particular way. Sometimes the narrator is a character within the story, actually telling the story, as is the case often in autobiography or in a novel or short story in which case the vision and knowledge of the narrator are limited to those of that particular character and bounded by time, space and social location. More usually, and

this is the case with Mark's gospel, the narrator is not a character within the story but is more a rhetorical device for getting the story told, in which case it can be difficult at times to distinguish the roles of author and narrator. When the narrator is anonymous and not a character in the story, he or she tells the story from a partially or totally omniscient point of view, knowing more about the individual characters than they do themselves, not only describing their words and actions but exposing even their secret thoughts and motives. This ensures that the reader has privileged knowledge and an advantage over the characters in the story. The narrator may remain hidden behind the narrative or may become obvious from time to time by breaking into the narrative with an explanatory remark, as for example, about a foreign place, custom or turn of phrase. Whether hidden or seen and heard the narrator ensures that the reader sees the narrative from his or her point of view. The gospel narrators are obviously Christians and see the story of Jesus from a believer's point of view. Imagine how different the story of Jesus would be if a narrator told it from the point of view of Caiaphas or Pilate or a spokesperson for the Pharisees and scribes! The narrator in Mark's gospel tells the story from the point of view of a believer who is carefully guiding the reader to share that same belief.

After a period of oral transmission of the remembered stories about the life, work, teaching, death and resurrection of Jesus, the written gospels present the traditional material in an overall story or narrative. This change from oral preaching and teaching, which was probably very disjointed and fragmented, to the written medium using narrative technique had far reaching consequences for the story being transmitted. Unlike the catechist or preacher, the narrator is not delivering a lecture, or assembling notes for preaching. The narrator is telling a story.

Telling a story, be it fictional or historical, demands planning if meaning is to be conveyed and convincing. Three essential elements in such planning are plot, character and setting and all three are enhanced by techniques of style and arrangement. The author of fiction has unlimited scope to invent on all these counts, the only constraints being credibility within the chosen genre. Writing history, however, the author is constrained by the known historical events, characters and outcome, and writes within the conventional boundaries of historical writing at the time of composition. Mark is not dealing with a fictional character, but with a real person whose life, death and resurrection has had a profound effect on human history. Furthermore, Mark wrote within living memory of the life of Jesus and possibly in and for a community where traditions about Jesus were well known. His narrative had to respect these historical parameters.

The Plot
The plot of a narrative is the ordered sequence of events, showing causality from one event to another, in an overall unified structure, moving towards a goal or end point and achieving emotional, psychological, moral, religious or artistic effects in the process, as more is being communicated than the bare storyline.[23] The plot is the author's interpretation of the unfolding story. The overall goal of Mark's narrative around which the plot is assembled is the establishment of the kingdom or reign of God by Jesus of Nazareth in spite of opposition and failure. The plot is supported by action, characterisation and thought. The narrator makes sure the reader is kept up to date with the story as it unfolds, properly informed about the various characters' motivation and duly instructed about unfamiliar terms or practices. The plot is arranged around Jesus' conflict with non-human evil forces, with human authority and with the obtuseness of the disciples. It is driven by these conflicts between belief and unbelief, understanding and misunderstanding, creation and relief of suspense, foreshadowing and fulfilment of events, inclusion and exclusion of persons, presence and absence of the kingdom. The reader's interest is engaged and sustained throughout by the suspense generated by these opposing forces. Furthermore, the narrator sees to it that the reader is led throughout the various twists and turns in the plot to identify with the desired goal of the story. The plot is consistent both in the narrator's point of view and portrayal of characters. There is a unifying interconnection of all parts of the narrative, achieved through the skilful use of literary techniques of repetition and arrangement of material. 'The unity of this gospel is apparent in the integrity of the story it tells, which gives a powerful overall rhetorical impact.'[24]

---

23. Aristotle's *Poetics* 1450b–1451b, speaks of order, amplitude, unity and probable and necessary connection.
24. D. Rhoads, J. Dewey, D. Michie, *op. cit.*, 3.

The Characters

In a certain sense the characters and the plot are two sides of a coin. The characters are the agents of the plot, causing it to take shape and unfold as a result of their motives, words and actions. On the other hand, the unfolding of the plot both reveals the characters and their motives and works on them to bring about change or confirm them in their motives or goals. The reader quickly sees in the character a determined force promoting or obstructing the overall goal of the narrative or an undecided and vacillating force awaiting further development and decision. In this way the reader may quickly come to identify with the character promoting the overall goal, adopt a hostile attitude to the character opposing the goal, and form a psychological and emotional companionship with the undecided character in the hope of accompanying him or her to a favourable resolution. In this way the reader is drawn into the plot and may even find himself/herself wondering with which character to identify, wishing to identify with a positive one but realising that an opposing or vacillating character may be a more accurate reflection of oneself.

The characters in a story are the 'creation' of the author and the narrator is 'omniscient' in their regard. The characters can reveal themselves in their actions and words, or the narrator can tell the reader about them. Since characterisation enables the 'omniscient' narrator to expose the character to the reader more profoundly and thoroughly than a person is exposed in real life, the readers of the gospel will have a better vantage point for observing and understanding Jesus than his followers and opponents had, both during his historical ministry and in the story world of the narrative. This is the difference between a real live person and a character. Nobody fully understands another person. An author, however, creates a character around his/her own understanding. Jesus in each gospel is a creation of the post-resurrection faith and understanding of each of the evangelists.

Characters can be of two kinds. There are 'round' or 'autonomous' characters with traits and personalities, whose strengths and weaknesses, thoughts and emotions, are like mini-plots in themselves. They are complex in temperament and motivation, in ways unpredictable and capable of surprising the reader with unexpected actions or patterns of behaviour. There are also ' flat' characters whose function is not to be interesting in themselves but to fulfil a role in the narrative. They are personifications of a single trait, or functionaries carrying out a task. These characters do not change, develop or suffer crisis. Groups can also function as round or flat characters. The characters in Mark's gospel display interesting elements of both types of characterisation.

Jesus, the protagonist, is a 'round' character whose humanity is not compromised by the fact that he is declared Son of God, empowered by the Spirit, prepared for by the Baptist and empowered with divine authority to establish the kingdom or reign of God. He is gifted with prophetic knowledge and wisdom, a superb teacher, healer and forthright challenger of arrogance and self interest in institution and leadership. He is heir to the prophets and sages of Israel and a significant player in the contemporary religious landscape. He inspires loyalty, love, curiosity, opposition and hatred. Though empowered by the Spirit and with divine authority over evil spirits, sickness and even the elements, he does not compel acceptance and faith. He respects the freedom of the individual to respond to him or to reject him and as such exposes his vulnerability and lack of power and authority on the 'human' plain. He displays a whole range of human emotions and reactions. He shows great compassion towards the sick, the possessed and the outcast and towards the crowd who were ' like sheep without a shepherd'. He displays great courage in facing the wrath of the Jewish and Roman establishments and experiences repeated frustration with the disciples' obtuseness and sullen silences. Finally, he is reduced to a state of extreme distress in Gethsemane and to a sense of abandonment on the cross. He is challenged by disappointments and crises and appears at the end of his life to have been destroyed by forces hostile to him and his mission. This Markan portrait of Jesus is a world apart from the more one-dimensional Hellenistic style portrait in John where Jesus, the pre-existent Word made flesh, comes into the world fully developed as a character and progresses from stage to stage in his life and ministry, always omniscient and always in control.

Some 'major' characters play a pivotal role in the development of the plot even though they may be 'flat' or one-dimensional characters. John the Baptist is the precursor preparing the way for Jesus' ministry, proclaiming his arrival and prefiguring Jesus' death in his own execution. Though he plays a major role his character is somewhat 'flat' or one-dimensional. He is the precursor and is clear about his mission and role. Judas facilitates the plot against Jesus by his enemies, but though he is of major importance to the plot he is also a flat, one-dimensional character and his development and motivation do not figure in the narrative. He betrays Jesus to the hostile authorities and his motives and possible regrets do not figure in Mark's story. Pilate is given a brief character sketch though he is a pivotal character in relation to the plot. He shows insight into the motives of the Jewish authorities in handing over Jesus, recognises Jesus' innocence, tries to reason with the authorities and the mob, but bows to pressure and hands over an innocent person to death.

Peter, however, is of major importance to the plot and is also a 'round' character. He responds instantly to the call to discipleship enabling the beginning of the mission, articulates the incipient faith of the disciples, reacts with alarm to Jesus' prediction of rejection and suffering and in doing so provides the context for Jesus' teaching on a discipleship of suffering and service. In his excitement at the transfiguration he blurts out the suggestion about building tents and the narrator points out that 'he did not know what to say' (Mk 9:6). He shows the willingness of a committed disciple. He is hurt and incredulous when Jesus predicts his forthcoming denials. He assures Jesus that even if all should fail, he would not. He discovers his own weakness in the context of Jesus' arrest and ends in denial of Jesus, and of his own role as disciple, resulting in bitter regret. However, the message from the Risen Lord on Easter morning, which promises a new beginning for the disciples, singles Peter out for special mention (Mk 16:7). The role of Peter in the gospel is central to the plot and to the theme of discipleship. Not only is he the pre-eminent disciple, he is the representative disciple and the paradigm of discipleship both in the story and for all subsequent readers. His 'failure' and 'restoration' are central to the good news, to the hope of restoration and salvation for those who fail.[25]

Many of the 'minor' characters in Mark's gospel make just a brief appearance. Their characters are determined by their responses and so they are one dimensional. For the most part the 'minor' characters do not interact with one another but fulfil a

25. For an examination of the importance of the role of Peter in the overall gospel, see A. Borrell, *The Good News of Peter's Denial. A Narrative and Rhetorical Reading of Mark 14:54, 66-72,* Atlanta: Scholars Press, 1998.

role in highlighting responses to Jesus during his ministry and in prefiguring future reactions to his followers in the time of the church. However, these 'minor' characters in the narrative are often the major players when it comes to acceptance of Jesus and the kingdom. In their faith and positive reactions to Jesus they show up the opposition, hesitation, fear and lack of understanding on the part of the 'major' characters. They exemplify often in their faith and determination the characteristics, attitudes and values that Jesus tried to instil in the Twelve. Often these 'minor' characters are individuals who stand out from their peer group (a good scribe, Jairus the good synagogue official, Joseph of Arimathea the good member of the Jewish authority). They also have a very important representative value rather out of proportion to the brevity of their appearances, and a symbolic value for the future mission of the church. The leper and the woman with the issue of blood represent the 'unclean' people cut off from social and religious life, yet full of faith and determination, whom Jesus restores to full participation in social and religious life. The Syro-Phoenician woman and the Gerasene demoniac represent the foreigners touched by Jesus' ministry and foreshadow the future mission of the church to the Gentiles. The blind man healed in two stages and the blind Bartimaeus represent different faith reactions to the healing ministry of Jesus and prefigure similar reactions to the future ministry of his followers. The woman who anointed Jesus at Bethany is representative of the 'outsider', the 'intruder' who understood more than the 'insiders' and acted on her convictions in spite of criticism. The centurion at the cross represents the powerful pagan persecutors brought to faith through the witness of the martyrs. Herod and Pilate in their dealings with John and Jesus represent those incipient or potential believers who hold positions of authority but do not have the courage of their own convictions when faced with opposition. They prefigure the political authorities with which Jesus' followers will contend in the days of the church.

There are also 'communal' characters constructed from identifiable groups such as the disciples, the women from Galilee, the adversaries, made up of various groupings of authority figures such as the chief priests, the elders and the scribes, the Pharisees, the crowd, those seeking help and healing and the demons representing a 'superior' power working to the detriment of the individuals they possess and to the destruction of the kingdom.

These communal characters function in the narrative as characterisations of the forces of support, misunderstanding, failure, opposition, hope and division. They also function as paradigms of discipleship and opposition, of 'insiders' and 'outsiders'.

The Settings

For Mark *place* is highly significant. First of all there is the biblical concept of the creation, comprising heaven, earth and underworld, wherein the drama takes place between God and the demonic forces. On the earthly level *place* signifies geographic location, socio-cultural, political and ethnic identity, hospitable or hostile territory and places of traditional religious significance. The introduction to the gospel takes place in the desert where the crowds have gone to be baptised by John and where Jesus is tempted by the devil and ministered to by the angels. There also he will go alone to pray, and there he will feed the multitude. The desert was the place where God, through the leadership of Moses, formed a covenant people at Sinai from the band of Hebrew slaves whom he had led out of Egypt, and it was through the desert God promised to make a way and lead the exiles safely back from Babylon. The desert was the place where prophets went for inspiration and sinners for repentance. It was where one depended totally on God. It was where wild beasts and evil spirits dwelt. The gospel opens very significantly with the Baptist's activity in the desert, when he was sent by God as precursor to prepare the way of the Lord. In the desert at the Jordan, with all its significance of the place of crossing into the Promised Land and the beginning of a new life for the people, Jesus was baptised, the Spirit came upon him and the voice from heaven proclaimed him 'my Son the Beloved'. In the desert the Beloved Son was tested and the angels ministered to him. In the desert he fed Jew and Gentile in 'messianic banquets' prefiguring the Eucharist and the eschatological banquet in the kingdom.

The *mountain* was the traditional place of theophanies, where God was encountered. There Moses received the Law. There the covenant was made. On the mountain Elijah heard the sound of the gentle breeze and wrapped his face in a mantle as the word of the Lord came to him. Jesus brings the disciples to the mountain to pray and there he is transfigured before them.

The *sea* was the place where the power of God was most

spectacularly in evidence. The biblical accounts of creation and reflections on creation emphasise God's order on chaos and God's control of the forces of the deep. The sea was seen as the dwelling place of demons and monsters who could churn up the winds and waves and threaten the order of creation. The combination of agitated sea, storm and darkness provide the setting for the terror of the disciples in the storm at sea. Significantly, Jesus showed how he has authority over the wind and waves. He saved the disciples from the raging storm at sea, and into that same sea the herd of pigs ran in terror as the demons took possession of them.

Public and *private venues* figure prominently in the narrative. Jesus carried on his public ministry in open spaces, desert places, synagogues, 'open' houses, and in the Temple and public places in Jerusalem. In these public places he preached, received the crowds, cured sick, exorcised the possessed and entered into controversy with his opponents. He withdrew with his disciples to instruct them further in private houses and in these private encounters we find also a good deal of the tension between Jesus and the disciples, arising from their failure to grasp the real significance of his ministry.

Galilee was the place where Jesus and the disciples were at home. There Jesus began his ministry, called his first disciples, preached his first sermons, healed and exorcised those who came to him for help. In Galilee the crowds flocked to him. Since Galilee was on the periphery of the 'Holy Land' and Jews lived there side by side with Gentiles, the Galileans were regarded with a certain amount of suspicion by the authorities in Jerusalem. Furthermore, in Roman eyes they were potential revolutionaries. From Galilee Jesus had easy access to the neighbouring Gentile territory of Tyre and Sidon to the north, and the Decapolis to the east (Mark makes no mention of Samaria to the south). Jews and Gentiles flocked to hear him and he fed them in the wilderness. In Galilee Jesus also experienced rejection by his own family and the people in his native place, and the long hand of Jerusalem authority reached into Galilee to observe and criticise himself, his disciples and his mission. Jesus' final message to the disciples through the young man at the tomb was that he would go before them into Galilee and there they would see him just as he had told them (Mk 16:7).

Between the ministry in Galilee and the ministry in

Jerusalem, Jesus and his disciples are *'on the way'*. 'The way' is the geographic path leading to Jerusalem, but it is also, and more importantly, the way of the Son of Man and the disciples' way of following Jesus to his destiny in the city and on the cross. It is the setting for Jesus' teaching on *the way of discipleship* and its requirements of denial of self, service of others and suffering along with the Son of Man.

Jerusalem was the Holy City, site of the Temple, centre of religious power and influence. From here Jesus' first critics came into Galilee. In Jerusalem Jesus challenged the religious powers and institutions, performed no healings or exorcisms and prophesied the end of the Temple and the end of the world as we know it. On his approach to Jerusalem he was received by an enthusiastic crowd proclaiming him as the one coming in the name of the Lord. In Jerusalem he was arrested, abandoned by his disciples, tried by Jewish and Roman authorities, rejected by a mob of his own countrymen, and executed. The powers he challenged defeated him. But God triumphed over those powers and raised Jesus from the dead, to lead his disciples back into Galilee.

Rhetorical Techniques

Various techniques in the use and repetition of words and phrases and the arrangement of material serve the purpose of making the story more interesting, hammering home the essential points, holding attention and presenting the story in such a way that it may be more memorable and easily repeated in whole or in part. The following are the more important techniques to observe in reading the gospel.

Dramatic Quality

Reading Mark's text, one quickly becomes aware of its definite dramatic quality. As in contemporary drama which was hugely influential throughout the empire in New Testament times, the protagonist and his/her background are introduced to the audience or readership at the beginning, and from this privileged position of inside knowledge the reader or audience observe the other characters as they interact and come to terms with the main character in the various situations and crises that arise. Mark paces the story like a drama. The ' inrush' or ' in-breaking' of the kingdom of God is dramatically captured in the first great section of the gospel, the ministry in Galilee, as everybody chases after Jesus and the repeated expression '(and) immediately' (more than forty times) conveys the sense of something wonderful happening at a really frenetic pace. 'It imparts to his narrative a sort of nervous random movement.'[26] The Galilean ministry is composed of three sections, each describing the powerful preaching and activity of Jesus. The atmosphere is charged with excitement and enthusiasm on the part of the crowds who flock to Jesus, but undercurrents of opposition, disbelief and misunderstanding are forming and threaten to sweep away the enthusiasm, as each of the three sections of the Galilee ministry closes on a negative note, emphasising violent hostility on the part of the authorities (Mk 3:6), lack of faith on the part of his own people and family (Mk 6:6), and lack of understanding on the part of his disciples (Mk 8:21).

The ministry in Galilee is followed by 'the way to Jerusalem', a geographical path which serves both as a setting and a metaphor for Jesus' teaching on 'the way of the Son of Man' and 'the way of discipleship'. Here the frenetic activity gives way to a walking pace, punctuated with Jesus' three predictions of the passion and the resulting fear and misunderstanding of the disciples. The atmosphere throughout this section is charged with hesitation, tension and foreboding. Jesus' focus of attention is now in very large measure on the instruction of the disciples and their preparation for sharing in his rejection, suffering and death.

In Jerusalem the pace slows further to a day by day account of Jesus' challenge to the institution (represented by the Temple and its authorities) and the teaching authority (Pharisees, Sadducees and scribes). The atmosphere is electrified with challenge and counter challenge ending in conspiracy. The pace slows further to an hour by hour account on the final day of Jesus' life as Jesus moves from the supper room to Gethsemane, to Jewish and Roman trials and on to crucifixion, death and burial. As Jesus sinks into the depths of human suffering and isolation, the God on whom he calls responds with the darkening of the heavens and the tearing open of the veil of the Temple. The words first spoken when the heavens were torn open at the baptism are re-echoed, not this time by the voice from heaven, but by the defeated powers of the world, in the person of the centurion, 'Truly this man was the Son of God'.

---

26. F. Kermode, *The Genesis of Secrecy*, 92.

Suspense/Tension

The creation of suspense is very important in a story. Mark is a master of suspense. He introduces a topic that begs an explanation and leaves the reader waiting and wondering until he returns to it again, maybe on several occasions, each time revealing a bit more and further whetting the appetite of curiosity and suspense. A case in point is the introduction of the enigmatic figure of the Son of Man. First introduced as the one who can forgive sins on earth, he is next spoken of as being master of the Sabbath, then as the one destined to suffer, to be rejected, put to death, and rise again, and in spite of such foreboding about him he will come in glory on the clouds. Other examples are the repeated predictions of the passion and resurrection, the foretelling of the betrayal by Judas and of the denials by Peter, and the flight of the disciples. All these create an expectation, produce tension and call for resolution by way of explanation and fulfilment. The eschatological or apocalyptic discourse (Mk 13) creates an ongoing suspense for all readers of the gospel.

Other common means of creating suspense in the gospel are challenges posed by his opponents when they set out to trap him in his speech or activity, in the hope of causing him to fall foul of the Jewish authorities, the religious movement of the Pharisees, the scribes who were the legal and biblical experts, the Roman authorities or the ordinary people.

Irony

Because of the privileged information that the reader is given in the prologue, it is possible to appreciate the dramatic irony of the gospel. The reader sees that things are not as they appear to the characters in the narrative or drama. The authority figures, the high priest, the priestly class and the elders seem to have real religious authority. Pilate represents the greatest political and military authority on earth. The scribes appear to know everything about law and scripture. The Pharisees are the devout and scrupulously observant members of society. Throughout the entire gospel these characters assert their authority and superior status and show off their learning and piety. Jesus in their eyes is a nobody, a layman, an uneducated, self-appointed teacher, a lawbreaker and no respecter of tradition in matters of Sabbath observance and ritual purity. To their disgust he also mixed and ate with the social and political outcasts, the ritually impure, the

Gentiles and anyone who came along in the crowd. The reader, however, knows the true identity of Jesus and the power of God behind his work establishing the kingdom. These two realities provide the dramatic irony of the gospel. The reader waits to see how the real power of God will exert itself against the apparent power of the opponents of Jesus and their apparent victory over him.

There is also the verbal irony when someone says something meaning quite the opposite and intending thereby to wound the target. The jeering references to Jesus' kingship, his messianic role and his prophetic statements are cases in point. They are examples of cynicism and satire at the level of the characters and of dramatic irony at the level of the reader, who knows the real truth behind the jeering comments.

Repetition
Though the gospel was written, it was still heard rather than read by most people, since most were illiterate and manuscripts were rare and very precious. The gospel, therefore, was read to them in liturgical or other gatherings. For that reason techniques of oral transmission and storytelling remain very important in the written work. Repetition of words, phrases, names, types of character and types of scene are very important. They hold a story together, keeping earlier parts of the story fresh in the mind as it progresses, and they relate various stories together. Repeated phrases also create a mood and prepare the listeners for what is to come. For example, in modern times when one tells a story to a child at bedtime the opening phrase, 'Once upon a time,' sets the child at rest, creates an atmosphere and raises a particular type of expectation. Similarly in the Bible, the expression, 'In those days', for example, creates the expectation that a significant event in salvation history is about to be related.

The gospel is like a tapestry and some of the main themes are like threads woven through the text, appearing with varying degrees of intensity in the repetition of key words with their cognates and word-roots, and their opposites, like *proclaim, good news, repent, believe, call, follow, understand, fear, forgive, hand over (betray), disciple, desert, loaf, cup, the appointed time, reject, suffer, raise/be raised, take hold of, it is necessary, kingdom (rule) of God, Messiah/Christ, Son of Man, Son of God.*[27]

27. See the article by J.Dewey, 'Mark as Interwoven Tapestry: Forecasts and Echoes for a Listening Audience,' *CBQ* 53(1991), 221-36.

Collections of previously independent sayings are often held together by a link word or phrase, for example 'in my name' forms a link between Jesus' acceptance of the unauthorised casting out of demons 'in my name' and the cup of water given 'in (my) name'.

Echoing and Foreshadowing
The frequently repeated words and phrases, like 'handing over' are very important in maintaining echoes of the earlier part of the story and foreshadowing what is to come. Echoes of Old Testament characters and events are regularly heard and foreshadowings and forewarnings of what will be experienced in the life of the church are already present in the ministry of Jesus, for example, his dealings with non-Jews foreshadow the mission of the church to the Gentiles

Double references
Mark likes to make double references to time, place, people, comments, events, questions and so forth. The second reference serves to make the first more explicit. It is common to find a general time reference followed by a more specific one, as 'early in the morning, before sunrise', or 'in the evening, after sunset'. With regard to place, one similarly finds a general reference followed by a more specific one as in the phrase 'outside, in a desert place'. So too in the case of people, the more general reference is followed by a more specific one. The woman whose daughter he heals is described as 'a Greek, a Syro-Phoenician by birth'. The widow putting her coins into the treasury, 'gave everything she had, her whole livelihood'. Questions also can be in two stages. The disciples asked Jesus after his remark about the destruction of the Temple: 'When will these things take place, what will be the signs?'

The gospel as a whole reflects this two stage approach. The gospel begins with the acknowledgement in the prologue that Jesus is the Christ and the Son of God. The first half of the gospel builds up to Peter's confession of Jesus as the Christ, then the second half of the gospel builds up to the centurion's confession of Jesus as Son of God. The double healing of the blind man at Bethsaida reflects this two stage approach of the gospel as a whole.

Triple Divisions, Actions and Statements
After the prologue, the body of the gospel covering Jesus' ministry is divided on a broadly geographical basis into three main parts – the ministry in Galilee, the way to Jerusalem and the ministry in Jerusalem. There are three major sections in the Galilee ministry, resulting in three parallel sequences of events ending in three negative responses. On the way to Jerusalem there are three predictions of the passion, similar in style, marking off the three sections of teaching on discipleship along the way. The final day of Jesus' life is divided into three periods of three hours.

Doing or saying something three times has a ring of completeness about it. There are three conversations between Jesus and the disciples in a boat and three disputes between them about bread. Three questions of a legal or scriptural nature are put to him in Jerusalem (concerning taxes to Caesar, the resurrection of the dead and the greatest commandment). Jesus prays three times in the garden of Gethsemane and three times finds the disciples sleeping. Peter denies his master three times. Pilate asks three questions of the mob and they three times reject Jesus, at the instigation of the authorities. Three groups mocked him as he hung on the cross.

Parables
The use of parables is one of the aspects of Jesus' teaching with which most readers are familiar. However, the term *parable* signifies a complex reality not as easily summed up as is often done with a simple statement like: 'A parable is a story with a religious or moral message.' Such a description is more suitable to Aesop's fables, each of which has a moral message, than to Jesus' parables. In Mark, and in all the gospels, the term 'parable' is used for short metaphorical sayings, similitudes, allegories, riddles, lessons for illustration and some longer narratives. They function as figures of speech which can at the same time both conceal the truth from the spiritually obtuse and reveal it to the spiritually open on the way to fuller understanding. Sometimes the parables are transparently obvious, other times they are not, and only yield their meaning later. Jesus often resorted to the use of parables when he was under pressure by way of criticism or outright attack, or when he wanted to go on the offensive against outright enemies or self righteous critics.

He also used parables to shock, provoke and stimulate his listeners into thinking through the implications of his words and actions. At times they were like a shot across the bows, at other times like a hard sweet on which to chew for a time.

Questions and Counter Questions/Controversies

Asking questions either from friendly or hostile motives is a common device in the gospel.[28] Responding to friendly questions leads on to teaching. Responding to hostile questions (or situations) with a 'no win' counter-question is another device. Asking the scribes whether it was easier to tell the invalid that his sins were forgiven or to tell him to arise and walk put his opponents into a dilemma of blaspheming, which was the source of their disquiet, or saying a miracle which they could not perform was easier (Mk 2:9). Similarly, asking if it were lawful to do good or to do evil, to save life or to kill on the Sabbath, put Jesus' opponents in the dilemma of saying either that doing good was wrong or doing wrong was good (Mk 3:4). Jesus at times initiates discussion with a question. He asks the disciples what they were discussing along the way and proceeds from that to a discussion on discipleship (Mk 9:33). He asks the crowd in Jerusalem how the scribes can maintain that the Messiah is David's son and leads from that into a discussion on the Messiah (Mk 12:35).

Structure of the Text

The organisation of the text is in itself part of the communication and explanatory process. The following are some of the more important techniques used by Mark.

Intercalation

Mark has a strong liking for 'intercalation' or 'sandwich technique' for achieving emphasis by inserting one story into the middle of another. Jesus' journey to the house of Jairus is interrupted by the encounter with the woman suffering from the issue of blood (Mk 4:21-43). The account of Jesus' family coming to take hold of him because they think he is mad is interrupted by the arrival of the scribes from Jerusalem who make accus-

---

28. For a study of the role of questions in the gospel see J. Dewey, *Markan Public Debate: Literary Technique, Concentric Structure, and Theology in Mark 2:1-3:6*, SBLDS 48, Chico: Scholars Press, 1980.

ations against him (Mk 3:21-35). The story of the unfruitful fig tree is interrupted by the account of the 'cleansing' of the Temple (Mk 11:12-25). The story of the plotting of the authorities and Judas' co-operation is interrupted by the anointing of Jesus by the woman in Bethany (Mk14:1-11). The Jewish trial of Jesus is set in the middle of the story of Peter's cautious following at a distance and his betrayals (Mk 14:53-72). These pairs of stories spliced together serve to mutually enhance each other by way of sharing a common theme or showing a sharp contrast. In the story of the woman with the issue of blood, which interrupts the story of Jairus and his daughter, the faith of both petitioners and the shared twelve years in which the little girl was growing into life and the woman was gradually losing hers, bind both stories thematically together. The anointing in Bethany, on the other hand, highlights by way of contrast the action of Judas and the loving action of the woman. Another sharp contrast is Jesus' courageous stand at his questioning before the powerful figures in the Jewish establishment and the simultaneous cowardly failure of Peter at his questioning by the relatively insignificant people in the courtyard.

Chiastic Structure (Concentric or Ring Pattern)
Literary structure or arrangement serves to highlight and interpret a text. In contemporary western society a storyteller, preacher or speechmaker tends to build up through a linear, logical argument to a climactic finale and the punch line comes at the end. Even if the main point has already been introduced and repeated we expect a climactic moment of emphasis to conclude the story or discourse. In biblical literature, on the other hand, the emphasis is regularly placed at the central point of a discourse, allowing for a step by step approach to the central point and a parallel series of steps departing from it, like mirror images reflecting and interpreting each other. The *chiastic* or *concentric* structure can be represented as A-B-C-D-C-B-A, where a series of scenes, A, B, C, leads up to, and a corresponding series of parallel scenes, C, B, A, leads away from, the central scene D. In this arrangement A and A, B and B, C and C reflect each other through similarities of personality, movement, language or theme.

Inclusion (Framing)
Passages which reflect one another in theme, language or loc-

ation are placed at the opening and closing of the text as a whole,
or they are used to section off a significant part of it. These
inclusions function like bookends at opposite ends of the entire
text or at the beginning and end of a significant portion within it.
For example, the rending of the heavens at the baptism of Jesus
with the voice from heaven proclaiming him the Beloved Son
forms a frame for the entire public ministry with the scene on
Golgotha when, in the aftermath of the darkening of the heavens
and the earth, the rending of the veil of the Temple is followed
by the confession of the centurion proclaiming the same message that the voice from heaven proclaimed at the baptism, that
this man was the Son of God (Mk 1:11; 15:39). An example of an
inclusion within the gospel is the healing of the blind man at
Bethsaida (Mk 8:22-26) and the healing of the blind man in
Jericho (Mk 10:46-52) which form a frame around the major section of the gospel dealing with the way to Jerusalem, the way of
the Son of Man.

The Importance of the Old Testament (The Hebrew Scriptures)
From the beginning the Christians went to the Old Testament to
find further insight into the meaning of Jesus' life, death and resurrection and a language in which to express it. The Old
Testament and commentaries on it served as a resource for the
first Christians as they reflected on the extraordinary life, terrible death and glorious resurrection of Jesus. Searching the scriptures helped them to come to an understanding of what had
taken place and supplied them with a dictionary of religious
language, theological terms and literary forms for proclaiming
their faith in Christ. They found that in Jesus they had the fulfilment of promises and prophecies, the making of a new
covenant, the climax of a historical process. They also found in
the Old Testament a dictionary of religious phrases and language canonised over centuries which they could use in articulating, explaining and defending their faith. They relied on patterns of storytelling already established in the Old Testament. In
particular, the stories of Moses and the people during the
Exodus and wandering in the desert provide patterns for the
telling of the stories of the miracles at sea and the feeding of the
multitudes in the desert. The raising, healing and feeding stories
in the Elijah-Elisha cycle in 1-2 Kings also provide models for the
telling of stories about Jesus. The promise of a new Exodus, a

new way or path through the desert under the protecting eye
and provident action of God, back to the Promised Land after
the exile in Babylon, is a major theme in Deutero-Isaiah (Isa 40-
55) and provides much of the imagery for the 'way of the Lord',
the 'way to Jerusalem' and the final gathering of the elect in
Mark's gospel. There are twenty two explicit quotations from
the Old Testament in Mark and numerous allusions to persons
and events. This intertextuality highlights the consistency and
continuity in God's work of salvation and points to the culmination of a historical development through the fulfilment in Jesus
of promise and prophecy in God's dealings with the people.[29]

New Testament writers and readers knew the Old Testament
from various sources. The Hebrew text had not yet been stan-
dardised as the Massoretic Text (MT) and therefore various
traditions of the texts were probably available.[30] After the Exile
the Jews for the most part became Aramaic speakers and, apart
from scholars, seem to have become unfamiliar with Hebrew.
The reading of Hebrew texts in the synagogue was therefore accompanied by an Aramaic translation-cum-interpretation of the
text, known as a *Targum* (pl. *targumim*). Many Jews in New
Testament times may have known their Bible stories from these
targumim and so they are often important for picking up allusions and references to the Old Testament as it was understood in
New Testament times.[31]

Story: Faith and History
The story of Jesus at one level fits the category of historical story,
in so far as it tells of a historical person, in concrete historical circumstances, surrounded by historical characters, the outcome of
whose life left an enormous mark in human history. At another
level it is a story that history cannot confirm or assess. His being
sent by the Father, his inner life and consciousness, his promise

29. For a study of the use of Old Testament quotations in the New
Testament, see B. Lindars, *New Testament Apologetic: The Doctrinal
Significance of the Old Testament Quotations*, London: SCM, 1961.
30. MT (The Masoretic Text) was produced by the Masoretes who were
scholars of the Masorah (tradition). They gave the Hebrew text its final
standard form around the 8th century AD. According to Jewish tradition this is exactly the same text as that edited by the rabbis in the period
after the Fall of Jerusalem (70-100 AD).
31. The *targumim* have been collected in the two great collections of rabbinic literature, the Palestinian Talmud and the Babylonian Talmud.

of salvation, his predicting the end of the world as we know it, his resurrection and glorification and the promised coming of the Son of Man in glory are matters beyond the competence of the historian. Yet they are a major part, in fact *the* major part, of his story. Putting the historical and ahistorical/transcendental together in one story so that the reader can understand is, to quote B. Witherington, writing about John, but equally true of Mark:

> ... an exercise in hermeneutics, the science of the interpretation and application of a foundational narrative, the taking of the story of Jesus and putting it into a language and form of narrative that will convey the significance and meaning of the Christ event ...[32]

VI
THE READER

The Reader/Reader Response Criticism
As the literary work itself, in this case the gospel of Mark, takes on a life of its own and becomes independent of, and outlives, the 'actual' as distinct from the 'implied' author and the author's originally intended/implied readers, 'real' readers, never envisioned by the author, take their place. Their horizons may be very different from those of the author and the ' implied' or intended readers. If we are to bridge the two horizons, we must realise that we live with a post-Enlightenment worldview of history and the cosmos, of society and religion, of individual and communal rights and obligations, very different from the worldview reflected in the gospels. Bridging the gap created by distance in time, place and culture is the task of the biblical scholar and commentator, who is first and foremost a reader who has engaged with the text and then aims to help other readers to grasp and understand the book, in this case the gospel of Mark. The text is like a music score, it remains a score until it is played, then it is music. So too, the text is a series of words on a page until it comes alive in the reading. The exegete/commentator is like the conductor who first studies and appropriates the music and then leads the players into a deeper understanding and appreciation.

---

32. Ben Witherington III, *John's Wisdom. A Commentary on the Fourth Gospel*, Westminster, John Knox Press, Louisville, Kentucky, 1995, 73f.

The reader, however, comes to the text with his or her own outlook, understanding, background, knowledge, strengths, weaknesses and prejudices. Author, text and reader all play a part in the interpretation of the text. A committed Christian, an agnostic and a committed atheist can read the same text and draw meaning from it. It is necessary, therefore, to acknowledge one's own 'position' as one approaches the text and presents one's understanding of it to others.

I write this commentary from the standpoint of one who sees the work as a whole, the text as it now stands (with its well known 'later' but 'canonical' longer ending). In dealing with sources, the 'historical' Jesus, and the nature and composition of the community in which the tradition was nurtured and transmitted, I do so only insofar as such information or speculation throws light on the text under examination and its place in the gospel as a whole. I refer to the other gospels, and particularly to the Johannine tradition which is the theological counterpoint of Mark, for the same purpose. The author has shaped the final text from the sources, oral and written, at his disposal and in the process has produced a text that is a marriage of content and form and stands on its own as a literary and theological whole.

The story of Jesus, according to Mark, is read by me, the listening reader, two millennia after its composition. I read, hear and retell it. It is Mark's story, the early Christians' story, but now it is my story and my retelling, and the readers of my words will make it their story. My reading is not 'the' reading, but one of many possible readings of a very subtly challenging text.

My hope is that I read it as *the good news* and succeed in communicating *the good news*. But how do I read the story? What hermeneutical grid is functioning in me as I read? What factors determine my approach?

As I have pointed out in other writings, I read St Mark's gospel as a practising Catholic, a priest and teacher of scripture for more than three decades. I read it in the context of faith seeking understanding, a faith that has been nourished in the liturgy and prayer and enriched by art, music and ritual. Above all, it has been honed on the anvil of teaching and learning from students seeking truth and life in the scriptures. I come to the gospel then with all the fascination of one whose life has been an absorbing of the 'polyphony' of faith expression. Within, and supported by, this faith context I bring academic training, reading and teaching experience to the understanding of the text. I question and analyse the text, not to deconstruct it, much less to deconstruct Jesus himself, but to enrich the overall impression, the form or *Gestalt*, with awareness of the rich diet of components that make up the gospel.[33] Furthermore, I see the gospel as an integral part of the whole canon of scripture, and consider exegesis as a science practised within the comprehensive view of the church. If one stands outside that comprehensive view one runs the risk of breaking up 'the indivisible unity of the figure of Christ'.[34] Hans Urs von Balthasar states it very clearly:

> Jesus' word can be understood by all, but only in the light of his testimony of being the Son of God does it become truly clear. Moreover, only in relation to his death and resurrection does it attain the fullness of its meaning: Jesus' entire being is one single Word. This perfect being becomes manifest only from the testimonials of faith … (which), all together, form a magnificent polyphony – not a pluralism in the contemporary sense … The more facets we can view, the better we can grasp the unity of the inspiration. The possessor of this inspiration is the church, the early charisma of which was to compose the New Testament and establish its canon. Only her eye of faith, guided by the Holy Spirit, could see the whole phenomenon of Jesus Christ.[35]

These are the co-ordinates on the grid of my hermeneutic as I set about commenting on the gospel according to Mark through the 'eye of faith'. That's me, the reader. But who is Mark? The questions relating to the identity of author and the date and place of composition are dealt with at the end of the commentary. I deliberately do not deal with them before reading the text, since it is an anonymous document, without reference to time and place of composition. To do so at the beginning may impose a grid through which the gospel would be filtered. Throughout the commentary I refer to the work as the gospel of Mark or simply Mark and refer to the other gospels in similar fashion.

Mark's gospel should be read on its own terms. The other gospels should not be used to 'fill out' or 'improve' Mark. Their theological perspectives should not be imposed on Mark. They

33. H. U. von Balthasar, 'Theology and Aesthetic', *Communio*, I, (1981), 64.
34. H. U. von Balthasar, *op. cit.*, 65.
35. *Ibid.*

can however be fruitfully used by way of comparison or contrast to highlight the different and distinctive approach and insight of Mark. Sometimes points of information, such as clarification of a word, custom, person, group or geographical reference, may be sought by way of reference to a clearer description in another gospel, but this does not impose or interfere with the distinctive character of the gospel of Mark.

Reading in Greek or in translation
Ideally a serious study of any of the New Testament documents should be conducted from, and accompanied by, a reading of the Greek text. In reality, however, most students are still learning New Testament Greek and many general readers have little, if any, knowledge of the language. As every translation is but an approximation to the original it is advisable, therefore, to follow more than one translation when making a serious study of the text. Words and expressions are very important in Mark and in translation they easily lose their impact and connotations. This is particularly true where a word group containing related noun, verb, adjective or adverb come from the same root, and are translated by very different words in English. In the commentary I frequently use italics for such related words. I also use italics for recurring words of particular significance, and for the transliteration into the Roman alphabet of Greek and Hebrew words and expressions. This last group I introduce gradually and translate until they should be quite familiar to the reader.

Chapter and verse
It should also be kept in mind that the original Greek text was not divided into chapter and verse, not to mention neat divisions into paragraphs with supplied headings and subheadings as in some modern printed Bibles. Chapter divisions were introduced into the Bible by Stephen Langton, Archbishop of Canterbury 1207–28, and the verse divisions were made by the Parisian printer and publisher Robert Estienne for his 1551 Geneva edition of the New Testament. The chapter and verse divisions are very useful for referring to the text but they can be very misleading at times if one wishes to follow the natural flow of the narrative. This is particularly true of Mark's gospel. In the commentary I endeavour to divide the gospel into its 'natural' sections as I see them and explain why I do so by way of reference to the indications in the text itself.

The Prologue Mk 1:1-15

1. The Plot

It was common practice in ancient literature and drama to begin a work with a prologue. It served to introduce the reader or audience to the plot, the characters, the issues and the outcome.[1] It gave privileged information of an authoritative kind which was not shared by the characters in the narrative or drama. The reader or audience, therefore, had the advantage over the characters in the story not only in understanding their relation to each other and to the plot as a whole, but also in having privileged access to their inner thoughts and motives and the influences to which they were subject. Matthew and Luke introduce their gospels with accounts of the birth and infancy of Jesus in which his true identity is revealed to the reader and his destiny foreshadowed. The prologue in St John's gospel serves the same function, introducing the Word made flesh as the *monogenês*, the 'only son'. Mark's prologue reveals the identity of Jesus and the sources of divine and demonic powers that will be working behind the scenes throughout his ministry. The 'omniscient' narrator sets the scene at the beginning, clearly showing the initiative of God in sending the messenger to prepare the way of the Lord, in confirming the identity of the Beloved Son and in empowering him with the Spirit. The narrator then carefully guides the reader or hearer of the gospel through the story, ensuring the acceptance of his (or her) own point of view.

The prologue begins with the announcement of the beginning of the good news of Jesus Christ, Son of God, and builds up to the proclamation of the good news of the Kingdom by Jesus on his return to Galilee. It roots the good news of Jesus in the plan of God revealed long ago in scripture and historically initiated by John who was sent by God to prepare the way of the Lord. The prologue underpins the authority of the protagonist, Jesus, with the account of the voice from heaven and the coming

---

1. See M. E. Boring, 'Mark 1:1-15 and the beginning of the Gospel', *Semeia* 52 (1990), 43-81; D. Dormeyer, 'Mk 1:1-15 als Prolog des ersten Idealbiographischen Evangeliums von Jesus Christus', *Biblical Interpretation* 5 (1997)181-211.

of the Spirit. It describes the beginning of the contest between the kingdom of God and the kingdom of Satan when the Spirit drives the protagonist, Jesus, into the desert to be tested by the antagonist, Satan, and to be ministered to by the angels. The prologue reaches its goal when Jesus emerges from the contest in the desert and proclaims the good news of the kingdom in Galilee, initiating an attack on the kingdom of Satan, laying siege to the house of the strong man. The final victory in the contest will be proclaimed at the empty tomb when the Beloved Son is vindicated by the Father.

Where does the prologue end?
Scholars discuss the exact extent of the prologue, whether it ends at verse 13 or 15. Verses 14 and 15 form an inclusion with Mk 1:1 in referring to the 'good news' and bringing the prologue to a conclusion or climax with the announcing of the good news by Jesus for whom the way has been prepared. At the same time these verses round off the career of the Baptist with the notice of his arrest. Furthermore the purpose of Jesus' coming from Galilee to be baptised results in his returning to Galilee announcing the good news, so his coming from and returning to Galilee are two parts of a single event in the prologue. For these reasons verses 14 and 15 seem to be an integral part of the prologue. However, looking at the overall structure of the gospel, Mk 1:14 to 3:6 forms a unit. It is one of three similarly formed units covering the ministry in Galilee and so verses 14 and 15 seem to belong also to the Galilee ministry. Furthermore, a definite change of time and place is indicated and a clear chronological separation of the ministries of John and Jesus is underlined in verses 14 and 15. These verses, therefore, are also an integral part of the Galilean ministry. For these reasons it is difficult to make a very clear division between the prologue and the beginning of the ministry in Galilee and it is best to see verses 14 and 15 as a bridge or hinge, rounding off the prologue and at the same time beginning the section Mk 1:14 to 3:6. The use of similar 'bridge' or 'hinge' passages will occur a number of times in the gospel. Furthermore, a number of bridge passages are summaries like Mk 1:14-15 which look back on what has been and look forward to what is to come.[2]

2. Furthermore, making a division between verses14 and 15 does not seem to be advisable as a solution because these two verses follow the

2. THE SUPERSCRIPTION / TITLE: MK 1:1

The first words of Mark's gospel, *Beginning of the good news of Jesus Christ, Son of God*[3] do not refer simply to the first words of the written text, as though the middle and end will be pointed out in due course. They refer rather to the whole gospel as an account of the origin and governing principle of the *euanggelion*, the good news brought about in the life, death, resurrection and glorification of Jesus Christ, Son of God, in whom it is very likely that the implied or originally intended readers or hearers had already come to believe.

Paul had already used the term *euaggelion*, 'good news', more than sixty times as a proclamation or a theological synthesis of the revelation and salvation brought about through the life, death and resurrection of Jesus Christ. As already seen in the introduction, for Paul and other New Testament writers the term *good news* was particularly apt for the gracious offer of salvation revealed in the life, death and resurrection of Jesus Christ, with its promise of a faith relationship in this life with the Risen Lord through repentance, baptism, forgiveness of sins and the gift of the Spirit, and the promise of an eschatological fulfilment when all things would be made new at Christ's return in glory.

In the Old Testament the equivalent Hebrew term for good news, *bsr*, was used especially in the Psalms and in Deutero-Isaiah with particular reference to the gracious act of God in effecting the return of the exiled or scattered people to Zion. The LXX (the Greek version of the Old Testament) used the verbal equivalent *euaggelizomai* for this saving work of God in preparing and opening up the way for their return from exile (Isa 40:9; 41:27; 52:7; 60:6; 61:1). Furthermore, the bringer of the good news, 'the joyful messenger to Zion' is a living sign or embodiment of the good news, of whom it can be said: 'How beautiful on the mountains are the feet of the one who brings good news, proclaims peace and says to Zion, " Your God reigns"'(Isa 52:7). The news is good in itself, and being the good news of God it ef-

---

typical Markan pattern of a general statement followed by a specific one: 'announcing the good news' is followed by the specific details of the nearness of the kingdom and the necessity of repentance.

3. There are variations in the text of the first verse, some manuscripts not having ' Son of God'. The presence of 'Son of God' in the important manuscript B, D, W, and the overall structure and theology of the gospel as outlined above, point strongly to the longer reading.

fects the good that it proclaims. No matter what human obstacles are in the way, the hearers are reminded that 'all flesh is
grass and its beauty like that of the wild flower, the grass withers, the flower fades but the word of our God endures forever'
(Isa 40:7,8).

In the Greco-Roman world the term *good news* was widely
used for the announcing of an important birth or significant
political or military victory. It was used for the pronouncements,
presence and performance of the 'divine' emperor. The messenger who brought good news was closely associated with the
good news he brought and honoured accordingly, as the good
news of a royal birth or important victory was announced with
pomp and ceremony. Conversely the bearer of bad tidings could
fear a reaction to himself as a consequence of his association
with the bad news he brought.

Mark's gospel marks a whole new departure in presenting a
narrative of the origin or beginning of the good news of Jesus
Christ, Son of God. From the very start the reader is drawn into
the story and senses a new beginning in the history of salvation.
The first word in the gospel of Mark is none other than the very
first word in the Bible itself, *beginning*. It re-echoes the first word
of the opening verse of Genesis which points to the origin and
governing principle of all God's work in creation and history.[4]
Using it here creates for the reader the sense of a radically new
initiative of God.

The good news of Jesus is not just the good news about him,
or the good news that he preached, but he himself is the embodiment of the good news. Throughout the gospel narrative the announcing of the nearness, presence or mystery of the kingdom
in the person, words and deeds of Jesus as he invites people to
repent, to believe in the good news and to follow him *on the way*,
constitutes the good news. In the narrative of the gospel the *good
news* takes on a whole new dimension at the climactic moment
when the young man sitting at the open tomb proclaims: 'You
seek Jesus the crucified Nazarene. He is risen. He is not here. Go
tell his disciples and Peter that he is going ahead of you into
Galilee' (Mk 16:8). Jesus, formerly the preacher and embodiment
of the good news of the kingdom, from that moment becomes

4. *Beginning* has no article, and as such the phrase *beginning of the good
news* resembles the Semitic construct case. The same word is used also
at the opening of John's gospel and *En archê* in Jn 1:1 also has no article.

himself in a whole new way the subject of the good news of salvation in the proclamation of his vindication by the Father in his
victory over Satan, death and the powers that brought about his
rejection and execution.

This first verse of the gospel introduces the main character
(the protagonist) in the story about to unfold on the human
stage. Jesus' role and true identity are proclaimed. The first half
of the gospel story builds up to Peter's proclamation of faith in
Jesus' as the Messiah/Christ, the expected anointed one of royal
descent (Mk 8:29). The second half contains Jesus' instruction
about the proper understanding of that role as it 'redefines messiahship in terms of suffering, death and resurrection. It replaces
the royal Davidic descendent who would defeat Israel's political
enemies with a Messiah who must fulfil his destiny as Son of
Man.'[5] The story comes to a climax when the centurion who presides over Jesus' execution, 'on seeing how he died' proclaimed
his faith in the identity of the one he has executed as he proclaims: 'In truth this man was the Son of God' (Mk 15:39), re-
echoing the superscription at the beginning of the gospel and
the declaration of the voice from heaven immediately after the
baptism of Jesus (Mk 1:11) and the voice from the cloud at the
transfiguration (Mk 9:7).

The reader, however, is given this privileged information
about Jesus' true identity and role at the outset and can therefore
appreciate the unfolding story from a privileged position, sharing in the 'omniscience' of the narrator and observing the reactions, difficulties and developing awareness of the characters in
the story. However, the reader also has to wait and be challenged along with the characters to see how the Father vindic-
ates the Son after his rejection and crucifixion. The Son is finally
vindicated by the Father when the young man at the tomb proclaims: 'He is risen. He is not here' (Mk 16:8).

5. M. Hogan, *op. cit.*, 61.

3. The Divine Plan: Mk 1:2-3

The established formula for quoting scripture, *it is written*, introduces the prime mover, God, into the story. The authoritative voice of God is heard through the teaching of the prophets in an adapted quotation rich in allusions to Isaiah, Malachi and Exodus, a quotation announcing the unfolding of a long awaited plan, foretold long ago (Isa 40:3; Mal 3:1; Ex 23:20). In the quotation God speaks through the prophetic voices to the protagonist Jesus, whom he addresses directly and to whom he promises to send a messenger to prepare the way: 'Behold I am sending my messenger before you to prepare *your* way.' The way (mentioned twice in the prologue) is described as 'the way of the Lord'.

Though the quotation is ascribed to Isaiah, the first part of the quotation re-echoes the prophet Malachi's prophecy that God will send a messenger, identified as Elijah, before 'the great and terrible day of *YHWH*' (Mal 3:1; 4:5). The second part of the quotation is from the Book of Isaiah and recalls 'the voice calling out in the wilderness: "prepare the way of the Lord".' The 'way of the Lord' is a powerfully evocative term in both Old and New Testaments. In Deutero-Isaiah 'the way of the Lord' refers to the way through the desert back to the Promised Land from the exile in Babylon, a physical way going hand in hand with the spiritual way of the Lord which the people will follow in response to God's gracious action on their behalf. The prophet to whom chapters 40 to 55 of the Book of Isaiah are ascribed, conventionally referred to as Second or Deutero-Isaiah, is the prophet of consolation, the 'joyful messenger to Zion', the prophet of the 'good news' for the people in exile. This good news was first heard during the exile as the 'voice crying out' to the people to prepare for their return home from exile in Babylon (Isa 40:3; cf Mt 3:2f; Mk 1:2f; Lk 3:4f.). It envisaged the end of the exile, a new exodus of the people and a passage through the desert, under the protection of God. In the Hebrew text of the Old Testament it was seen in terms of a physical journey, a real physical *path in the desert* and the path was described as the path *of our God*.[6] The imagery portrays God as the shepherd leading the people through the desert.

Here in Mark 'the way' refers to the way of Jesus, to God's

---

6. The MT has 'path in the desert', the LXX and NT have 'voice in the desert'.

way manifest in his life, death and resurrection. It is the way of
discipleship in which Jesus will call his followers to share his
destiny and walk with him on his divinely designated path. 'The
way' becomes a dominant theme in the section of the gospel
dealing with 'the way to Jerusalem' which is 'the way of the Son
of Man', Jesus' way to his passion, death and resurrection, and
which is at the same time the context for the teaching on 'the
way of discipleship' (Mk 8:27-10:52). By the time of the writing
of the Acts of the Apostles the term has become so established
that Christians are referred to as people 'of the way' (Acts 9:2).

In the New Testament the emphasis moves somewhat from
'a path in the desert' to 'a voice in the desert', so the way or path
can be seen, not only in geographical and physical terms but also
in spiritual terms, as the way of Jesus. This implies a new, spiritual, exodus, a calling of the people to the movement of repentance being carried on by John in the desert as a preparation for
'the way of the Lord'. The *voice in the desert* calls the people to
prepare *the way of the Lord*. The original physical journey is replaced by a spiritual journey signifying a return from spiritual
exile, a path in the heart that makes possible the approach of
God to his people, opening up their hearts, levelling their pride,
filling in their emptiness, if one applies the imagery to a spiritual
journey.[7]

'The way of the Lord' can be seen here both as 'the way of
God' made manifest in Jesus or 'the way of (Jesus) the Lord'. The
title 'Lord', *kyrios*, was used in the LXX as a translation of *adonai*,
used in the Hebrew Bible as a substitute for *YHWH*, since the
Jews regarded the name of God as too sacred to pronounce. The
title *kyrios* became a standard title for the risen and glorified
Christ in the early church. Though referring to Jesus as Lord is
not typical of the body of the gospel of Mark, it is not out of place
in the theologically and christologically rich prologue where he

---

7. The synoptics and John follow the LXX 'voice in the desert' rather
than 'path in the desert' but John takes an independent line from the
synoptics when he conflates the two elements of the LXX, which read
'prepare the Lord's road, make straight God's path' into 'Make straight
the Lord's path'. The synoptics have the two elements. The Qumran
community used this text to explain their living, waiting, preparing and
studying in the desert (I QS VIII 13-16). The synoptic narrators apply
this text to John the Baptist but in John's gospel he applies it to himself
in his response to the Jerusalem emissaries.

is called Christ, Son of God, Beloved Son, addressed by the voice from heaven, and invested with the Spirit. In Jerusalem at the end of his ministry Jesus will refer to the Messiah as Lord (Mk 12:35-37).

This part of the quotation, *the voice of one crying out in the desert to prepare the way of the Lord,* focuses on another very significant place and source of imagery in the Bible, 'the desert'. As pointed out in the introduction, the desert held a special place in the history and spirituality of Israel. It was the place where Israel became God's chosen people through covenant, when God liberated them from the slavery of Egypt 'with mighty hand and outstretched arm, with great terror and with signs and wonders' (Deut 26:8). It was also the place where they were tested, where they grumbled, complained, hesitated and suffered punishment and purification as they were led to the Promised Land. It was through the desert that God, in a new Exodus, would lead them back from the exile in Babylon, straightening the paths and making smooth the way.[8] The desert was seen as the place where the devout and repentant would withdraw to be with God and remake their lives. Elijah repaired to the desert in crisis. The Essenes went there to found an ideal messianic community when they withdrew from the illegitimate Temple authority in Jerusalem. It was therefore the ideal spot for a group like the followers of the Baptist to assemble in their quest for new beginnings and for straightening the spiritual paths and making smooth the ways on which they walked in their lives. Jesus himself after his baptism will be driven there by the Spirit to be tested by Satan. The desert is mentioned twice at the beginning and twice towards the end of the prologue, and in the ministry of Jesus it will be his place of retreat for prayer. It will also be the place where he will take his disciples to rest, and the place in which he will be moved to compassion to teach and feed the multitudes who come to the desert to be with him, to listen to him and to be healed by him. In doing so he will re-enact the caring and protecting activity of the Shepherd of Israel.

---

8. For an examination of the influence on Mark of Deutero-Isaiah's concept of 'the way of the Lord' as a new Exodus, a new return under the care and protection of a shepherding and warrior God, see R. E. Watts, *Isaiah's New Exodus and Mark,* Wissenschaftliche Untersuchungen zum Neuen Testament 2, Reihe 88, Tubingen: J. C. B. Mohr (Paul Siebeck), 1997.

4. Introduction of the Precursor, John the Baptiser Mk 1:4-6

The narrator introduces the precursor with all the solemnity of an Old Testament prophet. He uses the canonised LXX expression *egeneto*, often translated in the ritualised biblical language of English translations as 'it came to pass'. Though it makes for an awkward sentence, the solemnity would be well expressed by 'and it came to pass that John the Baptist was in the desert proclaiming ...' The messenger sent to prepare the way of the Lord, the one crying out in the desert, is identified as John the Baptist (lit. 'the one baptising').

John is preparing the way for the one coming after him. His baptism is a baptism of repentance for the remission of sins and it is sharply contrasted, by John himself, with the baptism in the Holy Spirit of the one coming after him. Baptism of repentance for the forgiveness of sins describes the nature and purpose of John's baptism. Unlike Matthew and Luke, the apocalyptic, fiery language of the wrath that is to come with the axe laid to the root of the tree and the burning up of the chaff is missing.[9] Missing also is the explicitly moralising tone of his preaching (Lk 3:7-14; cf Mt 3:7f). He calls for repentance, *metanoia*. This New Testament term signifies a change of mind, heart, attitude and direction as in reassessment of one's life and remorse for one's past. It is more or less synonymous with the Greek word *epistrephein*, 'to turn around', and the Hebrew word, *subh*, 'to turn back/return'. Turning round to face God in response and reconciliation, or returning to God and making a new beginning, are key concepts in the call to repentance. 'Repent' also captures the sense of the Hebrew *niham*, 'to be sorry'. Here in the prologue it represents the call back to God from the crooked paths on which one has strayed. The purpose of the exercise is the remission (*aphesis*) of sins. *Aphesis* (*aphiêmi*) signifies pardon, cancellation of a debt, release from captivity and remission of punishment. The people confess (*exomologoumenoi*) their sins. Confession of sins, in private and public, was reckoned as an important form of prayer/worship. This is obvious from the Old Testament, especially from the psalms, and from the apocryphal literature. Josephus Flavius states that God is easily reconciled to those who 'confess and repent', *exomologoumenois kai metanoousin*.[10]

9. Lk 3: 7, 9, 18; Mt 3:10-12. These verses are usually ascribed to the Q tradition which many scholars regard as a source for Matthew and Luke.
10. Ps 31 (32):5; 37 (38):18; 50 (51):3-5; cf Lev 5:5; *The Prayer of Manasseh*; Josephus, *War*, 5.415; cf *Ant.*, 18:117.

The account of John's movement emphasises the 'universal' character of the response to his call to repentance. '*All* the Judean countryside (*pasa*) and *all* the inhabitants of Jerusalem (*pantes*) went out to him.' This universal appeal on the part of the crowds in the context of the Baptist will be very characteristic of the response of the crowds to Jesus, particularly during his early ministry. In choosing the Jordan as the site for ritual baptism and inauguration into his movement, John the Baptist chose a place rich in associations with Israel's past. Crossing the Jordan dry shod behind the ark, which was carried in solemn procession into the promised land, was a pivotal moment in the history of the chosen people as they entered into the land to live there as God's covenanted people (Josh 3-4). Baptising in the Jordan river has the connotation of a spiritual crossing of the Jordan and it recalls the new life and dedication originally required of the people as they emerged from the desert wandering with its suffering and disaffection to the joyous occupation of the land of milk and honey. On that historic occasion they promised faithfulness to the covenant relationship with the God who had led them from the slavery of Egypt to the Promised Land. John's followers now come to the Jordan to renew that promise. The prophets had regularly called for repentance and for a return to the covenant way of life. Now John is the latest and final prophet in the former dispensation. His dress and deportment recall those of the prophets and of Elijah in particular (Zech 13:4; 2 Kings 1:8). His food consisted of locusts and wild honey. Locusts were one of the winged insects permitted in the Levitical code and featured in the Qumran diet (Lev 11:20-23; CD 12:14). Wild honey could be got from among the rocks, from trees and carcasses of animals (Deut 32:13; 1 Sam 14:25f; Jdgs 14:8f). The similarity to Elijah does not end with the description of John's clothes and diet. 'Preparing the way of the Lord' and announcing the coming of the 'stronger one' who will baptise in Holy Spirit and preparing for the one coming after him re-echo very strongly the expected return of Elijah to usher in the Messianic time. The gospel will show how the similarity with Elijah continues as John is arrested and put to death by a latter-day Ahab tricked by a scheming latter day-Jezebel (cf 1 Kings 19; Mk 6:17-29).

5. JOHN'S PROCLAMATION MK 1:7-8

Now after the narrator's introduction, John the Baptist's own voice is heard. Picking up on the solemn, prophetic note of proclamation (*kêryssôn*), the imperfect tense signifies ongoing and repeated activity. John was proclaiming (*ekêryssen*): 'the stronger one is coming after me'. The first word in the sentence is *erchetai*, 'he is coming'. 'The one who is coming' is an established messianic designation. The apocalyptic tradition speaks of the one coming from among the followers, from behind, to take over the leadership. Here *erchetai opisô mou*, 'there comes after me', alerts the reader to such a coming one, a follower who will take over the leadership, confirmed by John as he identifies the 'coming one' in terms of 'the one stronger than me', *ho ischuroteros mou*. The designation 'stronger one' not only alerts the reader to the relative strengths of Jesus and the Baptist but also recalls the divine visitation in Deutero-Isaiah where God will come 'with strength', *meta ischyos*. The God-given strength in the one coming will also be ' stronger' than the 'strong man', Satan, whose house he will spoil (Mk 3:20-27).

John'reference to the one whose sandal straps he is not worthy to bend down and untie, or carry, is common to all four gospels and Acts (Mt 3:11; Mk1:8; Lk 3:16; Jn 1:27; Acts 13:25). A disciple was expected to do for a teacher what a slave did for his master, except tend to his feet/untie his shoes, as it was regarded as too demeaning. Rabbi Joshua ben Levi states: 'All services that a slave performs for his master a pupil should do for his teacher, with the exception of undoing his shoes.'[11] John is here proclaiming that 'he is no more than a slave whose task is to untie his master's sandal; and he feels unworthy even of that'.[12]

To appreciate the significance of the contrast between their baptisms, which is highlighted by John the Baptist as he points to the one whose baptism in Holy Spirit radically surpasses his own baptism in water, John's baptism should be put in the context of the practice and understanding of baptism at the time.

The baptism of John fits into a wider context as is evident, for example, from the baptismal rituals of the Qumran community

---

11. *b.Ketuboth* 96a.
12. W. J. Harrington, *John, Spiritual Theologian*, 32. The remark about the sandals may be a reminder to those who continued to see John as the messianic figure, that John himself was the first to deny any such role for himself.

with which he may have had contact or by whom he may have been in some way influenced. Given the fact that he conducted his ministry in an area close to the monastery at Qumran it is quite possible that he was influenced in some measure by their asceticism, ceremonial practice and messianic expectation. Their Manual of Discipline is very definite, however, that mere washing cannot really make one clean. It can clean flesh, but only the submission of one's soul to God's ordinances can make one internally clean. It is only God who will finally purge all the acts of man and refine him by destroying every spirit of perversity in his flesh, cleansing him by a holy spirit and sprinkling upon him the spirit of truth like waters of purification to cleanse him.[13] The rite itself therefore was not seen as effecting forgiveness and purification and people could not use it to become like the holy ones. It was seen as an external expression of a sincere inner disposition of repentance. Josephus Flavius presents a similar view of John's baptism. He says that it was 'not to beg pardon for sins committed, but for the purification of the body, when the soul had previously been cleansed by right behaviour'.[14] Another possible influence may have been the process of proselyte baptism, signifying the cleansing process of a Gentile before entering into the spiritual heritage of Israel. These were the likely influences on John which he adapted for his purpose. Whatever the influences, however, John's practice of ritual baptism, as it stands here in the gospel, is unique to John in its broad scope and eschatological thrust.[15] He, however, emphasised the preparatory nature of his baptism and accentuated the contrast with the baptism by Jesus who will baptise in Holy Spirit A new era and a new baptism are about to be inaugurated with the rending of the heavens, the descent of the Spirit on Jesus and the voice from heaven proclaiming him 'My Son, the Beloved.'

6. INTRODUCTION OF THE PROTAGONIST. JESUS' BAPTISM MK 1:9-11

The same solemn word *egeneto*, 'it came to pass', is used to announce Jesus' entry into the story. It is here combined with another evocative expression, 'in those days', a phrase canonised

---

13. I QS 3:7-9; 4:20-22; I QH 16:12; cf 7:6; 17:26; fragment 2:9, 3. The influence of Ezekiel is evident here (Ezek 36:25-27).
14. Josephus, *Antiquities of the Jews*, 18:117.
15. J. P. Meier, *A Marginal Jew* 2, 53-55, sees John's baptism as quite original to John.

in biblical tradition as a description of the times in which some
great salvific event took place (Jdgs 19:1; 1 Sam 28:1). When
Jesus came from Nazareth in Galilee and was baptised by John
in the Jordan a new era was about to begin. As Jesus came up out
of the water the definitive salvific work of God began 'immediately' with the rending of the heavens and the descent of the
Spirit like a dove. This is the first instance of the use of the word
euthus, 'immediately'. Forty-seven times *euthus* (often *kai euthus*
and sometimes its adverbial variant *eutheôs*) is used, giving the
story of Jesus' ministry, especially in its initial stages in the
Galilee ministry, its sense of urgency as the kingdom rushes in
all around.

The rending or tearing open of the heavens described in the
immediate aftermath of the baptism of Jesus is an eschatological
sign, announcing the inauguration of the final definitive action
of God. It recalls the sentiment of Trito-Isaiah, ' O that you
would rend the heavens and come down ... to make known
your name to your enemies, and make the nations tremble at
your presence, working unexpected miracles such as no one has
ever heard before' (Isa 64:1-3; cf Isa 24:17-20; Rev 19:11).[16] Here
at the baptism scene the rending of the heavens and the heavenly
voice represent the divine presence, transcendent and immanent, joining earth and heaven, somewhat like the (Jacob's) ladder
image in John's gospel (Jn 1:51). J. Marcus explains the significance exceptionally well: 'God has ripped the heavens apart ir-
revocably at Jesus' baptism, never to shut them again. Through
this gracious gash in the universe, he has poured forth his Spirit
into the earthly realm.'[17]

The opening of the heavens and the descent of the Spirit
mark a completely new initiative of God in the economy of salvation. Contrary to the impression given by many works of
Christian art, the Spirit was not conferred on Jesus by the baptism of John but descended on him on the occasion of, and immediately following, the baptism, as he came up out of the
water. Mark (like Matthew) states that Jesus had already been
baptised and was coming up out of the water when the Spirit descended upon him (Mk 1:10; Mt 3:16). Luke further emphasises

16. The rending of the heavens is reflected in, and forms an inclusion
with, the rending of the veil of the Temple at the crucifixion, and both
'rendings' are followed by a declaration of the divine sonship of Jesus.
17. J. Marcus, *Mark 1-8*, 165.

the point when he says that he had been baptised and was at prayer when the Spirit descended on him (Lk 3:21). The gospel of John omits any reference to the actual baptism of Jesus and refers only to the descent of the Spirit showing him to be the Son/the Chosen One of God (Jn 1:32).[18]

Though the ministry of John is unique and the baptism of Jesus without parallel, still the narrative is rich in biblical allusions, setting it within the wider scope of salvation history. Many see in the figure of the dove appearing above the waters of the Jordan an allusion to creation with the Spirit of God hovering over the waters (Gen 1:2) or to the dove sent out by Noah heralding the ending of the flood, the completion of the punishment and the inauguration of a new covenant (Gen 8:8-12).[19] For the readers in the Hellenistic world, comparing the Spirit to a dove highlighted the divinity of the Spirit since the dove was regarded as a divine bird in the Hellenistic world.[20] The descent of the Spirit, therefore, points to the divine origin and power of the one about to be declared Beloved Son by the voice from heaven.

All these allusions point to the new initiative of God, a new creation and a new definitive reconciliation. Whereas the baptism of John was called a baptism of repentance (Mk 1:4), and could be graphically described as an empty hand stretched out to God for forgiveness, the baptism of Jesus signifies the beginning of a new era, a pivotal point in the economy of salvation, a new and final initiative of God in Jesus. This new era will be marked by the gift of the Spirit.[21] Baptism as an empty hand stretched out to God in repentance is now surpassed by the

---

18. In the synoptics this descent of the Spirit signifies the anointing of the Messiah and is interpreted by the witnessing voice of the Father (Isa 42:1; Ps 2:7). It signifies also the return of the quenched Spirit in a Spirit anointed Messiah (Isa 11:2; 42:1; 61:1) and the eschatological event heralded by the rending of the heavens (Isa 64:1). Furthermore the river has salvific significance in the biblical tradition where it can be seen to symbolise life (Ezek 47:1-12), forgiveness (LXX Ezek 47:3) and healing (2 Kings 5:14).

19. The hovering of the Spirit in Gen 1:2 is like the hovering of a bird above the nest inciting the young to fly. The bird in question was interpreted by the rabbis as a dove brooding above the nestlings. The song of the turtle dove in Song of Songs 2:12 was interpreted in the Targum on the Song of Songs as the voice of the Spirit.

20. R. H. Gundry, *op. cit.*, 4.

21. cf Acts 19:1ff as a practical manifestation of the promised reality.

promise of baptism in Holy Spirit, announcing the beginning of the eschatological time, marked by the return of the Spirit and the work of the Messiah. Baptism has taken on a whole new significance.[22]

After the end of the prophetic times, when the Spirit no longer spoke through the prophets, the rabbis spoke of the *bath qôl*, 'daughter of the voice', the faint echo of the divine voice uttered in heaven. This 'voice from heaven' at the baptism, accompanied by the return of the quenched Spirit is no faint echo, but the sound of the voice (*phônê*) of the Father, transcendent and immanent at this moment, addressing Jesus saying: 'You are my Beloved Son in whom I am well pleased' (Ps 2:7). There is a density of meaning here. First of all it recalls Psalm 2 which probably reflects an enthronement ceremony, where the metaphor of adoption as God's son (Ps 2:7) assures the royal prince of God's protection at his enthronement as Davidic King. However, this sonship transcends the general sonship of the anointed king, the righteous priest, prophet or prince and the suffering righteous one, or the collective sonship of the people. The term *agapêtos*, 'beloved', reflects the Hebrew *yahid*, 'unique', as in 'only son' (as *monogenês* in Jn 1:18) and therefore especially beloved, as in the case of Isaac (Gen 22:2, 12, 16). It also reflects the Hebrew *bakîr*, 'chosen', as in the appointment of the chosen servant of God, in whom God is well pleased and in whom he puts his spirit. This recalls the suffering servant, obedient to God to the end in spite of persecution, and suffering vicariously on behalf of others, taking their faults on himself and praying all the time for sinners (Isa 42:1-2; 52:13-53:12). The divine voice speaks in the second person addressing Jesus in the baptism scene, 'You are my Beloved Son ...' But later in the ministry, at the transfiguration, the voice will address the disciples speaking of Jesus in the third person: 'This is my Beloved Son ...'(Mk 9:7). Jesus is thus declared a messianic prince-king, a prophetic style servant, but above all the Beloved Son in a unique way.[23]

22. 'Baptism' can signify the beginning of a new life and a new state and similarly 'Baptism in a Holy Spirit' signifies the beginning of a new state involving a new and critical 'religious' experience (cf Acts 1:5; 11:16). It can signify a crisis and decision about one's response to the Messiah. Jesus himself used the metaphor of baptism for his impending passion and death (Mk 10:38; Lk 12:50).

23. Towards the end of his ministry in Jerusalem Jesus challenges the scribes' teaching that the Messiah is (merely) son of David and goes on

The 'installation' of Jesus in his role resembles (though in a much less dramatic way) that of Ezekiel who was also installed at the bank of a river as winged creatures (Ezek 1:1ff) appeared in the sky, and was then transported to another place by the spirit. The difference here is that Jesus does not become son at this point but his sonship is revealed to him, as it will be revealed to the three chosen disciples at the transfiguration (Mk 9:7). He is not sent on a mission, told what to say or do like the prophets of old, as in the case of Ezekiel eating the scroll or Jeremiah accepting that God would 'put my words in to your mouth' as he was sent 'to tear up and knock down, to build and to plant'(Jer 1:9f). Jesus' authority and mission spring from who he is, the Beloved Son, which has been declared to him and from the power of the Spirit, an integral constituent of his role as Messiah. His testing in the desert will show that the Spirit has not just paid him a fleeting visit, but in the words of John's gospel, the Spirit remains/dwells (*menein*) with him (Jn 1:32).

7. TESTING IN THE DESERT MK 1:12-13

The narrator has let the reader in on the private revelation of the Father to the Son and is now about to let the reader in on the private temptation or struggle of Jesus in the desert as he prepares for his ministry. Jesus Christ, Son of God, has been introduced to the reader. Now Satan, the source and personification of the forces of opposition throughout the story about to unfold, is introduced to the reader. The Spirit is mentioned three times in the prologue – in John's description of Jesus' future ministry, in the description of the descent of the Spirit on Jesus just after his baptism, and in the action of the Spirit in driving Jesus into the desert to be tested by Satan. The prologue thus introduces the divine powers behind the ministry of Jesus and the evil power, Satan, the arch-foe behind the opposition to him. At the same time the agents of divine support, the angels, are introduced. This brings out clearly at the outset that '… those who play a part in the rest of the book are not really the main characters in the drama about Jesus, but that hidden behind them there is another and more important struggle, of which the main figures are God and Satan'.[24] The Spirit is constitutive of the role of the

---

to point out that David himself calls him'Lord', elevating him to the divine plain (Mk 12:35-37).
24. B. van Iersel, *Reading Mark*, 34.

Messiah/Christ, the Anointed One, and when Jesus' role and the power behind it are challenged and he is accused of casting out demons by the power of the prince of devils, Jesus describes it as blasphemy against the Holy Spirit, and designates it 'an eternal sin' (Mk 3: 22, 29-31).

The breaking in and onrush of the kingdom is again highlighted by the expression 'and immediately', *kai euthus*, which opens the sentence describing Jesus' transportation into the desert. 'And immediately the Spirit drives him into the wilderness/desert'. The verb *ekballein* is the verb used for the driving out of demons and for other acts of coercion in the gospel. It reflects the power of the Spirit which will be active behind the scenes in Jesus' ministry. Forty days in the wilderness conjures up the memory of Israel's experience on escaping from Egypt and experiencing the presence of God in their midst leading them through the wilderness for forty years. It conjures up also the memory of their struggle in the desert between accepting the unfolding if yet unclear plan of God and the desire to return to Egypt. It echoes also the stories of many other figures going there to recapture the original experience of Israel before God in the wilderness. It recalls the experience of the forty day journey of Elijah to Horeb (Sinai) when he was assisted in his exhausted state by the angel (1 Kings 19:1-8).

The desert was the place of testing, of temptation, of fiery serpents. In popular imagination it was the place of threatening wild beasts, the home of demons and forces of destruction. It was the opposite of the Garden of Eden where harmony existed between God, humanity, the animals and the earth. Jesus was driven there by the Spirit. He was tested by Satan. He is like a new Adam, in harmony with God and at home with the wild beasts, a reminder of the prophetic promise that in messianic times the harmony of man and beast would be restored when 'the lion lies down with the lamb, the cow and the bear make friends and the infant plays over the cobra's hole' (Isa 11: 6-9). Here the battle lines are drawn between Satan, the strong man, and Jesus the stronger man in the gospel.[25] The narrator leaves

25. In Matthew and Luke the significance of the testing is spelled out in terms of the temptations to feed the crowd with physical food alone, to grasp at political power and to bypass the response in repentance and faith with miraculous proof. The tempter had begun his adversarial activity in Matthew and Luke by saying 'If you are the son of God …' Jesus' responses to the temptations in Matthew and Luke removed the 'if'!

the reader wondering about the exact nature of the testing/temptation and the exact identity of Satan. For the time being the reader is left to wonder. One thing, however, will become obvious very quickly in the narrative, and it is probably as a result of this initial testing. The demonic powers know who Jesus really is. The Beloved Son, empowered by the Spirit, has been tested and not found wanting.

The wild beasts also symbolise the evil powers that will threaten Jesus and his mission. But tradition, as seen in Ps 90 (91), also associates the protective care of the angels with the one present among the wild beasts. The Psalmist reflected: 'He will give his angels charge over you, to keep you in all your ways … on the lion and the viper you will tread and trample the young lion and the dragon …'(Ps 90 (91):11-13).[26] Daniel emerged from the lions' den with the affirmation, 'My God sent his angel who sealed the lions' jaws so they did me no harm since in his sight I am blameless …'(Dan 6:21-23). Similarly, the men tested in the fiery furnace were protected by the angel of the Lord (Dan 3:49). In his desert sojourn the angel came to the aid of Elijah in his hunger and weakness (1 Kings 19:1-8). St Luke speaks of the angel comforting Jesus in Gethsemane (Lk 22:43). Mark significantly closes his account of the testing (temptation) with the assertion 'and the angels ministered to him'.

The preparation of *the way of the Lord* is complete. The recognition, empowering and testing of the protagonist have taken place and the good news is now being proclaimed in a whole new mission in Galilee (Mk 1:41, 15). The prologue has achieved its goal. Mark emphasises the fact by confining the account of the Baptist's ministry to the prologue and introducing the ministry of Jesus with the words 'after John had been arrested'. The story of John's arrest and murder will be by way of reminiscence after his death (Mk 6:14-29). In contrast to the Johannine tradition which has a chronological overlap between the ministries of John and Jesus, the synoptics put a clear division between the two eras by having Jesus' ministry begin after John's arrest. However, though verses 14 and 15 form an inclusion with Mk 1:1 both in the reference to the *euaggelion* and to Jesus' continuing the call for repentance, a new era has already begun, and it is accompanied by a change of time and place as Jesus returns to

26. This psalm is actually quoted in the temptation accounts in Mt 4:6 and Lk 4:10.

Galilee whence he had come for the baptism of John and all that accompanied it. The activity at the Jordan and in the desert comes to a close. A new mission in a new area is about to begin.

The reader has now been led to see that God is the prime mover behind the good news of Jesus Christ, Son of God, the Lord for whom the precursor was sent to prepare the way. Jesus from Nazareth in Galilee is the Christ, the Son of God, the Lord on whom the Spirit descended at baptism and whom the Spirit subsequently drove out into the desert. He is the one whom the Father through the heavenly voice addressed as 'my Son the Beloved' and reassured with the promise 'my favour rests on you'. Satan represents the forces to be confronted and the protecting forces of God are represented by the presence of the angels. The reader is now equipped to read the story from a privileged position shared with the 'omniscient' narrator (though the narrator has a lot more to reveal). From the prologue one has acquired the necessary key to interpreting the gospel.[27]

8. THE GOOD NEWS PROCLAIMED BY JESUS

The introduction to the 'beginning of the good news of Jesus Christ, Son of God' is complete. Jesus, the embodiment of the good news of God, becomes the messenger of the good news of the kingdom as he embarks on his ministry in Galilee. Now he begins his own and the reader's adventure through his ministry as he comes into Galilee proclaiming the good news and calling on all and sundry to repent and believe in the good news (Mk 1:14, 15).

In the prologue we have a concentration of 'high' christological material, insight into the identity of Jesus and a privileged observation of the arrival of the Spirit and the voice from heaven. The rest of the gospel unfolds on a more 'earthly' plane, with the exception of the transfiguration (Mk 9:9) and some scenes with epiphanic or christophanic elements, such as the calming of the storm (Mk 4:35-41) and Jesus' coming over the water to the disciples (Mk 6:45-52). M. D. Hooker puts it very well:

> It is as though Mark were allowing us to view the drama from a heavenly vantage point (whence we see things as they really are) before he brings us down to earth, where we find characters in the story totally bewildered by what is going on.'[28]

27. See F. J. Matera: 'The Prologue as the Interpretative Key to Mark's Gospel', *JSNT* 34 (1988), 3-20.
28. M. D. Hooker, *The Gospel according to St Mark*, 32.

The Ministry in Galilee Mk 1:14-6:6a

Jesus reveals himself and his Mission

OVERALL PLOT AND OUTLINE

The ministry in Galilee is the first of the three major sections of the gospel dealing with the public ministry of Jesus. Here Jesus travels restlessly about the area. Here he gathers his inner group of disciples and a larger group of followers and wins the enthusiastic support of the crowds. He enters into controversy with the scribes and Pharisees on matters of authority such as the authority to forgive sins and on legal observance such as fasting laws, eating with tax collectors and sinners and Sabbath observance. He moves between house, synagogue, corn fields and open spaces. He retires to a lonely place, and has a special fondness for the shore of the lake, which is called here, unusually, the Lake of Galilee, again keeping the focus of attention on the 'local' character of the Galilee mission.[1]

The account of the ministry in Galilee is composed of three distinct and clearly defined sections. Like a drama it has three acts made up of smaller scenes or movements, each with a clear opening, development and conclusion. In each the opening consists of a summary, covering Jesus' ongoing activity. This is followed by a focus on the calling, commissioning or sending out of the disciples/apostles. The focus on the disciples/apostles is followed by Jesus' mighty words and deeds which produce a reaction of acceptance, rejection or misunderstanding. The conclusion in each case focuses on the negative reactions of hostility, non-belief and misunderstanding. In the first case, a coalition of religious and civil authorities from the opposite ends of the socio-political and religious establishments, represented by the scribes of the Pharisee party and the Herodians, plan to destroy him (Mk 3:6), then his own people in his native place refuse to believe in him (Mk 6:6a), and finally his disciples fail to understand him (Mk 8:21). This hostility, rejection and misunderstanding, together with Jesus' resolute response to it and his attempts to bring the disciples along with him in his resolve,

---

1. The more usual names for the lake were Kinneret or Gennesaret.

provide the ongoing dynamic which creates the tension and keeps the reader in suspense from the initial plan to destroy him (Mk 3:6) to its execution on Golgotha and God's response articulated through the young man at the tomb. The three sections of the Galilee ministry could be summed up thematically as follows:

A. Jesus with the crowds and the authorities. Mk 1:14-3:6.

Jesus calls for repentance and announces the imminent coming of the kingdom. He teaches with authority and matches his teaching with mighty action. He calls his first disciples. He breaks boundaries and engages in controversy. He evokes an enthusiastic response from the crowd and an increasingly hostile reaction from authority which ends in a decision to destroy him.

B. Jesus with his disciples and his family. Mk 3:7-6:6a.

Jesus chooses his new family of disciples. His family think he is mad and try to seize him. The scribes accuse him of working through the power of Beelzebul.He delivers the long parabolic sermon and performs miracles on sea and land. He is rejected in his native place and by his own people.

C. Jesus and the apostles/disciples. The Bread Section. Mk 6:6b-8:26

Jesus appoints the Twelve. The fate of John the Baptist is recounted. Then in two parallel series Jesus feeds the two multitudes, one predominantly Jewish, the other Gentile. He twice crosses to the other side of the lake, twice disputes with the Pharisees, gives general instruction and carries out healings of Jews and Gentiles. The section ends with a strong emphasis on the disciples' lack of understanding.

Jesus with the Crowds and the Authorities Mk 1:14-3:6 Set in Galilee: Initial Response and Reaction

1. PLOT AND OUTLINE

Mk 1:14-3:6 describes Jesus' arrival in Galilee and his proclam-ation that 'the time has come' and 'the kingdom of God is close at hand,' followed by his unconditional call to repentance and belief in the good news. This summary is followed by the calling of the first disciples and their immediate unconditional re-sponse. His first confrontation with the demonic forces takes place on the first Sabbath appearance in a synagogue, followed immediately by his overcoming of the forces of sickness in heal-ing Simon's mother-in-law and the crowds assembling around the door at sundown. His reputation spreads rapidly within and without the people of Israel. Then the leper comes and intro-duces another dimension, the outcast crosses the social and reli-gious boundary and presents himself to Jesus, begging to be healed. This is followed by a series of 'controversies' with mounting criticism and opposition on the part of authority fig-ures until the second appearance in a synagogue on the Sabbath when the hostility comes to a climax and results in a plan to do away with Jesus. This section, Mk 1:14-3:6, could be seen as the gospel story in miniature.

2. SUMMARY MK 1:14-15

After John had been handed over, Jesus came into Galilee. The era of John is completed. Jesus enters the public arena. *Handed over, paradothênai,* stands out at the beginning of Jesus' ministry as the fate of the one who initiated the story by preparing the way of the Lord. It prefigures exactly the fate of Jesus who is now beginning his public ministry. He too will be *handed over.*[2] He will warn his disciples and followers that the same fate may lie in store for them also.[3]

The summary in Mk 1:14-15 serves as a summary and also as an introduction both to the larger section of the gospel set in Galilee and surrounding regions (Mk 1:14-8:30) and to the im-

---

2. 'He is handed over into the hands of men ...' (Mk 9:31); 'He will be handed over to the chief priests and the scribes' (Mk10:33); 'one of you will hand me over' (Mk 14:18).
3. 'They will hand you over to sanhedrins ...' Mk 13:9.

mediate subsection (Mk 1:14-3:6). There are similar summaries
in Mk 3:7-12 and 6:6b. All three of them mention a change of
venue on Jesus' part, followed by a summary statement of his
activity. Known as 'summary statements' or 'transitional passages'[4] they function as hinges or bridges that sum up what has
gone before and set the programme for what follows.

Jesus came into Galilee *proclaiming the good news of God*. The
public nature of Jesus' proclamation stands out at the beginning
through the use of the verb 'proclaiming' (*keryssôn*) describing
the activity of a public herald (*kêryx*). Mark alone among the
evangelists adds 'of God' to the term 'good news', emphasising
its origin, as already emphasised in the prologue. Jesus' proclaiming of the good news will be both in word and deed, a
teaching with authority behind it. The time, the *kairos*, is fulfilled, that is, the time planned and laid out by God has been
'achieved', arrived at. The kingdom of God is imminent, in fact it
is arrived already. The immediacy of its arrival is emphasised by
the use of the perfect tense of the verb, *êggiken*. Jesus calls for an
unconditional response: 'repent (*metanoeite*) and believe (*pis-
teueite*) in the good news.'

Calling for repentance, Jesus is seen to be solidly within the
tradition of the prophets who time and again called on the people of Israel to turn from their evil ways and return to the God of
the covenant. Jesus' initial call is to the people Israel, but it is a
call that does not stop at the borders of Israel. It is a call that will
fulfil the prophecy of Isaiah that God's house will be a place of
prayer for all the nations (Isa 56:7; Mk 11:17). The repercussions
of Jesus' ministry will bring about a whole new religious scenario, like new wine which needs new skins, a new patch that
cannot be sewn onto old clothes (Mk 2:21f).

It is difficult to give a clear definition of the kingdom of God,[5]
partly because the term is used in different ways and partly because it is used for its evocative power. It is very rare outside the
synoptics where it is found on the lips of Jesus.[6] The actual term
is found only once in the Old Testament (Wisdom10:10) and was

---

4. Scholars regularly use the term 'Sammelberichte', a term coined by
German scholars for these summaries.
5. Matthew uses the term 'kingdom of heaven' to avoid using the divine
name. It refers to the same reality. Mark does not use 'kingdom of heaven'.
6. The two uses of the term in the Dialogue with Nicodemus in John's
gospel (Jn 3:3, 5) are unusual in the Johannine tradition.

not current in contemporary Judaism. W. J. Harrington says: 'The kingdom, though in its fullness still in the future, comes as a present offer, in actual gift, through the proclamation of the good news. But it arrives only on condition of the positive response of the hearer.'[7] In the parabolic discourse Jesus will state 'To *you* has been *given* the *mystery* of the kingdom …' (Mk 4:11). Three factors are important. The kingdom is a gift of God. It is given *to you*, that is to those open to receive and respond to it. It is described as a mystery, an unfolding plan of God, partly seen and partly hidden, partly present and partly in the future. Its presence issues in a challenge to respond here and now, its future beckons us to look beyond the here and now, beyond the world as we know it, to see all things in relation to their ending and reconstitution in the eschatological kingdom. This calls for a paradoxical outlook on life and the world with its established assessments and values.[8]

Bas van Iersel says of the kingdom:

It refers to a future event as yet unknown, as well as to a present reality one may already accept. In order to enter God's kingdom there are things in life you must do and other things you must leave undone, and in that sense it is intimately connected with the theme of 'the way'. The kingdom can be recognised but it is at the same time hidden. Likewise it is closely bound up with Jesus' presence and activity, his speaking and doing, and at the same time with the son of man who is to come when the end time, begun in Jesus, is one day fulfilled. So it is no accident that Jesus employs the language of parable, simile and metaphor when speaking about the kingdom of God.[9]

J. R. Donahue and D. J. Harrington comment in similar vein, saying that 'The recovery of Jesus' vision of the kingdom of God

---

7. W. J. Harrington, *Mark, Realistic Theologian*, 33.
8. S. Légasse, *L'évangile de Marc*, (Italian trans.), 222, states: *senza perdere la sua dimensione futura e finale e senza evolversi, come altrove nel Nuovo Testamento, verso un Regno di Cristo, il Regno di Dio è condizionato dal atto di seguire Gesù e la sua instaurazione definitiva e gloriosa coincide con la parusia … Infine, come nozione sintetica, esso ingloba tutto l'opera di rinnovamento e di salvezza inaugurata da Cristo.*
9. Bas van Iersel, *op. cit.*, 42; See B. T. Viviano, *The Kingdom of God in History*, Collegeville: The Liturgical Press, 1991, and B. J. Malina, *The Social History of Jesus. The Kingdom of God in Mediterranean Perspective*, Min.: Fortress, 2001.

was one of the great achievements of theology in the twentieth
century. And along with it comes the recognition that this demands a response that involves not only a change in attitude
('place your faith in the good news') but also a change of life ('repent'). In addition they emphasise the fact that the Kingdom is
'God's project'.

Most commentators hold that Mark in 1:15 presents an accurate summary of the main thrust in Jesus' ministry in word
and deed: the proclamation of God's kingdom and a change
of heart and faith as the proper human responses. However,
it is not easy to define the 'kingdom of God' because it is future in its fullness and transcendent in its origin. The kingdom is ultimately God's project ...

Jesus shared the belief of his Jewish contemporaries that
the fullness of God's kingdom is future, and yet, according to
Mark and the other evangelists, Jesus saw in his own person
and ministry the beginning or inauguration of God's reign:
'Now is the time of fulfilment; and the kingdom of God is at
hand' (Mk 1:15a). Whatever Jesus said or did was in the service of God's kingdom.[10]

Jesus is herald and agent, but the reign/kingdom belongs to
God. J. P. Meier, in his study of the historical Jesus, states that:
'The kingdom of God was simply Jesus' special and somewhat
abstract way of speaking of God himself coming in power to
manifest his definitive rule in the end time. God coming in
power to rule in the end of time: that is the point of Jesus'
phraseology.'[11]

In the Old Testament and other Jewish writings the term
'kingdom of God' is rare, but the related idea 'God is king' is
very frequent in references to God as Lord or primary agent in
history, at its beginning, throughout its unfolding course and in
the predictions of the consummation of creation and history
when God's definitive reign will be established. This is obvious
in the creation accounts, in the Exodus and wandering narratives, in the royal and enthronement psalms and in the eschatological writings of the prophets.

This idea of God as king, closely linked to the idea of God as
Shepherd of Israel who leads and cares for the flock, underpins
the concept of God's reign or kingdom as Jesus proclaims and

10. J. R. Donahue and D. J. Harrington, *op. cit.*, 72.
11. J. P. Meier, *A Marginal Jew, Vol 2*, 414.

seeks to establish it. Speaking of ' God's reign' emphasises the fact of God's activity, while 'God's kingdom' tends to emphasise the location or sphere of influence of that activity. Both dimensions are found in the gospel but the former is the more common. For those who are open to repenting and accepting the coming of the kingdom, there must be an acceptance of the sovereignty of God over all things, an awareness of the providence of God in their lives and a hope for a sharing in the fullness of the kingdom in the fullness of time.

Since the fullness of the kingdom is in the future, there is an unfulfilled aspect to it in the here and now. This leads to a sense of secrecy, a mystery or plan of God as yet undisclosed, and a resulting tension between the known and unknown, the already revealed and as yet hidden. The future therefore has a strongly determining influence on the present, setting the present 'given' nature of the kingdom in the greater eschatological perspective.

3. CALL OF THE DISCIPLES MK 1:16-20

After the summary statement the focus turns to the calling of the first disciples. These disciples, either the whole group, the Twelve or the inner group of Peter, James and John, will be 'with him' throughout his ministry until they abandon him in Gethsemane and take flight. Mark presents the call of the disciples as stark and sudden, like the calling of a prophet in the Old Testament, without forewarning. It is a reversal of the usual rabbinic procedure where the disciple seeks out the rabbi, and it resembles more the calling of the prophets (Isa 6:1-13; Jer 1:14-19; Ezek 1:1-3), where the parentage and profession of those called are often given together with their response. The details of leaving family and livelihood, though far less dramatic, are reminiscent of Elijah's call of Elisha, son of Shaphat, who left his family and his servants and sacrificed his oxen using the wood of the plough for the fire (1 Kings 19:19-21). Mark's account is in sharp contrast to the account in John's gospel which portrays a previous knowledge of the disciples on Jesus' part during the ministry of the Baptist, or Luke's account of the call after they have experienced Jesus' works, especially the miraculous catch of fish (Jn 1:35-51; Lk 5:1-11). Unlike Luke or John, Mark gives no hint of any preparation, just a stark call as in the case of the prophets.[12]

12. This resembles also the calling of some famous philosophers in the Greco-Roman world, such as the calling of Xenophon by Socrates who

Jesus' call is not a result of seeing some particular gift or aptit-
ude in those called, but a free act of graciousness on his part.

The two call narratives are in similar form. The first one describes Jesus moving (*paragôn*) along the shore and seeing the
prospective disciples and their work. It describes their relationship as brothers, recounts Jesus' call to them to 'come after me
(*deute opisô mou*) and I will make you fishers of men (people)',[13]
and their immediate response: 'and immediately (*kai euthus*)
they left their nets and followed (*êkolouthêsan*) him.' In the calling of the second pair of brothers Jesus is again described as
moving: 'having moved on a little' (*probas oligon*), he saw the
prospective disciples. The narrator tells their names and the fact
they were brothers, and names their father. He called them immediately (*euthus*) and 'leaving their father Zebedee in the boat
with the hired men they went after him (*apêlthon opisô autou*).'
The use of *euthus* stresses the immediate follow-up action of
Jesus in calling the second pair of brothers. In both cases the initiative is entirely with Jesus. He called whom he willed. The two
descriptions, 'they followed him' (*êkolouthêsan autô*) and 'came
after him' (*apêlthon opisô autou*) are two designations of discipleship which will be very important throughout the story.

The reader immediately sees a distinction between the second and the former pair whose father is not named. The former
pair are probably older, their father deceased, the second pair
younger, their father still alive. The first pair left their nets, symbols of their occupation and security, the second left their father
and his employees, pointing to the leaving behind the security
of family and occupation. Some commentators point to the different social background implied by the fact that the second pair
seem to come from a family business. 'The peer group's criteria
of success in life are abandoned: tools of trade (nets and boats)
and servants. Servants were a major sign of their success, as they
control a workforce.'[14] They had abandoned their power structure. They had left the security of family and livelihood. It is in-

said to him, 'Follow, then, and learn.' Diogenes Laertius, *Lives of
Eminent Philosophers*, 2:48.
13. See J. Murphy-O'Connor, 'Fishers of Fish, Fishers of Men', *BR* 15/3
(1999) and G. Fischer and M. Hasitschka, *The Call of the Disciple. The Bible
on Following Christ*, NY: Paulist, 1999.
14. F. J. Moloney, *The Gospel of Mark: A Commentary*, Peabody, Mass:
Hendrickson, 53.

teresting that the second pair will be inquiring of Jesus later on about positions of prominence in the kingdom, and even more significantly in ways is the fact that their mother will do the inquiring on their behalf in Matthew's parallel account (Mk 10:35-40; Mt 20:20-23). The call of Levi will follow the same pattern, but in his case it will be a calling of a controversial kind because he is a tax-collector, a very unpopular profession, putting him on the wrong side of the boundary of acceptability in Israel (Mk 2:13-14). The call narrative in each of these three cases could be illustrated as follows, with Jesus' act of calling at the centre:

    a. Jesus passes along.
        b. He sees them (him). Family/livelihood described.
           c. He calls them (him).
        b. They (he) leave (s) family/livelihood
    a. They (he) follow(s)/go(es) with Jesus.

By way of contrast, later on in the ministry, the calling of the rich young man, whose name is not given or whose parents are not mentioned, but whose personal dispositions and circumstances are described, will fail to elicit a positive response because of his attachment to wealth and possessions (Mk 10:17-22).

4. JESUS' MIGHTY WORDS AND DEEDS MK 1:21-3:5

As Jesus proclaims the kingdom, he confronts the demonic powers and brings forgiveness, restoration and healing to the victims of evil, sin, sickness, prejudice and ignorance. He communicates in words and deeds and by his powerful presence. His words come in many forms: instructions, prohibitions, appeals, parables, riddles, discussions and disputes. He teaches 'as one having authority and not like the scribes'. His power in word is matched by his power in deed, a new teaching combined with authority over unclean spirits (Mk 1:27). His words and deeds form a continuum. What he says is authenticated by the power manifest in his deeds and his deeds are themselves a teaching through action about the nature of the kingdom and a manifestation of the power of the Spirit in Jesus and his ministry.

Jesus' healings and exorcisms not only show his power over the forces of sickness and the evil spirits but they restore the ill or possessed person to full active participation in the people of God. Healing a sick or possessed person points beyond the physical healing to a healing of the destructive and alienating effects of sin and the gift of forgiveness. Healing the deaf and the blind are in themselves a call *to listen* to the word and *to see* the activity of the kingdom in the person and ministry of Jesus. There are also the miracles of calming the storm on the lake and the miraculous feeding of the multitudes in deserted places, recalling the God's power over creation and provision of food for the people in the desert, power now manifest in the person and work of Jesus. These are the so-called 'nature' miracles,[15] but M. D. Hooker very aptly points out that 'nature miracles' is 'hardly a good description, since it suggests a belief that in these particular cases Jesus was controlling nature, but that he was not doing so in the miracles of healing.'[16]

i. A Sabbath in Capernaum Mk 1:21-34

In the synagogue Mk 1:21-28

After the calling of the disciples Mark describes a 'typical' or paradigmatic Sabbath day[17] during the ministry of Jesus in Capernaum.[18] The verb, *edidasken*, 'he was teaching', is in the imperfect tense signifying ongoing or repeated activity, giving the impression of a typical or repeating pattern of behaviour. Whereas his calling for repentance and his proclamation of the coming of the kingdom cast him very much in the role of prophet, here in the synagogue we see him in the role of teacher, following in the tradition of the sages of Israel. He teaches 'as one having authority and not like the scribes'. His teaching is matched by his deeds. As the story of his ministry unfolds the reader will see how the people and his disciples will call him 'teacher' as he teaches them about the kingdom and about discipleship. His townsfolk will wonder where he acquired his wisdom and the 'professional' religious and legal teachers will be confounded by his teaching on the Sabbath, divorce, paying

---

15. For a recent study of the question of Jesus' miracles see: G. H. Twelftree, *Jesus the Miracle Worker. A Historical and Theological Study*, Downers Grove, Ill: Intervarsity, 1999.

16. M. D. Hooker, *op. cit.*, 72.

17. The expression 'on the sabbath' here at Mk 1:21 (and again in Mk 2:23, 25; 3:2, 4) is actually in plural form in Greek, *tois sabbasin*, whereas the *logia* in Mk 2:27,28 about the sabbath being for man and the Son of Man being master of the Sabbath use the singular, *to Sabbaton*.

18. The name means 'village of Naum'. Jesus' ministry in Galilee was centred on this important fishing town on the north-west shore of the lake. It was also a frontier town between Galilee and the Greek towns of the Decapolis, hence the presence of a toll collector.

taxes to Caesar, the reality and nature of the resurrection and the greatest commandment of the Law. In particular he will be portrayed as a teacher in parables.

Jesus, on this first occasion of a visit to the synagogue, preaches, casts out a demon, and shows the intimate connection between his word and deed. His authority in teaching is matched by his authority in action. The people were amazed at his teaching. The primary focus of their attention was not the miracle but the teaching that had such authority behind it. Teaching for the most part in this gospel (with the exception of the parabolic discourse in chapter 4 and the eschatological-apocalyptic discourse in chapter 13) is not conveyed in long sermons like those in Matthew or Luke or the discourses in John, but in short pithy sayings and 'parables' or 'riddles'. The teaching comes largely in the experience of the authority/power of his combined person-action-word which provokes the reactions of awe, fear, wonder, misunderstanding and hostility. These will be recurring themes throughout the ministry as the people are amazed at his preaching, healing, and exorcisms. The disciples will be awestruck at epiphanies and power over nature, and fearful at his predictions of rejection, suffering and rising from the dead. At the same time his power/authority will be a power exercised in service, suffering, failure, rejection and execution. Paradoxically it is in these examples he will finally show himself the 'stronger one', the *ischuroteros*. His authority, *exousia*, will be manifest in his power over the destructive elements that oppress and dehumanise people, whether they be the power of demons, sickness, death, oppressive religious structures and teaching, or the natural elements of wind and sea and the barrenness of the desert. His authority or power, however, is never exercised to coerce people into believing and following him. Human response must be free.

The exorcism

For the Jews of Jesus' time the power to drive out evil or unclean spirits was a very important element in the credentials of an agent of God. W. J. Harrington states: 'The exorcisms of Jesus are to be viewed in terms of an apocalyptic struggle. They show the inbreak of the rule of God.'[19] J. P. Meier states in his study of the historical Jesus:

19. W. J. Harrington, *op. cit.*, 88.

... it is fairly certain that Jesus was, among other things, a first-century Jewish exorcist and probably won not a little of his fame and following by practising exorcisms ... perhaps in no other aspect of Jesus' ministry does his distance from modern Western culture loom so large ... One can approach his exorcisms with greater sympathy if one remembers that Jesus no doubt saw them as part of his overall ministry of healing and liberating the people of Israel from the illnesses and other physical and spiritual evils that beset them ... If Jesus saw himself called to battle against these evils, which diminished the lives of his fellow Israelites, it was quite natural for him, as a first-century Jew, to understand this specific dimension of his ministry in terms of exorcism. All of this simply underscores the obvious: Jesus was a man and a Jew of his times.[20]

Jesus' first exercise of 'miraculous' power is against an 'unclean spirit', a force believed to be preternatural, part of the kingdom of Satan, and possessing more than human knowledge of Jesus' true identity and power. 'Unclean spirit' is the Semitic expression for what a Greco-Roman author would call a demon, *daimôn*. 'Unclean' in the biblical sense is the equivalent of 'unholy', something adverse to or not blessed by God. The possessed person is at one and the same time a victim and an instrument of the unclean spirit. In this case the unclean spirit shouts out: 'What is between us, Jesus of Nazareth (*ti hêmin kai soi*)?' Addressing Jesus by his personal name and referring to his place of origin can be seen as an attempt to seize control of the situation and put Jesus at a disadvantage and on the defensive. Normally knowing a person's name and origin gives a measure of control or at least a certain advantage in a situation. The expression 'what is between us' is a Semitic expression found in the Old Testament in the context of disputes (*mâ lî w'lakem*).[21] It is an expression designed to put the person addressed at the disadvantage of being responsible for what follows. It places an irreconcilable distance between the two disputants. The irreconcilable distance here is between this 'unclean' spirit and the one who received the Holy Spirit at the Jordan, was driven by the Spirit into the desert and was destined to baptise in Holy Spirit.

20. J. P. Meier, *op. cit.*, vol 2, 406, 407.
21. 2 Sam 16:10; 19:23;1 Kings 17:18; 2 Kings 3:13; Jdgs 11:12; 2 Chron 35:21.

It represents the dispute between the powers of evil and those of the kingdom. At the same time the unclean spirit acknowledges and feels the threat of defeat and destruction from Jesus' presence and superior power and he exclaims: 'Have you come to destroy us?' Whereas the people, the disciples, Herod and the enemies of Jesus, will continue throughout the ministry to struggle with the question of Jesus' identity, this 'preternatural' being recognises who he is: ' You are the Holy One of God.'[22]

Jesus rebuked, *epitimêsen*, (subdued/overpowered), and silenced the unclean spirit as he spoke his own healing word. No healing action is involved so there is no technical breach of the Sabbath observance! The verb *epitimêsen* translates the Hebrew *ga'ar*, used for exorcising evil spirits (Mk 2:13-14). Regularly in such healing and exorcism stories the disturbed condition of the possessed or ill person is emphasised by a final display or struggle which enhances the miracle that follows. Here the throwing down of the man and the great screech, heighten the tension and create a greater effect which emphasises the marvel and ensures the response of the onlookers and the readers. The focus of the account is on the unclean spirit and not on the possessed man, who does not really figure in his own right, but only as a victim and instrument of the spirit. There is no reference to the man's appealing to Jesus, to his faith or lack of it, or to his reaction to the healing. The focus of attention is elsewhere.

The amazement of the onlookers is directed toward the overcoming of the spirit rather than the healing of the man. They draw attention to the extraordinary authority behind Jesus' teaching. His mighty teaching is matched by his mighty deeds. The miracle has taken the usual form – problem posed, (implied appeal to Jesus), Jesus responds, the problem intensifies to heighten the tension, then Jesus performs the healing or exorcism, the problem is solved and the people react. They ask what this new teaching is, as they see the authority not only in the words but also in the deeds accompanying it. They are still not sure exactly what it is, but they are very impressed. Jesus' fame spread all through Galilee.[23]

22. Using the same expression as Peter in Jn 6:69 and the demon in Lk 4:34, ' holy one' acknowledges the special relationship with, and consecration by God.
23. See R. J. Dillon, 'As One Having Authority (Mk 1:22): The Controversial Distinction of Jesus' Teaching', *CBQ* 57 (1995), 92-113 and

In the house of Simon and Andrew Mk 1:29-32
The pace of the narrative to date has been breathtaking. Jesus is compulsively driven and continually on the move. The pace is conveyed by the repeated use of *euthus*, 'immediately' and *kai parataxis* (and ... and ... and). The pace continues as he leaves the synagogue: 'and immediately on leaving the synagogue they came to the house of Simon and Andrew together with James and John.' Simon's mother-in-law was laid low with fever and *immediately* they told him about her.

Following the overpowering of the demon in the synagogue Jesus now performs his first healing, as distinct from an exorcism, in the gospel. He heals a woman, the mother-in-law of Simon.[24] The language of 'taking control in power' (*kratein*) and the resurrection language of 'raising up' (*egeirein*) are used here and will continue to appear in other miracle stories.

Approaching the one who was 'laid low' (*katekeito*), he raised her up, having taken hold of her hand. The participles 'approaching' and 'having taken hold of' build up to the verb 'raised', *êgeiren*. Touch was a well established dimension of healing in biblical and extra biblical experience and literature.[25] Here, however, a very definite kind of touch is described, *kratêsas tês cheiros*, 'having taken her by the hand'. The verb *kratein* has the connotation of taking by force, taking control in power, and here emphasises power over the disease. The language of 'raising up' recurs in the gospel. It has connotations of restoring to health and wholeness and also of restoring the dead to life. Before the writing of Mark's gospel it was a long established term in the proclamation of the resurrection of Jesus whom 'God raised from the dead.' The immediacy and completeness of the cure is evidenced by the statement that she 'ministered to them', *diêkonei autois*, an activity requiring a level of

J. C. Iwe, *Jesus in the Synagogue of Capernaum: The Pericope and its programmatic character for the Gospel of Mark. An Exegetical-Theological Study of Mk 1:21-28*, Rome: PUG, 1994.
24. 1 Cor 9:5 may imply that Peter/Cephas brought his wife with him on his missionary journeys. Paul writes: 'Do we not have the right to be accompanied by a believing wife as do the other apostles and the brothers of the Lord and Cephas?'
25. Touching a woman, however, may have connotations of Jesus' breaking a taboo, as a rabbi or religious leader would not have done so. However, it was in the privacy of a home among friends and was not an issue.

energy not associated with someone who has just been in a
fever. A similar point will be made when Jesus tells the family of
Jairus to give food to the girl he has just raised – after such serious illness one's appetite usually returns only slowly and with
much encouragement and coaxing. There was no need for Jesus
to remind caring parents to feed their child, but in the circumstances reference to the child's appetite pointed to an instantaneous and complete cure (Mk 5:43).

'She ministered to them', *diêkonei autois*.[26] Here in this case
the verb *diêkonei*, does not have connotations of a 'servile' service but rather ties into the whole biblical idea of a ministry of
hospitality within home and community, particularly to the
ministers of the gospel (Mk 6:10f; Mt 10:11f; Lk 9:6;10:5ff). It is
also the verb used for describing the task for which the seven
were appointed in Acts 6:1-6. Like Martha in St John's gospel (Jn
12:2) the mother-in-law of Peter is said to 'serve/minister to'
(*diakonein*) her guests. In the mind of Mark and those for whom
he was originally writing, it was not a relegating of her to a
'menial' kitchen sink role but an elevation of her to what was
seen by them as an established, highly prized and important role
in the hospitality ministry of the community. Hospitality was
very important in early Christian communities. It should be kept
in mind that very early on there was a debate in the Jerusalem
church about the neglect of hospitality, in overlooking the
Hellenist widows. In response to the criticism the seven were
chosen for this service of hospitality. The apostles prayed over
them and laid hands on them (Acts 6:1-6). Furthermore, the criteria for enrolment as a widow in the First Letter to Timothy emphasises such hospitality. 'She must be a woman known for her
good works and for the way in which she brought up her children, shown hospitality to strangers and washed the feet of the
saints' (1 Tim 5:10). Some communities had an established order
of deacon already in New Testament times (Phil 1:1; 1 Tim 3:8,
12, 13; Rom 16:1).

At Sundown as Sabbath ended Mk 1:32-34
'As evening drew on, when the sun went down' is a typical

---

26. F. J. Moloney, *op. cit.*, 55 points out that in Jesus' time it may have
been a departure from custom, in fact a breaking of a taboo, to have a
rabbi or religious leader 'served' by a woman. However, by the time of
the writing of the New Testament that attitude had radically changed.

Markan double time reference where a second reference makes the first more specific. The reference is important because at sunset the Sabbath ended and its restrictions on work, movement and transportation were lifted so the crowds arrived around the door carrying all their sick and those possessed by unclean spirits so that the whole city was gathered around the door. The universal impact of Jesus' actions is emphasised by the hyperbolic use of '*all* the sick ...', 'the *whole* city ...' and 'many kinds of sicknesses' and 'he healed many sick and expelled many demons'. The Greek word for 'many', *polloi*, has much stronger connotations in the New Testament than its English translation, especially when translating from a Semitic usage such as *rabh* which has the connotation of 'a very large number'. Again the demons, with their preternatural knowledge, recognise him for who he is. He silences them. Why? The reader's curiosity is aroused. As in all good storytelling, the reader has to wait for an explanation.[27]

The end-of-the-day scenario provides a summary of Jesus' activity so far. He has overpowered the preternatural power and knowledge of demons and healed the scourge of sickness. But seeds of trouble have been sown. The people compared the teaching authority of their scribes unfavourably to the teaching authority of Jesus. As the scribes feel the sting and threat of such comments the reader expects, naturally, that they will turn up to hear, observe and possibly put the newcomer in his place.

ii. A Typical Morning and a Fresh Initiative Mk 1:35-39

Another double reference to time introduces the next scene. Jesus having risen 'early, while still very dark' used to go out and depart to a deserted place to pray in private, as a Jew should pray in the morning. The verbs build up a sense of determination and distance: *having risen*, he *used to go out* and *depart* to a deserted place and *pray*. The deserted place (*erêmos topos*) recalls the *erêmos*, desert, into which the Spirit had driven him earlier, and where he was with the wild beasts and the angels of God ministered to him. It was his special place for prayer. It was here

---

27. This is the attitude of Jesus which scholars have called 'the messianic secret'. Recognition of the 'messianic secret' as an important element in Markan redaction of the tradition was a key factor in realising that Mark too was an interpreter and theologian rather than a simple recorder.

in communion with the Father that he found and maintained the inspiration and energy for his mission.

On this occasion Simon and those with him sought him out. They had been chosen to 'follow him', to 'come after him' but here they display their lack of understanding by joining the crowd seeking him out. The verb *katediôxen* (*katadiôkein*) is commonly used for hunting a wild animal. In the context of a human being it has overtones of hostile pursuit, hounding and persecuting. Here it signifies a selfish and bothersome failure to give him time to himself. Simon tells Jesus, 'everyone is looking for you'. The verb *zêtein*, to look for / pursue, will later in the gospel signify a hostile seeking of Jesus by his enemies. Here in this scene the frenetic pursuing of Jesus begins because of his reputation as a wonder worker. The pursuit will continue, but it will change in tone and purpose as the disciples misunderstand him, the crowd hound him and enemies persecute him.

In response to this initial, uninformed or only partially informed enthusiasm on the part of the disciples, Jesus says: 'Let us go to the other villages round about to proclaim there, for that is why I came forth.' 'Let *us* go' points to the fact that Jesus is bringing them with him on his mission, including them in his ministry. His purpose in coming into Galilee was to proclaim the good news. 'He came forth' can signify his 'coming out' from private life into the public eye in his ministry, and also his coming forth from or being sent by God. Popular enthusiasm and the desire to detain, if not indeed to possess him, must not impede his 'going out' to proclaim the good news.

The initial response to Jesus has built up to a great climax, characterised by words like 'all', 'everyone', 'the whole town' and 'everywhere', to describe the universal excitement caused by his initial impact.

iii. Crossing the Boundary: Touching the Leper Mk 1:40-45

If Mark's gospel were a modern play or musical, the lighting and music would change to sober tones at this moment as a significant shift in the storyline breaks suddenly on the scene at Mk 1:40. The universal excitement and celebration give way to a solemn mood as something unexpected and socially unacceptable happens. Until now the socially acceptable were involved in Jesus' ministry. A mould of centuries is about to be broken and the breaking of this mould will stand as a rubric above the

entire narrative of the gospel. The approach of the leper signifies
that someone has taken Jesus really seriously. The good news is
for everyone. That message is now put to the test. A significant
boundary is about to be crossed in both directions. Leprosy was
just one of the factors which placed people in the category of the
unclean, the unholy or polluted and separated them from the
clean, the holy and the pure. The separation was strictly observed and violation of it was seen as an undermining of the appropriate social order. 'The purity system' made it very clear
who belonged to normal society and who did not, who were the
'insiders' and the 'outsiders', the 'clean' and the 'unclean'.
Unfortunately this sense of belonging or not belonging reached
beyond social and liturgical belonging and was regarded by
some strict observants as a pointer to acceptance and non-accep-
tance in the salvific plan of God. The rule of Qumran, for example, was very specific about who was excluded from the messianic community. Jesus' touching of the leper, his association
and eating with tax collectors and sinners, and his entering the
house of a Gentile are prophetic actions which challenge these
regulations and assumptions and in doing so proclaim that
everyone is welcome in the kingdom.

A leper crosses the boundary of convention as he comes to
Jesus, falling on his knees and saying to him: 'If you wish you
have it in your power to make me clean.'[28] Breaking the purity
rules, going against social custom, exploding the taboo, the leper
approaches Jesus.[29] Jesus responds in kind, reaching out to
touch the untouchable. The legislation in Lev 13:41ff, which follows a detailed description of symptoms of the disease and regulations for the examination of them by the priest, prescribed
that the leper wear torn clothes, keep dishevelled hair, live 'outside the camp' and cry out 'unclean, unclean'. This warned off

28. The participle *gonupetôn*, falling on (his) knees, is omitted in some
important manuscripts, such as the Western tradition and Codex
Vaticanus. However the manuscripts which contain ' falling on his
knees' are in line with the tradition as represented by Mt 8:2 and Lk 5:12.
29. There is an extensive section of legislation in Lev 13-14 dealing with
leprosy. Leprosy in the biblical sense may not be exactly the same as the
technical definition of leprosy in the modern world (Hansen's Disease).
In Greek the verb *leptein* means 'to peel off' and so the term *lepros*, could
cover a variety of conditions. The Hebrew term *sara'at* refers to the kind
of fungus growth one sees on clothes or a type of dry rot in houses, cf
Lev 13:47-58; 14:13-45.

the unsuspecting oncomer. Should another person touch the leper that person incurred the unclean state and its penalties. Leprosy meant isolation from social and religious gatherings, death of human relationships, and its pallor resembled that of a corpse, so it was regarded as a sort of death and curing it was seen as restoring life to one effectively dead (Num 12:10-12; 2 Kings 5:7). Leprosy was often seen as a punishment for sin.[30] Its effects in bodily destruction leading to death and a life of isolation from community paralleled the effects of sin. The rabbis used leprosy as a metaphor for sin and its effects.

The combination of *thelein* (wish) and *dunasthai* (to be able, have in one's power) in the leper's plea, ' If you wish you have it in your power to make me clean', highlights his perception of Jesus' power. In response Jesus says: 'I (so) wish, be cleansed.' The result is immediate. *Kai euthus* again appears. 'And *immediately* the leprosy left him and he was cleansed'. Most manuscripts say Jesus' action is motivated by compassion. 'Being moved to compassion (*splagchnistheis*), he stretched out his hand and touched him.' Some manuscripts, however, have 'being moved to anger (*orgistheis*), he stretched out his hand and touched him'.

The motive of compassion is in keeping with other actions of Jesus in the gospel. He will have compassion on the crowds because they are like sheep without a shepherd and will set himself to teach them at length (Mk 6:34), and he will also have compassion on them when they had been with him all day and had nothing to eat (Mk 8:2). Though the weight of manuscript evidence is in favour of compassion as the motive, it is unlikely that a reference to anger would have caused embarrassment to the point of causing a copyist to 'soften' the tradition by changing Jesus' motive from 'anger' to 'compassion'. The motive of anger must have been present already in an alternative and possibly earlier account.

The motive of anger is also a feature of Jesus' reaction to sickness and death in the New Testament. Anger is a common reaction of Jesus in the synoptics in the face of sickness and distress which are seen as a sign of the presence and power of Satan's kingdom. The equivalent scenario in John is the presence of death. In the face of sin and its consequences Jesus is angered, sometimes to the point of great anguish, as in the case of the

---

30. Num 12:10-15; cf Deut 28:27, 35; 2 Kings 5:25-27; 2 Chron 26:16-21.

death of Lazarus in John's gospel (Jn 12:27). The common belief
in biblical times was that there was a connection between humanity's sinful past and present and the suffering experienced in
the world. Sin was seen to be a root cause. It is not surprising
then that Jesus and others imply that sin is the remote cause of
suffering by issuing instruction not to sin again or pronouncing
forgiveness for sin in the context of healing. In the biblical mind-
set there is a broad association of sickness and death with sin
and the power of Satan.[31] Ps 106 (107) puts it very well:

> Some were sick through their sinful ways and because of
> their iniquities endured afflection. They had a loathing for
> every food; they came close to the gates of death. Then they
> cried to the Lord in their need and he rescued them from
> their distress. He sent forth his word to heal them and deliv-
> ered them from destruction. (Ps 106/107:17-20).

However, the undertones of anger are present in Jesus' dismissal of the healed man. 'Being moved to anger, *embrimêsa-
menos*, he sent him away.' The verb *embrimasthai* has the basic
meaning of expressing anger, 'snorting with anger'. It sounds almost like a reminiscence of an exorcism story from an earlier
stage in the tradition where Jesus expels the demon of leprosy,
'he cast him out.' Here it is used to describe Jesus' reaction in the
face of the evil of sickness, social exclusion and human misery.

Jesus' action in reaching out to touch the leper is a radical
step in proclaiming in action and attitude the inclusive nature of
the kingdom. Touch is a bridge, an embrace across the divide,
and in the embrace Jesus healed the leper. The story is reminiscent of, and yet very different from, the healing of Naaman
when he came to Elisha for healing of his leprosy. Naaman was
an 'outsider', an 'unclean Gentile' and he approached the
prophet in Israel, in faith that showed itself in his coming a journey and in his persistent manner. Elisha, however, did not touch
him but sent him to the river Jordan to bathe and be healed by
YHWH (2 Kings 5:8-14).

Returning to the story of Jesus and the leper, a double negative stresses the command of Jesus that he ' tell no one nothing',
mêdeni mêden, except of course the priest who was to witness the
healing and authorise his return to the community. Witnessing
to the healing was an elaborate process. The process for witness-

---

31. Gen 3:19; Ex 20:5; Deut 5:9; Job 3:3f; Mk 2: 5; Jn 5:14, 9:2f; Lk 13:2; cf
StB, II, 528f.

ing to healing shows that the term leprosy was used for a variety
of apparently similar conditions, which at that time were usually
regarded as incurable. The witnessing, according to Lev 14, was
an elaborate process of sacrifices, washings, shaving of head and
eyebrows, and a second and final examination confirming the
healing after seven days.

Jesus instructed the leper to tell no one. As mentioned already in the introduction to the commentary, he often instructed
the people he healed to remain silent about his action and he instructs the demons he confronts to remain silent about his identity. The 'messianic secret' as it has come to be called is in keeping with the thrust of the gospel, especially from Peter's confession of faith onwards where Jesus is interpreting the meaning of
his messianic role in terms of the suffering Son of Man who has
come to serve and to suffer, obedient to the divine plan. The
'secret' will not be fully disclosed until the young man at the
open tomb proclaims: 'He is risen. He is not here … He is going
ahead of you into Galilee.' Meanwhile the temptation is to see
Jesus in traditional terms as a political and social Messiah, a miracle worker whose powers should confound the opposition and
bring them to an acceptance of his claims. Hence the command
to silence. In so far as 'the secret' represents a fact of the historical Jesus' life it can be accounted for by a concern about false
messianic hopes of a political and social nature. In so far as it
was a matter of importance to the early Christian community it
may well reflect a certain anxiety about the fact that Jesus,
whom they now widely refer to as Christ/Messiah, did not himself make explicitly messianic claims during his ministry.

As the leper went to offer evidence of his healing he started
proclaiming, *kêrussein* (the word used already for the preaching
of John and Jesus) and spreading the word. Jesus had touched
him and could no longer enter any town, but had to stay outside
in 'deserted places', *erêmois topois*. Jesus, however, is already
quite at home carrying on his mission 'in deserted places', as
was John. 'And (*kai*) they kept coming (*êrchonto*) to him from
everywhere (*pantothen*)', again highlighting the continuous onrush and universal appeal of his mission at this stage. His touching of the leper has not dampened the enthusiasm of the crowd.

His movement, however, is now restricted. 'He could no
longer enter a town.' Is it because of the crowds and the political
sensitivities of Jewish and Roman authorities about crowds

gathering in urban areas and thus providing a cover or motivation for rebels? Or is it a more subtle reference to the fact that
the one who has touched the leper has taken on the condition of
the leper in the eyes of authority and of strict observants of custom and law? Is it a flight from those who gather all too easily in
urban areas for a 'spectacle' of healing that answers a certain
psychological and 'religious' need but in no way touches their
hearts and minds – the kind of activity which is portrayed, and
from which Jesus recoils, in the Matthean and Lucan temptation
accounts, and which he rejects in John's gospel with the statement, 'Unless you see signs and wonders you refuse to believe'
(Mt 4:1-11; Lk 4:1-12; Jn 4:48)? Though Jesus exercises full power
and control over evil spirits and diseases he does not exercise
such power over human hearts and minds to control how they
understand and receive his ministry.[32] All these elements are
probably present to some degree in the rich mix of human reactions.

Leprosy was regularly used as a metaphor for sin with its destructive effects on the person and on relations with society in
social and religious life. Significantly, the next scene in the narrative will deal with Jesus' power to forgive sin.

5. A Series of Controversies. Jesus' Authority

The gauntlet has been thrown down. Five conflict stories, the
Galilean controversy cycle, now trace the challenge of Jesus to
established religious and social attitudes and customs.[33] In these
controversy stories Mark 'puts the authority of Jesus on display.'[34] He forgives sins, chooses his companions from the outcasts, allows his disciples not to fast, and pronounces on the
Sabbath. At the same time the stories illustrate the deepening of
the reaction to him, beginning with unspoken criticism, mur-
murings in his critics' hearts, then progressing through criticism
spoken about him to his disciples, to two criticisms directed to

---

32. Klemens Stock, *Marco, Commento contestuale al secondo Vangelo*, 49,
puts it very well: *In un certo senso questo rivela i limiti della sua potenza: egli
può mondare (1:40), ma non può recarsi piú pubblicamente in una città(1:45);
ha potere su tutte le malattie, ma gli manca il potere sui cuori degli uomini, per
stabilire in che modo essi debbano accogliere quello che compie.*
33. See J. D. G. Dunn, 'Mark 2:1-3:6. A Bridge between Jesus and Paul on
the Question of the Law', *NTS* 30 (1984), 395-415.
34. R. H. Gundry, *op. cit.*, 6.

himself about his disciples. The reader expects the next criticism
to be about himself and made to himself. However, instead of
criticising him to his face and taking him head on in a discussion, thereby risking a loss of face themselves, the critics do not
criticise him to his face but watch for an opportunity to catch
him, hoping he will trap himself through a breach of Sabbath observance which would leave him open to serious criticism and
condemnation. When he outwits them they react with violent intent against him. The groups involved are first the scribes, then
the scribes of the Pharisee party, then the Pharisees, then the
Pharisees and Herodians. The story as it is unfolding shows a
mounting intensity in the criticism, ending in a plot to kill him.

These five controversy stories are arranged in concentric or
chiastic form and sandwiched into the middle is a teaching of
Jesus about the radical significance of what is really taking place
in his mission, together with a forecasting of the fate that awaits
him and his disciples. This central point is illustrated by three
'parables' (in the broadest sense of the term). A diagram shows
the pattern clearly:[35]

    a. Forgiveness of Sins. Jesus poses 'no win' question. Mk 2:1-12
      b. Unacceptable eating. Levi. Jesus' Logion. Mk 2:13-17
        c. Fasting: Bridegroom/Garment/Wineskins. Mk 2:18-22
      b. Unacceptable eating. Sabbath. Jesus' Logion. Mk 2:23-28
    a. Sabbath Observance. Jesus poses 'no win' question. Mk
    3:1-5

This chiasm or concentric ring structure shows how a series of
steps builds up to, and a corresponding series leads away from,
the central point. Framing the whole section (a) and (a) are two
of the great areas of controversy in Jesus' ministry, the forgiveness of sins and observance of the Sabbath. In both cases Jesus
confounds the leaders and scholars with a 'no win' question.
Then (b) and (b) focus on another area of controversy, Jesus and
the disciples eating in 'unacceptable' circumstances. Jesus eats
with tax collectors and sinners and the disciples pluck and eat
corn on the Sabbath. Both incidents end with a memorable pronouncement or *logion* of Jesus. In the central spot (c) between the
two controversies about eating there is an argument about fast-

35. These may have existed in a chiastic structure before Mark used
them. However, as now used they not only function as a chiasm pointing up the central teaching, but also they serve the plot in presenting a
sequential series of progressive criticism and reaction.

ing. Here at the centre of the chiasm, in response to the criticism of his disciples for not fasting, Jesus teaches by means of a 'parable' about the presence of the bridegroom and warns of the time to come when the bridegroom would be taken from them violently. In this he sums up the essence of his mission and looks ahead to his violent rejection. He then proceeds, by means of two further parables, to illustrate the radical change in the history of God's dealings with the people which his mission is bringing about.

The chiasm also has a linear, logical development. The criticism of Jesus moves from the unspoken criticism in the hearts of the scribes, through criticism spoken to Jesus' disciples, to criticism about the disciples spoken to himself and finally to unspoken criticism of himself manifesting itself first of all in passive aggression and then issuing in a plot to destroy him.

a. Forgiveness of Sins. Jesus poses 'no win' question. Mk 2:1-12
Following the healing (and resulting restoration to society and synagogue) of the leper, Jesus after some days again entered Capernaum and the report went around that he was in the house. The house is most likely that of Andrew and Peter.[36] Jesus' restless movement is still in evidence and his universal appeal is still strong, as one reads about the crowd around the door, just like on an earlier occasion at the end of the Sabbath in Capernaum. This time the bearers of a stretcher carrying an invalid fail to get near Jesus because of the crowd. Their dramatic action of 'unroofing' the building, stripping away the material and lowering the pallet on which the invalid was lying in front of Jesus, caused Jesus 'on seeing their faith' to address the crippled man with the words: 'Child, your sins are forgiven.'[37] A dramatic miracle story follows which strikes at the perceived root of all suffering when Jesus says to the man: 'Your sins are forgiven.' In saying this he gives offence to the scribes. This is the first of the controversy stories.

---

36. Reading the entire pericope one senses that it may originally have referred to a synagogue setting and contained also a Sabbath controversy since the scribes (some of them Pharisees) are sitting around and Jesus instructs the healed man to carry his sleeping mat/pallet as he does in St John's gospel at the pool of Bethesda, a symbolic infringement of the Sabbath in the context of emerging hostility to Jesus.
37. 'Faith', *pistis*, has connotations of their faith in Jesus and their fidelity to the sick person.

This provokes a reaction on the part of the scribes who were sitting there and, though their criticism is unspoken, Jesus reads it in their hearts. What has had all the appearances of being a typical healing/miracle story up to this point now becomes a typical controversy story, resulting not only in the amazement of the crowd at the healing but in the reaction of those who take offence.

The fact that there were scribes 'sitting around' as if in formal teaching position seems strange in a crowded house, and the description is possibly reminiscent of an occasion in the synagogue. They question in their hearts why this man (*houtos*) speaks like this (*houtôs*), thinking, 'He is blaspheming; who can forgive sins but God alone?' This first recorded criticism of Jesus in the gospel foreshadows the final, fatal criticism, the charge of blasphemy at his Jewish trial, which will signal his definitive rejection and condemnation by the Jewish authorities (Mk 14:64f).

Even the term 'this man' (*houtos*) has overtones of disapproval. Jesus immediately knew in his spirit that they thus thought to themselves and asked them: 'Why do you question so in your hearts?' Then he poses a question and places them in a no-win situation. He asks: 'Which is easier to say to the paralytic, "your sins are forgiven" or to say "rise up take up your pallet and walk"?' The verb 'rise up' re-echoes in this story the account of the healing of Peter's mother-in-law .[38]

Words are usually easy to say and they can equally easily deceive. Deeds are not. They are transparent. But in this case words are not easy as the only words possible would have been either: 'It is easier to say: "your sins are forgiven"' or 'It is easier to say "rise up take up your pallet and walk".' The first option was impossible because, if they said: 'It is easier to say "your sins are forgiven" ' it would implicate the critics in the very blasphemy that provoked their criticism. Their other option, to say: 'Rise up, take up your pallet and walk' would have exposed them to huge embarrassment and ridicule when, unlike the one they were criticising, they proved unable to match their words with deeds.

Then, having thus reduced his opposition to a shamed silence, Jesus showed the deeper meaning of his ministry and the

---

38. See Hunter, Faith and Geoffrey, 'Which is Easier? (Mk 2:9)', *Exp Times* 105 (1993), 12f.

words and deeds in which it found expression, deeper than just winning an argument. He said: '… in order that you may know that the Son of Man has power on earth to forgive sins (he addressed the paralytic), "I say to you, rise, take up you pallet and go to your home".' The well-established usage of 'and … and' (*kai parataxis*) together with 'and immediately' (*kai euthus*) emphasise the immediate healing and its results. And he *rose up* and having *immediately* taken up his pallet he departed in front of everyone, so that everyone was amazed and gave glory to God saying: 'We have never seen anything like this.' The enthusiasm of the crowd as they acknowledge the miracle as an act of God overshadows for the moment the criticism in the hearts of the scribes. But that criticism will smoulder and gradually assert itself openly. In the honour-shame consciousness of society, Jesus has scored a major victory and put his critics to shame.

The reference to the Son of Man who has power on earth to forgive sin is another example of a prolepsis, a gap leaving the reader to await further revelation before discovering who this Son of Man is and why he has power on earth to forgive sins, a prerogative of God alone. The original audience and the implied or original readers, may have had some knowledge of the Son of Man passages in Daniel and Ezekiel, but such knowledge would have served to whet the appetite rather than to explain the term and its function at this point in the narrative.[39]

The faith of the infirm man's friends figures in the story of the paralytic, giving them the role of a communal character manifesting a very positive attitude towards Jesus. They also represent, very likely, people in the Christian community who bring their sick for healing. Interestingly, the man himself does not figure as a character at all. There is no mention of his appeal to Jesus, his faith or lack of it, his response to his healing or the forgiveness of his sins. He merely fulfils a function. Perhaps his story was (and still is) important also for Christians who bring their sick, maybe unbelieving or sceptical family members or friends, for healing.

The critics of Jesus in this episode were the scribes. They were not a religious organisation or movement like the Pharisees, Sadducees or Essenes. The term is a professional one covering a broad array of people such as biblical scholars, legal

---

39. The Son of Man is mentioned fourteen times in Mark and thirteen in John, less often in Matthew and Luke.

experts and official secretaries of various kinds. They probably belonged to different religious and philosophical associations, as is evident from the reference to the scribes who belonged to the Pharisee party (Mk 3:6). However, their knowledge of scripture and law probably predisposed a larger number of them to be members of the Pharisee movement.[40] Significantly, the next group to criticise Jesus will be 'scribes of the Pharisee party'.

The Pharisees were the strict religious group, the guardians of law and tradition, and they are still remembered in Jewish circles as the saints and scholars of the period in question. The movement began in the second century BC as these observant Jews sought to 'separate' themselves from the aggressive influence of foreign culture, religion and way of life.[41] They proclaimed the sovereignty of God in every area of life, and for this they worked out in the greatest possible detail the implications of the law in every conceivable set of circumstances. A lay movement, they were not involved in the politics of the Temple priesthood. They believed in divine providence, judgement and life after death. They therefore lived strict lives, adhered both to the law and the oral tradition and were creative in their interpretation of the law. They were the real spiritual leaders of the nation, a fact borne out by their survival and their leadership in bringing the people together after the terrible events of 70 AD. They furnished the people with a whole new approach to Jewish life after the terrible destruction of the holy city and the Temple, which resulted in the loss of its atoning sacrifices and rituals and its central role as the goal and setting of the pilgrimage feasts.

In the ministry of Jesus they emerge as his critics and 'debating partners'. They do not figure in the passion account of Jesus, neither in his arrest or trial. They come across for the most part as friendly to the new Christian movement in the Acts of the Apostles. The post-70 situation, however, saw the beginnings of trouble between the Pharisees' revival and renewal programme and the Christian movement. At times this was quite fraught with threat and hostility and so the portrayal of the Pharisees, particularly in Matthew and John, is coloured by this later tension.

Jesus defended himself in this episode with a 'no-win' question addressed to his critics. He will pose similar 'no-win' ques-

---

40. For a study of the Scribes see C. Schams, *Jewish Scribes in the Second-Temple Period*, Sheffield: Academic Press, 1998.
41. Josephus, *War* II: 8.14; *Ant* XIII: 10.6; XVIII.1.3.

tions on a later date in the synagogue when he asks the question
about doing good or evil, saving life or killing on the Sabbath
(Mk 3:4) and later still when he asks about the origin of the baptism of John (Mk 11:27-33).

b. Unacceptable Eating. Call of Levi. Jesus' Logion. Mk 2:13-17

Jesus has just pronounced the forgiveness of sins (*hamartias*).
Now he calls sinners (*hamartôloi*) to discipleship in the kingdom
and gathers them around him, displaying an attitude that will
draw on him the criticism of the scribes of the Pharisee party. He
calls the toll / tax collector Levi. Here we again encounter the call
of Jesus, in a form akin to the calling of the Old Testament
prophets. The name of the addressee, his father's name, his
livelihood, and the location of the call, similar to the case of the
two pairs of brothers already called, are all given. This, however,
is a provocative gesture since the collectors of tolls or taxes were
seen as operating a system for a foreign government, often in the
interests of their own pockets and regularly carried out through
putting pressure on the more vulnerable members of society.
Needless to say the tax and toll collectors were held in disfavour,
or more accurately, they were greatly despised, by the people
generally.

Though Julius Caesar had discontinued the system of farming out the tax collecting to rich and often dishonest grasping
people, in Galilee under Herod the Great and his son Antipas
the tolls or taxes continued to be collected by royal officials, who
in turn sub-contracted minor officials to carry out the task. Tax
collectors get a bad press from Roman, Greek and Jewish writers
alike. Cicero and Dio Chrysostom link them with beggars,
thieves and robbers.[42] The Mishnah associates them with robbers, murderers and sinners.[43] In the New Testament they are
regularly associated with sinners in the phrase 'tax collectors
and sinners' (*telônôi kai hamartoloi*) (Mk 2:15; Mt 9:10; 11:19; Lk
7:34; 15:1) and sometimes with 'immoral persons' (*pornai*),
which signifies sinners in the area of sexual immorality, such as
prostitutes (Mt 21:31; Lk 18:11). Matthew also associates them
with Gentiles in a negative way (Mt 5:46; 18:17). The term 'sinners' did not apply primarily to people who committed occa-
sional transgressions, but rather those who lived outside the law

---

42. Cicero, *De Officiis*, 15-21; Dio Chrysostom, *Orations*, 14.14.
43. *m.Tohoroth* 7.6; *Baba Qamma* 10.2; *b. Nedarim* 3:4.

in a constant and fundamental way (e.g. 'Gentile sinners' in Gal 2:15).[44] The toll or tax collectors were despised as a class, regarded as sinners and considered outsiders in the community of Israel.

Jesus now takes the initiative and calls Levi, a toll/tax collector to follow him. He got up and followed him. Implied in the following of Jesus is the leaving of his desk, symbol of his profession and root of his sinfulness. Not only the unacceptable individual himself but the company he kept, the circle of associates in which he moved are now brought into the ambit of Jesus' acceptance as he dines with them. This time the criticism of Jesus does not remain unspoken in the hearts of his critics, identified on this occasion as the scribes of the Pharisee party, but it is spoken openly and challengingly to his disciples: 'Why does your master eat with tax collectors and sinners?' In the criticism the present tense of the verb 'eats' (*esthiei*) implies a habitual eating with such people. 'In his house' could refer to the house of Jesus or of Levi, but whichever is meant the point is the same. It could be a meal given for Levi and his associates by Jesus or, more likely, a meal given by them in Jesus' honour, since it was a common practice for wealthy people to give banquets for important teachers, philosophers and religious leaders.

The criticism this time is spoken and addressed to his disciples. This is the first use of the term *mathêthês* for 'disciple' (from the word *manthanein*, to learn), a term used to describe the process whereby a disciple became the pupil of a rabbi in order to learn his wisdom and knowledge. Jesus will later describe discipleship in a much more radical way.

The canonised wisdom as stated so clearly in Psalm 1 about not associating with sinners or sitting in the company of scorners is seen to be violated by Jesus. The traditional wisdom warned the just not to associate with the unjust for fear of contamination and becoming like them. The 'just' and the 'unjust' are regularly contrasted in moral discourse in the scriptures. Their paths and their destinies are contrasted. Psalm 1 contrasts the way of the just, like a tree planted by the waterside giving its fruit in due season, with the way of the wicked which leads to doom. Psalm 37 (36) is a treatise on the fate of the just and the unjust and Wisdom of Solomon states that ' the souls of the just are in the hands of God … but the godless will be duly punished for their reasoning' (Wis 3:1-12). Jesus reverses the

---

44. J. R. Donahue and D. J. Harrington, *op. cit.*, 102

maxim about the just not associating with the unjust by pointing out that in fact it is precisely those 'unjust' people who need a physician. The wisdom of Psalm 1 is reversed. The influence is going in the other direction, from the just one to the unjust. Jesus bridges this age old gap and reverses the process of influence, bringing the unjust into the sphere of influence of the kingdom of God.

Beginning again with the 'biblically sounding' expression *kai ginetai*, 'and it comes / came to pass', Jesus is described as 'reclining' in the house and many tax collectors are reclining (*synanekeinto*) with Jesus and his disciples. The historic present tense lends a sense of immediacy to the scene. The imperfect tense follows, 'for they were many and they were following him' (*êkolouthoun*). Again the use of the imperfect tense, and the 'many', representing his broader following of disciples, convey the impression of an increasing following *who kept on following him* (*êkolouthoun autô*).

These meals also display aspects of a Greco-Roman banquet at which the guest of honour, a philosopher, teacher or religious figure, would lead a symposium after the meal proper. Following a transition in which a libation was poured to a god, a hymn or prayer recited, the women withdrew to pursue their own company and interests and the men drank and discussed. In New Testament times many Jews had adopted and adapted this kind of meal for special occasions. Luke's account of Jesus' meal with Simon the Pharisee where he 'reclined' at table and a woman 'invaded' the male space, only to be defended by Jesus' pointing to her love and Simon's failure in hospitality and etiquette, is a case in point (Lk 7:36-50). Aspects of Greco-Roman practice, such as reclining for the meal, are mentioned twice in the pericope (*katakeisthai* is used of Jesus himself and *synanekeinto* of those dining with him). In such a setting Jesus would be expected to speak as a Jewish wisdom teacher, and his audience would function very much like the interlocutors in a symposium. In Greco-Roman society the symposium was the opportunity for establishing reputation and showing off social status. In this context, however, Jesus' presence and activity are countersigns to the 'status' game and the occasion for a very significant statement about the nature of his mission and of the kingdom he proclaims.

The criticism of Jesus may well have reached his ears already, since his attending such meals was a habitual practice. In the

manner of a Jewish wisdom teacher or Greco-Roman philosopher, he replied in a vein that would have been as natural to
Sirach as to Epictetus or Dio Chrysostom when he said: 'It is not
the healthy who are in need of a physician but those who are
sick.' Sirach commenting on medicine and illness wrote:

> Honour the physician with the honour that is his due, in re-
> turn for his services; for he too has been created by the Lord.
> Healing itself comes from the Most High, like a gift from a
> king … The Lord has brought medicines into existence from
> the earth, and the sensible man will not despise them. Did
> not a piece of wood once sweeten the water, thus giving
> proof of its virtue? (Sir 38:1-5. cf Ex 15:23-25).

The physician's place was seen as being with the sick and the
philosopher was often seen as a physician to those morally
sick.[45] Jesus' comment here in the gospel, 'It is not the healthy
who need the physician, but those who are sick', would have
been well received both in the Greco-Roman and the Jewish
world.

c. Fasting. Bridegroom/Garment/Wineskins. Mk 2:18-22
The next criticism, concerning his disciples, is directed to Jesus
himself by an unspecified group. He is challenged about fasting
when it is pointed out that the disciples of John and the
Pharisees were fasting and his disciples were not. Fasting regularly accompanied private prayers of petition, repentance and
devotion. The Day of Atonement, *Yom Kippur*, was a day of public fast. Other days of public fast could be proclaimed for particular reasons such as mourning, supplication in time of pestilence, famine or war, and repentance.[46] Waiting for the
promised one to come, and repentance by way of preparation
for his coming, would have been the order of the day among
some religious groups such as the Essenes and other pious
groups and individuals like the Pharisee in the Temple, in Jesus'
parable in Luke's gospel, who prides himself on his virtuous life
in contrast to the sinful tax-collector, and boasts about fasting
twice a week (Lk 18:9-14).

45. Dio Chrysostom, *Orations*, 3.2.14-30; Epictetus, *Discourses* 3.23, 30; cf
Plutarch, *Moralia*, 230f.
46. 2 Sam 12:23; 2 Chron 20:30; Joel 1:14; 2:12-15; Ezra 8:21; Jer 36:9; Pss
35 (34):13; 69 (68):10; Neh 9:1; Zech 8:19.

The disciples of the Pharisees were obviously people who followed, or were learning to follow, the devotional life of the Pharisees. The disciples of John are mentioned here and will be mentioned again when they come to bury his body after he has been beheaded, but these are the only references to them. This is quite a contrast with John's gospel where John's disciples are mentioned prominently, and some of them become the first disciples of Jesus. Again this shows Mark's emphasis on the break between the ministries of John and Jesus.

The criticism about his disciples' failure to fast is the cue for Jesus to reply in terms of his being the bridegroom of Israel. The imagery of the bridegroom is so well established in the Old and New Testaments that just a mention is needed in the gospel. As YHWH was the bridegroom of Israel in prophetic imagery, now in the New Testament the imagery shifts onto Jesus as bridegroom of Israel. However, Jesus here adds another radically new and ominous dimension: He begins with a statement that cannot be denied: 'Surely the bridegroom's attendants would never think of fasting while the bridegroom is still with them?'[47] This is an extremely significant claim about the nature of his presence and ministry. He is filling the role ascribed to YHWH in the Old Testament. Then he goes on to focus on a future violent event of eschatological significance. Using the established biblical phrase for a future significant event, 'days are coming' (*eleusontai hêmerai*) and the LXX phrase for the day of the coming of the Lord, 'on that day' (*en ekeinê tê hêmera*), Jesus points to the eschatological significance of his death. 'Days are coming when the bridegroom will be taken away from them, and then on that day they will fast.' Again the reader is left wondering and waiting for further clarification as the story unfolds.

Days will come when the bridegroom is taken away. The word ' taken away' (*aparthê*) signifies more than a simple departure. It warns of a forced or violent removal. The first shadow of the passion has now been cast. Here at the centre of the conflict

47. The significance of this pithy statement in Mark is brought out clearly in John's gospel where John the Baptist uses the imagery of the bride and bridegroom for Jesus and his following, an imagery long established for the covenant relationship of God and Israel. The one who has the bride is the bridegroom, the friend (the best man) stands by and rejoices at the voice of the bridegroom. John's joy is to see the stage set for that accomplishment as the bridegroom of Israel receives his bride, and John's task is accomplished (Jn 3:29f).

stories, Jesus' teaching pinpoints a future critical event that will usher in a new era and a new regime of fasting, an era known to the readers of Mark. The theme of his being taken away by force will be developed in the predictions of the passion in terms of his being rejected, handed over to the Gentiles and put to death (Mk 8:31; 9:31; 10:33f). It will be realised in the passion narrative. Mourning and repentance for the death of Jesus will call for fasting. The early Christian experience of fasting following the death of Jesus was a new departure unrelated to traditional Jewish practices. That the early Christians fasted on Wednesdays and Fridays is recorded in the Didache.[48] Mark here sets the precedent for their fasting in the saying of Jesus.

Now, however, it is a time for rejoicing as the groom claims his bride and the wedding feast is being prepared. The covenant was graphically described as a marriage bond between God and the people.[49] The restoration of the divine authority in the messianic time and the attendant blessings are encapsulated in the imagery of the kingdom (reign) of God. Jesus in his parables uses the wedding banquet as a metaphor for the kingdom, with all it entails by way of reconciliation, restoration and abundance.[50] Speaking of himself, rather than God, as the bridegroom is a whole new departure in Judaism, and having his disciples not fast while he is present not only says something very special about himself and his mission, but sets his disciples apart from other Jews and their traditions of fasting.

New Garment and New Wine Mk 2:21-22

Jesus uses two metaphors, or to use the word loosely, two 'parables' to focus on the radical newness of what is taking place in his ministry. What he is accomplishing cannot be fit neatly into, or contained within, the categories of the old dispensation, no more than a patch of unshrunken cloth can be sewn onto an old garment or new wine put into old skins. The inherent dynamism of the shrinking new cloth and of the fermenting wine is too powerful for the already shrunken garment and stretched wine-

---

48. *Didachê* 8:1.
49. Hos 2:19f; Is 25:6-8; 62:5; Jer 2:2; 3:14.
50. The Book of Revelation, for example, looks forward to the final establishment of the reign of God in terms of the eschatological banquet , the Wedding Feast of the Lamb (cf Mt 8:11) and the parables of the wedding feast appear in Mt 22:1-14; Lk 14:15-24.

skin and will cause damage, destroying the garment, spilling the
wine and ruining the skins.[51] Israel's traditions have done their
task as garment and wineskin, but something radically new is
happening and cannot be contained or imprisoned in the old. To
attempt to do so will destroy both the old and the new. Before
Mark's gospel appeared St Paul had already argued this same
case very vigorously in his discussions on circumcision and the
Mosaic Law.

b. Unacceptable Eating. Sabbath. Jesus' Logion. Mk 2:23-28

Jesus is now challenged, this time by the Pharisees, about the actions of his disciples whom they accused of breaking the
Sabbath by plucking grain in the cornfields and he responds
with a lesson from scripture. The lesson itself is crystal clear
even though the story differs in a number of ways from the
known texts of the Old Testament.

This Sabbath controversy arises from the fact that the disciples as they progressed[52] through the cornfield were plucking
ears of corn and eating them on the Sabbath. Plucking corn and
eating it as one passed through someone else's field was permitted, but putting a sickle into another person's corn was strictly
forbidden (Deut 23:25). The difficulty arose because they were
plucking the corn on the Sabbath and, in the eyes of the strict observants, it constituted harvesting work and was therefore a
breach of the Sabbath.[53]

Jesus' response is clear even if the biblical example is prob-
lematic. The story of David to which Jesus refers is found in 1
Samuel 21:1-6 (LXX 21:2-7). In both the Hebrew and Greek texts
of the Old Testament which have survived, Ahimelek, the father
of Abiathar and not Abiathar himself was the priest in question.
Furthermore, he was the priest, not the High Priest. No companions of David are mentioned, neither is there reference to their

---

51. The garment may conjure up the images of creation and community.
A new creation is unfolding and the untorn garment signifies a unified
community. The new wine conjures up the image of the kingdom, the
messianic time when the hills will flow with new wine (Amos 9:13). The
new reality being brought about should not to be hampered by hanker-
ing after the old.

52. *hodon poiein* seems remarkably like a Latinism for *iter facere*.

53. Ex 34:21; cf *m.Shabbat* 7:2; Philo, *Mos*, 2:22; CD 10:14-11:18. There
may be a concern also about not preparing their food prior to the
Sabbath. cf CD10:22.

being hungry and eating the bread of the presence, the twelve loaves baked specially to be set before the tabernacle every Sabbath and which were to be eaten only by the priests. This consecrated bread is often referred to as 'the bread of the presence' or 'shewbread'. The story as told here by Jesus may reflect a lost tradition of the Old Testament or a lost Targumic reflection on it. It may also reflect a New Testament tradition earlier than Mark's written gospel. The narrator, in keeping with other explanatory notes throughout the gospel which explain Jewish customs and traditions to non-Jews, adds the explanatory note about the bread, 'which it is not permitted for anyone except the priests to eat'.

The saying, 'The Sabbath was made for man (human being, *anthropos*), not man for the Sabbath', is a very pithy and clear saying which encapsulates what practical observation and wise counsel among the Jews had been advocating. Sabbath was for the benefit of the people of Israel and a badge of their identity among the nations rather than a command for all peoples.[54] Sabbath is a remembering (*zakôr*) of the creative and redeeming action of God. Celebrating it is a public acknowledgement of the sovereignty of God in creation and history.

The origins of Sabbath are obscure. Scholars have looked for evidence of such an observance among the Babylonians, the Canaanites and the Kenites. The Decalogue as it is now presented in Exodus and Deuteronomy, reflects the Priestly and Deuteronomic traditions and theology.[55] Maybe the earliest form of the Decalogue did not have the theological rationale with which the practice was subsequently invested. As with the feasts, older institutions were gradually historicised and invested with the memory of what God had done in creation and history.

The priestly tradition reflected in Exodus opens the Sabbath commandment with the injunction to 'remember' the Sabbath day, to keep it holy. The Hebrew *qds*, holy, emphasises separation, keeping person, place, object or time separated from the world and its pursuits, for the worship and service of God. The version of the command in Exodus emphasises the creation

---

54. Ex 20:8-11; Deut 5:12-15; CD 10:14-12:6; Jub 2:19, 21; 50:9-13. Mattathias and his companions had decided to fight on the Sabbath in order not to be wiped out by their enemies like their fellow Jews (1 Macc 2:34-38, 4).
55. Ex 20:7-11; Dt 5:12-15.

motif, recalling the priestly creation account, the first account in Genesis, describing how God rested on the seventh day from his creation and saw it was very good. This priestly theology is further evidenced in Exodus with the command, accompanied by the death penalty for infringement: 'Therefore the people of Israel shall keep the Sabbath, observing the Sabbath throughout the generations, as a perpetual covenant. It is a sign forever between me and the people of Israel that in six days the Lord made heaven and earth, and on the seventh day he rested and was refreshed' (Exod 31:15-17). The Sabbath is a sign of God's perpetual covenant with the people. This 'sign' value was of particular importance especially during the Exile when other institutions giving expression to their identity and facilitating their life of worship were destroyed.

The Deuteronomic tradition emphasised the dramatic event of God's intervention on their behalf in liberating them from the house of slavery in Egypt (Deut 5:12-15). They are exhorted in the Deuteronomic version of the Decalogue to 'remember', that is, to experience for themselves, the enormity of that event, as they celebrate the Sabbath.

Sabbath observance was therefore at the heart of the Torah and prescriptions for its observance were spelled out in great detail by scholars and legal experts. Thirty nine works were forbidden. These represent a certain relaxation of the practices such as those found in the Book of Jubilees and the Zadokite fragment.[56] Nine prescriptions referred to farming tasks, thirteen related to wool and thread tasks, seven to hunting and related tasks, two to writing, three to building and hammering, two to fires, two to baking, and finally one to 'taking out anything from one domain to another'.[57] Each of these prescriptions was subdivided to cover many activities, for example, in relation to the prescription about carrying a burden on the Sabbath, one could carry objects in one's private domain or four cubits in the public domain. Carrying a bed with an invalid on it was allowed, but carrying an empty bed was forbidden. Though on a small domestic scale, eating in the cornfield could be seen as an example of the relief of hunger and the sustaining of life in everyday circumstances, here in the story recounted by Mark it is taken by

---

56. *Jub* 50:8-12; *Zadokite Docm* 10-11.
57. *m. Sabb.* 7:2.

strict observants to fall within the thirty nine forms of work forbidden on the Sabbath.[58]

The rabbis noted the fact that God works on the Sabbath in sustaining creation, giving life and administering judgement, since children are born and people die on the Sabbath. Rabbinic interpretation allowed three classes of exception where situations took priority over Sabbath observance. They were cultic duties such as circumcision and work required for the Temple service like baking cakes for the cereal offering. Matthew's gospel refers to this: 'Have you not read in the law how on the Sabbath the priests in the Temple profane the Sabbath and are guiltless? I tell you, something greater than the Temple is here' (Mt 12:5-8). Defensive warfare, to defend oneself, was allowed, following the case where Mattathias decided the Jews could defend themselves if attacked on the Sabbath after he heard of a group of Jews, a thousand men, women and children, who were massacred because they refused to fight on the Sabbath (1 Macc 2:29-41). Saving life was also permitted. Rabbi Eleazar stated that since circumcision, which concerns one of man's 248 members, overrides the Sabbath, how much more must his whole body (if in danger) override the Sabbath.[59]

Challenging a legalistic approach to these prescriptions, Jesus opened a debate on the whole nature of the Sabbath and on the relationship of God to creation, to salvation history, to the chosen people, to social justice and humanitarian concerns. The synoptics and John all show Jesus challenging an interpretation of the Sabbath which failed to see it as a day for the celebration of creation, life, liberty and salvation. In challenging the prescriptions, Jesus is challenging a possessive human control over the life-giving relationship between God and humanity.

It is interesting to note that Mark uses the plural *tois sabbasin* 'on the sabbath' in Mk 2:23, 25; 3:2, 4, in the sense of the Sabbath day which recurs every week, whereas in the *logia* in Mk 2:27, 28 about the Sabbath being for man/humanity and the Son of Man being master of the Sabbath the singular *to Sabbaton* is used. This may be accounted for by seeing the *logia* as already established sayings included by Mark and the other references reflecting Mark's own usage. It also, and possibly more likely, signifies a

---

58. *m. Shabbat* 7:2, 18:3; 19:1.
59. *b. Yoma* 85b; cf *Mekilta Sabbata* 1.

difference between a day of the week devoted to Sabbath observance and a more abstract theological understanding of Sabbath
as a reflection of God's creative and salvific relationship to creation and humanity.

After the reference to 'man' (humanity), the term Son of Man,
follows naturally, as the Son of Man, already referred to in relation to the forgiveness of sins, is declared Lord/Master of the
Sabbath. The reader is again left to wonder who this Son of Man
is who has power on earth to forgive sins and how he is Lord of
the Sabbath, and in particular how the Jesus of the Galilean ministry relates to this figure.

a. Sabbath Observance. Jesus poses 'no win' question. Mk 3:1-6
In the dispute about plucking the grains of corn Jesus reminded
his accusers that the Sabbath was made for man (*anthrôpos*,
human being), not man for the Sabbath. Here in the synagogue
is a man, a human being. The term *anthrôpos*, a human being, not
anêr, a man as distinct from a woman, is used and it highlights
the connection with what has been said already and bears out
the saying that the Sabbath was made for man/humankind.
Jesus' teaching about the fundamental meaning of the Sabbath
as a remembering of the creative and liberating power of God
will be authoritatively illustrated in the healing and liberating
effects of his miraculous curing of the man (human being) with
the withered hand.

The final incident in this section of the gospel is as dramatic
as any found in the gospels. The atmosphere is charged with
tension as 'they' (identified at the end of the account as the
Pharisees) were observing Jesus to see if he would heal on the
Sabbath. The sense of the passage is that the unfortunate person
with the withered hand is either deliberately 'planted' or conven-
iently used in the synagogue as a bait to trap Jesus into an act of
healing on the Sabbath. In their 'religious' zeal and controlling
legalism they both degraded the person and abused the Sabbath
with their cunning approach. Jesus, however, realised the situation and threw down the gauntlet by asking a penetrating, 'no-
win' question which highlights the real significance of the
Sabbath and the 'anti-life' character of their legalistic approach.

Jesus said to the man with the withered hand: 'Rise up
(*egeire*), into the middle'. The use of the verb *egeire* is significant
since, as already seen, it is often used in the context of healing

with life-giving and resurrection overtones, as in the earlier cases of Simon's mother-in-law and the invalid at Capernaum (Mk 1:31; 2:9, 11, 12; 5:41; 10:49).

'They were watching'. The verb *paretêroun* is used of religious observance and medical observation. Jesus puts a question to those 'who were watching', giving them two parallel choices. Using the term *exestin*, ' lawful', (already used by critics against the disciples) Jesus asks them is it lawful to do good on the Sabbath or to do evil. The only possible answer is 'to do good'. But what does it mean 'to do good' and 'to do evil' in this context? His second, parallel phrase bears out the meaning: 'to save life or to kill'.[60] Not doing good when the opportunity presents itself and the need is obvious is in fact doing evil. Not saving life is in fact killing. Jesus now goes on to proclaim by his action that not healing is in fact doing evil as it is condemning the person to further suffering.

As the withered hand was most likely not life threatening, the description *exêrammenên* (withered) seems to suggest a long term condition, possibly from birth, Jesus is here pushing out the boundaries of standard practice. He is arguing from the greater 'saving of life' to the lesser 'restoring to full health' scenario. Matthew and Luke have a similar story in which Jesus explains his action by way of pointing to the concern shown for a sheep, donkey or ox that would fall into a well or hole on the Sabbath. In Matthew Jesus argues from the lesser case of an animal in difficulties to the greater case of a human being and says that a human being is more important than a sheep and so it is permitted to do good on the Sabbath (Mt 12:11; Lk 14: 5). Luke shows Jesus leaving his critics to draw their own conclusion in their confused embarrassment. In similar vein there is the case of lifting the burden from someone, as in Luke's story of the crippled woman, 'a daughter of Abraham whom Satan has held bound these eighteen years,' when Jesus asks rhetorically, 'Was it not right to untie her bonds on the Sabbath day?'(Lk 13:10-17). Mark is here reflecting a well attested attitude of Jesus to the Sabbath observance when he recounts how he healed the person with the withered hand.

60. See M. A. Tolbert, 'Is it Lawful on the Sabbath to do Good or to do harm?: Mark's Ethics of Religious Practice,' *Perspectives in Religious Studies* 23 (1996) 199-214. The law allowed for assisting people in danger of death on the Sabbath, such as a woman in labour or a man on whom a wall had fallen (*m. Shabbat* 18.3; *b.Yoma* 84; *Tosefta Shabbat* 15.14).

The silence of the critics provoked Jesus to anger. It is the silence of those who have been outwitted in their cunning and cannot afford to speak without bringing opprobrium or ridicule on themselves. It is, however, even more sinister. It is the passive aggression of critics who will not openly confront their target but are happy to scheme behind closed doors. Jesus' anger is a justified anger, reflecting the anger of God in the face of hardness of heart on the part of those closed to God's word and action (Ezek 3:7; Acts 28:27; Rom 2:5). Jesus further outwits the opposition by doing no action in the healing process and so incurs no technical breach of Sabbath observance. He simply tells the man to stretch out his hand. Obedience to his authoritative word brought about the healing. He thus follows his verbal victory with a clinching argument by way of healing the man with the withered hand and doing it without technically infringing the Sabbath observance. Defeated, his critics decide to annihilate their victorious opponent.

6. CONCLUSION. PLOT TO DESTROY JESUS. MK 3:6

In an honour-shame culture Jesus has throughout the controversy stories, and in a particular way here in the final one, 'shamed' his opponents and shown his own superior status and authority. They were reduced to silence. However, the familiar *euthus*, 'immediately', shows the haste with which the opponents come together to decide on putting a stop to Jesus' activity and have their revenge. When one hears of the Herodians one is immediately reminded of the fate of John the Baptist who was arrested and murdered by Herod Antipas and his guards, though his final fate has not yet been told in the gospel. These Herodians were most likely adherents of the ruler in Galilee, maybe sent to spy on Jesus as they obviously had done on the Baptist. Later they will be sent, again in the company of the Pharisees, to try to trap Jesus with the question about paying tribute to Caesar.[61] Again the Baptist's role as precursor, leading along the road Jesus is destined to follow, comes into view as his enemies appear on the scene. Jesus' question about doing good or evil, saving life or killing, is poignantly highlighted as he has done good on the Sabbath and in response his critics meet immediately and

---

61. Mk 12:13 // Mt 22:15-22. These are the only places where the Herodians are mentioned in the New Testament. Luke 20:20 speaks in this context of 'agents sent to pose as men devoted to the law'.

plot to kill him. Their scruples about infringing the holiness of the Sabbath did not cover plotting to murder.

The Pharisees who wished to remain cut off from all foreign influence and power join forces with the representatives of the opposite end of the socio-religious and political spectrum, foreshadowing Jesus' final destiny. The curtain comes down on the first section of Jesus' public ministry in Galilee. The dramatic effect is palpable as the reader/audience realises that the entire gospel has been foreshadowed in this first section. It remains to see it unfold.

As the public ministry opened in a synagogue in Galilee with Jesus preaching and overpowering the demonic powers, the people commented on him as teaching like one 'having authority and not like the scribes'. This section of the gospel reaches its climax in the synagogue where Jesus shows that same authority and his religious critics, the Pharisees, are so powerless they turn in frustration to the malevolent authority of the party who had destroyed the Baptist.

The end of the gospel is foreshadowed. Jesus has warned of the bridegroom being taken away and now the Pharisees and the Herodians have schemed about doing away with him. Later, the chief priests and the scribes will try to find some way of doing away with him after the 'cleansing of the Temple' when he tells the parable of the wicked husbandmen, and again at the approach of the Passover when they would have arrested him, but on each occasion they were afraid of the crowd (Mk 11:18; 12:12; 14:1). It will take the co-operation of a former 'insider', one chosen 'to be with him', to facilitate their plan. That story has yet to be told.

Jesus with his Disciples and Family Mk 3:7-6:6a
Set Around the Lakeside

1. PLOT AND OUTLINE

The second section of the Galilean ministry begins with a summary of Jesus' activity. The results of his ministry so far are becoming obvious. The enthusiastic response of the crowd continues as they gather from near and far. The demons continue to
identify him and their proclamations of his identity need to be
silenced. The authorities he has upset locally seem to have got
their message to headquarters in Jerusalem and the scribes come
from there to observe and condemn him. They cannot deny his
miraculous activity but ascribe it to demonic powers at work in
him. His frenetic activity causes his family concern and they
think he has become unstable and seek to take control of him.
The focus then moves to the disciples whom he chooses to be
apostles. They are appointed both to be with him, the standard
role of disciples, and also to be sent out to work on his behalf, the
role of apostles. There follows the first of the two major discourses in the gospel, the parabolic discourse, and this is followed in turn by Jesus' miraculous actions on sea and land
which provoke various responses and reactions. The section
comes to a close on the very negative note: 'A prophet is only despised in his own country and among his own relations and in
his own house; and he could work no miracle there, though he
cured a few sick people by laying his hands on them. He was
amazed at their lack of faith' (Mk 6:6a).

2. SUMMARY MK 3:7-12

Like the first section dealing with the ministry in Galilee, the second section also begins with a summary. The enthusiastic crowd
continue to pursue him and many with diseases wish to touch
him. He has to withdraw into a boat to address them and there
are no signs that the official attitude of hostility has rubbed off
on the crowd. Official criticism and hostility have not dampened
their enthusiasm. He continues teaching, healing and discomfit-
ing the unclean spirits who continue to recognise his identity.
They call out: 'You are the son of God,' and Jesus severely warns
them not to make him known. The summary begins as in the former section with a reference to Jesus moving from where he was

to the scene of his next activity, this time to the sea (of Galilee).
He goes there *with his disciples*.

As in section one when the crowds gathered around the door
at sunset, or blocked the entrance to the house in Capernaum
where Jesus was present when the people brought the invalid on
the stretcher, the enthusiasm of the large crowd, the *poly plêthos*,
twice referred to in the summary, and the magnetic attraction of
Jesus are highlighted by the reference to the wide extent of his
appeal and reputation. The people come from all the surrounding countryside because they have heard what he has been
doing. The crowd keep following him so that he cannot even
have a meal. From the holy city, Jerusalem, and its province
Judaea, from Idumea (the biblical Edom) in the deep south, and
Perea on the far side of Jordan right around to Galilee in the
north and out into Gentile territory to the north west, the fur-
thest limits of his ministry in Tyre and Sidon, the crowds come
to him.[1]

Withdrawing to the Sea of Galilee has overtones of seeking
seclusion, and perhaps also of seeking refuge from the threatening attitudes like those of the Pharisees and Herodians. He is accompanied by his disciples, a general term for all kinds of followers of his. The sea shore was also a convenient place for a
crowd of people to gather, where the speaker could withdraw
from the crush of the crowd by getting into a boat and addressing them from there (see also 4:1 and 6:2). In addition the voice
carries well over the water. Furthermore, the people could
spread out along the shore and they could buy fish when hungry. The double reference *poly plêthos* and *plêthos poly* give the
impression of a huge number, not just a crowd (*ochlos*) assembled
for an occasion, and it also transcends any ideas of 'a common
crowd' as in the Greek *hoi polloi* or the Latin *profanum vulgus*, so
despised by Horace, but much more of a *multitudo ingens*.[2]

They were drawn by the fact that he had already healed
many (and as pointed out already 'many' in biblical terms is a
stronger word than in English). He healed so many that all who
were afflicted (*hosoi eichon mastigas*, a reflection of the biblical
idea that sickness is a punishment of God) were trying to touch

1. Surprisingly there is no mention of people coming from Samaria in
this summary or anywhere else in Mark.
2. Some stylistic differences in manuscripts concerning the 'following'
by the crowd are of no importance to the meaning.

him. They manifest the common belief of the time that the spirit-filled body of the miracle worker possessed a communicable power, as will be seen in the story of the woman with the issue of blood who made her way through the pressing crowd to touch his garment (Mk 5:27) and on another occasion when the crowd try to touch the hem of his garment (Mk 6:56).

In the synagogue when he cast out the demon the people were amazed and marvelled at how the demons were subject in his name. Here the demons are seen not only to be subject to his 'rebuke' but they fall down before him, an attitude of prostration associated with being in the presence of the Divine or of some high official claiming divine or quasi divine status and authority. The action, though expressed in different words, is common in the Bible. Abr(ah)am prostrated himself on the ground before the Lord when he was told he would become the father of a multitude of nations (Gen 17:3). Nebuchadnezzar ordered all his subjects to prostrate themselves before the golden statue he had made (Dan 3:5). The Magi prostrated themselves before the royal child (Mt 2:11), and Satan required such obeisance in the temptations in the desert (Mt 4:9; Lk 4:7). The debtor pleaded for his life with his creditor with a similar gesture (Mt 18:26). In Luke's gospel the one leper who returned fell at Jesus' feet (Lk 17:16), as did Mary of Bethany on Jesus' arrival after the death of Lazarus (Jn 11:32). The arresting party in the garden in John's gospel fell to the ground when Jesus pronounced the *egô eimi*, 'I am' (Jn 18:6). It is therefore a very significant recognition of the identity of Jesus on the part of the demons when they prostrate themselves before him.

This gesture of the demons he expelled was accompanied by a 'preternatural' insight into his true identity, as in the former exorcism. They called him 'Son of God'. The angels, the people, the just one, and in a very special way the anointed king, were traditionally referred to as 'son of God'. Here, however, unlike the characters in the story, the reader who has been given privileged knowledge in the prologue can understand 'Son of God' in a whole new way, just like the preternatural beings whom Jesus 'rebuked' sternly, ordering their silence in regard to his sonship. This is a pivotal text in any understanding of the messianic secret. In Greek, *epitimân*, 'rebuke', is a judicial term signifying the placing of a penalty or charge against someone. In the LXX it translates roughly the Hebrew *ga'ar*, to signify exorcising or overpowering evil spirits (Zech 3:2, Pss 67/68:31; 105/106:9).

3. JESUS CALLS / APPOINTS THE TWELVE APOSTLES. MK 3:13-19

As in the introduction to the Sermon on the Mount in St
Matthew's gospel, and the multiplication of the loaves in St
John's gospel Jesus ascends *the mountain*, an unspecified mountain in Galilee associated also with the transfiguration in all
three synoptic gospels and with the final appearance of the risen
Lord in Matthew's gospel where he commissions the eleven to
make disciples of all nations.[3] On the mountain Jesus acts in
solemn sovereign fashion. The mountain is reminiscent of
Sinai / Horeb with its connotations of the presence and glory of
God, the gift of the Law to Moses and the gentle breeze heralding the word of the Lord to Elijah (Exod 19-20; 1 Kings 19). This
is a typical gospel setting for a teaching, healing, feeding or commissioning sequence (cf Mt 5:1ff; Mk 6:33f; Lk 9:12).

This call narrative emphasises both the initiative and the free
choice of Jesus. 'He called to himself those whom he wished.'
The deliberate intention of this action of Jesus is emphasised by
the use of two verbs, the 'fortified' verb to call *proskaleitai* (in the
Greek middle voice showing a certain reflexive meaning, 'call to
himself') and *êthelen* ('he wished'). Nine of the eleven verbs in
the pericope have Jesus as the subject, a further pointer to the deliberate choice and intensity of the action. Whereas the indicative, simple, unfortified active verbs *eipen autois* ('he said to
them') and *ekalesen autous* ('he called them') were used in the call
of the two pairs of brothers, the very deliberate nature of the action here makes the same point as the very explicit statements in
the farewell discourse in John's gospel: 'You have not chosen
me, I have chosen you and commissioned you to go out and bear
fruit' (Jn 15:16), and in the crisis following the discussion on the
bread of life when he says: 'Have I not chosen you Twelve, and
yet one of you is a devil', and the Johannine narrator goes on to
explain that he was referring to Judas Iscariot, one of the
Twelve, who was going to betray him (Jn 6:70f). Both traditions
emphasise the same point of Jesus' initiative and very deliberate
choice, even of the one who will betray him.

'He (made) constituted twelve', *epoiêsen dôdeka*, is stated
twice but the second statement is not in all manuscripts and

3. Mt 5-7, the Sermon on the Mount; Mk 3:13-19 / / Lk 6:12-16, the appointment of the Twelve; Mt 17:1-8 / / Mk 9:2-8 / / Lk 9:28-36, the
Transfiguration; Mt 28, the final appearance of the Risen Lord – all are
on the mountain in Galilee.

scholars debate the relative merits of regarding it as original. The meaning is unaffected either way. 'He called them apostles' does not appear in all manuscripts either, but the basic meaning of the text is entirely unaffected by its inclusion or exclusion. If included, it emphasises the points already made by the 'calling' and 'sending'. The repetition does not occur in the corresponding places in Matthew and Luke (Mt 10:1-4; Lk 6:12-16). The number twelve is symbolic. It is inspired by the number of the sons of Jacob after whom the tribes of Israel take their names and represents the fullness of Israel in the eschatological people of God. Here Jesus is embarking on a mission to renew Israel, not to establish 'a new Israel', but the renewal will have far reaching effects beyond the traditional boundaries of the people.

The Twelve are appointed *to be with him*, the standard requirement of a disciple, being with the master to observe and learn. Jesus will, however, push out the boundaries of discipleship and require them to be with him and share his fate in a very challenging way as he goes to Jerusalem and on to Golgotha/Calvary. 'Being with him' will also be the source of their authority and the context of their teaching. They will be 'with him' until they cease to be with him as they flee from him in the Garden of Gethsemane, where Judas will be 'with the arresting party' (Mk 14:43), and Peter 'having followed at a distance' will be 'with the guards' in the courtyard of the high priest (Mk 14:54).

They are *sent out* to proclaim, that is to be his heralds, and to have power to cast out demons, the very things Jesus himself was doing. 'Sending' them, *apostellein autous*, makes them 'apostles', representatives or ambassadors of Jesus, as well as disciples. To three of them he gave special names. To Simon he gave the name Peter, and to James and John, the sons of Zebedee, he gave the name 'sons of thunder'. Naming someone shows an authority over that person and when there is a change of name, or a new name is added to the old; it signifies a change of relationship, character, role, way of life or destiny. Significantly the three to whom Jesus gave new names are the three who will be with him as his intimate associates at the raising of the daughter of Jairus, at the transfiguration on the mountain and, together with Andrew, they will be the ones to whom he addresses the eschatological-apocalyptic discourse on the Mount of Olives. Finally they will be together with him as the inner group in the garden of Gethsemane. However, at this point in the narrative, these events are still in the future and again the reader is left wondering why Jesus gave them these new names when he chose them.

The list of the Twelve appears in all three synoptic gospels and in the Acts of the Apostles, but there are some minor variations in the lists (Mk 3:13-19; Mt 10:1-4; Lk 6:12-16; Acts 1:13). John mentions 'the Twelve' but does not supply a list of their names or a narrative of their call or appointment as a group of twelve (Jn 6:67, 70, 71; 20:24;). Paul mentions the Twelve but names only Cephas (Peter) in his list of appearances of the Risen Lord in 1 Corinthians (1 Cor 15:5). Every list begins with Simon (Peter) and the same four, the two pairs of brothers, Simon (Peter) and Andrew, James and John, are mentioned first. Every list ends with Judas Iscariot. In Matthew's gospel, at the point where Mark and Luke describe the call of Levi at the custom house (toll booth), Matthew calls the toll (tax) collector in question Matthew. In Luke's list Thaddeus is omitted and Judas, son of James is inserted. Nathaniel figures in the initial calling of disciples in John's gospel and tradition later identified him with Bartholomew.

The name Iscariot has been variously interpreted. The most straightforward meaning is 'ish Keriot, man of Kerioth, identifying him by his place of origin. Some see it as a condemnatory adjective describing his act of betrayal and derived from the Hebrew skr, which means to 'deliver', 'hand over' or 'betray'. Others speculate on a Semitic version of the Latin Sicarii, 'men of the dagger', a name for revolutionaries working to overthrow the Romans and their Jewish collaborators and so described from the short daggers they carried. Others think it may be derived from the Hebrew verb saqar, to act falsely. The New Testament writers generally heap opprobrium on Judas. His mind and motives have been a subject of discussion throughout history. Luke and John see the Prince of Evil at the root of Judas' actions. Both say that Satan entered into Judas (Lk 22:3; Jn:13:27), and John also says that Judas was a devil (Jn 6:70). This 'religious/philosophical' interpretation is accompanied by terms relating to what is often seen as the root of all evil, love of money. Mark and Luke show the chief priests tempting Judas with the offer of money. Matthew shows him demanding the money. John further develops this money loving weakness in terms of stealing from the common fund in his charge (Mk 14:11; Lk 22:5;

Mt 26:15; Jn 12:4-6). Since New Testament times historians, priests, poets, playwrights and many others have continued to speculate on his motives. Mark, probably very wisely, simply draws attention to the fact of the betrayal and avoids speculation on the motives.

Having called/chosen and constituted the Twelve, one is not really told, but left to figure out what exactly is the precise function of the Twelve that distinguishes them from the others. Several of those mentioned do not figure in any prominent way in the gospels or in the Acts of the Apostles. However, Matthew and Luke portray them as the eschatological judges presiding over the twelve tribes (Mt 19:28//Lk 22:28-30)[4] and the pressing desire to fill the vacancy left by Judas, signifying a vacancy 'on a bench' or 'college' of twelve is striking (Acts 1:15-26), as is the subsequent emergence of a volume of apocryphal literature that emerged in the early church in their names.

i. Jesus' Family: Old and New Mk 3:20-21

Contrast of 'Natural Family' and 'New family'
This section of the gospel sets the appointment of the Twelve, the enthusiasm of the crowds, the great 'parabolic' teaching of Jesus and his life-saving activity, against the background of scribal accusations of demon possession and mounting disbelief even on the part of his own people and his family. The concerned action of his family and the accusations of the scribes from Jerusalem are presented as an intercalation, the account of the scribes interrupting that of the family and their concern about Jesus' personal stability.

After several references to *proclaiming* and *preaching* the word, on the part of the Baptist, Jesus and his newly commissioned apostles, the focus now turns to hearing and listening to the word. Hearing/listening/paying attention to the word is essential to true discipleship. This is borne out by way of contrast between his unbelieving family who are 'near to him' (*par' autou*), bonded to him by ties of blood, and his close disciples, those who 'are with him' (*met' autou*), together with those

---

4. Mt 19:28//Lk 22:28-30 represents material the majority of scholars designate as coming from the Q source, the material common to Matthew and Luke which Mark does not share.

'around him' (*peri auton*), his broader followers and disciples, bonded to him by their response to the word.[5]

Rather ominously, however, his relatives do not believe in him, thinking he is mad. Even more ominously the scribes from Jerusalem claim that he casts out devils by the power of Beelzebul. What follows is the first example of an intercalation in the gospel. As described already in the introduction, an intercalation is an arrangement of material whereby a story is inserted into the middle of another in an A-B-A arrangement. Both stories serve to highlight each other by way of contrast or similarity. Sometimes also, as in the present example, the interruption of the first story provides the narrative time for a decision taken in the first part to take effect before or during the second part. In this case the interruption allows the family of Jesus the narrative time to come from his home in Nazareth to where he is preaching at the Sea of Galilee. Furthermore, the unbelieving attitudes to Jesus, evident in both stories, add up to a stark picture of growing rejection and hostility.

The two parts of the account dealing with Jesus' blood relations are divided and the account of his accusers inserted in the middle. The understandable concern of his unbelieving relatives, who believe he is mad, is mentioned in Mk 3:21. 'Those near him' (*hoi par' autou*),[6] that is his relatives, set out, very likely from Nazareth to the area around Capernaum, because 'they had been saying' he was mad. Who was saying it? His relatives? Or is it a general statement meaning 'it was being said', as in *Man sagt/on dit*. They set out to apprehend him, to take control of him by force. The verb *kratêsai* signifies a violent or forceful action as in arresting someone by force. It is the verb that describes Jesus' power over demons and sickness, and will be used to describe the arrest of Jesus in Gethsemane.

ii. Accusations of the Scribes. Mk 3:22-30

Turning to the accusations against Jesus of casting out devils by the power of Beelzebul,[7] we meet the most determined oppon-

---

5. See S. P. Ahearne-Kroll, 'Who are My Mother and My Brothers? Family Relations and Family Language in the Gospel of Mark', *JR* (2001) 1-25.
6. Sometimes this expression is translated as 'his disciples' but Greek usage and the second part of the account point in the direction of ' his relatives'.
7. The Syriac mss and the Vulgate have Beelzebub rather than Beelzebul.

ents of Jesus in Mark, the scribes from Jerusalem. They make a
two-fold accusation against him. They say that he is possessed
by Beelzebul (literally, he has Beelzebul) and that he casts out
demons 'by the prince of demons'. Having mentioned Beelzebul,
the narrator in typical fashion adds a description, 'the prince of
demons' which expands on the name. Who or what was
Beelzbul? The name is not found in the LXX for a demon. It occurs in the synoptics both in the triple tradition (Mk 3:22//Mt
12:24, 27//Lk 11:15) and in the double tradition, the material
usually designated as Q (Mt 10:25; Lk 11:15, 18f). There are some
variations in the name – Beelzebul, Beelzeboul, Beelzebub.
Looking for a possible origin of the name scholars point to the
likelihood that Beelzebul and Beelzeboul are variations on the
name of an old Canaanite god meaning 'Baal the Prince' or 'Baal
the exalted abode'.[8] The name Baalzebub ('Lord of the Flies') appears in the Second Book of Kings as a satirical version of the
name of the Canaanite god of Ekron and in the Testament of
Solomon Beelzeboul is a fallen angel who is called 'prince of
demons' and 'ruler of demons'.[9]

Responding to the charge, Jesus calls 'the prince of demons'
Satan. In the Book of Job Satan means 'adversary', much as we
would speak of 'devil's advocate' in a discussion. In this pericope in Mark, Satan is identified with Beelzebul, the prince of
demons. Satan is the tempter in the desert in the three synoptics
(Mk 1:13 and //s) and Luke says he departed from there to return at 'the appointed time', at 'his opportune moment' (achri
kairou) (Lk 4:13), generally seen as the moment of his entering
into Judas and motivating the betrayal (Lk 22:3; Jn 13:27). He is
seen in the New Testament generally as the adversary of Jesus.
In a more general way, any person operating against Jesus or inspired by thoughts and plans contrary to his could be regarded
as a 'Satan' figure, as Peter was when Jesus said: 'Get behind me,
Satan, your thoughts are not the thoughts of God but of men
(human beings)' (Mk 8:33).

Whatever the exact derivation of the names the accusation is
quite clear. Jesus is accused of having, in the sense of being possessed by, a leading spirit of a pagan pantheon who wields authority over other evil spirits, all of whom, by very definition,

---

8. J. R. Donahue and D. J. Harrington, *op. cit.*, 129, n.22.
9. *Ibid.* cf 2 Kings 1:3, 6. *Test. Sol.* 3:1-6.

operate against God and God's rule in creation and among his people.They are the forces opposed to the kingdom of God.

Jesus responds in metaphors, or 'parables' (using the term 'parable' in a very general way). He concludes with an oracular style judgement. The 'parables' take two different approaches, one looking at the accusation from the point of view of internal division in the kingdom of Satan, the other looking at it from the point of view of an attack from outside on that kingdom.

Using the image of a divided kingdom and a divided house, Jesus points out how neither can last. These examples are gnomic, proverbial, and applicable to all situations at all times, not depending on any particular set of circumstances for their validation. However, Jesus' audience would have seen how they reflected their own experience and Mark's audience would have plenty of contemporary examples to illustrate the maxims. The five emperors in the years 68-69 AD[10] with the empire-wide upheaval caused by military and dynastic rivalry was an example to everyone in the empire of the consequences of a kingdom divided against itself and the consequences when underlings seek the power of the *princeps*. So too the destruction of the house of Herod Antipas after he divorced the daughter of the Nabatean king Aretas in order to marry Herodias would have been well known. The powerful family that hounded John and Jesus had been destroyed from within by the time Mark's gospel was written.

The second image used is that of an attack from without. Jesus' coming is a great threat to the power of the strong, evil one and to his sphere of influence and power. John the Baptist introduced Jesus as *ischyroteros*, 'the stronger one.' Now the stronger one (Jesus) is attacking the strong man (Satan). Raiding the house of the strong man, the oppressor, is an established pattern in biblical thought. The Israelites 'despoiled' the Egyptians as they left in the Exodus (Ex 3:21f; 11:2f; 12:35f; cf Ps 104 (105): 37). God despoils the mighty of his captives and the tyrant of his prey. The servant of God divides the spoils with the mighty/ strong (Is 49:24f; 53:12).

Having delivered his response in 'parables' to the substance of the allegations made against him, Jesus now delivers a judgement in oracular language on the nature of the offence involved in making such allegations. In the synoptics a single 'amen' reg-

---

10. Nero, Galba, Otho, Vitellius and Vespasian.

ularly introduces a particularly solemn statement of Jesus. Matthew uses it thirty one times, Mark thirteen times and Luke six times. It leads into a significant statement that is intimately connected with what went before. It functions like the affirmation, 'Thus says the Lord' in the prophetic writings of the Old Testament. In the synoptics, a single 'amen' often introduces threat or promise, whereas in John, the double amen, which occurs twenty five times, is primarily a revelation formula.[11]

In response to the serious criticism and allegation of the scribes from Jerusalem, Jesus responds: 'Amen I say to you all sins and blasphemies will be forgiven the children of humanity.' This is a reaffirmation of a belief in God's universal forgiveness current among many of the people at the time. It is also a belief fortified and extended by the radical nature of Jesus' ministry in his embracing of people branded as sinners, and his inclusion of the marginalised and outcast.[12] Having stated the universal nature of God's forgiveness for all sins committed and blasphemies uttered, Jesus now highlights the heinous nature of the accusation made against him and his ministry by stating that there is a sin that can never be forgiven. As already seen in the gospel, Jesus' ministry is one of Spirit-empowered healing and forgiveness. He is the one on whom the Spirit descended at his baptism, the one driven into the desert by the Spirit and empowered by the Spirit as he ' baptises in Holy Spirit'. This ministry of Jesus, the baptism in Holy Spirit, has been branded by his accusers as the work of Satan. They have not only refused the gift, they have seen it as evil. Where else can they find forgiveness? They have refused it at source and condemned it. This has eternal consequences. It is no ' ordinary' blasphemy like uttering the Divine Name. The incident is rounded off by a reminder that the blasphemous dispute started because they were saying, 'He has an unclean spirit', which could be paraphrased as 'the spirit he has, which the reader knows is the Holy Spirit, is unclean'. There is nowhere else to seek forgiveness, no other power to forgive. The consequences are eternal.

---

11. 1QS,1:20, 2:10, 18 (after blessings and curses); cf 1QS 1-17. The double 'amen' is found at the end of a sentence in some Qumran texts, obviously under liturgical influence. The Johannine usage strikes the solemn liturgical note, creating a context for divine revelation, before Jesus pronounces *legô hymin (soi)*, ' I say to you'.
12. 1QS 11:11-14; cf also *The Prayer of Manasseh*.

Jesus' 'New Family' of Disciples Mk 3:31-35

The interrupted story about Jesus' relatives is resumed. The intercalation provides the narrative time for his family to have made their journey. His mother and brothers (and in some manuscripts sisters are included, as below at verse 35) arrive to rescue him and they send a message to him in through the crowd (Mk 3:31). Mentioning the crowd picks up on the introduction to the story where it stated that the crowds were gathering and it was impossible for him even to have a meal. It is another scene reminiscent of the last time he came home when the people crowded round the door at sunset, and of the occasion when the invalid was let down through the roof in front of Jesus because of the crowd.

It is noteworthy that Jesus' family send others in to him with the message that they are outside and seeking him. The references to 'others', 'outside' and 'seeking' emphasise the growing distance between Jesus' human family and his 'new' family. Already described as *hoi par' autou* (his relatives) in contradistinction to *hoi met' autou* (those with him), his relatives are now 'outsiders' and have to send for him into the group of 'insiders' *hoi peri auton*, a larger group 'around him' which by implication includes also those 'with him', *hoi met' autou*, his disciples. The crowd, here described as *ochlos*, are portrayed as sitting around him, in the manner of disciples listening to and learning from the teaching and preaching of the master.

When the message is brought to him that his mother and brothers are 'outside' seeking him, he asks 'who are my mother and my brothers (and sisters)?' Then looking around at those sitting in a circle 'around him' he uses the metaphor of family, mother, brother and sister and announces that his mother and brothers (and sisters) are those who hear the word of God and keep it. Commentators have noticed the absence of 'father' in the reply. Some have speculated on the fact that this is because Joseph was already dead and so the parallel with his human family did not include the father.[13] It is much more likely, though not explicitly stated in Mark, that the absence of a reference to 'father' reflects the understanding that his new family of disciples are the family of his Father in heaven. This understand-

---

13. Cf Mk 10:30. Fathers are not mentioned also in the restoration after persecution when the persecuted will be 'repaid a hundred times over with houses, brothers, sisters, mothers, children and land'.

ing forms the basis of a teaching in Matthew that 'You must call no one on earth your father, since you have only one Father, and he is in heaven. Nor must you allow yourselves to be called teachers, for you have only one teacher, the Christ' (Mt 23:10).

Earthly family ties have been replaced with the ties of the kingdom. This reminds one of the blessing of Elizabeth in Luke's gospel when she proclaimed that the mother of Jesus was blessed, not because she was his biological mother, but because she believed the word and thus became his mother: 'Blessed is she who believed that the word spoken to her would be fulfilled' (Lk 1:45).

4. JESUS' MIGHTY WORDS MK 4:1-34
i. He Taught in Parables

As the hostility shown to Jesus on the part of the authorities and the unbelief of his relations become more obvious, he concentrates on his 'new family', the Twelve, the disciples chosen 'to be with him' and the broader circle of 'those around him', the friendly crowd of followers who are disciples in the general sense. He withdrew to the shore of the Sea of Galilee and taught the crowd from the boat. In this tranquil oasis of calm, peace and harmony, after his frenetic movement throughout Galilee, he teaches the crowd in public and also withdraws to teach the Twelve and 'those around him' in private. Mk 4:1-2 is the longest and most formal introduction to a teaching sequence in the gospel, somewhat resembling the formality of the introductions to the Sermon on the Mount in Matthew or to the long discourses in John. Jesus was teaching them many things in parables, carrying on his customary practice of teaching (*edidasken*, the imperfect tense, is used for sustained or repeated action). The continuity of the pericope is enabled by *kai* 'and', often combined with *palin*, 'again' in the expression, 'and again' (*kai palin*), already used in Mk 2:1, 13; 3;1, (20). Mark begins the discourse with *kai elegen*, 'and he was saying', and repeats it a number of times, giving the discourse something of the flavour of a series of rabbinic instructions.[14]

The use of parables is one of the aspects of Jesus' teaching

---

14. At various points throughout the discourse the phrase *kai elegen*, 'and he was saying', is used (also the present *kai legei*). R. H. Gundry, *op. cit.*, 187, points to the likelihood that it is a reflection of the rabbinic usage in *m Aboth* of *hu' hayah 'ômêr '*(and) he was speaking/saying' with characteristic Semitic *w'* prefixed.

with which most readers are familiar. The Greek word for parable, *parabolê*, is made up of two words, *ballein*,' to throw', and
para, 'alongside', in the sense of throwing, or placing, two things
alongside each other as a means of comparison or contrast. In
Mark, and in all the gospels, the term 'parable' is used in a broad
and relatively loose sense and can refer to short metaphorical
sayings, similitudes, allegories, riddles, lessons for illustration
and some longer narratives. This ' broad' use of the term parable, *parabolê*, reflects the Hebrew *mashal* or the Aramaic *matla*,
capturing the more enigmatic element of *mashal/matla* which
covers various forms of speech and figurative discourse, parabolic narrative (Jdgs 14:10-18; Prov 1:1-7; 1 Sam 10:12), riddles,
proverbial sayings or aphorisms (Jdgs 14:10-18; Prov 1:1-7; 1
Sam 10:12), allegories (Is 5:1-7; Ezek 17: 3-24), satires and taunt
songs (Mic 2:4; Hab 2:6), apocalyptic revelatory texts (Dan 7:1-
28; 8:1-27; 1 Enoch 37-71) and so forth. All these function in the
Old Testament as figures of speech which can at the same time
both conceal the truth from the spiritually obtuse and reveal it to
the spiritually open who are on the way to fuller understanding.
In Mark the *parabolê* is used for short metaphorical sayings (Mk
3:23-27), longer narratives (Mk 4:1-9; 12:1-9), allegories (Mk:13-
20; 13:34-37), riddles (Mk 4:10-11; 7:17) and lessons or illustra-
tions (Mk 13:28).

Since parables function as figures of speech which can at the
same time both conceal the truth from the spiritually obtuse and
reveal it to the spiritually open on the way to fuller understanding, they are far more than stories with a straightforward moral
or religious message, which is how they are often inadequately
described. Such a description is more suitable to Aesop's fables,
each of which has a moral message, than to Jesus' parables. They
are unsettling confrontations with the realities of life. Sometimes
they are immediately obvious like the warning about the divided
kingdom. At times they can be like a shot across the bows, at
other times like a hard sweet to chew on for a time. Sometimes
they provoke an immediate response, as in the case of the parable of the wicked tenants where the immediate reaction is a desire to arrest Jesus (Mk 12:1-12) or a spontaneous exclamation on
the part of the listeners (Mt 21:33-46; Lk 20:9-19). At other times
they only yield their meaning later when the listeners have had
time to go away and think about them. In his book *The Parables of
the Kingdom*, C. H. Dodd described the parable as ' a metaphor or

simile drawn from nature or common life, arresting the hearer by its vividness or strangeness and leaving the mind in sufficient doubt about its precise application to tease it into active thought.'[15] F. Kermode puts it very well: 'The parable isn't over until a satisfactory answer or explanation is given, the interpretation completes it.[16]

A parable is like a weapon in the hand of a speaker. It can function as a shield to divert criticism and turn the tables on an adversary or it can sink a thought provoking shot into the mind and heart of the audience, causing a change of outlook and attitude, confronting the listeners with a decision that needs to be made. Jesus often resorted to the use of parables when he was under pressure by way of criticism or outright attack, or when he wanted to go on the offensive against his critics. He also used parables to shock, provoke and stimulate his listeners into thinking through the implications of his words and deeds.[17] In the overall context of this section of the gospel they are a catalyst, an important factor in identifying the 'insiders' and 'outsiders' and separating out the 'true family', the 'true disciples' of Jesus, those genuinely seeking the will of God (cf Mk 3:35).

ii. Outline of the Discourse Mk 4:1-34

The teaching in this collection of parables and explanations is well organised in a chiastic or concentric formation:

15. C. H. Dodd, *The Parables of the Kingdom*, New York, 1965, 5.

16. F. Kermode, *The Genesis of Secrecy*, 24.

17. In John's gospel this same aspect is evident and may throw light on the more enigmatic aspect of Mark. The metaphor of the Good/Model Shepherd in St John's gospel is called a *paroimia* in the text, a term used again three times in chapter sixteen (Jn 16:25 x 2; 29). The sense of Jesus' speech, at first hidden and obscure (Jn 10:6), becomes in a second moment more transparent as the parable is explained (Jn 10:7-16); it attains its greatest clarity at the moment of his glorification when Jesus will speak openly – *parrêsia laleo* – John 16:25 ,29 – when the Counsellor, the Holy Spirit will be sent, all things will be taught, all that he has said will be brought to remembrance (Jn 14:26). Not only the term itself but especially the way it is used, as opposed to speaking openly, shows some close similarity to the use of *parabolê* in the synoptics. cf M. Sabbe, 'John 10 and its Relationship to the Synoptic Gospels' in *The Shepherd Discourse of John 10 and its Context*, 91 . cf Mk 4:10-11//Mt 13:10-11//Lk 8:9-10.

a. Introduction: Teaching in Parables (Mk 4:1-2)
b.   Parable of Failed / Abundant Growth (the Sower) (Mk 4:3-9)
c.   The Mystery: Revealed and Hidden (Mk 4:10-12)
d.   Allegorical Interpretation to a small group (Mk 4:13-20)
c.   Secrets Revealed & Hidden. Lamp & Measure (Mk 4:21-25)
b.   Parables of Successful Growth (Mk 4:26-32)
a. Conclusion: Teaching in Parables. (Mk 4:33-34)

iii. The Discourse

a. Introduction. Teaching in Parables (Mk 4:1-2)
The scene by the sea with the crowds on the shore and Jesus entering the boat to speak from there is by now familiar to the reader. The emphasis on 'sitting' highlights the teaching position (as in 'the chair of Moses'). Here Jesus uses the boat as a 'chair of teaching' or pulpit. Grammatically the sentence is rather loose: 'entering the boat, he sat on the sea', but its meaning is quite clear. Getting into the boat and pulling out into the water kept him from being crushed and having his voice absorbed by the immediate section of the crowd in too close proximity. Furthermore, sound travels well over the water.

b. Parable of Failed & Abundant Growth ('the Sower') (Mk 4:3-9)
In his teaching he said: 'Listen!' That is a call to listen, in the sense of 'pay attention, hear and obey'. It is an appeal that must have rung in their ears like the Shema, ' Listen, O Israel', or reminded them of the 'Hear this word' oracles of a prophet like, for example, the oracles in chapters three to five of Amos. Jesus, having called for attention, went on to tell the parable usually called the parable of the sower. But should it be called the parable of the seed, or the parable of the ground, or the parable of failed growth, or the parable of the abundant harvest?[18] Just as Jesus begins the parable with an appeal to listen, so too he will conclude it with an appeal to listen: 'Listen, anyone who has ears to hear!' The repeated appeal to listen is the key to interpreting this parable as it comes across in Mark's redacted narrative. This will be confirmed in the allegorical explanation in Mk 4:13-20. Listening, however, is not just hearing and understanding intellectually. It is hearing and taking to heart what is heard in such a way that it becomes effective in one's life.

18. It is not introduced explicitly as a parable, but is later referred to as such in Mk 4:13.

Mk 4:3-9, usually though somewhat inaccurately called the parable of the sower, is the only 'parable story' in this collection.[19] Here in Mark's gospel it is really a parable story that contrasts frustrated growth, or failed harvest, with abundant harvest, though the emphasis may have been on the abundant harvest in an earlier stage of the tradition. In the pre-Markan tradition this was probably one of three straightforward parables of growth, the other two being the parables of the seed growing secretly and of the tiny mustard seed growing into a great plant. These other two parables follow shortly (Mk 4:26-32) but Mark has set the first one in his own redactional setting. To what or to whom does the parable refer? Several times already it has been said of Jesus as he set about his mission that 'he went out' (*exêlthen*). This is exactly what the sower does. He too 'went out' to sow. After the initial statement of 'going out to sow' there is no further emphasis on the sower. When the parable is taken together with the parable of the seed growing secretly and the parable of the mustard seed, all three are seen to focus on a growth beyond expectation. However, Markan redaction of this parable puts a good deal of emphasis on the impediments to that growth, a factor not present in the other parables. Three out of four sowings fail, the fourth produces abundantly, a triple abundance balancing the triple failure. Taken together with the introduction and conclusion which emphasise listening (in the sense of hearing, accepting and obeying) one will not be surprised to find that the allegorical interpretation, which follows shortly as a private instruction to 'those about him together with the Twelve', emphasises the different kinds of listening to, accepting and obeying the word. The crowd by the sea, however, who were also present when the 'parable story' was told, are left without an explanation and must think it through for themselves.

As a parable it is meant to present a comparison or contrast. The sower is the agent of the sowing but does not figure in any level of the comparisons (a further reason for not regarding it as 'the parable of the sower'). The manner of sowing, whether on ground subsequently ploughed or scattered widely on already ploughed ground, is not really relevant to the point of the story. It is not a teaching on good agricultural practice. The comparisons or contrasts come really in the nature of the ground and of

---

19. B. van Iersel, *op. cit.*, 71, uses the term 'parable story' to distinguish this classical parable from the other more general uses of the term.

the harvest produced. Of the four sowings there are three failures – instant failure on the path due to the birds, failure after an
initial growth on rocky ground due to the sun and poor roots,
and failure after more promising growth due to the choking activity of the thorns. The contrast comes with the fourth sowing
which produces a huge harvest from the good ground. The
triple failure is contrasted with the triple abundance. The one
point is clear. Seed on three kinds of bad soil fails, seed on good
soil produces thirty, sixty and a hundredfold. Jesus does not
spell out in detail at this point the possible applications to life of
the various types of ground and the images used. He will do so
shortly, in the house, turning the parable into an allegory where
various details have a meaning related to everyday experience.
He finishes the parable with the extended version of his initial
call to listen, that is, to pay attention, hear and obey. 'Let the one
who has ears to hear, listen.'

c. The Mystery: Revealed and Hidden. Mk 4:10-12
There is a sudden change of location and audience. The verses
that follow are among the most difficult in the New Testament.
They are inserted between the 'parable of the sower' and its explanation, but they deal with the explanation of the parables in
general. They interrupt the flow of teaching, as they introduce a
new audience consisting of an unspecified group, *hoi peri auton*, '
those around him,' (instead of the usual 'disciples' and 'crowd')
together with the Twelve, who are themselves now mentioned
for the first time since their 'appointment'. The phrase 'those
around him' is used to refer in a more general way to disciples
and followers who were in Jesus' company. In keeping with the
rabbinic practice of subsequently explaining to disciples a public
statement or teaching,[20] Jesus regularly takes his disciples aside
to explain further what he had been teaching in public (Mk 4:34;
9:28, 35; 10:10, 32; 12:43; 13:3). Again the biblical expression *kai
hote egeneto*, 'and when it came to pass', creates a mood of solemnity as it introduces an episode. 'And when it came to pass that
they were alone, those around him (*hoi peri auton*), together with
the Twelve, asked him about the parables.'

They asked Jesus to explain the meaning of the parables.
Though it may at first appear, because of its position in the text,
to be an inquiry about the parable that he had just told, and an

20. D. Daube, *The New Testament and Rabbinic Judaism*, 141-50.

explanation of that parable will follow shortly, the question and Jesus' answer actually address the use of parables in general. In fact the introduction to 'the parable of the sower' mentioned a more extensive teaching in parables (Mk 4:2). Using the term 'parable' in its broadest sense the reader has already heard the 'parables' of the bridegroom, the unshrunken cloth, the new wineskins, the divided kingdom, the house of the strong man and now the parable usually called the parable of the sower. This question about the meaning of the parables and Jesus' answer facilitate the insertion into the Markan narrative at this point of the *logion*: '*To you* has been given the secret mystery (secret) of the kingdom of God, but *to those outside* all is in parables (riddles)'. Mark sets this *logion*, which was most likely present already in the pre-Markan stage of the tradition, in this context and further redacts it with the loose quotation from, or allusion to Isa 6:9,10.[21] The same passage from Isaiah (Isa 6:9f) is used, very possibly because of Jewish and Christian disputes and the rejection of Christian claims that the kingdom had come in a definitive way in Jesus, in two later Christian documents explaining the rejection of Jesus' claims (Jn 12:40) or his followers' claims on his behalf (Acts 28:26f).

Insiders and Outsiders
Who exactly are the 'insiders' and 'outsiders'? Most interpreters reject the opinion of some scholars that, for Mark, the 'insiders' are those in the house or in the boat with Jesus receiving the private instruction from the master, while the 'outsiders' represent the crowd outside the house or along the shore for whom the parables are esoteric teachings which they do not understand. This appears to be the meaning in the parallel texts in Mt 13:11 and Lk 8:10. M. J. Lagrange strongly rejects such an opinion with the observation that the division is not one of accidental location but of principle,[22] an opinion shared by J. R. Donohue and D. J. Harrington who state that 'outside' is not simply a spatial term but can also describe a relationship to Jesus.[23] Furthermore, the

---

21. D. Daube, *ibid.*, suggests it may have its origin in a liturgical setting.
22. M. J. Lagrange, *Évangile selon Saint Marc*, 26, explains: '*Ce ne sont pas ceux qui sont sur le rivage, par opposition à ceux qui sont dans la barque, repartition de pure circonstance, car ici il est question d'une repartition de principes.*'
23. J. R. Donohue and D. J. Harrington, *op. cit.*, 140.

relationship does not reflect a neat division between the 'disciples' and the 'crowd'. The most widely accepted opinion sees
the 'outsiders' as those who are the adversaries of Jesus, like his
critics, his unbelieving relatives and, *a fortiori*, his accusers
among the hostile authorities who have not accepted him.[24]
Jesus earlier declared that his brother and sister and mother
were 'whoever does the will of God,' while his natural family
stood 'outside' looking to apprehend him. On that occasion he
looked at those around him (*tous peri auton*), the same designation of the group that is found here with the Twelve, and he
called them his brother, sister and mother.

B. van Iersel sums up the situation very well:

It remains to point out that in order to establish the identity
of the outsiders, we should not go beyond Mark. If 'outsiders' must be assigned in the book, it would be first of all
those who have shut themselves out, like the Pharisees and
scribes, and those who refuse to enter where Jesus is, like his
own relatives. But it is perhaps even more sensible to confine
the opposition between insiders and outsiders implied by
this chapter to the characters that appear in it. Within the
framework of this chapter, then, the outsiders are people
who do not want to listen to the word of Jesus or are unwilling to live up to it, while the insiders are those who ask Jesus
for an explanation.[25]

In the context of the developing narrative of the gospel, Jesus is
now surrounded by his 'new family' in contrast to his unbelieving natural family and his adversaries. Their 'listening' is bearing fruit. They are asking questions, seeking further understanding because they have become engaged with him in a positive
way. The 'outsiders' have not done so and therefore it all remains a riddle to them. To those on the outside everything is in
'parables'. This use of the term 'parables' here resembles the biblical use of the *mashal/matla* as a riddle or puzzle, so that everything comes across to 'those outside' as a riddle or puzzle – it
partly reveals and partly hides the truth contained in it. F. J.
Moloney puts it succinctly:

24. C. Focant, *L'Évangile selon Marc*, Commentaire biblique: NT 2, 167,
says: *'La question de l'identification de "ceux du dehors" a été abondamment
discutée. Le contexte narratif oriente vers les scribes et la famille de Jésus ... la
plupart des exégètes ... pensent que l'expression de Marc fait plutôt reference à
des adversaires de Jésus ...'*
25. B. van Iersel, *op. cit.*, 82.

The mystery of the kingdom is partly uncovered for those 'outside' as they both hear and see Jesus in and through parable. However, they do not perceive, nor do they understand. But there is no immediate reason to believe that all is lost.'[26]

All is not lost for 'the outsiders', however, at this point in the gospel narrative, because it is not yet clear who will eventually turn out to be the 'insiders' or 'outsiders' and this may very well account for the indeterminate nature of the expression *hoi peri auton*, 'those around him'. The 'insider-outsider' division is not yet finally settled in the narrative and in many respects the difference between 'those inside' and 'those outside' will take many a turn during the rest of the story. Peter himself, for example, will stand 'outside' and deny his master and his own discipleship at the critical moment when Jesus is facing his accusers in the Jewish trial!

The Mystery of the Kingdom

Jesus tells those about him with the Twelve: 'The mystery of the kingdom of God has been given to you', that means, 'God has given it to you'.[27] The mystery of the kingdom 'is given', that is, it is a gift of God. Significantly, the term 'given' rather than 'revealed' is used and so the 'revelation' of the mystery is still taking place and will be understood or misunderstood, accepted or rejected, as the story unfolds.[28] The fact that the mystery of the kingdom is given is noted, but its exact nature is still to be revealed. J. Jeremias put it succinctly:

> ... 'the secret of the Kingdom of God' which constitutes God's gift must not be understood as implying information about the kingdom of God, but ... a particular piece of information, the recognition of its dawn in the present.[29]

Jesus began his ministry by announcing the good news, proclaiming that the time is fulfilled, the kingdom of God is drawing near, and calling for repentance and belief in the good news. Following his initial proclamation, his mighty words and deeds

26. F. J. Moloney, *op. cit.*, 89.
27. Jewish concern about predicating direct action of God often results in the use of the 'divine passive'.
28. R. H. Gundry, *op. cit*, 197, points out how 'given' rather than 'revealed' implies that there is a possibility of non-understanding.
29. J. Jeremias, *The Parables of Jesus*, (revised edition), SCM Press, London, 1972, 16.

manifested the power of God working through him as he expelled and silenced the demonic powers, overcame the power of sickness and displayed power to forgive sin, all manifestations of the presence of the kingdom (reign) of God in the world. There is a 'givenness' about Jesus and his ministry to date, but it is a pointer to the greater reality of the as yet to be revealed 'mystery (secret) of the kingdom of God.' It is a gift, as yet unwrapped.

The 'mystery' is described here in Mark in terms of 'the mystery of the kingdom of God.'[30] What is that mystery? The term 'mystery', *mystêrion* (from *myein*, to be silent) is a Greek word which is used in the New Testament with a very different set of meanings to its general usage in the Greek language of the time. Outside the New Testament it was used (often pejoratively) of the 'mystery' religions, like those of Mitras, Isis and Osiris, Cybele and Attis and others. It conveyed the sense of the secret rites and initiations into enlightenment that the devotees conducted away from the gaze of outsiders. In the Bible, however, the term *mystêrion* is used to convey a very different and thoroughly biblical meaning. Daniel, for example, had used the Hebrew equivalent, the term *raz*, 'mystery', for the hidden purposes of God (Dan 2:18f; 27-29; 30, 47). In the Pauline writings, the term *mystêrion* is used twenty-one times and with different shades of meaning. It refers to the hidden salvific plan of God made manifest in the Christ event (1 Cor 2:7; 4:1; Rom 16:25f; Eph 3:9). It appears as a summary term in the Christian proclamation (Col 2:2; 4:3; Eph 3:4; 6:19; 1 Tim 3:9, 16) and Paul also uses the term *mystêrion* to describe the incomprehensible rejection of Jesus by his own people which must in some way fit into the divine scheme of things (Rom 11:25). He also describes the Christian preachers as 'stewards of the mysteries of God'(1 Cor 4:1).

The formerly hidden plan of God for salvation is being made manifest in the mighty words and works of Jesus. His subsequent parables and mighty deeds will continue to manifest a good deal about the nature and presence of the kingdom and of the identity of Jesus himself, the one in and through whom it is being established. But there is much more of the mystery to be revealed. As usual the reader is being kept in suspense for the further revelation of the mystery.

30. For an overall treatment of the question see J. Marcus, *The Mystery of the Kingdom of God*, S.B.L Dissertation, Atlanta, 1986.

The rejection, suffering, trial, execution and resurrection of the one in and through whom the kingdom is being established have yet to take place. These events will present not only 'the outsiders' but the apparent 'insiders', 'those around him,' together with his disciples and the Twelve, with the mystery of a kingdom founded on an apparently failed, rejected and shamed Messiah. It is a kingdom looking to a glorious eschatological fulfilment in the future, but taking root in the present in circumstances that seem to deny its power, glory and heavenly nature. When Jesus introduces the first prediction of the passion with the phrase 'it is necessary (*dei*) that the Son of Man should suffer', he will set the suffering in the context of the salvific plan or mystery of God. 'It is necessary' (*dei*) is the established expression for speaking of the necessity of carrying out the will or plan of God. The will of God expressed in the divine plan for a rejected and suffering Messiah will be the acid test for deciding who are Jesus' 'brother and sister and mother' who accept the will of God. The paradox of a failed, rejected and crucified Messiah and the challenge of seeing the kingdom (reign) of God present in human suffering, failure and disgrace, will be the test of 'insider' and 'outsider'. It will cause his disciples to flee from him and Peter to stand 'outside', literally and metaphorically, during his trial. It will be the great cause of making people, in the language of Isaiah, blind and deaf to the mystery of the kingdom (Mk 4:12; Isa 6:9f); 'so that (*hina*) they may see and see and not perceive and hear and hear and not understand lest/unless (*mêpote*) they turn (convert) and be forgiven' (Mk 4:12; Isa 6:9,10).

So that they may see ... and not perceive ... (Isa 6:9f)
These verses of Isaiah which are loosely quoted, or alluded to, in Mk 4:12 are the most difficult verses of the gospel, and certainly among the most difficult in the whole New Testament. The difficulties focus both on the wording itself of the quotation (or allusion) which differs significantly from the MT and LXX[31] and also on the possible translations of the two Greek words, *hina* (so that) and *mêpote* (lest/unless).

---

31. These difficulties certainly alert one to the problems of translating subtleties from a very concrete Semitic language or mindset to the logical clarity of Greek language and thought, particularly when the accuracy of Classical Greek has given way to the more fluid usage of Koinê Greek. It also alerts one to the fact that Jews in Jesus' time were as likely to know their biblical texts from sources other than the text behind the MT or the LXX.

The wording of the 'quotation' itself causes difficulty. It differs from both the MT (Hebrew) and the LXX (Greek) and is closer to the Targum of Isaiah. For this reason one could refer to it as an explicit allusion rather than a quotation.[32] Furthermore, much of the sting is removed from the original text of Isa 6:9, 10 by the omission of references to hardening of the heart, stopping of the ears and closing of the eyes.[33]

The second difficulty arises in understanding and translating *hina* (so that) and *mêpote* (lest/unless). In translating *hina* one must decide whether 'so that (*hina*) they may see and see and not perceive and hear and hear and not understand' refers to the purpose or the result of teaching in parables. The word *hina* in Classical Greek signified purpose or intent, but in Koinê Greek it has a looser usage. It can signify either purpose or result, or the outcome of a command or wish.[34] This possibility of a looser use of *hina* signifying a result, cause or explanation rather than a purpose has meant that many scholars shy away from the implications of a scenario reminiscent of the 'hardening of the heart' theology of the Old Testament.[35] Matthew avoids the problem (Mt 13:10ff) by using *hoti* (because) instead of *hina* and this turns the parables into Jesus' response to the negative reaction and resistance of the listeners and not the cause. ('He taught

32. In the MT (Hebrew text), Isa 6:9-10 uses two imperative verbs in the second person for seeing and hearing and the LXX (Greek text) has two future tenses in the second person. Mark, however, uses two subjunctives in the third person and in this he is in line with an underlying Aramaic usage in the Targum of Isaiah, which though probably later than the New Testament, may well share a common understanding. In addition both Mark and the Targum have 'be forgiven' rather than 'be healed' (both are 'divine' passives, meaning 'God will forgive' or 'God will heal'). Cf J. J eremias, *op. cit.*, 15.
33. C. Focant, *op. cit.*, 166.
34. An examination of the text of Mark shows a variety of uses. In Mk 3:9 *hina* is used of a wish or command where Jesus tells the disciples to have a boat ready. In Mk 5:18 it is used of a desire on the part of the formerly possessed man to remain with Jesus. In Mk 6:8 it is used of Jesus' instruction to the Twelve about taking nothing with them on their missionary journey and in Mk 9:9 it is used when instructing the inner group of disciples to tell nobody about the 'transfiguration'.
35. This was prominent in the story of God's hardening of the heart of Pharaoh in the lead up to the Exodus when Pharaoh was 'predestined' by God to reject the pleas of Moses to let the people go (Ex 4:21; 8:15, 32; 9:34).

in parables, because, seeing they do not see …'). Matthew's use of *hoti* in this context may well have resulted from an awareness of the ambiguity in the tradition as reflected here in Mark or from an embarrassment at the idea of a deliberate attempt to make the teaching obscure and so predestine some hearers not to understand.

Some scholars, among them J. Jeremias, have suggested that *hina* is shorthand for 'in order that what was spoken by the Lord through the prophet, (or some similar expression for the citation of scripture), might be fulfilled.'[36] This would be a very neat resolution of the difficulty surrounding any hint of predestination, replacing it with prophetic foreknowledge, but it is not universally accepted as a solution. It has been objected to on the grounds that elsewhere Mark uses an introductory formula for introducing quotations from scripture. However, it must also be said that the 'quotation' is more an allusion than a quotation and does not need an introductory formula.

Translating *mêpote* is equally difficult. In Classical Greek it is a conjunction expressing negative purpose as in 'lest ever' or 'in order that not', but in Koinê Greek it can also mean 'perhaps' or 'unless'. J. Jeremias suggests that it reflects the underlying Aramaic word *dilema* used in the Targum which means 'unless'.[37] This is one of the better suggestions, even in the face of the criticism that elsewhere Mark explains such Aramaic words. However, against this criticism it can be argued that an Aramaic word or phrase is not used but an underlying idiom or formula is taken as understood.

The purpose of the giving of the secret of the kingdom is the putting before the hearers of the choice which demands acceptance or rejection, and rejection leads on to a failure to repent. In this sense also there are connotations of both purpose and consequence in the 'negative finality' of *mêpote*. The failure to 'hear/accept' leads to the failure to repent and be forgiven.

God's intervention through Moses and the prophets always seemed to provoke reactions of acceptance and rejection. God's intervention in Jesus was no different, and the New Testament writers face up to the fact that, whereas many within Israel and in the larger world accepted God's intervention in Jesus, very

---

36. J. Jeremias, *op. cit*, 17 suggests that *hina* is shorthand for *hina plêrôthê to rhêthen hypo tou Kyriou dia tou prophêtou*.
37. J. Jeremias, *ibid*.

significant numbers of the people of Israel and of the larger
world did not. In the words of Simeon in Luke's infancy narrative the child was to be 'a sign to be contradicted' (Lk 2:34). In
the language of the Johannine tradition, the acceptance or rejection of the Word is itself the judgement, and results from one's
knowing God and having the proper dispositions towards the
Father and the Son whom he sent. One's dispositions enable one
to be drawn to the Father and the Son, summed up in the
Johannine statement: 'No one can come to me unless the Father
who sent me draws him'(Jn 6:44). It is very different language to
that of Mark but the underlying reality is the same. The Word
came into the world so that the blind would see and those who
see would turn blind (Jn 9:39). The purpose of the coming was to
separate them, but which side of the separation one found oneself on was not determined by God but by the dispositions of the
hearers. Those with the right dispositions were drawn to God
and consequently to God's envoy (and vice versa).

To sum up it can be said that the divine intervention always
has the purpose of provoking decision which results in division
into those who accept and those who reject. As Jesus explains his
reason for speaking in parables, it may appear at first glance that
he does so in order to deliberately confuse people and then condemn them for not understanding. In fact his preaching is designed to divide people into those who accept and reject. It is,
however, the disposition of the listeners that does not allow
them to understand the parables and that divides them into
those who see only riddles or those who question and seek further insight and clarification.[38] In this sense, the *hina* is both final
and consequential. It is a catalyst provoking a reaction which results from the dispositions of the hearers. This differs essentially
from divine predestination or the revelation of a long-hidden
secret to privileged witnesses while others remain in ignorance,
a scenario reminiscent of the apocalyptic tradition in which select
privileged persons or groups are given privileged knowledge.

The 'outsiders' for the moment in the narrative are those who
do not listen to the word, or reject it out of hand, or fail to live up

38. C. Focant, *op. cit.*, 166, states: *Il ne peut en aller autrement, non pas `a cause de l'émetteur qui voudrait envoyer un message brouillé, incomprehensible, mais parce que l'attitude de ces récepteurs ne leur permet pas de comprendre les paraboles, alors que celles-ci constituent pour l'heur le seul moyen de communication approprié `a la transmission du mystère du Règne de Dieu.*

to its demands. The ' insiders' are those who are open to further listening and are well disposed even though they will encounter misunderstanding and failure which will blur the distinction between 'insiders' and 'outsiders'. For the present the 'insiders' are eager to question and to hear the explanation of the parable of the sower with its references to the seed, the ground, the failure and the growth.[39]

d. Allegorical Interpretation of 'the parable of the sower'. Mk 4:13-20
Jesus now returns to the parable of the sower. He begins by saying: 'Do you not understand this parable?' or 'You do not understand this parable!' depending on whether one sees the remark as a question or exclamation, as is often the case in translation since the New Testament writers did not use punctuation marks. Then Jesus asks: 'How will you understand any of the parables?' There is an implication here that the parables form a coherent whole and that this parable is pivotal and provides the key to understanding all the parables. It means also that the reader has to wait until he/she has read all the parables before seeing the overall picture.

As 'the parable of the sower' is redacted by Mark, it refers to hearing and accepting the word sown by Jesus in his ministry. It must also reflect the reaction to the word sown by the Christian preachers in the Markan community, and among the Markan readership. The allegorical interpretation turns the parable into an allegory on listening, hearing, accepting and persevering in the word. Using allegory most probably reflects a Greco-Roman or Diaspora Jewish readership which would have been quite familiar with allegory since it was very common among Greco-Roman writers and popular also among the Jews at Alexandria where it was to become the dominant Christian method of biblical interpretation. In the case of the parable, the hearer applies it to life; the allegory, on the other hand, is a form of teaching in which the teacher rather than the hearer makes all the practical connections between the story and its application to life. The parable is a conversation between teller, parable and hearer. It challenges the hearer to think, respond or react. The allegory

---

39. In the light of what has been said, Mk 4:10-12 should not be taken, as it often is, together with Mk 4:33-34 simply as a 'parable theory' in the sense that Jesus' teaching in parables is always enigmatic and meant to keep the outsiders in a state of confusion.

seeks to give significance to the various details of the story rather than to emphasise the simple thrust of the comparison or contrast which often builds up to a punch line at the end.

The allegorical interpretation most likely does not have its origins with Jesus, but Jesus' explanation to a Semitic audience is translated into a genre or idiom more familiar to a Greco-Roman readership of the gospel. M. D. Hooker makes the point very clearly: 'Parables spoken by a wandering teacher in Galilee sounded very differently when recited as words of the Master whom the community acknowledged as risen Lord. Inevitably parables took on a new meaning in a new situation, and inevitably, in the process, their relevance sometimes seemed obscure.'[40] This is very likely the reason why a preacher or teacher explains them in allegorical fashion.

In this explanation Jesus begins with the seed and interprets it as the word and then interprets the condition of the ground as the disposition of the listener. By implication the sower is the preacher, and as already pointed out the sower '*goes out* to sow' as Jesus 'went out' on his journeys to preach and as Christian preachers continued to do, following the example of Jesus and those whom he sent.

There is a significant history of using the imagery of 'sowing' in the Bible. Already in the New Testament Paul used sowing as a metaphor for preaching in 1 Cor 3:5-9. In the Old Testament it is used as a metaphor for planting the law among the people (4 Ezra 9:30-37). It is used for moral living, for sowing righteousness and reaping love (Hos 10:12), and sowing virtue and reaping a solid reward (Prov 11:18). It is also used for negative actions and their consequences, for sowing the seeds of grief and reaping the results (Job 4:8).

The fate of the seed represents the response to the word. The seed is healthy but the ground can be unhealthy because of its composition (rocky) or circumstances (overgrown with thorns or trampled into a path and exposed to the birds). Three failures in sowing are followed by three outstanding successes. The birds that eat the seed on the path are interpreted as Satan taking the word from the heart of the listener. Interestingly, demons were portrayed as birds in apocalyptic tradition. In 1 Enoch 90:8-13 and in *Jubilees* Prince Mastema, a Satan like figure, sets the crows to eat the seed that is being sown. The seed on the rocky

---

40. M. D. Hooker, *op. cit.*, 120.

ground, *petrida*,[41] does better initially but there is no root and it
dies under the heat of the sun, like those who after several initial
displays of enthusiasm, fell away or were scandalised, under the
threat of persecutions and trials on account of the word. The
seed among thorns is interpreted as those who have heard the
word and have an initial positive response, but the worries of
the world and the lure of riches choke the word. Interestingly,
thorns were seen as a metaphor for the irrational passions by
Philo in his comments on the thorns in Gen 3:18.[42] All categories
heard the word initially and made an initial positive response
but, depending on their inner disposition or external circumstances, they responded with different degrees of commitment.
The triple failure is more than compensated for by the seed that
fell on good ground. This represents the people who heard the
word, accepted it, and produced a harvest thirty, sixty and a
hundredfold.

In its original form the parable of the sower would most likely
have been a single-point explanation of the huge harvest that
comes unexpectedly from successfully sown seed in spite of the
failure of the other seed. Like the parables of the seed growing
secretly or the insignificant mustard seed which follow, the emphasis was probably on the successful result of the planting.

Mark translates Jesus' explanations in good catechetical style
into the language and usage of his audience. This explanation of
the parable not only comes in the form of an allegory but contains a group of failings akin to those in the lists of vices which
were common in primitive Christian catechesis and secular literature. Wealth, power and worldly concerns are obstacles to the
challenge proposed by Jesus throughout the gospel. A similar
catalogue is obvious in this gospel when Jesus describes the
evils that come out of a man in terms of a catalogue of vices,
common to New Testament and secular writers (Mk 7:21f).[43]
Teaching morality and ethics by way of lists of virtues and vices,
a method referred to by scholars as catalogical *paraenesis*, was

---

41. Some commentators say *petrida* may also contain a pun on Peter and
his falling away under pressure.
42. Philo, *Legum Allegoria*, 3.248.
43. V. Taylor, *The Gospel According to St Mark*, 2nd ed. 1972, 88. V. Taylor
sees these two examples as pointers to the formation of a primitive
catechism in the Roman community.

widespread, both in biblical and secular literature.[44] Virtue lists are also used in a variety of contexts and have great variety in content.[45] They are fewer in number and even more general in nature than the vice lists. They also relate to traits and characteristics rather than to deeds. In the handing on of the tradition it is quite possible that Jesus' original explanation has been translated / transformed into this list of vices, evil inclinations and failures which would have been a familiar style of teaching for the Markan audience, where the teacher makes the practical connections with life, while maintaining the essential meaning.

Both the allegory and the vice list would be familiar to a Greco-Roman or Jewish Diaspora audience. The story of the rich young man who refuses the call because of his great wealth is a particular case in point (Mk 10:17-22). Similarly Herod was pleased to listen to the preaching of John but when he came under pressure, he soon forgot what he had heard with enthusiasm (Mk 6:14-29). Like David listening to Nathan's parable about the lamb (2 Sam12:1-6), the listeners must have found themselves challenged to ask: 'Which kind of ground am I?'

The crowd on the shore, however, who were not present for the subsequent allegorical interpretation of the parable, were left to think over its possible implications and respond accordingly.

c. Secrets: Revealed and Hidden. Lamp and Measure. Mk 4:21-25
The narrative continues with: 'And he said to them …' To whom is Jesus now speaking? Is he still speaking to 'those around him with the Twelve' or is this a continuation of the general address to the crowd from the boat which was interrupted after the parable of the sower? The context suggests the former, as it parallels Mk 4:10-13 above with its reference to the mystery of the kingdom which was being disclosed or hidden. Here there is reference to hidden things that are being made known and secrets disclosed.

Expecting a resounding answer 'no!' prompted by the Greek *mêti*, 'surely not !' Jesus says: 'Surely the lamp does not come in

44. The vice lists appear at Rom 1:24, 26; 29-31; 13:13; 1 Cor 5:10f; 6:9f; 2 Cor 12:20; Gal 5:19-21; 3:5-12; Eph 4:31; 5:3-5; 1 Tim 9f; 6:4f; 2 Tim 3:2-5; Tit 3:3; 1 Pet 2:1; 4:3f; Jude 8:16; Rev 9:20f; 21:8; 22:15; Mt 15:19 / / Mk 7:21f. The most common evils mentioned in the vice lists are fornication (8 times) and idolatry (5 times).
45. The main virtue lists are found in Mt 5:3-11; 2 Cor 6:6f; Gal 5:22f; Eph 6:14-17; Phil 4:8; 1 Tim 3:2f; 6:11; Tit 1:7f; Jas 3:17; 2 Pet 1:5-7.

order to be put under a bushel or under a bed!' The reference is to the coming of Jesus, and the image of the lamp was already an established metaphor for a prophet. It was used of Elijah in the book of Sirach and is found on the lips of Jesus in John's gospel referring to John the Baptist (Sir 48:1; Jn 5:35). Though not as pronounced in Mark as elsewhere, 'the one who comes' is a messianic designation. Jesus says of himself in the gospel that he has not come to call the just but sinners (Mk 2:17), and the Son of Man has not come to be served but to serve (Mk 10:45). The fact that *hina*, 'in order to', is stated four times points to the fact that the emphasis is on the purpose of the coming of the lamp, that is, the coming of the prophet or teacher. The very open and indeterminate nature of the sentence, *mêti erchetai ho lychnos*, 'surely the lamp does not come …' leaves the 'coming' and 'the lamp' without a stated destination until the bushel and the bed are mentioned. The lamp does not come in order to be put under a bushel, a measuring bowl, probably used to quench a lamp and contain the smoke of a rush oil lamp from filling a small airless room. So the lamp does not come in order to be extinguished, but to perform its task of shedding light. Neither is it meant to shine its light where it cannot be seen, as under a bed. Light is to reveal, not to conceal. The light comes to shine for everyone. This is very interesting as it comes after the recent statement that those inside would be given the mystery, others would remain outside and see everything in riddles. However, the follow up statement seems to counter the idea of purely esoteric knowledge for the few: 'There is nothing hidden that will not be disclosed and nothing kept secret that will not come to light.' The emphasis has been very much on the verb *akouein*, to listen to the word, which for Mark is 'the good news'. Now the emphasis on word and hearing is being complemented with the imagery of light and seeing. The proclamation of the kingdom is made to be heard and its establishment can be seen and this is again reinforced by restating the call to listen, and take note, in an expanded form: 'Let the one who has ears to hear, listen' and this is immediately followed by: 'Look at (take note of) what you hear (*blepete ti akouete*)!' The reception of the word, especially in the prophets, is often described in terms of 'seeing' rather than 'hearing', as 'seeing' is a verb that expresses a very full perception of the truth that is being revealed, combining the elements of hearing, seeing and understanding (cf Amos 1:1; Mic 1:1; Hab 1:1; Zech 1:7,8).

Mark again uses for his own redactional purposes in this collection of teachings about listening (and seeing/watching) a
traditional 'measure for measure' saying or image.[46] In Mark the
'measure for measure' image reflects closely the point of the
parable of the sower and the surrounding teaching on listening
(and seeing/watching). The positive response will not just 'get
as good as it gives' but an immeasurably greater reward. The
ones who listen, in the sense of listening, understanding and
obeying the word, will progress in seeing, understanding and
commitment as the kingdom comes more and more to take root
in their lives. Those who don't really listen, just hear superficially
and do not observe, understand or obey, will gradually loose interest and commitment and find it has vanished completely
from their sight. 'Those who listen with their hearts will receive
understanding, but those who do not will eventually stop listening altogether.'[47] As the birds picked the seed from the path or
the stony ground left it wither or the thorns choked it, so the
seed of the word will disappear. For 'the one who has not', the
measure will not remain static, but will grow immeasurably
worse, till none is left. This saying in Mark, directed first of all at
those who listened superficially to Jesus and then fell away, is
equally relevant to the Markan community, and intended readership, who were falling, or had fallen away, possibly during the
threat or actual experience of persecution.

b. Parables of Successful Growth Mk 4:26-32
'And he used to say' (*kai elegen*) seems to imply a return to the
customary teaching of Jesus, as if picking up on the teaching in
the boat to the original general audience. There follow the only
two parables, or more accurately similitudes, explicitly associated
in the text with the kingdom. These are the parable of the seed
growing secretly and the parable of the mustard seed. They are
introduced respectively with the words: ' Thus is the kingdom
of God' and 'How can we compare the kingdom of God, what
parable can we use to describe it?' The emphasis in both is on

---

46. In Matthew and Luke this image is used at the end of a teaching on
judging: 'the judgement you give is the judgement you get' (Mt 7:2; Lk
6:38). It is used also at the end of the parable of the talents/pounds (Mt
25:29; Lk 19:26) and also as an example of the Golden Rule: 'Do to others
as you would have them do to you' (Mt 7:12; Lk 6:31).
47. B. van Iersel, *op. cit.*, 76.

growth, and they probably went together as a pair, possibly forming a trio of parables with an earier form of the parable of the sower in pre-Markan tradition.

The seed growing by itself

The rhythm of waking, working and sleeping, together with nature's rhythm of sowing, sprouting and growing, is well replicated in the rhythm of the sentence with the multiple use of *kai*, 'and', showing the passage of time and the inherent power of growth independent of the sower's ongoing attention, as the seed bears fruit 'of its own power', *automatê*. The sickle is then 'sent into' the harvest. There are nuances of the harvest of the kingdom and those sent to reap it. The seed grows inevitably in spite of human endeavour. The word, once sown, grows inevitably, the kingdom makes inroads, in spite of the good or bad efforts, even in spite of the subsequent failure and betrayal of the those who sowed the seed. The imagery is close to that in Joel 4:13 which speaks of putting the sickle into the harvest on the day of the judgement of the nations. An even closer parallel is found in John's gospel when Jesus speaks of the fields white to harvest, and says to the disciples 'one sows, another reaps. I sent you to reap a harvest you had not worked for' (Jn 4:35-38). The guaranteed harvest is the result of the gift of God in the life-giving power of seed or word, irrespective of the qualities of the sower or preacher of the word.

The mustard seed

The parable of the mustard seed emphasises first of all the tiny size of the mustard seed from which (with literary exaggeration) the largest of the plants grows.[48] The plant in fact grows to a height of two to six feet and was common along the shore of the Lake of Galilee. It was noted for spreading in an invasive way and could quickly take over a garden.[49] The image of a great tree was often used as the symbol of a nation and its power or the beauty of its terrain. The cedars of Lebanon are proverbial as symbols of power and beauty. Daniel describes the power and personal status of Nebuchadnezzar in terms of the great tree 'under which lived the beasts of the fields, and in its branches

48. In Mt 17:20 the tiny size of the mustard seed shows that even the tiniest amount of genuine faith can work miracles.
49. Pliny, *Natural History*, 19:170-171.

dwelt the birds of the sky' (Dan 4:19-21). Even closer to the imagery in Mark is the statement in Ezekiel that God will take a sprig of a great cedar and plant it to produce fruit and become a noble cedar under which 'every kind of bird will live; in the shade of its branches every kind of winged creature' (Ezek 17:22f). Jesus thus portrays the kingdom where every creature will find refuge. But in the irony of the gospel, the great tree is in fact an intrusive bush grown from the tiniest of seeds. From insignificant beginnings the greatest of kingdoms, the kingdom of God, will emerge, because the gift of God's life-giving power is in its beginnings and in its process of growth. 'For the dominion of God is like the word: paltry in appearance, but hiding a tremendous divine potency behind its apparent insignificance.'[50]

a. Conclusion. Speaking in Parables Mk 4:33-34

Mk 4:1-34 is a paradigm of Jesus the teacher. He teaches the crowds by the lakeside and the smaller group of 'the Twelve and those around him' in the privacy of the house. He calls for responsive, productive listening and careful, perceptive observation.

Mk 4:33-34 serves now as a summary of that paradigmatic day of typical teaching. The verb *elalei* is the imperfect tense, signifying continual or repeated action. The verb *lalein* is a change from the now familiar *elegen. Lalein* has overtones of prophetic speech. 'The word' (*logos*) is a general term for all his teaching. 'He spoke (used to speak) the word to them in many such parables, as they could listen'. The parables were partly plain and partly obscure, so the listening varies according as they were able to hear. 'He did not speak except in parables but he explained everything to his disciples when they were alone' like a rabbi or teacher explaining his public statements subsequently to his disciples.

5. JESUS' MIGHTY DEEDS MK 4:35 -5:43

The mighty preaching of Jesus in the parable discourse is followed by a series of mighty deeds which show his power over nature, demons, sickness and death.

Jesus' first session of teaching in the synagogue in Capernaum on the first great day of his ministry when the people commented on his teaching authority was followed by a

50. J. Marcus, *Mark 1-8,* The Anchor Bible 27, 323.

mighty deed in which he showed that authority over the unclean spirit, and this was followed immediately by a number of
other healings (Mk 1:21-34). Authority in word and deed went
hand in hand as a continuum, so that the people could speak of
his authority in word and deed. Now after Jesus' great day of
teaching the crowd by the lakeside and teaching the smaller
group in private, his authority in word will again be matched by
his authority in mighty deeds. The teaching and mighty deeds
are linked together here also by a time reference in a typical
Markan double reference, 'on that day, as evening came on'. The
phrase functions as a time and theme link. The reference also
carries connotations of 'that fateful, important day in the plan of
God and the ministry of Jesus.'

The typical double time reference, 'on that day, as evening
came on,' the second reference making the first more explicit,
brings this great day in the ministry of Jesus, a day of teaching,
to a close, and links it to the beginning of the next day which
technically begins at sundown. It will be a day of mighty deeds
showing his authority over the forces of nature, over the demonic
forces and over the forces of sickness and death. After the first
Sabbath Jesus had said to those who sought him in the early
morning: 'Let us go on to the other towns ...' and they went all
through Galilee (Mk 1:38f). Here he says 'Let us go to the other
side (of the lake)' (Mk 4:35). They are now heading for Gentile
territory, a whole new dimension in the ministry.

i. Stilling the Storm Mk 4:35-41

After leaving the crowd behind they took him in the boat 'just as
he was,' just as he had been sitting there teaching the crowd.[51]
Mention of the other boats 'with him,' *met' autou*, (the phrase
used for being a disciple) point to other followers who would
experience the storm, the calming and its effect on their understanding of Jesus though they do not really figure in the story
which focuses on the people in the boat with him. Mention of the
other boats is often used as an argument for the eyewitness
nature of this story as a reminiscence of Peter but it can also be
argued that it is part of the vivid narrative skill of Mark. In
Mark's redaction these boats are full of disciples gathered

---

51. This is probably another indication that the section dealing with
those around Jesus and the Twelve was inserted into an earlier narrative.

around to hear him, after the crowd had been left behind on the land.[52] The image of the boat, providing not only security for Jesus from the crush of the crowd, but also providing a seat of teaching, a pulpit for preaching, a vehicle for travelling between Jewish and Gentile territory and now a platform for a mighty deed, runs like a thread through the whole section from Mk 4:1-41. Being in the house with Jesus is a pointer to being a disciple and enthusiastic follower. But the house is a comfortable and safe place. Being in the boat with him at night is a far greater test when the little boat, open to the elements, is battered by wind and sea. Against all odds it did not break up and sink. The power of God protected it in spite of the superior forces ranged against it. Commentators see in the boat with its endangered, troubled passengers and sleeping, but protecting Jesus, an image of the church in a troubled, and persecuting world.

When Jesus said, 'Let us cross to the other side', the disciples 'took Jesus along with them just as he was' into the circumstances of their own lives with the accompanying stresses and dangers of fishing and sea-faring. Their story provides a paradigm for all followers in the church who bring Jesus with them in the difficult circumstances of life but may be tempted to think he is asleep and unaware or uncaring about the difficulties they experience.

A violent storm (*lailaps megalê anemou*) broke upon them. The lake was notorious for sudden storms as the land cooled after the heat of the day and tornado-style whirlwinds resulted from the difference in air temperatures over the lake and the surrounding land. The waves breaking over the boat create the sense of chaos emerging from the disturbed sea, often seen in biblical times as the home of the primeval monster and the forces of chaos. The vivid description sets the scene for the terror of the disciples and Jesus' powerful word of command to the wind and the sea.

The terror of the disciples stands out in great contrast to the untroubled sleep of Jesus – manifesting his lordship over life, death and chaos and his awareness of the power and protection of God, expressed so clearly in the psalms of confidence: 'I will

---

52. These boats would be about twenty-six feet long and eight feet wide, holding twelve to fifteen people. cf J. R. Donohue and D. J. Harrington, *op. cit.*, 157, quoting John J. Rousseau and Rami Arav, *Jesus and His World.*

lie down in peace, and sleep comes at once, for you, Lord, make me rest in safety' and 'Now I can lie down and go to sleep, and then awake, for YHWH has hold of me'(Pss 4:8; 3:5 inter al.). The description of Jesus asleep in the boat is reminiscent of the account of Jonah sleeping in the ship during a violent storm when the other passengers were terrified and calling on their gods until the boatswain woke Jonah up in a less than gentle manner and commanded him to call on his god: 'What do you mean by sleeping? Get up. Call on your god! Perhaps he will spare us a thought and not leave us to die' (Jonah 1:4-6).[53] Both Jewish and Gentile readers of Mark would be aware of the power of the sea and Jewish and pagan literature has many stories of travellers calling on the god of the sea.

In this, their first address to Jesus in this gospel, the disciples address him as 'teacher', as is fitting at the end of a day dedicated to teaching. Using the present tense brings out all the urgency and sense of immediate danger as they say accusingly in their terror: 'Is it not of concern to you that we are perishing?' They fail to see his lordship and to understand his identity as they 'accuse' him. Their address 'teacher' falls far short of the terms Lord, Christ and Beloved Son, which the reader has learned in the prologue together with the titles Son of God and Holy One of God, which the preternatural creatures know and use as an address.

Jesus rose up. The fortified verb, *diegertheis*, conveys the powerful picture of Jesus rising up in the stern of the boat where he had been sleeping, to confront the life-threatening forces of wind and sea. Seeing them in personalised terms as forces to be controlled, he rebuked the wind and spoke to the sea: 'Be silent! Be stilled!' 'Rebuking' (*epitimêsan*) is the verb already used in the gospel for rebuking the demons and silencing them. Here Jesus rebukes the wind and speaks to the sea, so often seen as the abode of monsters and demons. As he already in the gospel story compelled the demons he exorcised to be silent, so now he compels the silence of the sea and the wind. 'Be stilled' is a form of curing the agitated state of the sea, stirred up by the power of the wind (and the sea monsters?) just as the demoniacs and sick

53. By way of contrast, Jonah was on his way west to avoid his God-given mission to the Gentile Ninivites. Jesus was on his way east to the Gentiles' side of the lake to carry on his mission in Gerasene territory, when they encountered the storms.

people are agitated by their demons. The great storm, *lailaps megalê*, becomes a great calm, *galênê megalê*.

Exercising this power over wind and wave casts Jesus in the role of one having extraordinary possession of the divine powers evident in control over creation. God's creative power is seen at its most spectacular in the control of the sea. The control and separation of the waters at creation and the leading of the people through the waters of the sea as they fled from the Egyptian army at the Exodus stand at the foundation of biblical understanding of God's role in creation and in their own history as a people.[54] This biblical awareness of the divine presence in, and power over creation, especially as manifested in the case of the angry sea, is found all through the Bible. Job affirmed: 'He alone stretched out the heavens and trampled the sea's tall waves' (Job 9:8), and Deutero-Isaiah proclaimed: '… the redeemed pass over the depths of the sea … *I am, I am*, the one comforting you, how then can you be afraid …'(Isa 51:10, 12).[55]   The psalms have many references to God's control over the sea and his protection of those threatened by its power: 'You strode across the sea, you marched across the ocean but your footsteps could not be seen' (Ps 76/77:19). 'Some sailed to the sea in ships … they cried to the Lord in their need and he rescued them from their distress. He stilled the storm to a whisper; all the waves of the sea were hushed. They rejoiced because of the calm and he led them to the haven they desired' (Ps 106/107:23-30). 'You control the pride of the ocean, when its waves ride high, you calm them' (Ps 88/89:8f). 'When the waters saw you, O God, they recoiled, shuddering to their depths' (Ps 76/77:16). This understanding of God's power over the sea permeated the thinking and prayer life of the people of Israel. Here, to the amazement of the disciples, Jesus shows that same divine power emanating from his command to wind and sea.

Jesus, who had chosen the disciples 'to be with him,' responds to their plea in the boat and challenges them about their timidity and lack of courage.[56] 'Why were you fearful/cowardly/

---

54. cf Gen 1:6-8; Ex 14; 15; Deut 7:2-7; Job 38:16; Pss 29:3; 65:8; 77:20; 89:10; 93:3f; 51:9f; Isa 43:1-5; 51:9f.

55. *I am, I am*, the one consoling/comforting you. LXX *ego eimi, ego eimi ho parakalôn se.*

57. In Matthew's parallel account the point is well made by simply having Jesus address them while the storm is still raging. 'Why are you so

timid?' Have you no faith? Their fear is a result of their not having adequate faith, their not yet realising who Jesus really is in
spite of his authority in word and deed already made manifest
to eyes of faith (and also, unlike the reader, they had not read the
prologue!). The reaction of the disciples is one of great fear (they
feared a great fear/*ephobêthêsan phobon megan*). This 'fear' is
somewhat ambivalent. On the one had it highlights a 'negative'
fear showing itself in lack of understanding, faith and courage,
and on the other it contains a more positive element of awe, associated with a manifestation of divine power in an epiphany or
christophany.[57] The 'negative' fear will be in evidence as a mark
of failure throughout the gospel and will be the final comment in
the gospel (before the non-Markan ending) as the women leave
the empty tomb and fail to proclaim the miracle of the resurrection, 'for they were afraid' (*ephobounto gar*). Fear, in fact, is the
opposite of faith, and the great barrier to belief and discipleship
in Mark's narrative.

In the story of Jonah, after the people in the boat experience
the calming of the storm by YHWH, the God of Jonah, 'they
were seized with dread of YHWH; they offered a sacrifice to
YHWH and made vows' (Jonah 1:16). The people of the Greco-
Roman world would have been familiar with prayers to the
gods of the sea, sky and earth for protection. The disciples in the
boat with Jesus have an even more awe-inspiring experience as
they see that power of YHWH exercised by their teacher in the
boat. Their awesome terror prompts them to ask the central
question of the gospel, 'Who indeed is this for the wind and sea
obey him?' The question will be asked again and again until it is
finally answered by the centurion who presides over his execution. 'Obey' (*hypakouein*) is a reinforced form of *akouein*, to lis-

---

frightened you men of little faith?' he asks them in their mortal peril
(Mt 8:26). In John's account of the disciples' distress on the lake rowing
against the head wind, Jesus addresses them in terms essential to an
epiphany/christophany: 'Do not be afraid!' The focus in John is not on
the miracle of calming the storm but on the epiphany conveyed
through the divine name, 'I am', and the accompanying reassurance
'Do not be afraid.' Mk 6:47-52 parallels John's account.

57. Fear of the Lord in the Wisdom tradition is seen as ' the beginning/
foundation of wisdom' (Prov 1:7; 9:10; 15:33; Job 28:28; Pss 1:7; 111
(110): 10; Sir 1:11-20). There may be an element of this kind of fear in the
story; the elements of awe and especially of negative fear are the dominant ones.

ten/hear. After a day's teaching in which Jesus called on his audience to listen, hear and obey his word, the disciples now see
the wind and sea, the violent forces of nature, listening, hearing
and obeying his word. The whole story thus comes to a climax in
the christological question which points to the identity of Jesus
and the nature of the kingdom he proclaims.[58]

The demons speaking through the possessed man whom
they encounter immediately on landing in pagan territory will
have no such problem knowing Jesus' true identity!

ii. The Gerasene Demoniac Mk 5:1-20

Jesus and his disciples have reached the other side of the Lake of
Galilee. The goal of Jesus' journey has been achieved, facilitated
by his saving action on the water. They have arrived safely in
pagan territory. The troublesome distance between Jewish and
pagan territory has been well experienced in the dangers of the
storm, and will be further highlighted in Jesus' reception on the
other side.

In the handing on of the story of the Gerasene demoniac, confusion about the exact location has crept into the accounts. Most
manuscripts of Mark speak of 'the territory of the Gerasenes',
some Markan manuscripts, and Matthew, speak of the territory
of the Gadarenes, and Luke speaks of 'the territory of the
Gerasenes which is opposite Galilee'. Some manuscripts have
'Gergesenes'. Furthermore Gerasa (modern Jerash) is thirty-
seven miles from the sea, and Gadara which is five miles from
the sea, has no steep cliffs. Both sites are therefore problematical.
Maybe 'territory of the Gerasenes (or Gadarenes)' refers to territory where they shepherded their flocks in summer months
away from their homes, as was customary with nomadic people,
and the presence of the herd of swine seems to support this
view. However, the purpose of the story and its place in the
overall narrative of the gospel are the important points and the
exact location is of purely academic interest, except in so far as it
points to a location in Gentile territory.

On his disembarking from the boat, a man with an unclean

---

58. Even though the story was important for the first Christians as a
consolation in the midst of persecution, pointing to the fact that an apparently sleeping Jesus was still very much with them in their suffering,
and in control, still, as it is told here in the gospel, the point of the story
is primarily christological rather than an allegory on persecution.

spirit immediately accosted Jesus. He is referred to as *anthrôpos* not *anêr*, (like the man with the witherd hand in Mk 3:1ff), emphasising the fact that he was a human being rather than a male of the species. This man's unfortunate condition results from his being possessed by an unclean spirit, *en pneumati akathartô*, so called in Mk 5:2, 8. His condition is referred to as 'demon possessed' *daimonizomenos* in Mk 5:15, a term used in Mark only once, whereas 'having an unclean spirit' is a common term. Here 'unclean' is particularly appropriate because of the ritual uncleanness associated with Gentile territory and especially with tombs and dead men's bones, the presence of the pigs and the possible proximity of pagan shrines round about in the mountains. The reference to the hilltops has overtones of pagan worship and all kinds of unacceptable rituals and demonic presences. Isaiah criticised the 'rebellious people' who imitate pagan rituals, sacrificing on the hills to gods who are demons and sleeping in tombs and eating swine's flesh (Isa 65:3, 4, 7, 11). Though the circumstances here are quite different to those envisioned by Isaiah, the mood and environment are similar.

Powers greater than death bind this man. He lives in the tombs, from which he emerged, and day and night he went about among the tombs. These tombs are mentioned several times. His was a living death. The tombs were probably cave-tombs in the mountains. He roamed the mountains screaming and slashing himself with stones. Living in tombs and burial sites, and running about in the night and tearing one's clothes were seen by the rabbis as signs of madness.[59] Chains could not restrain him, so great was the demonic power driving him. The multiplication of negatives, *oudeis, oude,* and *ouketi,* 'nobody, nothing and never', highlight the hopelessness of his case in spite of many efforts to restrain him. 'Nobody was strong enough to subdue him' (Mk 5:3). They bound his hands and feet but he broke the chains. The power possessing him was greater than that of the chains with which he was bound. The description builds up the tension before Jesus' mighty deed of healing / exorcism. Two Markan themes are very much in evidence. Firstly, the man is restored to the community from living outside as one unclean, unholy and effectively dead. Secondly the house of the strong man is attacked and spoiled as the demons, who were believed to be territorial, are driven from their occu-

---

59. Strack-Billerbeck, 1:491-2.

pation of the man, and having begged to be left in the area and finding their new home in the pigs, they are then destroyed in the sea.

The reader remembers the parable about 'binding up the strong man' (Mk 3:27) as Jesus 'the stronger man' now approaches the scene and the possessed man sees him from afar. He prostrates before him in an act of obeisance appropriate for a divine or semi-divine person. Like the man with the demon in the synagogue (Mk 1:24), he cries out: 'What is in common between me and you, Jesus, Son of God the Most High?', thus issuing a challenge and an address similar to the former demon's challenge and identification of Jesus as 'the Holy One of God'. Then, in an ironic twist, it is not the exorcist who invokes God before the exorcism, but the demoniac himself. He has, however, done homage to Jesus by giving him his divine title, in keeping with other demons who show preternatural knowledge of his identity. He begs not to be tortured, as in the eschatological judgement, when Satan and the demons will be judged and finally overcome and eternally punished. The verb *basanizein*, to torture/punish, is used in Mt 18:34 of eschatological judgement and in Lk 16:23, 28 of the damnation of the heartless rich man.

'What is your name?' Jesus asks, for to know the name is to facilitate address and thereby gain access and control. The exorcist needs to know the name in order to address the demon and to call on God to expel him. (In the former exorcism in the synagogue the demon tried to seize the initiative by calling Jesus by name and saying he knew who he was.) In the Testament of Solomon, Solomon asks a demon its name and the demon responds: 'If I tell you his name, I place not only myself in chains, but also the legion of demons under me.'[60]

In answering, the demonic voice within proclaims the presence of a legion of demons. The term *legion* is borrowed from Latin, signifying a company of about six thousand soldiers. However, it seems that it is used here to emphasise the large number of demons working in co-operation in the demon kingdom that have taken possession of this man, not as a veiled reference to the forces of Roman occupation, as sometimes alleged.

60. *Test. Sol.* 11:5; 5:1-13; 13:1-7. Even if *Test. Sol* is later than and dependent on Mark, still the remark highlights the significance of the name in the practice of exorcism. cf J. R. Donahue and D. J. Harrington, *op. cit.*, 165.

It may, however, have a certain pejorative political ring even though the incident takes place outside the Jewish territory where there was not the same resentment against the Romans. Jesus avoided 'politics', and the portrayal of Roman soldiers, outside the scene of mockery in the passion, is consistently good throughout the gospels. (This gospel comes to a climax with the profession of faith of a Roman centurion. Mark's original readership, however, may have had a different, negative, experience of the Roman military.)

The earnest request, as to a superior power, not to be sent away out of the territory reflects the ancient belief that demons were territorial. Being in the district would facilitate other possessions there. The request is repeated by way of asking to be allowed to enter the pigs.[61] The abode of the demons is being plundered! The superior status and power of the stronger one, Jesus, the *ischuroteros*, are seen in his allowing the transfer. Appropriately the 'unclean' spirit (or legion of demons) enters what to the Jews were the uncleanest of the unclean, a herd of pigs. Not alone were Jews forbidden to eat pig meat, they were forbidden to keep pigs and swineherding was seen like tax collecting as an unacceptable occupation for a Jew. Minding the pigs for a Gentile was the ultimate degradation for the Prodigal Son (Lk 15:15f).

The demons get their new abode but they are 'sold a dummy'. Some say that the folkloric motif of the 'duped demon' may be present here in the story.[62] Their presence causes even the unclean animals to go into such a frenzy that they rush down the hill into the very water from which Jesus has so recently saved his disciples. He has consigned the demons to their place in the deep with the forces of chaos. Of significance also is the fact that demons were reputed to be afraid of the sea. R. H. Gundry detects a note of humour in the telling of the story as the demoniacs, having been reduced to 'grovelling supplication' are described as 'drowning' (*epnigonto*), the imperfect of the verb functioning as a humourous 'slow-motion playback.'[63]

So far the story has followed the usual form of an exorcism story – a meeting with Jesus, the demon cries out in fear, the

61. See the article by D. H. Juel, 'Plundering Satan's Household: Demons and Discipleship' in D. H. Juel, *A Master of Surprise. Mark Interpreted*, 65-75.
62. J. R. Donohue and D. J. Harrington, *op. cit*, 166.
63. R. H. Gundry, *op. cit.*, 9.

demon identifies Jesus and tries to control him, Jesus controls and expels the demon, and the possessed person is restored to health and a position in society. Usually there follows a command to silence. That does not happen here. Instead of the usual brief statement about the effect of the miracle on the people who observed it, the reactions to the extraordinary happening are told at greater length than is customary in a healing or exorcism story. The herdsmen 'fled' and 'announced/publicised' it in the city and the countryside and the people came to see what had happened. Now the change to historic present tense takes the reader right into the story as one reads: 'They come to Jesus and they see the demoniac sitting, clothed and rational, making sensible conversation, the very one the legion had possessed.' The 'seated', 'clothed', 'sensible (rational/wise)' condition of the man contrasts dramatically with his earlier running wildly around the mountain, shrieking loudly. The people were struck with fear (*ephobêthêsan*), just like the disciples when Jesus silenced the wind and calmed the waves.

In a great gesture of irony they ask Jesus to leave the very countryside that the unclean spirits had sought permission from him to inhabit, but from which Jesus had caused them to be expelled in the fleeing unclean animals. Why then did the people ask Jesus to leave? Some have speculated that the loss of the pigs was an economic blow which they did not want repeated – the price of the man's healing was the loss of the pigs! It is much more likely that the fear/awe with which they were struck in the presence of this Jew who had come over the lake (a person driven and empowered, as the reader knows, by the Holy Spirit), was too much for pagan people to handle at the time. (Is Mark conscious of this kind of experience being repeated in the case of some of the first Christian missionaries among the pagans?)

The incident comes to a close again with a reference to the boat: 'As Jesus was getting into the boat, the formerly possessed man *begged* him that he might 'be with him', that is, that he might become one of his disciples. But Jesus chooses his disciples on his own initiative. This is the fourth use of the verb 'beg' (*parakalein*) in the story, showing the recognition of the authority of Jesus. The unclean spirit(s) *begged* to be allowed to stay in the district and *begged* to be allowed enter the pigs. The people *begged* him to leave the district. Now the cured man *begged* to be with him. However, unlike the disciples of the rabbis, the disci-

ples of Jesus do not seek him out to become his disciples. Jesus
chooses them on his own initiative. In this case, however, he
chooses the cured man to be his herald and sends him to proclaim among the Gentile inhabitants of the area what the Lord
had done for him and how he had shown him mercy.

Significantly, Jesus restores him to normal society and family
as he did with the leper and will shortly do with the woman
with the issue of blood. He also sends him as an apostle to his
own home and relatives and tells him to announce (*apaggeilon*)
what the Lord had done for him, and how he had shown mercy
on him. The man departed and began to proclaim (*êrxato kêrussein*), in the Decapolis, what Jesus had done for him. The same
verb, *kêrussein*, was used of the Baptist, of Jesus, of the disciples
and of those healed, and was to become the term for the first
preaching of the church.[64] Here we see the pagan 'proclaiming'
in pagan territory. Being sent by Jesus to tell the people what the
Lord had done, he told them what Jesus had done. As in the
preaching of the church he identified Jesus as Lord.

Mark mentions that he proclaimed his message in the
Decapolis. The term refers to the federation of ten Hellenised,
Greek-speaking, pagan cities across the Jordan. There is evidence of early Christian missionary work there and a tradition
that the Christians fled from the Palestine area to Pella at the
outbreak of the Jewish War against the Romans.[65] The names of
the ten cities are given by Pliny the Elder as Damascus,
Philadelphia, Raphana, Scythopolis, Gadara, Hippos, Dion,
Pella, Gerasa, and Canatha. Sending the man to preach to his
own people is similar to the scene in St John's gospel where the
woman of Samaria becomes the missionary to her own people
(Jn 4:28f; 39-42). Both stories reflect an incident in Jesus' ministry
which foreshadows an important mission of the early church.

The familiar response closes the scene. They were all amazed
at what Jesus had done for him. The preaching of the man and
the wonder it provokes serves to replace the fear of the people
on that side of the lake. Did this also foreshadow a fear of the
early Christians and their mission, caused through misunderstanding or prejudice, which was dispelled when their message
was preached and heard?

64. Mk 1:4, 7; 14; Mk 1:38, 39; Mk 3:14; 6:12; Mk 1:45; 5:20; 7:36; Mk 13:10;
14:9, respectively.
65. Eusebius, *Eccl. Hist.* 3.5.2-3. There are critical questions about the
accuracy of this tradition.

iii. Jairus' Daughter (1) Mk 5:21-24

Jesus returns to his own side of the lake and assumes his now familiar position on the seashore, surrounded by a large crowd. Along the sea shore he had called the two pairs of brothers, and Levi, and given his discourse in parables. Now the distraught father of a critically ill child enters the familiar scene, and while Jesus is on his way to the house another ill woman approaches him, interrupting the crisis with her own. The two stories are placed together as an intercalation or 'sandwich' highlighting each other. They come at the climax of a series of miracle stories where Jesus overcomes various powers. Both recount the healing of a woman. Both very significantly recount very great faith on the part of two people at the extreme opposite ends of the social and religious scale. Jairus is a man with a name in a patriarchal and androcentric society, a person of considerable religious and social standing as one of the officials of the synagogue and a man surrounded by family and friends who show concern for him in his trouble. His fatally ill daughter is at home surrounded by family and friends. By way of contrast, the woman is unnamed, alone, chronically and probably fatally ill, frightened, and excluded from the synagogue and the society of the chosen people because her constant bleeding made her ritually impure and socially excluded. Both come to Jesus displaying great faith. Jairus, 'on seeing him', abandoned the dignified stance of his high office and humbled himself by falling, or throwing himself down, at Jesus' feet. The woman braved serious disapproval by touching with her ritually impure hands the garment of an important religious figure surrounded by his disciples and followers. Jesus puts his saving, life-giving power ahead of any considerations of ritual impurity or taboo in both stories. The woman's story is broadcast in the midst of a thronging crowd. The girl's story is to be kept secret. The twelve years of the woman's illness correspond to the twelve years of the girl's growing to womanhood.

Both stories highlight each other in the telling. The process of intercalation in this case heightens the dramatic tension as the urgent movement towards the house of the ill child is delayed, and also heightens a contrast of the little girl growing into life for twelve years as the older woman gradually loses her life force in the issue of blood during the same period of time. The older woman has lost her life-giving power of motherhood and

the girl is just arriving at the age of motherhood and legal marriage. 'In these two narratives Jesus not only rescues these two
women from death but also restores to them their life-giving
capacity. Both can bring forth life from their bodies, one once
racked with disease, the other deprived of life itself.'[66]

Jairus,[67] the father of the girl, pleads earnestly with Jesus,[68] a
pleading emphasised by the gesture of falling at his feet. The
father is 'one of the leaders of the synagogue', an *archisynagogos*,
one of the officials charged with overseeing the physical and
financial welfare of the synagogue. He is one of two people who
came to Jesus for help whose personal names are given in this
gospel. The other is the blind beggar, Bartimaeus (Mk 10:46).
Jairus begs Jesus to come to his 'little daughter' or 'dear daughter'[69] who was 'on the point of death' (*eschatos echei/in extremis*)
and lay his hands on her so that she may be saved, that is, saved
from the power of death, and live. Laying hands on someone, in
this positive sense,[70] is in line with biblical usage where the laying on of hands can signify blessing, consecration, sacrificial ritual, healing and exorcism.[71]

Forming an inclusion with the opening of the story and
preparing for the interruption caused by the insertion of the
other story, Jesus is said to be accompanied by a large crowd
who were pushing against him. The verb *synethlibon* (cognate of
thlipsis, distress, suffering) has the connotation of pushing
against him in an annoying or uncomfortable way.

iv. The woman with the Haemorrhage Mk 5:25-34

There now emerges from the thronging crowd a woman whose
rounded character and personal medical history are described
in a way somewhat unusual for the gospels where 'minor' characters often tend to be stereotyped. She has been afflicted with a
'flowing of blood' for twelve years, suffered much (*polla*) at the

66. J. R. Donahue and D. J. Harrington, *op. cit.*, 181.
67. The words *onomati Iairos*, 'by name Jairus', are missing in Old Latin
manuscripts and D.
68. *parakalei auton polla*, literally 'he pleads repeatedly / in many ways.'
69. 'dear' daughter' would be the translation if the diminutive *thugatrion*
from *thugater* is seen as endearment rather than referring to her young
age.
70. Laying hands on someone can at times signify doing them harm.
71. Acts 8:19; Lev 8:10; Exod 29:10; Lev 4:15; 16:21; 2 Kings 4:34; Mk 16:8;
Acts 9:12; 28:8.

hands of many (*pollôn*) physicians and spent all her resources, and rather than improving, her condition was getting worse. The double use of *polla/pollôn* emphasises her suffering condition and the desperation it provoked.[72]

Having heard about Jesus she is the first woman to approach him in public and her example of forthrightness stands as a reproach to the faltering disciples and as an example for all followers.[73] Coming from behind in the crowd, she touched his garment, for she was saying, 'If I can but touch the hem of his garment I shall be saved.' Healers were considered to be possessed of spiritual power which was channelled to the person being healed, and the laying on of hands or touching the sick person was the means of channelling that power. Here the woman in her desperation and determination 'short circuits' the process by touching the healer herself. Immediately the bleeding stopped and she was aware that her affliction was cured. Jesus immediately knew that power had gone out of him and he turned round in the crowd asking who touched his clothes.

The spotlight moves momentarily onto the disciples who are already beginning to show their lack of understanding and obtuseness generally in regard to Jesus and his ministry. They have seen his cures. They have been saved by his power over the raging elements of wind and sea and seen his power over the demon legion, and still they are surprised at his knowing that someone has been cured by his power. They see only the external factor of a crushing crowd and the confusion it generates. Their question to Jesus about how he can ask, 'Who touched me?' when so many are crowding around him, seems even to have a note of ridicule or mockery in it. Jesus, however, persisted in looking around the crowd for the person.

The spotlight moves back on to the woman. 'Aware of what had happened to her', meaning very likely a deeper awareness than that of knowing she had met a healer, she came forward 'in fear and trembling' (*phobêtheisa kai tremousa*), that is, 'completely

---

72. At this point Luke simply says 'she could not be healed by anyone', a point often used in the argument that Luke himself was a physician, and is here showing a little professional loyalty. (Lk 8:43)
73. See the study by Marla J. Selvidge, *Woman, Cult and Miracle Recital. A Redactional Critical Investgation on Mark 5:24-34*, Lewisburg, NJ: Bucknell University Press,1990.

awestruck' as in the presence of divine power.[74] She fell down
before him, telling the whole truth. Hers was a tragic truth. For
twelve years she had an ongoing bleeding, a gynecological problem, resulting in vaginal bleeding, which rendered her ritually
impure and socially excluded, sexually impotent and gradually
facing certain death from her complaint. She had braved the ritual impurity and social taboo which may have been the reason
for not coming face to face with Jesus in the presence of onlookers, and showed great determination and courage in physically
pushing herself through the crowd. Now she tells the whole
truth, her own tragic story and its wondrous outcome. Hisako
Kinukawa, writing from a feminist perspective, points out how
the woman and her condition symbolise 'the burden put on us
women because of our femaleness' and goes on to point out that
she had taken an initiative which led Jesus to demonstrate the
breaking down of the male-female barrier.[75]

Jesus addressed her as 'daughter'. It is reminiscent of his remark to his critics in Luke's gospel when they criticised him for
healing a long suffering woman on the Sabbath. He spoke of her
as a daughter of Abraham (Lk 13:16). It reminds the reader of the
statement about the mother, brothers and sisters in the kingdom
(Mk 3:31-35). Like the 'dear daughter' of Jairus, this woman too
is a daughter. It is a familiar address in the midst of an awe-inspiring experience. He tells her 'Your faith has saved you' and
dismisses her in peace with the imperative 'Be (remain) healed
of your affliction.'

The daughter of Jairus (2) Mk 5:35-43

The story of Jairus and his daughter now resumes with the arrival of the messengers bringing news of the girl's death. The resumed narrative is connected to the 'interrupting' narrative with
the words, in a genitive absolute (*autou lalountos*), 'as he was still
speaking'.

The news of the death of his daughter and the recommend-

74. Mk 4:41; 5:15; Phil 2:12f; Eph 6:5; Exod 15:16; Ps 2:11; Jer 33:9; Dan
5:19; 6:26.
75. Hisako Kinukawa, *Women and Jesus in Mark: A Japanese Feminist
Perspective,* Maryknoll, NY: Orbis 1994, 49, quoted in Donohue and
Harrington, *op. cit.,* 182. See also Hisako Kinukawa, 'The Story of the
Hemorrhaging Woman (Mark 5:25-34) read from a Japanese Feminist
Context,' *Biblical Interpretation* 2 (1994) 283-93.

ation of the messengers that Jairus should not trouble the teacher any further, create another scene of apparent hopelessness. In so doing the tension is heightened and the scene set for the drama that follows, showing once again the extraordinary power of Jesus over life and death.

Overhearing the remark about the death of the girl, or deliberately ignoring it (both translations of *parakousas* are possible) Jesus says to the synagogue official, 'Do not be afraid, only have faith.' The fear in this case is not the awe-inspired fear in the presence of the divine, but the natural anxiety and anticipation of a distraught parent in these circumstances. Reference to faith or the lack of it is a recurring theme in relation to all Jesus' wondrous actions.

He allowed no one to come with him except Peter, James and John, the brother of James. These are three of the first disciples called, to whom he gave special names. They will be with him on the mountain of transfiguration (Mk 9:2ff), and (together with Andrew) they will be with him on the Mount of Olives when he delivers his eschatological-apocalyptic address (Mk 13:3ff). Finally they will form the inner group he brings closer to be with him in the garden of Gethsemane (Mk 14:33ff). They are with him to experience these key moments of his ministry.

He came to the house and on seeing all the weeping and wailing, asked its purpose, stating that the child was not dead but sleeping. The scene reflects the elaborate mourning rituals common both to Jewish and Greco-Roman society. Lamentations, funeral dirges, keening women, flute players, fasting, rending garments, scattering ashes and so forth were all part of the process. Into such a scene Jesus enters and clears out the whole company. They ridicule his remark about sleeping. Though sleeping was a common euphemism for death, it also carried the nuance that no one is dead to God. In the New Testament death is seen as the sleep from which the believer will waken. This is most likely the meaning of Jesus' remark. Some scholars point out that the girl was not really dead and that Jesus' remark is pointing out that fact to the mourners. If that were the case would the story have been significant enough to command such attention in the gospel, in fact in all three synoptics? (Mt 9:18-26; Lk 8:40-56). Were the messengers, the mourners and the family all mistaken? In the case of Lazarus in John's gospel Jesus says he is sleeping and then has to correct the mistaken view of the disciples who think that he is simply asleep (Jn 11:11f).[76] Would the healing of a seriously ill child have caused him to issue such a strict order about keeping the matter secret (Mk 5:43)? The scoffing of the mourners may reflect also some experience of the early Christians of scoffing reaction to their belief in resurrection. Scoffing and mockery of the believer are a common motif in biblical literature and Hellenistic miracle stories.

Raising the dead would not have seemed as incredible to people in Jesus' time as it would in our day. The biblical stories of Elijah and Elisha raising the dead would have been known and believed (1 Kings 17:17-24; 2 Kings 4:18-37). Matthew, Mark and Luke tell the story of Jairus' daughter (Mt 9:18-26; Lk 8:40-56). Luke tells the story of the raising of the widow's son at Naim (Lk 7:11-17) and John tells the story of the raising of Lazarus (Jn 11:1-44). Jesus' response to the messengers of the Baptist includes 'the dead are raised' (Mt 11:2-6; Lk 7:18-23) and Jesus' programmatic statement in his sermon in Nazareth refers to Elijah and the widow at Zarephath (Lk 4:26; 1 Kings 17:8-24), an indirect reference to raising the dead during his ministry.

Jesus took the father and mother of the child, and those with him (the three disciples) and entered where the child lay. As in the case of touching the leper, Jesus takes the child by the hand and in so doing breaks a very serious taboo incurring ritual impurity for touching a corpse. As already seen, the verb *kratêsas* has strong connotations of power, so it may be translated, 'having taken her hand in power' (as he did with Peter's mother-in-law). He addresses her with the Aramaic expression, *talitha koum*,' little lamb, arise', which is then translated into Greek as *korasion*, 'young lady or young woman', the diminutive of *korê*, maiden. 'I say to you, rise.' 'I say to you' emphasises the power of Jesus' word. *Egeire*, means 'rise up', 'wake from sleep', 'stand up', and as already seen the verb is very much associated with resurrection from the dead.

'And *immediately* the young lady got up and walked about, for she was twelve years old.' Following the familiar *immediately*, the statement that 'she walked about' seems to say something more than that she took some steps across the room because it is followed by the clause 'for she was twelve years old'.

---

76. 1 Thess 4:13-18. ' Sleeping', *koimesis*, becomes a common Christian word for death and the related word 'cemetery' is used for the place of such sleeping.

Throughout the Bible and related literature 'walking' and 'path' are regularly used as metaphors for living and behaving. Here it seems to mean she took the first steps back to her normal healthy life now at the legal age of twelve when she would be embarking on marriage and childbearing.

'*And immediately* everyone was ecstatic with a great ecstasy'. The familiar 'and immediately' introduces the reaction of the witnesses, in this case expressed in a particularly striking form, 'they were ecstatic with a great ecstasy' (*exestêsan ecstasei megalêi*).

And he ordered them sternly (lit.'repeatedly / in many ways', *polla*) that no one should know this, the clearest 'secrecy' command in the gospel. He ordered them to give the girl something to eat, a sign of her full, instantaneous recovery, since usually after serious illness it takes time, and friendly persuasion, to recover one's appetite.[77]

There are echoes of the raising of the son of the Shunammite woman by Elisha (2 Kings 4:25-37) in the account of the raising of Jairus' daughter. The pleading and faith of the parent, the announcement of the death of the child by a servant, the going privately into the room where the child lay and the restoration of the child to the parent are points in common to both stories.

There is a further symbolic and literary level of meaning. In this gospel which puts so much emphasis on feeding and food, and customs and taboos around who, where, when and how people eat, the theme of feeding the child will resonate in the next healing of a girl, this time the healing of the daughter of a non-Jewish parent, the Syro-Phoenician woman. The healing of that child will follow a discussion on giving food to Gentile children from the table of the Jewish children, a metaphor for the ministry of Jesus to both Jew and Gentile (Mk 7:24ff). Jesus has just 'ordered' the feeding of a Jewish child in the context of his healing ministry. The Syro-Phoenician woman will tell him in no uncertain terms (even if using metaphors) that Gentile children also need to be fed. Like the Shunammite woman in the story about Elisha this foreigner will also approach the Jewish

---

77. Various less likely explanations for this have been given, from seeing it as an example of the practical thoughtfulness of Jesus (as if her parents and carers were not thoughtful!), to showing that she is really alive and not a returned spirit. Like the serving hospitality of Peter's mother-in-law it shows the instantaneous nature and completeness of the restoration to life, health and strength.

prophet and not take ' no' for an answer. He has addressed the woman with the haemorrhage as 'daughter' and raised the daughter of Jairus. The next 'daughter' healed will be a Gentile.

6. REJECTION BY HIS OWN PEOPLE IN HIS NATIVE PLACE MK 6:1-6A

From 'that place', the place where he had raised the daughter of Jairus, he went to his home town 'and his disciples followed him', though they do not figure in the story about to unfold.[78] Mark considers Nazareth as Jesus' home town, as is obvious from his statement that he came from Nazareth to be baptised by John (Mk 1:9) and from the number of references to him as a Nazarene. His origin in Nazareth is mentioned by a demon (Mk 1:24), by the people around the blind Bartimaeus (Mk 10:47), by the servant challenging Peter in the court of the high priest (Mk 14:67), and by the young man at the tomb (Mk 16:6).

He began to teach on the Sabbath in the synagogue. It was the prerogative of any layman to teach in the synagogue if invited to do so by the synagogue officials. It was in the synagogue in Capernaum that he first made a deep impression on the people by his preaching with authority, an authority further manifested in his expulsion of the demon (Mk 1:21ff). On that occasion his preaching was seen to overshadow that of the scribes, a comment that struck a note of praise and warning. Later he healed the man with the withered hand on the Sabbath in a synagogue and in reaction the Pharisees and Herodians plotted how to destroy him (Mk 3:1ff). Now he is preaching in the synagogue in his home town but he will meet with total rejection among his own people.

At first the people in the synagogue in Nazareth were astonished (*ekplessein*) at his preaching. This same verb is used for the very positive reaction to his preaching in his first synagogue appearance in Capernaum, and again such positive amazement at his teaching on the part of the crowd will be the reason restraining the authorities from taking strong action against him in the immediate aftermath of the 'cleansing of the Temple' and making it necessary for them to plot how to capture him away from the gaze of the people (Mk 1:22; 11:18; .14:1f). But the initial response of positive amazement in Nazareth turns sour. The crowd (*hoi polloi*, the many, or maybe the *profanum vulgus*), ask a

---

78. *Patris* could be translated ' home country' or 'home town'. The context favours 'home town'.

series of five questions, each charged with hostility. The biting cynicism of the first question is difficult to render directly into English. It is just three words in Greek, *pothen toutô tauta*, literally meaning 'whence to this fellow these things?' It could be translated as, 'Where did the likes of this fellow get the likes of all that?', seeing 'this *fellow'(toutô)* as a cynical comment on someone who had risen above his station. Then comes the question: 'What is the wisdom given to this fellow?'(again the cynical 'this fellow') or 'what kind of wisdom could a fellow like this have?'[79] This is followed by: 'What (or whence) are the mighty deeds accomplished through his hands?'[80] These questions fit into an overall pattern of speculation on the origin of his teaching and power to do mighty deeds, not only in Mark but in all gospels, and very likely also they reflect ongoing questioning during the early years of the church.

The other questions are about his background and origins. 'Is not this fellow the manual worker (craftsman, carpenter), the son of Mary and brother of James and Joses and Judas and Simon? Are not his sisters with us?' In a number of manuscripts he is not called 'the carpenter' but 'the son of the carpenter'.[81] In either case it is probably meant as a slur, implying that he has no distinguished background and no education or training other than using his hands for his trade. How can he teach us! There follows the typical statement of jealous small mindedness which could be summed up as, 'sure we know all his people and all about them!'

Identifying Jesus as 'the son of Mary', the only reference to Mary by name in Mark's gospel, has caused commentators to speculate on this reference to Jesus, identifying him by his mother's name. Some point to the fact that it is because Joseph was already deceased. Maybe so, but persons can be identified by reference to a deceased parent in a local community, particularly if that person was well known, as Joseph would have been as a

79. This is the only reference to ' wisdom', *sophia*, in Mark.
80. The syntax of the Greek is difficult and one has either to understand an unstated *so that* mighty deeds are accomplished, or understand 'and what are?' or 'whence the mighty deeds?'
81. The reading 'son of a carpenter' may be a scribal harmonisation with Mt 13:55. This scribal change may be due to the same attitude which caused Origen to deny that any gospel describes Jesus as working with his hands (*Contra Celsum*, 6:36).

local tradesman. Some say there may have been a hint at illegiti-
macy, and in that case mentioning him as son of his mother
could be seen as an insult. Maybe Mary was well known in the
community, as for example Mary of Bethany in John's gospel,
where the village itself could be called the village of Mary (Jn
11:1). Or, and this seems the most likely, in the case of a man
being married more than once, the children are identified in relation to the mother, especially if she is well known, as in the
case of the women mentioned in Matthew's genealogy of Jesus.
In this way they are distinguished from the children of the other
wife (wives). Even in multiple marriage families all are still
called brothers/sisters as in the case of the twelve sons of Jacob/
Israel. The reference here to Jesus' family members really serves
the purpose of showing how ordinary he was in the eyes of the
people among whom he grew up and who now think he has
risen above his station.

The brothers and sisters of Jesus are mentioned, and the
brothers are identified by name as James, Joses, Judas and
Simon. The dominant Catholic understanding, held also by
many other Christians, has been that Mary was 'ever virgin' and
so these brothers and sisters of Jesus were not children of Mary
and Joseph but children of an earlier marriage of Joseph. This
would also point to the reason for referring to Jesus as son of
Mary. Another tradition of interpreting the reference is to understand it as referring to cousins, members of the extended
family, possibly children of Mary's sister.[82]

The outcome of their speculations about Jesus' background
and family is 'scandal', a stumbling block to belief that anyone
so like themselves, one of their own, about whom they knew
everything, with nothing in background or education to recom-
mend him, should be so possessed of power to preach and work
wonders. This poses for them a 'scandal', 'a stone causing them
to stumble'. They reject him.

82. In the ancient church Hegesippus (2nd cent), Tertullian (2nd-3rd
cent) and Helvidius (4th cent) held that they were the biological children of Mary and Joseph, an opinion held by many 'non-Catholic' scholars and by some recent Catholic commentators, such as J. P. Meier, *A
Marginal Jew*,1:327-32 and Rudolf Pesch, *Markusevangelium*, 1:322-24.
This question does not touch on the question of the virginal conception
of Jesus. See also J. P. Meier, 'The Brothers and Sisters of Jesus in
Ecumenical Perspective' *CBQ* 54 (1992) 1-28; R.Bauckham, 'The Brothers
and Sisters of Jesus: An Epiphanian Response', *CBQ* (1994) 686-700.

Jesus is now in the tradition of the rejected prophet,[83] the servant of God without honour,[84] the wisdom teacher not listened to.[85] He responds: 'A prophet is only without honour (*atimos*) in his native place, among his own relations and in his own house.' The sentiment is reflected across the gospels. Luke reports the saying as: 'No prophet is accepted in his native place' and John has: 'A prophet does not have honour in his own native place' (Lk 4:24; Jn 4:44). Similar experiences and sayings are found among philosophers and healers in the wider world. Among those in Hellenistic literature is the comment in Philostratus' *Life of Apollonius of Tyana*, that it is the universal opinion of philosophers that life is difficult in their native land.[86] The gospel of Thomas reflects a combination of New Testament and broader sayings: 'A prophet is not acceptable in his home town, a doctor does not heal those who know him.'[87]

In the corresponding pericope in Luke, Jesus realises that they expect him to perform the same mighty works in his home town that he has been doing in Capernaum (Lk 4:16-30) and after heated exchanges they end up wanting to throw him over the brow of the hill on which the town was built, a form of stoning by throwing the victim onto rocks. At this point in Luke Jesus sets out (*eporeueto*) on his journey which eventually takes him to Jerusalem.

He was unable to do any mighty work (*dynamis*) there, except that he laid his hands on a few sick people and cured them. The reason for his inability is given in the next sentence. It was because of their lack of faith, at which he was shocked (*ethaumasen*). This 'inability' to do any mighty work in the face of a lack of faith is a pointer to the fact that Jesus was not a wonder worker performing mighty deeds in order to convert people to his cause. There is no compelling of people into belief. The temptation narratives in Matthew and Luke dramatise this truth in the neat stylistic presentation of Jesus' response to the main factors that will bedevil his ministry – the pressure to respond to

83. 2 Chron 24:19; 36:16; Neh 9:26, 30; Jer 35:15; Ezek 2:5; Hos 9:7; Dan 9:6, 10.
84. Is 53:3 (LXX), the suffering servant is *atimos*, without honour.
85. Significantly Mark uses the term *sophia* for Jesus' teaching only here in the gospel, in the context of the rejection of his teaching.
86. Letter 44, quoted by J. R. Donahue and D. J. Harrington, *op. cit.*, 185.
87. *Gospel of Thomas* 31; *P. Oxy.* 31:1-2, quoted by Donahue and Harrington, *ibid.*

physical need such as hunger for food instead of seeing the deeper needs of people for the word of God, to grasp at political power and influence and to perform compelling religious signs (Mt 41-11; Lk 4:1-13). These would satisfy people and win them to his cause but they would not open them to the word of God, and the call to conversion, repentance and belief. This truth is clearly seen here in Mk 6:5f where healings are said to follow faith, not the other way round.

'He marvelled at their unbelief.' The same verb *ethaumasen* has already been used of the people who marvelled at his works. This section of the gospel ends on this very negative note. He will not be found preaching in the synagogue again.

Looking back over this section of the ministry in Galilee and surrounding areas (Mk 3:7-6:6a), one can see the positive elements being overshadowed by the negative elements emerging in the plot. Jesus chose his Twelve Apostles 'to be with him'. He suffered the allegations of the scribes from Jerusalem that he was possessed and was casting out demons by the power of the prince of devils. He suffered also the non-belief of his family and relations who tried to capture / restrain him. He spoke of his followers as his true family. His preaching in parables and his mighty power over nature, demons, sickness and death were presented in a paradigmatic series of teaching and miracles. Now he has returned to base and picked up on the negative vibes that had come from his own people, originally from his family. He is the rejected prophet, without honour in his native place, among his relations and in his home. In the first section he was rejected by the authority figures. Now he is rejected by his own people. The next section of the Galilee ministry will focus on his relations with his 'new family' of disciples, and will end with an emphasis on their failure to understand.

The reader by this time is very impressed by Jesus' teaching and miraculous deeds, showing his power and compassion, but is also growing more and more aware of the opposition and disbelief, and hoping that the 'new family' of disciples whom 'he chose to be with him' will emerge in better light and counteract the negativity.

Jesus and His Disciples / Apostles: The Bread Section
Mk 6:6b-8:21

Touring the Villages / Feeding in the Desert

1. THE PLOT AND OUTLINE

As in the two former sections of the account of the ministry in Galilee, this section also begins with a summary which is followed by a focus of attention on the disciples / apostles / the Twelve. Jesus calls the Twelve to him, gives them a commission with authority and tells them how to behave as his representatives. Their authority comes from him and this is borne out by the binding effect of the multiple use of paratactic *kai* throughout the pericope, twelve times between Mk 6:6b and 6:13. It ties their mission to Jesus' mission and to his giving them authority. It also binds the various elements of the passage together. The sending of the Twelve and their return form an intercalation with the story of John the Baptist and Herod. The news of their mission and the resulting opinions circulating about Jesus lead into the story of John the Baptist and Herod. Their report on the mission is held over until the 'apostles', ' the ones who had been sent', (the only use of the noun apostle in Mark) return and report to Jesus, thus forming the intercalation. Again, after focusing on the apostles / disciples there follows, as in the two former sections, a series of mighty words and deeds of Jesus, this time in two parallel series in which bread / food / eating is a recurring theme. These two parallel cycles of events follow each other, beginning in each case with a feeding of the multitude and ending with a healing. Again, this third section ends on a very negative note with Jesus' exasperated comment on the disciples' lack of understanding. Their failure to understand is graphically illustrated by the healing of the blind man in two distinct stages, the first ' failed' attempt illustrating the failure of the disciples to understand Jesus clearly, the second 'successful' attempt a summary preview of the second half of the gospel where Jesus will instruct the disciples in the meaning of discipleship and prepare them (or, more accurately, will endeavour to prepare them) for his passion, death and resurrection. The healing of the blind man at Bethsaida, approximately half way through the gospel, functions as a vantage point from which to look back over what has been and to look forward to what is to come.

The following outline illustrates the overall contents of the section (Mk 6:6b-8:26) and the two parallel cycles which make up the 'Mighty Words and Deeds'. The healing of the blind man which completes the parallel in the series also forms an inclusion with the healing of the blind Bartimaeus at the end of the next major division of the gospel (Mk 10:46-52).

Overall Outline:
1. Summary. Mk 6:6b.
2. The Twelve/Apostles: Herod & the Baptist (Intercalation) Mk 6:7-31.
3. Jesus' Mighty Words and Deeds: Two Bread Cycles. Mk 6:32-8:26.
4. Conclusion: Failure of Disciples Mk 8:14-26.

2. SUMMARY MK 6:6B

Like the first two major sections of the Galilee ministry, this third section, often referred to as 'The Bread Section', also begins with a summary: 'He made a tour round the villages teaching.'

3. THE MISSION OF THE TWELVE APOSTLES, HEROD AND JOHN MK 6:7-31

This section of the gospel sets the appointment and sending out of the Twelve, and the feeding of the multitudes, against the background of the murderous banquet in the house of Herod Antipas.

i. Commissioning of the Twelve Mk 6: 7-13

Jesus summoned the Twelve (*proskalein*) to come to him and sent them out (*apostellein*) with authority over unclean spirits. They are sent out in twos. In addition to any consideration of prudence concerning their safety and well being, there was a long tradition of seeing two persons as necessary for juridical witness (Deut 17:6; 19:15; Num 35:30; 2 Cor 13:1). Representing Jesus, acting in his name and with his authority, is a bearing of witness to him and to his mission to establish the kingdom. This concept of 'witnessing' is brought out clearly in Jesus' farewell and commissioning at the beginning of Acts when he tells the disciples: 'You will be my witnesses not only in Jerusalem but throughout Judaea and Samaria and to the ends of the earth'(Acts 1:8).[1] The sending of the seventy two in Luke also emphasises their going

---

1. The term *martyros*, martyr, witness, was to become the term used in the church for those who were put to death for witnessing to Jesus.

in pairs (Lk 10:1). This was also very likely the practice of the early church. Barnabas and Paul went together, and when they fell out, Paul brought Silas on his missionary journey and Barnabas brought John Mark (Acts 15:39f). Peter and John went together to Samaria (Acts 8:14-17).

There follows the 'mission charge' for the way (*eis hodon*), and *hodos* may well have a double meaning here, the missionary journey in a physical sense and the disciples' journey in a spiritual sense.

The missionaries must be detached, relying on the providence of God who sent Jesus whose representatives they now are, and on the hospitality of those to whom they minister. They therefore are to bring no bread, no bag (*pera*), no money in their belt, and no spare tunic. The *pera* mentioned is very likely a ' begging bag' like that used by wandering Cynics or philosophers, or begging priests and officials of pagan deities and their shrines, the latter described in antiquity as 'pious robbers with their booty growing from village to village'.[2] Jesus' ambassadors, however, were sent out by him on a very different mission.[3]

Further emphasising this point of dependence on providence and hospitality, Matthew emphasises that they are to bring no staff and no sandals (Mt 10:10) and Luke states that they are to bring no staff (Lk 9:3). Matthew further makes the point by including Jesus' saying: 'the Son of Man has nowhere to lay his head' (Mt 8:20). E. Schweizer puts it succinctly: 'Messengers who wish to provide for every emergency do not have faith. Messengers are not to be believed if they rely on their own resources (material or spiritual) rather than on the One whom they proclaim.'[4] M. D. Hooker points to a passage in the Mishnah which forbids entry to the Temple Mount with staff, sandal or wallet, or with dust on one's feet. Jesus' instruction to the apostles resembles this instruction about respecting the sacred nature of the Temple Mount and T. W. Manson suggests that Jesus' instruction similarly reflects the sacred nature of their mission.[5]

2. Quoted by W. Barclay, *The Gospel of Mark*, 143.
3. The nature of their mission is described by J. A. Draper, 'Wandering radicalism or purposeful activity? Jesus and the sending of messengers in Mark 6:6-56', *Neotestamentica* 29 (1995) 183-202.
4. E. Schweizer, *The Good News According to Mark*, 130.
5. M. D. Hooker, *op. cit.*, 156, quoting *m. Berakoth* 9.5., and T. W. Manson, *The Sayings of Jesus*, London, 1949, 181.Though the *Mishnah* was codified later than the New Testament, it must reflect traditions formed over a long period of time.

The witness across all three synoptics points very clearly to dependence on God's providence and the generosity of the recipients of the gospel in the sacred task of representing Jesus and the kingdom he preaches. However, though all three emphasise the same overall understanding of the nature of the mission task, Mark differs from Matthew and Luke on the instruction about not bringing a staff or wearing sandals. According to Mark Jesus tells them to bring a staff and to wear sandals (Mk 6:8f). One asks, 'why the difference?' Is it a practical suggestion for those who may have taken the original command too literally at a cost to their health and safety? That may be partly the case, but there is probably a more theological reason, one which highlights the nature of the mission without in any way compromising the dependence on providence and generosity as already outlined. The restless movement of Jesus throughout his ministry in Galilee and his fateful journey to Jerusalem paint a picture of a wandering prophet and teacher, a charismatic wanderer. F. J. Moloney points out that the staff and sandals symbolise very well such a wandering lifestyle. Almost every pericope begins with a verb of motion. The staff and sandals are the symbols of the missionary lifestyle into which the Twelve are now being commissioned.[6] Furthermore, the shepherd's staff was a symbol of the shepherd's role and care, and was widely used even by political rulers in the secular cultures of the east. The staff of God's envoy symbolised the authority and power conferred for the mission or office. Moses and Aaron used the staff to demonstrate their power (Ex 4:20; 7:9-20; 8:16f; 14:16). Gehazi, the servant of Elisha was told to place the staff of Elisha on the face of the Shunammite woman's son prior to the healing (2 Kings 4:29-37).

Similarities have been pointed out between Jesus' mission charge to his apostles and the 'mission' of the Cynics. Their setting out without food, clothing and other accessories is similar but their purpose and behaviour are quite different. The Cynics shunned company and hospitality, rejected tradition and authority and addressed people in an aggressive manner, decrying the system and society wherever they saw the need to challenge the smug and the arrogant. The work and attitude of the Twelve was to be very different in spite of superficial similarities.

---

6. F. J. Moloney, *op. cit.*, 122.

The Twelve are told to stay in the same house while in a place/area of preaching. Hospitality is a mark of the God-fearing person and the hospitable household is a sacred congregation in itself into which one did not take staff, begging bag or money belt, just as one left them outside the Temple. They are not to move from house to house. Stability within an area is necessary for good communication. But there is a deeper reason. Hospitality once offered should not be rejected, especially in the interests of better accommodation or more interesting company. To do so would reject and demean the goodness of those who first showed hospitality and such an action would put material and social concerns ahead of the missionary way of life. Their lifestyle should reflect their preaching.

Inhospitality is the mark of a non God-fearing people. Where they meet inhospitality they are instructed to treat that area symbolically as 'a pagan place', shaking the contaminated pagan dust from their feet, the gesture they used on returning from Gentile territory into the Holy Land

They set out and did exactly as Jesus did himself and had instructed them to do. They preached repentance, exorcised demons and anointed sick people with oil and cured them. Anointing with oil is a ritual not evident in Jesus' own cures. However, it was common practice in the Greco-Roman world to anoint sick people with oil. Here there may also be a reflection of the practice of the early church as evidenced in the Letter of James (James 5:14).

ii. Herod and John the Baptist Mk 6:14-29

The newly commissioned missionaries are now following in the footsteps of Jesus and John the Baptist in calling for repentance. Their activity caused people to ask about Jesus and to discuss his identity and the nature and purpose of his mission. They associated Jesus with a return of John the Baptist, Elijah or one of the prophets. The reference to John provides the cue for introducing at this point in the narrative the story of his imprisonment and execution and the fear (remorse, repentance of a kind?) of Herod. According to Mark the Herod family had been very disturbed by John's preaching of repentance. Their subsequent actions in his arrest and death gave much additional reason for their needing repentance. Herod's earlier fascination with John and his execution of him will now come back to haunt him. The

reference to Elijah is also very apt since he too fell foul of a royal
family because of his outspoken criticism, but escaped their
murderous intent. The discerning reader may begin to wonder
at this time if the stories of John (as the returned Elijah), and
Elijah, and indeed of the prophets generally, are a warning that
Jesus and his representatives will follow in their footsteps when
powerful people turn against them.

The story of John's arrest and death forms an intercalation
with the thoroughly Markan pericopes of the sending out of the
Twelve and their return to report to Jesus. In this intercalation
the account of John's execution allows the narrative time for the
new missionaries to have carried on their mission before reporting back to Jesus.[7] The story of John's murder is an extended,
vivid and artistically constructed narrative, different in style
and vocabulary from the surrounding Markan material.
Scholars have classified its literary genre in various ways, as
popular folktale, legend and midrashic exposition.

As the Twelve spread out on their mission the name of Jesus
became well known. The general discussion that ensued among
the people about Jesus' identity and role reflects some of the
messianic expectations current at the time, somewhat similar to
those articulated in St John's gospel by the messengers sent by
the Jerusalem authorities to question John the Baptist: 'Are you
the Christ ... Elijah ... the Prophet?' Though the exactness of the
Johannine formula, especially in relation to 'the Prophet', is not
seen here in Mark, the variable character of the expectation is in
evidence. The speculation that Jesus was John the Baptist risen
from the dead, or that the spirit of John was in him, and that was
why miraculous powers were at work in him, was probably
prompted by John's widespread appeal and by popular revul-
sion at the violent cutting short of his fiery mission which resembled, even in his dress and appearance, that of the equally fiery
Elijah whose return was expected. The New Testament in fact
presents the mission of John the Baptist in terms of the return of
the spirit of Elijah (Lk 1:17; Mt 17:9-13; cf Mk 9:13; 1:4-8).

Others thought of Jesus in terms of the return of Elijah because he was expected to reappear in order to usher in the final
time. This expectation was fuelled by the story in 2 Kings about
Elijah's ascent into heaven in a fiery chariot and the account in 2

7. M. Hooker, *op. cit.*, 158, writes: 'The somewhat artificial insertion provides an interlude for the disciples to complete their mission.'

Chronicles which speaks of the reception of a letter from him after the event, suggesting that he was alive (2 Kings 2:11; 2 Chron 21:12). There was a strong post-exilic expectation of his return before the Day of the Lord. Malachi speaks of the angel coming to prepare the Way of the Lord, and this angel is identified in a later addition as Elijah (Mal 3:1; 4:5; 3:23f).[8] Sirach speaks of Elijah as 'designated in the prophecies of doom to allay God's wrath ... to turn the hearts of fathers towards their children, and to restore the tribes of Jacob' (Sir 48:10f; cf Lk 1:17). In Enoch the animal allegory of history portrays Elijah's return before the judgement and the appearance of the great apocalyptic lamb (Enoch 90:31; 89:52; cf Jn 1:29.36).[9]

There were others who thought of Jesus in terms of a prophet like one of the prophets of old. This rather general idea of a prophet lacks the same focus, but probably emerges from the same tradition that lies behind the expectation of the prophet in the Johannine tradition. The Johannine expectation is based on the prophet figured in the Deuteronomic legislation drawn up for various functionaries such as judges, kings, priests and prophets. The text contains the statement: 'a prophet like me (Moses) will the Lord, your God, raise up' (Deut 18:15-18). This came to be interpreted as a prediction of the coming of a 'prophet-like-Moses'. The Essene community at Qumran were told to cling to the Torah and the laws of community till a prophet (like Moses?) comes.[10] The Samaritan woman at the well reflects a similar expectation among the Samaritans about the function of 'the one to come' when she hopes he will clarify the issue of the legality of the Temple worship on Gerizim (Jn 4:20-25). In the Acts of the Apostles Jesus is identified as the prophet-like-Moses in Peter's address in the Portico of Solomon (Acts 3:22). However, here in the Galilean context of Jesus' time, as portrayed by Mark, where the ordinary folk did not share the precise knowledge and studied formulae of the educated Jerusalem classes and the Qumran scholars, the people had a more general, less clear idea of an expected prophet. Their discussion, however, and the worried conscience of Herod, serve to advance the debate in Mark's gospel about the identity of Jesus.

---

8. Circa 450 BC.
9. The dress and behaviour of John, particularly as portrayed in the synoptics, recall that of Elijah (Mk 1:6; cf 2 Kings1:8).
10. 4 Q *Testimonia*; 1QS 9:11; 4 Q *Flor*.

As the people talked about Jesus, Herod (Antipas) heard
about him 'for his name became known'.[11] What did he hear? It
was being said (lit. ' they were saying') that John the Baptist had
risen from the dead and that was why these powers were at
work in him. Others were saying it was Elijah. Herod, on hearing it, said: 'It is John whom I beheaded. He is risen.' Herod's
troubled conscience propels him into debating Jesus' role and
identity and its possible connection with a return of the Baptist.
This in turn gives the narrator an opportunity for telling the
story of the Baptist's murder. His troubled conscience is understandable as the story goes on to explain that Herod knew he
was a just and holy man. He gave him his protection. He 'was
afraid of (in awe of?) John', and when he heard him speak he
was greatly perplexed[12] and liked to listen to him. However, like
the seed that fell on rocky ground, Herod heard the word, received it with joy, but had no root in him, or like the seed among
thorns when its initial growth showed promise it was choked by
the worries of the world.

Herod Antipas was a son of Herod the Great and succeeded
his father as tetrarch (not king) of Galilee and Perea. Matthew
and Luke give him his proper title, but Mark calls him a king.
Some scholars see this as a straightforward mistake or the result
of editorial fatigue. It is more likely that it reflects popular usage
and here in Mark it may be deliberately used as a literary association with the stories of king Ahab and queen Jezebel (1 Kings 19
& 21) and the king in the Esther story (Esther 5), both of which
have strong echoes in the Markan narrative. Furthermore, Mark
and his intended readers very probably knew that his downfall
some years later resulted from his ambition to be king, so there
is a great irony in calling him 'king'. His own, and particularly
his wife's, ambition that he be made king caused him to be dismissed and sent into exile by the emperor Caligula shortly after
his accession to the imperial throne circa 38-39 AD. His downfall
was brought about in large measure at the jealous instigation of
Herodias' brother, Herod Antipas' nephew, Agrippa, who laid
charges against him. Furthermore the dark irony continues as

11. From a grammatical point of view the verb does not have a direct
object but a paratactic *kai elegon hoti*, 'and they were saying', serves as
the object, as the *kai* is equivalent to 'for' / ' because'.
12. Some mss read 'when he heard him speak he did many things',
epoiei instead of *êporei*.

the would-be king's murderous banquet for the nobility in his palace will be followed by the real but discreet king's compassionate messianic banquet for Jew and Gentile in the desert.

It may appear at first glance that this is a story in the gospel that does not directly relate to or directly concern Jesus and his ministry. That, however, would be an understanding that misses the point. John is the precursor. He began the process of preaching repentance and the forgiveness of sins as preparation of the way for the one who would baptise in the Holy Spirit. Jesus stepped into the breach when John was arrested and carried on the mission of preaching and now his representatives are going about Galilee preaching. John, the first of the preachers, now meets the fate which will await Jesus and the others. In his death, therefore, he is also the precursor, preparing the way. Shortly Jesus will begin speaking about a similar fate awaiting himself, and possibly also awaiting his representatives.

As Elijah condemned Jezebel for her patronage of the cult of Ba'al and subsequently for the murder of Naboth and the impounding of his vineyard, so John criticised the incestuous marriage of Herodias and Herod Antipas. As Jezebel was wont to force her will upon her weaker and vacillating husband King Ahab, and Elijah only luckily escaped her murderous designs, so too Herodias tricks Herod Antipas, against his will, into serving up the head of the Baptist on a dish at his birthday party (1 Kings 19 & 21). Jesus also will be put to death by a ruler, Pilate, who recognises his goodness, but is trapped into giving in to pressure, and unable or unwilling to extricate himself from authorising his execution when a hostile authority and angry mob pressurise him into crucifying Jesus in spite of his initial unwillingness to do so (Mk 15:6-15).

As the Baptist began by preparing the way for Jesus through his preaching and baptism, now he prefigures in his arrest and execution, the fate of Jesus (and his new missionaries). John's role as precursor preparing the way continues until, and includes, his death. The age old story of the rejected and persecuted prophet continues.

The beheading of John Mk 6:17-29
The story of the beheading of John bears all the marks of a consummate biblical storyteller whether it had been composed prior to Mark's inclusion of it in the gospel or whether he com-

posed it himself. It is based on some essential historical facts relating to the preaching, arrest and beheading of John. The reasons for the arrest given by Mark are religious and moral, relating to his preaching against Herod Antipas' incestuous marriage.[13] The reasons given by the historian Josephus are political,
relating to the fears surrounding a popular figure who draws
crowds that may encourage or give cover to revolutionaries.[14]

Several words rare in Mark and in the New Testament are
used in the story and give it its exotic and vivid character. This is
particularly so in verses 21-26. This in part can be explained by
the rare nature of the story[15] but there is also an uncharacteristic
use of participles throughout the pericope, two of them in genitive absolute phrases.[16]

Though Mark very frequently uses the historic present tense
to give the sense of immediacy to his narrative, here in this long
account it is noticeably absent. A variety of tenses are used. The
scene is set with a series of imperfect tenses in verses 18-20
which describe a prolonged and repeated series of actions and
attitudes which characterised the fraught relationship between
John, Herod and Herodias. 'John was saying … Herodias was
furious and wishing to kill him … and unable … because Herod
was in awe (feared) John … he protected him … he was confused ... he listened gladly.'

The triple use of participles adds to the vivid nature of the
story as they describe the movement of the characters. The girl
'having entered, having departed, having entered' (*eiselthousês*,

---

13. See the extended note at the end of the commentary on the intricacies of the Herod family marriages.
14. Josephus, *Ant* 18:109-119.
15. The main examples are: *enechein*, to be furious, *dikaios kai hagios*, just
and holy, *synterein*, to protect, *aporein*, to be hesitant, unsure how to
react, *eukairos*, opportune, *genesia* here meaning birthday, *megistan*,
magnate, *chiliarchos*, commander of a thousand soldiers, *orcheisthai*, to
dance, *areskein*, to please, *hemisus*, half, *exautês* meaning *exautês tês horas*,
this very hour, immediately, *pinax*, dish for serving food, *perilypos*, very
sad, distressed (cf 14:34 of Jesus in Gethsemane), *spekoulator*, body-
guard, agent, here 'executioner', (*hapax* in NT, Latinism from *speculator*,
spy, scout), *apokephalizein*, to behead.
16. The participles are: *eidôs*, *akousas*, *exelthousa*, *eiselthousa*, *legousa*,
genomenos, *aposteilas apelthôn*, *aposteilas*, *akousantes*. Two participles appear in genitive absolute phrases, *genomenês hêmeras eukairou*, *eiselthousês tês thugatros*.

exelthousa, eiselthousa). The triple use of the indicative has a similar effect, describing the delivery of the head of the Baptist: 'he brought it on a dish, he gave it to the girl, the girl gave it to her mother' (*ênegken ... edôken ... edôken*). There is a similar triple action of the disciples of John on hearing of his death: 'they came, they took the body, they placed it in the tomb' (*êlthan ... êran ... ethêkan*). In all these cases the vividness, pace and elegance of the Greek can be easily lost in translation.

The wording of the story is striking. Rare words and expressions, several New Testament *hapax legomena* (words used only once in Mark or in the New Testament), word plays and a Latinism are all present. The birthday of Herod is described as his *genesia*, a very likely word play because *genesia* was used frequently for the anniversary of death. Now the birthday of Herod is the anniversary of John the Baptist's death!

Entrances and exits lend pace and drama to the story. The dancer's entrance is portrayed as sudden and unexpected with the use of the genitive absolute (*eiselthousês tês thugatros autês*[17] *tês Herodiados*). She 'pleased' Herod and his fellow diners. The verb *êresen/areskein*, pleased, has the meaning of 'entertained' in a non-erotic sense, though popular representations of the scene usually take it in the erotic sense. The promise of half his kingdom, a promise with its antecedent in the Esther story (Esther 5), may be a highly ironic statement on the part of the narrator because Herod was a client ruler under Rome and did not have power to do any such thing and furthermore, as seen above, he was not a king and did not have a kingdom to divide! On the part of Herod himself or of the original storyteller, or on the part of Mark, the expression may well be seen as a popular way of making a big generous and indiscreetly boastful gesture such as promising a lover the moon and the stars. But in the circumstances it was a lethal mistake. The solemn oath to make a generous gift was very serious. In Jewish culture it invoked the Holy One with all the solemnity that such a gesture entailed. In

17. Some of the mss of Mk 6:22 describe the dancer as 'his daughter' rather than 'her daughter', reading *thugatros autou Herôdiados* instead of *thugatros autês Herôdiados* which translates as 'his daughter Herodias' rather than 'daughter of the same Herodias'. In the light of the story as a whole the better reading is 'her daughter' and also the // Mt 14:6 points to the reading Herodias' daughter. Josephus gives her name as Salome. She would have been Herod Antipas' stepdaughter, and therefore in a broad sense his daughter.

Hellenistic culture a royal oath was the pinnacle of binding oneself in honour and to Christian ears it was similar to the Jewish
religious obligation. The 'king' realised how badly he had been
trapped and he was *perilypos*, very distressed, the same verb
being used only one other time in the gospel, for Jesus' distress
in Gethsemane (Mk 14:14).

Biblical stories tend to follow well established patterns and
this story fits the pattern of the stories of strong wives of kings. It
re-echoes the steely determination of Jezebel, offended on behalf
of her vacillating husband, King Ahab, by the refusal of Naboth
to sell him the vineyard, her frustration with the fiery condemnations of the prophet Elijah, and her lethal intentions in his regard (1 Kings 21). The story recalls also the clever ploy of Queen
Esther when she entered the presence of the king without being
duly summoned, for which she could have been put to death.
Feigning weakness on entering, thereby moving the king to concern and compassion, she motivated him to offer her half his
kingdom and promise to spare her people from the threatened
persecution and to come to the banquets she had prepared to
trap her tormentor (Esther 5).

Beheading brings dishonour to the victim and to the victim's
followers and family, a very serious concern in a culture with an
honour-shame consciousness and value system.[18] The beheading of John was a blow struck against his person and his following and a threat also to the reputation and standing of the one
for whom he prepared the way and for whom he bore solemn
witness in public. His disciples, however, remained faithful to
him. They came, took the body and placed it in a tomb. Jesus'
disciples will have abandoned him and a member of the authorities whom the reader would expect to be his enemy will come to
bury him.

The reference to the disciples of John is but a small window
on the phenomenon of John's baptism and mission. The New
Testament seems to be in constant unease with the fact that
many people still believed that John was the Messiah. All the accounts of John in the New Testament insist on John's own admission of the superiority of Jesus' baptism, person and mission

18. Josephus, points out that Anthony beheaded Antigonus to dishonour him and diminish his fame among the Jews (*Ant.* 15:9f) and he
points out also that beheading is similar in that intent to crucifixion
(*War* 2.241).

over his own. Josephus has a significant comment on the influence of the Baptist, and the Acts of the Apostles speaks of people as far away as Ephesus having received the baptism of John (Acts 19:1-7).

This banquet of the rulers, military authorities and upper classes, *megistantes, chiliarchoi, prôtoi*, opens the 'bread/food' section of the gospel. It stands in great contrast to the open air banquets for the ordinary people which follow where the little food available feeds the masses at the command of Jesus. The murderous banquet of the elite that comes to a climax at the command of the host, the ruler of the people, with a dish bearing the head of the prophet, is followed by the banquets for Jew and Gentile at the command of the one who had compassion on the people because they were like sheep without a shepherd.

iii. The Return of the Twelve Mk 6:30-31

As the reader pictures the disciples of John gathering to give a fitting burial to their murdered leader, the spotlight turns to Jesus' apostles as they rejoined him and told him all they had done and taught. Here they are called 'the apostles'. They were sent out as 'the Twelve', but the sending makes them apostles, 'the ones sent'.

The 'apostles', 'the ones sent out' and empowered by Jesus tell Jesus all *they* had done and taught. The emphasis in their report seems to be on themselves, what 'they' had done. The usual comment in such circumstances throughout the Bible would focus on *what God had done* through their preaching and activity. When Jesus sent the Geresene demoniac back to announce the good news of his cure to his own people he told him to 'tell them all that the Lord in his mercy has done for you' (Mk 5:19). Peter, Paul and Barnabas announce to the assembly in Jerusalem *what God has done* in their mission activity (Acts 15:7-12). Here, in the case of the Twelve, has the initiative of Jesus, his calling, commissioning, and empowering of them been overlooked? Have they forgotten that their authority comes from being 'with him?' Two sentences from St John's gospel could sum up the situation. 'You have not chosen me, I have chosen you' (Jn 15:16) and 'Without me you can do nothing' (Jn 15:5). Significantly, Jesus will take them aside to his own place of prayer, and later again he will instruct them that their failure to heal was due to a lack of prayer – and by implication, an over reliance on themselves (Mk 9:29).

Jesus' response to their report is to invite them to come aside to a lonely place to be by themselves and rest for a while. 'To a lonely place' (*eis erêmon topon*) is twice mentioned, and again recalled further on in the remark, *erêmos estin ho topos*, 'the place is a desert' (Mk 6:35). It recalls the place where Jesus went after his baptism in the Jordan and where he went in the early morning to pray. Jesus is instructing the apostles in his own pattern of life. However, the desert place sought for solitude will be peopled with the enthusiastic crowd who guess where they are going and arrive before them. This will create a scenario reminiscent of the needs of the people of Israel wandering in the desert and provoke a response recalling the activity of Moses.

3. JESUS' MIGHTY WORDS AND DEEDS MK 6:32-8:26

Two Bread Cycles

The reaction to Jesus' own 'doing and teaching' had resulted in the crowds coming to his door at sunset (Mk 1:33), to the assembling of the crowds around the door in Capernaum that hindered the entry of the man on the stretcher (Mk 2:2) and of the crowds that kept him from even taking a meal (Mk 3:20). Now the apostles are beginning to experience something similar, with crowds coming and going and their being unable to take a meal themselves. Jesus shows concern for them as he takes them aside to a lonely place (*eis erêmon topon*) to be by themselves and rest a while. The subject of food has again been introduced into the narrative with the reference to their being unable to take a meal, and it will become a dominant theme, both in Jesus' actions and in his teaching.[19] The 'Bread Section' is composed of two parallel cycles of actions and teachings of Jesus, beginning in each case with a feeding of the multitude, followed by a sea crossing,[20] a dispute with the Pharisees, a teaching on the theme of bread and concluding with a healing of hearing or sight. The restoring of eyes that see and ears that hear, point to the important themes of 'seeing' and 'hearing' (Mk 4:12; 8:18). The multiplication of the loaves and fishes is one of the few miracles recounted in all four

---

19. See the studies by G. van Oyen, *The Interpretation of the Feeding Miracles in the Gospel of Mark*, Turnhout: Brepols, 1999 and A. Grassi, *Loaves and Fishes: The Gospel Feeding Narratives*, Collegeville: The Liturgical Press, 1991.

20. Luke's account stands alone among the six accounts in not having a sea crossing following the multiplication.

gospels (Mt 14:13-21; 15:32-39; Mk 6:35-44; 8:1-10; Lk 9:12-17). In fact there are two accounts in Mark and Matthew, both of whom have two 'bread cycles' in their gospels. Whether or not Mark inherited from the tradition a cycle of miracle stories containing two catenae[21] or lists with doublets, he has used the two 'bread' cycles with great skill to highlight the messianic banquet for Jew and Gentile, placing one in Jewish territory and the other in Gentile territory.[22]

Outline of the Two Parallel 'Bread' Cycles:

Feeding of 5000 (Mk 6:30-44)	Feeding 4000 (Mk 8:1-9)
Sea Crossing (Mk 6:45-52)	Sea Crossing (Mk 8:10)
Healings(Mk 6:53-56)	
Dispute/Teaching (Mk 7:1-23)	Disputes/Teaching (8:11-21)
Syro-Phoenician Woman (Mk 7:24-30)	
Healing: Deaf and Dumb (Mk 7:31-37).	Healing:Blind (Mk 8:22-26)

The First Bread Cycle Mk 6:32-7:37

Here in St Mark's gospel, Jesus' compassion for the flock casts him in the role of shepherd, reminiscent of the caring activity of God, the Shepherd of Israel, for the people in the desert. It is reminiscent of the role and leadership of Moses as he fed the people in the desert and provided them with the Torah. It highlights the two great messianic activities of Jesus, his response to the two great hungers, the hunger for teaching, for which the metaphors of food, manna and bread were widely used (Prov 9:5; Sir 15:3; 24:19), and the physical hunger for food. His compassion, manifesting itself in his teaching and feeding activity makes Jesus a worthy leader, a true shepherd whose role is often associated with the role of king, and particularly with David the divinely appointed shepherd king. Jesus' compassionate feeding of the multitude in the desert stands out in severe contrast to what has taken place at the banquet in the palace of the earthly 'king' at which the prophet's head was served on a dish. Jesus challenges the Twelve to share in this shepherding work by feeding the crowd themselves. One feels that there is a double

---

21. See P. J. Achtemeier, 'Toward the isolation of pre-Markan miracle catenae' in *JBL*, 89 (1970), 265-91.
22. The overall structure of the section and its theme and atmosphere point to Gentile territory even though, as M. D. Hooker points out (187ff), the specific references do not definitely specify a Gentile location.

meaning to feeding throughout. As well as the physical feeding the Twelve are commissioned to feed the people with the word.[23] This double aspect of Jesus' 'feeding' activity is developed at great length in the sixth chapter of St John's gospel.

i. The Feeding of the Five Thousand Mk 6:32-44

Jesus and his disciples went off in a boat to a lonely place to be alone and to rest. As the people guessed their destination they set out from every town and reached it on foot before them. They seem to have stayed on the same side, the Jewish side, of the lake. A new theme is introduced as Jesus took pity on the crowd and set himself to teach them at length as they were like sheep without a shepherd. The comparison of the crowd to 'sheep without a shepherd' (Mk 6:34) is a powerful evocation of the scattered and uncared for flock, a leaderless people. The understanding of God as Shepherd of Israel is deeply rooted in biblical and apocryphal tradition. Psalm 22 (23) opens with: 'The Lord is my shepherd there is nothing I shall want' and goes on to describe God as a shepherd leading the flock to pasture and as a host preparing a feast.

The sentiment of Moses' prayer in the desert is recalled when Jesus had compassion on the crowd who followed him out in the countryside, because they were like sheep without a shepherd (Mk 6:34).[24] Moses prayed: 'Let the Lord ... appoint someone over the congregation who shall go out before them and come in before them, who shall lead them out and bring them in, so that the congregation of the Lord may not be like sheep without a shepherd' (Num 27:16f). Micaiah son of Imlah, contradicting the lying spirit of the false prophets, proclaimed to the kings of Israel and Judah: 'I have seen all Israel scattered on the mountains like sheep without a shepherd' (1 Kings 22:17). Both Jeremiah and Ezekiel severely condemn the shepherds of the people and echo each other in the promise of God to raise up good shepherds for them. Ezekiel proclaimed that for want of a

---

23. This teaching dimension is picked up and greatly developed in the sixth chapter of St John's gospel which develops the idea of the Bread of Life, both as Word and Eucharist.

24. cf Mt 9:36, 'they were harassed and dejected like sheep without a shepherd' and Lk 12:32. Luke portrays Jesus' comforting words: 'There is no need to be afraid, little flock, for it has pleased your Father to give you the Kingdom', a saying that evokes the image of a shepherd-king.

shepherd the people were scattered and had become prey to any wild animal (Ezek 34:5) and promised a new David who would be a true shepherd to the sheep. 'I mean to raise up one shepherd, my servant David, and to put him in charge of them … I, YHWH will be their God, and my servant David shall be their ruler' (Ezek 34:23f; cf Ps Sol 17:40f). A similar sentiment is expressed in Jeremiah, where God promises to raise up shepherds for the sheep who have been abandoned by bad shepherds and left to wander uncared for and become dispersed (Jer 23:1-4).

The role of the shepherd is to protect, care for, feed and gather together the flock, to seek the lost and not lose any of the flock. The imagery of the shepherd, shepherding and the shepherd-king, was widely applied to religious and secular leadership in the ancient world and in the Bible. Jesus now responds as a true shepherd to the crowd who followed (or rather, preceded) himself and his disciples to the deserted place. Like Moses he both taught them and fed them in the desert. He will expect his disciples to do likewise, a fact that will be made plain when he instructs them to 'give them something to eat yourselves' and when he tells them to get the people seated on the grass and hands them the bread to give it to the people.

When the apostles tell Jesus to send the crowds away to buy food and Jesus responds that they should give them something to eat themselves they reply in desperation to Jesus: 'Are we to go and spend two hundred *denarii* on bread for them to eat?' They hear and respond on the 'earthly' level.[25] Jesus emphasised that they should feed the people (Mk 6:37, 41). The circumstances of the Exodus-wandering with its large groups of people needing food in the wilderness and the dominant figure of Moses spring to mind. The reader remembers the desperation in Moses' questions to the Lord in the desert: 'Where am I to get meat to give all these people?' and 'If all the flocks and herds were slaughtered would that be enough for them? If all the fish in the sea were gathered (LXX *synagein*) would that be enough for them?' (Num 11:1-3, 13, 22). This same theme is reflected in the psalm: 'They even spoke against God. They said, "Is it possible for God to prepare a table in the desert?" '(Ps 77 (78):19). But the Lord said to Moses, 'Behold I will rain bread from heaven for you, and the people shall go out and gather a day's portion every day' (Ex 16:4). The provision of the bread from heaven, the

---

25. A denarius was a day's wages.

manna, (Exod 16; Num 11) not only fed the people physically
but it also became a metaphor for teaching, for Wisdom and
Torah, and in Christian understanding became a pointer to the
Eucharist. All these aspects are present as undercurrents in
Mark (though they are developed at much greater length in Jn
6).[26] According to the prediction of Deutero-Isaiah the miracle of
feeding the people during the Exodus-wandering would be repeated during the return from exile in Babylon: 'They shall be
fed along the way ... they shall not hunger, nor shall they thirst'
(Isa 49:9ff).

The multiplication of the loaves also conjures up the memory
of the Elijah-Elisha cycle with its promise of the return of Elijah.
It recalls the multiplication of the barley bread by Elisha, succes-
sor to Elijah: 'Give it to the people to eat,' said Elisha to a man
from Baal-Shalishah, ' they will eat and have some left over.' The
hundred men ate the twenty barley loaves and had some left
over (2 Kings 4:42-44). The barley bread in the Elisha story was
cheaper than wheaten bread and so regarded as the bread of the
poor. John's gospel speaks of barley bread in the context of the
multiplication. Mark does not, but in his reference to the twelve
baskets he uses the term *kophinos* which was the basket of the
poor Jews in Rome satirised by Juvenal.[27] (This may be a pointer
to an intended Roman audience for Mark. The Jews in Rome
were widely satirised for their poverty.)[28] In the second multiplication account, Mark uses the regular term *spuris* for basket
(Mk 8:1-10).[29] As the Elijah-Elisha and the Mosaic-Exodus traditions are recalled, the coming of the prophet like Moses[30] and
the return of Elijah both spring to mind. This double allusion
probably reflects the conflation in the popular opinion of first
century Jews, especially in Galilee, who did not share the clear
division of personalities and roles of 'the coming one' unlike the
educated Pharisees and Qumran devotees. Even as early as the
writing of the First Book of Kings there was a merging of the

---

26. This is brought out clearly in the teaching of Vatican II in *Dei Verbum*
which speaks of 'the table of the Word of God and of the Body of
Christ'.
27. Juvenal, *Satires*, 3:14; 6:542.
28. M. Mullins, *Called to be Saints, Christian Living in First Century Rome*,
Veritas, Dublin, 1991, 65-67, 19-20.
29. F. J. Moloney, *op. cit.*, 132.
30. Deut 18:15-18; 1 Macc 4:41-50; 14:41; 4 Q *Testimonia*; Acts 3:22.

Mosaic, Messianic and Elijah figures (1 Kings 19). The reader wonders if the Twelve will pick up on the allusions and sense what is really taking place.

Jesus issues the instruction to the Twelve to heighten the awareness of the problem and to create an appreciation of the gift which follows and its sign value. The shepherding role of Jesus, so evident in his compassion, is met by a severely rational 'common sense' economic argument on the part of the Twelve. Instead of sharing Jesus' compassion for the flock, and faith in providence, they consider the cost and say that the crowd should look after themselves. They completely miss the point that they should share in the shepherding role of Jesus who had commissioned them with an admonition to bring no bread and no money in their purse but to rely on providence and generosity. Jesus sends them to find out how many loaves they have. There is no mention of the little boy with the loaves and fish who appears only in John's account (Jn 6:9) but whose presence has become an established part of the popular telling of the story in harmonised versions and works of art. This points to the fact that the disciples themselves have the bread and fish. (Is this meant to reflect negatively on the fact that in spite of Jesus' admonition to them to rely on providence and hospitality, they have brought provisions for the journey?) They answered that they had five loaves and two fish. They were perturbed at the small amount of food, and had not even considered the possibility of sharing it. Then Jesus issued another command: 'Make the people sit down, *symposia symposia*, usually translated as 'in groups.' This recalls the organisation of companies of hundreds and fifties during the wandering in the desert (Exod 18:21-25; Num 31:14; Deut 1:15).[31] The community at Qumran organised their assemblies in similar groups, so the desert tradition was well known. It also reflects the *symposion* context of the early Christian Eucharist as the assembly reclined to eat.[32] There is a reference to the green grass, an allusion to Psalm 22 (23) with its

32. Exod 18:21-25; Num 31:14.
31. When the Qumran community lost faith in the governing structure in Jerusalem centred on the Temple and priesthood which they regarded as illegitimate, they withdrew to their desert retreat where they organised themselves along the lines of the 'ideal' congregation of Israel, formed after the fashion of the desert wandering period into groups of a thousand, a hundred, fifty and ten. cf 1QS 2:21-23; 1QSa1:14-15, 28-29; 2:1; 1 QM 4:1-5,16-17; CD 13:1.

emphasis on green pasture, rest after a journey and safety under the caring eye of the shepherd as they ate and had not only their fill but had food left over. 'The Lord is my *shepherd* I shall *not want*, fresh and *green* are the pastures where he gives me *repose* ... he prepares a *banquet* for me ... my cup is *overflowing*.'

Jesus' words and actions reflect the words and actions by then established in the eucharistic liturgy. *Taking* the five *loaves*, *looking up* to heaven, *saying the blessing, breaking* the loaves, *distributing* them, all are actions and words familiar from the liturgy. So too is the word *symposia*, for the assemblies, as already seen. The focus of attention is on the bread rather than the fish, because the allusion to the eucharistic celebration is highlighted.[33] The account of the multiplication reflects the established practice of the eucharistic liturgy and in the narrative points forward to the institution of the Eucharist at the last supper and the eschatological banquet in the kingdom.

The fish are not mentioned in Mk 8:18-21 when Jesus reminds the disciples of both multiplications. Furthermore a word usage in John may throw light on the custom of eating bread and fish. The term *opsaria*, a double diminutive, is used there for the fish and points to the fact that what was probably meant by fish was a savoury to put in a sandwich of bread. It would therefore have been absorbed in the bread as one piece of food like a sandwich, and not receive much notice in its own right (Jn 6:9).

The gathering of the fragments (*klasmata*) recalls the gathering of the manna and with it the desert scenario of Moses and the Exodus-wandering when the people gathered the manna each day, until they had what they needed (Ex 16:8, 12, 16, 18, 21). The account emphasises the compassionate response of God to the people's plea for food, the gift of God and the fact that whether a person gathered less or more manna, everyone had enough. Unlike the manna, however, which was not to be stored for another day and any manna hidden away perished (Ex 16:19f; 27), the *klasmata* are gathered after the multiplication so that none may be lost. It remained in the twelve baskets. It is to

---

33. Bread was not usually eaten on its own but would have some 'filling' as in a sandwich. In John *opsarion*, a double diminutive, was used to describe such a filling. It literally means 'a small, little fish'. Combined with bread such a ' filling' is referred to as 'food' or, in the more general sense of the term, 'bread'. The' fish' is not therefore left 'redundant' in the narrative.

continue to be available to future believers who want to share in
the food which Jesus provides. The noun *klasmata* has overtones
of the breaking into shared pieces of the eucharistic bread and is
so used to signify the eucharistic fragments in the First Letter of
Clement of Rome, in the *Didache* and in the letter of Ignatius of
Antioch to Polycarp.[34] The mention of twelve baskets, however,
shifts the focus of attention from the food to the people, pointing
to the complete number of the tribes of Israel, thus referring to
the completeness of God's people, a number used also in the
choice of twelve apostles, like the twelve sons of Israel (Jacob),
and now signifying the full number of believers in Jesus (Mk
6:43; Mt 14:20; Lk 9:17).

This first multiplication of loaves and fishes has a very
Jewish character. The idealised time of Israel's sojourn in the
desert, fed by the Shepherd of Israel at the hands of Moses, was
recalled in the compassion for their plight and in the organising
of the groups for the purpose of feeding. Telling the confused
disciples to feed the crowd was like YHWH telling a very distraught Moses to feed the people in the desert and draw water
from the rock. The location, the fact that they came from all the
towns on the Jewish side of the lake, the allusions to Ps 22 (23)
and the significance of the twelve baskets (the other multiplication will have seven) and the *kophinos*, basket of poor Jews, all
point to a Messianic banquet for the Jews, the expected repetition of the miracle of Moses, to be carried out by the Messiah.

The multiplication of the loaves is both a christological and
eucharistic miracle. Unfortunately its significance on both
counts has been overlooked and its many rich seams of meaning
have been diminished by rationalistic attempts to explain away
the miraculous. J. R. Donahue and D. J. Harrington comment as
follows:

> One way not to actualise the passage is to say that the people
> were so moved by the preaching of Jesus that they divided
> their food with others. This 'nice thought' interpretation goes
> back to the nineteenth century rationalistic attack on miracles
> but has now achieved a strong foothold in mainline Christian
> preaching. Rather, the narrative offers a picture of Jesus as
> compassionate towards the leaderless people and concerned
> about their physical hunger. A church that invokes the name
> of Jesus must be concerned about the spiritual and physical

34. 1 *Clement* 34:7; *Didache* 9:3,4; Ignatius, *Polycarp*, 4:2.

hungers of people today. The location in a desolate place
evokes God's care of the Jewish people during the wilderness
wanderings. Since Vatican II has chosen 'pilgrim people' as
one of the central metaphors for the church, this aspect of the
narrative can readily be actualised.[35]

ii. The Sea Crossing. (Epiphany / Christophany) Mk 6:45-52

Following the multiplication of the loaves there is a scene on the
sea where Jesus comes to the disciples in distress. The double action, the feeding of the multitude and his saving presence on the
sea, re-echo the double action of Moses in feeding the people in
the desert and leading them through the sea.

Mark (like Matthew) describes Jesus sending the disciples
away in a boat to Bethsaida as he himself dismisses the crowd
and goes to the mountain to pray. As seen already in the introduction to the commentary, going to the mountain has deep res-
onances in the history of salvation. The mountain was the special place associated with the Divine Presence (Gen 22:14; Exod
3:1; Deut 11:29; Josh 8:70) and with encounters with the Divine.
Moses encountered YHWH on the mountain (Exod 19:3, 16, 24)
and the word of the Lord came to Elijah on the mountain (1
Kings 19:9-18). Moses returned from the mountain bathed in
light and his altered appearance terrified the people (Exod
34:29f). On this occasion Jesus will come from the mountain and
the disciples will be terrified by his appearance as they see him
coming over the water. He will later be transfigured on the
mountain in the presence of Peter, James and John (Mk 9:2-13)
and on the Mount of Olives he will deliver his apocalyptic discourse to Peter, James, John and Andrew (Mk 13).

In Mark (and Matthew) Jesus is very swift and deliberate in
his sending the disciples away from the scene of the multiplication. 'He immediately forces them' to embark.[36] The implied
reason may well be his desire to remove them from the misguided
messianic enthusiasm of the crowd caused by the feeding of so
many in the deserted place. John's account spells out such an enthusiastic reaction from which Jesus himself escapes from the
crowd into the hills alone to avoid their taking him away to declare him king, and later in the evening the disciples went down
to the sea and embarked (Jn 6:15-17).

---

35. J. R. Donahue and D. J. Harrington, *op. cit*, 211.
36. *kai euthus/eutheôs ênagkasen … embênai.*

As Jesus goes to the mountain alone to pray, especially in the wake of the Mosaic-Exodus allusions in the story of the multiplication of the loaves, the reader now picks up on the imagery of Moses going to the mountain alone to encounter the Lord. Similarly Elijah went to the mountain to encounter the Lord and there he encountered the gentle breeze heralding the word of the Lord and beginning the tradition of classical prophecy (1 Kings 19).

The 'Mosaic' action of feeding the multitude is now followed by another great miracle reminiscent of the Passover-Exodus event, the safe passage through the sea, guaranteed by the divine name and presence. The focus is not on the miracle of calming a storm or stilling a difficult head wind. It is on the terrified state and perplexity of the disciples at the sight of Jesus coming towards them over the water, an epiphany interpreted through the divine name, *I am,* with its accompanying reassurances, *have courage* and *do not be afraid.*

As evening fell the boat was out in the middle of the sea (lake) and Jesus was alone on the land. He observed that they were distressed from rowing for the wind was against them. He came to them walking over the sea, about the fourth watch (between three and six o'clock in the morning). 'He wished to pass by them', *êthelen parelthein autous,* does not mean simply he was going to pass them by and go on his way. It is a phrase canonised in the tradition of the theophany/epiphany.[37] It signifies 'passing by' in the sense of 'passing in front of, and in view of them'. It recalls Moses' plea to God: 'Show me your glory, I beg you' and the response: 'I will let all my splendour pass in front of you and I will pronounce before you the name YHWH' (Exod 33:19) and 'The Lord descended in a cloud, and Moses stood with him there. He called on the name of the Lord. The Lord passed before him and proclaimed, "The Lord, the Lord, a God of mercy and compassion, slow to anger, rich in loving kindness and faithfulness"'(Exod 34:5f). The theophany is marked by God

---

37. J. P. Heil, *Jesus Walking on the Sea. Meaning and Gospel Functions of Matt 14:22-33; Mark 6:45-52 and John 6:15b-21,* Rome, Biblical Institute Press, 1981, 70; E. Lohmeyer, *Das Evangelium des Markus,* 17th ed., Meyers Kommentar, Göttingen: Vandenhoeck& Ruprecht, 1967, 133f; R. Pesch, *Das Markusevangelium,* Herders theologischer Kommentar zum Neuen Testament II / 1-2, 2 vols, Freiburg: Herder 1976-1977, I:361-63.

'passing by' or 'passing in front of' Moses and pronouncing the Divine Name.[38] As Jesus 'passes by them' the disciples were terrified thinking he was a ghost. They all saw him and were terrified. They cried out in fear. He responded to their terrified state with: 'Have courage. I am / It is I. Do not be afraid.' (*Tharseite, egô eimi, mê phobeisthe*). Jesus thus fulfils the role of the comforting saviour, pronouncing the *egô eimi*, 'I am' and exhorting the disciples not to be afraid. Having repeated the miracle of Moses in feeding the people in the desert, a sign expected to herald the arrival of the messianic age (2 Baruch 29:8), he proceeds to repeat the other Mosaic miracle of leading his followers through the water. However, unlike Moses, Jesus himself pronounces the 'I am' and issues the exhortations to have courage and not to be afraid.

The context, following the Mosaic-Exodus allusions, alerts the reader to the deeper significance of *ego eimi*, 'I am' which is significantly more than a simple self identification such as 'It is I' meaning, 'This is Jesus whom you left on the shore a few hours ago.' When God's name was revealed to Moses in the words usually translated as 'I am who I am', the revelation was followed by the command to go to the people and say: '*I am* sent me to you' (Ex 3:14f). Isaiah develops this *I am* designation for God in several passages, and the LXX use of *ego eimi* for the Divine name springs immediately to mind,[39] as for example, 'I am, I am, the one comforting you' (Is 51:12), and 'therefore my people will know my name on that day because I am he, the one (who is) speaking to you (Is 52:6).'[40] D. M. Ball, writing about the use of *ego eimi* in John, makes a point equally relevant to its use here in Mark. He states the case clearly as he points out how the single phrase containing *egô eimi* may alert the implied reader to an entire thought world, which is shared with the implied author since they are within a shared cultural framework. The implied reader, therefore, would automatically understand the implications of the words *egô eimi*, which is clear from the fact that

---

38. Translating the verse as 'He wished to pass by', as though unnoticed, in keeping with the 'messianic secret' theme, misses the point and is further refuted by the revelation which follows.

39. Isa (LXX) 41:4; 43:10; 46:4; 48:12; 51:12.

40. Isa 51:12 *ego eimi ego eimi ho parakalôn se;* Is 52: 6 *dia touto gnôsetai ho laos mou to onoma mou en tê hêmera ekeinê, hoti egô eimi autos ho lalôn soi.* (*egô eimi autos,* in Hebrew, *ani hû*).

they are not explained. Furthermore when Jesus uses these words, it is not only the words themselves but also the thought world to which they point which helps to explain what he means.[41] He also points out that: 'The absolute use of "I am" in the Old Testament is striking as the only conclusive parallel to the use in the New Testament. However … it is not only in the words *egô eimi* that John points back to Isaiah, but also in the way that those words are presented.'[42] This is equally true of Mark. The *egô eimi* is in the context of an epiphany and enclosed between the standard expressions used in an epiphany / theophany, 'have courage', and 'do not be afraid'. This epiphany reflects the biblical awareness of the divine presence in, and power over, creation, especially as manifested in the case of the angry sea, seen already in relation to the calming of the storm (Mk 4:35-41).[43]

The egô eimi statement of self identification and reassurance is inextricably linked to the words 'Have courage' and 'Do not be afraid'. This injunction not to be afraid is a recurring feature of Old Testament theophanies. YHWH spoke to Abram, saying: 'Do not be afraid, Abram, I am your shield' and went on to promise him the land from the Wadi of Egypt to the Great River (Gen 15:1,18). In the apparition to Isaac at Beersheba, YHWH said; 'I am the God of your father Abraham, do not be afraid for I am with you' (Gen 26:24). To Jacob YHWH said: 'I am God, the God of your fathers, do not be afraid of going down to Egypt, for I will make you a great nation there' (Gen 46:3). The injunction not to be afraid is found in Isaiah, 'I am holding you by the right hand; I tell you do not be afraid, I will help you', and 'Do not be afraid for I have redeemed you; I have called you by your name, you are mine. Should you pass through the sea I will be with you, or through rivers they will not swallow you up … do not be afraid for I am with you' (Isa 41:13f; 43:1-5). Several times Jeremiah is assured that he has no need to fear his enemies, because YHWH will be with him (Jer 1:8,17; 42:11; 46:28).[44]

41. D. M. Ball, 'I Am' in John's Gospel: Literary Function, Background and Theological Implications', *Journal For the Study Of The New Testament. Supplement Series*, 124, Sheffield Academic Press, 1996, 177.
42. Ibid.
43. Ps 106 (107):9, 30. cf Ex 14; 15; Deut 7:2-7; Job 38:16; Pss 29:3; 65:8; 77:20; 89:10; 93:3f; 51:9f; Isa 43:1-5; 51:9f.
44. In the annunciations to Zachary and Mary the angel tells them not to be afraid (Lk 1:13, 30). Before performing some of his healings Jesus

The disciples, without Jesus in the boat, were tossed about on the sea making little progress towards the point to which they were heading. Jesus comes to them over the water. They react to his epiphanic appearance with terror at first, thinking he is a ghost though they should have known him and understood his power over nature and other forces from their experience of being with him when he calmed the wind and the sea. However, the narrator points out that they failed to recognise him precisely because 'they had not understood about the loaves (*epi tois artois*)', for their heart was hardened.'[45] Obviously the miracle of the loaves was meant to communicate something very important to them about the identity of Jesus. Jesus himself will refer to their failure to see the significance of the multiplication of the loaves when they are discussing having only one loaf in the boat (Mk 8:14-21) and on that occasion he will point to their serious failure in perception and understanding.

'Their heart' is in the singular and so represents a communal response, or rather, lack of response. This expression has already been used by Mark in relation to the hardness of heart of the group of Pharisees and Herodians who tried to trap him in the synagogue (Mk 3:5). Hardness of heart is reminiscent of the attitude of Pharaoh in response to Moses' appeals to let the people leave Egypt throughout the drama of the plagues.[46] A similar understanding comes across in Isaiah 6:9-10, a text used in John, Acts, 2 Corinthians and Ephesians to explain the rejection of Jesus (Jn 12:40; Acts 28:26f; 2 Cor 3:14f; Eph 4:18).

This is the second of the three episodes at sea in Mark. In the first one Jesus comments on their fear by asking: 'How is it you do not have faith?'(Mk 4:40). Here in the second one the narrator comments on their *kardia pepôrômenê*, 'hardness of heart' (Mk 6:52). The third episode will find Jesus himself severely chastis-

---

told the petitioner not to be afraid (Mk 4:40; 5:36; Lk 8:50) and in the resurrection appearances the terrified or perplexed recipients of the appearance are told not to be afraid (Mk 16:6; Mt 28:5, 10; Lk 24:5).

45. Mk 6:52-53 has been the subject of a textual debate since Jose O Callaghan proposed in 1972 that a small fragment of text from Cave 7 at Qumran (7Q5) represents these verses. The suggestion has not been generally accepted. See S. Enste, *Kein Markustext in Qumran: Eine Unterschung der These: Qumran-Fragment 7Q5=Mk 6:52-53*, Göttingen: Vandenhoeck & Ruprecht, 1999.

46. Exod 7:13, 14, 22; 8:15, 19, 32; 9:7, 12, 34, 35; 10:1, 20, 27; 11:10; 14:8.

ing them when they are worried because they had forgotten to take bread along in the boat. He will warn them to beware of the yeast of the Pharisees and the yeast of Herod, and he will ask them are their hearts hardened (Mk 8:17) before going on to remind them of the two multiplications of loaves, the significance of which seems to have eluded them completely. His reprimand will bring this section of the gospel to its negative conclusion with the words: 'Do you still not understand?' (Mk 8:21).

iii. Healings at Gennesaret Mk 6:53-56

Having completed their journey, they landed at Gennesaret and tied up. Their journey did not take them across the lake but to another part of the western shore, the fertile ground on the north west shore between Tiberias and Capernaum. The area, known as Gennesaret, was a thickly populated area referred to by name only in Mark. The summary that follows shows the magnetism of Jesus and the enthusiasm of the crowds. They came from 'the whole region', like the people coming from 'the whole of Galilee, from all the cities,' described earlier, a universalising impression continued in the use of *hopou*, 'wherever' and *hosoi*, 'as many as' (whoever/everyone) touched him were healed (Mk 1:28, 33, 39). They brought the sick on stretchers (straw sleeping mats) to wherever they heard he was. The word was being proclaimed and they came in response. Their enthusiasm makes a contrast with the fear and misunderstanding arising in the disciples from their hardness of heart.

The universalising character of the report/summary is further strengthened by the reference to the different centres where people lived in this very populated area of villages, cities and country areas (clusters of farms/hamlets). They put down the sick in the *agora*, the public square (the forum, the market place, the commercial centre and the place of public religious activity). It is the place where the scribes like to walk about in long robes and to be greeted obsequiously and the place from which the Pharisees would not return without washing their hands (Mk 12:38; 7:4). Bringing the sick to Jesus here was a very public gesture, giving him a significance far beyond that of a simple rural itinerant preacher. 'The *agora* is now the centre of the healing power of God, and not simply the locus of political and economic power.'[47]

---

47. J. R. Donahue and D. J. Harrington, *op. cit.*, 218.

The verb *parakalein* is used of their request to Jesus to heal the sick. Literally it means 'to call alongside', and is usually translated as 'to beg, to implore'. It is a pointer to Jesus' acknowledged power and status among the people. *Parakalein* was used in this sense of the leper's appeal (Mk 1:40), of Jairus' appeal (Mk 5:23) and here it is used of the people's appeal to Jesus in the *agora* (Mk 6:56). The verb is used four times in the story of the Gerasene demoniac (Mk 4:10, 12, 17, 18). Like the woman with the issue of blood who believed that touching his garment would bring her healing, they begged him that by touching the hem (fringe or tassel) of his garment they would be saved/ healed. They too saw the holy man as a reservoir of power.[48]

iv. Dispute and Teaching. Purity Laws and Tradition

Dispute with Pharisees and Scribes Mk 7:1-13

Jesus' feeding of the crowds with loaves in an open place where, because of its location in Galilee of the Gentiles, there may have been Gentiles among the predominantly Jewish crowd is a significant background for a discussion about Jewish attitudes to ritual purity concerning the cleanness or uncleanness of places, things and food, and Jewish association with the Gentiles.

On a sociological level the discussion is very much about boundaries and who imposes, controls and abolishes them. The boundaries were clearly laid down and there were plenty of people to guard them in the name of religion, health and hygiene, political and cultural identity and social order. Infringement was regarded with great suspicion. The rules were there and could be used 'as potent weapons to include or exclude.'[49] Jesus crossed these boundaries to show the all-embracing nature of the kingdom of God.

A controversy begins when the Pharisees and some of the scribes who have arrived from Jerusalem gather around him and criticise some of the disciples for eating with 'unclean' hands. At the mention of the Pharisees and some of the scribes

48. *Kraspedon*, fringe, tassel, can refer to the tassels prescribed to be worn by Num 15:38f and Deut 22:12. Like the woman with the issue of blood, they believed that touching his garment would bring healing.
49. J. H. Neyrey, 'Clean/Unclean, Pure/Polluted, and Holy/Profane: The Idea and System of Purity' in R. Rohrbaugh, (ed), *The Social Sciences and New Testament Interpretation*, Peabody: Hendrickson 1996, 83.

that arrived from Jerusalem gathering around Jesus, the reader expects a confrontation because of their former appearances in the gospel.[50] Scribes had already accused Jesus of blasphemy when he told the paralytic his sins were forgiven (Mk 2:6f). Scribes of the Pharisee party had questioned his disciples about his reason for eating with tax collectors and sinners (Mk 2:16). The Pharisees had questioned him about his disciples' breaking of the Sabbath in the cornfield (Mk 2:24). Then they watched him to see if he would heal on the Sabbath and conspired with the Herodians about how to do away with him (Mk 3:1-6). Scribes *from Jerusalem* had already accused him of casting out demons by the power of Beelzebul. The Jerusalem powers were already casting a shadow. They seem to have wanted to maintain tight control on matters religious and reacted to any stirrings of messianism, as is obvious from the questioning of the Baptist as it comes across in John's gospel. This time the scribes from Jerusalem complain that some of his disciples eat 'loaves', *artous*, with unclean hands. This sparks one of the longest controversy pericopes in Mark's gospel. It begins with a comment on 'washing', moves to a discussion on the role of tradition in relation to Torah and then on to a discussion on 'clean and unclean foods' in the context of external and internal cleanness in people. Jesus addresses three audiences. His first audience is made up of the critics themselves, the second is made up of the people he gathered around himself, and finally the disciples form the third audience in the privacy of the house.

The Dispute
The text says 'some of the disciples' were eating with unwashed hands, so others were obviously following the tradition. It may even point to (acrimonious?) divisions among the disciples themselves. This pointer to differences in custom among the disciples themselves may also be intended as a second level of reading reflecting the different customs in the early church, like those with which Paul had to deal.

The narrator gives a list of customs of the Pharisees, and of

---

50. Some scholars wonder if the Pharisees also came from Jerusalem since they are not sure about the presence of Pharisees in Galilee in Jesus' time. However, Paul was a son of Pharisees and was born in Tarsus in Cilicia, much farther from the centre of Pharisaic movement.

the Jews generally (Mk 7:3f).[51] The list refers to washing oneself
before eating and on returning from the marketplace, and washing cups, bowls and bronze kettles.[52] (Some manuscripts add to
the list the washing of beds, very likely because of contamination from bodily fluids). How widespread were these customs?
The Mishnah codified the oral traditions and rituals later than
the New Testament and it gives a unified picture, but the customs in Jesus' time were probably not so uniform. The Pharisees
had their strict code, as had the Essenes, but the Sadducees did
not accept oral tradition and this probably led to differences in
practice. There were probably differences also from area to area,
as between the more rural population of Galilee and the more
urban population of Jerusalem. Some scholars think that only
the priests and some groups of Pharisees followed these regulations. The narrator's comment is therefore a generalisation
made later in the light of ongoing debate about these matters. In
speaking of 'the tradition of the elders' the narrator is probably
referring to biblical texts like Num 18:8-13 and Lev 11-15 which
deal with things consecrated to God and things 'clean and unclean' respectively, and to the tradition that had developed relating to their practical application. 'Unclean' is designated as
koinos, which literally means 'common', that is 'in common secular use', 'tainted' by contact with the world, as distinct from
hagios, blessed by, or dedicated to God (hagiazein/qaddes).[53] The
'tradition' (paradosis) was an unbroken chain of teaching stretching from Simeon ben Gamaliel in the late second century BC
back to Moses.[54] Josephus points out that the Pharisees had in-

---

51. See R. P. Booth, *Jesus and the Laws of Purity: Tradition History and
Legal History in Mark 7. JSNTSS* 13, Sheffield: JSOT Press,1986; C. Focant,
'Le rapport à la loi dans l'évangile de Marc,' *RTL* 27 (1996), 281-308.
52. The washing of the hands before meals appears differently in the
mss. In some it says 'wash the hands, *pygmê*, which can mean with the
fist, i.e. with a fistful of water, or 'to the wrist', sometimes translated as
'up to the elbow'; another reading is 'wash the hands *pykna*' which can
mean often or thoroughly. The overall meaning is the same whichever
reading and translation one adopts.
53. *Koinos* means 'common' and in classical Greek is the opposite to
idios, private, but is used of unclean animals in 1 Macc 1:47, 62 and of
unclean food in Acts 10:14, 28; 11:8; and Rev 21:27.
54. m. *Abot* 1:1-18.

cluded traditions of the fathers not found in the Book of Moses
and the Sadducees rejected these additions.[55]

The Pharisees put a question to Jesus about why his disciples
did not follow 'the tradition of the elders'. This challenge put to
Jesus gives him the opportunity to play the role of the prophet
who challenges stringent tradition that kills living religion. In
the only use of the verb 'prophesy' among the many references
to Isaiah in this gospel Jesus recalls the major prophetic theme of
external rituals that do not reflect internal dispositions. Ritual
without internal moral and spiritual dispositions is performance
(*hypokritein*), so he calls them 'performers', persons who play a
part, act out a role. The Greek *hypocritês* does not necessarily
carry the connotations of deviousness and deception that 'hypo-
crite' carries in English. Its connotation is more that of 'empty
performance', 'going through the motions', 'lip service', rather
than 'deliberately deceiving.' It is an attitude well summed up
by Isaiah: 'This people honours me with their lips, but their
heart is far from me, the worship they offer me is worthless' (Isa
29:13; Mk 7:6f).

The second part of the Isaian quotation or (more accurately)
allusion, moves the discussion from 'empty performance' to the
relative values of divine command and human tradition. The
quotation is closer to the Hebrew text than to the LXX Greek
text, but even at that it adapts the original 'teaching human precepts and doctrines' to 'teaching as doctrines the precepts of
men (human beings)' and adds 'you cling to the tradition of men
(human beings) casting aside the commandment of God.' Jesus
points his remark directly at his critics: 'Well (*kalôs*) do you lay
aside (*akurountes*) the commandment of God, in order to preserve your tradition.' The verb *akuroô* means to nullify in the
legal sense. The word *kalôs* has a really sarcastic sting in it which
might be paraphrased with an expression like: 'how neatly or in
what a polished way you manage to do it!'

To prove the point about putting their tradition ahead of the
Mosaic Law, he takes the example of honouring parents (Ex
20:12; Deut 5:16; Ex 21:17; Lev 20:9). The prescriptions of the
Mosaic Law or Torah were seen as the commandments of God,
not simply the commandments of a pivotal figure like Moses. So
when Jesus equivalently says: 'Moses said … but you say' he really
highlights their arrogance or blindness. He quotes the example

55. Josephus, *Ant* 13.297 and 18.12.

of the Corban. The exact meaning, extent and practice of Corban
is unclear and the particular practice criticised here by Jesus is
elsewhere unknown. Corban is an Aramaic word whose basic
meaning is 'an offering made to God with an oath'.[56] What Jesus
is here criticising therefore seems to be either the allowing or en-
couraging of a practice in the name of religion which denied due
support to parents by dedicating to the Temple with an oath
what would have been necessary for their support, or refusing
to permit someone who makes a hasty or ill-judged oath of dedication to Corban to annul it later in the interest of due concern
for the parents. In fact the Mishnah, codified later than the New
Testament but very likely reflecting practices of the New
Testament period, allows for the setting aside of a vow that con-
travenes a biblical precept, especially in the case of consequent
neglect of parents.[57] It is at least a possibility that this Mishnaic
excusation clause arose in response to something similar to what
Jesus was here criticising.[58]

Teaching the crowd and the Disciples Mk 7:14-23
A change of audience signals a further shift in the argument. 'He
called the people again', so the Pharisees and scribes from
Jerusalem are no longer the sole audience. 'Listen to me all of
you and understand'. Again the call to listen recalls the Shema:
'Listen, O Israel,' and also reiterates the call to listen already emphasised at the teaching in parables. The original point of dispute was how they should eat. The argument now moves to
what they should eat. The saying is referred to as a parable when
Jesus is in discussion with the disciples but it is really an aphor-
ism or riddle, a *mashal/matla*. 'Nothing that goes into a man from
outside can make him unclean; it is the things that come out of a
man that make him unclean.' This *logion* or saying introduces
the next stage of the argument and in some manuscripts it is reinforced by Jesus' call for listening and understanding. ('If anyone has ears to hear let him listen to this' is omitted in many
manuscripts and translations. If included it reinforces the call to
listen already made in verse 14).

The audience changes again as Jesus enters the house with

---

56. Josephus speaks of Corban as a gift offered to God, *Ant* 4.73; *Against
Apion* 1:167.
57. m. *Nedarim* 9:1;11:11.
58. cf F. J. Moloney, *op. cit.*, 140f.

the disciples. When they are alone he explains the meaning of the parable to them. This is reminiscent of the occasion when he explained the purpose of the parables and gave the explanation of the 'parable of the sower'(Mk 4: 10ff).

When they ask him the meaning of the parable Jesus responds quite sharply to their question by asking them: 'Are you so lacking in understanding (*asynêtoi*)?', a reprimand repeated in, 'Do you not know that …(*ou noeite*)?' Then he explains that things from outside do not enter the heart but pass through the stomach into the drain. However, what is in the heart is manifest in what comes out of the heart, in what one does and says. Using a list of vices, Jesus then spells out the bad things that come from the heart.

Jesus explains the 'parable' or image in terms of food from outside passing through the digestive system and then out into the sewer without making any negative moral impact on the person. Originally the saying 'what goes into a man' may not have been in the context of a dispute about clean and unclean food, but an independent *logion* emphasising the contrast between external influences and the true state of one's 'heart' (*kardia*). The heart is mentioned three times in the pericope, signifying the centre of one's life, the seat of one's emotions, convictions, motivation and actions, in short, one's character. The heart is often portrayed in the Bible as the arena or battleground where good and evil forces confront one another. There are many positive and negative examples throughout the Bible, summed up in terms such as learning wisdom in the secret of the heart, giving praise from the heart, rending the heart and not the garment, evil thoughts arising in the heart, plotting malice in the heart, being hard of heart and so forth.

In Mk 4:19 the narrator, or an editor, gives Jesus' saying a clear practical application related to circumstances arising in the community: 'He thus pronounced all foods clean.' If such a clear directive had come from Jesus himself it would surely have rendered unnecessary much of the subsequent soul searching, debate and disagreement on the issue of food, evidenced for example in the letters of Paul and in the Acts of the Apostles. The comment obviously addresses the situation at the time of Mark's gospel, when much reflection on what Jesus had said and done had already taken place. This comment seems to respond to the same question addressed in the Acts of the Apostles. Acts 10 and

11 deal with Peter's experience in seeing the sheet let down from heaven. He was told to kill and eat, against which he reacted saying he never ate anything unclean. He was then told that what God has declared clean he had no right to regard as unclean (Acts 10:15). Following this, and consequent on its impact, he goes to the house of Cornelius, and subsequently he boldly defends his action in doing so both to the other disciples in Jerusalem and later again at the Jerusalem meeting following the crisis in Antioch. Paul had to address the question of food laws when writing to the Romans in 57/58 (Rom 14:2, 14, 20, 21) and in Galatians he speaks of the serious dispute between Peter and himself on the question of Jews and Gentiles eating together (Gal 2:11-21).

Jesus' response to the disciples' request for clarification spells out the dispositions of the evil heart with a catalogue of vices. As seen already in connection with the explanation of the parable of the sower, teaching morality by way of lists of virtues and vices, a method referred to by scholars as catalogical paraenesis, was widespread, both in biblical and secular literature.[59] Virtue lists are also used in a variety of contexts and have great variety in content.[60] They are fewer in number and even more general in nature than the vice lists. They also relate to traits and characteristics rather than to deeds. In the handing on of the tradition it is quite possible that Jesus' original explanation has been transformed into this list which would have been a familiar style of teaching for the Markan audience, where the teacher makes the practical connections with life, while maintaining the essential meaning.

Beginning with the emphatic phraseology 'for it is from within, from out of the heart that "evil machinations" (*dialogismoi*)[61] come', Jesus goes on to spell out the significance and re-

---

59. The vice lists appear at Rom 1:24, 26; 29-31; 13:13; 1 Cor 5:10f; 6:9f; 2 Cor 12:20; Gal 5:19-21; Eph 4:31; 5:3-5; 1 Tim 9f; 6:4f; 2 Tim 3:2-5; Tit 3:3; 1 Pet 2:1; 4:3f; Jude 8:16; Rev 9:20f; 21:8; 22:15; Mt 15:19//Mk 7:21f. The most common evils mentioned in the vice lists are fornication (8 times) and idolatry (5 times).

60. The main virtue lists are found in Mt 5:3-11; 2 Cor 6:6f; Gal 5:22f; Eph 6:14-17; Phil 4:8; 1 Tim 3:2f; 6:11; Tit 1:7f; Jas 3:17; 2 Pet 1:5-7.

61. cf Mk 2:6, 8 for verbal cognate used for the critical/hostile thoughts rising in the hearts of the scribes as they secretly accuse Jesus of blasphemy and Mk 8:17 where Jesus criticises their faithless, (obtuse, failing to remember) 'discussion' about not having any bread .

sults of the 'evil machinations' or 'designs of the heart' in terms of a list of twelve vices or evil actions and dispositions. Six of them are in the plural signifying 'acts of' fornication, theft, murder, adultery, avarice and malice and six are in the singular signifying dispositions or qualities of actions such as deceit, licentiousness, envy, slander, pride and folly. All except the general *dialogismoi*, machinations, and *ophthalmos ponêros*, 'the evil eye' signifying envy, are found in the Pauline lists of vices. The point being made is abundantly clear. People are not made unclean by 'external' factors like eating certain foods. They are unclean because of their 'inner' state and motives which result in external actions.

Jesus has just made the point that what a person eats does not make that person clean or unclean. This is an important consideration when one remembers that one's attitude to clean and unclean food was a pointer to one's religious affiliation and ethnicity. It provides a good lead into the following story which will focus very clearly on questions of ethnicity, religious affiliation and food.

The controversy with the Pharisees and scribes and the teaching to the crowd and to the disciples are now followed in turn by the mission of Jesus to Gentile (and potentially hostile) territory, the region of Tyre and Sidon. There he will encounter a Syro-Phoenician woman, hold a discussion with her about food and feeding Gentile children, heal her daughter, heal a deaf man and feed a crowd in Gentile territory. The feeding of the four thousand will be a messianic banquet for Gentiles, paralleling the earlier one for Jews in Jewish territory (even if some Gentiles were among the crowd). This second multiplication of 'loaves', in a Gentile area, will obviously involve a predominantly, or exclusively, Gentile crowd, signified not only by the place, and the absence of the very Jewish allusions to Exodus and the Shepherd Psalm 22 (23) so obvious in the first multiplication, but also in the symbolic numbers used for the crowd and the baskets of fragments.

V. HEALING OF GENTILES

The Syro-Phoenician Woman's Daughter Mk 7:24-30

The striking introduction, 'Rising up from there he departed to the territory of Tyre,' introduces a new phase in the protagonist's progress. He is now about to heal and feed Gentiles in

Gentile territory. Even though he was already rejected in his own town and by his own people he had subsequently carried on a mission and miraculously supplied food to the crowds in a desert area in Jewish territory. Since it was in Galilee of the Gentiles and crowds were probably coming from the surrounding Gentile areas, he may well have fed Gentiles together with the Jewish crowd in what had all the appearances of a Messianic Banquet for the Jews. Now he leaves the land of Israel and travels into thoroughly Gentile country to the north as he heads for the region of Tyre (some manuscripts add 'and Sidon', as Sidon is subsequently mentioned in Mk 7:31 and in / / Mt 15:21). Tyre is not only Gentile territory but the inhabitants were particularly hostile to the Jews, a fact borne out by their imprisoning and killing many Jews at the outbreak of the Jewish war against the Romans in 66 AD.[62] However, Mark already mentioned Tyre and Sidon as areas from which the crowds were coming to Jesus, so his name was known there among the people (Mk 3:7f).

He is now in Gentile territory and enters a house there, not wishing anyone to know, but he is unable to remain unnoticed. The Markan penchant for Jesus' desire for secrecy is in evidence but his reputation has already spread into (potentially hostile) Gentile territory. The boundary of 'cleanness' has been twice crossed, on entering Gentile territory, and on entering a Gentile house. A woman approaches him and he dialogues with her.[63] There is no mention of anyone else being present. Two more boundaries, therefore, have been crossed – the woman approached a strange man and they dialogued alone. The text can be read on two levels. On one level Jesus crosses and is provoked into crossing, boundaries between Jew and Gentile and on another level there is the parallel experience of the Christian readers of Mark. The houses where the healings, teachings, fellowship across boundaries, and controversy about boundaries take place in Jesus' ministry foreshadow the house churches of the first Christians. Though the story begins as a miracle story, a plea for help, a description of the disease or possession suffered by the girl, it becomes a debate on the appropriateness of helping the Gentiles and thereby letting them into the arena of God's saving work.

---

62. Josephus, *Against Apion*, 1.13; *War* 2.478.
63. See J. Dewey, 'Jesus' Healings of Women: Conformity and Non-Conformity to Dominant Cultural Values and Clues for Historical Reconstruction', *BBT* 24 (1994) 122-31.

This story of the woman coming to Jesus, receiving a less than hospitable reception and challenging Jesus in response, resembles the story of the royal official in St John's Gospel (Jn 4:46-54) who came to Jesus and was greeted with the remark: 'Unless you see signs and wonders you do not believe.' That father (most likely also a Gentile) and the woman in this story matched Jesus' 'theological' reaction with the determination of a desperate parent. In both cases Jesus heals at a distance. A similar story, which may be a variation of the story in John, is that of the centurion with the ill servant. It also describes a non-Jew entering into dialogue, showing determination, faith and humility, and on being told to go home, returning home to find the servant cured from a distance. The account of the healing and the comment of Jesus, 'I tell you, not even in Israel have I found faith like this' helped to root in the ministry of Jesus his approval of the mission to Gentiles (Mt 8:5-13; Lk 7:1-10).[64] Many of the miracles for Gentiles are at a distance, symbolic of their coming 'from far away' and emphasising the faith of the person who has come a distance to seek Jesus' help. All these stories of Gentiles approaching Jesus helped to root the church's mission to the Gentiles in the ministry of Jesus.

The woman in this Markan story is described as a Greek, a general term for a non-Jewish person of Hellenistic culture. Typical of Mark, the general description is followed by a more specific one. By birth she was a Syro-Phoenician, that is a Phoenician from Syria as distinct from a Libo-Phoenician from North Africa.[65] The repetition of the word 'woman', *gynê*, and the adversative, *de*, 'but', for emphasis, together with the description of her background, and her obvious self assurance and articulate line of argument, point to her being a lady of some class.[66] Furthermore her comfortable domestic circumstances are obvious from the fact that her daughter is lying on a *klinê*, a dining couch, rather than the ordinary bed, *krabattos*, the sleeping mat usually described in the New Testament.[67] It is interest-

---

64. This is the only miracle story from the material usually ascribed to Q.

65. Carthage was founded and peopled by Phoenicians, hence the word Punic, as in Punic Wars.

66. In later church tradition she is given the name Justa and her daughter as Bernice in Pseudo-Clementine *Homilies* 2.19; 3.73.

67. This was the bed of the poor. cf Mk 2:1-12; 6:55; Jn 5:8, 9, 10, 11. It is spelled *krabaktos* in Egyptian documents.

ing that before the narrator tells us that she was a foreigner, he
describes her in exactly the same way as if she were a Jewish
parent coming and falling at Jesus' feet (like Jairus), showing the
same level of faith and the same desperation of a distraught parent.

Her approach to Jesus has the marks of determined action. A
woman of substance and decision sets about her task. 'But immediately on hearing of him ... she came and prostrated herself
at his feet', showing her faith in action just as Jairus and the
woman with the issue of blood had done (*euthus akousasa ... elt-
housa prosepesen*). Her swift action is matched by her pleading
gesture, manifesting the depth of her plea and her respect for
and faith in the one she approached. She begged him to cast the
unclean spirit from her daughter. 'Unclean' or 'impure' in the
biblical sense refers to the influence of forces destructive of the
person. It signifies a removing of the person from the goodness
and health associated with the 'holy' and 'pure' and the living of
a normal life in society.

The form of the story is the usual miracle format with two
differences.[68] In the usual form a problem is presented, a request
made, a response or reaction of Jesus is described, a healing or
exorcism follows and then there is a reaction of amazement on
the part of the onlookers. One difference here is the lack of response on the part of the onlookers since the miracle is described
as taking place in the privacy of a house. The other difference is
Jesus' response, or perhaps more accurately, his reaction to the
request and the dialogue it provoked between himself and the
woman.

It is surprising, in fact it goes against the thrust of the narrative so far, that Jesus, having deliberately set out on a journey
into Gentile territory, would be hostile to the Gentiles as such, or
that he would have regarded a mission to the Gentiles as something to be undertaken after, and only after, a total mission to
the Jews.[69] The crowds had been coming from the neighbouring
pagan territories since his first appearance in Galilee and he had
already exorcised, healed and restored to normal life the

---

68. See D. Rhoads, 'Jesus and the Syro-Phoenician Woman in Mark. A
Narrative-Critical Study', *JAAR* (1994) 343-75.
69. Matthew brings out a certain explanation in his parallel version of
the story, 'I was sent only to the lost sheep of the house of Israel' (Mt
15:24; cf 10:6).

Gerasene demoniac in pagan territory. The reader is therefore shocked that Jesus' reaction to a desperate parent of a sick child sounds so rude, racist and removed from any compassion: 'The children should be fed first because it is not right to take the children's food and throw it to the little dogs.' In the mixed Jewish and Gentile population of Tyre where relations were often strained, this expression may have been characteristic of attitudes and remarks. It may even reflect a proverb or quotation. If so, using it in this way Jesus highlights the prejudice. The forthright exchange which ensues between the woman and Jesus will lance the boil of bigotry.

The word used here is *kunaria*, a diminutive of *kuôn*, dog. It seems to mean 'pups', offspring of dogs, as distinct from the offspring of the householder. In the context of the story the children of the householder are the children of God, the Jews. 'Dog' was a pejorative term applied by some Jews to the Gentiles. In Jewish eyes dogs were unclean animals, and being touched by them was a contamination.[70] In the Sermon on the Mount Jesus says, 'Do not give to dogs what is holy' (Mt 7:6). Dogs had a very bad press and the term dog was very insulting when applied to persons with whom one disagreed. The 'dog language' here is symbolic of the deep chasm between Jew and Gentile. In the light of Jesus' recent controversy and discussion on 'clean and unclean' it is more than surprising to find him make such a re-

70. The pathetic description of Lazarus at the rich man's gate is crowned with the descriptions of his desire to eat the scraps left for the dogs and of the dogs licking his sores (Lk 16:19-22). The threat to Ahab and Jezebel was that the dogs would eat Jezebel in the Field of Jezreel, and that those of Ahab's family who die in the city, the dogs would eat (1 Kings 21:23-24). Other disparaging remarks about dogs are found also in 1 Sam 17:43 where the Philistine says to David 'Am I a dog that you come against me with sticks?' and Isa 56:10-11 which describes the 'greedy dogs that are never satisfied'. In 1 Sam 24:14f David sees himself as being treated by Saul like a dead dog (cf 2 Kings 8:13). Job laments that he is the laughing stock of his juniors whose fathers he did not consider fit to put with the dogs that looked after his flock (Job 30:1). Hazael in a show of humility asked Elisha: 'How could this dog achieve anything so great?'(2 Kings 8:13). New Testament writers show a similar attitude to dogs when Paul warns the Philippians: 'Beware of dogs. Watch out for the people who are making mischief', and the Second Letter of Peter describes false teachers and opponents in the words of Proverbs as 'dogs returning to the vomit' (Phil 3:2; 2 Pet 2:22 quoting Prov 26:11).

mark. But the remark serves to reflect a general prejudice which will be successfully challenged in the discussion it provokes. There is no basis for trying to soften the remark by saying it is a diminutive, 'little dogs' and possibly even an endearing term, as though someone would be less offended or feel less belittled by being considered 'a little dog' or 'a dear little dog' rather than a dog. Saying that Jesus said it with a smile or in a jocose or play-ful way, even if it is true, is not suggested by the text and there is no evidence for Jesus behaving in such a manner elsewhere in Mark or in any of the gospels.

What did Jesus mean by his remark about dogs? The narrator shocks the reader and thus prepares for something dramatic or very significant to follow. M. D. Hooker makes what seems to be the most apt comment: 'In its present context, the term is a chal-lenge to the woman to justify her request.'[71] Why would a Gentile come to a Jew for healing? Was it because she saw in him, for example, some magical power or exceptional natural healing power? Was it because of some level of religious faith in the God of Israel and in Jesus as God's prophet or envoy? Is it a recognition of the special role of the Jews in the history of God's dealings with humanity? If so, it is the exact point made by Jesus in John's gospel in his conversation with the Samaritan woman when he says: 'Salvation is from the Jews, but the hour is coming … when the true worshippers will worship the Father in Spirit and in truth'(Jn 4:22f). Jesus is challenging the Syro-Phoenician woman to justify her request with some articulation of the faith that prompts her request to a Jewish prophet-preacher and ex-presses itself in her reverential approach in falling at his feet.

As in other cases in the New Testament where Jesus initially reacts against petitioners and brings out their faith in an open and clear demonstration, this woman professes her faith in recognising the priority of the Jews in the history of salvation but she asserts also the rights of the Gentiles. The Jews are the children (of God) but the Gentiles also belong to the household of God, even if in a different capacity. She finds a role in the household for those regarded as outsiders and unclean, as the 'little dogs.' They can eat the crumbs from the children's table.[72]

71. M. D. Hooker, *op. cit.*, 183.
72. See study by J-F Baudoz, *Les Miettes de la table. Étude synoptique et socio-religieuse de Mt 15:21-28 et Mc 7:24-30.* E.B.n.s. 27. Paris: Gabalda, 1995.

The story plays out in the ministry of Jesus a debate still alive and controversial in the early church and very possibly among the first recipients of Mark's gospel. The story is therefore unfolding on two levels. It brings the debate about 'clean and unclean' to its ultimate conclusion with Jesus face to face with a Gentile woman, in a conversation dealing with table-fellowship, food, religion and racism. In her faith the Gentile woman breaks through all the boundaries. She acknowledges who she is, who Jesus is and the priorities in the history of salvation with regard to Jews and Gentiles. Her story prepares for the second multiplication of the loaves in Gentile territory, and prefigures a debate about the relations of Jew and Gentile in the early church, very much in evidence, as seen already, in the letters of Paul and in the Acts of the Apostles.[73]

Gentiles did not have a ' hang up' about dogs. The woman's reply was straight to the point. Children share the food given to them with the little dogs under the table. The rather domestic scene of throwing food to the little dogs eating the crumbs of the little children under the table in the house stands out in contrast to the possible negative connotation of throwing food to dogs in the street. Interestingly the children and the little dogs share one house and one table. Together they constitute an overall domestic scene. The reference to the children reminds one that throughout their history the people of Israel saw themselves as God's children. The woman implies that the scraps from the table of God's children can be given to the Gentiles, 'the little dogs' or 'the Gentile children'.

The children of Israel have been fed in the first multiplication of loaves. The words *artos* (loaf) and *chorthasthênai* (to be fed) figure in the first multiplication and are found again here in this dialogue, tying both stories together thematically. The debate following the multiplication showed how very abstemious some of the children of Israel could be when it comes to eating. At a social level the distinction between Jews and Gentiles was very obvious in the context of eating because of the dietary regulations whereby some foods were unclean to the Jews, but were eaten by the Gentiles, who were thereby seen to reflect the uncleanness of the foods they ate. The distinction between Jew and

---

73. Paul on his missionary journeys in Gentile territory explains his approach as 'to the Jew first, then to the Greek', though his mission to both was simultaneous. The priority was not chronological.

Gentile was therefore often symbolised by reference to food. Interestingly the healing is preceded by a dialogue about feeding Gentile children. When Jesus raised the daughter of Jairus he followed the miracle with the instruction about feeding the Jewish child. But the Syro-Phoenician woman leaves Jesus in no doubt that God has other children, whatever their position in the household, and they too need to be fed.

Jesus' responds: 'because of what you have said, go home, (lit. 'because of this word, go') the demon has gone out of your daughter.' 'Because of this word' seems somewhat enigmatic but Matthew spells out the meaning in the corresponding passage as 'woman, great is your faith' (Mt 15:28) and this reflects the various places in Mark's gospel where miracles are related to faith (Mk 2:5; 5:34; 9:22; 10:52). Her word was a word of faith. She showed a level of appreciation for the gift of God that was absent in the critics of Jesus among his own people and not understood by 'those with him'. Jesus heals her daughter at a distance.[74] In fact, as already noted, many of the miracles performed for Gentiles in the Bible are at a distance, symbolic of their coming 'from far away'.

Again the story is told with an eye to the Old Testament, specifically to the Elijah and Elisha cycle of stories. Jesus alone is mentioned and is not portrayed as being surrounded by disciples as he is in Matthew's parallel account (Mt 15:21-28). Mark portrays him as a lone prophetic figure in a pagan land like Elijah or Elisha as he enters into dialogue and accedes to the request of the distraught and forthright mother. Elijah 'rose up' and went to Zarephat, 'a Sidonian town' (just as Jesus 'rose up' and went to the regions of Tyre in this story) and miraculously fed the woman and her son. When the son died the woman challenged the prophet, and after performing the life-giving miracle he finally said 'your son lives' (1 Kings 17:8-24). Elisha raised the son of the Shunammite woman, a woman persistent like the Syro-Phoenician as she grasped the feet of the prophet to implore his help. This story also happens after a miraculous feeding by the prophet (2 Kings 4:18-37). Another re-echo of the Elisha (LXX) story in the account of the Syro-Phoenician woman

---

74. Healing at a distance appears in both Jewish and Gentile traditions. The Talmud contains the story of the healing of the son of Rabban Gamaliel by Hanina ben Dosa (b. *Berakot* 34b) and Philostratus tells of a healing by Apollonius of Tyana in *Life of Apollonius* 3:38.

is the use of the term *klinê* for a bed. These stories bring out the repeating pattern and consistency in God's plan of salvation for Jew and Gentile.

The Deaf and Dumb Man Mk 7:31-37

The opening words, 'And again setting out (*kai palin exelthôn*) from the regions of Tyre he travelled by way of Sidon', set the scene for a new initiative, as Jesus goes more than twenty miles further north to Sidon and then east to pass through the middle of the Decapolis region on his way to the eastern shore of the Lake. Tyre and Sidon are regularly mentioned together as representing the whole southern Phoenician territory. Mark already mentioned Tyre and Sidon together as one of the areas from which the crowds were coming to Jesus, so he was known there already (Mk 3:7f; cf Acts12:20; Joel 3:4; Zech 9:2, 2 Esdra 1:11). He was known also in the Decapolis. The Gerasene demoniac had seen to that after his cure! Jesus had sent him to tell his own people what the Lord had done for him.

They (the people in the Decapolis) bring to him a man who is deaf (*kophos*) and 'speaks with difficulty' (*mogilalos*) and they beg him to lay his hand on him. The change in tense to the historic present lends vividness to the narration and engages the reader, before returning to the aorist participles and indicative for the actions of Jesus. The familiar verb *parakalein* is again used for 'beg' and sets the scene for a healing action. The usual form of a miracle story is followed. The problem is presented, a request is made, Jesus responds, a cure follows and the onlookers are amazed.

A triple emphasis on secrecy is conveyed by taking the man aside (*apolabomenos*), from the crowd, (*apo tou ochlou*), by himself, (*kat' idian*). Jesus will similarly take the blind man at Bethsaida aside to cure him.[75] This Markan emphasis on secrecy will continue until Peter's confession of faith in Jesus as Messiah. Then the secret is out, so to speak, and Jesus will spend the rest of the gospel explaining the true meaning of his messianic role in terms of the Son on Man who was sent to serve and destined to suffer, to be put to death and to rise again.

Jesus touched the deaf and dumb man by putting his hands in his ears – perhaps a sign of unblocking them. Then he spit and

---

75. Mk 8:26. These two cures have been used as evidence in the case for the 'messianic secret'.

put saliva on his tongue, a sign of healing. Saliva is a universal sign of healing. One's cut finger finds its way spontaneously to one's mouth! An animal spontaneously licks its sores and tends to its young with its tongue. In the gospel of John Jesus heals the blind man at the Pool of Siloam with a paste made of spittle and clay (Jn 9:6). In the Greco-Roman world healing with saliva/spittle was known. A blind man at Alexandria begged the emperor Vespasian to put spittle on his eyes, according to Tacitus' account of the 'miracles' of Vespasian.[76]

'Having looked up to heaven,' a typical gesture accompanying prayer, Jesus sighed (in the sense of sighing deeply) and said, 'Ephphata'. Scholars have speculated on the reason for, or meaning of, his sighing. Sighing was known to be part of the technique of miracle workers in the Hellenistic world, but it was not a regular practice in the case of Jesus, at least not in Jewish territory. Now he is in Gentile territory and he may be adopting a familiar custom, or a storyteller could have told the story using a familiar pattern. In John's gospel Jesus is greatly moved and shudders before the tomb of Lazarus, a reaction to the power of Satan's realm of death and unbelief (Jn 11:33, 34, 38). Here it may be a less dramatic example where Jesus sighs in distress at the sight of someone bound in this way, in the biblical mind-set, by the power of Satan.[77]

The word *ephphata* is translated into Greek by the narrator as 'be opened'. Its rare sound seems almost like an incantation lending colour and drama to the account. Again Jesus may have adopted the local custom and/or a storyteller could have told it in familiar fashion. The etymology of the word, however, is greatly debated. J. R. Donohue and D. J. Harrington sum up the debate:

> A few authors claim that this is the Greek vocalisation of a Hebrew *niph'al* imperative, but most see it as the vocalisation of the Aramaic *'eppatah,* the imperative of *petah* ('open'). Though the use of foreign words (*rhêsis barbarike*) as an incantation is a frequent motif in magical papyri and in exorcisms, such words often take the form of unintelligible 'abracadabras'.[78]

His ears (lit.' hearings') were opened, the binding of his speech

76. Tacitus, *Histories* IV.81f;6:18; and Suetonius, *Vespasian*, 7. cf Pliny, *Natural History*, 28:4,7; Jn 9:6.

77. M. Dibelius, *From Tradition to Gospel*, 84-86.

78. J. R. Donohue and D. J. Harrington, *op. cit*, 240, n.34.

(the impediment/the tying of his tongue) was loosed, and he spoke properly (*orthôs*). Jesus then ordered them to tell nobody but the more he insisted the more they proclaimed it (*ekêrusson*). Now the people of the Decapolis are 'proclaiming'. Their proclamation: 'He has done all things well (*kalôs*). He makes the deaf to hear and the dumb to speak,' echoes the messianic prophecies of Isaiah who had prophesied about the day of salvation: 'Then the eyes of the blind shall be opened, the ears of the deaf unsealed, then the lame shall leap like a deer, and the tongues of the dumb sing for joy' (Isa 35:5f). A similar sense of fulfilment is proclaimed by Jesus himself in the gospels of Matthew and Luke. In replying to the Baptist's question, Jesus tells his messengers: 'Go and tell John what you have heard and seen, the blind see again, the lame walk, the lepers are cleansed, the deaf hear, the dead are raised and the poor have the good news preached to them' (Mt 11:2-5; Lk 7:22).[79] Here in Mark this first proclamation of Jesus' messianic potential in line with these prophetic expectations comes on the lips of the Gentiles. It forms a striking contrast with the hostility he encountered on the part of the Jewish authorities, the disbelief of his family and the hesitancy, misunderstanding and fear on the part of the disciples.

The first 'bread cycle' is now complete. It consisted of the multiplication of the loaves (which probably included Gentiles in the mainly Jewish multitude), the sea journey with the epiphany in the boat, the various reactions to Jesus, the 'clean and unclean' dispute arising from the disciples eating 'the loaves' with unwashed hands, the discussion with the Syro-Phoenician woman on feeding the Gentile children, and the healings in Jewish and Gentile territory. The cycle has shown a movement of Jesus' ministry in the direction of the Gentiles. That movement will be even more in evidence as the second 'bread cycle' opens with the feeding of a Gentile crowd in Gentile territory.

Jesus is the one who brings the Messianic/Eucharistic Banquet to Jew and Gentile alike, as he demonstrates and foreshadows in the feeding of both multitudes. Jesus chose the disciples 'to be with him'. The other side of that coin is that he is with them in their distress on the various occasions in the boat. This will be very important for Mark's readers in the early church as

---

79. Mt 11:2-5; Lk 7:22. The response of Jesus is a medley of allusions to Isaiah. Isa 26:19; 29:18f; 35:5f; 6:11; cf Lk 4:18-19 quoting Isa 61:1f.

they struggle with the external pressure of persecution and the
internal turmoil as questions of sharing the table with Jew and
Gentile arise, as seen both in Acts and the letters of Paul (Acts
10-11;15; Gal 2:11-21).

The Second Bread Cycle Mk 8:1-26
i. The Feeding of the Four Thousand Mk 8:1-9

The solemn biblical style of introduction, 'In those days' (*en
ekeinais tais hêmerais*), rather than the more usual 'and' or 'and
immediately' (*kai* or *kai euthus*), not only links the section to
come with what has been taking place, especially in relation to
the Gentiles, but it also alerts the reader to expect a new departure or significant event. The description of the crowd is a reminder of the crowd that gathered before the first feeding, a link
brought out explicitly by the use of *palin*, 'again'. In the first
feeding Jesus had compassion on the crowd because they were
like sheep without a shepherd. In good Mosaic fashion he responded first with a teaching. Then the entire feeding passage
reflected the Shepherd of Israel theme. In the account of the first
multiplication Jesus' compassion was reported in the third person by the narrator but here in the account of the second multiplication his compassion comes in his own words when he says:
'I have compassion on the crowd because they have been with
me for three days and have nothing to eat. If I send them away
hungry they will collapse on the way for many have come a
great distance' (Mk 8:1-3). The mention of three days is a pointer
to the extent of his involvement in teaching and healing, and the
mention of the long distance they have come shows the expan-
sion of Jesus' reputation and ministry among the Gentiles.
'Coming from afar' is a recurring theme in the Old Testament
used for the Gentiles who come to learn about, and worship, the
God of Israel,[80] a theme that comes to the fore in the New
Testament in the coming of the Magi (Mt 2:2,12), the coming of
the Greeks (Jn 12:20f) and the gathering of all the peoples at
Pentecost (Acts 2:39). The compassion of Jesus for this Gentile
crowd is the dominant theme, a straightforward humanitarian
concern motivating Jesus to respond to the Gentile crowd with
the same divine authority with which he responded to the

---

80. Josh 9:6, 9; Isa 2:1-4; 60:2-22; 40:4; Mic 4:1-3; Ps 71 (72):10f; Mt 2:2, 12;
Jn 12:20f; cf also Acts 22:21; Eph 2:12, 17.

hunger of the flock of Israel. The question of the disciples: 'Where would anyone get bread in a deserted place?' resonates, as in the first feeding, with the desperation seen in the accounts of Moses' wondering how to feed the people in the wilderness.

The numbers of loaves, of people and of baskets of left-overs are different from the first feeding and their use here highlights the importance of symbolic numbers in biblical narratives. Seven, the number of loaves and of baskets of food left over, is a number very much associated with the Gentiles. It is the number of commandments in the Noachic covenant with all humanity before the call of Abraham (Gen 9:4-7), the number of the pagan nations of Canaan (Deut 7:1; Acts 13:19), the number of Hellenists chosen as deacons (lit. 'to serve')(Acts 6:3) and the number of churches in Revelation (Rev 2-3). The number 4000 is probably a combination of the use of the 'four' and 'thousands'. Since there was no word in the Hebrew vocabulary for 'infinity', 'thousands' tended to be used for huge numbers. The multiple four was probably intended to reflect the four points of the compass, the four winds, the four corners of the universe, from which the Gentiles were gathering, so 'four thousand' signifies a vast number of Gentiles from all directions.

In this multiplication account the disciples again ask: 'Where could anyone get bread to feed these people in this deserted place?' Jesus again puts the question to them about how many loaves they have. (They have to admit again that they have bread in their possession in spite of his injunction about providence and relying on hospitality.)

The eucharistic 'ritual' is reflected here as in the first feeding, though the initial 'looking up to heaven' is omitted. Taking the bread, saying the blessing and/or giving thanks, breaking the bread and distributing it are the actions and words of the eucharistic celebration. The first feeding in Matthew and Mark and the feeding in Luke have 'said the blessing', *eulogêsas* (reflecting the Hebrew *berekah*) as the prayer over the bread. This is the expression used by Matthew and Mark in the 'institution' of the Eucharist narratives at the last supper (Mt 14:19; 26:26; Lk 9:16; Mk 14:22). The second feeding accounts in Mark and Matthew use 'giving thanks', *eucharistêsas*, for the prayer over the bread, as do Luke and Paul in their accounts of the institution of the Eucharist (Mt 15:35f; Lk 22:19; 1 Cor 11:23f). The first account does not include a prayer over the fish but the second account does, for which the more Semitic term *eulogêsas*, 'having said the blessing' is used.

They ate as much as they wanted ('they were satisfied'), as after the first feeding, but here there is a heightened awareness of their having been well fed because of the emphasis at the beginning of the account on their hunger and the danger of their collapsing on their way home without food. Now Jesus has fed both Jew and Gentile, a significant follow up to the challenge of the Syro-Phoenician woman's comment on the need to feed not only the children of the household but also the 'little dogs' under the table (also part of the household).

ii. The Sea Crossing Mk 8:10

After both multiplication accounts in Mark and Matthew, and the account in John, when the crowd are dismissed and disperse there follows a sea crossing. Here Jesus crosses to 'the region of Dalmanutha', a place-name that appears only here in the New Testament and about which scholars have made various suggestions of a textual, translation, transliteration and geographical nature. Matthew's parallel account has 'mountains of Magadan' at this point but it is equally obscure and no help in identifying the exact location. In spite of the difficulty in identifying the place exactly, the point being made is that Jesus and his disciples now return to the western side of the lake, the Jewish side.

iii. Dispute with the Pharisees about signs Mk 8:11-13

The Pharisees emerged and began to argue with him, seeking a sign from heaven to test him. It is slightly strange to read about the Pharisees 'emerging', as they have already been in evidence many times in the gospel. It was the scribes of the Pharisee party who challenged Jesus' disciples about why their master was eating with sinners and tax collectors and it was the Pharisees who challenged Jesus about the disciples eating grains of corn in the fields on a Sabbath. It was they who plotted with the Herodians about how to destroy him after he healed on the Sabbath. It was the Pharisees and some of the scribes from Jerusalem who commented on how some of the disciples ate without first washing their hands. The scribes from Jerusalem who said he cast out devils by the power of the prince of devils were probably also of the Pharisee party, since their rivals, the Sadducees did not believe in angels and spirit, and so were unlikely to bother much about evil spirits either.[81] The statement that, 'The Pharisees emerged ...' therefore has the marks of a summary statement relating a pervasive, overall attitude not related to any specific incident. The verb, 'they began', *êrxanto*, has the meaning 'they started and continued on in a persistent way.'[82] The verbs 'to dispute, seeking, testing', *synzêtein, zêtountes, peirazontes*, reinforce their hostile, demanding and probing tone.

Why do the Pharisees emerge at this point in the narrative for such a brief encounter? Firstly, placing this encounter with the Pharisees at this point provides the cue for Jesus' warning to the disciples about the leaven of the Pharisees as the narrative moves towards its depiction of the disciples' ongoing failure. Secondly, it forms part of the parallel with the structure of the first bread cycle where a dispute with Pharisees follows the boat journey. It very probably represents also an early tradition which put these events together, as the same combination (feeding, boat journey and seeking signs) is found in the Johannine tradition where the multiplication is followed by an incident in the boat and subsequently by the crowd calling for a sign (Jn 6:1-34).

Looking for 'signs' is in line with the tradition of Old Testament prophets and their authenticating signs. The Deuteronomic prescription concerning true and false prophets presumes that prophets demonstrate their authenticity by predicting some happening (Deut 18:20-22). The prophetic message was often confirmed by a divine sign as when Isaiah predicted the receding shadow of the sun as a confirmation of his message to Hezekiah, and the birth of the Immanuel child as a sign of God's protection during the Assyrian war and the Syro-Ephraimite coalition.[83] The crowds reacting to the multiplication of the loaves in John's gospel see it as an authenticating sign and say 'this is really the prophet that has to come into the world', even though the crowd on the following day are demanding an authenticating sign 'so that we may believe in you' (Jn 6:14f, 30).

In seeking a sign, *sêmeion*, the Pharisees are looking for a sig-

---

81. The Sadducees' focus of attention was on their power and position arising from their association with the religious, civil and economic powers.

82. The English idiom 'Don't start me on that !' or 'When he gets started on that topic ...!' conveys something of the sense of *êrxanto* in this context.

83. 2Kings 20:8f; Isa 7:11-14; 55:13; cf also Ezek 12:11; 24:27, inter alia.

nificant proof of the divine authority behind Jesus' teaching and actions. What is being asked of Jesus here is a 'sign from heaven,' a periphrasis for 'a sign from God', an 'authenticating sign' rather than an apocalyptic sign in the heavens. Political agitators and charlatans from time to time tried to trick the people with phoney signs, *semeia kai terata*, resulting in tragic consequences. Gamaliel names two such persons in his speech to the Sanhedrin, Theudas and Judas the Galilean (Acts 5:36f) and the historian Josephus strongly condemns such characters.[84] Jesus will warn about them in his eschatological-apocalyptic discourse (Mk 13:22).

However, in the New Testament the seeking of signs is regarded as a negative attitude in all gospel traditions. Here in the Markan tradition Jesus replies to the demand for a sign that 'no sign will be given'. The Matthean tradition adds 'except the sign of Jonah' to the response 'no sign shall be given' and develops this further into a lesson on reading the signs of the times and a comparison between Jonah's time in the belly of the whale and the time the Son of Man would spend in the belly of the earth (Mt 12:38-42; 16:1-4). Luke expands on it with reference to Jonah's preaching to the people of Nineveh (Lk 11:29-32; 16). Paul reflects critically on the Jews' penchant for signs: 'The Jews seek signs and the Greeks seek wisdom ...' (1 Cor 1:22). In the Johannine tradition Jesus did not trust himself to the enthusiastic crowd who were impressed with him in Jerusalem on his first visit because of the 'signs' he performed. Back in Galilee he responded to the request of the royal official with the saying 'Unless you see signs and wonders you refuse to believe', and later in the ministry he refused to go to the Feast of Tabernacles with his brothers because they were urging him to perform signs in Jerusalem (Jn 2:23-25; 4:48; 7:2-8). The overall New Testament witness is consistent in its negative attitude to the seeking of signs.

'Having sighed in his spirit' Jesus responds negatively to the demand for a sign. This verb 'having sighed' (*anastenaxas*) is a *hapax* in the New Testament. It represents a deep sigh, and is reinforced with 'in his spirit' so it means something like 'a deep inward sigh', almost a 'groaning in spirit', or a 'plumbing of per-

---

84. Josephus, *War*, 2.259; *Ant.* 20.168. See R. A. Horsley and J. H. Hanson, *Bandits, Prophets and Messiahs. Popular Movements at the Time of Jesus*, San Francisco: Harper and Row, 1985.

sonal depths' both in response to the challenge and as a solemn preface to his significant question and solemn, 'Amen I say to you' statement that he is about to make. He asks: 'Why does this generation demand a sign?' 'This generation' is a pejorative reference to a generation represented by those who are now trying to trap him (*peirazontes auton*), which Jesus will shortly spell out explicitly as 'this evil, adulterous and unbelieving' generation (Mk 8:38; 9:19). His mighty words and works (*dynameis*) have manifested the reign of God taking root in his ministry for those open to it. These critics, and the generation like them, have not been open to what was taking place. In fact they saw his mighty deeds and said they were done through the power of Beelzebul. Jesus is not now going to jump to their command and perform to their requirements.

'Amen I say to you' introduces a solemn statement, usually signifying a threat (Mk 3:28; 8:12; 9:1; 13:30; 14:18, 30) or a promise (Mk 9:41; 10:15, 29; 11:22; 12:43; 14:9, 25).[85] Using this solemn formula, 'Amen I say to you,' Jesus makes clear that no sign will be given, a 'divine passive' meaning, 'God will give no sign.' In fact the structure of the sentence is pretty unique. Literally it reads: 'Amen I say to you, if a sign is given to this generation …!' The sentence is not finished, and scholars see it as resembling an oath formula: 'If so and so happens, then …' Here it has all the marks of a statement of total disbelief that it would happen. 'Amen I say to you, if God gives a sign to this generation …!' It also preserves the prerogative of God. Jesus does not actually say God will or will not give a sign, but makes it clear that he is absolutely convinced God will not.

Having dismissed them (the questioning Pharisees), and having embarked again he departed to the other side. 'Dismiss' captures well the superior authority of Jesus, who has silenced

---

85. A single 'amen' occurs in the synoptics where Matthew uses it thirty one times, Mark thirteen times and Luke six times. It leads into a significant statement that is intimately connected with what went before. It resembles in some measure the prophetic tradition of promise and threat or beatitude and woe. The double 'amen' at the beginning of a sentence is peculiar to John where it occurs twenty-five times. The double 'amen' is found at the end of a sentence in some Qumran texts, obviously under liturgical influence, cf 1QS, 1:20, 2:10, 18 (after blessings and curses); cf also 1QS 1-17. The Johannine usage strikes the solemn liturgical note, creating a context for divine revelation, before Jesus pronounces *legô hymin (soi)*, 'I say to you'.

222   THE GOSPEL OF MARK

his adversaries. This is Jesus' last sea journey in the gospel. It
will bring him to Bethsaida and to a new audience. The journey
itself brings this third and final section of the ministry in Galilee
and surrounding areas to a climax, and as in the case of the first
two sections this third section ends on a negative note. The
Pharisees and Herodians conspired how to destroy him at the
end of the first section (Mk 3:6), his family and the people of his
native area rejected him at the end of the second (Mk 6:6a), and
here at the end of the third section, a very negative note is struck
as the failure of the disciples themselves to remember and understand becomes patently obvious (Mk 8:21).

iv. Boat Scene. The Disciples' Obtuseness Mk 8:14-21

Having already read the accounts of two extraordinary events
on the sea, when Jesus accompanied and came to the aid of the
disciples in their boat, the reader may now expect another
epiphany or miracle of some kind. Was this scene originally an
account of an epiphany or miracle that has been transformed
into a setting for a teaching with a focus on the total failure of the
disciples to understand? Or is the reader put into the same position as the disciples, possibly expecting a miracle, and not seeing
the christological an eucharistic miracle that has taken place and
is now present symbolically in the boat?

The theme of bread continues. The narrator tells us that the
disciples had forgotten to take any loaves (*artous*) with them in
the boat. Then he adjusts the remark with a reference to their
having only one loaf with them (*hena arton meth' heautôn*). The
shortage and the reference to loaves (*artous*) immediately recall
the two multiplication accounts. Two dimensions are pointed
out by scholars, the christological and the eucharistic. The first
one focuses on the person, identity and power of Jesus and the
failure of the disciples to grasp his identity even after he has
miraculously fed Jew and Gentile in a messianic banquet.[86] The
second dimension focuses on the 'one loaf' to be shared among
many, Jews and Gentiles, a prefiguring of the Eucharist and at
the same time a recalling of the multiplications with their eucharistic language and ritual. The account focuses on the fact
that there is one loaf (*artos*) in the boat. The next reference to a
single loaf will be at the institution of the Eucharist during the

86. See J. B. Gibson, 'The Rebuke of the Disciples in Mark 8:14-21,' *JSNT*
(1986), 31-47.

last supper when Jesus identifies himself with 'the loaf' (*artos*), (Mk 14:22). Jesus is the one loaf uniting Jew and Gentile into a single messianic people.

Jesus gave them a very stern warning. 'He warned them, saying: "Observe, watch out for the leaven of the Pharisees and the leaven of Herod!"' The end of the first section dealing with the Galilean ministry showed the machinations of the Pharisees and the Herodians and here at the end of the third section the Pharisees are mentioned again, not this time with the Herodians, but with Herod himself, as the ministry in Galilee draws to a close with this sea journey.

The metaphors of bread and banquets were regularly used in the Bible for Torah, Wisdom and the Word of the Lord. The metaphor of leaven, the essential ingredient in making bread is now used as a critique of the Pharisees and Herod. It carries a double meaning full of irony. Leaven is an essential ingredient in making bread, but in fact it is in itself a corrupting agent in the fermentation process. It causes the bread to rise and expand. It does so, however, by a decaying process during fermentation, which eventually causes the bread to become stale and mouldy and thereby unhealthy and unpalatable if not eaten soon after baking. St Paul used leaven as a metaphor for a morally corrupting influence or agent (1 Cor 5:6-8; Gal 5:9) and in so doing was in line with Greco-Roman writers like Plutarch and Perseus.[87]

What then is meant by the leaven of the Pharisees and of Herod? Mark leaves the question open, though Matthew focuses on the teaching of the Pharisees (Mt 16:12), and instead of mentioning the leaven of Herod he focuses on the leaven of the Sadducees (Mt 16:16), since Herod was not involved in teaching. Mark leaves the readers to draw their own conclusion from what has been taking place in the narrative. The emphasis throughout on listening to the teaching of Jesus and the clash between his teaching and theirs leads the reader to understand the leaven of the Pharisees as the mindset by which their teaching is processed, whereby good teaching is allowed to grow stale, unpalatable and lacking in nourishment, resulting in a feeling of threat from anything new and challenging. From this there springs their questioning attitude, outright hostility and mur-

---

87. Plutarch, *Quaestiones Romanae*, 109 and Persius, *Satires*, 1.24. Leaven can also connote the idea of being 'puffed up', having what in colloquial idiom may be called 'a swelled head', an inflated opinion of self.

derous intent towards Jesus, their failure to understand him and
their demanding a sign from heaven when someone has the
nerve to oppose their teaching.[88] The leaven of Herod seems to
be an inability to be decisive in his response to what he perceives
to be sound teaching, as in the case of John the Baptist. Herod's
weakness of decision and lack of understanding seem to have
been manipulated by stronger characters leading, in the Markan
narrative, to the execution of John at the instigation of the very
determined Herodias who had a violent and destructive attitude
towards him. This attitude is reflected also in the Herodians, the
party who had already schemed with the Pharisees about doing
away with Jesus (Mk 3:6).

The disciples immediately proved the aptness of Jesus' warning by completely failing to understand what he was talking
about and they said: 'It (his warning) is because we have no
bread.' Jesus responded to this comment of theirs by asking why
they were discussing having no bread, and he goes on to say:
'Do you not grasp or understand what has happened, is your
heart still hardened? Having eyes do you not see, having ears do
you not hear? Do you not remember? Do you still not understand?' The 'hardness of heart' was already used to describe
their lack of understanding following the first multiplication in
Mk 6:52. The general failure to grasp, understand, see and hear
is summed up and focused on their concern about having only
one loaf, in spite of having Jesus with them in the boat, especially
after witnessing his miraculous feeding of the two multitudes.
Here Jesus sees in the disciples the same lack of positive response, eyes that do not see, ears that do not hear, as that encountered long ago by Jeremiah, Ezekiel (and Isaiah) (cf Jer 5:21;
Ezek 12:2; cf Isa 6:9f). The disciples are on the same slippery path
as the Pharisees and Herod. It forebodes badly for them. As the
readers of Mark hear Jesus saying, 'Do you not remember, do
you not understand?', they too are challenged to remember
Jesus' feeding of Jew and Gentile and his presence with the disciples in the boat.

---

88. Matthew interprets it as referring to their teaching. This is in keeping with his overriding concern about teaching and his portrayal of
Jesus as the teacher *par excellence*. Matthew has Pharisees and
Sadducees in this scene, not Pharisees and Herod, probably because
both groups were involved in teaching, whereas Herod was not.

4. CONCLUSION

The Disciples' Obtuseness

In reminding them of the two feedings of the multitudes Jesus again uses the eucharistic language when he speaks of 'breaking the loaves' among the five thousand and the four thousand and when he asks them how many baskets of *klasmata*, 'remainders' they gathered up. They answered 'twelve' and 'seven'. These *klasmata* signify the Eucharist overflowing into the world of Jew and Gentile, represented by the numbers twelve and seven. Jesus rather severely asks them: 'Are you still without perception?' This stinging criticism of the disciples brings the narrative movement of this section of the gospel to its conclusion, ending on a negative note like the first two sections. The Pharisees and Herodians plotted to get rid of him at the end of the first section (Mk 3:6), his own people rejected him at the end of the second section (Mk 6:4-6), and now at the end of the third, his disciples who are his 'new family', his supposed supporters, 'the would-be insiders', show that they really have not understood anything about him and his mission because their perception is dulled, their hearts hardened. Ironically, the Gentiles, historically, socially and religiously 'outsiders', have shown a better response throughout, both individually and communally than many who would be considered, or consider themselves, 'insiders'.

The Healing of the Blind Man at Bethsaida

Both 'bread cycles' or 'feeding sections' of the gospel are rounded off with a healing story (Mk 7:31-37 and Mk 8:1-20). Both healings have several points in common. They are introduced impersonally with the phrase *pherousin autô* 'they bring (the one in need of healing) to him.' There is no reference to demons, nor is there any reference to faith. Both refer to the use of spittle, almost like a human healing process rather than a miracle. Together the healings have the cumulative effect of showing how Jesus fulfilled the prophecies of Isaiah and the prophets about opening the eyes of the blind, loosening the tongue of the dumb and unstopping the ears of the deaf (Isa 35:5-6; 29:18-23; 32:18; cf Ezek 24:27). Both stories are peculiar to Mark. D. E. Nineham speculates that Matthew and Luke may have omitted them because of the physical nature of the healing process which may not have been in keeping with their understanding of the dignity and miraculous character of Jesus' person and work. It is likely also that they were sensitive to the apparently syncretistic influences in the account, or embarrassed at the failure of the first attempt to heal the blind man.[89] However, for Mark this healing is at a pivotal point in the plot, as the story of the gospel takes a definitive turning. It functions like a parable in action, highlighting the difficult path to faith and understanding on the part of the disciples.[90]

The healing of the blind man at Bethsaida forms an inclusion with the healing of the blind man, Bartimaeus, in Jericho (Mk 10:46-52). These two healings function like bookends enclosing between them the major section of the gospel dealing with 'the way', that is the physical way to Jerusalem and the way of discipleship. The section dealing with the ministry in Galilee ends with the two-stage healing of a blind man, without any reference to faith, but the section dealing with the way to Jerusalem, the way of discipleship, will end very differently with the blind man receiving full sight instantaneously and proclaiming faith in Jesus as Son of David, becoming a disciple and *following* Jesus *on the way*.

---

89. D. E. Nineham, *op. cit.*, 202.
90. See J. Marcus, 'A Note on Markan Optics', NTS 45 (1999), 250-256.

The Pivot of the Gospel Mk 8:22-30

1. Healing of the Blind Man Mk 8:22-26

The healing of the blind man at this juncture in the narrative functions both as a pointer to the results of the ministry so far and as a foreshadowing of what is to follow in the rest of the gospel. Furthermore, from a literary point of view it functions like a turnstile in the plot, supplying the miracle to end the second bread cycle on a similar note to the first (Mk 7:31-37) and at the same time providing a frame or inclusion for the following section of the gospel which both opens and closes with the healing of a blind man, the unnamed blind man at Bethsaida, and the blind Bartimaeus at Jericho (Mk 8:22-26; 10:46-52).

The healing

They came to Bethsaida[91] and people brought a blind man and begged Jesus to touch him. The verb 'beg', *parakalein*, is again used and so also is the verb to touch, *haptein*. The blind man had to be brought to Jesus who took him by the hand and led him outside the village. As in the case of the deaf and dumb man he used spittle, putting it on his eyes, and laid his hands on him. So far it seems like a regular miracle story where the healing is carried out in a manner similar to that of the wonder workers of the day.[92] However, to the reader's surprise, when Jesus asks him, 'Do you see anything?' he receives the reply that he can see but in a very unclear and confused manner. He sees people like trees walking. This kind of response was sometimes experienced by the wonder workers.[93] The healing brought the man from a state of non-seeing to a state of partial seeing. Then Jesus, without any reference to the use of spittle or incantations, simply laid his hands on the man's eyes and he could see everything clearly. He was cured, and the narrator repeats and expands his confirmation of his being able to see clearly: 'He could see everything

---

91. Bethsaida was a village. Some scribes 'corrected' the mss to read Bethany.

92. Tacitus, *Histories*, 481, Suetonius, *Vespasian* 7:2-3, and Dio Cassius 66.8 relate Vespasian's cure of a blind man in Alexandria, in similar fashion.

93. D. E. Nineham, *op. cit.*, 219, quotes a Hellenistic parallel. Alcetas of Halice was cured of blindness by the god and 'the first things he saw were the trees in the Temple precincts' (*Sylloge Inscr. Graec.*, iii, 1168).

plainly and distinctly.' Jesus sent him home and said to him: 'Do not even go into the village.' Again 'the messianic secret' is imposed.

The healing of the blind man in two stages symbolises the two stages of understanding in the gospel. Jesus' disciples have but an unclear vision of what he has been teaching and revealing in word and deed. That is why he said: 'Do you still not understand?' when they argued about not taking sufficient bread in the boat in spite of their having witnessed the feeding of the two multitudes. This failure to understand is graphically illustrated in the first attempt of Jesus to heal the blind man. He sees in a confused way. The second stage in the healing now foreshadows what Jesus will undertake in the second half of the gospel by way of trying to bring the disciples to a full understanding, a clear vision of who he is what his mission really entails. The next healing of a blind man, Bartimaeus, will be instantaneous and he will not only see clearly but also follow Jesus 'on the way'. Meanwhile Jesus will endeavour to bring the partially seeing disciples further along the path of understanding, in the way of discipleship, as they head for Jerusalem.

The next major section of the gospel, describing the way to Jerusalem, the way of the Son of Man, provides the framework for instruction on the way of discipleship as the way of service and suffering. The' way' will be punctuated by three predictions of the passion, each followed by a reaction of the Twelve/the disciples, and teaching on service and suffering. The way to Jerusalem, the way of the Son of Man, provides the context for Jesus' teaching that discipleship entails suffering, service and sharing with him in the destiny awaiting him, and them, in Jerusalem.

PETER'S PROFESSION OF FAITH MK 8:27-30

The healing of the blind man at Bethsaida and Peter's profession of faith in Jesus as the Christ/Messiah taken together form an inclusion with the healing of the blind Bartimaeus in Jericho and his profession of faith in Jesus as Son of David.

The 'double' healing at Bethsaida, producing at first an unclear vision, and then a clear one, symbolises the unclear vision of the people generally,of the disciples and of Peter in particular at this point and the attempt of Jesus to bring about a clear vision in the teaching that follows in the second part of the gospel. The unclear vision is manifest in the responses to Jesus' double question: 'Who do people say that I am?' and 'Who do you say that I am?' The second half of the gospel will deal with Jesus' attempt to lead them into a clear vision, but it will come on the lips of the executioner, the centurion who saw how he died (Mk 15:39).

The discussion about Jesus' identity leads up to the first prediction of the passion and resurrection. The discussion reflects the earlier opinions of the people, now reported to Jesus by the disciples when he himself poses the question: 'Who do people say that I am?' This is a question that effectively asks who do the ordinary people who have seen, heard or heard about Jesus and his ministry, say that he is. Throughout the first major period of the ministry, in Galilee and its environs, the impact of the person, words and works of Jesus caused people to ask questions about, and comment on, his identity and the source of his power. Already in chapter six, as the apostles spread out on their mission throughout Galilee, Herod (and the reader) became aware of the opinions of the people about Jesus. Some were saying he was John the Baptist risen from the dead and that was why miraculous powers were at work in him. Others were saying he was Elijah or one of the prophets of old (Mk 6:14-16). Their incipient positive but unclear faith in him is expressed in terms of the great people of the immediate and distant past, but as already seen, these opinions reflect different and relatively unclear expectations of a precursor and or/messianic figure on the part of ordinary folk.

Having ascertained the opinions of the people, Jesus then puts the question directly to his disciples: 'But you, who do you say that I am?' Jesus' question could be paraphrased: 'In the light of what has gone on to date in the ministry, you who have been chosen to be with me and have been sent out to represent me, you who have heard my public and private teaching, and seen my works, you who should be "on the inside", to whom the mystery of the kingdom of God has been given, who do *you* say that I am?' Their spokesperson, Peter, answered, saying: 'You are the Christ (Messiah)'. The first-time reader of the gospel, particularly if that reader had already read Matthew's gospel, is in for a shock when Jesus reacts to Peter's profession with a solemn warning to tell no one about him. An even greater shock is to follow.

Had the reader not read the prologue introducing Jesus as Christ (Messiah), Son of God and Lord on whom the Spirit de-

scended, the one whom the Spirit had driven into the desert,
Peter's response may have seemed very adequate, if not even
praiseworthy and deserving of a favourable response from a satisfied Jesus (as in Mt 16:17f). This is especially so in the light of
the popular response to the ministry in Galilee and surrounding
areas. However, Jesus does not deny the truth or accuracy of the
designation, but in keeping with what has been called the 'messianic secret' of the gospel he warned them not to tell anyone
about him. The already familiar verb *epetimêsen*, 'he warned',
used earlier for Jesus' orders to the unclean spirit and the elements (Mk 1:25; 4:39) carries a strong note of censure or rebuke.

Why did Jesus issue such a warning/rebuke, particularly
when Peter's answer was in fact correct (as is borne out in the
first verse of the prologue of this gospel where Jesus is introduced as Christ/Messiah)? Jesus' further comments explain the
reason. Peter's response involves a partial understanding, confused by popular expectation, hampered by 'what people think',
and by Satan's prompting, as Jesus points out when he says: 'Get
behind me Satan.'[94] Though he is Messiah his Messiahship is
very different from popular expectations. Whatever ideas the
disciples, and the people, had of the Messiah, however unclear,
all had one thing in common. For them the Messiah, the anointed
one, would be chosen and empowered by God. 'Power is none
the less power for being directly supplied from heaven – he
would be a glorious and manifestly victorious figure to whom
defeat and suffering would be entirely foreign.'[95] For them this
God-given power of the Messiah would confound the forces of
moral, political or social evil experienced by the people, even if
assessed differently by different individuals or groups. However,
Jesus' understanding of Messiah runs counter to all three –
moral, political and social forces will appear to overpower him –
his fate will be one of ignominy, defeat and suffering.

Jesus' rebuke in large measure changes the nature of the
'messianic secret' approach which persisted while the people
were discussing his identity. From now on Jesus speaks plainly
about his identity as the Son of Man who will be rejected, treated
violently and put to death, but subsequently divinely vindicated.
Jesus' rebuke marks the beginning of this new revelation about

---

94. See G. Claudel, *La confession de Pierre, trajectoire d'une péricope évangelique*, Paris, Gabalda, 1988.
95. D. E. Nineham, *op. cit.*, 235.

himself and his destiny. It marks the beginning also of the private and intense instruction of the disciples on the way of discipleship, both of which will be spelled out on the way to Jerusalem. The reader (who knows more than the characters in the story) is also included in this 'you' and challenged by the question about Jesus' identity. The shocked disciples (and readers) are embarking on a steep learning curve as they are confronted both with the central question of the gospel: 'Who do you say that I am?' and with the implications for their own lives of Jesus' response.

Peter's profession and the voice at the transfiguration stand mid-way between the baptism and the crucifixion-resurrection. Mark opens the gospel with the reference to Jesus Christ, a designation soon followed in the prologue by the heavenly voice proclaiming him 'Beloved Son' (Mk 1:11). Here, approximately half way through the gospel, Peter's proclamation of Jesus as Christ will be followed very soon by the voice from the cloud at the transfiguration proclaiming him Beloved Son (Mk 9:7). The profession of faith of the centurion, the executioner, at the end of the gospel will proclaim him Son of God (Mk 15:39) and the young man at the tomb will shortly afterwards proclaim his vindication in the resurrection (Mk 16:5-7). So why the command to silence at this point? The answer comes in the shocking announcement that Jesus will have to suffer, be rejected and put to death, and on the third day rise again. And in addition, the disciples will be expected to share in his destiny.

Jesus' command to silence is neither a denial of his Messianic role nor a pointer to the fact that historically Jesus did not see himself in messianic terms. Were it so it is most unlikely that Matthew would have given such a high profile to Jesus' praise of Peter for his profession of faith (Mt 16:13-20). Furthermore, in all the gospel traditions the messianic role and/or its related royal status is an issue in his trials by the Sanhedrin (Mk 14:61; Mt 26:63; Lk 22:67) and Pilate (Mt 27:11; Mk 15:2; Lk 23:2f; Jn 18:33, 37; 19:3). It appears on the official notice of his crime placed on the cross and as a source of mockery at his trials and crucifixion (Mk 15:2, 18, 26; Mt 27:29, 37, 42; Lk 23:35, 37, 38; Jn 19:15, 19, 21).

The Way to Jerusalem Mk 8:(22-) 27-10:52

After sending the formerly blind man of Bethsaida to his home and commanding him not to enter the village, Jesus again 'departed' (Mk 8:27). The verbs of motion, 'came', 'set out', 'departed', and 'entered' have been used several times to indicate a fresh initiative with change of place, action, teaching and audience. Here Jesus 'departs' for the villages of Caesarea Philippi, that is, the settlements clustered around the city, like suburbs in a modern town or city. The city was near Mount Hermon and the source of the Jordan. The emperor Augustus gave the city, formerly called Panion after the pagan god Pan, to Herod the Great. It was rebuilt by the tetrarch Philip, son of Herod the Great and renamed after the emperor and himself as Caesarea Philippi.

For the first time Jesus is described as being 'on the way'. This 'way' will take him via Caesarea Philippi, the Mount of Transfiguration, back through Galilee, and from Capernaum on through the Jordan valley to Judea and beyond the Jordan and then to Jericho and finally to his destination and destiny in Jerusalem. Just as Jesus three times predicts his forthcoming passion, death and resurrection in Jerusalem whither 'the way' takes them (Mk 8:31; 9:31; 10:32-34), so too the narrator will repeatedly remind the reader that Jesus and the disciples are 'on the way'(Mk 10:17, 46, 52; 11:8; 12:14). This is a whole new departure in the gospel and this major section of the gospel is focused on Jesus' forthcoming fate in Jerusalem and his teaching about a discipleship of service and suffering. In contrast to his ministry to date there will be only two healings on the way to Jerusalem, that of the (epileptic) boy with a dumb spirit (Mk 9:14-29) and the restoration of sight to the blind man, Bartimaeus, in Jericho (Mk 10:46-52).

The healing of the blind man at Bethsaida stands as a bridge between the two major sections of the gospel, the ministry in Galilee and environs and the way to Jerusalem. It forms an inclusion with the healing of the blind man in Jericho which concludes the way to Jerusalem and in turn forms a bridge with the ministry in the city. The following diagram shows the outline in three 'stages' of the way to Jerusalem, the way of the Son of Man and the way of discipleship.

Outline of Mk 8:22-10:52

Inclusion: Mk 8:22-26 / 27-30.
Blind Man at Bethsaida; Peter's Profession.

The Way. *Stage 1.* Caesarea Philippi. Mk 8:31-9:29
1. First Passion Prediction. Mk 8:31f
2. The Reaction of Peter. Mk 8:32f
3. Teaching on Discipleship.
    i.   Teaching the Crowd and the Disciples. Mk 8:34-9:1
    ii.   Transfiguration. Mk 9:2-13
    iii.   Teaching when the Disciples failed to heal. Mk 9:14-27

The Way. *Stage 2.* Galilee, Judea and Beyond the Jordan
                 Mk 9:30-10:31
1. Second Prediction of the Passion. Mk 9:30f
2. Reaction of the Disciples. Mk 9:32
3. Teaching on Discipleship.
    i.   Instructing the Twelve. Mk 9:33-50
    ii.   Instructing Pharisees, Disciples and Crowd. Mk 10:1-16
    iii.   Obstacles to Discipleship. Riches: Poverty. Mk 10:17-27
    iv.   The Reward of Discipleship. Mk 10:28-31

The Way. *Stage 3.* Going up to Jerusalem, Jericho. Mk 10:32-45
1. The Plot.
2. Third Prediction of the Passion. Mk 10:32-34.
3. Reaction of the Disciples. Mk 10:35-40
4. Instructing the Twelve/Servant/Gives his life Mk 10:41-45

Inclusion: Mk 10:46-52.
Blind Man at Jericho: Bartimaeus' Profession.

The healing of the blind man at Bethsaida and Peter's profession
straddle the central point of the gospel and so they figure in both
outlines. The major section describing 'the way', the way to
Jerusalem, the way of discipleship, the way of the Son of Man, is
enclosed between the two healings of blind men which function
as 'inclusions', like bookends holding the section together. Both
healings are closely aligned to a profession of faith, the profession of Peter and that of Bartimaeus. The section is punctuated
by the three predictions of the passion (Mk 8:31; 9:31; 10:32-34),
each predicting an official rejection of Jesus' claims, a violent
death and a resurrection. Each of the predictions begins a sub-

section which follows a common pattern of passion prediction, reaction of the Twelve/the disciples, and teaching on discipleship, focusing on perception, suffering and service in sharing the way and the fate of Jesus, the way of the Son of Man.

The Way: Stage One. Caesarea Philippi Mk 8:27-9:29

1. FIRST PREDICTION OF THE PASSION MK 8:31-33

The expression 'He began to teach them' (*êrxato didaskein autous*) points to the beginning of a habitual or repeated teaching. He was teaching them that,' it is necessary (*dei*) for the Son of Man to suffer many things, to be rejected by the elders and the chief priests and the scribes, and to be put to death, and after three days to rise again.' This first prediction of the passion and resurrection is presented in indirect speech in the third person, and it is presented as a summary of ongoing or repeated instruction. Furthermore the narrator tells us that Jesus was speaking the word openly. Underlining this understanding of his identity, role and destiny, so very different from the expectations of the people and the disciples, Jesus does not use the title Messiah of himself, but in the context where one would expect him to do so he uses 'Son of Man' as he speaks of his destiny in Jerusalem.[1]

Jesus' use of the Son of Man title as a term to indicate his messianic role as one who suffers sets the Danielic Son of Man imagery (Dan 7:13f) in an ironic position of one who, instead of receiving all authority over men, suffers at the hands of men before being glorified at the resurrection and coming on the clouds in glory to gather the elect.

2. THE REACTION OF PETER MK 8:32-33

The expression 'it is necessary', *dei* (he must suffer many things) reflects a theme in apocalyptic literature that certain future events were part of the firmly decreed will of God. Asking him to shrink from such a divinely decreed event is therefore asking him to disobey the will of God. This explains Jesus' response to Peter, 'Get behind me Satan', with the comment that his attitude is that of human beings and not of God. It reflects the human de-

---

1. See H. F. Bayer, *Jesus' Predictions of Vindication and Resurrection*, Tûbingen: J. C. Mohr (Paul Siebeck), 1986.

sire for the Messiah to carry out his work and win people by spectacular means not involving suffering or a change of heart through repentance and faith. This reflects closely the point of the temptation narratives in Matthew and Luke where Jesus is tempted by Satan in the wilderness (Mt 4:1-11; Lk 4:1-13; cf Mk 1:13).

Peter's reaction is not just a failure to understand intellectually but an indication of not wanting to see Jesus fail, and to find that he himself and the other disciples are followers of a failure, 'a loser'. These are naturally very human thoughts, 'the thoughts of men and not of God', to quote the response of Jesus. Peter has already spoken in the name of the disciples. Jesus, now looking at the disciples, is concerned about their overhearing Peter's response that showed a wrong understanding and attitude on the part of their spokesman and leader. He therefore instructs Peter on discipleship. When Jesus tells Peter, who has taken Jesus aside to advise him as though he were the master, to 'go behind me', (*hypage opisô mou*), he is in fact telling him to resume his position as a disciple, one of those 'following', 'coming after Jesus', as designated in the original call to 'come after (follow) me' (*deute opisô mou*). Thinking like Peter's is an obstacle in the way on which Jesus (together with the disciples) has embarked. The hardening of their hearts, the power of Satan and the lure of the world and its way of thinking hamper the disciples' response, like the impediment to growth in the case of the seed falling on the path, the rocky ground or among the thorns.

The passion predictions in the synoptics are like neat, tightly expressed summaries of what actually came to pass. These 'formulae' are obviously the result of repeated telling and are most likely influenced by the actual historical outcome.[2] However, there is a real experience of threat behind the formula. Already the Pharisees and Herodians have conspired about how to destroy him (Mk 3:6). After the parable of the wicked husbandmen the Jerusalem authorities will have similarly lethal intentions in his regard (Mk 12:12) and finally the chief priests and scribes will plot against him and accept the help of Judas in handing him over (Mk 14:1, 2, 10, 11). In St John's gospel, which is so different in many ways to the synoptics, there is a striking parallel to the sense of foreboding and future vindication contained in

2. There are also the references to resurrection and to the suffering of the Son of Man in Mk 9:9, 12.

the synoptic predictions. Time and again there are attempts to arrest, stone or kill him but they are unsuccessful because *his hour* has not yet come.[3] After the raising of Lazarus, Caiaphas announced to the Sanhedrin that it was better for one man to die for the people than that the whole nation should be destroyed (Jn 11:50). Jesus' pronouncements about 'being lifted up' are somewhat equivalent to the synoptic passion predictions but they are set in thoroughly Johannine theology: 'When you have lifted up the Son of Man then will you know that I am' and 'When I have been lifted up from the earth I shall draw all to myself' (Jn 8:28). In the parable of the good/model shepherd Jesus speaks of laying down his life for his sheep and laying it down and taking it up of his own accord (Jn 10:11, 15, 18). These references in John and the predictions in the synoptics toll like a bell throughout the gospel signalling the oncoming salvific event.[4]

'And he said this plainly' also has a parallel in John's gospel where the disciples say 'now you are speaking plainly and not in metaphors' and Jesus goes on to warn them that 'the time will come when you will all be scattered leaving me alone ...', a prediction which also has a close parallel in Mark with Jesus' comment about the striking of the shepherd and the scattering of the sheep (Jn 16:29-33; Mk 14:27).

Looking at this very varied material from different gospel traditions it is obvious that there is a solid historical basis for Jesus' expectation of a violent death and his faith in a divine vindication. It is quite possible that Jesus, like the prophets, had a clear prophetic insight into the outcome of his ministry. But even from the point of view of a shrewd human being he must have had an awareness of the forces lining up against him, together with his faith that God would ultimately have the last word. M. D. Hooker sums the case up very well:

> ... it seems incredible that Jesus should not have foreseen at least the likelihood (if not the inevitability) of his death. The conviction that suffering was likely may well have arisen from the hostility of the authorities and would have been confirmed from his reading of scripture, where obedience to God frequently involves suffering. The pattern of suffering

3. Jn 5:16-18; 7:20, 25f, 30, 32, 44, 46; 8:20, 59; 10:30-33, 39; 11:8, 49, 57.
4. J. Ernst, *Markus*, 59 writes: *Die drei Leidenankundigungen Jesu sind wie das Wetterleuchten vor dem Drama der Passion. Der Weg nach Jerusalem hat durch die Todessignale eine klare Orientierung erhalten.*

of the righteous and prosperity for the wicked is especially prominent in the psalms ... Although the details of the passion predictions may be *vaticinia ex eventu*, there seems no reason to deny that he spoke of his rejection in general terms.[5]

3. TEACHING ON DISCIPLESHIP MK 8:34-9:1

After Peter's strong reaction to Jesus' prediction of his forthcoming rejection, suffering and death, three important 'moments' of instruction follow. First of all Jesus teaches the crowd and the disciples. Secondly he brings the inner group, Peter, James and John, to the mountain where they experience the transfiguration. Thirdly he gives further instruction following the disciples' failure to heal the epileptic/possessed boy.

i.Teaching the Crowd and the Disciples

Jesus summoned the crowd, together with the disciples, to him and spoke to them about the conditions for following him as his disciples. The disciple must follow Jesus who renounced messianic glory to follow the path of the rejected and suffering Son of Man, by renouncing self, taking up one's cross, losing one's life for the sake of, and never being ashamed of Jesus and the good news.

Whoever wishes ...
The invitation to discipleship is both individual, emphasised by the use of the singular *tis*, 'if any person wishes' (*ei tis thelei*) and universal, emphasised by the use of the more indefinite 'whoever may wish' (*hos gar ean thelê*).

The nature and personal cost of discipleship are spelled out in a collection of sayings which may have existed as individual sayings or *logia* prior to their being collected and edited by Mark or someone before him during the process of transmission prior to the writing of the gospel. The collection builds up to the promise of eschatological reward by the vindicated, glorious Son of Man for those who persist in discipleship, or rejection for those who feel ashamed and deny their discipleship. All people are afraid of pain and suffering and ashamed of failure, and of appearing foolish before others. The challenge of discipleship is

5. M. D. Hooker, *op. cit.*, 204f.

to follow Jesus through these 'negative' experiences to a sharing of his final glorious vindication.

Taking up one's cross
The first saying (Mk 8:34) is about renouncing self, taking up one's cross and following Jesus. It arises directly from Peter's rejection of suffering. 'If anyone wishes to come after me (i.e. to follow me, to be my disciple), let him deny himself and let him take up his cross and follow me (i.e. persist in following me in spite of the cross)' (Mk 8:34).[6] Denying oneself means taking oneself out of the centre of the picture and selflessly placing oneself at the service of Jesus and the good news. Speaking of taking up the cross reminds the reader of Jesus' own carrying of his cross. However, the reference does not necessarily have to have its origin in the post Good Friday recollection of Jesus' own carrying of the cross because crucifixion was a common experience, as was the sight of the victims carrying the crossbeam to the place of execution. This fact is borne out by Plutarch's remark in his work on punishment and providence that every criminal who is executed carries his own cross.[7] Carrying one's cross and following Jesus is a very apt description of discipleship at this point in the narrative as Jesus sets out on the fateful way to Jerusalem together with his disciples, a way that will end in his carrying of his cross to Calvary, and the enlisting of a stranger to assist him after the disciples have left him and fled.

Saving and losing one's life
The second saying (Mk 8:35) is a paradoxical teaching about saving and losing one's life. 'Whoever wishes[8] to save his/her life will lose it and whoever loses his/her life for the sake of me and of the good news will save it.' The word 'life' (*psychê*) in this context has posed problems for translators. The Greek word should

6. This is an example of a sentence where the impact and clear focus of the original masculine form, intended inclusively, is slightly dulled in translation by the need to translate inclusively, especially when the translator uses the plural. An attempted inclusive translation would be: 'If anyone wishes to come after me, let that person deny self, and let that person take up his/her cross and follow me.' Also, some mss have 'come' instead of 'follow', probably a scribal attempt to harmonise with Mt 16:24.
7. Plutarch, *De sera numinis vindicata*, 9.554b.
8. *hos gar ean thelê*, lit., 'If anyone would wish', 'whoever might wish'.

not be taken in the philosophic Platonic sense of soul as distinct from body. Neither should it be taken in the straightforward sense of life just as we know it in this world, the biological life between birth and death. It is more the Hebrew concept of the essential person, the *nephes*, with the connotation of the survival of that which is essential to the person after death. Saving one's life and then losing it implies directing all one's energies to preserving, securing and enriching one's own life for this world only, and missing out on something far more fundamental, the final sharing in the glory of the vindicated Son of Man. Losing one's life implies an acceptance of suffering, rejection, death, loss and failure 'for the sake of me and the good news' and being prepared to appear foolish to people for living such a way of life.[9] Such an apparent loss of life results in 'saving one's life', that is, it brings the 'essential person' to the glory of the vindicated Son of Man.[10]

What price for one's life?

The third saying (Mk 8:36) is couched in the commercial language of the world: profit, loss, gain, exchange. 'What does it profit a human being to gain the whole world and suffer the loss of one's life (*psychê*) or what can one give in exchange for one's life?' (Mk 8:37). Jesus poses the question as a challenge to make them think about what possible profit it is to someone to gain the whole world and lose one's life (that which is most essential to their person, and which will survive this present biological phase of life), or what can one give in exchange for (as a price for) one's life.

Ashamed of Jesus and his words?

The fourth *logion* (Mk 8:38) picks up on such attitudes. 'If anyone is ashamed of me and my words in this adulterous and sinful generation, the Son of Man will be ashamed of him / her when he comes in the glory of his Father with the holy angels.' Being ashamed of Jesus and his words[11] and the way of life they de-

9. Some mss have 'for the sake of the good news' rather than 'for the sake of me and of the good news'. Matthew and Luke have 'for the sake of me' without the reference to the good news.

10. See D. Rhoads, 'Losing Life for Others: Mark's Standards of Judgement,' *Int* 47 (1993) 358-369

11. Some mss have 'ashamed of me and mine' rather than 'ashamed of me and my words'

mand will lead to exclusion from the glory of the vindicated Son of Man who will be ashamed of the one who was ashamed of him, 'when he comes in the glory of his Father with the Holy angels'. The offer of life which is a sharing in that glory will have been lost in the pursuit of transitory life in this 'adulterous and sinful generation'. A similar insight is contained in John's gospel where acceptance or rejection of the Son, the light of the world, contains in itself the judgement with eternal consequences (Jn 3:18f). This description of an 'adulterous and sinful generation' is reminiscent of the prophetic condemnations of the people for turning away from YHWH and involving themselves in Ba'al cult and social injustice, regularly classified as fornication or adultery since it broke the covenant or marriage bond with God, the bridegroom of Israel.

The Son of Man, who could forgive sins on earth and who was declared master of the Sabbath, is now presented as one who will be rejected and then vindicated through resurrection and a second coming in glory in the power of the Father and accompanied by the holy angels. The 'gaps' in the story of the Son of Man are beginning to be filled in, but the reader must wait for further revelation which will come in Jesus' eschatological-apocalyptic discourse' and in his statement about coming in glory to gather the elect which he utters at his Jewish trial (Mk 13:26 and 14:62).

J.R.Donahue and D.J.Harrington give an excellent summary of this teaching on discipleship:

Mark 8:27-38 is a rich resource for those who seek to make Mark's gospel come alive in the lives of Christians today. It sets before us the basic question of Mark's gospel and indeed of the entire NT: Who do you say that I am? It confronts us with the mystery of the cross and challenges us to integrate the reality of Jesus' suffering (and our own) into our understanding of Jesus and discipleship. And it spells out the demands, value and rewards of faithful following of Jesus. In a sense Mark 8:33, with its contrast between God's thoughts and human thoughts, is the nub of the gospel. Mark presents his first readers and today's reader with an exercise in 'right thinking' about suffering.[12]

---

12. J. R. Donahue and D. J. Harrington, *op. cit.*, 266.

Seeing the Kingdom
The chapter division between Mk 8:38 and 9:1 is not only artificial but also misleading. The verse 'Amen I say to you' (Mk 9:1)
seems to flow from the final verse of chapter eight about the Son
of Man coming in glory with the angels. It therefore belongs to
the preceding collection of sayings and furthermore there is no
change of audience, time or place mentioned. However, it forms
a bridge with the transfiguration account which follows. The
collection of sayings comes to a climax with the prophetic
promise, articulated with all the solemnity of a pronouncement
beginning with 'Amen I say to you' and going on to declare:
'There are some people standing here who will not taste death
until they see the kingdom of God come in power.' The reader is
left to ponder on this prediction.

ii. The Transfiguration Mk 9:2-29

The transfiguration scene which follows can be seen as a first in-
stalment on the glory of the Son of Man, whether one sees it in
terms of the resurrection or the second coming (*parousia*). Both
are aspects of the coming vindication of the Son of Man over the
imminent rejection, suffering and death which he has foretold.
The prophetic oracle or promise, 'Amen I say to you there are
some people standing here who will not taste death until they
see the kingdom of God come in power' functions as a bridge,
being both a climax to the teaching on following Christ and an
interpretative opening to the account of the transfiguration.

The Transfiguration/Transformation of Jesus Mk 9:2-10
Approach and Interpretation
Dashed hopes, Jesus' rebuke, a menacing future for Jesus and
probably also for the disciples in the short term, and the promise
of a final coming of the kingdom of God in power set the scene
for the transfiguration. The scene itself is unique in the gospels
and the lack of other examples for the purpose of comparative
study makes it difficult to interpret. It is set between the promise
that some here present with Jesus will see the kingdom of God
come in power and the prediction about Jesus' resurrection from
the dead and the statement that Elijah has already come and has
been badly treated. These utterances will help to interpret aspects of the transfiguration.[13]

13. See J. P. Heil, *The Transfiguration of Jesus: Narrative Meaning and*

Lines of Interpretation

Three lines of approach to the interpretation of the transfiguration have been taken by scholars. Firstly, some emphasise the actual historicity of the event, with various degrees of attention to the details. Secondly, others in the tradition of Bultmann see in the transfiguration a post-resurrection story placed back in the ministry. Thirdly there are those who see it as an apocalyptic vision in the style of the visions in Daniel, Ezekiel and other apocalyptic books such as 1 Enoch, 4 Ezra and 2 Baruch. However, though there are certain points of contact with all three types of experience, serious reservations must be kept in mind when dealing with all three.[14]

Firstly, seeing it as an actual historical event, a transcendental experience during the ministry of Jesus, one must remember that such experiences are not usually available to historical scrutiny. Even for those who have these experiences the subsequent task of understanding, articulating and communicating the experience is quite a challenge whether the experience was internal or visual and/or auditory. The narrative, thought categories, literary genre and imagery of well known experiences in biblical and related literature provide a ready made language for communicating the meaning of what has been experienced. Failure to appreciate the use of such 'established' imagery and language in communicating the experience can lead to an over literal approach. It is also necessary to remember that analysing and commenting on the literary and theological language and imagery used in the account is not an attack on the historicity of the actual experience itself.

Secondly, the approach of Bultmann, followed by others, that this is a post resurrection appearance narrative, an account of an appearance of the Risen Christ set back in the ministry of Jesus, falls short on a number of crucial points. The resurrection appearance narratives in the gospels and Acts show Jesus himself taking the initiative in appearing to and addressing the disciples. In these appearances he speaks on his own behalf, and is not assisted or vindicated by a voice from heaven or a famous figure from the past like Elijah or Moses. The resurrection ap-

Function of Mark 9:2-8, Matt 17:1-8 and Luke 9:28-36, Rome, Biblical Institute Press, 2000.

14. See J.Murphy-O'Connor, 'What Really happened at the Transfiguration?', *Bible Review*, 3/3, (1987) 8-21.

pearance narratives also contain a commissioning and empowering of the disciples of Jesus and a sending of them into the world to carry out a mission in his name – an extension of the commissioning during the ministry. Furthermore, none of the resurrection narratives speak of Jesus' dazzling appearance and clothes. On the part of the disciples in the post-resurrection appearance narratives, they doubt and fail to recognise Jesus. The transfiguration does not resemble a post-resurrection appearance in any of these essential aspects. However, the scene is a *foretaste* of the glorified Christ and in this sense it is, to a certain degree, a preview of God's vindication of Jesus in the resurrection.

Thirdly, the changed states of consciousness and alteration of appearance, the cloud of divine presence, the heavenly voice from the cloud, the appearance of heavenly beings, all are characteristic of apocalyptic visions. The transfigured state of Jesus can be seen as a foretaste of his second coming at the *parousia*, and a confirmation of his role in the bringing in of the kingdom in its fullness of power and glory.[15] Furthermore, on their descent from the mountain Jesus instructs the disciples to tell no one 'what they had seen' (*ha eidon*) (Mk 9:9). This is close enough to Matthew's description of the event as 'the vision' (*to horama*) (Mt 17:9). In this sense there is an apocalyptic flavour to the transfiguration. However, seeing the transfiguration in terms of an apocalyptic vision (*horama*) runs into the difficulty that it does not conform to the general pattern of such visions which are of a particular genre in which there is a narrator who describes the vision in the first person (Rev 1:9) or an angelic person who interprets the vision (Rev 1:17). The transfiguration also departs significantly from the apocalyptic genre in not speaking in strange language, using esoteric images or prophesising spectacular or terrifying happenings.

A Revelation during the ministry for the sake of the disciples
The scene involves the three disciples to whom Jesus gave special names, Peter, James and John. As pointed out already, these are the three who accompanied him to the house of Jairus, the synagogue official and the same three (together with Andrew) who will be the recipients of the eschatological-apocalyptic dis-

15. For a study of the transfiguration as a foretaste of the *parousia* see G. H. Boobyer, *St Mark and the Transfiguration Story*, Edinburgh 1942.

course on the Mount of Olives and whom he will associate closely
with himself in the garden of Gethsemane (Mk 3:16f; 5:37;
14:33f). The whole scene about to unfold seems to be directed at
them, and here lies the key to its interpretation. The whole
experience is for the benefit of the central group of disciples at
this critical juncture in the ministry and for this reason it must be
seen as an experience during the ministry rather than a reloc-
ation of a post-resurrection experience. The reader has already
been given the essential information that Jesus is the Beloved
Son. Here that information is being given to these chosen disciples. R. H. Lightfoot points out:

> ... the whole event, from first to last takes place solely for the
> sake of the three disciples. 'He was transfigured *before them*';
> 'there appeared *unto them* Elijah and Moses'; 'there came a
> cloud overshadowing *them*'; 'this is my only Son; hear *ye*
> him'; 'and suddenly, looking round about, *they* saw no one
> any more, save Jesus only *with themselves*'.[16]

This corporate experience may in large measure be explained as
a mystical experience of a group associated with Jesus and
caught up in his intimate prayer with the Father in which the
reality of his nature and identity shines through his changed appearance. It confirms his status and authority and lays the
ground for their acceptance of his assertion of the necessity of
his suffering, death and resurrection.

The narrative of the transfiguration is, however, very symbolic, and the Old Testament imagery and typology is striking,
even if not always clearly spelled out and therefore difficult to
interpret exactly. Its overall purpose and impact is nonetheless
clear. In the words of M. D. Hooker:

> For Mark's readers, the story spells out the truth about Jesus
> and confirms their belief in him as God's beloved Son. For a
> brief moment, the three disciples are said to have a shared
> vision of the understanding of Jesus which belongs to the
> post-resurrection situation.[17]

This is borne out by the fact that Jesus commands the disciples to
tell no one about it until the Son of Man is risen from the dead,
when presumably the experience could be put into the context
of his vindication by the Father as proclaimed by all believers.

M. D. Hooker points out that the best explanation for this

---

16. R. H. Lightfoot, *op. cit.*, 44.
17. M. D. Hooker, *op. cit.*, 214.

experience of the disciples, subsequently presented in the traditional language and categories canonised in the Old Testament is:

> … an historical 'happening' of some kind has been interpreted with the aid of Old Testament allusions to produce the narrative as we have it, but the two have been so fused together that it is impossible for us now to separate the two … The true nature of Jesus is a hidden mystery which breaks out from time to time, and for Mark these revelations do not require explanations.[18]

The Account: Examining the Old Testament allusions

Looking at the Old Testament language, allusions and categories one is immediately struck by the mention of six days. 'After six days …', is somewhat unusual in Mark's gospel as a measure of time between events.[19] It is significant in that it binds the event about to take place to the preceding material.[20] Taken at face value it may refer back to one or all of the preceding conversations – Peter's profession of faith, Jesus' rebuke, his teaching on the suffering in store for the Son of Man, his teaching on discipleship, and his affirmation about the coming of the Son of Man and the kingdom of God. However, this mention of 'six days' most likely has a deeper symbolic significance.

'Six days' traditionally represented the time for preparation and self purification before an encounter with the divine (cf Exod 24:15-17) and in the original form of the story some period of preparation may have been implied or described.[21] The narrative so far has been rich in allusions to the foundation events in the formation of Israel at Sinai and during the sojourn in the desert. Symbolically this story contains echoes of Moses' ascent of Mt Sinai when he and his servant Joshua spent six days on the mountain, when the glory of the Lord settled on Mount Sinai and the cloud covered it for six days, before God called to Moses from out of the cloud on the seventh day (Exod 24:12-18). It recalls also the story of Moses and his preparation of the people in the desert for the revelation of the glory of God *on the third day*

---

18. *Ibid.*

19. Matthew (17:1) and Mark mention 'six days later' but Luke (9:28) speaks of 'eight days later'.

20. The only other example in the gospel is at Mk 14:1 where there is a reference to events 'two days before the Passover'.

21. D. E. Nineham, *op. cit.*, 234.

(Ex 19:9-25).[22] 'Go to the people and consecrate them today and tomorrow … and prepare for the third day, because on the third day the Lord will come down upon Mount Sinai in the sight of all the people' (Exod 19:10f). *The third day* subsequently became a 'canonised' term for the day of God's presence in glory when he gave the people the gift of the Law. The memory of the event at Sinai came to be celebrated at Pentecost on the third day of a three day preparation as described in the Exodus narrative. Later still these three days of immediate preparation were preceded by four days of remote preparation, creating a six day period of preparation for the manifestation of the glory on the seventh day.[23] Echoes of such a preparation may very well be present in the six days mentioned here.

There follows the reference to the 'high mountain.' Jesus brings Peter, James and John, by themselves, up a high mountain, an unspecified mountain in Galilee familiar to readers of the synoptics and John[24] and reminiscent of Sinai/Horeb with its connotations of the presence and glory of God, the gift of the Law to Moses and the gentle breeze heralding the word of the Lord to Elijah.[25] The mountain has been variously identified as Mt Hermon, Mt Carmel and Mt Tabor. Since the fourth century Mt Tabor has been the most frequently accepted venue, probably due to its location, and nowadays it is to the church at its summit that pilgrims are taken to commemorate the event. However, the New Testament does not specify the location as to do so would take from the whole symbolic meaning of the

22. Exod 19:9-25. The phrase 'the third day' occurs four times in the passage.

23. In St John's gospel a four day period comes to a climax with Jesus' promise to the disciples that they will see greater things with the rending of the heavens and the vision of the angels of God ascending and descending on the Son of Man (Jn 1:51). Then the climax of the inauguration narrative comes at Cana 'on the third day' when Jesus manifests his glory and his disciples believe in him; that is, after a six day period of preparation (Jn 2:1). See J. Potin, *La Fête juive de la Pentecôte*, 314-317.

24. Mt 5-7, the Sermon on the Mount; Mk 3:13-19//Lk 6:12-16, the appointment of the Twelve; Mt 17:1-8//Mk 9:2-8//Lk 9:28-36, the Transfiguration; the final appearance of the Risen Lord (Mt 28) – all are on a mountain in Galilee, and so too is the multiplication of the loaves in Jn 6:3ff.

25. Ex 19-20; 1 Kings 19. Traditionally the Mount of Transfiguration has been identified as Mt Tabor, but it is really the symbolism of 'the mountain' that is important rather than the identity of the location.

mountain with its connotations of the divine presence and the encounters on Sinai/Horeb.

Jesus was transformed, transfigured, *metemorphôtê*. 'He had a change of form.' Commentators point out that this probably refers to a manifestation of the glorious form he would assume after death, resurrection and exaltation in glory to the right hand of the Father. It is a foretaste, a glimpse beforehand of Jesus in the final state of Lordship and glory to which he would finally be exalted. It is 'conceived as actual ethereal substance ... the sort of body generally supposed to belong to heavenly beings and indeed to be the vesture of God himself.'[26]

Matthew (Mt 17:2) and Luke (9:29) mention that Jesus' countenance shone like the sun. Mark does not refer to his countenance but describes the gloriously shining garments. The concept of garments reflecting glory was common, as seen from the comment in 1 Enoch: 'The elect will be clothed with garments of glory from the Lord of spirits, and their glory shall never fade away' (1 Enoch 62:15f). It is found also in 2 Enoch: 'Take Enoch from his earthly garments and clothe him in garments of glory (2 Enoch 22:8).'[27] In the vision of the heavenly court in Daniel the heavenly being is described in terms of brightness and having a robe white as snow (Dan 7:9f). In the Book of Revelation the martyred saints are described as those clothed in robes washed white in the blood of the lamb (Rev 6:11; 7:13f).

There are, however, other factors to be taken into account such as the appearance of Elijah and Moses, and why Mark mentions Elijah before Moses, unlike Matthew and Luke who mention Moses first. The mention of Elijah and Moses sets Jesus in the context of salvation history. Both figures are associated with divine encounters on the mountain of Sinai/Horeb (Exod 19:16-25; 24;12-18; 34;1-28; 1 Kings 19:11-18). The presence of Elijah and Moses testifies to Jesus in the face of those who accuse him of being a false prophet. The Law and the Prophets are represented by these two central characters who are in conversation with Jesus,[28] and bear witness by their presence to the authentic nature of his mission as the one whose coming is heralded by

26. D. E. Nineham *op. cit.*, 234, quoting G. H. Boobyer, *St Mark and the Transfiguration Story*, 23.

27. cf Rev 4:4; 7:9; 3:5 inter al.

28. Luke specifies that they were speaking about his 'exodus', i.e his passion, death, resurrection and ascension.

Elijah and fulfils the promise that a prophet like Moses will appear. Moses represents the Law but was also seen as the prophet *par excellence*.

There was a belief in Jesus' time that prominent figures from the Old Testament would appear in the end time and play a part in the kingdom.[29] Particularly from the time of Malachi Elijah's name is most frequently used. Malachi prophesied: 'Know that I am going to send you Elijah the prophet before my day comes, that great and terrible day' (Mal 4:5f). The end time would also be a time when false prophets abound (Mk 13:5f; Mt 24:4f; Lk 21:8).

Both Moses and Elijah are also associated with ascensions into heaven.[30] Elijah ascended in a fiery chariot (2 Kings 3:9-12), an incident that received much consideration in subsequent biblical and extra-biblical writing.[31] Moses' death is recorded but his burial place is unknown (Deut 34:5-8) and later tradition associated his death with ascension into heaven as reported in the apocryphal *Ascension of Moses* (11:5-8), in Josephus, (*Ant* 4:8.48) and in Philo, *Moses* (2.288, 291f). Their presence therefore is also symbolic of Jesus' future ascension to the glory of the Father and the holy angels, mentioned in Jesus' recent remark to the disciples (Mk 8:38), but only after his rejection, suffering, death and resurrection.

However, unlike Matthew (17:3) and Luke (9:30) who mention 'Moses and Elijah' in straightforward conjunctive phrases, giving priority to Moses as a figure, Mark mentions Elijah before Moses. If putting the more significant figure second after *syn* (with) as in 'Elijah with Moses', as J. P. Heil suggests, is Mark's purpose, then the intention of all three synoptics is to see Moses as the more important figure.[32] Why then does Mark mention Elijah first, even if he wishes to keep the priority of Moses as a biblical figure?

It may be due to the fact that Elijah has figured prominently in the discussions about Jesus' identity (Mk 6:15; 8:28) and will

---

29. Mt 8:11 and Lk 13:28f speak of the role of Abraham, Isaac and Jacob in the kingdom.

30. Some scholars see a connection with the two eschatological witnesses sent by God in Rev 11:3-13.

31. Further reflection on this takes place in Sir 48:9; 1 Macc 2:38; 1 Enoch 89:52; 93:8; Josephus, *Ant.*, 9:28.

32. J. P. Heil, 'A Note on "Elijah with Moses" in Mark 9:4', *Bib* 80 (1999), 115.

be central to a discussion just after this scene as they come down from the mountain when Jesus will point out how John the Baptist as precursor fulfilled the role of Elijah. The reader has already been introduced to the Baptist in the prologue in a way that recalls the person and mission of Elijah. The disciples will be instructed in the Baptist-Elijah connection as they descend from the mountain.

Placing Moses second, even if maintaining his premier role in the Old Testament, while highlighting the role of Elijah, may also reflect an attempt to avoid making Jesus simply another Moses figure. The reference to his face shining like the sun in Matthew and Luke, may be omitted by Mark again to avoid too close a comparison with Moses whose countenance shone so brightly with the reflected glory of his encounter with God on Sinai (Exod 34:29). Jesus' glory, unlike that of Moses, is not just reflected glory!

The reaction of the disciples, again articulated by Peter, shows their continuing obtuseness and fear in the face of what is taking place. Peter's address 'Rabbi' may point to a primitive account of the event or more likely to Mark's deliberate showing that Peter's faith is still underdeveloped, seeing Jesus as a rabbi who teaches in the tradition of Moses and the prophets, having not yet taken in the significance of the conversation at Caesarea Philippi or the event taking place around them at that moment. Peter says: 'It is good to be here.'[33] Does this refer to the three disciples, to the three disciples and Jesus, or to the three disciples, Jesus, Elijah and Moses? He goes on to say: 'Let us build three tents (skênai), one for you, one for Moses and one for Elijah.' (Moses precedes Elijah in this reference, confirming the fact that it was Mark's editing procedure that put Elijah first in the earlier reference, unlike the parallel synoptic accounts where Moses appears first.) The inappropriateness of the remark about building tents (booths) is highlighted by the narrator's comment: 'He did not know what to say, for they had become frightened.' Misunderstanding and fear, instead of understanding and faith, are again highlighted as the dominant reactions of the disciples.

What exactly had Peter in mind by offering to build tents (booths)?[34] He is suggesting the building of a permanent dwelling

---

33. Lit erally: 'It is good that we are here.'
34. St John's gospel speaks of the Word becoming flesh in terms of 'pitching tent among us', eskênôsen en hêmin (Jn 1:14).

place or shrine for the transfigured Jesus and his heavenly companions, to preserve the moment forever. It ignores the fact that they will have to come down from the mountain, leaving the extraordinary experience behind and face into the rigors of daily life as disciples and the fateful journey to Jerusalem and what it holds in store, in short, all that Jesus has said about his having to suffer rejection, ignominy and death. It also seems to put all three, Elijah, Moses and Jesus on a par, overlooking the unique identity of the Beloved Son (which the reader already knows, and the disciples are just about to be told).

The reference to the cloud that enveloped them recalls the intervention of God in the life of the people of Israel, the cloud by day in the desert, the cloud on Sinai, the cloud on the Tent of Meeting and the cloud covering the Temple at its dedication, associated also with the 'glory' of the Lord's presence.[35] The cloud became a circumlocution for God's presence, the *shekinah*, (from *shakan*, 'to dwell'). 'The cloud covered them,' appears to mean it covered Jesus, Moses and Elijah, as the disciples experienced the voice coming from out of the cloud.

The divine command: 'Listen to him!'
The voice comes out from the cloud just as on Sinai Moses heard the voice from out of the cloud (Ex 24:16) and Ezekiel heard the voice speaking in the vision in which the light of the glory of the Lord was like the bow in the clouds on a rainy day (Ezek 1:28). The voice of God commands them to listen to the Beloved Son, just as Israel's foundation creed begins with the commanded to: 'Listen, O Israel' (*shema' Israel*) and when the people were promised a prophet like Moses they were told: 'YHWH your God will raise up for you a prophet like myself, from among yourselves, from your own brothers; to him you must listen' (Deut 18:15). Jesus himself has many times called on them to listen. Now the voice of the Father identifies Jesus as 'my Son the Beloved' and instructs them to listen to him.

The truth of Jesus' messianic role and status as Son is confirmed by the voice from out of the cloud saying: 'This is my Beloved Son', a repetition of the words spoken at the baptism but this time spoken to the disciples in the context of a manifestation of his glory (the reader already overheard the address of the Father to the Son at the baptism). The heavenly voice raises

35. Exod 13:21f; 24:16; 33:7-11; 34:5; 40:34f; 1 Kings 8:10f; Ezek 1:28; 11:23.

Jesus above the prophets and shows him to be more than the 'prophet like Moses' (Deut 18:15, 18f) or the returned Elijah (Mal 4:5f), but far above both in that he is God's own Beloved Son to whom they are commanded to listen. This is very significant given the fact that soon the authoritative voices claiming to speak with the authority of the law (Moses) and of the prophets (Elijah) will accuse him of being a blasphemer at his trial precisely when he affirms that he is Son of the Blessed One. In doing so they will imply that he is a lawbreaker and a false prophet. They will reject him and his claims. However, their religious authority and judgement are rendered void in anticipation by the authority of the Father's voice from the cloud. This voice from heaven also, and very significantly, commands the disciples, the very people who such a short time previously found Jesus' teaching about the nature of his messianic role and the suffering it will entail so unacceptable, to 'listen to him.' It will be important also, not only for the characters in the story, but also for the readers of the gospel to listen to the voice of Jesus amid contending voices and claims.

The disciples then find themselves alone with Jesus in his usual state/form. The moment has passed. The reader wonders if the disciples have learned anything or come to a deeper understanding of Jesus and the good news. That has yet to be revealed by the narrator.

The injunction, as they came down the mountain, to tell no one what they had seen until the Son of Man is risen from the dead is sometimes seen as a fourth prediction of his resurrection, with his suffering and death implied (Mk 9:9). The injunction continues the 'messianic secret' theme and also links the experience with the future vindication of Jesus over death. Showing an ongoing failure to understand, the disciples seize on the saying and discuss among themselves what rising from the dead might mean.

Elijah and John the Baptist Mk 9:11-13
In an abrupt change of theme the disciples ask Jesus why the scribes say that Elijah must first come. The reference is very likely to the scribes' teaching about the prophecy in Malachi 4:4-6 which states: 'Remember the teaching of my servant Moses to whom at Horeb I prescribed laws and customs for the whole of Israel. Know that I am going to send you Elijah the prophet before the coming of the great and terrible day…' Mark, or an older

tradition or source, may well have had this passage in mind and wanted to show both the presence of Moses and Elijah together, and at the same time present this fleeting glimpse of Elijah as his promised reappearance. Mark therefore inserted the transfiguration between Jesus' assertion or promise that 'some standing here will not taste death till they see the kingdom of God come with power' and the disciples' question about the return of Elijah. This also may explain his being mentioned before Moses in the account of their appearance together. Maybe in an older tradition or source the disciples' question came immediately after Mk 9:1 where Jesus' promise would have caused them to wonder about the expected coming of Elijah 'before the great and terrible day of the Lord' as promised in Malachi 4:4-6.

As the text now stands, the return to the question of Elijah is an abrupt transition and leads to a different conclusion. Elijah returned, by inference, in the person of the Baptist (an association made quite explicit in Mt 17:9-13). Elijah was expected to carry on a mission of repentance and reform expressed in terms of turning the hearts of fathers to their children, a text applied specifically to John by Luke (Lk 1:17). John carried out such a mission of repentance which drew all Jerusalem and Judea to him confessing their sins. People also came from Galilee as one can see from the presence of Jesus. In addition Elijah had to suffer, as seen in the treatment and attempt on his life in 1 Kings 19:1-3, and John the Baptist suffered imprisonment and execution. Both Elijah and John prefigure the suffering about to fall on the Son of Man. They are forerunners, precursors in suffering just as in glory.

iii. Teaching when the Disciples failed to heal Mk 9:14-29

When Jesus and the three disciples came from the mountain and rejoined the other disciples, they entered into a situation fraught with argument and debate. On their arrival the crowd were astonished on seeing Jesus and they ran to greet him. The verb *ekthambeomai* appears in the New Testament only in Mark and signifies very great emotion. In Mk 14:33 it describes Jesus' overwhelming sorrow in Gethsemane, and in Mk 16:5, 6 it describes the astonishment of the women at finding the empty tomb and the young man in white sitting there. Here it signifies much more than their excitement at Jesus' anticipated or unexpected appearance. It re-echoes the reaction of the crowd to Moses when he came from the mountain reflecting the light of God's presence (Exod 34:29f).

The Disciples arguing with the Scribes: The Possessed Boy
A large crowd had gathered around the disciples and they were arguing with the scribes. When Jesus asked the subject of the argument, it was not the disciples or the scribes (who do not figure any further in the story) who answered but a nameless man in the crowd. He was the father of a 'possessed' boy and he immediately drew Jesus' attention to the failure of his disciples to heal him. His desperation caused him to regard as irrelevant the actual nature of the exchanges between the disciples and the scribes that arose on the occasion of their failure. This is a tantalising gap in the narrative. The disciples have failed in the very mission they were given, 'to have authority over unclean spirits' (Mk 6:7). Their earlier reporting to Jesus was a reciting of 'what they had done' (Mk 6:30), not 'what God had done through them'. Their arrogance has now been exposed, their pride has led them to a fall. The disciples were asked to perform the healing/exorcism because it was assumed they would exercise the same power as their master. He had, after all, sent them out to do this very work, and specifically to cast out demons, which they had failed to do. Were the scribes now jeering at their failure, saying it pointed back to their master, showing him to be a fraud? One can only speculate as the narrative does not deal with the issue and goes on to focus on the desperation of the parent describing the spirit of dumbness that took hold of his son and caused him to suffer symptoms similar to those we now associate with epilepsy.

In a reaction that parallels Jesus' reaction to the Syro-Phoenician woman (Mk 7:27) or to the royal official in John's gospel (Jn 4:48), Jesus responds with an apparently harsh reply which in turn brings a statement of faith from the petitioner. Jesus exclaims: 'You faithless generation, how much longer must I be with you?' However, he says 'with you', *pros hymas*, in the plural. Jesus' reaction of criticism targets a broader audience than the father or the disciples, as in the case of the royal official in Jn 4:4:48. Already the authorities have been shown to be hard of heart and the lack of faith in Jesus' home area resulted in his failure to work any miracles there. That was not because of a lack of power on his part but because of their lack of faith, which caused him astonishment (Mk 6:1-6). The failure of the disciples puts them in the company of those lacking in faith. As Jesus condemns 'this faithless generation' for their failure to respond, the reader recalls the Song of Moses in which he laments over the faithless people (Deut 32:20).[36]

As the man asks him for help, with the proviso 'if you can', Jesus responds that all things are possible to the one who has faith. This remark points first of all to Jesus and then to those open to sharing his faith, in this case to the father, who surpasses the disciples in openness to, and understanding of Jesus.

The story has the marks of a conflation of two original accounts. There are two crowds, the crowd already present, and the crowd that gathers. The boy's condition is described both as a demonic possession and also as an illness. There are two descriptions of the illness (Mk 9:18, 20), and though he is said to have a dumb spirit (Mk 9:17) and a deaf and dumb spirit (Mk 9:25), the illness is twice described in terms very similar to an epileptic seizure. The story therefore may be a conflation of more than one story. There is a focus on the need for faith for a healing in such circumstances, and a focus on the need for prayer. Two lines run through the story, the father's admission of his little faith together with his openness to Jesus in which he acquires strong faith, and the disciples' inability/lack of power, and their being associated by Jesus with the 'generation without faith' (and in the discussion that follows, with those without prayer).

The basic outline of the story is that of a miracle, a healing or exorcism story where a problem is presented, Jesus first reacts and then responds, the demon makes a determined show of strength which heightens the tension, then Jesus heals and/or exorcises the demon, the miracle is observed and causes admiration. However, in this case the story of the disciples' ineptitude and Jesus' instruction are woven into the story of the healing/exorcism. This means that the focus is not so much on the power of Jesus as on the lack of power on the part of the disciples and their failure in this case fits into the overall portrayal of their lack of understanding and underdeveloped faith. This furnishes Jesus with the opportunity of giving them an instruction on the source of power, as he points to their lack/neglect of prayer.

The father of the boy, unlike the disciples, recognises his own underdeveloped faith, and responds to Jesus', recognising his

---

36. At this point Mt 17:17 and Lk 9:41 use the term 'perverse' which is the actual term used in Deut 32:20.

shortcomings and asking for help: 'I do believe, help my unbelief.'

Asking the father how long the boy had suffered the recurring symptoms highlights the gravity of the case and the impressive nature of the cure. The gravity is further emphasised by the description of the 'seizures' and the reference to the danger of his being thrown down into fire or water. The problem is then graphically illustrated by the violent seizure that actually takes place as Jesus is in conversation with the father. As in the case of the healing of Peter's mother-in-law and the raising of Jairus' daughter, the language used in the healing/exorcism is resurrection language. After the boy had taken on the aspect of a corpse and the onlookers proclaimed he was dead, 'Jesus took him by the hand and raised him up.' Jesus healed him, not only of the current attack, but ordered the spirit not to enter him again.

Jesus' Teaching
In spite of the disciples' failure, Jesus keeps them 'with him' and continues to instruct them privately, indoors. In response to their question about being unable to heal the boy/to cast out the demon, Jesus told them that this kind can be driven out only by prayer.[37] Jesus himself spent time in prayer, in communion with the Father who sent him. The disciples need to learn the same lesson about the source of power.

The Way: Stage Two
Galilee, Judea and beyond the Jordan
Mk 9:30-10:31

1. SECOND PREDICTION OF THE PASSION MK 9:30-31

Beginning with a reference to leaving that place and making their way through Galilee, the theme of journeying towards Jerusalem is kept in play. Now, however, the emphasis is very heavily on Jesus' private instruction of the disciples, so no one is to know his whereabouts. 'He was instructing his disciples.'

37. Some mss such as Vaticanus and Sinaiticus add 'and fasting'. This probably reflects the early church's emphasis on prayer and fasting. Maybe also it is a spelling out of what is seen as the proper dispositions for prayer, as prayer and fasting regularly went together as a single spiritual/penitential exercise.

The instruction again begins with a prediction of the passion, his second and shortest prediction. 'The Son of Man will be delivered into the hands of men; they will put him to death and three days after he has been put to death he will rise again' (Mk 9:30). It is introduced with *edidasken*, the imperfect tense signifying an ongoing or repeated teaching activity. The 'persecutors' are not specified as 'the elders, the chief priests and the scribes,' but simply as 'men' (human beings). Similarly the verb *paradidômi*, 'hand over', is used in a general sense here, not yet in its specific sense of 'betrayal' by Judas. The general nature of the prediction and the (divine?) passive 'handed over' seems to refer to God's divine plan rather than to any specific human agency. Some scholars speculate that this may be the most primitive form of the prediction which has been expanded in the other two predictions, while others think that they are three independent primitive sayings. As already noted these predictions serve a similar function to the references to the hour (*hôra*) and the time (*kairos*) of Jesus in John's gospel where his *hour* and his *time* signify his glorification when he will be lifted up from the earth and draw all to himself. There are many references in John to the hostility Jesus experienced which result in the desire to arrest, stone, interrogate and kill him, a desire frustrated throughout the gospel until his *hour/time* had come.

2. REACTION OF THE DISCIPLES MK 9:32

Again the disciples show their inability to understand, their confusion and fear, for 'they were afraid to ask'. Were they afraid of a possibly frustrated Jesus reacting in anger at their obtuseness, as already they were afraid to let him know about their shortage of bread in the boat, or were they afraid of what they were beginning to suspect may happen in Jerusalem, as appears to be the case in Mk 10:32 when they display fear along the road?

3. TEACHING ON DISCIPLESHIP MK 9:33-10:31

'Leaving from there and making their way through Galilee' further emphasises the journey motif. The use of the imperfect tense in 'continued teaching … and saying' emphasises the ongoing, continuous teaching activity of Jesus during the journey. Another milestone in the journey is signalled as they come to Capernaum.

i. Instructing the Twelve

When they were in the house Jesus asked them what they had been arguing about on the way. The private nature of Jesus' instruction is highlighted by his being in the house with the disciples, his sitting down and calling the Twelve to him, and his inquiring into their own 'internal' discussion/dispute. They are supposed to be on the way to Jerusalem and all that it entails by way of preparation for sharing in Jesus' rejection, suffering, death and resurrection, but they still think in terms of some kind of messianic kingdom in which they will achieve recognition and status. The instruction that follows is a collection of sayings illustrating Jesus' teaching on discipleship (Mk 9:33-37). His teaching role is emphasised with the reference to his sitting position, the official position for those 'in the chair of Moses'.

The disciples' discussion 'on the way' was about personal status and importance in the group. Jesus asked them what they were discussing 'on the way' but was answered with an embarrassed (or obstinate?) silence. Silence can result from embarrassment or it can be used as a strategy. When Jesus put the question about doing good or evil on the Sabbath to his critics in the synagogue they responded with a silence that Jesus read as thorough obstinacy, a hostile passive aggression (Mk 3:1-6). Here the silence is possibly due to embarrassment before Jesus and also through inner tensions in the group.

The two references to 'on the way' highlight for the reader, who knows well that they are 'on the way' to an ominous encounter in Jerusalem, the fact that the disciples are exceedingly 'out of touch' as they discuss the pecking order of importance among themselves. Jesus countered their idea of greatness with a description of greatness which was as foreign to them as the idea of a powerless, suffering Messiah.

Whoever wishes ...
After the first prediction of the passion Jesus spoke of the need to deny oneself and to take up one's cross. Now after the second prediction he speaks of the need to serve. True greatness, being first, belongs to the one who considers the other rather than the self, and seeks to serve the other. 'If anyone wishes (*ei tis thelei*) to be first, he/she shall be last of all and servant of all' (Mk 9:35). This 'saying' or *logion* of Jesus was probably a *logion* floating in the tradition without a remembered context and used here to il-

THE GOSPEL OF MARK

lustrate the teaching. Variations on this *logion* are found in Mt 23:11, 'the greatest among you must be your servant' and in Lk 22:26, 'the greatest among you must behave as if he/she were the youngest, the leader as if he/she were the one who serves.'[38] Mark returns to this theme in the instruction following the third prediction of the passion, when he reacts to the ambition of the sons of Zebedee: 'Anyone who wants to become great among you must be your servant, and anyone who wants to be first among you must be slave to all' (Mk 10:43//Mt 20:26).

Following the saying about being last of all and servant of all, Jesus illustrates his message with his placing a child in their midst, whom he embraces, and then says: 'anyone who accepts (*hos an ... dexêtai*) one of these little children in my name, accepts me.'[39] The mark of genuine humility and service is being of service to those who are unimportant, poor and inconsequential in the eyes of the world and who are therefore not in a position to reciprocate one's service or generosity.

The child was the outstanding example of a person without influence or means, and to 'accept' or 'receive' the child, in the sense of rendering service to the child is the great example of the person who opts out of a system of status, show and expectation of reward or recognition, to be of service to the little ones. The term 'accept' or ' receive' is used four times in the one verse (Mk 9:37). The emphasis is on the acceptance of the little child in my name (*epi tô onomati mou*). Welcoming the little child in Jesus' name points to the fact that these 'little ones' belong to Jesus, a fact highlighted in the last judgement scene in Matthew's gospel where Jesus uses the term 'little ones' in a transferred sense for all his followers who are without worldly power and influence: 'In so far as you did it to one of the least of my brothers you did it to me / in so far as you neglected to do this to one of the least of my brothers you neglected to do it to me.' (Mt 25:40, 45). Further on in the instruction Jesus again uses the example of the child, this time as a model of openness and acceptance in the face of the kingdom (Mk 10:14f).

---

38. A similar example of a floating *logion*, maybe a variation of the same *logion*, is used in Mt 20:16 in the context of the labourers in the vineyard.
39. Some scholars, following Matthew Black, *An Aramaic Approach to the Gospels and Acts*, 218-23, see an original pun in Aramaic on the word *talya* which can mean child or servant (or lamb) and so forming a link with ' servant' in the *logion* in the previous verse.

Whoever accepts …
'The one who accepts' functions as a link phrase with the next *logion*. Jesus now states that the one who accepts him accepts the One who sent him (Mk 9:37). It is a basic tenet of political, social, synagogue and church practice that the one sent, the emissary, ambassador or apostle is treated with the respect due to the one who sends him/her. To deny such respect and acceptance is to deny respect to the one who sent the emissary.[40]

'In my name' now serves as a linking phrase with John's complaint about the 'unofficial exorcist' who casts out demons in Jesus' name'.

In Jesus' name: The Unofficial Exorcist Mk 9:38-40

John poses the question about the 'unofficial' use of Jesus' name in the exorcisms carried out by someone who 'did not follow them'. There is a great irony in the story. The 'official' disciples/apostles who earlier boasted to Jesus of what they had done, without any reference to 'in Jesus' name' or 'by God's power', are now confronted with the situation of someone who was not an 'official' disciple/apostle but who is succeeding in casting out demons 'in Jesus' name', the very thing they had so recently failed to do when approached by the distressed parent of the possessed/epileptic boy. Probably they saw that person as a threat to the status they were already discussing. In fact John's complaint, stated twice, is 'He did not follow us,' that is 'He was not a follower of ours.' Probably they felt that person should have consulted them, even done the work in their name. Significantly they did not say to Jesus, 'He is not one of yours, he did not follow you, you did not commission him.' Jesus responds that anyone who works a miracle in his name is unlikely soon afterwards to speak ill of him. Jesus then uses another *logion*, which also may have floated about in the tradition and been given a definite context here by Mark. The *logion*, 'He who is not against us is for us' fits the context very well. There is an interesting parallel in the Book of Numbers in the story of Eldad and Medad who prophesied 'unofficially' in the camp of the Israelites. Joshua asked Moses to stop them but he replied that it would be desirable if all God's people were prophets with the spirit of the Lord upon them (Num 11:26-29).

40. This is a central theme of St John's gospel where it is strongly emphasised that rejection of the one sent results from not knowing, not hearing and not obeying the Father who sent him.

In Jesus' Name: Generosity in Jesus' name Mk 9:41
'In the name' again provides the link for another *logion*, concerning service and generosity to one of Christ's followers. The
solemnity of the pronouncement is emphasised with 'amen, I
say to you'. 'If any person (*hos gar an*) should give you a cup of
water because you belong to the Christ, (lit. in the name that you
are of the Christ), amen I say to you, that person will certainly
not (*ou mê*) lose his/her reward.'

The Little Ones: Scandal Mk 9:42-48
'Little ones' is the link with the next *logion* about scandalising
'the little ones who are believers.' It picks up on the theme of
children mentioned above. 'Scandalise' is a verb related to the
noun 'scandal' which means in Greek a stone that causes someone to trip on the way. Applied to a person's life it means something that causes one to lose faith, to fall into sin, and in this context here, where the whole passage deals with discipleship, it
means to cause one to trip up on the path of discipleship. To do
so is a very serious matter, and it is graphically described as
being worse than drowning in the sea with a donkey's millstone
round one's neck.[41] Drowning was a form of capital punishment
practised by the Romans, and not unknown in Galilee.[42] Jesus is
pointing out that execution is better than scandalising the little
ones.
     'Scandalising' or 'causing one to stumble' is the link with the
next *logion* or group of *logia*. Following the capital punishment
of drowning, Jesus follows through on other forms of punishment such as deprivation of hand, foot and eye (Mk 9:45-47) and
says they are preferable to 'stumbling'.[43] Mentioning the hand,

---

41. *Mulos onikos*, a donkey's millstone, i.e. a large millstone turned by a
donkey.
42. Josephus *,Ant* XIV,15.10.
43. Josephus speaks of cutting off the hands for forgery and sedition,
Life 34f; *War II*, 21:10. D. Derrett, *Studies in the New Testament*, I, 4-31,
points out that these punishments were known in other nations. Loss of
hand or foot was a punishment for theft, and of eyes for adultery.
Donohue and Harrington, *op. cit.*, 290, point to the discussion among
some moral theologians who see in these references a connection with
rabbinic teaching as seen in the Babylonian Talmud, *b. Niddah* 13b,
about sexual sins of child abuse (the little ones), masturbation (the
hand), adultery (the foot), lustful glances (the eye). See R. F. Collins,
Sexual Ethics and the New Testament: Behaviour and Belief, New York:

the foot and the eye, all three essential to life in the world, Jesus points out in three similar statements that if any one of them is a cause for leading one into sin it would be better for that person to be at the loss of it and living in the kingdom than able-bodied and excluded from it. Hand, foot and eye together seem to have been regarded as the basic essentials for healthy living. Job, for example, sees the health of the person in terms of purity of eyes, foot and hands (Job 31:1, 5, 7). Loss of any or all of them is therefore a serious loss of life, but it is preferable to loss of life in the kingdom. The sayings are a general statement on the cost of discipleship, in the words of F. J. Moloney: 'The sayings are, therefore, a strong affirmation of the life offered by following Jesus, cost what it may.'[44]

It is possible that Mark meant the sayings here to have also a communal application in relation to removing certain members from the community. Commentators point to the widespread use of the body as a metaphor for the functioning of a social unit or organisation. The Roman general Agrippa used it to restore harmony in the army during the threat of a mutiny. St Paul used it in his discussions on the community as the body of Christ, and his appeals for the community to work in harmony as the parts of the human body (1 Cor 12:12-26). Paul also advocated the expulsion of certain elements from the body, the community, lest they corrupt the whole (cf 1 Cor 5:1-5).

The opposite to entering into the kingdom is 'going away' (*apelthein*) to Gehenna or 'being cast', *blêthênai*, into Gehenna, the former used once, the latter twice for the damnation to Gehenna 'where the worm will not die nor the fire go out.'[45] Gehenna is a name derived from the Valley of Hinnom, a deep gorge that surrounded Jerusalem on the southern and western sides, adjoining the village of Silwan/Siloam. It had a notorious reputation in

Crossroads,2000, 62-72 and W. Deming, 'Mark 9:42-10:12, Matthew 5:27-32 and *B.Nid* 13b: A First-Century Discussion of Male Sexuality,' *NTS* 36 (1990), 130-41. Donohue and Harrington are in agreement with R. E. Collins, however, that as Mark uses these sayings here they convey a general statement about discipleship rather than a comment on specific sins.

44. F. J. Moloney, *op. cit.*, 191, n.93.

45. The quotation from Isa 66:24 in verse 48 about the unquenchable fire and the worm that dies not was included by some scribes after the warnings in verses 43 and 45. The better mss exclude them, i.e., they omit verses 44 and 46.

the time of the Judean kings as the forbidden religious rituals were performed at a forbidden 'high place', the Topheth, where even human sacrifices by fire were carried out (2 Chron 28:3; 33:6; Jer 7:31; 32:35). Jeremiah had issued a devastating oracle against it which gave rise in time to the imagery of hell as the place of death, fire and abandonment where sinners go for punishment (1 Enoch 27:2; 4 Ezra 7:36, Mt 5:22, 29f; 23:33; Lk 12:5). Jeremiah complained:

> And they go on building the high place of Topheth, which is in the valley of the son of Hinnom, to burn their sons and their daughters in the fire ... the days are coming, says the Lord, when it will no more be called Topheth or the valley of the son of Hinnom, but the valley of Slaughter ... the corpses of this people will be food for the birds of the air, and for the beasts of the earth, and none will frighten them away ... and they shall not be gathered or buried; they shall be as dung on the surface of the ground. Death shall be preferred to life by all the remnant that remains of this evil family ... (Jer 7:31-8:3).

The reference to the fire that does not go out and the worm that does not die comes from a similarly devastating oracle at the end of the Book of Isaiah describing the fate of those who have rebelled against YHWH. It comes in the context of the eschatological ingathering of the peoples, both Jew and Gentile, at the appearance of the new heaven and the new earth. The enemies of YHWH will not just be annihilated they will be subjected to eternal punishment.

> From new moon to new moon, and from Sabbath to Sabbath, all flesh shall come to worship before me, says the Lord. And they shall go forth and see the dead bodies of the people who have rebelled against me; for their worm shall not die, their fire shall not be quenched; and they shall be an abhorrence to all flesh (Isa 66:23f).[46]

The concept of fire and worms as instruments of punishment are spelled out in the description of the day of judgement in Judith.

> Woe to the nations who rise against my people! The Lord Almighty will take vengeance on them on judgement day. He will send fire and worms in their flesh and they shall weep with pain for evermore (Jdt 16:17).

The teaching of Jesus on the heinous nature of scandal, causing

---

46. The allusion to Isa 66:23f is omitted from the parallel passage in Mt 18:8f.

others to lose faith, is highlighted by drawing on these graphic descriptions and allusions to the punishment awaiting the scandal givers. The loss of some faculty or advantage in life pales before the heinous crime of scandal and the punishment it deserves.

Fire and Salt Mk 9:49-50

The reference to fire serves as a link with the next three sayings, all dealing with the imagery of salt and its uses. The first 'salt' saying, 'Everyone will be salted with fire,' draws on the imagery of salt which can be used as a purifying agent or disinfectant and its effects are here compared to those of the purifying effects of fire. The biblical imagery of gold tested in the fire, signifying the testing of character in tribulation, comes to mind. Sirach wrote: 'Gold is tested in the fire and those found acceptable in the furnace of humiliation' (Sir 2:5; cf Ezek 16:4; 43:24). As salt purifies and disinfects, it destroys impurities but it preserves life and health. The followers of Jesus will be tested in many ways in the world, not least in suffering and persecution. The purifying effects of the testing, the *peirasmos*, will prepare them for their reception of the kingdom and ultimately for the eschatological judgement when the Son of Man comes to gather the elect.

The copyists may have had difficulty in understanding the exact meaning of this saying for there are a number of variant readings which interpret it by way of reference to the use of salt in sacrifice: 'Every sacrifice will be salted with fire.' This smacks of a testing of the nature of worship to see that it reflects the genuine dispositions of the worshipper.

The second salt saying states: 'Salt is good, but if the salt becomes insipid, how will you season it?' 'Salt is good' is almost an understatement since salt is needed for the proper functioning of the body and its vital presence in the body is witnessed in blood, sweat and tears. In New Testament times before the invention of the refrigerator it was vital for preserving food and keeping it healthy and edible. Salt also seasons food and makes it palatable and attractive to eat. It was used also to preserve wounds from becoming infected. So vital was it that soldiers were often paid in part with a ration of salt, hence the saying 'worth one's salt', and the modern term 'salary'. The imagery points to the follower of Christ as a person who is penetrated with the life, vision and message of Christ. Such a person's spiritual presence, expressing itself in teaching and example is an agent of health and preservation in society, and it 'seasons' living with the good news of the kingdom made known in Jesus' ministry. Such a presence and influence are aptly described as 'salt of the earth' in the Sermon on the Mount in Matthew (Mt 5:13). Salt actually never becomes insipid in itself but if it is 'watered down' sufficiently it loses its effectiveness. So too, there is nothing 'insipid' about the following of Christ, but if the following is 'watered down' it loses its effectiveness.

Finally, the third saying, 'Have salt among yourselves and be at peace with one another' alludes to the ritual use of salt in making covenants with one another to maintain hospitality and peace in the community, which reflect the covenant with God maintained and celebrated through sacrificial worship (Mk 9:50).[47] In middle-eastern culture to this day, eating bread and salt with someone signifies the forming of a friendship and a bond of mutual respect and help for life.

ii. Instructing Pharisees, Disciples and the Crowd Mk 10:1-10:31

Again the journey motif is stressed as Jesus leaves that place and comes (*erchetai*) into the regions of Judea and beyond the Jordan.[48] The crowds again gather/come together to him (*synporeuontai*). The use of the historic present gives the narrative a vivid character and involves the reader. The well established pattern of his teaching the crowds is emphasised by the use of the imperfect 'he was teaching' (*edidasken*) and reinforced by 'as was his custom' (*eiôthei*). The second use of 'again' (*palin*), 'he was again teaching them (the crowds)' is due to the fact that for most of the journey to Jerusalem so far his teaching has been concentrated on the disciples.

The Pharisees and Divorce Mk 10:1-12
The Pharisees questioned him (or, according to some manuscripts, an indefinite *they* questioned him) about divorce.[49]

47. 'salt of the covenant with God.' cf Lev 2:13a; Num 18:19; 2 Chron 13:5.
48. The mss have slight variations 'regions of Judea and beyond the Jordan', 'regions of Judea beyond the Jordan' and 'regions of Judea through beyond the Jordan'. This is a longer route but was regarded as safer because they saw Samaria as bandit country. cf Josephus, *Antiquities* 20:118; *Jewish War*, 2:232.
49. R. F. Collins, *Sexual Ethics and the New Testament: Behaviour and Belief*, New York, Crossroads, 2000, 22-41; See also R. F. Collins, *Divorce in the New Testament*, Collegeville: The Liturgical Press, 1992

However, the reference to Pharisees here is in harmony with the parallel passage in Mt 19:3 and also reflects the concerns about divorce which were a live issue among the Pharisees at the time. There was a divergence of opinion on the grounds for divorce between the strict school of Shammai and the more liberal school of Hillel. The question was not a genuine seeking of opinion or knowledge. It was a 'testing' of him in a negative way. This is very obvious when Jesus responds by asking them what it says in the law and they immediately respond with exact scriptural knowledge of Moses' regulation in Deut 24:1 about drawing up a writ of dismissal and so, by implication, allowing divorce. They already knew the answer but hoped to show him up as being unorthodox in his teaching or attitude and opposed to scripture with regard to Moses' prescription about the provision of a writ (certificate) of divorce. In Deut 24:1-4 Moses is not actually giving an instruction on divorce itself. He is in fact forbidding the first husband from remarrying his former wife if she has contracted another marriage in the meantime and has been subsequently divorced or widowed.

The writ of divorce was a legal document showing the proof that the marriage had ended and the husband had no further legal rights. The former wife had protection from further claims on his part (as for example, concerning financial matters like a dowry). The writ showed a prospective new husband that the woman was free to marry again and protected him also from any claims of the first husband.

Seeing the prescription of Moses as a compromise made necessary by their 'hardness of heart' (*sklêrokardia*), Jesus appeals to the scriptures that deal with creation where the ideal of marriage is laid down. In this he is not attacking either the scriptures or Moses since the creation accounts were also part of the Book of Moses, the Torah. 'Hardness of heart' is mentioned here by Mark and also by Matthew in the parallel passage where Jesus comments on divorce (Mt 19:8). The term captures the idea frequently used in the Old Testament for resistance to God's word or plan, as in the case of Pharaoh who refused to let the people go from Egypt or in the case of the Israelites in the desert when they hardened their hearts at Meriba, as recalled in Psalm 94 (95), a prayer in which the people are asked not to harden their hearts.

Moses' concession to human weakness or hardness of heart is countered by Jesus' appeal to the ideal enshrined in creation. Jesus has come to restore the harmony of creation, as seen from his 'being with the wild beasts and the angels ministering to him'(Mk 1:13). He counters Moses' 'allowing' divorce (in a society of hardened hearts where it was necessary to ensure that the divorced partner be treated with justice), with a clear statement of what God 'willed' in creation.

Mark records Jesus' recourse to Gen 1:27 and 2:24, 'God made them male and female', and 'That is why a man leaves his father and mother (and joins himself to his wife) and they become one body.'[50] He adds that they are no longer two but one body. What God has joined man must not separate. He is in fact re-establishing the ideal and re-anchoring the definition of marriage. After the public discussion, when Jesus is alone with the disciples in the house, he tells them that divorcing a wife or husband and remarrying is committing adultery.

The Pharisees most likely came to contend with Jesus on the issue of divorce because they knew his position. This is a reasonable assumption from their attitude, though Jesus has not already spoken on the issue in this gospel. Following the public exchange with the Pharisees Jesus goes indoors and explains to the disciples in the house that marriage to a divorced person is adultery. However, he makes an equal case for men and women, implying that women can initiate divorce. This raises a question about the audience for whom Mark is writing and interpreting Jesus' message. In the Palestine of Jesus' day women did not initiate divorce. They were the vulnerable partner. It was not so in Rome and the Roman cities under Italian law which gave them the same system as the mother city. There huge changes in the role, status and legal rights of women had taken place since the inception of the empire, and powerful Roman matrons regularly divorced their husbands. The implication in both cases is that a more powerful or influential partner, whether that be the man or the woman, does the other an injustice, and the person marrying that person who has been put away compounds that injustice.

Women in Roman society had traditionally played a role of subservience to men. The patriarchal organisation of society had its *paterfamilias* at the centre with rights and duties in regard to the womenfolk. But this had changed with the death of the Republic and by the second century AD nothing but the memory

---

50. Some mss of Mark omit the words 'and be joined to his wife'. The omission is probably due to a mistake on the part of a copyist, since it leaves the quotation unfinished.

remained of the principles on which the patriarchal family of ancient Rome had been based, relationship through the male line
(*agnatio*) and the unlimited power of the *paterfamilias*.[51]

Relationship, however, was now recognised through female
descent and extended beyond legitimate marriage. Traditional
moral values of family life and marital fidelity fell simultaneously
with the old order. Augustus reacted with his programme for
moral reform, the Julian Laws. They were unsuccessful against a
tide of 'liberalisation' and the creation of legal fictions to avoid
their enforcement.[52] Horace did the public relations work for
their success with his 'Roman Odes', highlighting traditional
moral values in love and marriage, but Juvenal's satires are an
equally eloquent testimony to the onward march of 'liberalisation' and ' feminism'.[53] The adding of the prohibition against
the woman initiating divorce has all the marks of an adjustment
or 'spelling out' of the implications of Jesus' teaching on divorce
for a (Greco-)Roman society very different to that in Palestine.

Jesus and the Children Mk 10:13-16
Having dealt with Jesus' attitude to husbands and wives in the
marriage and divorce discussion, it is a natural step to follow on
with his attitude to the children. The people were bringing
children to him so that he might touch them, since blessing
could be obtained by contact with the holy person through an
action like the laying on of hands or through the invocation by
the holy one of a blessing from God.[54]

The lack of understanding on the part of the disciples is again
in evidence as they try to stop the people from bringing the
children to Jesus. The severe expression 'they rebuked them',
epetimêsan autois, is used, emphasising their obtuseness. Jesus reacts angrily. He had similarly strong reactions of anger, compas-

51. J. Carcopino, *Everyday Life in Ancient Rome*, Eng Trans., 1956, 89; M.
Cary, *A History of Rome*, 456f; M. Mullins, *Called To Be Saints: Christian
Living in First Century Rome*, Dublin, Veritas, 1991, 17-19.
52. J. J. O'Rourke, 'Roman Law and the Early Church', *The Catacombs
and the Colosseum*, ed S. Benko and J. J. O'Rourke, 180.
53. *Ibid*.
54. This story of Jesus and the children has been consistently used as an
argument in favour of infant baptism. See J. Jeremias, *Infant Baptism in
the First Four Centuries*, Philadelphia: Westminster, 1962; F. Beisser,
'Markus 10:13-16 (parr) – doch ein Text für die Kindertaufe,' *Kerygma
und Dogma* 41 (1995), 244-51.

sion or frustration on encountering the leper (Mk 1:43), on seeing the stubbornness of his critics when he asked about healing
the man with the withered hand in the synagogue on the
Sabbath (Mk 3:5), on being challenged by the Pharisees to show
a sign from heaven (Mk 8:12), on complaining to the disciples
that they failed to see the significance of the two multiplications
of the loaves (Mk 8:17-21) and when they failed to heal the boy
with the spirit of dumbness (Mk 9:19). Now he is provoked to
anger by their obtuseness in stopping the people bringing the
children to him.

As Jesus rebuked them for preventing the children coming to
him, he told them that the reason for his displeasure at their action in stopping the children was because 'of such is the kingdom of God.' 'Amen, I say to you' introduces his solemn pronouncement that anyone who does not receive the kingdom of
God like a child may not enter it. Whereas earlier the attitude *towards* the child was the subject of Jesus' teaching, here the subject is the attitude *of* the child. The child's attitude to parents,
family, society and the world is one of dependence and vulnerability. The child receives everything as gift, earns nothing and so
depends on others for food, clothes, protection and all the other
necessities of life. The child makes no display of self sufficiency,
much less of arrogance. The child's whole life is one series of re-
ceptive activities, seeing, hearing, touching as it embraces the
world. In the face of the kingdom we are all like children because we are all receivers and should display attitudes of receptivity, dependence and humility, rather than self sufficiency,
righteousness and arrogance.[55]

Jesus proceeded with the activity the disciples had tried to
prevent as he took the children in his arms and blessed them,
laying his hands on them.

iii. Obstacles to Discipleship.Riches and Poverty Mk 10:17-31

This is the longest single treatment of an ethical issue in this
gospel. It was probably put together from four elements that
were separate before being edited together by Mark. They illustrate important aspects of wealth, poverty and status. First of all
the story of the rich man shows how a good, pious, law abiding

---

55. This attitude is summed up in the first beatitude in Matthew's
Sermon on the Mount: 'Blessed are the poor in spirit, theirs is the kingdom of heaven' (Mt 5:3).

Jew finds the attraction of wealth too strong to give it away and become a benefactor of the poor and a disciple of Jesus (Mk 10:17-22). Secondly Jesus instructs his disciples on how difficult it is for the rich to enter the kingdom of God (Mk 10:23-27). Thirdly Jesus promises the disciples a hundredfold reward for following him and forsaking the things of the world, while also predicting persecution (Mk 10:28-30). Fourthly there is the *logion* about being first and last and how these positions will be reversed (Mk 10:31).

The Rich Young Man Mk 10:17-22

'Setting out on the way' reminds the reader again of the journey on which Jesus and the disciples are embarked. 'A certain man' (*eis*) ran up and, like the leper in Mk 1:40, knelt before him.[56] He asked him: 'Good master (teacher) what shall I do to inherit eternal life?'

Jesus' response, 'Why do you call me good? No one is good but God alone!' leaves the reader asking what he meant. Is it a criticism or a probing question? If it is a criticism, did he suspect an insincere motive such as flattery or hostile intent as in an attempt to lead him into a thorny discussion? Or is it a critical reaction on Jesus' part to an apparent over equating of the one sent with the God who sent him? On the other hand, since 'good' is applied to other than God in the OT, as for example it is applied to all aspects of creation in the creation account (Gen 1:4, 10, 12, 18 *et al.*) it is unlikely that the question or criticism arises from seeing Jesus as 'good' in an 'ordinary' sense of the word. It obviously touches on the goodness that belongs to God alone.

If, on the other hand, it is not a rebuke but a probing question designed to make the young man reflect more deeply on his intuition about Jesus, it could be seen as an invitation or challenge to probe further the real relationship between Jesus and God.[57] This may well be the case since 'good' (*agathos*) in this context could well mean something like 'gracious', reflecting God's faithful loving kindness, truth and compassion,[58] the unique aspects of God's covenant relationship with the people which the young man may have seen reflected in Jesus' ministry.

---

56. The parallel passage in Mt 19:22 has ' a young man / a youth / an adolescent (*neaniskos*); Lk 18:18 has 'a ruler' (*archôn*).
57. See J. C. O'Neill, '"Good Master" and the "Good" Sayings in the Teaching of Jesus', *Irish Biblical Studies* 15 (1993), 167-78.
58. *hesed* and *emet/charis, alêtheia, eleos.*

Jesus spells out for the young man the commandments of the Decalogue which cover actions towards other people, not, interestingly, the ones dealing with attitudes or actions directed towards God. F. J. Moloney points out that:

> These are the commandments that a rich man might be prone to violate. Ritual obligations toward God may be in place (see Exod 20:2-10; Deut 5:6-15), but one's weaker neighbour is dealt with sinfully. However, this is not the case; the man replies that he has always lived according to these commandments, from his youth.[59]

On hearing his reply Jesus' attitude now changes from questioning, possibly somewhat harshly, and laying down the law, to admiration and affection for a person who has kept the commandments all his life. Now he poses the great challenge to a man who has much wealth (*chrêmata*) and many possessions (*ktêmata*).[60] He tells him to sell what he has, give to the poor and have treasure in heaven and 'come follow me'. This is a call to discipleship like that issued at the beginning of the gospel to the two pairs of brothers and to Levi. They left everything and followed Jesus. This man failed to rise to the challenge and leave everything to become a disciple because of his wealth, and went away sad.

This call to poverty in Mark's gospel is not a call to asceticism as such, or to a hostile attitude or approach to the things of the world, but rather a call to the itinerant lifestyle of an apostle, as pointed out by J. R. Donahue and D. J. Harrington:

> Being with Jesus and sharing in his mission of teaching and healing demand the adoption of the simplest possible way of life ('one staff, no bread, no bag, no money') and subordinating one's personal comfort to the mission. The kind of poverty envisioned in Mark's gospel is apostolic or mission-oriented rather than ascetic in the sense that self-denial becomes an end in itself. The man's rejection of Jesus' invitation arises from his unwillingness to adopt the simple and itinerant lifestyle suited to Jesus' ministry and the conditions of first-century Palestine.[61]

---

59. F. J. Moloney, *op. cit.*, 199.
60. The mss differ in their use of *chrêmata* or *ktêmata* at this point.
61. J. R. Donahue and D. J. Harrington, *op. cit.*, 307.

Jesus' Teaching on Riches Mk 10:23-27

Jesus looked around at his disciples and spoke of the problem of riches. The word *chrêmata*, wealth/riches, is stronger than the word *ktêmata*, possessions, and has the connotation of the pressures put on some by wealth which needs protection, care, planning and general expenditure of time and energy, distracting from more important aspects of life and living. Furthermore wealth has an addictive character making one seek more and more. Paul used the term *pleonexia*, avarice, the need for more that is never satisfied, which he describes as *eidôlolatria*, idolatory (Col 3:5; cf Mk 7:22).[62] The biblical 'remedy' for wealth was to use it for good purposes, such as the relief of poverty. In biblical thought the good person prospers and becomes a benefactor, 'making friends with the mammon of iniquity', ensuring a welcome in the kingdom from the recipients of one's generosity (Job 1:1-5; 29:1-25; Lk 16:9). There follows from this the understanding that 'the poor' are privileged in so far as they, unlike the rich, are not enslaved to wealth and worldliness and so Luke can write, 'Blessed are you poor' and 'Woe to you who are rich …' (Lk 6:20, 24). The receptivity of the poor to the gift of God is seen in the Magnificat: 'He puts down the mighty from their thrones and raises the lowly/He fills the starving with good things, and sends the rich away empty' (Lk 1:52f).

The image of the camel passing through the eye of a needle is as striking as it is hyperbolic. But it is no mere hyperbole. It states a plain fact. Riches are a diriment impediment to entry into the kingdom. Suggestions that the eye of the needle is a gate in the walls of Jerusalem through which the camels had great difficulty in passing, or the replacing of the word 'camel' (*kamêlon*) with the word 'rope' (*kamilon*) in some mss serve only to rob the image of its powerful effect. F. J. Moloney sums up:

> The practical examples of marriage (10:1-12) and possessions (10:17-22) teach that God's ways are unlike human ways. All human effort to enter the kingdom is like trying to get a camel through the eye of a needle. It cannot be done. For human beings, entry into the kingdom is impossible, but God sees to it that even the impossible becomes possible: all things (*panta*) are possible with God. The 'all things' must be taken seriously.[63]

62. Mark includes avarice in the list of evils that come out of a person (Mk 7:22).
63. F. J. Moloney, *op. cit.*, 202.

The call to poverty in Mark differs from that in Luke-Acts with its emphasis on ideal communities sharing all goods in common. It is a poverty geared in a very practical way towards an itinerant missionary life. It is very well described by J. R. Donahue and D. J. Harrington:

> The kind of poverty promoted by Mark and other NT writers is not simply monastic community of goods or a primitive form of communism as envisioned in the Qumran *Rule of the Community*. Rather it is first and foremost poverty undertaken voluntarily in the service of proclaiming and witnessing to the kingdom of God. It is intended to contribute to an appreciation of the centrality of God's kingdom by minimising the distractions involved in becoming and staying rich, and it promises rewards not only in the world to come but also in the present. Mark's addition of 'with persecutions' in 10:30, however, is a sobering reminder of the reality of the world in which Mark's community lived and worked ...[64]

iv. The Reward of Discipleship Mk 10:28-31

This section is a response to Peter's question to Jesus asking about the disciples' reward for leaving everything to follow him. Jesus promises that their reward will be experienced both in this life and in the age to come. Responding with the solemn formula, 'Amen I say to you', he promises that their leaving of house, brothers, sisters, fathers, mothers, children or land 'for my sake and the gospel's sake' would be rewarded a hundredfold with houses, brothers, sisters, mothers, children and land in this life and with eternal life in the world to come. The replacement of natural family with 'spiritual' family may well reflect the emergence of the house churches and communities where equality among members as brothers and sisters, and the presence of mothering care replaces the patriarchal authoritarian structure of family life. The 'new' family as described by Jesus does not mention the father figure! Neither did his statement about his family being those who do the will of God (Mk 3:34). Maybe it is because the new community will have no father but their Father in heaven! The community thus formed will however, suffer persecution!

Having or sharing a heritage has a well established history in the bible. The LXX uses *meros* to translate the Hebrew *hêleq*, her-

---

64. J. R. Donahue and D. J. Harrington, *op. cit.*, 308.

itage. Originally it referred to the God-given heritage of Israel, where each of the tribes except Levi received a heritage or share in the Promised Land (Num 18:20; Deut 12:12; 14:27). Later it came to signify a share in the afterlife and it is used in this context in Revelation (Rev 20:6; 21:8; 22:19). In St John's gospel when Peter objects to having his feet washed Jesus points out that not only is the footwashing necessary, but emphasises that he (Jesus) himself must perform it. 'If I do not wash you, you will have no heritage (*meros*) with me' (Jn 13:5-9). The ' heritage' is described specifically as a heritage with him, and this is subsequently spelled out in the farewell discourse as 'where I am you also may be' (Jn 14:3). In Mark the heritage is spoken in terms of 'houses, brothers, sisters, mothers, children and land in this life and eternal life in the world to come'.

Reversal of Status Mk 10:31

Jesus' *logion*: 'Many who are first will be last, and the last first' appears in the parallel passage in Mt 19:30 and at the end of the parable of the labourers in the vineyard (Mt 20:16). It also appears in Luke at the conclusion of the parables on final salvation (Lk 13:30). It is obviously a well remembered *logion* or saying of Jesus which has outlived its original context and has been used in differing contexts to give the conclusion a punch line. It may even be the case that Jesus used it himself in different contexts for that very purpose. It emphasises the reversal of values, status, roles and destinies in the final arrangement of the kingdom.

The Way: Stage Three
Going Up to Jerusalem. Jericho
Mk 10:32-52

1. THE PLOT

This section (Mk 10:32-52) follows the same lines as the two previous sections: a passion prediction, a focusing on the blindness of the disciples and a call to discipleship with relevant instructions. It ends with the healing of a blind man, forming an inclusion with the healing of the blind man at Bethsaida which concluded the ministry in Galilee and opened the journey to Jerusalem.

The way to Jerusalem and the way of discipleship are emphasised again in the phrase 'they were on the way going up to

Jerusalem.' Jesus is going ahead, the disciples following, a physical position symbolising the roles of the master and his followers, but also emphasising both Jesus' acceptance of what lies in
store as he forges ahead to his destiny, and the confusion and
anxiety of the disciples as they follow on behind. Jerusalem is
now explicitly mentioned as the goal of the southward journey.
It has been the real centre of hostility to him throughout the ministry and he is now deliberately setting his face to go up to
Jerusalem. No wonder his followers are puzzled and afraid even
if they are not too sure why.

'They were on the way, going up to Jerusalem, and Jesus was
going ahead of them and they were alarmed / distressed, and the
ones following were afraid' (Mk 10:32). Who are the subjects in
these sentences? Are the first group the disciples (the Twelve)
and the second group a more general group of followers, or are
the first mentioned a general group and 'those following' the
disciples who had left all to follow him, as remarked by them in
Mk 10:28? In form this is a typical Markan construction, as in
time references, where a general description is followed by a
more specific one, except that it is unclear exactly who is the
subject in each case. It makes little difference to the overall
meaning, however, as the point being made is clear. Jesus forges
ahead. All the others have difficulty in doing so.

Why were they distressed and afraid? The verb describing
their being alarmed (distressed / confused) (*ethambounto*) reflects
the verb used for the distress of Jesus in Gethsemane (*ekthambeisthai*). The alarm and fear are the reactions of those who face
the possibility of persecution and martyrdom, and Mark may
well have his readers' own experience in mind as he tells this
story of Jesus and his original followers.

Because of the position of Jerusalem on the central highland
ridge, the phrase 'going up' to Jerusalem was long established
and became associated with the pilgrim path to Jerusalem and
the Temple. This, however, is a pilgrimage of a different order
and Jesus is leading the way. He is set apart from the others in
his deliberate intention of carrying out God's plan and submit-
ting to it in obedience even with the foreboding and foreknowledge that it will entail suffering and death. The others are following, again symbolising both following him on a physical
journey and following him 'on the way', the way of discipleship,
as they follow and are called to share in his fate. The reference to

'on the way' here at the beginning of this section forms an inclusion with the end of the section where Bartimaeus follows Jesus 'on the way'.[65]

2. THIRD PREDICTION OF THE PASSION MK 10:32-34

As so often in the gospel, particularly in this section dealing with 'the way', Jesus calls the Twelve aside to instruct them, and now for the third time he predicts his fate in Jerusalem, again referring to himself as Son of Man. The detailed nature of this third passion prediction points to Mark's intention of making the description more detailed as Jesus came closer to his fate. In so doing he may well be reflecting a tradition from the liturgy or from a catechism on which he drew.[66] E. Schweizer points out that the emphasis on 'being handed over to the Gentiles' (this is the first mention of the Gentile involvement in his predicted death) and the details of how they treat him may well point to a Jewish-Christian tradition, possibly in Palestine.[67] It is interesting also that the prediction speaks of 'killing' rather than 'crucifying' the Son of Man, whereas Matthew has 'crucify' in the parallel passage. The prediction reads like a programme for the dramatic events of Jesus' last day alive – being handed over to the chief priests and scribes; condemned to death; handed over to the Gentiles; being mocked and spit upon; being scourged; put to death and then raised after three days. D. E. Nineham states:

> This prediction, which makes no reference to the other two, is much fuller than either of them and exhibits greater literary art. It has been described as 'reading like a printed programme of a Passion Play' and the six stages on the way to the cross are clearly defined. In its present form it is regarded by almost all commentators as a 'prophecy after the event', especially as the vocabulary is characteristically Markan. It has been noted that in this prediction Jesus appears far more active in the determination of his destiny than in the other two.[68]

65. Mk 10:52. cf Acts 9:2 where 'the way' is a designation for the followers, the church.

66. E. Schweizer, *op. cit*, 217.

67. *Ibid.*, 216.

68. D. E. Nineham, *op. cit.*, 278; See also R. McKinnis, 'An Analysis of Mark X 32-34', *NovT*, 18 (1976), 81-100.

3. REACTION OF THE DISCIPLES MK 10:35-40

As in the case of the two earlier predictions the disciples react with a mixture of misunderstanding, incomprehension and apprehension when they realise that this prediction may apply to their own lives as well (Mk 8:32f; 9:33ff). In the case of each prediction there followed a focus on the disciples' failure to understand. Peter's failure to understand resulted in his telling Jesus, 'this must never happen to you,' after the first prediction. After the second prediction the disciples failed to understand and were afraid to ask him what he meant. They resorted to discussion among themselves about status. This third prediction is set in the context of their anxiety and fear and the sons of Zebedee, James and John, show how they have not understood anything of what Jesus has been saying but keep thinking in terms of earthly status and importance.

The misunderstanding, or total obtuseness, of the disciples, is highlighted by the request of James and John to have the places at the right and left side of Jesus in the kingdom. (In Mt 20:20 the request comes on behalf of the brothers from their mother!) What were they expecting and why were the ten indignant with them? They were nearing Jerusalem and the end was in sight. They may have expected the great revolution and the establishment of the kingdom along the lines of the kingdom of David. Their request then would have been to share the thrones of political power with the newly proclaimed messianic–warrior king. Or it may have been a reflection of the same thinking that manifested itself in the Qumran community where there was a detailed approach to where everyone would sit at the messianic banquet. Whichever it was, the other ten protested, probably not out of high moral principle, but because their own ambitions were being cut across as the brothers got their applications in ahead of them![69]

4. INSTRUCTING THE TWELVE MK 10:35-44

Places in the Kingdom

Jesus' immediate response to the sons of Zebedee was to say, ' You do not know what you are asking'. Sharing with Jesus meant sharing in his rejection, suffering and death. Those who

---

69. C. Focant, *op. cit.*, 398, puts it succinctly: *Le lecteur ne peut pas deviner si leur indignation est intéressée ou verteuse.*

were eventually on his right and left side were in fact those crucified with him![70] The readers of Mark then, and now, know that
sharing with Jesus means sharing in persecution and martyrdom. Ironically James was to die at the command of Herod (Acts
12:22). There are various accounts of John's martyrdom but also
a contrary tradition of his living to old age in Ephesus. If he lived
to old age in Ephesus, he certainly knew of the persecution by
Nero in Rome and would live to see the persecution by
Domitian in Asia Minor, the area in which he was living.
Furthermore, Mark and his intended readers may have been
aware of tensions about status and privilege in the church/com-
munity and so in recounting this story he indirectly addresses
the issue.

Jesus asks them if they can drink the cup that he has to drink
and be baptised in the baptism with which he is to be baptised.[71]
The cup signifies what God has in store for a person. 'Drinking
the cup' is a well established image in the Bible. It can signify
something good, as in 'my cup is overflowing' (Ps 22/23:5), but
it usually refers to suffering.[72] In the second century AD the
apocryphal *Martyrdom of Isaiah* speaks of the cup in terms of
martyrdom: 'For me God has mingled the cup of martyrdom.'[73]

Speaking of the baptism he asks them if they can be baptised
with the baptism with which he is to be baptised (the word bap-
tism/baptise being emphasised by its triple occurrence in the
sentence). *Baptizô* in Greek can mean 'I drown' and the passive
baptizomai signifies 'I am drowned.' Isaiah states 'Unrighteous-
ness baptises/submerges me' (Isa 21:4, LXX). Water can be a
symbol of disaster, in the sense of being drowned or flooded in
disaster, being drowned at the bottom of the sea (Pss 41/42:7;
68/69:1f; Isa 43:2). The significance is highlighted somewhat by
a parallel statement in Luke where Jesus emphasises the distress
such baptism causes. 'There is a baptism with which I must be
baptised and how great is my distress until it is accomplished'
(Lk 12:50). Here in Mark it is a parallel image to that of the cup of
suffering.

The disciples had already argued about precedence and

---

70. M. D. Hooker, *op.cit*, 247.
71. Ritual baptism such as that practised by the Baptist or the Qumran
community or the Christian rite of initiation is not what is in mind here.
72. Isa 51:17, 22; Lam 4:21; Ps 75:8, Jn 18:11 and Mk 14:36//Mt 26:42//
Lk 22:42.
73. *Martyrdom of Isaiah*, 5:13.

earned a rebuke from Jesus for so doing (Mk 9:33f). Jesus again, as so often before, calls his disciples together after their failure and begins yet again to instruct them. This time his reaction is to summon them and talk to them about the nature of worldly power, or more exactly (and ironically), the appearance of worldly power, since he refers to *hoi dokountes archein*, 'the ones who appear to rule'. There is a great irony in this comment, and furthermore the terms used for exercising power *katakurieuousin* and *katexousiazousin* are rare and point to an oppressive exercise of power which weighs heavily on people.[74] God's power is the real power and it often works in a way completely opposite to human expectations and practices. Jesus himself submits to the will of the Father as he accepts the fact that 'it is necessary' for the Son of Man to suffer. He does not seek earthly power and status but accepts the role of one who serves and suffers. As he accepts the will of the Father, not determining his own status and glory, so must his followers accept the will of Father and the positions in the kingdom which are determined not by the one sent, but by the One who sent him. 'To sit at my right or left hand is not mine to give, but it belongs to those for whom it is prepared (i.e. for whom God has prepared it).'

As one who serves
The paradoxical nature of leadership and greatness in the kingdom is again stated.[75] It has already been touched on in Mk 8:35, 9:35 and 10:31. After the first passion prediction Jesus spoke about denying oneself, taking up one's cross and following him, and losing one's life for his sake and the sake of the gospel (Mk 8:30-35). After the second prediction he said that the one who wishes to be first must be last and servant of all (Mk 9:35). Now after the third prediction he states that the one who wants to be great (*megas*) or first (*prôtos*) must be servant (*diakonos*) and slave (*doulos*) of all (Mk 10:43f). Jesus does not teach this in the abstract or from a safe distance. He himself leads the way. In all three predictions of the passion he speaks of his forthcoming death as the death of the Son of Man. Here he now speaks of the Son of Man as one who serves. This is a far cry from the picture of the glorious Son of Man in Daniel coming in splendour to subject

---

74. C. Focant, *op. cit.*, 398.
75. See D. Seely, 'Rulership and Service in Mark 10:41-45,' *NovT* 35 (1993), 234-50.

the nations to his rule (Dan 7:14, 27), a role which would elicit thoughts of one who came to be served and to save others from death rather than one who comes to serve and submit to death.

The Danielic picture of a glorious saviour of the nation, a conquering hero on their behalf, comes from a period of persecution, represented also in the stories of the Maccabees and the great persecution the nation suffered at the hands of Antiochus IV (Epiphanes). Now, however, Jesus' final statement, or *logion*, in this collection of sayings allies the Son of Man with the persecuted rather than with the saviour-warrior. He sums up the teaching on discipleship in terms of service to the point of giving one's life. 'For the Son of Man himself did not come to be served but to serve, and to give his life as a ransom for many' (Mk 10:45).

In a corresponding collection of sayings a similar instruction to the one given here is given by Jesus at the last supper in Luke's gospel following a dispute among the disciples about who was the greatest (Lk 22:24-27). The teaching about 'greatness' in Lk 22:27 represents Jesus as stating simply: 'Here am I among you as one who serves'. Some scholars see the Lukan version as the older one going back to Jesus himself and they see the Markan version as introducing a whole new theological dimension into the teaching, as he goes on to explain the significance of his death as 'a ransom for many'.

In Mark's gospel Jesus renders this service as *lytron anti pollôn*, usually translated as 'a ransom for many'. In the words of V. Taylor, 'This saying is one of the most important in the gospels.'[76] But what exactly does it mean? It is somewhat out of harmony in context and without parallel in Mark.[77] Each of the three words has provoked scholarly discussion. Here in Mark it represents a very sudden and radical departure in terminology since elsewhere during Mark's account of the ministry Jesus does not speak of his death in terms of ransom (*lytron/lytroô*), as in paying the price for the release of a captive or the emancipation of a slave (Lev 25:47-55), or in ritual terms like the sacrifice offered in place of the first-born (Exod 13:13-16). Furthermore, the LXX never associates *'asham* (an offering for sin) and *lytrôn* (ransom).

76. V. Taylor, *op. cit.*, 444.
77. See also A. Y. Collins, 'The Signification of Mark 10:45 among Gentile Christians', *HTR* 90 (1997)371-82 and B. Lindars, 'Salvation Proclaimed. VII. Mark 10:45: A Ransom for Many,' *ExpTim* 93 (1981-82), 292-95.

The preposition *anti*, 'for', can be translated as 'in favour of', 'for the benefit of' or 'instead of'. Its meaning in this context depends on one's interpretation of *lytrôn*. As seen earlier 'many' in the Greek usage of the gospel is a translation of the underlying Hebrew or Aramaic 'many' which serves for 'the multitude', 'a limitless number', 'all the people', an expression used in the Dead Sea Scrolls for 'the people of God/the community'.[78] In the Pauline tradition a parallel statement is translated as 'all' in the phrase *antilytron hyper pantôn*, 'ransom on behalf of all' (1 Tim 2:6).

This concept of 'ransom for many' picks up on the 'saving the people' motif of the Son of Man in so far as it speaks of the salvation of the people, and it may reflect also the understanding of the deaths of martyrs as compensation for the sins of the people (1 Macc 2:50; 6:44; 2 Macc 7:17ff; 4 Macc 6:29; 17:21f). But it seems closest to the Christian community's reflection on the death of Jesus and its significance for salvation, as seen first in the Pauline letters and also in the emerging Johannine tradition of service and laying down one's life for flock or friend, though not necessarily dependent on these traditions. In the Pauline tradition a parallel statement is found in the phrase *antilytron hyper pantôn*, 'ransom on behalf of all' (1 Tim 2:6). The correspondence between them is obvious also in the verbal similarities in *antilytron* and *lytron anti*. A corresponding idea is found in various New Testament documents using the related term *apolytrôsis* (Rom 3:24; 8:23; 1 Cor 1:30; Eph 1:7, 14; Heb 4:30; 9:15; 11:35).

In John the washing of the disciples' feet casts Jesus in the role of one who serves and in interpreting the gesture Jesus points to the necessity of accepting his servant model of salvation and he instructs the disciples to follow his example, since 'I who am Lord and Master have washed your feet, you should wash each other's feet … no servant is greater than his master' … 'greater love no one has than to lay down one's life for one's friends' (Jn 13:3-16; 15:13). Earlier in John Jesus had spoken of the ideal shepherd as one who 'lays down his life for his sheep'(Jn 10:11, 15, 17, 18). It appears that the connection between service and giving one's life was well established as the traditions of Jesus' teaching developed in the light of his saving death and resurrection. John also records the words of the high priest 'prophesying' that Jesus would die for the nation (Jn

---

78. *1 QS* 6:1, 7-25; *CD* 13:7; 14:7.

11:50, 51). Underlying both the synoptic and Johannine developments of the theme, is the basic concept of a service given by one
who is prepared to render that service even if it is given at the
cost of one's life.

The vicarious suffering of the Suffering Servant in Isa 52-53
as a background to 'ransom for many' has been both affirmed
and denied by scholars. Some point to the fact that the LXX does
not use *diakonos/diakonein* for 'servant/serve' but renders the
Hebrew *ebed* (servant) as *pais*, sometimes as *doulos*. On the other
hand the 'ransom for many' does at least resonate with the vicarious suffering 'for many' and 'praying all the time for sinners' of
Isa 53:4, 5, 10-12. One must remember, however, that ideas and
images can persist and influence each other even if different vocabulary is used, especially when an idea is remembered in an
oral context without immediate access to a written text, and
above all when it is translated into another language. In this way
a *logion* or an idea can be established in popular tradition.

D. E. Nineham wisely sums up: 'Different people will obviously evaluate these considerations differently.'[79] What is not in
dispute is the call to service of others, in imitation of the Son of
Man who rendered that service to the point of paying for it with
his life. Whatever the earlier history of the *logion*, it is set here in
the Markan context of the rejected, suffering, Son of Man who
goes to his death in accordance with the plan or will of the
Father, looking forward in faith to a vindication by God for himself and those who follow him. R. H. Gundry sums up very well:

> Jesus interprets his approaching death as supremely self-sac-
> rificial for the saving of many other's lives. Thus the Marcan
> apologetics of miraculous ability, of didactic authority, and
> of predictive power metamorphoses into an apologetic of
> beneficial service. The cross will not bring shame to its vic-
> tim, but salvation to his followers.[80]

5. Healing of Blind Bartimaeus Mk 10:46-52

The healing of the blind man which takes place as Jesus leaves
Jericho with the disciples and a large crowd (citizens of Jericho

---

79. D. E. Nineham, *op. cit.*, 281; See also R. E. Watts, 'Jesus and the
Suffering Servant' in W. H. Bellinger Jr and W. R. Farmer, eds, *Jesus and
the Suffering Servant. Isaiah 53 and Christian Origins*, Harrisburg, Penn:
Trinity Press International, 1998, 125-52;
80. R. H. Gundry, *op. cit.*, 581.

and probably also pilgrims bound for the festal celebrations in Jerusalem) is the last of the healing stories and it fulfils an important function in the gospel. It rounds off the major section of the gospel dealing with 'the way to Jerusalem' which was punctuated with the three passion predictions and replete with instructions for the uncomprehending disciples about the way of discipleship. Bartimaeus stands out at the end of this major section of the gospel dealing with discipleship as an example of a man who receives sight, manifests faith, understanding and courage, and becomes a disciple, following Jesus willingly to Jerusalem and proclaiming his faith in him as son of David.

The story of the healing of Bartimaeus forms an inclusion with the healing of the blind man at Bethsaida at the beginning of this major section dealing with 'the way' and it stands out in contrast to it as this blind man at Jericho comes immediately to full sight and spontaneously leaves behind his cloak and follows Jesus 'on the way'. His cloak was both his beggar's uniform by day and possibly his blanket by night. It was probably the instrument of daytime earning as he spread it on the pavement for people to throw their alms on it. Leaving his cloak is therefore akin to the first disciples leaving the security of home, boats, nets and counting house to follow Jesus.

This is one of very few healings where the personal name of the petitioner, in this case, Bartimaeus, is given.[81] Jairus is another, but even there the name of Jairus' daughter is not given. The location of the story emphasises the fact that Jesus is now only fifteen miles or so from Jerusalem and from here on 'going up to Jerusalem' is literally a journey from the lowest point on the earth's surface up the incline to Jerusalem, built on the central ridge of the highlands.

The story contains the first public recognition of Jesus in what could be called a messianic title or acclamation to go unrebuked by Jesus. This confession of him as son of David also forms part of the inclusion framing the journey to Jerusalem as it balances the 'underdeveloped' and more private confession of Peter at the start of the journey. The confession of Peter earned a rebuke by way of a command to silence. Here the crowd order

---

81. *Bar* in Aramaic means 'son', like *ben* in Hebrew, so Bar-Timaeus means son of Timaeus. One can ask if Mark gives the name because the man became well known in the community, or because it is an eye-witness account that survived in the tradition.

the man to be silent, and they are countermanded by Jesus with his request to 'call the man' to him.

The story reminds the reader of the healing of the blind man in John's gospel (Jn 9:1-41) and the comments of Jesus about blindness and sight, the only other place in the New Testament where the description 'beggar' (*proaitês*) is used (Jn 9:8). Here in Mark, as in the Johannine story, there is more attention paid to the blind man than to Jesus and a clear statement of his imperviousness to the people (including the disciples who merge with the crowd in this story) who wanted to silence him. He is told that Jesus of Nazareth (the 'everyday' name of Jesus, identifying him by his place of origin, implying no special role on his part or faith on the part of the people using the name) is passing by. As in the story in John, the blind man here also sees the truth in a way that the sighted people around him do not. He responds to the presence of Jesus with a faith-filled address: 'Son of David, have pity on me.' Like the Syro-Phoenician woman and the man with the dumb (epileptic)/possessed son, he calls out to Jesus for mercy, calling out from the margins, bringing nothing to his call but faith.[82] His 'calling out' to Jesus increases after the crowd rebuke and try to silence him. It is the first public address to Jesus in what could be taken for a messianic title. Jesus responds immediately to his address and cry for mercy. Instead of silencing him, as he earlier silenced others, he rebukes, not the blind man, but the crowd who were trying to silence him.

Jesus says *'call* him' and 'they *called* him' saying: 'Courage, rise up, he is *calling* you', three mentions of the verb 'call' with all its significance of calling to discipleship. Responding to the call Bartimaeus left his cloak, symbol of everything he possessed, and followed Jesus 'on the way' in a spontaneous manner reminiscent of the response of the first disciples at their calling as they left family and livelihood to follow Jesus. Together with the verb 'call', the instruction to 'rise up' (*egeire*) has connotations of resurrection, as in the story of the healing of Simon's mother-in-law (Mk 1:31), the raising of Jairus' daughter (Mk 5:41) and the healing of the man's son after the descent from the Mount of Transfiguration (Mk 9:27).

The blind beggar, without sight, status, position or posses-

82. See M. A. Beavis, 'From the Margin to the Way: A Feminist Reading of the Story of Bartimaeus', *Journal of Feminist Studies in Religion*, 14 (1998), 19-39.

sions, sat stationary on the margins, not 'on the way' with Jesus, the disciples and the crowd heading for Jerusalem. Sitting 'beside the way' he was stuck in the helplessness of blindness and poverty, a nobody in the eyes of the onlookers and an embarrassment on a public occasion with an important person 'passing by'. After the triple call of Jesus and the instruction to 'rise', he immediately follows Jesus 'on the way'. The story sparkles with the words which sum up the essential elements of Christian discipleship – *compassion/mercy, call, faith, save, rise up, follow, the way,* and it is therefore a key text in the interpretation of the gospel.[83]

Bartimaeus' confession also sets the tone for what follows in the triumphal approach to Jerusalem as the crowds hail Jesus in terms of a royal son of David, and prepares the reader for what follows by way of Jesus' authoritative action in the Temple, his disputes with religious leaders and his debates with teaching authorities, coming to a climax with his question about why the scribes say that the Messiah is son of David.

Prior to this in Mark, such confessions were on the lips of demons, or emerged from the confused understanding of people and disciples. This confession comes in the context of increasingly intense appeals for compassion as the man calls out: 'Jesus, son of David, have mercy / compassion on me.' Jesus responds to the confession-based appeals with a healing. In the light of Jesus' subsequent discussion on the Messiah as son of David in a somewhat negative and confrontational way with the authorities, one asks what the meaning of the title is here, and why Jesus responds so spontaneously and positively to it. J. P. Meier shows how compassion and healing are an apt context for such a confession as he points out that the title was applied to Solomon who was seen as a healer in first century writings.[84] Furthermore, the expectation of a messianic son of David is reflected in the Psalms of Solomon 17, contemporary with the New Testament, in the prayer: 'See, Lord, and raise up for them their king, the son of David, to rule over your servant Israel in the time known to you, O Lord.' This contemporary 'royal-mes-

---

83. See the article by H-J Eckstein, 'Markus 10:46-52 als Schlüsseltext des Markusevangeliums,' *ZNW* 87 (1996) 33-50.
84. J. Meier, *A Marginal Jew,* 2:689f; Josephus, *Ant.,* 8:46-49; *Test. Sol.* 20:1; cf F. J. Moloney, *op. cit.,* 209.

sianic' understanding gives a context for the enthusiasm of the crowd as Jesus approaches Jerusalem.

Bartimaeus spontaneously joins the disciples and the crowd (and the reader) as they accompany Jesus on the final stage of the way to Jerusalem.

Last Days in Jerusalem Mk 11-13

A Historical Note

Apart from the reference in St Luke's gospel where Jesus is brought to Jerusalem at the age of twelve by his parents (Lk 2:42ff), the synoptics do not recount any presence of Jesus in the Holy City prior to his final, fateful visit. In Mark and the other synoptics, all the traditions dealing with his Jerusalem ministry are therefore arranged in this one visit. The acclaim Jesus receives on his approach to the city, the provocative action in the Temple, the clashes with the supreme authority of the chief priests, elders and scribes, the reactions of the Jerusalem crowd and his scoring legal and theological points over the Pharisees, Sadducees, and scribes are all telescoped into the final week of his life. In St John's gospel, on the other hand, Jesus goes to Jerusalem on a number of occasions to attend and carry on his ministry at the pilgrimage feasts so the traditions dealing with Jerusalem are spread over a number of visits.

Historically Jesus seems to have visited the city on a number of occasions, as John describes, and there are even indications that his final visit may have been of longer duration than may appear from the synoptic and Johannine accounts. That he died during the Passover celebrations is clear but there are some indications that his 'triumphal' entry may have taken place either during the autumn Feast of Tabernacles or the winter Feast of Dedication/Hanukkah. The waving of branches and palms was a prescribed ritual in these festivals. These branches were usually gathered outside the city (as is specifically stated in Mk 11:8) and the palm, mentioned only by John (Jn 12:13), was brought from the area around Jericho, pointing to its not being a spontaneous gathering of the branches on the occasion but a using of those branches already collected for the feast of Tabernacles or Hanukkah. This may indicate a longer final visit to Jerusalem or a 'triumphal' entry on an earlier visit. D. E. Nineham suggests that possibly the early church was already celebrating a Holy Week and therefore Mark fits the various elements into the framework of one final week.[1]

---

1. D. E. Nineham, *op. cit.*, 289.

As Jesus arrives in Jerusalem the final period in his earthly life and ministry has begun. This Jerusalem visit consists of two major sections, his activity in the city and environs in chapters 11 to 13 and the passion and Easter narrative in chapters 14 to 16.

PLOT AND OUTLINE

The predictions of the passion have been presented in Mark in stylised 'oracular' formulae en route to the Holy City. They create a real sense of foreboding. At the same time they provide the opportunity for instructing the disciples in the necessity of fulfilling the divine plan for the suffering and serving Son of Man, and for calling on the disciples (and the reader) to be prepared to share the suffering and serving roles of the master.

The reader therefore has two contending impressions as Jesus approaches the city – the long term foreboding created by Jesus' own predictions of what lies ahead and the short term enthusiasm of the crowd surrounding his approach to the city from his leaving Jericho to his arrival at Jerusalem.

These three chapters (Mk 11-13), though composed from previously independent materials, form a single overall unit covering the ministry of Jesus in Jerusalem. The unity is emphasised by the recurring references to the Temple, the Temple area, the view of the Temple and the destruction of the Temple.

The section is contained within an inclusion which focuses on the first and second comings, the coming of the royal son of David, coming in the name of the Lord, humbly riding on a colt, amid the enthusiastic shouts of the people, and the prediction of the coming of the Son of Man on the clouds with great power and glory, sending out his angels to gather the elect (Mk 13:7ff; 26f). The first coming is followed by the ominous sign of the withered fig tree and the second is heralded by the promising sign of the fig tree coming into bloom (Mk 11:13, 14, 20, 21; 13:28).

The entire section has the character of a denouement. The royal, messianic visitation of the city heralds a radical change, an ending of Temple worship (Mk 11:1-25) and teaching authority (Mk 11:27-12:44). The visitation is carried out by one who not only manifests an authority greater than the Temple and greater than the teaching authorities, but one who prophesies also the destruction of the Temple (Mk 13:1-23), the universal mission of the gospel, the end of the world as we know it, and the coming of the Son of Man in glory to gather the elect (Mk 13:24-37).

Whereas the emphasis throughout the section dealing with
'the way to Jerusalem' has been on the predictions of the passion
and resurrection, with a very heavy emphasis on instructing the
disciples about their calling to a discipleship of suffering and
service, the entry into Jerusalem marks a significant departure
as a new dynamic and energy come into play. The disciples remain in the background as the focus again becomes thoroughly
christological.

Jesus acts and teaches with an authority that manifests his
superiority over the religious administration and teaching authority. A significant turning point in the section occurs when
Jesus puts to an indeterminate and all inclusive audience of listeners and readers of the gospel the question about the teaching
of the scribes that the Messiah is the son of David. Having already discredited their authority, he now points to an authority
greater than the traditional authority of the Messiah as son of
David. It is the authority of one whom David addresses as Lord
(Mk 12:35-37), a title that reminds the reader of the divine commission to the Baptist who was sent as a 'messenger to prepare
the way of the Lord' (1:3). From this point to the end of the section Jesus is building up to his prophecy of the coming of the
Son of Man in glory to gather the elect. He adopts the mantle of
eschatological-apocalyptic prophet and predicts the end of the
Temple and of the world, and the coming in glory of the Son of
Man to gather the elect when the universal mission to preach the
good news to all nations is complete.

Outline of Mk 11-13
1. Royal Visit and Prophetic Visitation Mk 11:1-25
The royal son of David comes to city and Temple. It is a visitation resulting in a judgement on the sterility of the Temple and
its impending demise, symbolised by the withering of the fig
tree.
2. Clash of Authorities Mk 11:27-12:44
In the Temple area Jesus, in a series of controversies, manifests
an authority greater than the institution and the teaching authorities. The Messiah is Lord, not just the son of David.
3. Eschatological-Apocalyptic Discourse Mk 13:1-37
Jesus leaves the Temple. He predicts the fall of the Temple, the
universal mission, and the end of the world. The Son of Man will
come in glory to gather the elect.

Royal Visit and Prophetic Visitation

1. ROYAL VISIT TO THE CITY

i. Preparing to enter the City Mk 11:1-7a

The reader of the gospel has been brought along the way with Jesus and the disciples and is now full of anticipation and foreboding as the goal of pilgrimage, the city of destiny, draws near. Bartimaeus struck an important note with his 'son of David' confession, and as Jesus and his party ascend and the city comes into view, Bethphage and Bethany are reached.[2] The frequent use of the historic present tense (they draw near ... he sends ... he says) keeps the reader in the midst of the unfolding action. The anticipation is heightened by naming the villages of Bethany and Bethphage, like milestones along the way, and as they are reached the narrator points out that they are nearing the Mount of Olives. Mention of the Mount of Olives is, however, more than a pointer to another milestone on the way because a formal or ceremonial entry into the city from the Mount of Olives is an action laden with biblical significance.

It is of great significance that Jesus approaches the city from the Mount of Olives. Approaching from the Mount of Olives conjures up the imagery of the day of the eschatological battle and judgement. Coming from the Mount of Olives has strong echoes of divine judgement. Zechariah described the coming of YHWH for the eschatological judgement of Jerusalem and the nations: 'A day is coming for YHWH ... On that day his feet will rest on the Mount of Olives, which faces Jerusalem from the east' (Zech 14:1, 4). Malachi also had prophesied about the Day of YHWH when there would be a divine judgement on the Temple (Mal 3:1, 2). This echo of judgement will run not only through the immediate approach to the city and Temple but right throughout the ministry in Jerusalem.[3] The association of the Mount of Olives with the coming of the Messiah is reflected in Josephus, both in the *Jewish War* and the *Antiquities*.[4]

Old Testament and current Jewish expectations of a royal

---

2. In fact Bethany would have been reached first though Mark mentions Bethphage first. This has led some scribal copyists to 'correct' Mark's topography by dropping the reference to Bethphage.

3. J. Radermakers, *La Bonne Nouvelle de Jésus selon saint Marc*, 304.

4. Josephus, *War* 11, 13, 5; *Ant* 20, 8, 6.

Messiah fired the minds of the Jews at the pilgrimage feasts, especially at Passover. The authorities, Jewish and Roman, had to be
very alert to the presence of any messianic figure and the prospect
of revolutionary activity when crowds assembled for the pilgrimage feasts, especially for Passover with its connotations of liberation from slavery in Egypt and the defeat of their powerful op-
pressing enemy. Jesus now takes the initiative and prepares to
make his own statement by the manner of his approach as he responds to the messianic expectations of the crowd and of his disciples (who seem to be still without understanding) as he carefully
plans the nature and circumstances of his approach.

The royal visitor is approaching the city. His careful preparation results in an approach to the city that is like a prophetic *ôt*,
a sign worked out in mime.[5] The prophets regularly made use of
symbolic gestures which were really parables in action to highlight their message and set people thinking. Often a symbolic
gesture (*ôt*) or mime was bizarre or designed to shock. Isaiah
walked barefoot and naked through Jerusalem to highlight the
forthcoming defeat of Egypt and Cush by the Assyrians (Isa
20:1-6). For Jeremiah the spoiling of the loincloth, the breaking
of the yoke on his neck and the buying of the field, all had significant political messages (Jer 13:1-11; 28:1-17; 31:1-15). For Ezekiel
the eating of the scroll and his dumbness signified his prophetic
role. His portrayal of the city under siege in illustration on a
brick and the shaving of his hair foretold what lay ahead in the
horrors of the siege (Ezek 2:1-33; 4:1-4; 5:1-4). Jesus now engages
in a prophetic style dramatic action to proclaim and illustrate
the nature of his kingship.

Pilgrims entered the holy city on foot, and Jesus himself
walked everywhere. Now, however, he sends two of his disciples to the village opposite (Bethany or Bethphage?) to requisi-
tion a colt on which he will enter the city.[6] This very deliberate
action, involving the commissioning of two disciples to bring

---

5. Jesus prepares carefully for approaching the city just as he subsequently, in a parallel passage, prepares for the celebration of the
Passover meal (Mk 14:12-16).
6. *pôlos* can mean the offspring of various animals, donkeys, horses,
crossbreeds, camels. I translate as donkey because of the Zech 9:9 text
which is being acted out, and is actually quoted in the parallel passage
in Mt 21:2, 7. Matthew, takes the biblical parallelism of Zech 9:9 rather
literally and speaks of two animals.

the colt (young donkey), points out that he is making a very definite statement by the manner of his approaching the city, reminiscent of Zechariah who prophesied concerning the entrance to the city of the royal Messiah: 'your king comes to you; he is victorious, he is triumphant, humble and riding on a donkey, on a colt, the foal of a donkey' (Zech 9:9).

In the mythology of the Ancient Near East the donkey (or mule) was at times associated with representations of the gods, very likely because it was the domestic animal *par excellence*, the one sharing the human burden of work and the opposite to the horse, used since the time of Solomon as a mount for the warrior heading for war and seen as a symbol of power and prestige. Furthermore, the donkey was long since closely associated with the ruler that would arise from the tribe of Judah, and so it had associations with the house of David. Concerning the ruler from the House of Judah, the blessing of Jacob had proclaimed: 'Binding his foal to the vine and his donkey's colt to the choice vine, he washes his garments in wine and his robe in the blood of grapes' (Gen 49:10f).

A significant historical incident also needs to be kept in mind as a background to Jesus' action. Towards the end of David's troubled reign the disputed succession to the throne was decided finally in favour of Solomon when David sent for the priest Zadok, the prophet Nathan, and Benaiah son of Jehoiada and commanded them: 'Take with you the servants of your lord and have my son Solomon ride on my own mule, and bring him down to Gihon. There let the priest Zadok and the prophet Nathan anoint him king over Israel' (1 Kings 1:32-34). Then Solomon and his entourage went up to the city as the people accompanied them with loud rejoicing and the usurper Adonijah and his entourage broke up and fled as they heard that Solomon was made to sit on the king's mule, anointed king and entered the city to tumultuous rejoicing to sit on the throne of David (1 Kings 1:44).

Jesus is therefore preparing to approach the city in a highly significant way. As he sends the two disciples to acquire the colt the reader may ask whether his knowledge of where they will find the colt is the result of divine foreknowledge, prophetic insight, prior arrangement or good guesswork arising from prior local knowledge, but in the context the nature of his knowledge is really secondary to his intention. Like the passion predictions and the preparation of the Passover meal, which follows later, it sets Jesus' 'foreknowledge' in the context of his obedience to the unfolding divine plan.

The message sent by Jesus to those who might inquire about their reason for taking the colt was: 'The *kyrios* has need of it (*autou chreian echei*) and will send it back directly.' Does it mean it is needed for the plan of God (understanding *kyrios* as referring to God)? Or is it a declaration that Jesus is *ho kyrios autou*, 'his master/owner', referring to the animal and implying a divine ownership, or a royal right since Jesus as king has the right to lay claim to it? Or is it a straightforward application of the title *kyrios* to Jesus? The use of *kyrios* to refer to Jesus during the ministry is not typical of Mark's gospel. Luke, however, uses the term *kyrios* eighteen times in speaking as a Christian writer of Jesus during his ministry, but the title comes from the pen of Luke rather than from the lips of Jesus. For Luke it is a telling of the story of Jesus using a title born of the post-resurrection faith in the Risen Lord. Has Mark used it in that way here? Is it a setting down of a marker for his forthcoming statement in Jerusalem that the Messiah is Lord? He was, after all, introduced in the prologue as *kyrios*, in the phrase 'prepare the way or the Lord' (Mk 1:3) and in Jerusalem he will state that the Messiah is not just son of David but *kyrios* (Mk 12:35-37). At the same time the promise to send it back straight away is the action of an observant Jew concerned to fulfil the legal requirement of a loan of someone else's property, and this is a pointer to the fact that it is not referring to its actual owner/master (*kyrios autou*) who may be already in the company of Jesus. The overall impression given is that a divine plan is unfolding.

As Jesus now prepares to enter the city seated on a donkey's colt he acknowledges his royal status but with a gesture that interprets it in line with biblical expectations different to those uppermost in the mind of the enthusiastic crowd and disciples and the possibly jaundiced eye of the authorities who may witness or come to hear of the event. In royal fashion he approaches the city seated on a beast of burden, symbol of the king coming in peace. Jesus' action illustrates not only the 'humble' dimension as prophesied by Zechariah, but the whole symbolism of coming on the colt is a demonstration of the peaceful nature both of his coming and of his kingship/kingdom. The warrior king would come on a war-horse! The gesture is a parable in action emphasising the peaceful nature of the coming of the king/ prophet. Jesus thus acknowledges but significantly reinterprets the popular view of his kingship.[7] This is a far cry from the national liberator in the tradition of the Maccabees, and the revolutionary leader or warrior expected by many of Jesus' contemporaries, against whom the Jerusalem authorities and the Roman occupiers were constantly on guard, especially on the occasion of Passover and the other major pilgrimage feasts.

The action recalls not only Solomon, the son of David, entering the city to sit on the throne, but also recalls the prophecies of Zechariah and Zephaniah who speak of the victorious warrior-king humbly approaching the city proclaiming a message of peace. Though Mark does not actually quote these prophets the symbolism and allusions are evident. Matthew does in fact quote the prophecy from Zechariah and John has a fusion of quotations from Zechariah and Zephaniah (Mt 21:1-11; Zech 9:9; Zeph 3:16f; cf Lk 19:28-40; Jn 12:12-19). The passage in Zechariah reads:

> Rejoice greatly, daughter of Sion! Shout aloud, daughter of Jerusalem! See now your king comes to you: he is victorious, he is triumphant, humble and riding on a donkey, on a colt, the foal of a donkey. He will cut off the chariots from Ephraim and horses from Jerusalem; the bow of war will be banished. He will proclaim peace for the nations. His empire shall stretch from sea to sea, from the river to the ends of the earth' (Zech 9:9).

This peaceful aspect, and the reassuring words of peace are explicit in John where the mixed quotation/allusions from Zechariah and Zephaniah call for rejoicing and having no fear. Though Mark is more understated his symbolism is there to be seen by those who can, or when they can.[8]

---

7. As he does in his trial before Pilate in John's gospel when he says: 'My kingdom is not of this world' (Jn 18:36f).
8. The expectation of the Messiah coming in glory or riding on a donkey lived on in Jewish circles and about 250AD Rabbi Joshua ben Levi remarked that if Israel was worthy the Son of Man would come 'on the clouds of heaven', and if not, he would come 'lowly and riding upon a donkey'.

ii. The Triumphal Approach to the City Mk 11:7b-10

At the beginning of Jesus' final ascent to the Holy City, the blind
beggar in Jericho, Bartimaeus, proclaimed him son of David, a
title full of royal messianic significance. What Bartimaeus said in
faith may have been heard and taken up in misplaced messianic
enthusiasm by the disciples and the crowd. Mark speaks of
'those who went before and those following', a scene that could
be regarded as a description of Jesus and his entourage coming
on pilgrimage to the sanctuary of the Lord, like the rejoicing
crowd coming on pilgrimage, described in Ps 67/68:25: 'cantors
marching in front, musicians behind'. However, there is a great
irony in Mark's account. The disciples are meant to 'follow'
Jesus to Jerusalem and to all the rejection and suffering that
awaits him (and them) there, but here they are going ahead of
him, rejoicing with false expectations of messianic glory. The
disciples, who had been called to *follow* him are now going before him! The formerly blind beggar, Bartimaeus, on the other
hand, is *following him on the way!*

Meeting a royal visitor, a king or emperor, outside the gates
and escorting him into the city was a custom in the Greco-
Roman world. The usual term used for a pilgrim's approach to
Jerusalem is 'going up' to Jerusalem but here Jesus is hailed as
'the one who comes' to the city (*ho erchomenos*). This emphasises
the royal and messianic nature of his visit, or more accurately
perhaps, of his visitation. The triumphal approach of Jesus, followed by his solitary entry into the city and his looking around,
followed next day in Mark's gospel by the action in the Temple,
set the 'judgemental' tone for all that follows.[9]

The Davidic kingship has been proclaimed by Bartimaeus
and the crowd proclaim the coming of the kingdom of 'our father
David'.[10] The enthusiastic crowd put garments on the colt,
decorating it as a throne and placed garments and 'a carpet of
greenery' (*stibas*) on the roadway. Placing garments on the roadway is a gesture of homage to a royal person, as seen in the case
of the proclamation of Jehu as king: 'They all took their cloaks

9. For background to the 'triumphal approach of a warrior or king to the
city see P. B. Duff, 'The March of the Divine Warrior and the Advent of
the Graeco-Roman King. Mark's account of Jesus' Entry into Jerusalem',
JBL 111 (1992), 55-71.
10. An unusual way of referring to David, since the term 'father' was
used more or less exclusively of the Patriarchs.

and spread them for him on the bare steps; and they blew the trumpet and proclaimed, "Jehu is king".' (2 Kings 9:13). *Stibas* is the term usually applied to greenery and straw used for bedding. In the accounts in the other gospels the crowd wave the branches, and John alone specifies that it was palm. Carrying such branches which they gathered or cut outside the city, and palm which was brought from the area around Jericho, was a custom at the Feasts of Tabernacles (*Sukkot*/Booths) and Dedication (*Hanukkah*) (2 Macc 10:7).

The line from the psalm, 'Blessings on the one who comes in the name of the Lord' was probably used as a prayer or blessing by the priests as they greeted the pilgrims on arrival at the Temple (Ps 118:26). Here the blessing is given a messianic connotation and directed towards Jesus and it is accompanied by the blessing on 'the coming kingdom of our father David'. The messianic expectation in New Testament times, in terms of a prince from the House of David, is clearly expressed in the Psalms of Solomon: 'See Lord, and raise up for them their king, the Son of David, to rule over your servant Israel in the time known to you, O Lord (*Pss Sol*. 17). 'Hosanna in the highest' is a paraphrase of Job 16:19 and Ps 148:1 which literally means, 'Save us, we pray, you who dwell in the highest', but here it is more in the nature of a joyous acclamation or greeting in the form of a shout of praise to God who dwells in the highest heaven. In the context of Jesus' entry into the city, 'Hosanna' is more an exclamation of joy and homage, an affirmation of what is taking place rather than a prayer of petition or simply a calling down of a blessing on the recipient. It was associated with the enthusiastic waving of the palm fronds and sheaves of foliage at the festivals and so the *lulab* or bunch of foliage was often called a 'hosanna'.[11] The quotation, 'He who comes in the Lord's name' is from Psalm 117 (118), one of the Hallel Psalms associated with the entry to the Temple at Passover and Tabernacles. Here it emphasises the messianic significance of 'the one who comes.'[12]

The 'one who comes', 'the one who is to come' or the 'coming

11. *Sukka* 37b. At Tabernacles as the Psalm 117 (118) was chanted the males present waved the *lulab*, the bunch of greenery, at the words 'Blessed is he who comes in the name of the Lord' (verses 25, 26).
12. Ps 117 (118):26. Throughout the scene the crowd act almost like the chorus in a Greek play voicing the background issues, providing a stimulus and an interpretation of the event.

one' is an established term in the gospels for the awaited messianic figure. Here the coming is associated with the coming to the city and is reminiscent of Malachi whose words were used to define the function of the Baptist at the beginning of the gospel: 'Look, I am going to send my messenger before you to prepare your way' (Mk 1:2). Jesus' approach to the city and Temple now recalls in action the next verse of Malachi's prophecy: 'The Lord you are seeking will suddenly enter his Temple; and the angel of the covenant whom you are longing for, yes, he is coming, says Yahweh Sabaoth. Who will be able to resist the day of his coming? Who will remain standing when he appears?' (Mal 3:1, 2). Jesus' entry into the city is followed shortly, though not immediately as in Matthew and Luke, by the judgemental action in the Temple. This interval between entering the city and the 'cleansing' of the Temple in Mark's gospel serves the purpose of making a distinction between both episodes, the royal approach to the city and the prophetic, judgemental action in the Temple.[13]

There are a number of points of contact between the accounts as told in the three synoptics and John (Mk 11:1-11; Mt 21:1-11; Lk 19:28-40; Jn 12:12-19). All four gospels record the enthusiasm, the approach or entry on a beast of burden, the royal overtones, the citation of, and/or allusions to scripture. Matthew, Mark and John prefix 'Hosanna' to the citation from Psalm 117 (118), 'Blessed is he who comes in the name of the Lord' and John adds the suffix 'even the King of Israel' (Ps 117 (118):25f). This royal dimension is reflected in Mark's 'Blessed is the kingdom of our father David that is coming' and in Matthew's reference to 'son of David'(Mk 11:10; Mt 21:9).

The other synoptic gospels and John paint a larger canvas of pilgrims and citizens greeting Jesus. John knits into the crowd of pilgrims and citizens, those who saw Lazarus being raised and those who came to see the one who was raised. These larger crowds naturally draw the hostile attention of the authorities in the other gospels. In Mark the approach is not quite so spectacular and the crowd has dispersed before the actual entry of Jesus into the city.

---

13. Again Mark and John are in agreement in making this distinction.

iii. The Solitary Entry into the City Mk 11:11

The final sentence in the sequence describes Jesus' entry into the city. Significantly the verb *eisêlthen* is in the singular, emphasising his lonely entry into the city and Temple, leaving the enthusiasm outside at the approach. It reads almost like a summary statement about a tourist's first visit to the city but in fact 'looking around' has a much deeper significance. Its purpose will come to light when Jesus returns to the Temple. Meanwhile he returns to Bethany, his base of operations during this visit.[14] The coming to the city and coming to the Temple are thus kept apart as two separate episodes, one a royal visit, the other a prophetic visitation.

In Mark's account the entry does not immediately cause a re-action as the action in the Temple is on the next day. Like the other accounts, however, the action in the Temple will provoke a questioning of the authority by which he does these things. This questioning in turn provides the context for Jesus' display of a greater teaching authority than those who challenge him. His action in the Temple and his disputes with the religious and legal experts all reflect a negative judgement on the central institution and leadership of Israel very much in line with the prophecy of Malachi: 'Who will be able to resist the day of his coming? Who will remain standing when he appears' (Mal 3:1,2)?

2. PROPHETIC VISITATION OF THE TEMPLE MK 11:12-19

i. The Barren Fig Tree

The story of the barren fig tree provides a frame for the account of Jesus' action in the Temple, generally referred to as 'the cleansing of the Temple'. This passage is a classic example of an intercalation, or sandwich, where one story is inserted into another and they mutually throw light on each other. Inserting the story of Jesus' action in the Temple into the story of the fig tree points to the fact that the fig tree in some way interprets the action.[15]

---

14. The modern name for Bethany is Al Azariah, a name that associates the place with the story of Lazarus (Jn 11).
15. See C. Böttrich, 'Jesus und der Feigenbaum. Mk 11:12-14,20-25 in der Diskussion,' *NovT* 39 (1997), 328-59 and W. J. Cotter, 'For it was not the Season for Figs,' *CBQ* 48 (1986), 62-66.

Why would Jesus, a native of a land where figs grow, look for figs at a time when figs were not in season, and react so strongly when he found none? The reader's first reaction is to regard it as a pointless exercise and a very unreasonable reaction. Did he inspect the tree in early spring to see if it had the early indications of a good harvest to come or, as has already been suggested as a possibility, did he enter the city at the autumn Feast of Tabernacles or the winter feast of Dedication when he may have sought some late fruit? Is the phrase 'was not the season for figs', an explanatory comment added subsequently to the story in the course of transmission? It may well be that the fig tree as its decaying process had taken hold put out a final unhealthy but apparently lush growth, as often happens with decaying vegetation. This appearance of healthy growth may have led Jesus to seek fruit or to go through the motions of seeking fruit as a parable in action for the disciples.

The story of Jesus' cursing of the fig tree has raised many an eyebrow among those who see it as an action out of character for Jesus, and out of character with the canonical gospels generally, though quite in line with some of the stories in the apocryphal gospels. Some see it as an aetiology, a story composed to explain the phenomenon of a withered fig tree. Others wonder if it was a misunderstanding on the part of the disciples or if the story began as a parable like that of the unfruitful fig tree in Luke 13:6-9, and was later transformed in the course of transmission from a parable into an account of an action. Others see it as a parable in action or prophetic sign (ôt) like the actions of the prophets in the Old Testament described above in connection with the 'triumphal' approach to the city.

One can only speculate on the historical question. Its significance for Mark has to be sought within the gospel itself. Whatever the origin of the story and the history of its transmission, the significance of the story here in Mark's gospel lies in its relation to the action in the Temple. Mark uses it in this specific context and invests it with definite meaning.

As with the approach to the city, this story of Jesus and the fig tree is like a prophetic ôt and to understand its significance the reader needs to hear the Old Testament echoes that would have been heard by the original audience to the story, possibly before the writing of the gospel, and by the intended readership. In the Old Testament the fig tree and the vine (or vineyard) were used as metaphors for Israel (Isa 5;1-7; Hos 9:10; Mic 7:1; Jer 8:15). When God sought grapes or figs and found none it was a prelude to divine condemnation. Isaiah speaks of the condemn-ation of the vine(yard): '(God) expected it to yield grapes but sour grapes were all it gave … I will lay it waste, unpruned, undug, overgrown by the briar and the thorn' (Isa 5:1, 2, 6). Jeremiah articulates a similar condemnation: 'I would like to harvest there, says YHWH, but there are no grapes on the vine, no figs on the fig tree, even the leaves are withered' (Jer 8:13). John uses this same imagery evocatively in his passage on the vine and the branches: 'Every branch in me that bears no fruit he (my Father) cuts away '(Jn 15:2). For John the fruit comes through the life-giving power of Jesus, the vine. The parable of the wicked tenants of the vineyard who refused to give the fruits of the harvest to the owner, and maltreated his messengers, is another case in point and in fact will shortly be told in the gospel, broadly speaking in relation to the cleansing of the Temple and Jesus' authority for acting as he did (Mk 12:1-12// Mt 21:33-46//Lk 20:9-19). The fig tree had special messianic sig-nificance. Israel should welcome the Messiah with a harvest of figs. Its absence is an impediment to the reception of the Messiah and the arrival of the messianic age, and results in condemn-ation. M. D. Hooker sums it up succinctly:

> … in the messianic age the fig tree will bear fruit. The fig tree is an emblem of peace and prosperity: hope for the future is expressed in terms of sitting in security under one's vine and one's fig tree (e.g. Mic 4:4 and Zech 3:10) and gathering fruit from them (Hag 2:19). William Telford *(The Barren Temple and the Withered Tree)* argues that the fig tree would have been understood as a symbol for Israel, which should have borne fruit in the messianic era: yet when Jesus comes to the city, the tree is without fruit, and judgement inevitably follows.[16]

Here in Mark's gospel, therefore, the 'cursing' of the fig tree is not just a reaction of pique on the part of a hungry and tired Jesus when he finds no figs on the tree. It is not just a cursing of a tree but a prophetic symbolic condemnation of Israel for not producing fruit and for not recognising 'the one who comes'.

---

16. M. D. Hooker, *op. cit.*, 262.

ii. The Cleansing of the Temple Mk 11:15-19

In the synoptic accounts Jesus' action in the Temple takes place at the end of his ministry and is presented as the final challenge to official authority, bringing into sharp focus the question of his own authority, and setting in motion the events leading to his trial and execution. By way of contrast the incident takes place at the beginning of the ministry in St John's gospel and serves as a programmatic statement and a throwing down of the gauntlet to the establishment from the outset (Jn 2:13-22). What really matters, however, is not the timing but the meaning of the event in Mark's gospel. It comes across as a prophetic-style action or demonstration. It provides the motive and generates the energy for pursuing Jesus and bringing him to trial. One of the accusations at his Jewish trial will focus on an alleged threat to the Temple (Mk 14:58; Mt 26:61) and similar accusations about Jesus will be made at the trial of Stephen (Acts 6:14).

Since there is but one journey of Jesus to Jerusalem in the synoptic gospels the reader can see that the event had to be placed in the context of his final days. However, the fact that this action, according to all four gospels and the Acts of the Apostles, attracted such hostile attention from the authorities and resulted in their questions about Jesus' authority, makes it likely that if the event took place early in the ministry it would have proved an obstacle to continuing his ministry, especially in Jerusalem and above all in the Temple area. One therefore is inclined to think that the synoptic location of the event towards the end of the ministry is well placed historically. It may well be that historically Jesus had an ongoing attitude to the Temple during a number of visits, and it boiled over or came to a head at the end of the ministry. It is clearly placed early in John's gospel for theological and literary reasons where it functions as a programmatic event setting the tone of the ministry and offering a challenge, a catalyst provoking a reaction by way of a decision for or against Jesus (Jn 2:13-22).[17]

It is not surprising that Jesus would have a strongly critical attitude to the Jerusalem authorities and to the Temple which was their centre of power and influence. The long hand of Jerusalem authority had already reached out to his ministry in Galilee, accusing him of being possessed by Beelzebul and cast-

---

17. John's gospel portrays the raising of Lazarus as 'the final straw' for the authorities. Here again theological concerns are uppermost.

ing out demons by the prince of demons. According to St John's gospel, it had already reached out to interrogate the Baptist (Jn 1:19-28). The Jerusalem authorities were obviously very jealous of their authority and prerogatives and did not take kindly to mavericks or messianic 'pretenders'.

Jesus was not alone in his own day in having a strongly critical attitude towards the Temple. The Hellenists were less than enthusiastic and the Samaritans were quite hostile in its regard. The Essenes had opted out of the whole Temple-based religious life of Jerusalem and the Qumran community saw itself as the messianic community in waiting, seeing a renewed people of God as the true Temple. In having a critical attitude, Jesus would also have been in direct line of descent from the prophets. The four accounts of Jesus' 'cleansing' of the Temple stand in continuity with this prophetic tradition. It was commonplace for the prophets to adopt a critical stance on the Temple, its worship, its authority and its ongoing role in the life of the people. They issued stern reminders of the holiness of the Temple. They pointed out that it should be a place free from all kinds of corruption and venality, a place of true inner worship and a place which God would visit at some future time.

Hosea had condemned rituals performed by unworthy people and stressed the need for proper inner dispositions on the part of those who worship. 'For I desire steadfast love and not sacrifice, the knowledge of God rather than burnt offerings' (Hos 6:6a). Exhortation at times gave way to warnings of dire consequences. Amos threatened that God 'would strike the capitals so that the whole porch is shaken' (Amos 9:1). Micah had predicted the destruction of the Temple: 'Zion will become ploughland, Jerusalem a heap of rubble, and the mountain of the Temple a wooded height!' (Mic 3:12). Jeremiah said the Temple had become 'a den of thieves' and the Lord would destroy it as he did the sanctuary at Shiloh, making it 'a curse for all the nations of the earth' (Jer 7:11; 26:6). Furthermore, Jeremiah paid dearly for his attitude with persecution and attempts on his life. The persecution of Jeremiah for speaking against the Temple foreshadows the persecution and passion of Jesus and supplies the New Testament writers with a storyline to emulate and a scripture to quote (Jer 7:11; cf Mt 21:13; Mk 11:17; Lk 19:46).[18] Such prophetic conviction, often leading to persecution, prompts the

18. Jer 7:11 quoted in Mt 21:13; Mk 11:17; Lk 19:46.

psalmist to say, 'Zeal for your house consumes me', a text (quoted in Jn 2:17) which may well refer to the case of Jeremiah himself.[19]

From the time of the Exile the prophets looked to an ideal future with a reformed, ideal Temple. Ezekiel spoke of this future ideal Temple from which the water of life would flow to bring life to all that was dead in the land (Ezek 47:1-12). Trito-Isaiah said the Temple would be a place of prayer for all peoples (Isa 56:7). Zechariah looked forward to the Day of the Lord when all would be holy and no merchant would be found in the Temple (Zech 14:21). Malachi predicted that the Lord would suddenly enter his Temple after it was chastised for abuses in Levitical worship (Mal 3:1). He went on to prophesy that the judgement would be a purification, not in terms of ritual only but of up-rightness of life: 'I mean to visit you for the judgement and I am going to be a ready witness against sorcerer, adulterer and perjurer, against those who oppress the wage earner, the widow and the orphan, and who rob the settler of his rights'(Mal 3:5).[20]

Historically there had been three far reaching reforms which included 'cleansings' of the Temple, the first two by the reforming kings Hezekiah and Josiah under the influence of the prophets, and the third by the Maccabees in reaction to the desecration of the Temple by foreign persecutors, the forces of Antiochus IV, Epiphanes, and their Jewish collaborators. Hezekiah closed down the 'high places', destroyed the brazen serpent and repaired the Temple (2 Kings 18:3f; 2 Chron 29:1-36). Josiah cleansed Jerusalem, the Temple and the surrounding areas of all vestiges of 'idolatry', removing pagan altars and deposing priests (2 Kings 23:1-20; 2 Chron 34:29-33) and the Maccabees swept away the 'abomination of desolation' erected

---

19. Ps 68 (69) is one of the most quoted psalms in the NT. Scholars see it as originally referring to the persecution of Jeremiah, or to the Maccabees, or to the sufferings preceding the time of Ezra.

20. This connection of ' ritual' with 'moral' considerations is spelled out by Matthew in the criticism of scribes and Pharisees by Jesus in Mt 23:23, 'You who pay your tithes of mint and dill and cumin and have neglected the weightier matters of the Law – justice mercy, good faith', and in Mt 5:23, '… if you are bringing your offering to the altar and there remember that your brother has something against you, leave your offering there before the altar, go and be reconciled with your brother first, and then come back and present your offering', and also in Mt 23:18, 'You who say… If a man swears by the altar it has no force, but if a man swears by the offering that is on the altar he is bound.'

by Antiochus Epiphanes and there followed the rededication of the Temple in 164 BC (1 Macc 4:36-59).

A public judgemental action or statement of a high profile religious leader in relation to the Temple and its functioning came therefore laden with historical precedent and allusion. All four gospels record the action of Jesus in the Temple and the inevitable questioning of his authority which it provoked. Among the synoptic accounts Mark's is the longest. It speaks of Jesus casting out the buyers and sellers, upsetting the tables of the money changers and the stools of the pigeon sellers, and not allowing anyone to carry anything through the Temple area. Matthew speaks of casting out the buyers and sellers and upsetting the tables of the money changers and the stools of the pigeon sellers (Mt 21:12f) and Luke speaks of driving out those who were selling (Lk 19:45). Carrying things through the Temple and taking a short cut through its precincts were forbidden in the Mishnah, and the carrying of money bags was specifically forbidden.[21] Jesus' reaction to carrying things would have been a reaction to the general carrying of things related to commerce, and that would necessarily have involved carrying quite a deal of money. All three synoptics include the statement that the Temple should be a house of prayer but they had made it 'a den of thieves'.

Coins with the emperor's or other rulers' heads and inscriptions which, as graven images, would have been offensive in a sacred place, were exchanged for Jewish or Tyrian coins by the money changers. These acceptable coins could be used for buying the birds, animals, grain, wine and oil for various sacrificial rites, and also for giving as offerings to the Temple treasury and for paying Temple tax and dues. Birds were on sale for purchase by the poor who could not afford more expensive animals for the sacrifices. Pigeons or turtledoves were offered as sacrifices by women after childbirth if they could not afford a lamb (Lev 12:6-8; cf Lk 2:22-24) and lepers were to offer one pigeon or turtledove as a sacrifice for sin, and another as a holocaust (Lev 14:22).

Jesus' statement about the 'den of thieves', quotes the condemnatory phrase of Jeremiah against this commercial activity (Jer 7:11). John's gospel hammers home this point by saying they were turning the Temple into an *emporion*, a market (Jn 2:16).

---

21. m. *Berakot* 9.5.

Not only is the commercialism condemned but there is also a very strong implication of dishonesty in the expression 'den of thieves'. In the light of Malachi's prophecy (Mal 3:5) of the future purification when the Lord enters his Temple and brings and end to the oppression of the wage earner, the widow and the orphan, the reader wonders if there is not also an implication that these vulnerable people are being robbed of their hard earned money in the payment of taxes and offerings to the Temple. If so, Jesus' action could be seen also as a criticism of extortion on the part of the Temple authorities or priests in regard to fees for religious services or a very rigorous attitude on the part of the Temple establishment with regard to the purity of offering, the unblemished character of animals, the nature of the coinage used and so forth, perhaps putting a burden on the poorer people, and so meriting the phrase used by Jeremiah against the Temple, 'a den of thieves'.[22]

However, with regard to the 'cleansing of the Temple' one asks if the action was simply a 'cleansing' of the Temple in line with the historical criticisms of the prophets and the reforms mentioned already or did it have a deeper significance? Is it simply a reaction to the commerce and possible extortion being carried on in the outer court of the Temple even if it was legitimate and in the service of the various rituals?[23] At first glance, at least, the reader is most likely to see Jesus' action as a prophetic protest against this commercialisation and secularisation of the Temple complex through the carrying out of commercial activity. Such activity should have been done outside the Temple complex itself out of respect for the sacred character of the Temple precincts and the prayerful atmosphere that should have been preserved.[24] But has it a further and even more radical significance?

Furthermore, the reference to 'a house of prayer for all the nations' not only emphasises the purpose of the Temple as a place of prayer, and not of commerce and dishonest or extor-

---

22. See C. A. Evans, 'Jesus and the " Cave of Robbers": Toward a Jewish Context for the Temple Action,' *Bulletin of Biblical Research* 3 (1993) 93-110.
23. For a recent comment on the action of Jesus against the money changers see the article by J. Murphy-O'Connor, 'Jesus and the Money Changers (Mark 11:15-17; John 2:13-17),' *RB* 107 (2000) 42-55.
24. J. R. Donahue and D. J. Harrington, *op. cit.*, 332. See also D. Seely, 'Jesus' Temple Act,' *CBQ* 55(1993), 263-83.

tionist dealings, but written into its very 'constitution' according to the prophecy of Isa 56:7 was the programme for a revolutionary new order when the 'pagan' nations would look to the centre of Judaism as their place of prayer. But was that universal dimension possible in the context of the Temple as it was functioning or was a whole new order necessary? Mark's insertion of the account into the midst of the story of the barren fig tree about to wither, alerts the reader to the fact that the present order, like the fig tree, is about to pass away.

The action in the Temple is much more than a straightforward cleansing and reform. Like the fig tree, the Temple is doomed. It may well be, as pointed out above, that the fig tree as its decaying process had taken hold put out a final unhealthy but apparently lush growth. So too the feverish activity around the sacred precincts was like the lush growth giving the impression of life and health while underneath the plant is doomed and no longer producing fruit.

This question about the deeper meaning will be answered clearly in the eschatological-apocalyptic discourse. Mark, in fact all the synoptics, record Jesus' saying that 'not a stone will be left upon another. All will be destroyed', in response to the disciples' comments on the magnificence of the Temple buildings (Mt 24:1-3; Mk 13:1-4; Lk 21:5-7). In the parable of the wicked tenants he will speak of the stone rejected by the builders becoming the cornerstone (referring to the cornerstone of the new Temple) and in the discourse on the Mount of Olives he will predict the preaching of the good news to all the nations (Mk 12:10f; 13:10), which the reader can appreciate as a fulfilment of the prophecy of Trito-Isaiah that 'my house' would be a house of prayer for all the nations (Isa 56:7), in spite of the loss of the Temple.

The incident in the Temple leads eventually to Jesus' arrest. This is not surprising given the central role of the Temple in the life of the people, especially the people of Jerusalem. Not alone did the Temple function as the central place for worship, the exclusive location for sacrifice and the goal of pilgrimage, it also played a crucial role in the socio-economic life of Jerusalem and its citizens and was central to the power, prestige and welfare of the Jewish religious and civil authorities.[25] Jesus' attitude would

---

25. This socio-economic dependence was typical of all 'shrines', e.g. the centrality of the Temple of Artemis-Diana in Ephesus, as seen from the riot of the silversmiths, Acts 19:23-41.

therefore have made a deep impression on the citizens and
badly stung the establishment. This will be obvious when Mark
(like Matthew) records Jesus' attitude to the Temple as one of
the accusations made against him at his trial (Mk 14:58; Mt 26:61)
and a source of mockery at his crucifixion (Mk 15:29; Mt 27:40).
The Acts of the Apostles records similar accusations about Jesus
at the trial of Stephen (Acts 6:14). The statements about destroying and rebuilding the Temple are heard on the lips of false accusers and mocking enemies.[26]

iii. Faith and Prayer: The New Temple Mk 11:20-25

The following morning as they passed along Peter drew Jesus'
attention to the fact that the fig tree was withered to the roots.
The surprise of the disciples at the fulfilment of Jesus' promise
(prophecy or curse) that the fig tree would bear no more fruit
was a pointer for them that the power of God was working
through him. Jesus' response points to prayer as the source and
locus of all divine power in human life and activity. Jesus' statement about the power of prayer is very significantly placed here
in the gospel, and expressed in typical Semitic hyperbole.
Moving mountains was a common metaphor used by rabbis for
doing things of great difficulty, and a rabbi who could explain
particularly difficult passage of scripture was regarded as a

---

20. In St John's gospel, however, these statements are not heard on the
lips of opponents, but form the basis for a high christological statement,
or *logion*, on the lips of Jesus himself, and they serve the purpose of raising the issue onto another plane. Matthew uses another *logion* in the
context of the dispute about breaking the Sabbath. Having pointed out
that the Temple priests are blameless in 'breaking' the Sabbath by carrying on their ministry, Jesus makes a profound christological statement in the *logion* 'something greater than the Temple is here', and then
goes on in true prophetic style to quote the text: 'What I want is mercy,
not sacrifice', before making a second christological statement in the *logion*, 'The Son of Man is master of the Sabbath.' The synoptics thus portray Jesus breaking the mould and transcending the institutions and
practices of Israel's past. In all the gospels his attitude to Temple, Torah
and Sabbath is of central significance and displays his greatest claims to
divine authority. The many variations on the statement point to a widespread diffusion of the theme which therefore must have sprung from
historical reminiscence rather than from the creation of a midrashic
style commentator.

'mountain-remover'.[27] Confidence in prayer, born of faith, opens the way for God to act in our lives and world. In return, we must, in words reflecting the 'Our Father' (Lord's Prayer) in Matthew and Luke (Mt 6:12; Lk 11:3) have an open and forgiving attitude to others.[28] His action in the Temple, its symbolic representation in the fig tree and Jesus' pointing to the centrality of prayer and its power, point forward to the fact that in Jesus there is a new way to God, a new way of faith, prayer and forgiveness replacing the Temple and its sacrificial and atoning rituals.

When challenged about his action in the Temple Jesus will tell the parable of the wicked husbandmen and round it off with the reference to the stone rejected by the builders becoming the 'cornerstone', that is, by implication, the cornerstone of a new Temple.[29]

---

27. D. E. Nineham, *op. cit.*, 305; See also the article by C. W. Hedrick, 'On Moving Mountains. Mark 11:22b-23 / Matt 21:21 and Parallels', *Forum* 6 (1990) 219-37.

28. Mk 11:26: 'But if you do not forgive, your Father in heaven will not forgive your failings either', is regarded by scholars as a later scribal interpolation from Mt and Lk and not part of the original Markan text, even though it was included by Estienne in his numbering of the verses for his 1551 Geneva New Testament.

29. John's gospel depicts Jesus speaking of this new Temple in terms of 'a new Temple' of his risen body.

3. CLASH OF AUTHORITIES: JERUSALEM DISPUTE CYCLE
MK 11:27-12:37

Jesus' approach to the city showed a possible potential for revolutionary activity and his action in the Temple implied a level of authority that challenged the establishment. From the beginning of the gospel his authority in word and deed had been commented on. 'He speaks as one having authority, not like he scribes', the people in the synagogue in Capernaum had said at the very beginning of his ministry (Mk 1:22). 'He does all things well, he makes the deaf to hear and the dumb to speak', the people in the region of the Decapolis said when he cured the deaf and dumb man (Mk 7:37). His authority provoked the question of his true identity and the nature of his mission. 'Who can he be? The wind and sea obey him,' the disciples said after the calming of the storm (Mk 4:41) and the people in Capernaum asked, 'What is this? ... the demons obey him!' (Mk 1:27).[1]

In Jerusalem the religious authorities, administrative, priestly and scholarly, will now question publicly the nature and source of his authority for acting as he does. They will put his authority in teaching to the test, in the hope of discrediting him publicly before his followers. Jerusalem had already stretched its long hand of authority into Galilee during his ministry scrutinising his activity and teaching. The scribes from Jerusalem had declared that Beelzebul was in him and that through the prince of demons he was casting out demons (Mk 3:22). They had criticised his disciples, and by implication, himself, for not washing their hands before eating (Mk 7:1). Other references to Pharisees and scribes who had dogged his path may imply that they came from Jerusalem even though it is not specifically stated, since both groups are more closely associated with Jerusalem and the surrounding area than with the rural areas of Galilee. From John's gospel one learns that the Jerusalem authorities had earlier scrutinised John the Baptist and asked about his identity and his authority to baptise. This is a clear pointer to their keeping a close eye on anything they do not initiate and control themselves. Mark clearly assumes that this attitude was known to Jesus' audience and would be known or deduced by his intended readers.

---

1. Jesus' authority has significant implications for social, political and religious life and organisation. See A. Dawson, *Freedom as Liberating Power. A socio-political reading of the exousia texts in the Gospel of Mark*, Fribourg: Universitätsverlag, 2000.

Five 'controversies', containing challenges and responses, centred on the issues of forgiveness of sins, association with sinners, fasting, plucking corn on the Sabbath and healing on the Sabbath were set into the opening controversy narrative which marked the beginning of Jesus' ministry in Galilee (Mk 2:1-3:6). Five 'controversies' now form the centrepiece of a day of controversy which marks the opening of his Jerusalem ministry (Mk 11:27-12:37). They take place on a single day, the day that opened with the discovery of the withered fig tree. They all take place in the area of the Temple. Unity of time and place give form, strength and authority to the section. Jesus' two highly significant gestures, his royal approach to the city and his prophetic action in the Temple, provoke the officials to question him about his authority, and then the other debates or 'controversies' follow suit as the leaders of the various religious, scholarly and political groups challenge and are in turn silenced by him.[2] The five central controversial issues concern the authority of the Baptist, the payment of taxes to Caesar, the resurrection of the dead, the greatest commandment and the teaching about the Messiah as son of David. These were probably well established as a Jerusalem 'controversy' tradition prior to the writing of the gospel. Mark puts his own stamp on them. He treats the question of the greatest commandment in a 'non-controversial' manner and adds other material such as the parable of the wicked husbandmen, the condemnation of the scribes (and other religious leaders) and the story of the widow's mite.

i. The Chief Priests, the Scribes and the Elders. Mk 11:27-33

Jesus' authority and the authority of the Baptist
In the Johannine tradition the emissaries from Jerusalem cross questioned John the Baptist in severe fashion about his authority and his baptism (Jn 1:19-28). This questioning is not recorded in the synoptic tradition but it can be deduced that their attitude to John proved to be an ongoing embarrassment to them, and that Jesus did not shrink from reminding them of their obtuseness in this regard when they began to question his own authority. His

---

2. The entire section Mk 11:27-12:44 has close parallels in the other synoptics (//Mt 21:23-23:12; Lk 20:1-47; 10:25-38; 11:37-52) and therefore points to an already well established block of material which J. P. Meier has called ' The Jerusalem Dispute Cycle.' cf J. P. Meier, *A Marginal Jew*, 3, 414f.

public question to them about the source of John's authority left them the stark choice of admitting their own failure or facing the hostility of the people.[3]

This group of chief priests, scribes and the elders representing the priestly, scholarly, legal and administrative authority of the Sanhedrin challenges Jesus to tell them what authority (*exousia*) he has and who gave authority to him to do these things. They are the people with responsibility for keeping order in Jerusalem and for the running of the Temple and its affairs. Jesus' royal approach to the city and his prophetic action in the Temple naturally provoked a reaction on their part. Great tension is in the air and the reader will now remember with a certain amount of alarm that this is the very combination of characters mentioned in the first passion prediction when Jesus said he would be rejected by the chief priests, the scribes and the elders and put to death (Mk 8:31).[4] They are now trying to trap him into publicly laying claim to divine authority. Their challenge and the response it provoked from Jesus leave them publicly exposed as not being able to identify divine authority even when they encounter it, as in the case of John the Baptist, even though the ordinary people whom they are supposed to lead and teach had recognised it.

The question of Jesus' own authority is intimately linked to that of the Baptist. Jesus' revelation as Beloved Son, the descent of the Holy Spirit on him and his being driven into the desert by the Spirit as a preparation for his ministry, all happened in the context of John's baptism. It was John who 'prepared the way' and proclaimed the arrival of the 'stronger one' following him, the strap of whose sandals he was not worthy to untie, the one who would baptise in Holy Spirit (Mk 1:7f). A positive response to the question of John's authority would therefore have huge implications for the question of Jesus' own authority and vice versa.

Jesus' counter-question to them presumes knowledge on the part of the listeners (and readers) of their attitude to John the Baptist. As he did in Capernaum when challenged about forgiv-

---

3. When they questioned his own authority he responded with the question about their assessment of the authority of the Baptist, Mk 11:27-33 and //s.

4. They will be the main agents in the Jewish trial and the handing over of Jesus to the Romans (Mk 14:43, 53; 15:1).

ing sin, and in the synagogue in Galilee when he was under
scrutiny in the matter of Sabbath observance, Jesus responds in
rabbinic style with a searching ('no win') question designed to
embarrass and undermine his challengers. If they answer his
question (and whichever way they answer they will lose), he
will answer theirs. Either a positive or negative response would
have very serious consequences for themselves and their standing with the people. Asking them about the source or nature of
the Baptist's authority was 'very close to the bone' and in doing
so Jesus scores two points.

First of all, they are put in the position of having to answer a
'no-win' question. If they say John's baptism was from God they
will admit to their own obtuseness in his regard and their failure
to see what the ordinary people saw clearly. If they say it was
'from man' they will deny what they have now come to realise,
and also provoke a hostile reaction from the crowd who had enthusiastically followed John, as Mark pointed out, 'All Judaea
and all the people of Jerusalem made their way to him, and
being baptised by him in the river Jordan, confessed their sins'
(Mk 1:5). Their very embarrassment reveals their unacknowl-
edged belief in the divine origin of the Baptist's mission and
their failure to accept it at the time. To save face they have to
admit (or pretend?) 'we do not know'. This was a huge admission and embarrassment on their part.

Secondly, they are now shown up as behaving in the same
way towards Jesus, not having learned from their mistake. Jesus
leaves them to their devices by saying; 'Neither will I tell you by
what authority I act like this.' Since they do not answer his question neither does he answer theirs.

Their 'authority' as institutional figures has now been challenged by the charismatic, prophetic roles of John the Baptist
and Jesus as heralds of the kingdom. The classic challenge between prophecy and institution is in evidence. The classical reaction of institution is also in evidence. The gospel speaks of
Herod Antipas' arrest of John because of his attitude to his marriage to Herodias, but Josephus reports that he had felt a threat
from the Baptist because of his popularity with the crowds and
had moved against him as a protection against civil unrest.[5]
Now the Jerusalem authorities are similarly fearing the crowds
and possible civil unrest if they allow Jesus to continue his highly

5. Josephus, *Ant*, 18.118.

significant activity, and equally fear unrest if they try to apprehend him.

John the Baptist, the precursor who prepared the way, the
Elijah figure foretold by Malachi, has been mentioned now for
the last time in Mark's gospel. It was he who baptised Jesus and
proclaimed his coming as the coming of one greater than he, the
thong of whose shoes he was unworthy to untie, the one bringing baptism in Holy Spirit. After his arrest Jesus had taken up
the baton and as his ministry began to make an impact the
crowds and Herod himself thought John's spirit had come back
in Jesus. The discussion of his authority brings his role to the
fore again as the gospel approaches its denouement. His role as
precursor foreshadows also the arrest and execution of Jesus,
the one for whom he had prepared the way.[6]

The Parable of the Wicked Tenants Mk 12:1-12
Having turned the tables on the interrogators and reduced them
to a state of public embarrassment, Jesus now goes on the offensive. He follows on with a parable about bad leadership.[7] He
regularly tells a parable when challenged, criticised or disappointed. It is meant to provoke thought, either immediately or
later as one reflects on it. Sometimes a parable is like a shot between the eyes which provokes an immediate response or
exclamation. Such is the case with this parable of the wicked tenants. Having referred to the case of John the Baptist and the reception he received, Jesus now tells a parable that illustrates the
long history of such rejection of God's messengers. This parable
is no riddle with a mysterious or secret message for the few, but
a blatantly transparent allegory on the history of leadership in
Israel.

As seen already in the case of the fig tree, the fig tree and the
vine or vineyard are long established metaphors for the people
of God (Isa 5:1-7).[8] God expects fruit from them at harvest time.

---

6. For an overview of John the Baptist and his role, see W. Wink, *John the Baptist in the Gospel Tradition*, Cambridge: Cambridge University Press, 1969.

7. For recent study of the parable see K. Snodgrass, 'Recent Research on the Parable of the Wicked Tenants: An Assessment,' *Bulletin of Biblical Research* 8 (1998) 187-215.

8. See W. J. C. Weren, 'The Use of Isaiah 5:1-7 in the Parable of the Tenants (Mark 12:1-12; Matthew 21:33-46),' *Bib* 79 (1998) 1-26.

In this parable the people responsible for the vintage/harvest and its fruits have not only failed miserably but have ill-treated those who demanded the fruit of the harvest on behalf of the Lord of the harvest. The killing of the son in the hope of making the vineyard their own is the final failure, and outrage. As Jesus reaches the culmination of the story and asks the listeners what the lord of the harvest will do, the listeners exclaim spontaneously that the lord of the harvest will make an end of the tenants and give the vineyard to others. This is a spontaneous condemnation of the leaders on the lips of the listeners.

The parable is like the Bible or the history of salvation in miniature. It illustrates what the prophets would call the *hesed adonai*, the faithful loving kindness and concern of God for the covenant partner, Israel, as God keeps appealing to them even in the face of repeated infidelity (Hos 2:2, 14-20; Jer 3:11-14; Ezek 16:59-63). It reflects on the part of the covenant partner what Isaiah would call the hardness of heart whereby the eyes do not see nor the ears hear (Isa 6:10). The parable reflects closely the complaint in 2 Chronicles where the heads of the priesthood are condemned for defiling the Temple:

> All the leading priests, and the people too, added infidelity to infidelity … defiling the Temple that the Lord had consecrated for himself in Jerusalem. The Lord, the God of their ancestors tirelessly sent them messenger after messenger, since he wished to spare his people and his house. But they ridiculed the messengers of God, they despised his words, they laughed at his prophets, until at last the wrath of the Lord rose so high against his people that there was no further remedy (2 Chron 36:14-16).

The parable of the tenants uses a well known scene. Building the fence to keep out animals, digging the pit for pressing the grapes and building the tower as a shelter and lookout post, set the scene for a well-run operation which the absentee landlord entrusts to his stewards. They in turn are expected to work the operation, make a living from it, and ensure the profit due to the owner at the proper time (*tô kairô*). The vineyard with its operation and care, together with its production of a good vintage, was a long established metaphor for Israel and its spiritual harvest.

This parable of the vineyard and those charged with working it shows a process of development or clarification in transmission.

In Jesus' time the vineyard would have clearly represented the people of Israel and the *geôrgoi*, the 'land workers', represented the people charged with their spiritual welfare, answerable for their spiritual fruits to the God of Israel. The succession of messengers sent to remind them of the fruits that were due to the owner represent the prophets and other messengers who were so often badly treated.

As Jesus himself told the parable he may well have focused on John the Baptist as the last of the prophets, maybe even seeing him as the son in the parable, particularly if the parable was originally told in connection with the question about his authority. However, as the parable comes to Mark and is portrayed by him, the reference to striking the head of the second messenger may well be an allusion to the beheading of the Baptist, and Jesus is clearly the son who was killed and cast out.[9] This would fit the christology of the gospel with the heavenly declaration at the baptism and transfiguration where he is described as 'the Son, the Beloved' (Mk 1:11; 9:7).[10] They killed the son and threw him outside unburied, to get possession of the vineyard, and thereby maintain their own control, authority and interests. But Jesus asks the question: 'What will the owner of the vineyard do?' He will make an end of the tenants and give the vineyard to others. So they lost the inheritance they coveted by killing the son and suffered a similar fate to the one they had inflicted on him.[11]

However, the *logion*, a quotation from Psalm 118:22f (LXX),'The stone which the builders rejected became the cornerstone (*kephalê gônias*)', illustrates how God's choice and God's marvellous work are achieved in spite of human rejection.[12]

---

9. Heb 13:12f speaks of Jesus as 'suffering outside the gate'.

10. There are echoes of Abraham's beloved son Isaac and Jacob/Israel's beloved son Joseph against whom his brothers conspired: 'Come let us kill him' (Gen 22; 37:20).

11. For a discussion on the identity of the son and the other characters see A. Milavec, 'The Identity of the "Son" and "the Others": Mark's Parable of the Wicked Husbandmen Reconsidered,' *BTB* 20 (1990) 30-37.

12. *Kephalê gonias* has been interpreted as the cornerstone in the foundation, the capstone on top or the keystone in the arch. Whichever understanding is taken, the point is the same. It fulfils a vital function in the whole edifice. This may well be one of a number of *Testimonia* or proof texts assembled from the OT to illustrate particular points. Note how it is spoken of as *graphê*/writing/ text, whereas Mark usually introduces

Some scholars think that perhaps the similarity in sound between the Hebrew words *ben* (son) and *'eben* (stone) prompted the joining of the *logion* to the parable. It was probably placed here by Mark as a reflection on the parable. The experts in the dressing of vines and the dressing of stones are both shown up very badly. They failed to identify the identity, value and quality of the person they rejected but God's purpose was achieved in spite of them. The rejected Son, the rejected stone, survived to become the cornerstone of the new Temple.

The question concerning the Baptist and the parable of the wicked tenants reduce the chief priests, scribes and elders, the leaders of the people, to silence before the people, largely due to the fact that the people show discernment. The unwarranted superior attitude of the authorities and their failed interrogation technique turn now to hostility and aggression. They would have liked to arrest Jesus but they were afraid of the crowd. This same fear will cause them to seek a means of arresting him away from the festal crowd and Judas will come to their aid in facilitating the arrest.[13]

Having challenged the authority of the powerful leaders of the Temple priestly and political-religious class, Jesus is now drawn into a series of controversies which deal with questions of law and scripture. David Daube, in his study of Rabbinic Judaism and its influence on the New Testament, pointed out how the following 'debates' reflect the groupings of questions in rabbinic literature, even though they do not follow the same order.[14] Twelve questions were put to Rabbi Joshua ben Hananiah, as reported in the Babylonian Talmud.[15] Three of the questions were concerned with *Hokmah* (wisdom) in the interpretation of *Halakah* (legal questions arising from legal texts), three with *Haggadah* (non legal questions dealing with apparent contradictions in scripture), three with *Bôrut* (ridiculing the opponent's belief in the resurrection) and three concerned with *Derek 'Erets* (matters of moral conduct). Though the Jerusalem

---

quotations from the OT with *gegraptai*, 'it is written.' cf 4 Q 175-177 as anthologies of proof texts from the OT about the Messiah, the future consolation of Israel and the last days.

13. John's gospel points to several occasions in Jerusalem when they wished to arrest him.

14. D. Daube, *The New Testament and Rabbinic Judaism*, 158-169. J. Radermakers, *La bonne nouvelle de Jesús selon Marc*, 2, 313f.

15. *B. Nid.* 69b-71a. J. *Pesah* 10:37d.

and Babylonian Talmudim are later than the New Testament they reflect an established pattern of debate and controversy. This division of questions is followed in the debates (controversies) here in Mark, but significantly the *Haggadah* question dealing with apparently contradictory scriptural texts, here dealing with the son of David, is kept until the end, as a climax in the arguments and a turning point or pivot in the overall section.

ii. The Pharisees and Herodians: Tribute to Caesar Mk 12:13-17

'They sent', that is, the chief priests, the scribes and the elders, having been beaten themselves in their attempt to entrap Jesus and discredit him with the crowd, now enlist the help of the Pharisees and the Herodians. These unlikely partners have already conspired against Jesus during the early days of his ministry in Galilee and Jesus later warned his disciples against 'the leaven of the Pharisees and the leaven of Herod' (Mk 3:6; 8:15). The Pharisees were the saints and scholars of Palestinian Judaism, careful about the law, the traditions that grew up around its interpretation and its strict observance in every aspect of life. They were a foil for Jesus in his public ministry, and in the period after the destruction of the Temple they were the driving force in the reconstruction of the Jewish way of life.[16] In their way of seeing things Jesus was not an observant Jew in regard to the Sabbath observance. He also fell short in instructing his disciples in purity regulations. Furthermore, the scribes who thought he uttered blasphemy in pronouncing the forgiveness of sins may well have been of the Pharisee party. It was in their interest to undermine the influence that such a person had on the common people. Though no friends of the House of Herod and its Roman associations, they made common cause with the Herodians in the face of this common, but probably differently viewed, threat or nuisance.

The Herodians, on the other hand, were supporters of the house of Herod, in this case, the house of Herod Antipas. Josephus points out how Antipas was worried about the influence that John the Baptist had with the ordinary people in case it would boil up into revolution against himself or the Romans.[17]

---

16. The tensions that arose in that later period probably influenced their negative portrayal in the gospels of Matthew and John, particularly in Matthew, especially in Mt 23.
17. Josephus, *Ant*, 18:118.

This concern may well have been transferred to Jesus and his following after the elimination of John, and may in part account for Herod's desire to see Jesus during his visit to Jerusalem for Passover, when he was sent to him by Pilate, as Luke reports (Lk 23:5-12). Herod Antipas was particularly careful not to let anything happen in his jurisdiction that would upset the Romans lest they depose him as they had deposed another of the Herodian family, Archelaus, and divided his jurisdiction. Anxiety about Jesus' influence with the people would have made Antipas nervous of Rome, but an obvious move against Jesus could have brought about the very disturbance that he tried to avoid. Maybe enlisting the support of the Pharisees with their religious and nationalist reputation would soften the blow in the eyes of the people if they could undermine him. This may well account for the unlikely association. Conversely the Pharisees probably saw in the Herodians an arm of the law that would control this unconventional preacher and his following. They were not on good terms with the Sadducees who had their hands on the levers of Jerusalem Temple authority, so the Herodians were a tactical option and they held sway also in Galilee where Jesus had started his mission and had a large following.

Whether this alliance is mentioned here to give an overall historical picture of the wide range of opposition experienced by Jesus, or a more literary highlighting of the coming together of even the most unlikely groups from opposite ends of the political, religious and social spectrum in the face of a perceived threat from Jesus, the combination is striking.

An honorific address, *didaskale*, 'teacher', and feigned praise about his honesty and reputation for giving straight answers in keeping with the way of God and not 'respecting' personages, was an attempt to 'set Jesus up', in order to trap him with feigned praise, a *captatio benevolentiae*. It failed to trap him and he unmasked their hypocrisy. Their real plan was to trap him through pretended praise of his sincerity and forthrightness into responding to their question, which was presented as a typical example of seeking *hokmah* (wisdom) in relation to a question that required a *halakah* (legal) response, about whether or not it was right to pay tribute (*kênsos*) to Caesar.[18] It was an attempt to make public his attitude.

---

18. The *kênsos* was a tax imposed on Samaria, Judea and Idumea in 6BC when they became Roman provinces.

On the one hand, if Jesus had said it was lawful to do so (*ex-estin* – it is lawful according to the Mosaic Law), he would very likely have been seen as a collaborator and alienated the Jews among his followers who resented the Roman intrusion into their country, imposing taxes, dividing the country into Judea, Samaria and Idumaea as areas of Roman administration, and importing a pagan coinage with the emperor's head, all of which contributed to the resentment from which the Zealot movement was born.[19]

On the other hand, if he said it was not lawful, then there would have been an obvious case against him for treason against the emperor and his appointed administration. Such a case against him would have been easily believed by the Romans because he came from Galilee, home of the Zealot movement. The words Galilean and Zealot were almost synonymous in many people's minds. In that case the Romans could move against him. Furthermore, the two parties asking the question were on opposite sides of the issue. If he said a straight 'yes' at least some of the Pharisees in the questioning group would have taken umbrage, if he said 'no' the Herodians in the same group, supporters of the house of Herod who were clients of Rome, would have seen it as treason. He could not please both elements in the questioning party. He would fall foul of one or other group whether he answered 'yes' or 'no'.

Even among the Pharisees themselves this may have been a divisive question. Throughout their history they resisted foreign and pagan influences of any kind. They 'built a hedge' of detailed prescriptions around the law to protect it from infringement. Their instincts would have been anti-Roman, and particularly opposed to the portrayal of the emperor's head and the inscription claiming divine or quasi-divine status for the present and past emperors (Exod 20:2-6; Deut 5:6-11). However, the Pharisees may have had some concerns about the obligation of paying for the services of administration and security provided by the Romans, services for which, according to the Pharisees, the Romans too would have to render account since all authority came from God.[20] They may also have preferred to keep the *status*

19. Josephus, *Ant.*, XVIII.1.1,6.
20. J.Radermakers, *op. cit*, 317f. *Les pharisiens s'en accomodaient pratiquement, estimant que les gouvernements païens recevaient aussi de Dieu leur autorité de gardiens de l'ordre, dont ils auraient à lui rendre compte.* This is similar to the advice of Paul, a former Pharisee, in Rom 13:1-7.

quo rather than risk the consequences of an open rebellion.[21]
Their question therefore put Jesus in a really difficult situation
even with the Pharisees themselves. On all fronts it seemed to be
a win-win situation for Jesus' opponents, and a lose-lose situation for himself.

Again Jesus did not answer the question, at least not on the
terms in which it was asked. He responded to the question about
tax with a counter-question about the coin in which the tax was
paid. He asked them to produce the coin used in the tribute.
Jesus was not carrying a coin with the image of a pagan ruler on
it in the Temple precincts, but obviously someone among the
questioners was! As they produced the coin used in the tribute,
the denarius (*dênarion*),[22] he asked them a question which made
them admit that the image and inscription on the coin which
they were so happy to use, and many did not want to part with
by way of taxation, were in fact Tiberius' head and the inscription read: *Tiberius Caesar Divi Augusti Filius Augustus* (Tiberius
Caesar, Augustus, Son of the Divine Augustus). They lived in
Caesar's world and engaged in the commerce and life of his
world. Caesar provided the administration, the security and the
economic and financial system. The coin and all it stood for was
Caesar's. Therefore they should 'give back' to Caesar what was
Caesar's, pay it back as a debt that was owed, as pay for the services provided by Caesar's system.[23] Jesus did not comment on
the rights or wrongs of the political system whereby they belonged to Caesar's world, so he did not upset the people who resented Caesar's rule. Neither did he upset the Romans by opposing
the payment of the tax. Instead of a 'win-win' the opponents had
lost out on both counts. Small wonder they were taken completely by surprise.

Then Jesus adds, like a sting in the tail, awakening the listeners to a very different level of reality, 'and give to God the things

---

21. M. D. Hooker, *op. cit.*, 280. See also 'Numismatik und Neues
Testament ,' *Bib* 81 (2000) 457-88 and C. H. Giblin, 'The "Things of God"
in the Question Concerning Tribute to Caesar (Lk 20:25; Mk 12:17; Mt
22:21),' *CBQ* 33 (1971) 510-27.
22. The denarius was regarded as the equivalent of a day's wages.
23. This is a similar attitude to that of Paul in Romans 13:1-7, esp. 6, 7,
and in 1 Peter 2:13-17. Subsequent persecution by Nero and Domitian
brought about a very different attitude to the Romans, as evidenced in
Revelation where Rome is described as the scarlet whore drunk on the
blood of the martyrs and saints, Rev 17:1-7.

that are God's.' This was no pious afterthought. It was a brilliant stroke in a situation provided by his opponents. It drew a clear line of distinction between the kingdoms of the world and the kingdom of God. The opponents were using a question about the coinage of the world and its kingdoms, under the guise of religious concern, to frustrate the one coming to announce the kingdom of God and its concerns. The first part of Jesus' reply focused on the kingdoms of the world and one's obligations towards political authority. They owed to Caesar a debt for organising, governing and protecting the world they lived in, even if they would prefer to organise and govern it themselves. 'Give to Caesar what belongs to Caesar.' Earthly government and its rights, duties and obligations are the proper concern of the rulers of this world. The second part of the reply draws a clear line between what was owed to Caesar and what was owed to God.

One is left to chew over the question of 'what belongs to God' in the context of Jesus' reply. In the light of what has been taking place in the immediate context of the gospel, true and fruitful worship, unlike the commercialism and possible exploitation of the Temple system, and acceptance and proper treatment of the people sent by God to gather the fruits of the vineyard, in this case the Baptist and Jesus himself, could be regarded as the fundamental attitudes required.

The growing trend, however, of regarding the emperor as 'divine', *divus*, and *filius divi Julii* (son of the divine Julius) or *filius divi Augusti* (son of the divine Augustus), a trend that developed into full-blown emperor worship in the days of Caligula, Nero and Domitian, is a trespassing into the area of God's domain. The human agent should not trespass on the divine prerogatives or the exclusive right of God to receive divine worship. The Jewish and Christian difficulty with emperor worship may well be a sub-text in Mark's reporting of this saying of Jesus.[24]

iii. The Sadducees. Resurrection Mk 12:18-27

As the Pharisees and Herodians disappear defeated from the story, not to return, the Sadducees now try their hand at trapping him. The Sadducees were members of the Jewish priestly aristocracy, people of high standing in the socio-religious order

24. Emperor worship eventually became a matter of life and death for Christians, in the days of Domitian.

of their day. Taking their name most likely from the High Priest Zadok who lived in the time of David and Solomon (2 Sam 8:17; 15:24; 1 Kings 1:8), and enjoying also a happy similarity of name with the term *saddiqim*, the righteous ones, they were conservative and suspicious of change and innovation in belief and practice. They were theologically opposed to the Pharisees, especially on the questions of the resurrection of the dead and the existence of angels and spirits,[25] and they recognised the written law of Moses only, unlike the Pharisees who followed not only the written law but also the oral tradition that grew up around the law and its interpretation. They regarded the Prophets and the Writings as having less authority than the Torah (Pentateuch), and in the opinion of some scholars they completely disregarded them. They liked to enter into debate with distinguished teachers about their teaching and their memory lived on in rabbinic literature where they function as foils for discussions with the Pharisees. Being quite removed from the ordinary people they were of limited influence with them.[26] Being prosperous and comfortable in this life they did not see the necessity of looking to an after-life existence.[27] Their children would perpetuate their name when their mortal life had ended, a belief strongly supported by the obligation of the levirate law about the brother of a childless dead man taking his wife and raising offspring to carry on his brother's name (and probably ensuring also that land and wealth remained within the family).[28]

This is the only exchange between Jesus and the Sadducees in this gospel. In fact it is their only appearance in the gospel and after the exchange they disappear from the story. It is interesting that during this exchange Jesus adopts the theological position of his more usual adversaries, the Pharisees. The Sadducees ask Jesus a question, not because they want or respect his opinion,

25. Paul stirred intense passion between them by raising the issue of resurrection in Acts 23: 6-10.
26. Josephus, *Ant*, XIII, 10,6; XVIII, 1,4,16; *War* II, 8.14.
27. See the treatment by J. P. Meier, 'The Debate on the Resurrection of the Dead: An Incident from the Ministry of the Historical Jesus?' *JSNT* 77 (2000) 3-24. See also E. Main, 'Les Sadducéens et la resurrection des morts: comparaison entre Mc 12:18-27 et Luc 27-37,' *RB* 103 (1996) 4111-32.
28. Deut 25:5f. *Levir* is the Latin term for a brother-in-law, hence the term 'levirate law' for the regulation instructing the brother of a dead man to take his wife and raise children to carry on his brother's name.

but in order to undermine the belief in resurrection by making it look ridiculous. This is a typical *Bôrut*, a question introducing a discussion designed to mock the belief of the opponent. Quoting the levirate law and citing the authority of Moses that lay behind the law, they put forward an argument that seems to make belief in the resurrection of the dead look ridiculous. The levirate law (so called from the Latin word *levir* which means ' brother-in-law') lays down that: 'If brothers live together and one of them dies childless, the dead man's wife must not marry a stranger outside the family. Her husband's brother must come to her and, exercising his levirate, make her his wife, and the first son she bears shall assume the dead brother's name; and so his name will not be blotted out in Israel' (Deut 25:5-10).[29]

The Sadducees put to Jesus the case of a woman who has had seven husbands and ask which will be her husband 'at the resurrection when they rise again'.[30] The authority of Moses stands solidly behind their interpretation of the levirate law and the question arising from its scrupulous application seems to highlight the ridiculous nature of belief in resurrection where the woman would have seven contending former husbands. Jesus' response elaborates critically on their interpretation of scripture and their understanding or, more accurately, their not understanding the power of God to raise the dead, and elaborates also on the nature of the resurrection.

Jesus' reply to the questioners opens and closes with a statement that they are wrong (Mk 12:24,27). The verb *planân* means 'to lead astray', and it is here used in the passive meaning 'you are led astray, you are wrong/mistaken'. They are wrong on two counts. They do not understand the scriptures or the power of God (to raise the dead). Jesus appeals to both authorities in his response to their question and in his refutation of their underly-

---

29. The story of Judah and Tamar in Gen 38 arises from Judah's failure to respect this law and Tamar's action which ensures the continuation of the line of the promises. The story of Ruth and Boaz similarly shows the woman's action ensuring the continuation of the line through a relative (Ruth 2-4), an extension of the levirate law.

30. Some mss do not have 'when they rise again', neither do the parallel accounts in Mt 22:28 and Lk 20:33. However, the pleonastic approach 'at the resurrection, when they rise again', is quite in keeping with Mark's penchant for adding a clarifying phrase or clause to a stated time, e.g. 'that evening , after sunset,' 'early in the morning, long before dawn,' inter al., Mk 1:32, 35.

ing misunderstanding. He answers their questions in reverse order to the two mistakes he points out. He begins by talking about the power of God to raise the dead and then deals with the interpretation of scripture.

Having pointed to their two mistakes Jesus deals with the second one first. They have not understood the power of God. God has power to raise the dead to a new way of life. This new life at the resurrection is a communion of life with God. It is not just a resuscitation of the present life, a continuation of the present physical existence with marriage and giving in marriage.[31] It is a whole new life in communion with God, and it is in God's power to bestow this new life. It is a different mode of life, 'like the angels in heaven' (an undermining of another theory of the Sadducees, that there are no angels!).

Jesus is confirming a long tradition of belief in an afterlife and presents it in terms of a sharing in the life of God. The Psalms speak a lot about an 'afterlife' but it is an ill-defined, shady, 'limbo-like' existence. Isaiah has a clearer statement, 'Your dead shall live, their corpses shall rise' and Daniel says, 'Many of those who sleep in the earth shall awake, some to everlasting life ...' (Isa 26:19; Dan 12:2f). The Wisdom tradition speaks of the rewards of a good and bad life after death: 'The souls of the just are in the hands of God, no evil shall ever touch them ... they are at peace ... grace and mercy await those he has chosen ... Not so the wicked ...' (Wis 3:1-12). There is a much clearer hope of eternal life in the speech of the mother in 2 Macc 7:29, 36. 'Make death welcome, so that in the day of mercy I may receive you back in your brothers' company ...' and in the words of the youngest son: 'our brothers drink of ever flowing life by virtue of God's covenant'. In New Testament times Martha declares to Jesus that she believes her brother Lazarus will rise on the last day, a reflection of the belief of the ordinary people, in line with the belief of the Pharisees (Jn 11:24). The

31. The active and passive forms of the verb *gamein* were used of the man and woman respectively in regard to contracting marriage. Radermakers, *op. cit.*, 319f, comments: '... *celui que forgent les sadducéens apparaît singulièrement théorique: il révèle, de plus, une conception de l'au-delà calquée sur les réalités terrestres, où les joies de l'union conjugale apparaîtraient comme la suprême bénédiction divine ... Les relations sexuelles appartiennent à la condition charnelle de l'homme terrestre, il ne faut pas les transposer imaginativement au monde de la résurrection. La loi du lévirat est donc transitoire.'

Thanksgiving Hymns of the Dead Sea Scrolls, the *Hodayoth*, reflect the belief in an angelic style existence in the heavenly court, celebrating the heavenly liturgy, an image reflected in the Book of Revelation (Rev 14:3ff, 13). Significantly, Jesus, though he speaks of his resurrection in the passion predictions, does not base his teaching in this discussion with the Sadducees on his own resurrection, a pointer possibly to the fact that the tradition of this discussion goes back to Jesus' ministry and has not been influenced by later teaching in the light of Jesus' own resurrection.[32] St Paul, however, emphasises the fact that resurrection will lead to a life that is not just a continuation of the present life but a whole new existence, 'what is sown a perishable body will rise imperishable and what is sown a physical body will rise a spiritual body' (1 Cor 15:42-44). Paul, however, roots his teaching in the resurrection of Jesus and the believer's participation in it.

The other point on which the Sadducees are mistaken relates to their misunderstanding of scripture. Here Jesus engages in a rabbinic style argument from the scriptures. He chooses a well known pivotal text in the Old Testament, the passage about Moses and the burning bush in which the God addressing Moses identifies himself as 'the God of Abraham, Isaac and Jacob', the Patriarchs who had died many centuries earlier (Exod 3:6, 15, 16; cf 4:5).[33] Jesus uses this central text to illustrate his point. God is not just the God of dead heroes of the past. M. D. Hooker explains the biblical argument: '...if God is the God of the Patriarchs (and of those who came after them), he does not cease to be their God at their death; experience of fellowship with God demands belief in some kind of continuing relationship with him.'[34]

The encounter ends not with a statement of the reaction of the onlookers as is customary in Mark, but with a repetition of Jesus' telling his questioners that they are very much mistaken.

---

32. For a treatment of Jewish belief in resurrection in the intertestamental period as a background for understanding New Testament issues and innovations, see G. W. E. Nickelsburg, *Resurrection, Immortality, and Eternal Life in Intertestamental Judaism*, Cambridge, Mass: Harvard University Press, 1972.

33. A belief was current that the Patriarchs were still alive, as is seen from 4 Macc 7:19; 16:25.

34. M. D. Hooker, *op. cit.*, 285.

iv. The Good Scribe. The First Commandment. Mk 12:28-34

The reader is likely to expect that the scribe who now comes forward with a question has hostile intent like the previous questioners. This is especially likely since the scribes were allied with the chief priests and elders in Mk 11:27 when they questioned Jesus about his authority after the cleansing of the Temple, and they appeared several times throughout the gospel as his critics, at times allied with the Pharisees. The scribes from Jerusalem were named specifically as the ones who said he was possessed and cast out devils by the power of the prince of devils (Mk 3:22). In fact the parallel accounts of this story in Matthew and Luke describe a hostile attitude on the part of the questioner. Matthew speaks of a Pharisee putting the question 'in order to disconcert him' (Mt 22:35) and Luke speaks of a lawyer who wished 'to disconcert him' (Lk 10:25). Surprisingly the encounter in Mark's gospel is not only friendly but also mutually complimentary on the part of Jesus and of the scribe.[35]

Mark here introduces the sole example of a leader in Israel who agreed with Jesus, 'a good scribe' representative of those scribes who listened to him, and subsequently to his followers. The scribe approaches Jesus in positive mood like a student approaching a well established master, because he was impressed with how well Jesus had responded to his questioners / critics.

The question introduces a discussion which deals with the *Derek 'Eretz*, 'the way of righteousness', the fundamental principles of moral conduct. It is about 'the first of all the commandments' and it is not so much a question about the most important commandment among all the others, as a commandment that encapsulates some basic principle that underpins and runs through the vast array of commandments that were later organised by the rabbis into the 365 negative and 248 positive commandments, a total of 613 in all. Here two commandments are brought together to form one great commandment.

In giving a single, combined commandment Jesus is stating an underlying principle that runs through all commandments.

---

35. Scholars discuss whether the Markan or Lukan approach is the more primitive. Both show signs of development. J. Gnilka, *Das Envangelium nach Markus*, 2.163, points out how Mark has used a traditional story and linked it (with verses 28 and 34) into the present sequence of discussions. He sees the pericope as a product of the Hellenistic Jewish Christians disputes.

He is also at the same time issuing a challenge to the approach to
law which lost sight of the central insights of the law and considered it necessary to legislate for every possible circumstance in
everyday living, leading at times to an overburdening of people
with obligations (and consequently with guilt).

Being asked about one commandment, Jesus takes two commandments and knits them together as one great commandment or principle. First of all there is the commandment to love
God, and then, following on that the commandment to love
one's neighbour, typical of biblical religion where moral injunc-
tions flow from religious worship and doctrine.[36]

Although Mk 12:29-31 consists almost entirely of verbatim
quotations from two Old Testament passages (Deut 6:4, 5 and
Lev 19:18 – both fully emphasised and commented on by the
rabbis and scholars), 'the combination of these two widely
separated texts as taking us to the heart of religion is clearly an
original and creative achievement of the highest order'.[37] Was
Jesus the first to combine them? It is worth noting that whereas
Mark and Matthew portray Jesus as combining them in his answer to the question about the greatest commandment put to
him by the scribe, Luke places the combination on the lips of the
scribe and maybe in so doing reflects a tradition that was in
vogue and is drawn on and highlighted by Jesus (Lk 10:25-28).
Luke portrays the scribe as asking the question: 'What must I do
to inherit eternal life?' Jesus responds, 'What is written in the
Law? What do you read there?' to which the scribe responds
with the double commandment of love of God and neighbour.
Jesus responds that he has answered right and if he acts accordingly, 'life is yours'. In spite of the negative introductory note
about his trying to disconcert Jesus, the scribe in Luke's account
also represents a tradition of 'good' scribes whose openness and
perspicacity bring them close to the essential teaching of Jesus.
The combination of the two commandments is also seen in a number of places in the Testament of the Twelve Patriarchs, a work
generally regarded as having come under Christian influence.[38]

36. E. Lohmeyer, *Das Evangelium des Markus*, 258, points out how the
two commandments in effect sum up the two tables of the Decalogue,
the first dealing with our relationship with God, the second with neighbour.

37. D. E. Nineham, *op. cit.*, 324.

38. *Dan* 5:3; *Issachar* 5:2; 7:6.

The commandment to love God is taken from Deuteronomy and begins with the command to 'listen/hear', the *Shema*, recited morning and evening by the Jews as their prayer and renewal of commitment. 'Listen, O Israel, the Lord our God is the one Lord' (Deut 6:4f, 9; cf 11:13-21; Num 15:37-41). Following this declaration/profession of faith, in the Hebrew text there follows the command to 'love the Lord your God with all your heart, with all your soul and with all your strength' (Deut 6:5). In the text of Mark and Matthew 'with all your mind (*dianoia*)' is added to 'with all your heart, soul and strength', probably reflecting an attempt, under Hellenistic influence, to cover every aspect of the human person's personal response. Luke adds 'with all your mind' (*synesis*) and omits 'all your strength'. This also resembles an attempt to cover the response of the whole person.

The commandment to love one's neighbour is a quotation from Leviticus 19:18. The standard measure for love of neighbour is love of self. 'It assumes that people naturally love themselves enough to care for themselves, protect themselves, and look after their own interests. The challenge is to show the same kind of love to others.'[39] In Leviticus 'neighbour' is seen in terms of family, kin and friend. Gradually a broader concept emerges and this is hammered home by Jesus in the parable of the Good Samaritan in Luke's gospel where being a neighbour is defined in terms of response to anyone in need, of whatever race or background, even someone from a background hostile to one's own, a traditional and national enemy (Lk 10:29-37).

It was not uncommon for a master to be asked questions about the relative seriousness of various commandments. Some were regarded as 'light', others as 'heavy'. In the Sermon on the Mount Jesus speaks of 'the least' of the commandments (Mt 5:19).[40] Sometimes, too, a master would be asked a question such as, 'could the entire body of law be summed up in a sentence, or

39. J. R. Donahue and D. J. Harrington, *op.cit.*, 355.
40. I. Abrahams, in 'The Greatest Commandment' in *Studies in Pharisaism and the Gospels,* First Series, Cambridge: Cambridge University Press, 1917, 18ff, is of the opinion that the attempt to isolate the basic principle(s) underlying the law caused fear among some rabbis that this could result in regarding some laws as less important, whereas they regarded all the law as important. He suggests that the original intention of the question put to Jesus was to see where he stood on the issue. See, D. E. Nineham, *op. cit.*, 324f.

recited while standing on one foot'. A famous example is that of
Hillel, quoted in the Babylonian Talmud.[41] Shammai and Hillel
were two of the most well known rabbis who were more or less
contemporaries of Jesus (mentioned already in connection with
the debate on the grounds for divorce). The former was regarded
as more strict, the latter as more liberal in interpretations of the
law. A Gentile approached Shammai promising to become a
proselyte if he could teach him the whole Torah while he stood
on one foot. Shammai chased him away with a stick. He came to
Hillel who responded to the same request with what has been
called the 'silver rule' of Hillel, 'What you yourself hate, do not
do to anyone; this is the whole law, the rest is commentary; go
and learn it.' This reflects very closely a maxim stated in Tobit:
'Do to no one what you would not want done to yourself' (Tob
4:15).

Whereas the 'silver rule' was stated in negative terms, saying
what should not be done, Jesus' 'golden rule' is stated in positive terms, stating what should be done. The 'golden rule' of
Jesus in Matthew's gospel is spoken in the context of an underlying principle in the teaching of the law and the prophets: 'So always treat others as you would like them to treat you, that is the
meaning of the law and the prophets'(Mt 7:12). In Luke the
'golden rule' is included as one of a series of maxims in the sermon on the plain. St Paul quoted it in his letter to the Galatians:
'The whole Law is summarised in a single command: "Love
your neighbour as yourself"'(Gal 5:14) and in his Letter to the
Romans: 'The one who loves his neighbour has fulfilled the law
… All the commandments … are summed up in this single command: "You must love your neighbour as yourself. Love is the
one thing that cannot hurt your neighbour; that is why it is the
answer to every one of the commandments"'(Rom 13:8-10).

Returning to Mark, the scribe repeats Jesus' words in praise
and affirmation about the joint commandment of love, and adds
that 'it is more important than any holocaust or sacrifice' (Mk
13:33). This addition, very apt in the Temple area and following
Jesus' 'attack' on the Temple and its worship, is itself a summary
of an insight which appears in many of the traditions in the Old
Testament concerning worship. One reads in the First Book of
Samuel: 'Is the pleasure of YHWH in holocausts and sacrifices
or in obedience to the voice of YHWH ? Yes, obedience is better

41. b. *Shabbat* 31a.

than sacrifice, submissiveness better than the fat of rams' (1 Sam 15:22). Hosea proclaimed: 'What I want is love, not sacrifice; knowledge of God, not holocausts' (Hos 6:6) and Micah remarked: 'What is good has been explained to you, O man. This is what YHWH asks of you; only this, to act justly, to love tenderly and to walk humbly with your God (Mic 6:8). The Book of Proverbs states: 'To act virtuously and with justice is more pleasing to the Lord than sacrifice' (Prov 21:3) and David's Psalm of Repentance affirms: 'My sacrifice is a contrite spirit, a humble, contrite heart you will not spurn' (Ps 50 (51):17). In St John's gospel the question of the contending locations of Mt Gerizim and the Temple as the place of worship is shifted by Jesus from a Jew-Samaritan debate about belonging to the holy people and the true place of worship to an emphasis on worship 'in spirit and in truth' (Jn 4:20-24). St Paul reflects a similar approach in the Letter to the Romans when he speaks of 'offering your living bodies as a holy sacrifice, truly pleasing to God' (Rom 12:1).[42]

Jesus commends the scribe for answering wisely (*nounechôs*),[43] not only because he understood and accepted what Jesus said about love of God and neighbour, repeating Jesus' response as a sign of his acceptance, but showing how he understood the scriptural emphasis on the superiority of love over holocausts and sacrifices.[44] The scribe was obviously open to, and appreciative of, Jesus' authority in teaching, and so he was open to what Jesus was doing and saying by way of establishing the kingdom. In the words of Jesus, he was 'not far from the kingdom of God.'

The section closes with a double negative emphasising how Jesus had outclassed and silenced his critics and proved his worth to the open-minded. 'After that nobody (lit.'nobody … never) dared to question him any more' (Mk 12:34).

42. Cf also Isa 1:11; Jer 7:22f.
43. *Nounechôs* is a *hapax* in the NT.
44. For further study on the 'love commandment' see, J. R. Donahue, 'A Neglected Factor in the Theology of Mark', *JBL*, 101 (1982), 563-94; P. Perkins, *Love Commands in the New Testament*, New York: Paulist, 1982; V. P. Furnish, *The Love Command in the New Testament*, Nashville: Abingdon, 1972.

v. Jesus takes the Initiative Mk 12:35-37

The Question about the son of David

Having silenced the opposition Jesus now has centre stage as he continues to teach in the Temple.[25] The location adds a note of solemnity to his teaching, combined with a sense of challenge to the authorities there. It is now Jesus' turn to ask a searching question. He addresses the crowd, criticising the teaching of the scribes: ' How do the scribes say that the Messiah is the son of David?' Challenge and criticism are implied in this opening re-mark. This question was probably very important for the early Christians as they debated among themselves and with the Jews how best to understand, articulate and argue the identity, role and status of Jesus. Being well established in the tradition, the debate finds its way into the three synoptic gospels with some differences of setting and audience. In the parallel passage in Matthew's gospel Jesus puts the question to the Pharisees about whose son the Messiah/Christ is. They answer, 'David's' (Mt 22:41-46). In Luke's account he appears to address the scribes (Lk 20:41-44).

The Messiah/Christ, 'the anointed one,' was 'the one who is to come', variously expected to be a prophet, priest or prince/ king. Prior to the Exile the kings were seen to be descended from David, in the words of Isaiah, a shoot from the stump or root of Jesse (David's father) (cf Isa 11:1, 10). Jeremiah spoke of God raising up 'a branch from the root of Jesse' (Jer 23:5). Ezekiel looked to the day when God would raise up a new David, a shepherd-king to look after the flock of God (Ezek 34:23). After the Exile the expectation developed in different ways. As the people struggled with the remnants of what had been, some looked to a complete apocalyptic destruction and a new begin-ning; others looked to an ideal future with the hope of restoring the kingdom of David and Solomon when God would raise up a judge, king or warrior to establish it. The Psalms of Solomon 17 from the century before Christ testify to the expectation. The devotees at Qumran expected two, possibly three, persons to fulfil the priestly, prophetic and princely roles of the expected

---

45. There is a shift in vocabulary from controversy back to an emphasis on 'teaching', possibly reflecting older tradition, but it is set within the overall context of the controversies.

Messiah.[46] In John's gospel the questioning of John the Baptist by the emissaries sent by the Jerusalem authorities shows a triple expectation of 'Christ, Elijah and the Prophet' though this neat formula may be influenced by subsequent Christian reflection (Jn 1:19-28). A messianic figure, a descendant of David, was expected, but the terms 'son of David' and 'Messiah' do not seem to have been closely associated in common usage.[47]

This general and possibly diverse and unfocused expectation of a Messiah hung heavily in the air at Passover, and attached itself to Jesus in a very definite way on the occasion of his triumphal approach to the city when he was hailed as son of David by Bartimaeus and the crowd called down blessings on 'the one who comes in the name of the Lord' and on 'the coming kingdom of our father David' (Mk 11:9f).

Now Jesus is posing a question, or rather issuing a challenge, about the identity of such an anointed figure. He quotes the opening verse of Psalm 109 (110) which guarantees the assistance of God to the king at his enthronement, as though he sits with God in the heavenly court: 'The Lord said to my Lord, "Sit at my right hand, I will make your enemies a footstool under your feet".' Both Jesus and the listeners associate the psalm with David as author, and accept its authority as inspired scripture. Both he and his audience are also accustomed to hearing verses of scripture quoted 'out of context', taken on their own and presented as oracles or proof texts. The verse is quoted here in Mark without reference to the footstool: 'I will put your enemies beneath your feet.'[48] Here however, as God is seen to inspire the

---

46. On the Qumran material see J. J. Collins, *The Sceptre and the Star: The Messiahs of the Dead Sea Scrolls and Other Ancient Literature*, ABRL, New York: Doubleday, 1995, and also his article 'The Nature of Messianism in the Light of the Dead Sea Scrolls' in *The Dead Sea Scrolls in their Historical Context*, (eds T. H. Lim, L. W. Hurtado, A. Graeme Auld, and Alison Jack), Edinburgh: T&T Clark, 2000, 199-219. See also the essays in J. H. Charlesworth (ed), *The Messiah: Developments in Earliest Judaism and Christianity: The First Princeton Symposium on Judaism and Christian Origins*, Minneapolis: Fortress, 1992.
47. Cf F. J. Moloney, *op. cit.*, 243, text and note 145.
48. In the ancient world, as is evidenced, for example, from some of the artefacts from the Egyptian tombs, it was customary for the victor to paint the image of his conquered enemy on his footstool. Putting his feet on the footstool then represented having his foot on the neck of his enemy, the sign of victory in combat. Mark and Matthew (Mt 22:41-46)

oracle through divine inspiration of scripture, and David articulates it in the psalm, a third person, understood here to be the Messiah, is seen to be the addressee.

The argument made by Jesus is even more striking when seen against the background of the Greek text, *eipen ho kyrios tô kyriô mou*, 'The Lord said to my Lord'. The term Lord had become a standard translation for *adonai*, which was in turn a substitute for YHWH in the reading of the Hebrew scriptures where, out of reverence, the Divine Name was not pronounced. In the Greek of the Septuagint and of the New Testament therefore the same title is used for God and the one to whom the psalm is addressed, the Messiah, in Jesus' interpretation. It could be paraphrased: 'God said to my Lord, through the words of David's psalm.' David, speaking of the Messiah, in this understanding of the psalm, describes him as 'my Lord', thus putting him on a different plain altogether to any son or descendant of his own. Sitting at God's right hand and having his enemies (a footstool) under his feet became for the Christians the great expression of Jesus' glorification and victory over sin and death (Mk 14:62; Col 3:1; Heb 1:3; 1 Cor 15:25).[49] The verse is actually quoted in Acts 2:34f and Heb 1:13. It is quoted in the context of Peter's speech at Pentecost in Acts, and followed by the remark: 'For this reason the whole house of Israel can be certain that God has made this Jesus whom you crucified both Lord and Christ.' In Hebrews 1:13 the author says: 'God has never said to any angel: "Sit at my right hand and I will make your enemies a footstool for you".'[50] As the Christians proclaimed Jesus Lord, they did so in a world, and often against a background of persecution, where the emperor was seen as Lord/*kyrios*/*Dominus*. By the time of Domitian they will be required to choose between Jesus as Lord and God (the great faith profession of John's

drop the LXX reference to the footstool and simply state 'under your feet'. Luke maintains the reference to the footstool (Lk 20:41-44). The point being made is the same with or without the reference to the footstool. 'Underfoot' is understood in both renderings and signifies 'vanquished'.

49. Artists have often pictured the risen Jesus with his foot on the tomb as a sign of his victory over death.

50. See W. R. G Loader, 'Christ at the Right Hand. Ps CX.1 in the New Testament', *NTS* 21 (1974-1975) 81-108; and D. M. Hay, *Glory at the Right Hand. Psalm 110 in Early Christianity*, SBLMS 18. Nashville: Abingdon, 1973.

gospel on the lips of Thomas in Jn 20:28) and the emperor
Domitian as *Dominus et Deus, Kyrios kai Theos*, Lord and God.
Mark's gospel represents a step on the way towards this public
clash of lordships.

All three synoptics have an account of this discussion about
the son of David. All three accept the importance of the Davidic
descent of Jesus. The genealogies and infancy narratives in the
gospels of Matthew and Luke (Mt 1:1-16, 20; Lk 1:27, 3:23-38)
carefully emphasise the Davidic descent of Joseph who gave
Jesus his legal paternity and all four gospels highlight the
Davidic element in the enthusiastic (even if misguided) reception of Jesus at his triumphal entrance into Jerusalem. Mark also
emphasises the Davidic confession of Bartimaeus in Jericho as
Jesus begins the final ascent to Jerusalem. Apart from Jn 7:42
where the crowds are discussing the fact that Jesus came from
Galilee whereas the Messiah must be descended from David
and come from Bethlehem, there is no denial of Jesus' Davidic
descent in the New Testament. The oldest references are those in
Paul's letter to the Romans where he writes: 'This news is about
the Son of God who, according to the human nature he took was
a descendant of David: it is about Jesus Christ our Lord who, in
the order of the Spirit, the Spirit of holiness that was in him, was
proclaimed Son of God …'(Rom 1:3) and in Rom 15:12 he applies
Isaiah's designation 'the root of Jesse' (David's father) to Jesus.
In 2 Tim 2:8 Jesus is described as ' sprung from the race of David.'

The discussion about the 'sonship of David' is not an attempt
to deny the Davidic descent on the human level, but rather an
opportunity to emphasise that he is more than the son/descen-
dant of David, modelled on him and his role. He is far superior
to David himself and to any of the expected political messianic
figures of contemporary Jewish hopes. As the reader knows,
Jesus is Messiah/Christ and Lord, Beloved Son of the Father, in
him the Father is well pleased, and on him the Spirit descended
at the Jordan. The triumphal approach to the city and the action
in the Temple of one publicly celebrated by the rejoicing crowd
as 'son of David', in fulfilment of their political hopes, is but a
faint prelude to the 'coming' in glory of 'the Son of Man' when
city, Temple and the world as we know it have passed away, as
Jesus will go on to point out in the eschatological/apocalyptic
discourse' (Mk 13:26f) and in his Jewish trial (Mk 14:62). To sum
up in a phrase borrowed from Paul, Jesus 'according to the

human nature he took was a descendant of David' (Rom 1:3).
But he is something much more. He is Lord.

The power and status of the scribes rested on their knowledge, understanding and interpretation of the scriptures and the
Law. Jesus has now shown them to be unreliable in their own
profession. He has outclassed them in their own field, thereby
undermining their power and status among the people. In a
society conscious of honour and shame, this victory for Jesus
and defeat for his opponents had huge significance.

The Temple and its worship, the leaders of the people represented by the chief priests, elders and scribes, the religious
movements represented by the Pharisees and Sadducees and
now the scribal tradition have all been scrutinised and found
wanting. The setting in the Temple provided Mark with a redactional framework for bringing all these elements together, ex-
tending even to the discussion with the good and wise scribe
who shines out in an otherwise very dark scenario.

As is often the case in the gospel, the scene ends with a reference to the reaction of the crowd. Here it says that the crowd listened to him eagerly. This concluding remark serves also as the
opening of the next scene, providing the audience for Jesus'
comments on the scribes (and others?).

Condemnation of the Scribes (and Others?) Mk 12:38-40

The good, wise scribe stands out in the gospel against the background of a more negative portrait of his colleagues.[51] They
were critical of Jesus during his ministry in Galilee and allied
themselves with the chief priests and elders in Jerusalem in their
opposition to him. They will again be allied with them in their
plot to kill him (Mk 11:18, 27; 14:1). Having praised the good,
wise scribe Jesus then challenged the scribes' teaching on the
Messiah as son of David according to their interpretation of
Psalm 109 (110). Now as he continues to teach in the Temple
Jesus condemns their conduct and behaviour, criticising them
for being unduly conscious of their status and unduly dependent on the praise and admiration of the people.[52] He criticises
them for seeking attention and admiration, as they ostentatiously

---

51. See H. T. Fleddermann, 'A Warning about the Scribes (Mark 12:37b-
40),' CBQ 44 (1982) 52-67.
52. This seems to be taken from a longer collection of criticisms, as for
example, the tradition behind the criticisms in Matthew 23.

parade themselves in long flowing robes, *stolai*, probably a reference to the *tallith*, the long ceremonial robe, and for seeking the places of prominence in religious and social gatherings. The front seats in the synagogues may have been facing the congregation and so they would have been seen and admired as persons of importance, just as happened when they were given the important couches, signifying the places of honour, at banquets.[53]

Jesus then condemns an offence more drastic than the rather silly pride of dress and status. He condemns those who 'swallow the property of widows, making pretence of long prayers'. A much greater punishment awaits the perpetrators of this kind of injustice than that awaiting the egotistical, foolish but, from the point of view of injustice and harm to others, relatively harmless practice of dressing up, showing off and wanting to be admired.

Throughout the Bible, the legal, prophetic and wisdom traditions single out the widow, the orphan and the stranger or wayfarer as being in greatest need of protection and fair play, and because of their vulnerability God is seen as their special defender.[54] In this the Bible reflects the broader concerns of the Ancient Near East. The exploitation of these three classes of people is severely condemned by the prophets.[55] Here in this condemnation by Jesus the practice of 'devouring the property of widows' refers to the exploitation of widows through the use of religion for ulterior purposes. Widows, those who had lost a husband and had no near relative to see to their protection and welfare were socially, economically and emotionally very vulnerable, being without a legal *persona* themselves. Furthermore they were often without social security and welfare, and disadvantaged as women in a patriarchal and androcentric society.

---

53. The scribes were not a religious movement as such, but were affiliated to the different groups like the Pharisees and Sadducees. Their expertise in biblical and legal matters of a spiritual and moral nature would have made many of them sympathetic to the Pharisee movement, and they seem to have survived the disaster of 70AD as they are associated with the Pharisees in the criticism of Mt 23. Their legal expertise and business acumen would have involved others in the intricacies of political, economic and social life in Jerusalem, bringing them closer to the Sadducee movement and the priestly class.
54. Ex 22:21-24; Deut 14:29; 24:17,19-22; 27:19; Isa 1:17; Jer 7:6; 49:11; Pss 68:5; 146:9.
55. Isa 1:17, 23; Jer 7:6; Ezek 27:7; Zech 7:10; Mal 3:5; Ps 146:9; Prov 15:25.

Who would be in a position to 'devour their property'? The scribes were theologians, lawyers and experts in the Torah but they were also the educated people who were trained to read and write and so they were engaged in the business of drawing up documents and legal contracts which could be a very lucrative affair. In their reputation for piety and their enjoyment of the salutations in the marketplace they easily built up a clientele for their legal business and won their way into the confidence of the vulnerable people like the widows who were so dependent on their services. This may be the reason for long prayers, not so much a false piety as a confidence trick on the part of some to win the confidence of these vulnerable people and exploit them in their dealings on their behalf. Josephus condemns the Pharisees (probably meaning scribes of the Pharisee party) who sponged on people of limited means.[56] Scribes often came from the poorer classes and hospitality towards them was regarded as an act of piety.[57] They are seen to exploit this piety, in this case, on the part of vulnerable and less well off people, with the pretence of long prayers. Jesus says that for this,' they will receive the heavier judgement/punishment.'

Are the scribes the only targets of this condemnation or does it also include other religious personnel like the priests and Temple officials?

The grammar of the sentences shows a definite break between the condemnation of the scribes, who like to wear the long robes and get preferential treatment in the synagogue and on social occasions, and the condemnation of those 'devouring the property of widows'. The sentence: 'Watch out for those scribes who desire to walk about in long robes and (desire) salutations in the marketplaces and the front seats in synagogue and pride of place at banquets' (Mk 12:38, 39) contains the Greek genitive construction following the admonition 'to watch out for.'[58] Though it is a very particular construction it is not followed through in the next condemnation. Instead there is a clear

---

56. Josephus, *Ant.*, 17: 41-45. See J. D. M. Derrett , 'Eating Up the Houses of Widows: Jesus' Comment on Lawyers,' *NovT* 14(1972) 1-9 and *Studies in the New Testament*, 1, Leiden 1977, 118-27 for a treatment of those who exploit their positions as trustees and guardians appointed to look after estates.

57. J. Jeremias, *Jerusalem in the Time of Jesus,111ff.*

58. *blepete apo grammateôn tôn thelontôn* (watch out for the scribes who desire...)

grammatical change introducing the next sentence (Mk 12:40) with the nominative article and participle, 'the ones who devour …' and following through with the nominative participle, 'praying', in the phrase 'praying long prayers for show.'[59] Does such a sharp change in grammatical structure indicate a change in subject, implying a change in the target of the criticism, or is it a joining together of two independently composed criticisms of the scribes? In the immediate context the criticism comes together with a number of other criticisms of the scribes (their dressing up for show and seeking places of honour, following on the criticism of their faulty understanding of scripture about the son of David). These criticisms are directed at a group who throughout the gospel have come across consistently in bad light because of their hostility to Jesus, and their being allied both with the Pharisees and with the Jerusalem priestly authorities in opposition to him. The context seems to make up for the lack of clarity of the syntax at least in so far as it seems to point to the scribes as a target in this condemnation. But are they the only target?

Has the condemnation a broader scope? The criticisms of the scribes after all come in the context of a wider criticism of Temple authorities, priests, elders and scribes, already mentioned in the disputes with Jesus, and with whom the scribes are usually associated in descriptions of the Jerusalem authorities. Following the earlier criticism of the Temple and its commercial activity, are the priests who collect the money in the name of a Temple system already condemned by Jesus, also included among those who are being accused of the swallowing the property of widows? The following story about the widow putting all she had to live on into the treasury may well be another example of the exploitation of the widow which Jesus is condemning.

Praise (and lamentation) for the (exploited) Widow Mk 12:41-44

Now Jesus takes up the case of the widow paying into the treasury (*to gazaphylakion*). The treasuries at the temples in ancient cities often functioned as banks and treasuries and so were often targeted by robbers and invading armies. Here the term *gazaphylakion* could mean the treasury or a collection receptacle. The Mishnah speaks of thirteen trumpet shaped chests in the sanctuary which were used for different offerings.[60]

---

59. *hoi kathesthiontes … proseuchomenoi.*
60. m. *Sheqalim* 6:5.

Copper coins would reverberate as they dropped into the receptacle and so draw attention to the gift and the giver. As the rich gave from their abundance their coins would make a significant jingle in the receptacle and so draw admiring glances. This corresponds to the seeking of admiration of the scribes already criticised. By way of contrast the poor widow put in a small offering which would have little impact by way of attracting admiration. Her contribution consisted of two *lepra*, the smallest denomination in coins, the equivalent of a *kodrantes*, the Greek term for the Roman *quadrans*, quarter of an *as*, a Roman denomination.[61] But she gave from her very need, all she had to live on, a total commitment. It appears that her offering was for the upkeep of the Temple.

The sentence: 'Jesus summoned his disciples and said to them', builds up to the solemnity of the pronouncement formula introduced by 'Amen I say to you ...' His solemn pronouncement about the value of the poor widow's contribution points to it as an example of true religion and one worthy of sincere praise. Traditionally it has been seen (and used!) in this light. But is the reader meant to understand it also as a lament for her exploitation as she puts all she has to live on into the treasury of a Temple whose religious life Jesus has severely condemned and whose destruction he has hinted at already and will shortly predict in clear terms?[62] Are there echoes of Malachi's prophecy about the Lord suddenly entering his Temple 'when they will make the offering to YHWH as it should be made' and when judgement will be passed 'against those who oppress the wage-earner, the widow and the orphan and who rob the settler of his rights ...' (Mal 3:1-5)?

The model of discipleship, seen when the first disciples left their families and livelihood, was the 'leaving all things' to follow Jesus. Here the disciples see in the poor widow an example of such total dedication to God. But her example also highlights

---

61. The explanation of the value of the coin in terms of the *kodrans-quadrans-as*, together with several other Latinisms, is taken by many scholars as a pointer to the fact that the gospel of Mark was written with the Roman audience in mind.
62. See the following articles for more detailed treatment. A. G. Wright, 'The Widow's Mites: Praise or Lament? A Matter of Context,' *CBQ* 44 (1982) 256-65; R. S. Sugirtharajah, 'The Widow's Mites Revalued,' *Exp Times* 103 (1991) 42-43; E. S. Mallon, ' The Poor Widow in Mark and Her Poor Rich Readers,' *CBQ* 53 (1991) 589-604.

the exploitation by those who 'devour the property of widows' and the emptiness of those who contribute for show from the abundance of their wealth, two improper uses of religion.

4. The Eschatological-Apocalyptic Discourse Mk 13:1-37

i. Introduction to the Discourse

Though a significant turning point is reached as Jesus left the Temple precincts and moved to a new location, the Temple theme and setting are carried on from the vantage point of the magnificent view of the Temple and city from the Mount of Olives. In fact the view of the Temple from the Mount of Olives would have given an overview of the whole complex and of the city not possible from within or in close proximity to the Temple. The change of location also reflects the movement of the narrative, combining the dominant view of the Temple with Jesus' leaving it for the last time. The location, steeped in biblical tradition, also facilitates the ongoing theme of denouement, this time predicting the end of the Temple and of the world.[1]

As Jesus leaves the Temple and city and takes up a position on the Mount of Olives, the reader remembers Ezekiel's description (Ezek 11:23) of the 'glory of the Lord' rising up from the middle of the city and coming to rest on the mountain east of the city (the Mount of Olives) in a prophecy of an imminent destruction of the city and scattering of the people, and a promise of a long-term gathering together again of the scattered people and their return to the land of Israel (Ezek 11).

The setting for the discourse is the magnificent view of the Temple across the Kidron valley from the Mount of Olives which runs parallel to the eastern side of the city.[2] The area was steeped in allusions to the Day of YHWH, the day of judgement and the final victory of God. As already seen in reference to Jesus' entry into the city, Zechariah had prophesied that God

---

1. For an examination of the role of Mk 13 in the overall plan of the gospel see B. van Iersel , *op. cit.*, 158-70.
2. He is overlooking the city from where he began his 'triumphal' entry into Jerusalem passing close to the traditional sites of the graves of some of the later prophets. Jesus in Luke's gospel (Lk 19:41-44) wept over the city that rejected its opportunity for the peace that God had offered, and predicted the forthcoming tragic events of the siege. The spot today is marked by the church of the *Dominus Flevit*, ('The Lord Wept'), constructed in the shape of a tear.

would set his feet on the Mount of Olives and the intervening valley would be the setting for the final victory of God over the enemies of Israel (Zech 14:4). The view from here was ideal for contemplating the promise of Malachi that the Lord would suddenly enter his Temple on the day of judgement (Mal 3:1ff). Josephus highlights the ongoing awareness of these associations and of the continuing expectation that the Messiah would come from the Mount of Olives to liberate the people, when he tells the story of an Egyptian prophet who persuaded the crowd to follow him to the Mount of Olives where he would issue a command and the walls of Jerusalem would tumble down.[3]

Though Jesus addresses the discourse to the four original disciples, Peter, James, John and Andrew, he finishes it with a universal appeal or warning: ' What I say to you, I say to all: "Watch!"' (Mk 13:37). The 'you' addressed by Jesus throughout the discourse includes not only those original four disciples, but also all readers and hearers of the gospel. Furthermore, the narrator makes this clear as he addresses the reader directly ('Let the reader understand' in Mk 13:14).

The discourse is not typical of Mark as it is a connected, coherent discourse with a unifying theme (in spite of the fact that it was most likely composed from earlier materials). Unlike the other long teaching section in Mark, the parable discourse in chapter four, this has a single unchanging audience and location, and does not come across as a collection of materials each introduced with 'and he said (says) to them' but it is a discourse that is developed step by step in a logical progression. Many volumes have been written on the possible sources, traditions, editing processes and interpretations of the discourse.[4] Our interest, however, is primarily in the discourse as it now appears in Mark's gospel, and in other considerations in so far as they throw light on the text as it now stands.

The plot of the gospel is temporarily suspended. The spotlight moves from Jesus and his imminent fate, and from the growing lack of understanding and increasing confusion of the

---

3. Josephus, *Ant.*, XX.169-72; *War* II.262.
4. An overview of critical approaches to the study of Mark 13 can be found in G. R. Beasley-Murray, *Jesus and the Last Days: The Interpretation of the Olivet Discourse*, Peabody: Hendrickson, 1993 and K. D. Dyer, *The Prophecy on the Mount: Mark 13 and the Gathering of the New Community*, ITS 2; Bern: Peter Lang, 1998.

disciples. The story is put on hold as an important message is communicated. It is a message for future followers of Jesus who for the most part do not figure in the actual narrative of the gospel. It has a two-tier audience, one in the very near future, between the ministry of Jesus and the writing of the gospel, the other in the long term life of the church. The first group had already experienced, or were experiencing, the predicted distress (*thlipsis*) in the short term. The narrator speaks directly to them ('let the reader understand') though his aside is somewhat puzzling to later generations of readers as it lacks specificity. The second group consists of all generations of believers until the end of the world when the Son of Man will come to gather the elect.

Jesus speaks with authority about the future. However, because his message 'contains elements that are quite foreign and perhaps even unpalatable to present-day readers, Jesus' apocalyptic discourse is often felt to be a strange and even disturbing element in the book.'[5]

ii. Classifying the Discourse

Eschatological Discourse
First of all, how should the discourse in Mark 13 be classified? Because it deals with 'the last things', in the sense of the ending of the Temple and the world and the final coming in glory of the Son of Man to gather the elect, it can be classified as an eschatological discourse. But 'eschatological' does not fully describe this discourse because it also deals at length, and with repeated emphasis, on life in the world between the tribulations to come in the 'short term' (most likely, though not explicitly stated, surrounding the fall of the Temple and city, resulting in the scattering of the people), and the events in the ' long term' heralding the end of the world and the coming of the Son of Man to gather the elect.[6]

Prophetic Discourse
The discourse could also be seen in terms of a prophetic con-

5. B. van Iersel, *op. cit.*, 158.
6. For a recent study on eschatology in the early Christian period see V. Balabanski, *Eschatology in the Making: Mark, Matthew and the Didache*, SNTS Monograph Series 97, Cambridge, Cambridge University Press, 1997.

demnation of the Temple and warning of things to come. It fits
well into prophetic tradition, already discussed in relation to the
'cleansing of the Temple', as one recalls the predictions of Micah
and Jeremiah against the first Temple. Micah prophesised that,
'Zion will become ploughland, Jerusalem a heap of rubble, and
the mountain of the Temple a wooded height' (Mic 3:12).[7]
Jeremiah said the Temple had become a 'den of thieves' and the
Lord would destroy it as he did the Temple at Shiloh, making
the city 'a curse for all the nations of the earth' (Jer 7:11; 26:6).
Jesus is clearly within the prophetic tradition of predicting an
end to the Temple even if the actual historical experience of the
Roman destruction of Temple and city subsequently coloured
and added detail to the prophecy, giving it the appearance of a
prophecy after the event, a *vaticinium ex eventu*. Apart from
Jesus' prediction there seems to have been a sense of foreboding
abroad about the Temple and its future,[8] and this would make
the authorities very wary of remarks about the destruction of the
Temple. Rabbi Johanan ben Zakkai had predicted the destruction of the Temple some forty years before it took place, according to a tradition in the Talmud.[9] According to Josephus Jesus,
son of Ananus, had predicted the destruction of the Temple before the Jewish War.[10] As seen already, attitudes to the Temple
and its authorities among the community at Qumran and the
Samaritans were very negative and the Hellenists were not overly
enthusiastic in its regard. In such an atmosphere hostile action
like the 'cleansing' of the Temple or negative comments and predictions about it from a popular preacher like Jesus would have
been quite threatening to the authorities. Such action and words
cast Jesus very clearly in the role of the prophets.

On a broader canvas also Jesus is following in the tradition of
the prophets as he predicts difficulties and troubles in the time
to come. The entire book of Amos is a warning about disaster to

7. cf Jer 26:18 which quotes Mic 3:12.
8. For a more detailed treatment see the article by C. A. Evans,
'Predictions of the Destruction of the Herodian Temple in the Pseud-
epigrapha, Qumran Scrolls, and Related Texts,' *JSP* 10 (1992) 89-147.
9. b. *Yoma* 39b
10. Josephus, *War*, 6.301: 'a voice from the east, a voice from the west, a
voice from the four winds; a voice against Jerusalem and the temple; a
voice against the bridegroom and the bride; a voice against the whole
nation.'

come, but includes a hope of restoration in the promise of the remnant and in the addendum at Amos 9:11-15. Isaiah speaks of wars between nations (Isa 19:2) and earthquakes (Isa 13:13) but promises the birth of a child who will bring peace through establishing the authority of God over the nations (Isa 9, 11, 2). Jeremiah warns of drought, famine and war (Jer 14) but buys the field as a sign of hope for the future restoration of the people (Jer 32). Ezekiel speaks of the scattering of the people as a punishment and the gathering of them together and bringing them back to the land of Israel 'with a new heart and a new spirit' (Ezek 11). As Jesus speaks of the destruction of the Temple and the end of the world he warns his followers not to be afraid, promises a universal preaching of the good news, and builds up to the promise of the coming of the Son of Man in glory to gather the elect. In all these respects the discourse is solidly in the prophetic tradition.

Apocalyptic Discourse

Because the discourse reflects aspects of the apocalyptic literature like Dan 7-12, 4 Ezra 13, 1 Enoch and 2 Baruch, dealing with the course of history leading to a climactic cosmic event, it can also be described as an apocalyptic discourse. Apocalyptic and prophetic literature have features in common such as condemnation of the *status quo*, predictions of forthcoming disasters and hopes for, or predictions of, a better time to come. However, unlike the prophets, the apocalyptic writers tend not to focus on reform in the present world as we know it but to focus rather on a heavenly vision in which they are shown a complete destruction of the world as they know it and a whole new world order coming into being. Within a narrative framework the human visionary is promised an eschatological salvation from the present world of persecution, alienation, national disaster and powerlessness. Furthermore, the heavenly vision and the predicted destruction and new beginnings are usually expressed in bizarre coded images and language.

Apocalypse (a Greek word meaning 'revelation') emerged as the coded language of people subjected to persecution and dispossession, religious discrimination and cultural upheaval, and was well established by New Testament times. The persecution by the forces of Antiochus Epiphanes, 168-164 BC, forcing the Jews to worship *Baal Shamin*, 'Lord of heaven', at the altar they had desecrated in the Temple, and to abandon the Torah and their traditions, was a major factor in the emergence of classical apocalyptic literature in the Old Testament. The Book of Daniel had its origin in this persecution. In a heavenly vision a history lesson about the period from the Babylonian destruction of the Temple and city and the captivity of the people (587 BC), until the persecution under the Seleucid Antiochus IV, Epiphanes, (168-164 BC), is presented in the guise of prophecy beforehand of the future when God would vindicate his people after their ill treatment by the empires of the Babylonians, Medes, Persians and Greeks. Its bizarre language and imagery was followed in other apocalyptic writings.

This apocalyptic tradition was ready-made for the early Christian writers as they reflected on their own experience of the many crises they suffered in the first two generations after Jesus' crucifixion. Stephen, Peter and Paul and their companions, and James suffered the trials, imprisonment, persecution and even death, which Jesus predicted for his followers. The crisis provoked for Jew and Jewish Christian alike by the attempt of Caligula to erect a giant statue of himself in the guise of a pagan god in the Temple in 40 AD, and/or the erection of the standards with the emperor's image by Titus caused them to focus on the reappearance of 'the abomination of desolation.'[11] Nero's very savage persecution of the Christians in Rome would have been another important factor in focusing Christian attention on Jesus' forewarning of trials and persecution. The apocalyptic tradition continued to develop in Christian circles after Mark and by the time the Book of Revelation was written, Domitian (c. 95 AD) was demanding worship as Lord and God, and persecuting those who refused it. This was probably the catalyst for the production of the 'great apocalypse' (The Book of the Apocalypse or Revelation). At the same time the worship of the goddess Roma, the personification of the empire, was also demanded and this was probably the catalyst for the description of Rome as the scarlet whore drunk with the blood of the saints, and the blood of the martyrs of Jesus' (Rev17:6).

The Jewish War was also a devastating experience ending in the destruction of the Temple and city (70 AD) and the scattering

---

11. Josephus, *Ant*, 18.261. See N. H. Taylor, 'Palestinian Christianity and the Caligula Crisis,' Part 1, *JSNT* 61 (1996) 101-24; Part 2, *JSNT* 62 (1996), 13-41.

of the people who survived into exile, as refugees, prisoners or
slaves. On the broader world scene the earthquake of 62 AD destroyed the cities of Pompeii and Herculaneum and the surrounding areas and, within a decade of Mark's gospel, they
were rebuilt just in time to be wiped out by the eruption of Mt
Vesuvius in 79 AD with its horrific devastation of the cities
around the bay of Naples. These widely known disastrous
events focused attention on cosmic signs and forces. Any or all
of these factors could have been catalysts for the apocalyptic emphasis of the gospels and the Book of Revelation. Commentators
have speculated at length about their influence on the formation
of the apocalyptic traditions in the New Testament and have attempted to date the New Testament writings accordingly.

Scholars also debate about the possible existence of a 'little
apocalypse',[12] a Jewish-Christian or Jewish document that
emerged during the crisis of 66-70 AD, which preceded Mark's
gospel and may have been used as a source by Mark.[13] If such a
document, or something similar by way of an oral tradition
emerged, it could well account for the transforming of Jesus'
original teaching into apocalyptic style language and imagery.

The discourse in Mark 13 reflects this apocalyptic tradition in
speaking of warnings, tribulation, cosmic signs and a final cosmic event bringing about a new order. Three dimensions or
phases of apocalyptic discourse are present: the forewarnings or
birthpangs (*hai ôdines*), the tribulation (*hê thlipsis*) and the end or
consummation (*to telos*). On the other hand Mark 13 is unlike the
apocalyptic tradition in so far as it does not deal with a heavenly
vision and concentrates on the long term life of the followers of
Jesus in the present world, and though building up to the climactic coming of the Son of Man in power and glory it does not
focus on the *parousia* and final judgement.[14]

Farewell Discourse/Valedictory
Coming as it does at the end of the ministry, and preparing his

12. The term is used in contradistinction to the 'great apocalypse' i.e.
the Book of the Apocalypse or Revelation.
13. This theory was proposed in 1864 by T. Colani, supported at the
time by C.Weizsäcker, and later popularised by R. Bultmann.
14. For an examination of the apocalyptic language of the discourse see
the article by A. Y. Collins, 'The Apocalyptic Rhetoric of Mark 13 in
Historical Context,' *Biblical Research* 41 (1996), 5-36.

followers for the time between his departure and his coming in glory at the end of the world, the discourse serves the function also of a farewell discourse or valedictory. In ancient literature, biblical and secular, the farewell discourse or valedictory played a very significant part. It acquired a particular weight and poignancy from the situation in which it was delivered and it was the final trump card in the hand of the departing prophet, teacher, leader or head of tribe or family. Gathering together the central insights and primary motivation of his life, the departing person entrusts them to the guardians of his legacy. The farewell discourse is often accompanied by a memorable gesture such as a last meal together, a blessing or, as in the case of St John's gospel, a footwashing, shared meal and final prayer. The emotional state of the hearers (in this context one of foreboding) and the reinforcement of the advice with a blessing or curse, promise or warning, reinforce the message. The discourse often includes a prophetic statement about the future of certain courses of action.[15] The final days of Jesus' ministry follow this tradition with the eschatological-prophetic-apocalyptic discourses in the synoptics (Mk 13; Mt 24; Lk 21) and the farewell discourse at the final meal in St John's gospel (Jn 14-17).[16] Jesus before his final rejection and execution instructs his disciples, and through them, his followers, about their life after his departure. The farewell discourse in Jn 14-17 has the same themes of suffering, rejection, trials and persecutions in the world after his departure as Mark 13 though expressed in very different language. In both traditions there is a strong note of caution, combined with the

---

15. The Old Testament contains the farewell discourses of Jacob (Gen 47:29-50:14), Joshua (Josh 32:1-24:32), Moses (Deut 1-4; 31-34), Samuel (1 Sam 12) and David (1 Kings 2:1-9; 1 Chron 28:1-29:28). Some books, such as *Deuteronomy, The Assumption of Moses, Jubilees* and *The Testaments of the Twelve Patriarchs* are structured as farewell discourses / valedictories. In the New Testament as well as the 'synoptic apocalypse' (Mk 13; Mt 24; Lk 21) there is the farewell discourse of Jesus in John's gospel (Jn 14-17). Paul's speech at Miletus to the elders of Ephesus summed up his ministry and issued warnings for the future about false teachers (Acts 20:17-38). The Second Letter of Peter and the Second Letter to Timothy are both valedictories. In secular literature, for example, Oedipus spoke of the future of the city, in Sophocles' *Oedipus at Colonus*, 1518-55. Cambyses reinforced his message to the Persians with a blessing and a curse.
16. Mk 13:1 -37; Mt 24:1 -25:46; Lk 21:5-36; Jn 13-17.

optimism that God has all things in control, even though they will suffer in the world. Jesus in Mark's account endeavours 'to cool down end-time excitement and to urge cautious discernment in the face of dramatic cosmic events'[17] and Jesus in John's gospel says: 'In the world you will have tribulation, but be brave, I have overcome the world' (Jn 16:33). Both traditions may well have their origin in the remembered farewell advice of Jesus to his disciples. The evangelists in turn would have edited the tradition(s) in the light of the actual experience of adversity and persecution and in the case of Matthew, Luke and John (and possibly Mark) following the actual experience of the destruction of the city and Temple.

iii. Outline of the Discourse

The discourse deals with two periods of tribulation, one in the near future, the other at the end of the world as we know it. Between them there is a period of the universal mission of the church, which will be carried out in the context of persecution. The overall presentation is in the form of a chiasm, a 'concentric' arrangement whereby a series of steps leads into a central point and a parallel series leads away from it. In this arrangement the universal mission of the church and the experience of persecution occupy the central spot. At the same time the entire discourse, though concentric in arrangement, builds up to the climax of the coming of the Son of Man. There are therefore two focal points, one at the centre emphasising the universal mission and persecution, the other at the conclusion of the chiasm when the whole process comes to a climax with the coming of the Son of Man to gather the elect. The following outline shows the 'concentric' arrangement which I follow in the commentary.

a. Observe the doomed magnificence of the Temple (Mk 13:1-4)
   b. Beware! False Prophets/Messiahs (Mk 13:5-6)
      c. Dot be alarmed! Wars and Rumours of Wars (Mk 13:7-8)
         d. Beware! Persecution. Universal Mission (Mk 13:9-13)
      c. Take Flight! Wars and Rumours of Wars (Mk 13:14-20)
   b. Beware ! False Prophets/Messiahs (Mk 13:21-23)
a. Observe the Son of Man coming in power & glory (Mk 13:24-37)

---

17. J. R. Donahue and D. J. Harrington, *op. cit.*, 369.

IV. THE DISCOURSE

a. Observe the doomed magnificence of the Temple (Mk 13:1-4)

As Jesus was leaving the Temple one of the disciples remarked on the huge stones and the huge buildings. This remark about the magnificence of the stones and of the buildings, reflecting the impressive nature of the reconstruction of the Temple buildings by Herod the Great and the huge stones used in the work, provides the cue and sets the tone for the discourse that follows.[18] Jesus' shocking reply predicting that it would all be destroyed strikes like a thunderbolt. It is recorded in all three synoptics (Mk 13:2; Mt 24:2; Lk 21:6):[19] The double negative *ou mê* emphasises the point. This is no simple prediction of a future event. It is 'a judgement on the nation in whose midst the temple stands.'[20]

In response to their question about when these things which he had just predicted would take place Jesus assumes the sitting position of the teacher (and judge) and instructs privately the four disciples he had originally called. These four original disciples are representative of all disciples. Furthermore, in the apocalyptic tradition, the secrets of the future are usually revealed to a representative individual or small group. Three of these, Peter, James and John, were with Jesus at the raising of Jairus' daughter and on the mountain of transfiguration, and they will be brought as a group into close contact with him in Gethsemane, also located on the Mount of Olives, in the same general area where they now listen to his eschatological, prophetic, apocalyptic, farewell discourse.

When they ask Jesus, 'When will all these things take place?' the reader naturally expects Jesus to talk about the destruction of the Temple, the subject which prompted the question, but the expression, 'all these things' (*tauta panta*) indicates that the destruction of the Temple is part of a broader complex of issues.[21]

18. Josephus, *Ant*, XV.11.5, 6,1 1; *War* V.5, comments on the extent of the building project, the size of the stones, the marble and gold façade which reflected the rays of the sun. The work was begun in 20 BC and believed to be still in progress in Jesus' time.

19. See L. Gaston, *No Stone on Another: Studies in the significance of the Fall of Jerusalem in the Synoptic Gospels*, NovT Sup 23, Leiden: 1970.

20. G. R. Beasley-Murray, *Jesus and the Last Days: The Interpretation of the Olivet Discourse*, Peabody: Hendrickson, 1993, 381.

21. The Greek *tauta panta* points to the fact that in the tradition the de-

The reader, therefore, has to wait until some general warnings are first given before the specific question relating to the Temple is answered. Jesus first issues warnings and talks in general about the future experience of his followers in the world after his departure.

After Jesus assumes the sitting position of the teacher in this panoramic, historic and highly symbolic place, the typical Markan phrase, 'he began to speak' opens the discourse.[22] The verb *blepein*, 'to watch out for', 'to be aware of', in Mark is consistently used in the sense of a call to discernment. Having already told them to ' beware of' the leaven of the Pharisees and the leaven of Herod' (Mk 8:15) and to 'beware of the scribes who like to parade in long robes' (Mk 12:38) he now uses the expression 'to beware/watch out for', four times in the discourse: watch out lest anyone lead you astray; watch out for yourselves (because) they will hand you over to sanhedrins; watch out (because) I have told you all these things; watch out, be on your guard and pray (Mk 13:6, 9, 23, 32). These calls to beware punctuate the discourse, sometimes opening, sometimes closing a section, and come to a climax with a final, related and possibly stronger word than beware, *grêgoreite*, 'be watchful/be on your guard!'[23]

Jesus' prediction of the destruction of the Temple in Mark's gospel serves to introduce his comments on the greater cosmic dissolution. Matthew and, even more obviously Luke, set the prediction of the destruction of the Temple in the context of the fall of Jerusalem.[24] Mark's text is more general and enigmatic

struction of the Temple is part of a complex of events. Mt 24:3 has the disciples ask the larger question, adding to their inquiry about 'these things' a question about 'the sign of your coming and the end of the age'.
22. This construction appears 26 times in Mark.
23. See the study of these 'watchwords' by T. J. Geddert, *Watchwords: Mark 13 in Markan Eschatology*, Sheffield: JSOT Press, 1989.
24. The prediction about the Temple in Luke's gospel is accompanied by the prediction that Jerusalem would be 'surrounded by armies and soon laid desolate' and in Matthew's gospel it is contained within clearly prophetic references, preceded by the lamentation-cum-threat: 'Jerusalem, Jerusalem, you that kill the prophets and stone those that are sent to you ... your house will be left to you desolate' and the prediction of the desperate flight from Jerusalem when 'you see the abomination of desolation of which the prophet Daniel spoke set up in the Holy Place ...' (Lk 21:5, 6, 20; Mt 23:37, 15ff).

and, apart from the introductory prediction about the forthcoming destruction of the Temple, the fall of Jerusalem is not clearly stated, but may be encoded in the imagery of the 'abomination of desolation' and flight of the people. However, comparison with the other two synoptics, together with the introductory remark and question, have generally led scholars to understand the forthcoming tribulation, *thlipsis*, as the fall of Jerusalem, though some strongly deny the connection.[25]

b. Beware! False Prophets/Messiahs Mk 13:5-6

A typical Markan phrase, 'Jesus began to say to them ...' introduces the warning against false prophets (messiahs): 'Watch out lest anyone lead you astray.' Jesus issues the warning in v 5, and having described the activity of false messiahs he repeats it in v 6 saying, 'they will lead many astray'. 'Watch out', *blepete*, is a call for discernment, a scrutinising of what lies behind their plausible words and deceptively impressive signs. Jesus warns that 'Many will come' in his name. 'Coming' had a messianic significance prior to Jesus' ministry relating to the expectation of 'the one coming into the world', and later for Christians 'coming' was related to the return of Jesus as the glorified Son of Man. Here Jesus is warning about pretenders 'who will *come* in my name'. 'Coming in the name of Jesus' can signify usurping his position and dislodging him from his messianic status, or it can mean coming in the name of Jesus pretending to be his representative, or even coming with the claim to be Jesus risen from the dead. Such claimants may use the *egô eimi* formula which Jesus used as he came to the disciples over the troubled waters. The designation *egô eimi*, 'I am/I am he', is rare in the synoptics but all pervasive in John's gospel where it designates the divine status of both the revealer and the revelation.[26] Here in Mark's ver-

---

25. For a strong argument in favour of linking Mk 13:5-23 to the fall of Jerusalem and the destruction of the Temple see J. Marcus, *Mark*, 33-37 and his article 'The Jewish War and the Sitz im Leben of Mark,' *JBL* 111 (1992), 446-48. For a similar position see W. A. Such, *The Abomination of Desolation in the Gospel of Mark: Its Historical Reference in Mark 13:14 and Its Impact in the Gospel*, Lanham: University of America Press, 1999. For a contrary argument see M. Hengel, *Studies in the Gospel of Mark*, London: SCM Press, 1985,14-28.

26. Mk 6:50. The injunction 'do not fear' is a recurring theme in theophanies/epiphanies. On the storm tossed water it accompanies and highlights the solemnity of the self designation of Jesus as *ego eimi*, 'I am',

sion of the apocalyptic discourse Jesus uses it to warn his disciples about the very serious, even divine, claims that will be made by the false messiahs. G. Beasley-Murray points out that the affirmation 'I am he', (*ego eimi*) since it relates to the Messiah who comes with his kingdom (or comes again in his kingdom) almost certainly carries with it the implication that the last times have now arrived and the apocalyptic denouement has begun.'[27] As Jesus warns the disciples, the warning is directed also to the readers of Mark who are very probably aware of the many false messiahs who preceded Jesus and of the many such figures who emerged in the crisis of the war against the Romans and the siege, capture and destruction of Jerusalem and the Temple.[28] The Acts of the Apostles and Josephus give accounts of these persons.[29] They will be referred to again during the discourse (Mk 13:21-23).

c. Do not be alarmed! Wars and Rumours of Wars (Mk 13:7-8)

Another theme is introduced with Jesus' exhortation to the disciples not to be alarmed (*mê throeiste*) when they hear of wars and rumours of wars. In prophetic and apocalyptic literature they were seen as a necessary part of the upheaval that preceded the end time and necessitated divine intervention (Jer 4:16-17; Zech 14:2; 4 Ezra 8:63-9:3). Wars, earthquakes and famines were traditional elements in prophetic and apocalyptic representations of the end and the approach of the end. They were seen as judgements and punishments experienced in connection with the Day of YHWH. The wars and rumours of wars, however, do not necessarily signify the imminent arrival of the end but they are part of God's overall plan as affirmed in the *dei genesthai*, 'it must be so'. As already seen the verb *dei* ('it must, it is necessary') is widely used in the New Testament to express the necessity of fulfilling God's will/plan.

Wars and such troubles were often seen in the Old Testament prophetic and apocalyptic traditions as punishment by God in

modelled on the Divine self designation in the Old Testament. cf Ex 3:14; Deut 32:29; Isa 41:4; 43:10; 45:18.
27. G. R.B easley-Murray, *op. cit.*, 392.
28. Even as late as 132 AD Bar Cochba, (a name meaning 'son of the star', a messianic designation) led a revolt against the Romans.
29. Acts 5:36f; Josephus, *Ant.*, 17.261-85; 20:167-72; *War* II.433-34, 444, 652; 613; 7.29-31.

the process of chastising the people (Jer 4:16f; Zech 14:2). Wars
and revolutions were part and parcel of the prophetic and apocalyptic expectation (Isa 19:2; 4 Ezra 13:31).[30] Earthquakes too
were to be expected (Isa 13:13; Jer 4:24; 1 Enoch 1:6f) and famines
(Isa 13:13; 14:30; Jer 4:24; Joel 1; 1 Enoch 1: 6f; 2 Baruch 27:6).
Ezekiel describes four deadly acts of judgement of the Lord,
sword, famine, wild beasts and pestilence (Ezek 14:21). They
would continue throughout history as nation rose against nation
and kingdom against kingdom after the present troubles were
over. These present troubles are only the beginning, the 'birthpangs'. The pangs of childbirth had been used as an image by
the prophets for the sufferings accompanying a momentous act
of God in history, a judgement on the sinfulness of the people
and a looking to a new future.[31]

These wars and rumours of wars are not yet signalling the
end. Life goes on after them and will be marked by nation rising
against nation and kingdom against kingdom. The words of
Jesus to the disciples: 'Do not be alarmed!' (*mê throeisthe*), assur-
ing them that the end was not yet, would have issued a very significant message to the intended readers of Mark who may well
have thought the end was nigh as they lived through the terrible
times from the fire of Rome in the year 64 to the fall of Massada
in 73 AD. It was a time when Christian, Jew and Pagan alike witnessed the apparent collapse of the world they knew and the
sweeping away of the authority, institutions and communities
that gave meaning, shape and security to their world.[32] The verb
throeisthai, 'alarmed', is the same as that used to calm the fears of
the Thessalonians (*mêde throeisthai*) when false rumours were
abroad that the day of the Lord had already arrived (2 Thess
2:2). More will be heard about these wartime troubles in Mk
13:14-20.

d. Beware! Persecution. Universal Mission Mk 13:9-13
Having already warned his disciples to beware, to 'watch out
for' false prophets (messiahs) Jesus now, at this central point in

30. 4 Ezra 13:31 states for example: 'They shall plan to make war against
one another, city against city, place against place, people against people, and kingdom against kingdom.'
31. Isa 26:17f; 66:8f; Hos 13:13; Mic 4:9f. The rabbis spoke of the sufferings that would precede the end as 'the birthpangs of the Messiah', a
phrase that probably had gained a good deal of currency.
32. See the essay, 'The World of Mark' at the end of this commentary.

the discourse, exhorts them again to beware, this time to 'watch yourselves'. They will need to watch their own faith, courage, patience and endurance in the universal mission, because they will be persecuted by Jewish and Gentile people and authorities 'for my sake' and they will be called on to bear witness to their persecutors. Jesus had already warned the disciples about the possibility of having to lay down their lives (Mk 8:34-37), of the coming of the Son of Man and the required dispositions of people at his coming (Mk 8:38), and of the coming of the kingdom before the living generation had passed away (Mk 9:1). He is now dealing more explicitly with these subjects.

The first readers of Mark were aware that the prophetic warning of Jesus about persecution had become a reality before the gospel was written.[33] Jesus warned that his disciples would be brought before the *synedria*, the local Jewish courts in each town with powers of discipline to beat them, carried out in the synagogue.[34] In this regard, Peter and his companions were flogged in Jerusalem (Acts 5:40). Paul states that he was given the 'forty lashes less one' five times and beaten three times with rods on their authority, the punishment laid down in Deuteronomy (Deut 25:1-3; 2 Cor 11:24). According to Jesus' warning they would also be brought before pagan courts, before governors and kings 'to bear testimony to them.' The reader thinks of Paul bearing testimony before Felix, Festus and Agrippa (Acts 23:24; 24:27) and being sent under guard to Rome where he was held under house arrest. All these had taken place before the writing of Mark's gospel.

The verb 'hand over' (*paradidômi*) in the sentence 'when they hand you over' is a 'loaded' term in the New Testament generally and in Mark in particular. It is used in the second passion prediction (Mk 9:31), it appears ten times in the passion narrative, and Paul uses it in Rom 4:25 and 8:12. It reverberates with the fate of the Baptist who was handed over to Herod Antipas, the would-be king, and with Jesus' predictions of being handed over himself to his fate. The readers are aware that Judas handed Jesus over to the Jewish authorities who handed him over to Pilate and Pilate handed him over to be crucified.[35] The disciples

33. Matthew has the parallel to verses 9, 11 and12 in the instructions to the Twelve in Mt 10:17-21.
34. *Sanh* 1:6.
35. Mk 9:31; 10:33, and in all four gospels. Matthew has these verses in the instructions to the Twelve in Mt 10:17-21.

are destined to follow Christ in his passion, and the readers of
Mark had directly or indirectly experienced the fulfilment of
Jesus' prophetic warning. Tradition places the martyrdoms of
Peter and Paul in Rome, together with the 'huge number' who
died in the Neronian persecution and are referred to by Clement
of Rome and Tacitus.[36] These may well have been known to
Mark's readers.

Jesus predicts that in the councils, in the synagogues, and before governors and kings they 'will bear witness to them.'
Though some commentators see this as a bearing of witness
against them before the court of heaven, it most probably means
that they would bear witness to their persecutors about Jesus
and the good news. This prediction about bearing witness before governors and kings leads into Jesus' statement about the
universal mission, the preaching of the good news to all nations.

Universal Mission Mk 13:10
Before advising them about how to behave when they are handed
over and brought before the courts, Jesus states: 'And first it is
necessary (*dei*) that the good news be preached to all nations.'
This statement which seems to interrupt the flow of the discourse in mid-course, sets the persecution of disciples in the context of the universal mission. It is heavily laden with Markan
theology and vocabulary. Beginning with the paratactic *kai*, it
has three favourite words or concepts of Mark, *dei, kêruchthênai*
(*keryssein*) and *euaggelion*, ('the good news must be preached')
focusing on the necessary divine plan for the proclamation and
the good news. Furthermore, the Gentile mission is given a profile somewhat uncharacteristic of the overall gospel so far. It
may well be Mark's editing of an earlier tradition or 'little apocalypse' for the purpose of setting persecution in its mission context. The necessity (*dei*) of the unfolding of the divine plan for
the evangelisation of all nations is being stressed, much as Paul
stressed it in his correspondence with the Romans where he
speaks of the blindness of one section of Israel 'until the full
number of Gentiles come in' (Rom 11:25f). The 'insertion' of the
remark about the universal mission into the discourse, like
Paul's remark in Romans, serves to offset expectation of an immediate end, and draws attention to a prolonged mission
among the Gentiles. The preaching of the gospel to all nations

---

36. 1 *Clement* 5; Tacitus, *Annals*, xiv, xliv.

must first (*prôton*) take place. It emphasises the fact that between the present troubles and the end the gospel, the good news, will be preached to all nations but such a universal mission will not take place without suffering hostility from without and apostasy and betrayal from within the followers.

Persecution Mk 13:11-13

Continuing with the focus on persecution Jesus warns the disciples not be frightened about what to say 'when they lead you away to hand you over'. Facing the court would have been a very terrifying experience particularly for so many early Christians who would not have been well educated or well off people able to afford an advocate or call on influential friends. Jesus promises that 'it will be given (i.e. God will give) to them what to say.' This is reminiscent of God's promise to the anxious prophet: 'I am putting my words into your mouth' (Jer 1:9f). Witnessing to the nations was also the task of Jeremiah into whose mouth God placed the words to enable him to 'tear up and to knock down, to destroy and to overthrow, to build and to plant' (Jer 1:9f). Jesus promises his followers that it will not be themselves who are speaking but the Holy Spirit. The Spirit will give them what they should say. In John's gospel this role of the Spirit as Paraclete/Advocate is further developed and spelled out in terms of a divine comforter and advocate who will defend them in the face of an unbelieving and hostile world, and lead them into understanding, and cause them to recall all that Jesus had said and done (Jn 14:16, 26; 15:26; 16:7). The promise is here in Mark in a less elaborate form.

The warning about hostility from society in general is followed by a warning about hostility within the family circle. Warnings about family division figured in prophetic condemnations of the corruption of the people and also in Jewish apocalyptic imagery.[37] Jesus' prediction that 'brother will hand over brother to death and the father his child, and children will rise up against parents and have them put to death' reflects the description in Micah: ' For the son treats the father with contempt, the daughter rises up against her mother, the daughter-in-law against her mother-in-law; your enemies are members of your

---

37. Mic 7:6; Jub 23:19; 4 Ezra 5:9; 6:24; 2 Bar 70:3.

own household' (Mic 7:6).[38] It is also quoted in *m. Sotah* 9:15b as part of a passage on 'the footprints of the Messiah' after 'children will shame elders, and elders will stand up before children.' Mark's first readers may well have seen a fulfilment of Jesus' prediction in the betrayal and handing over of family members during the Neronian persecution. Tacitus describes how some of those arrested betrayed their fellow Christians and Clement of Rome reflects on the disastrous results of fanatical zeal.[39]

Predictions about general hostility and family divisions are followed by a very strong prediction of universal hatred. 'You will be hated by all on account of my name.' The farewell discourse in St John's gospel conveys a similar message. Jesus says to the disciples: 'If the world hates you remember that it hated me before you … because you do not belong to the world … therefore the world hates you' (Jn 15:18f). He also says: 'If they persecuted me, they will persecute you too' and '… the hour is coming when anyone who kills you will think he is doing a holy duty for God' (Jn 15:20; 16:2). The evangelists had good reason for emphasising the reality of persecution, hostility and hatred. Tacitus, for example, reflects the hostile opinion of society in his description of the Neronian persecution. He described the victims as 'the notoriously depraved Christians' and described the movement as a 'deadly superstition'.[40]

In Jewish and Christian tradition patience (*hypomenê*) is seen as a necessary virtue which accompanied one's waiting 'to the end', *eis telos*, that is ' to the full unfolding, 'to (the) end or completion' of the divine plan (Dan12:12; 4 Ezra 6:25; 7:27; Rom 5:4f). The one who thus endures with patience will be saved, not just saved from persecution and suffering, but saved in the sense of spiritual and eschatological salvation.

c. Take Flight! Wars and Rumours of Wars Mk 13:14-20
In keeping with the concentric arrangement, there is now a return to the former topic of wars and rumours of wars. However, in keeping with the ' linear' movement towards the climax, the mood and pace of the discourse change. Instead of caution, calm and waiting with patience, a note of urgency and alarm sets the tone for the recommendation to flee with all haste. The disciples' question: 'When will these things take place?' is now partly an-

---

38. cf similarities with Mt 10:35, Lk 12:53.
39. Tacitus, *Annals*, XV,xliv; 1 *Clement* 6:1.
40. Tacitus, *Annals*, XV,xliv.

swered with an ominous warning: 'When you see the abomination of desolation standing where it (he) should not be ... then
... flee.'

The 'wars and rumours of wars' mentioned already are now
spelled out at greater length in Mk 13:14-20. The implied or originally intended readers of Mark are most likely aware of the persecution of Nero and the empire-wide upheavals which followed on his forced suicide as contending armies fought to establish their candidates on the imperial throne. They must have
been aware also of the events that would, or already had, culmin-
ated in the destruction of Jerusalem and the Temple, and the
flight of the people from the city and surrounding area. The
original readers would therefore be very alert to Jesus' words to
the disciples, and the narrator ensures that they take note, by directly inserting the comment into the text: ' let the reader under-
stand/take note.' They realise that when one event takes place
the other follows. When they see the 'abomination of desolation'
(to bdelygma tês erêmôseôs) then the flight of the people will follow.

The 'abomination of desolation' or 'the desolating sacrilege'
originally referred to the altar to Ba'al Shamen, an oriental version of Olympian Zeus, set up on the altar of burnt offering by
the Seleucid king Antiochus IV (Epiphanes) on the 25th day of
Chislev 168, on which sacrifice was offered to Zeus (1 Macc 1:54-
59).[41] It appears from Dan 9:27 that a statue of Zeus, made in the
image of Antiochus, was erected in the Temple.[42] This was part
of his programme of forced imposition of religious uniformity
along Hellenistic lines throughout the Seleucid lands. He forbade the traditional Temple sacrifices and rituals, forbade the
people to follow the laws and customs of the ancestors and
burned copies of the Law. Incense was offered at the doors of
houses and in the streets and pagan altars were set up in the surrounding towns of Judah. This action provoked the armed revolt of the Maccabees, the literary reaction of the Book of Daniel
and the increase in numbers of holy people leaving the city to
live outside as Hasidim.

41. 168 or 167 BC. There is a one year discrepancy in determining
Maccabeean dates.
42. There are, however, some differences of opinion about the exact interpretation of the verse.

The term used in the Book of Daniel,'abomination of desolation' (Dan 9:27; 11:31; 12:11 LXX), seems to be a play on the name of the aforementioned deity Ba'al Shamen (Lord Shamen). The term 'abomination of desolation', *shiqqus somem* or *mesomem* is made up from *shiqqus* which means 'an abomination' and *shomem* or *meshomem* which means 'desolation' (probably also a cynical word play on the Hebrew *shamayim*, which means 'heaven') (Dan 12:11). The sacrilege defiled the Temple so no Jewish rituals could take place, thus rendering it desolate until its purification after the Maccabees' victory on the 25th Chislev 164 which ended its desolation. The Feast of Dedication or The Feast of Lights (in Hebrew, *Hanukkah* or in Greek, *Enkainia*) celebrates the rededication. Sometimes it is called 'The Feast of Tabernacles of the month of Chislev', because of similarities in the rituals of the feasts.

To what is the narrator drawing the reader's attention in so specific a manner in the parenthesis,'Let the reader understand.' The reference has been interpreted by scholars in different ways. As it draws the reader's attention to the image of the 'abomination of desolation' drawn from the Book of Daniel, it could be seen as an imaginative way of illustrating in general the difficulties of living under pagan or anti-Christian rule and comparing it to the experience under the Seleucid persecution. It appears more likely, however, to be a reference to some specific event or person, as though to say: 'The reader knows quite well to what or to whom I am referring.' This second possibility seems to link well into a grammatical anomaly by which the narrator may be pointing to something very specific.

The reference to 'the abomination of desolation standing where it (or he?) should not' contains a grammatical feature which gives rise to a question about the exact nature of what is meant by the 'abomination of desolation' as Mark uses the term. In Greek, 'abomination' is a neuter noun. However, the participle 'standing', which qualifies and should be in agreement with it, is masculine, in the accusative singular case (*hestêkota*). Unless Mark made a grammatical error, which is not in keeping with his general ability in writing Greek, one thinks of the abomination in terms of a person. Is the personal nature of the abomination determined by an original image of Olympian Zeus placed in the sanctuary, an outrage very nearly repeated by the threat of placing the (standards and) statue of Caligula in the Temple in 39-40 AD, an action that would possibly have sparked the war with the Romans a quarter of a century earlier than it happened?[43] Or is it a reference to the standard and possibly the image, or person of Titus in the Temple, where he received the homage of his troops? Could it be a similar generalised reference to an Antichrist figure, like the one referred to in 2 Thessalonians as 'the man of lawlessness … who … takes his seat in the Temple of God, declaring himself to be God' (2 Thess 2:3f), in this case an emperor claiming divine status and honour. Whichever option the reader follows, it is obvious that the reference to the 'abomination of desolation' points clearly to a happening in the Temple known to the implied reader, which will result in the desolation and flight of the people.[44] The references to Daniel and the general mood of the passage reflect the prophetic warnings of Jeremiah and Ezekiel about the desecration and destruction of the Temple, the fall of the city and the devastation and scattering of the people (Jer 26:1-19; Ezek 7-11).

As the discourse speaks of 'sufferings like none ever seen before or will ever be seen again' the reader recalls the descriptions of the plagues of hail (Exod 9:18), of locusts (Exod 10:14) and of the weeping for the first-born of the Egyptians (11:6) which were similarly described. So too the treatise on the conflict of nations and heavenly powers in Daniel 10-11, is followed by the statement, 'There shall be a time of anguish such as never occurred since nations first came into existence' (Dan12:1). Mark expands on this quotation to cover the whole period from the beginning to the end of creation, 'Those days shall be a tribulation such as has not been from the beginning of the creation that God created until now and never will be' (Dan12:1; Mk 13:19).[45] However, though the time of testing and waiting for the coming of God's kingdom is a time of stress, God seems to have a worked-out schedule of events (Dan 12:7, 11, 12) and so another theme of the apocalyptic tradition is then introduced as Daniel goes on to introduce a note of hope.[46] 'But at that time your people shall be delivered, everyone who is found written in the book' (Dan

---

43. Caligula was murdered on the Palatine Hill in 41 AD, so there was no further trouble about the statue.
44. G. R. Beasley-Murray, *op. cit.*, 411.
45. Josephus, *War*, proem 4, uses a similar expression to describe the suffering of the people at the destruction of Jerusalem.
46. 1 Enoch 82:2; 83:1; Baruch 20:2.

12:1). Mark similarly points to an act of God's mercy in the cutting short of that difficult time as Jesus declares, 'On account of the elect he shortened the days.' God is Lord of history and out of mercy for the elect who would otherwise run the risk of falling away, of breaking under persecution and suffering, he has put a limit on the suffering. God thus ensures the survival of the elect, as he ensured the survival of the faithful remnant of Israel. God will not allow his people to be exterminated. The repetition of shortening the days emphasises the point, but history will continue until the gospel is preached to all nations.[47]

This general apocalyptic and prophetic vision and language of destruction, together with the actual experiences of the Markan community, combine to give the discourse its vivid character. Scholars debate about the exact relation of the events of 66-70 AD to the references in the discourse, but from the point of view of the gospel story itself they are of secondary importance. Jesus is issuing a dire warning about the destruction to come, and flight is the appropriate and urgent response.[48] So urgent is the flight that those on the roofs, flat roofs where they often slept, ate, worked, prayed and relaxed in summer months, and those in the fields where they worked should not return indoors to gather their belongings or their outer garments. The reader remembers the instruction 'not to turn back' at the flight from Sodom (Gen 19:17). Such a flight will be particularly difficult for pregnant and nursing mothers. If it occurs in winter it will be particularly difficult because of the rains producing mud, flooded wadis, rising water in the Jordan and flash floods typical of the region, with no fruit or crops to sustain them in

---

47. 'The beginning of creation that God created' and 'the elect whom he elected' are examples of Markan repetition.

48. A pre-Markan tradition of a flight in 67 AD in the depths of winter may well colour the narrative, a tradition later historicised and appearing differently in Eusebius' *Historia Ecclesiastica* 3.5.3 and in Epiphanius' *Panarion* 29.7.7f and *De mensuris et ponderibus* 15, as a flight of the Christians to Pella and more generally to areas around Perea. A flight in the later stages of the war would have meant leaving the city to go to surrounding areas already occupied by Roman military, and Jerusalem itself, being on the central ridge, it seems unlikely that 'fleeing to the mountains' would be an exact historical reference. The 'abomination of desolation' and 'the flight' are brought together here in what seems to be a simplification of a more complex series of frightening events.

their flight. These warnings to flee create a very definite mood and sense of urgency.

b. Beware ! False Prophets/Messiahs (Mk 13:21-23)

In keeping with the concentric arrangement the discourse now returns to the issuing of further warnings about false messiahs and false prophets (with their followers who will draw attention to them, thus gathering a following). As in the earlier warning in Mk 13:6, again there is emphasis on the need to cool overheated messianic and end time expectations. Josephus testifies to the fact that several false messiahs (*pseudochristoi*) had appeared and caused little harm to the Romans but brought great slaughter on the people.[49] The actual use of the term' false christs' (*pseudochristoi*) occurs only here and in the parallel passage in Mt 24:24, whereas the term 'false prophets' (*pseudoprophêtai*) occurs much more frequently, showing a more widespread concern about the latter. False prophets were an ongoing phenomenon in the history of God's people and had been legislated for in Deuteronomy (Deut 18:20, 22; cf Mk 13:1-5). The stock in trade trick in the bag of the false prophets in the Old Testament was a display of signs and wonders towards which one must have a discerning and sceptical attitude, and the New Testament has a similar aversion to their tricks. In fact Jesus, particularly in John's gospel (Jn 4:48), has a particular aversion to a faith that depends on *sêmeia kai têrata*, signs and wonders, and the Second Letter to the Thessalonians issues very strong warnings against the Rebel and the false signs and wonders (2 Thess 2:1-12, esp. 9f). If they had their way God's plan for the elect, for preaching the gospel to all nations, would be thwarted.

Jesus winds up this part of the discourse with another warning to 'watch out' and emphasises that he has told them everything beforehand. In John's gospel Jesus tells the disciples during the farewell discourse that he has told them all these things beforehand so that when they happen they will remember that he had told them (Jn 16:4). This should help them to stay calm and remain on their guard.

a. Observe! Watch for the coming in power and glory (Mk 13:24-37)

Throughout the discourse so far there has been a clear distinction drawn between the tribulation, (probably the destruction of

49. Josephus, *Ant*, 17.285.

the city and Temple) and the end of the world. The disciples are told that 'the end will not be yet,' that 'the gospel must first be preached to all nations,' that 'you will be hated by all on account of my name,' and finally that 'the one who stands firm to the end will be saved' (Mk 13:7, 8, 10, 13). They are warned specifically about the false messiahs and prophets who will proclaim the end prematurely (Mk 13:5, 6, 21, 22).

Beginning with the biblically loaded phrase, 'But *in those days* after that *tribulation (thlipsis)'*, the discourse looks to the end time and picks up on the questions of the four disciples about the signs preceding these things and when they will take place. The adversative *alla* ('but'), the phrase 'in those days' and the reference to *that tribulation* just endured *(thlipsis)*, implying that another *thlipsis* is to come, all strike a particularly ominous note for what is to follow. In this mood the discourse goes on to address the question of the end of the world as we know it and the coming in power and glory of the Son of Man on the clouds to gather the elect from the four winds, from the ends of the earth to the ends of heaven.

Before the tribulation, there were frightening portents of an earthly nature. Now after that tribulation one looks to the portents preceding the end time. These portents will be of a cosmic nature and are described in imagery taken from Isaiah (Isa 13:10; 34:4) and reflecting widespread biblical and extra biblical apocalyptic and prophetic style language and imagery for the end of the world as we know it. 'The sun will be darkened, the moon will not give its light, the stars will fall from heaven and the powers of the heavens will be shaken.'[50] The imagery should not be taken literally as an exact physical description of the final dissolution, but as an imaginative representation of the end of all things as we know them.

The description reflects also the great reaction of nature described in the context of an Old Testament theophany, where great natural and cosmic phenomena mark the Day of YHWH. The imagery is drawn from various Old Testament passages. The Book of Amos opens with the menacing words announcing the theophany: 'YHWH roars from Zion and makes his voice is heard from Jerusalem. The shepherds' pastures mourn and the crown of Carmel withers' and its description of the Day of

---

50. cf Isa 13:2-10; Joel 2:10-3:4; 4:15f; Amos 8:8f; Rev 6:12f; 4 Ezra 5:4, *inter alia*.

YHWH emphasises its cosmic dimensions: 'That day – it is the Lord who speaks – I will make the sun go down at noon, and darken the earth in broad daylight' (Amos 1:2; 8:9; cf Joel 4:15). The Psalms have cosmic imagery of God's activity, borrowed probably from other ancient literature, for example, Ps 67 (68):4 describes YHWH as the one who 'rides on the clouds.'[51] Joel speaks of the day of battle when the 'earth quakes, the skies tremble, sun and moon grow dark and the stars lose their brilliance' and of the Day of YHWH when 'the sun will be turned into darkness and the moon into blood … and all who call on the name of the Lord will be saved' (Joel 2:10, 31). In his oracle against Babylon Isaiah says: 'the Day of YHWH is coming, merciless with wrath and fierce anger … for the stars of the sky and their constellations shall not let their light shine; the sun shall be dark at its rising and the moon will not shed its light' (Isa 13:10, cf 34:4). This imagery persists into the New Testament in passages like 2 Peter 3:10-12 which speaks of the Day of the Lord coming 'like a thief when the sky will vanish with a roar, the elements will catch fire and fall apart and the world and all it contains will dissolve in flames.' The Book of Revelation speaks in similar language of the cosmic reaction to the breaking open of the sixth seal (Rev 6:12-14). The cloud is the great symbol of the presence of YHWH. Moses entered the cloud on Sinai, the pillar of cloud covered the tabernacle by day and a fire shone through it by night; the cloud covered the Temple when the Ark was placed there (Ex 24:16; 33:9; 40:36-38; 1 Kings 8:10f). At the transfiguration the cloud covered the mountain and the voice from heaven was heard from the midst of the cloud. The cloud both reveals and conceals the glory of YHWH (Mk 9:7 and//s).

This wealth of cosmic imagery is now transferred to the time of the coming of the Son of Man, emphasising its cosmic significance, and the end of the world as we know it. In the midst of this cosmic dissolution 'the Son of Man will come in the clouds with much power and glory.' The cosmic imagery is that of the Day of YHWH. The 'one like a Son of Man coming with the clouds of heaven' is modelled on the description in the Book of Daniel. Stating that the one coming is 'like a son of man/a human being' implies that in fact he is both like and at the same time very different from 'a son of man' in the sense of a human

---

51. An image possibly borrowed from the Canaanite storm god, Ba'al, described as 'cloud rider'.

being. In Daniel he is the one sent with the power to give life and to judge, two divine prerogatives, as he comes to vindicate the holy ones of God (Dan 7:13f).

Already in Mark's gospel, the Son of Man title or role was used by Jesus to justify his forgiveness of the infirm man's sins when he was let down through the roof in Capernaum (Mk 2:10) and again when he replied to the charge of breaking the Sabbath with the statement that 'the Son of Man is master of the Sabbath' (Mk 2:28). The future coming of the Son of Man in glory was already mentioned when he spoke of the predicament in store for those who are ashamed of him now in this adulterous generation when he comes in the glory of his Father with the holy angels (Mk 8:38), a glorious coming he will mention again at his trial before the High Priest when he looks to the future when the Son of Man will be 'seated at the right hand of the Power (God) and coming with the clouds of heaven' (Mk 14:62). He commanded the disciples to be silent about the transfiguration until the Son of Man was risen from the dead (Mk 9:9). However, the title is most frequently associated with Jesus in his predictions of his passion, talking about his being betrayed, his giving his life as a ransom for many and in his call to suffering and service as the marks of real discipleship (Mk 8:31; 9:31;10:33, 45; 14:21 (x2), 41).

Now Jesus declares that the coming of the Son of Man will be an event of great cosmic significance for he will come 'in clouds with much power and glory'. His coming will be heralded by a great cosmic cataclysm as the sun is darkened, the moon does not give its light, the stars fall from heaven and the powers in the heavens are shaken. This reflects the Day of YHWH imagery and the cosmic Christ of Colossians who has subjected all powers under his feet, and the Christ of Galatians who has freed the believers from the slavery to the *stoicheia tou kosmou*, the elemental spirits of the universe who were believed to control the fate of people, often with capricious and malevolent intent.[52]

The long history of God's care for the elect, especially those who had been scattered throughout the world, 'to the four winds' is a common theme in the Old Testament (Ezek 36:19; Zech 2:6). The promise to gather them together from wherever they have been scattered and to bring them back to their own

---

52. Col 2:8, 20; Gal 4:3; 2 Pet 10, 12 speak of the elements melting in the heat when the world dissolves in flames.

land to dwell in peace, plenty and security is a recurring theme, especially in the prophetic books.[53] The language and imagery of the scattering and gathering back together of the 'elect', 'the chosen', is now transferred to the larger cosmic community of the elect of the Son of Man, which will be gathered from the whole of creation, 'from the end of the earth, to the end of heaven.'[54] The angels will be the agents of the gathering and they will gather the elect 'from the four winds', that is from the entire world.[55] It will not be simply a gathering of the people of Israel into their ancestral homeland but an eschatological gathering of all peoples, since by then the gospel will have been preached to all the nations.

In a certain sense the prophecy of the coming of the Son of Man in glory (Mk 13:26) already hinted at in Mk 8:38 and later repeated at his Jewish trial (Mk 14:62), is the climax of Jesus' 'revelation' of his identity and ultimate purpose.

vi. Conclusion: Two Parables about Watching Mk 13:28-37

Learn from the Fig Tree Mk 13:28-31

'From the fig tree learn the parable'. The term 'parable' is used here in a general sense. It is really a similitude, though it is not introduced with the standard phrase introducing a comparison, such as 'it is like ...' Here it refers to observing the annual cycle of the fig tree and observing the signs of the things that are happening or about to happen. In a land whose climate disposes it to the growth of many evergreen trees, the fig tree stands out as a tree that loses its leaves in winter and appears rigid and dead, and its becoming supple and putting out new leaves is a sign of the arrival of spring and the approach of summer. Like the leaves of the fig tree announcing the approach of summer 'these things happening' will announce the approach of the Son of Man. (Already the withered fig tree was used as a pointer to the ending of the life and rituals of the Temple.) To what does the expression 'these things' refer – to the death, resurrection and

53. Isa 11:11, 16; 27:12; 60:4; Ezek 36:24; 39:27; Deut 30:3-5.
54. Deut 13:7 and 30:4 use these expressions about the end of earth and the end of heaven.
55. In Matthew's gospel the angels gather those who are to be judged and separate the wicked from the just and they consign the wicked to the blazing furnace where there will be weeping and gnashing of teeth (Mt 13:49f).

glorification of Christ, the siege of Jerusalem and the destruction
of the Temple or the end of the world and the judgement? 'He is
at the gates' could signify a general leading the army to capture
a city (as at the siege of Jerusalem) or a royal visitor approaching
in procession (as the Son of Man coming to the elect). What will
the keeper of the gate do? The next parable will address that
question.

Jesus then pronounces a solemn statement introduced with
the 'Amen I say to you' formula: 'Amen I say to you this generation will not pass away until all these things take place.' Is the
reader to understand 'this generation' as referring to the generation of Jesus or the generation of the evangelist? Whichever is
meant, the message is clear. 'These things' would happen in the
near future. The reference is not so much a 'time reference',
borne out by the following remark about nobody knowing it,
but rather an emphatic call for readiness, a notification that there
is no time for prevarication and postponing decisions.[56] D. E.
Nineham puts it well:

> Did this (verse 30) come originally immediately after verse 27
> and form the conclusion of the discourse proper? This gener-
> ation is to be taken literally but just possibly the saying re-
> ferred originally to some specific event, such as the destruc-
> tion of Jerusalem. However, in view of 9:1 and Matt 10:23, it
> more probably referred originally, as it does in effect here, to
> the *parousia*. If so, it is an example of that 'foreshortening of
> the perspective' so frequent in the prophets. 'When the pro-
> found realities underlying a situation are depicted in the dra-
> matic form of historical prediction, the certainty and in-
> evitability of the spiritual process involved are expressed in
> terms of the immediate imminence of the event.'[57]

The word of the Lord throughout the Old Testament stands unchanged in the changing circumstances of the people's history. It
remained as the sole foundation of their faith, identity and hope
for the future when all other institutional expressions of their
identity as a people had collapsed in the Exile. The prophet, conventionally known as Deutero-Isaiah proclaimed in the midst of
the Exile that there would be a new Exodus and immediately
followed his proclamation with the assurance, 'All flesh is grass

56. F. J. Moloney, *op. cit*, 269.
57. D. E. Nineham, *op. cit*., 360, and quoting C. H. Dodd, *Parables of the
Kingdom*, 71.

and its beauty like that of the wild flower, the grass withers, the flower fades but the word of our God endures forever' (Isa 40:8). He also prophesied that: 'the heavens will vanish like smoke, the earth will wear out like a garment … but my salvation shall last forever and my justice have no end' (Isa 51:6). Jesus uses similar imagery: 'Heaven and earth will pass away but my words will not pass away.'

The Returning Householder. That Day and Hour Mk 13:32-37
'About that day or hour no one knows, neither the angels in heaven, nor the Son, but only the Father.' This seems to subordinate the Son to the Father as did Jesus' response to the sons of Zebedee when he said that the places at table in the kingdom were not his to give (Mk 10:35-40). Mentioning the 'Son' rather than the ' Son of Man' or ' Son of God' (or indeed any other title such as Messiah/Christ) and speaking of 'the day' and 'the hour' places the saying in a category of Son-Father sayings, the majority of which dominate the theology of St John's gospel where the ' hour' and the '*kairos*' (equivalent of Mark's 'day and hour'?) are determined by the Father. A similar statement occurs there which seems to imply subordination of Son to Father. During the farewell discourse he tells the disciples that they should rejoice that he is going to the Father because 'The Father is greater than I' (Jn 14:28). Seeing these statements in the light of the trajectory that finds such a fuller development in John's gospel one can agree with the comment of J. R. Donahue and D. J. Harrington on the Markan text: 'These sayings are not the kind of material that early Christians would have created on their own, and so they may well represent the authentic voice of Jesus and provide an important perspective on the incarnation.'[58]

These texts have been the subject of christological debate but to discuss them on the level of later christological controversies is to miss the point of what is actually being said in the synoptic apocalyptic discourse or the Johannine farewell discourse. The main thrust of the Johannine text is the return of the one sent to the One who sent him. The relationship of sender and the one sent was already spelled out for the disciples after the footwashing, when Jesus affirmed that 'no servant is more important than his master; no messenger is more important than the one who sent him'(Jn 13:16. cf Mt 10:24; Lk 6:40). This observation made

58. J. R. Donahue and D. J. Harrington, *op. cit.*, 376.

in regard to Jesus and his disciples is replicated in relation to
Jesus and his Father. The Johannine statement relates to the
Logos become *sarx* rather than the '*Logos* with God', or the only
Son 'ever at the Father's side'. It is the Father who brings everything to fulfilment. It is he who sent the Son because he loved the
world so much. It is he who has determined the hour and the
time, the *hôra* and the *kairos*. It was from him that the Son
learned everything that he said and did. The emphasis on the
Son as agent, as the one sent, focuses attention on the role of the
Father who sent him. The Son's 'obedience' to the Father is seen
as a harmony of wills rather than 'obedience' in the sense of a
servile submission of will, and so the words and works of Jesus
are by definition the words and works of the Father. This is func-
tional subordination of Son to Father. Now the Son returns to
the Father, to the one who sent him. This later and more developed theology/christology of John helps to throw light on the
developing tradition in the earlier Markan texts. However, these
Markan texts (together with those in John) provided ammuni-
tion throughout the centuries for those who question Jesus' divinity and equality with the Father in the Trinity.[59]

Several aspects of Jesus' teaching are recapitulated in this
'parable', or more accurately, similitude, introduced with the
formula *hôs*, 'just as/like'. It compares the need to be vigilant to
the vigilance required of the doorkeeper (and servants) waiting
for the expected return of the master, the uncertainty of the time
of return, the need to be alert and watchful, the note of praise or
blame (judgement) on his return depending on their disposition
and readiness.

The setting of the parable resembles that of the talents or
pounds in the gospels of Matthew and Luke where the emphasis
is on the good or bad use to which they were put in the master's
absence and his reaction to their use on his return (Mt 25:14f; Lk
19:12f). By way of contrast the Markan parable emphasises the
readiness of the servants to open the gate to the master at his return. Opening the gate to an exhausted traveller and being
ready to tend to his needs (and those of his travelling companions, servants, horses or other beasts of burden) was a very important service to the master whether he was exhausted after the
heat of the day, after a journey lasting into the midnight hour, or
throughout the night to the early hours, maybe even until dawn

59. *Ibid.*

or later. Mark mentions these four 'watches' into which the Roman day was divided. The gatekeeper did not know in which watch the master would return. Unbroken vigilance was therefore required if he was to be properly attended to on his arrival. Otherwise the master might find him sleeping (and the house and stables and their attendants not ready to render the required service). The reference to the 'hours' or Roman 'watches' of the night sets the scene and forms a link with the passion narrative which follows.

Jesus finally addresses his original audience of Peter, James, John and Andrew and tells them to 'Watch' and not only they themselves are to watch, but all are to watch. This universal command ties this parable to the warnings of the coming of the Son of Man who is already at the gate. But a more imminent 'hour' is about to break upon the sleeping disciples who failed to keep watch in spite of the repeated exhortation to 'watch and pray' in Gethsemane before Jesus declares that the hour has come (Mk 14:32-41).

The Passion Narrative

The Nature of the Narratives

The purpose of the passion narrative in all four gospels is not the preservation of detailed historical information for its own sake.[1] Its purpose is primarily religious and theological, and secondarily apologetic. R. E. Brown makes the point very well in the introduction to his book, *A Crucified Christ in Holy Week:*

> ... we should reflect on what Jesus' passion meant to Christians of the NT period, using the gospels as a guide. It is noteworthy that many features depicted by later artists and writers have no place in the gospel accounts, for instance elements of pathos and emotion, and a concentration on pain and suffering. On Calvary, the evangelists report laconically 'they crucified him' without reference to the manner. Strikingly, however, they pay attention to the division of his garments and to the exact placement of the criminals crucified with him. Such details were important to the early Christians because they found them anticipated in OT psalms and prophets. Not biography but theology dominated the choice of events to be narrated, and the OT was the theological source book at the time. (This approach is far more likely than the skeptical contention that the Christians created the details of the passion in order to fulfill the OT.) The evangelists were emphasising that through the scriptures of Israel God had taught about His Son. Their emphasis also had an apologetic touch against Jews who rejected the crucified Jesus precisely because they did not think he fulfilled scriptural expectations.[2]

Not only were the accounts composed with 'an apologetic touch

---

1. For a comprehensive study of the passion narratives and related material in the New Testament see the monumental work by R. E. Brown, *The Death of the Messiah: From Gethsemane to the Grave. A Commentary on the Passion Narratives in the Four Gospels,* New York, Doubleday, 1994. See also the four volumes by D.Senior, *The Passion of Jesus in the Gospel of Matthew, The Passion of Jesus in the Gospel of Mark, The Passion of Jesus in the Gospel of Luke, The Passion of Jesus in the Gospel of John,* Michael Glazier: Wilmington, Delaware.,1984.

2. R. E. Brown, *A Crucified Christ in Holy Week,* 18.

against Jews who rejected the crucified' as pointed out in the above quotation from R. E. Brown, but all four gospels are equally careful to make it quite clear to the Romans that Jesus and his followers were not political revolutionaries or common criminals, a false portrayal perpetrated in Roman circles even as late as eighty years or so after Jesus' death when Tacitus wrote his *Annals*.[3] Pilate is carefully presented in the gospels as declaring Jesus' innocence of any political crime, a declaration which by implication declares also the innocence of his followers.

Dealing specifically with the passion in Mark's gospel, D. Senior, in his book *The Passion of Jesus in the Gospel of Mark*, points out how the cross comes as no stunning surprise since Mark has prepared the reader throughout the gospel for Jesus' death by weaving allusions to the passion into the body of his gospel. He states:

> The cross is not a final arbitrary act in the Jesus drama. It takes on meaning from the commitment of Jesus' life and vision. Mark's gospel demonstrates how the character of Jesus' ministry provoked the opposition and misunderstanding that built into a hostile and death-dealing force. The Jesus of Mark's gospel is no mere victim, passively accepting an unjust death. He 'takes up the cross' not by morbidly choosing death, but by choosing a way of life that would ultimately clash with those who could not see Jesus' way as God's way.[4]

In the light of the terrible history of anti-Semitism any writing, teaching or preaching on the passion narrative should include a very clear caution against a facile blaming of 'the Jews' for the death of Jesus. Jesus' story is a universal story and the factors that happened to manifest themselves in a Jewish context would have manifested themselves in any human society. Jesus was *handed over* by a faithless disciple and friend turned enemy, a jealous, manipulating, religious authority, a judge who failed to administer justice and a hostile mob. The failure of discipleship, the abuse of friendship, the jealous protection of religious status, the ignoring of justice, the mindless hatred of a mob, the political expediency of an occupying power and the 'dutiful' obeying

3. Tacitus, *Annals* XIV.
4. D. Senior, *The Passion of Jesus in the Gospel of Mark,* 15. See also A. Y. Collins, 'The Genre of the Passion Narrative,' *Studia Theologica* 47 (1993) 3-28 and W. H. Kelber, ed, *The Passion in Mark: Studies on Mark 14-16,* Philadelphia: Fortress,1976.

of orders by the military, all contributed to the handing over of
'the King of the Jews' to a horrible and shameful death. All
human life was there just as it has been in all societies throughout history.

Ironically Pilate emphasised Jesus' kingship, however he understood it and for motives known only to himself. (Was it to
tease the Jews who gave him this headache on the politically
fraught festive occasion?) All the gospels capitalise on the irony.
He also clearly acknowledged Jesus' innocence but gave in to
the mob that called for him to be crucified. This is the first reference in Mark to his being crucified in the gospel, as the predictions simply spoke of his being put to death.[5] Whatever construction one puts on Pilate's motives and predicament, the man
in authority *handed over* an innocent man, declared innocent in
his own public judgement, to be put to a most cruel and inhu-
man death by the military under his own command.

In the irony of the gospel, the King of the Jews is finally rejected by a mob from among his own people manipulated by a
hostile authority who probably wanted a king of the Jews, after
their own liking, in place of the Romans, and who did not scruple
to use the Romans to kill this 'pretender'. In so doing they facilitated the release of a representative of the very people who, in
the effort to establish an earthly kingdom, will provoke the violence which will sweep away the city and the Temple and undermine the freedom of the Jewish people, as the nation is sub-
dued and the people scattered in the terrible events between the
outbreak of the Jewish-Roman War in 66 and the Fall of Massada
in 73 AD. However, the kingdom proclaimed by the crucified
'King of the Jews' was very different, an eschatological kingdom, already present, but not yet fully, and it embraced Jew and
Gentile alike in the family of God.

The Reader

The religious, social, cultural and political background of the
readers for whom the gospel was originally intended would
have influenced the formation of the narrative. Once written the
text took on a life of its own and generations of readers from
New Testament times to the present day bring different back-

---

5. Unless one sees the reference to carrying one's cross (Mk 8:34) as a
reference to his crucifixion, but it is not so much a direct prediction as a
maxim for living.

grounds and perspectives to the reading of the text. Prior to reading this gospel the original readers may well have heard the stories of the arrest, trial and execution of Jesus circulating in the oral tradition of the community and celebrated in the liturgy. The gospel interprets in the light of its own theological insights the events which may have been already familiar to the originally intended readership. It also sets the implied readers' own experience of Jewish and Roman hostility in a framework rooted in the experience of Jesus and his contemporaries. Pilate and the Jewish authorities are prototypes of these forces hostile to the first readers. This is true not only for the implied, or original readers, but for readers of all generations. For present day readers Pilate and the religious authorities can function in the narrative as prototypes of contemporary influential forces working against the believer.

2. OUTLINE OF THE NARRATIVE

In dealing with the formation of the passion narrative some scholars point to the emergence of a shorter passion narrative beginning in Gethsemane which was then developed into a longer narrative beginning in Bethany with the anointing of Jesus. In effect this would mean that the passion narrative falls into two distinct parts, the introduction leading up to the arrest in Gethsemane (Mk 14:1-53) and the passion account proper describing the events from Gethsemane to the tomb (Mk 14:54-16:8). In the longer account, as I outline it below, there are nine 'scenes' or 'units', seven in the account proper. Mark, however, has woven the entire passion narrative into a single piece which represents a series of nine 'units', each of which is structured somewhat like an intercalation or at least a central story within an obvious inclusion. The dramatic effect and movement are aided by the changes of place and the indications of the passage of time. If one looks at the longer account, the central scene (no 5) deals with the choice of Barabbas and the call for the crucifixion of the King of the Jews. If one looks at the shorter account the central scene (no 4) deals with the crucifixion and mockery of the King of the Jews. In both cases 'King of the Jews' occupies a central role in the entire account. This is true also of the Johannine tradition. The following outline highlights Mark's overall arrangement of 'units' or 'scenes' which are either intercalations or have an iternal arrangement very like an intercalation (a-b-a).

I   a. Jewish leaders plot to kill Jesus (14:1-2)
    b. Jesus anointed for burial (14:3-9)
  a. Judas facilitates the leaders' plot (14:10-11)

II   a. Jesus prepares the Passover meal (14:12-16)
    b. Jesus predicts the betrayal by Judas (14:17-21)
  a. Jesus shares the Passover meal. (The Eucharist) (14:22-25)

II a. Jesus predicts the disciples' flight (& Peter's denials):
    Going to Gethsemane (14:26-31)
    b. Jesus in Gethsemane (14:32-42)
  a. The disciples' flight at the arrest of Jesus: Leaving
    Gethsemane (14:43-53)

IV a. Peter 'follows' Jesus at a distance (14:54)
    b. Jesus' Jewish trial (14:55-65)
  a. Peter denies knowing Jesus and being his disciple (14:66-72)

V a. The authorities hand over Jesus to Pilate (15:1-5)
    b. Crucify the King of the Jews! (15:6-11)
  a. Pilate hands over Jesus to crucifixion (15:12-15)

VI a. Mockery of the King of the Jews by Gentiles (15:16-20)
    b. The King of the Jews is crucified (15:21-27)
  a. Mockery of Christ, King of Israel by Jews (15:29-32)

VIIa. Darkness over the earth and the cry of Jesus (15:33-36)
    b. The death of Jesus (15:37)
  a. The Temple veil torn and the cry of the centurion(15:38-39)

VIII a. The women watching the crucifixion (15:40-41)
    b. The deposition and burial (41-46)
  a. The women watching the burial (15:47)

IX. a. The Women come to the tomb (16:1-2)
    b. The young man's good news and commission (16:3-7)
  a. The women flee from the tomb (and tell nobody) (16:8)

I have included these units under the following headings in the commentary:

I. Betrayal and Anointing; II. Passover/Eucharist and Betrayal; III. Gethsemane: Jesus' Prayer and Disciples' Flight; IV. Jewish Trial and Peter's Denials; V. Roman Trial and Call for Crucifixion; VI. Mockery and Crucifixion of the King; VII. Portents and Cries: The Death of Jesus; VIII. The Watching Women: Deposition and Burial of Jesus; IX. The Empty Tomb and Terrified Women.

3. THE NARRATIVE

i. Betrayal and Anointing

a. Jewish Leaders plot to kill Jesus

The ministry is drawing to a close and the shadow of death looms large. In setting the story of Jesus' passion, death and resurrection within the context of the Passover and the Feast of Unleavened Bread,[6] even specifying the days of the festal period,[7] Mark not only gives a context and creates a mood, but also introduces them as an interpretative backdrop for the unfolding events. As with the Temple and the teaching authority, Jesus will invest the festal life of the people with a new meaning, bringing to completion the older promise of the feasts and opening them onto a new future springing from the gift of new life in his death and resurrection, a (new) covenant established in his blood.

The first 'unit' is a composite of scenes of hostility and betrayal, love and service. The plot against Jesus is no surprise to the reader. Although the conspirators are trying to operate in secret, (*dolos* has all the overtones of secrecy and underhandedness), their hostility and lethal intentions towards Jesus are already well known. In his early ministry the long hand of Jerusalem authority had reached into Galilee proclaiming that

---

6. The history and significance of these two feasts, combined before the time of Jesus, are explained in an extended note at the end of the commentary.

7. Two days before the Passover and the Feast of Unleavened Bread in the Semitic way of counting the days probably refers to the 13th, the day before the eve of the feast, the 14th Nisan which will be the next time indicator when Jesus sends the disciples to prepare the Passover Meal (to take place in the evening as the 14th becomes the 15th at sunset). John follows a different chronology, having Jesus crucified on the day before the feast (the 14th).

Beelzebul was in him and that he cast out demons by the power
of the prince of devils. The Pharisees and Herodians had discussed how to destroy him (Mk 3:6) though in the long run the
Pharisees do not figure in the actual death of Jesus. In Jerusalem
after his action in the Temple the chief priests and the scribes
sought some way of doing away with him (Mk 11:18) and the
authorities who felt attacked by the parable of the tenants would
have arrested him there and then except for their fear of the
crowds (Mk 12:12). In the passion predictions in Mk 8:31 and
10:33 the chief priests are the main agents of Jesus' downfall.[8]
His popularity with the crowd is the very reason they now give
for needing to 'get hold of him (*kratesantes*) by stealth in order to
kill him'[9] and not *en tê heortê*, a phrase that could be translated as
either 'during the festival', or 'among the festal crowd' who
were present and in enthusiastic mood about Jesus and the
hopes they had pinned on him.[10] The element of secrecy and
plotting heightens the tension in the narrative and throws even
more bad light on the conspirators and the betrayer. Jesus is
now well and truly in the predicament of the rejected prophet,
like Jeremiah, 'the gentle lamb led to the slaughter' (Jer 11:18f),
the faithful, suffering servant, 'oppressed and afflicted ... led
like a lamb to the slaughter, dumb before the shearers' (Is 53:7);
like the just person calling out to God in the psalms that 'a company of evildoers surrounds me ... they stare at me and gloat'

8. The priesthood was hereditary through male membership of a priestly
family and as the numbers of priests increased a hierarchy of authority
and influence emerged. Some were poor and powerless while others
were very wealthy, powerful in their own circle and influential with
the Romans. The chief priest in the 'hierarchy' was the High Priest, sup-
posedly chosen for life, but the Romans gained control of the office,
kept the ornamental vestments in the Antonia fortress and released
them for specific occasions. The Romans used the High Priest and his
council as their 'go-between' with the Jews and were prepared to dismiss him if he did not co-operate. This accounts for the stinging remark
in Jn 11:49, 'Caiaphas was High Priest that year', though it was an office
for life! The family of Annas and Caiaphas were highly political and
several of them held the office of High Priest.
9. *Kratêsantes* signifies more than a legal process of 'arrest'. It could be
translated 'get the better of him', 'take hold of him', 'capture him'.
10. In St John's gospel there is a parallel and even more pointed repetition of the desire of the authorities or others to arrest or stone him: Jn
5:16; 7:20, 30, 32; 10:39; 11:49-54, 57.

(Ps 21 (22):16f), a state of distress strongly represented in Pss 41 (42) and 55 (56), and the targeted righteous one in Wisdom, 'Let us lie in wait for the righteous man' (Wis Sol 2:12). The passion of Jeremiah, prophet of the fall of the Temple and the captivity of the people (Jer 37-38) and Zechariah's passion of the rejected, murdered messianic shepherd-king (Zech 9-14) are in the background throughout the unfolding events of Jesus' passion.

Popularity of a prophetic or messianic figure always posed a problem for the Jewish authorities who feared the Roman reaction against themselves if they seemed to lose control of the situation. This was the reason Josephus gives for the arrest of the Baptist. It was also the reason for the concern of Caiaphas in Jn 11:49f when he said it was better for one man to die for the people than that the whole nation should perish. It is now a similar situation here in Mark's gospel as they plot the arrest of Jesus. The pilgrimage feasts, especially Passover, were highly charged with religious and national fervour and messianic expectations. As the population of the city multiplied during the festal period the festivities and the presence of the crowd could provide opportunity and cover for revolutionary activity against the Roman administration.[11] The authorities could not risk a riot which could easily ensue if they arrested him in public. To operate by stealth they needed an 'inside' collaborator.

b. Jesus Anointed for Burial Mk 14:3-9 (//Mt 26:6ff; Jn 12:1-8)
In a classic use of intercalation Mark now places the story of the anointing of Jesus by an unnamed woman in Bethany (in the house of a leper!) between the two parts of the account of the plot to arrest Jesus and his betrayal by one of his closest associates, Judas Iscariot.[12]

In Mark's (and Matthew's) gospel, the anointing takes place between the authorities' seeking an opportunity to arrest Jesus and the offer of Judas to arrange it. Sandwiched between the scheming of the authorities and the betrayal by a disciple, the noble action of the woman stands out as a gesture of love and discipleship. Having already said the gospel will be preached to

---

11. Josephus, *Antiquities of the Jews*, 17.213-218; 20.105-112; *Jewish War* 2.255; 2.280f; 5.244.
12. See the extended note at the end of the commentary on the different accounts of the anointing in Bethany, the story of the woman with the bad reputation in Lk 7, and the confusion with Mary Magdalene.

all nations (Mk 13:10), Jesus will now go on to say that wherever the gospel is preached the action of this woman will be told in memory of her.[13] The Markan/Matthean and Johannine settings of the anointing seem to reflect an early tradition in which a dark frame or context highlight the noble action of the woman.[14] D. Senior describes this intercalation succinctly when he says it is like 'soiled paper around a jewel'.[15]

In contrast to the plotting of the authorities and the treachery of Judas, there stands out in high profile the striking action of the woman who invades the male space at the banquet, breaks the alabaster jar of ointment and pours over the head of Jesus its contents of pure nard, an extremely expensive perfume, made from a plant grown in northern India, and costing in this case three hundred denarii, a year's wages.[16] For the woman of Bethany it was the sacrificing of something very precious, an action akin to that of the widow who put 'all she had to live on' into the treasury. It was the action of a devoted disciple demonstrating her faith in, and love for, Christ. Her action mirrors the anointing of a Messiah or King. Earlier, at Caesarea Philippi Peter had confessed his belief that Jesus was the Messiah (Christ) only to earn a stern rebuke because of his mistaken notion of the role and destiny of the Christ. The note of kingship had been struck by Bartimaeus as they began their ascent to Jerusalem, and the crowds had proclaimed it enthusiastically at Jesus' approach to the city. But it is only now that the real significance of Jesus' anointed messiahship-kingship is authentically proclaimed as Jesus himself puts words on the woman's action and says, 'she has anointed my body beforehand for burial', setting her action in the context of his forthcoming death. Her silent proclamation-in-action is in line with Jesus' own predictions of his passion which were first spoken as a corrective to Peter's mistaken notions of messiahship. As Jesus moves forward to-

13. See the article by C. S. Barton, 'Mark as Narrative. The Story of the Anointing Woman (Mk 14:3-9),' *ExpTim* 102 (1991) 230-34.
14. In John's gospel Judas is introduced into the anointing scene as the one who voices criticism of the anointing and the remark is included that he was the one who was to betray Jesus.
15. D. Senior, *The Passion of Jesus in the Gospel of Mark*, 42.
16. A denarius a day was the usual pay at the time. Taking Sabbath days and holy days into account there were approximately three hundred working days in the year. Women sometimes wore small flasks of nard around their necks with which to freshen up.

wards death from this point in the narrative his anointed kingly
status emerges more and more clearly. The 'noble action' is in
fact 'one of the good works', that is, the fitting burial of the dead.
Jesus' words about his forthcoming death link the story of the
anointing to its dark frame and at the same time they inform the
reader that the plotting and treachery will succeed.

Jesus has already said that the gospel will be preached to all
nations and now as he praises the action of the woman he states
that, 'Wherever the gospel is preached in the whole world, what
she has done will be told in memory of her' (Mk 14:9).[17] This unnamed woman in Mark's gospel, like the unnamed widow, the
unnamed Syrophoenician woman and the blind Bartimaeus are
those who may well have been seen as outsiders but who in fact
become and behave as 'insiders', while the 'insiders' become
more and more like outsiders as they in turn move towards their
moment of betrayal, denial and panic-filled flight from Jesus.

In responding to the criticism of her action, Jesus points out
how she was taking responsibility beforehand for his burial. The
reader can see here the action of a disciple for the master, a
prophetic action in proleptically anointing his body for burial.
Her faith and generosity stand in stark contrast to the behaviour
of Judas. Anticipating the burial of Jesus, she becomes the first
disciple to understand the significance of his death.[18] She does
beforehand what the disciples of John had done for their murdered master, and what the disciples of Jesus will fail to do for
him, as they will already have left him and fled. She prepared
him for a fitting burial.

Those who saw it as a waste are not specified by Mark but
one suspects the disciples were involved, a suspicion made explicit in Matthew's account where he says it was the disciples
who complained, and John's account points specifically to
Judas. They covered their avarice with false concern for the
poor, a bluff called immediately by Jesus who reminded them

17. John reflects a similar understanding as he points out that the aroma
filled the house (Jn 12:3). The reference to the aroma may reflect the
same tradition as that in *Midrash Rabbah* on Eccles 7:1 which says: 'The
fragrance of a good perfume spreads from the bedroom to the dining
room; so does a good name spread from one end of the world to the
other.' This parallels the saying, 'Wherever the gospel is preached in
the whole world, what she has done will be told in memory of her' (Mk
14:9).
18. W. J. Harrington, *op. cit.*, 64.

that the poor were always present and in need of help, a remark very likely charged with the implied question and reprimand: 'What have you done for them before, and what will you do for them in the future? Don't be using them as an excuse!' Mark and Matthew describe Jesus' reprimand and state in addition that Jesus said the woman had done a *good work*. The Jews divided *good works* into almsgiving and charitable deeds, the latter including among other pious works the fitting burial of the dead. Then he explained that she had prepared him for burial. He said that they will always have the poor present, but will not always have him. This is a reminder of Jesus' earlier comment, 'The days will come when the bridegroom will be taken away and then they will fast' (Mk 2:19).

a. Judas facilitates the leaders' plot Mk 14:10-11

The narrator emphasises the nature of the betrayal by identifying Judas Iscariot as one of the Twelve, and going on to say that he went to the chief priests in order (to plan how) to hand Jesus over to them (and the reader has already seen the very hostile attitude of those to whom he is to hand Jesus over). The reader senses their perverse joy (*echarêsan*) on hearing of the planned betrayal and they promise Judas money and arrange the 'handing over.' Mark and Luke say the chief priests tempted Judas with the offer of money. Matthew says he demanded the money. John further develops this money loving weakness in terms of stealing from the common fund in his charge (Mk 14:11; Lk 22:5; Mt 26:15; Jn 12:4-6). This interpretation portrays Judas' weakness in terms of what is often seen as the root of all evil, love of money. Luke and John see the Prince of Evil at the root of Judas' actions. Both say that Satan entered into Judas, and John also says that Judas was a devil (Lk 22:3; Jn 13:27; cf 13:2; 6:70). The mind and motives of Judas have continued to be a subject of discussion throughout history. Since New Testament times historians, priests, poets, playwrights and many others have continued to speculate on his motives. However, Mark does not dwell on Judas' motives but portrays him as the example of a failed disciple, the one called 'to be with Jesus' who joins with those who are not only against him but in fact violently opposed to him, and Judas will arrive with them to betray and arrest Jesus. He is a vital link in the chain of people involved in the 'handing over' (*paradidonai*) of Jesus. At the same time he functions as a human instrument in the great design of God, 'as it is written'.

ii. Passover / Eucharist and Betrayal

a. Jesus prepares the Passover Meal Mk 14:12-16

In the second 'unit' the announcement of the betrayal by Judas is the centre of an intercalation, being set poignantly in the midst of the Passover meal at which the Eucharist was instituted, the meal signifying Jesus' total gift of self in his body and in his blood 'poured out for many'. It is placed between the preparation and the celebration of the meal. Mark describes the Day of Preparation (14th Nisan) as 'the first day of the Feast of Unleavened Bread' though the Paschal meal with the Paschal lamb, would have been eaten that evening, when the new day (15th Nisan), the first day of the feast began at sunset. This 'inaccuracy' was probably a 'concession' to a non-Jewish audience / readership for whom the day already began in the early morning. On the preparation day 'they were sacrificing' (or 'used to sacrifice,' *ethuon*) the Paschal lambs.[19] In the original legislation, which had the extended family celebration in mind, it was prescribed that the sacrifice should take place between the two evenings, that is, in the twilight between sundown and darkness (Exod 12:6).[20] In Jesus' time, however, following various reform movements, Passover was a pilgrimage feast and the sacrifices took place in the Temple. The huge numbers attending the feast necessitated the slaughtering / sacrificing of the lambs from noon onwards.

The disciples asked Jesus where he wished them to go and make preparations so that 'you can eat (*phagês*) the Passover meal'. The singular verb emphasises the fact that it is Jesus' Passover meal and so the others would join him in his Passover meal, Jesus being the *paterfamilias*, the head of the group / family. The question / request addressed to the householder will bring this out: 'The teacher says, "Where is my guest room where I am to eat the Passover meal with my disciples?"' The term 'disciples' is used during the preparation, a term signifying a group broader than the Twelve. However, when they assemble for the meal the group is described as the Twelve.

The account of the preparation of the meal shares the same literary form and theological perspective as the preparation for

19. The word 'lambs' is not in the Greek text but is implied by the context.
20. For the biblical background to the legislation and customs see Exod 12:1-20; Lev 23:5-8; Num 28:16-25.

Jesus' approach to the city. In an instruction and a scene very
similar to the instruction and scene when he sent the disciples to
acquire the colt on which he rode into Jerusalem, Jesus now
sends two disciples to acquire the room for the supper. His
prophetic words about seeing a man carrying a jar of water are
fulfilled to the letter. This is striking because it was unusual for a
man to carry water in a jar. Women drew the water in jugs and
jars for domestic purposes, and men carrying water for a journey or into the fields would do so in a leather bottle. His predictions about entering a house where they will find 'a large room
well decked out and ready' are also fulfilled. Describing the
room as *anagaion mega* points to its being 'a large upper room,'
coenaculum magnum, above a shop or other business along the
street front. Describing it as 'decked out/well furnished', *estrô-
menon*, refers to its being well furnished with coverings such as
carpets, cloths/drapes. The corresponding verb *estrôsan* described the laying of garments on the ground for Jesus to pass
over on his entry into the city.

The ' prophecy' about what they would find in the city is fulfilled exactly, as in the preparation for his approach to the city,
enhancing Jesus' authority and status. The deliberate nature of
the preparation also highlights the fact, which Jesus will subsequently make known at the meal, that Jesus is preparing the opportunity for Judas to betray him, in the very context of a betrayal
of table fellowship. Jesus is master of the situation as he prepares
to respond to God's will, though the unfolding events will appear to master him. F. J. Moloney puts it succinctly:

> The events that are about to happen transcend the expected,
> and Jesus goes into them knowing what lies ahead, and
> makes suitable arrangements for the first of the events of his
> passion.[21]

Because the pilgrims were expected to eat the Passover meal in
the city, the inhabitants were expected to make available their
suitable spare rooms and accommodation for the many pilgrims. (Does Jesus say '*my* guest room' because, historically, he
had been there on previous occasions for the festal celebrations,
and the historical reminiscence remains in the remembered saying?) The term used here for 'guest room' is *katalyma*, the word
used by Luke in describing the plight of Joseph and Mary who
could not find a place in the *katalyma*, 'inn/guest house' (Lk 2:7).

---

21. F. J. Moloney, *op. cit.*, 283.

Furthermore, the night of the Passover was to be spent within the city boundaries and because of the crowds of pilgrims the boundary had been extended to include the Mount of Olives.

b. Jesus predicts the betrayal by Judas Mk 14:17-21

The Twelve are said to form the company of Jesus for the meal. From now on they are seen in increasingly negative light, one betraying him to his enemies, another denying him, and all leaving him in the garden and fleeing. The meal is overshadowed by the prophecy of Judas' betrayal and will be followed by the prophecy of the disciples' desertion and Peter's denials, a dark shadow of negativity on the part of the disciples shrouding the meal which will come to symbolise the total self-giving of Jesus 'as he reclined with them' (*anakeimenôn met' autôn*).

Jesus arrived in the evening with the Twelve and they reclined to eat the meal. The Passover meal was begun between official sundown and the onset of darkness. Though originally it was eaten standing up in the manner of persons in a hurry, staff in hand and dressed for flight (Ex 12:11), by Jesus' time it was celebrated in the manner of a Greco-Roman banquet with the guests reclining on mats, leaning on one elbow. This may also have had the significance of emphasising their status as free people after liberation from the slavery of Egypt, since slaves did not recline to eat.

Now Jesus shocks the Twelve with a revelation of something known to the reader since Judas was introduced as the traitor when the Twelve were chosen and named, and again clearly revealed to the reader in his dealings with the enemies of Jesus who were seeking a way to capture him away from the crowd. Now the Twelve are confronted with the shocking news, proclaimed in a solemn 'amen I say to you' formula by Jesus. The heinous nature of betrayal is highlighted by the multiple references to table-fellowship: 'while they were reclining and eating', 'one of you', 'the one eating with me', 'one of the Twelve' and 'one dipping into the dish with me'. The sense would be well rendered into English if the word *you* were emphasised and the sentences read as: 'Amen I say to you, one of *you*, yes, one of *you*, one of *you* who is actually here and now eating *with me*, will betray me.'

The shock of the Twelve is described in terms of their distress and sorrow that one of them should behave thus towards Jesus,

and their anxiety articulates itself in the chorus of dissociation
from the heinous act as one after another they protest: 'Not I,
surely!' The Greek *mê* emphasises the fact that they expected a
negative answer. Maybe they protest too much. Throughout the
gospel they have been unaware of the significance of the events
unfolding around them and unsure of themselves and their reactions. Are they now completely unnerved? Do they realise
their own vulnerability and potential for betrayal? Or are they
still obtuse enough to believe that Jesus may even be mistaken?

Jesus responds to their initial reaction with a reaffirmation of
the fact that it is 'one of the Twelve, one dipping with me into
the dish'. He emphasises the close bond of table fellowship, the
betrayal of which is seen in biblical eyes as one of the greatest of
all forms of betrayal. One psalmist decries the evil intentions of
enemies who say: 'How long before he dies and his name per-
ishes' and goes on to say, 'even my closest and most trusted
friend, who shared my table, has lifted his heel against me' (Ps
40 (41):5, 9) and another laments: 'Were it an enemy who insulted
me I could have put up with that ... but you, my equal, my companion, my familiar friend with whom I kept pleasant company
in the house of God' (Ps 54 (55):12-14).

Jesus now proclaims: 'The Son of Man goes forth as it is written of him.' This is almost like a summary and recapitulation of
the three predictions of the passion to be endured by the Son of
Man, the first of which was introduced with the statement of divine necessity or decree, *dei*, 'it is necessary that the Son of Man
should suffer many things ...' (Mk 8:31; 9:31; 10:33f). Three more
sayings during the passion narrative will emphasise his suffering (Mk 14:21x2; 41) and one will proclaim his future coming in
power and glory (Mk 14:62). The divine necessity or decree is
represented here by the authoritative word of scripture, 'It is
written.' The willing obedience of the Son of Man to that divine
plan is emphasised in the choice of words 'he goes forth' (*hy-
pagei*). He is not captured, constrained or dragged along. He
goes willingly.

From early on in their Christian lives the first followers of
Jesus, to borrow the phrase from the Acts of the Apostles,
'searched the scriptures' and found in them the passages that
enabled them to see and accept the divine will and economy at
work in the events surrounding the death and resurrection of
Jesus. Paul could write to the Corinthians that he was handing

on to them what he himself had received, 'that the Lord Jesus died for our sins *according to the scriptures* ... that he rose on the third day *according to the scriptures*' (1 Cor 15:3-5). By the time the Acts of the Apostles was written the words *foretold, foreseen, foreknowledge, predetermined* were the stock in trade vocabulary for showing the divine plan in Jesus' suffering and death.[22] Mark, however, like the other evangelists, does not excuse Judas' deliberate action in cutting himself off from Jesus and plotting his downfall, even though it fits into God's overall plan. Mark reports Jesus' prophetic style lamentation: 'Woe to one by whom the Son of Man is handed over; it would be better for him that he had never been born' (Mk 14:21).

The 'woe' (*ouai*) recalls the warnings of the prophets. Throughout the Bible there are many examples of blessing and woe (curse) alternatives. On entering the Promised Land Moses sets before the people a blessing and a curse (Deut 11:26-28). There is a blessing on those who keep God's law, who walk in the way of the righteous, who care for the poor, and so forth. There is a curse on those who do not keep God's law, who do not walk in the way of righteousness and who ignore the plight of the poor. In the prophetic literature these alternatives are frequently spelled out in the beatitudes and woes: 'Blessed are those who ... ' and 'Woe to those who ...' The emphasis is usually on the nature of the attitude and activity being praised or blamed. Here in typical prophetic style the activity of the betrayer is condemned in a fashion that mirrors the 'woe' statements of the prophets.[23] The attitude/activity is a declaration of total failure to grasp what Jesus had done and taught, a total closing off from what he offered. In some ways it resembled the sin against the Holy Spirit for which there is no forgiveness (Mk 3:28f). It is like the one who has gained everything and lost his life (Mk 8:35f). In prophetic words, it resembles a saying about those who deny the Lord of Spirits in 1 Enoch, 'It were better had he never been born' (1 Enoch 38:2).

a. Jesus shares the Passover Meal. The Eucharist Mk 14:22-25
Mark presents the meal as the Passover meal though there is no detailed account of the overall ritual and there is no mention of

---

22. The Acts of the Apostles was probably written in the early eighties.
23. Hos 7:12-14; Amos 5:17-19; 6:3-5; Mic 2:1-2; Isa 5:7-23; 28:1f. cf Mt 23:13-32; Lk 6:24-26.

the principal dish, the lamb. Jesus is the lamb and the emphasis
on his blood brings out his significance as the Passover Lamb.
The sharing of the cup and the mention of 'covenant' emphasise
the Passover dimension, as does the hymn singing at the conclusion of the meal. The reference to the blood is a reminder of the
escape from the slavery of Egypt when the blood of the lamb
was sprinkled on the doorposts in Egypt marking out the
Israelites as the children of God (Ex 12:1-14), and of the blood of
the sacrificial animals half of which was poured on the altar and
half sprinkled on the people as a sign of the sealing of the
covenant at Sinai between God and the recently liberated chosen
people (Ex 24:6-8).

At one level the ritual of taking the bread and the cup, saying
a blessing or giving thanks, then breaking and distributing the
bread, and handing around the cup of wine reflects the action of
the *paterfamilias* at a festal meal. On another level it reflects the
stylised ritual action and language of the early Christian eucharistic celebration, a ritual reflected already in the two accounts
of the multiplication of the loaves in Mark, and in the parallel accounts in the other gospels (*labôn arton/potêrion, eulogêsas/eu-
charistêsas, eklasen kai edôken*) (Mk 6:41; 8:6 and / /s).[24] Though the
bread was probably unleavened bread, *azymos*, and the reference to the Feast of Unleavened Bread has already been made in
the introduction to the passage, still the term *artos*, ordinary
leavened bread, is used, again a reflection of eucharistic language. The Jewish custom of praising God and giving thanks at
the beginning of the meal is reflected in the use of *eulogêsas* and
eucharistêsas, again two terms that became established ritual expressions in the eucharistic celebration. Mark and Matthew have

---

24. The monumental work of J. Jeremias, *The Eucharistic Words of Jesus*,
New York: Scribner's, 1966, has been of huge influence in reconstruct-
ing the historical ritual and language of the Passover Meal and examining its setting and interpretation in the New Testament. However,
scholars have pointed out that the information drawn from the
Mishnah and Talmud on which it relies sometimes reflects a situation
somewhat later than the New Testament, when significant changes had
been brought about by the dramatic events of 66-70 AD and their aftermath. See also M. Casey, 'The Original Aramaic Form of Jesus'
Interpretation of the Cup,' *JTS* 41 (1990) 1-12; D. B. Smith, 'The More
Original Form of the Words of Institution,' *ZNW* 83 (1992) 166-86; G.
Ossom-Batsa, *The Institution of the Eucharist in the Gospel of Mark*, Bern-
Frankfurt: Lang, 2001.

both terms but Luke and Paul kept to *eucharistêsas*, giving thanks, probably because it was better suited to the language of their Gentile audiences.[25] However, Mark (and Matthew likewise), unlike Luke and Paul, does not include the injunction to repeat the action in his memory (Lk 22:19; 1 Cor 11:24f) as Mark's focus at this point in the narrative is not on showing the beginning of the church's eucharistic practice but rather on emphasising the salvific nature of the total self gift of Jesus' body and blood, 'the blood of the covenant which is poured out for many.' The 'self-giving' of Jesus represented in the giving of his body and blood is juxtaposed to the 'handing over' of Jesus by Judas.

During the meal, literally 'as they were eating',[26] having taken bread, having said the blessing, he broke (it) and gave (it) to them and said: '*Take. This is my body.*' He took the cup and having given thanks he gave (it) to them and they all drank from it. And he said to them, '*This is my blood of the covenant, which is poured out for many.*' Some manuscripts have 'the *new* covenant',[27] but with or without the word 'new' the concept of something new taking place is obvious from the context. The addition of the word 'new' in some manuscripts may be under the influence of the parallel Lukan text and/or the eucharistic text in Paul's First Letter to the Corinthians (Lk 22:20; 1 Cor 11:25).

'My body' and 'my blood' are two parallel, rather than complementary, ways of saying 'myself' or 'my life', each pointing to the fullness of the identity and life of Jesus in his gift of himself/his life.[28] 'The many' in Hebrew means 'the multitude', 'a number beyond counting', 'all and sundry', an all-inclusive term, rendered in Greek by *hyper pollôn*, (but losing some of its all inclusive import in the English version 'for many'). Jesus already spoke of giving his life as 'a ransom for many', *lytron anti pollôn*, (Mk 10:45). Paul emphasises this vicarious/salvific theme

---

25. Mk 14:22ff; Mt 26:26ff; Lk 22:19f; 1 Cor 11:23ff.
26. This is a genitive absolute, though in strictest terms of Classical Greek it should be dative agreeing with *autois*, and not a genitive absolute. In Koinê Greek, and in Mark in particular, this looser use of the genitive absolute is regularly found.
27. Important mss like Vaticanus and Sinaiticus just say 'covenant'.
28. John on the other hand in the eucharistic section of his Bread of Life treatise uses *sarx* and *haima*, the flesh and blood as separated in sacrificial rituals, and therefore complementary (Jn 6:53ff).

in several letters. In addition to his handing on the tradition of
the last supper and the institution of the Eucharist in First
Corinthians, he wrote to the Romans that 'Christ died for us
while we were still sinners,' and 'God did not spare his own Son
but gave him up for the benefit of us all.' To the Galatians he
wrote: 'Christ … sacrificed himself for our sins' and 'the Son of
God sacrificed himself for my sake' (1 Cor 11:24; Rom 5:8; 8:32;
Gal 1:4; 2:20). Mark's ' for many' is a Semitic equivalent of this
universal language of Paul.

Passing the cup (*potêrion*) around for all of them to drink, and
the statement that all drank from it, has the triple significance of
sharing the wine in fellowship, entering the (new) covenant in
his blood and accepting the cup of suffering. The blood is the
blood of the covenant, established in his name. The cup has
overtones of the fate of Jesus, his suffering and death. Jesus'
prayer in Gethsemane for the cup to be taken away from him
will emphasise this. Those who are about to betray, deny and
flee from him are all invited to participate in the meal, in the suffering and in the covenant. The salvific death of Jesus is for all. St
Paul brings out the significance: 'The blessing cup that we bless
is a communion with the blood of Christ, and the bread that we
break is a communion with the body of Christ. The fact that
there is only one loaf means that, though there are many of us
we form a single body because we all have a share in this one
loaf' (1 Cor 10:11f).

'Covenant' is central to the experience of Israel. The covenant
with Abraham established YHWH as the patron God of Abraham
and promised a future for his offspring and for all nations who
would be blessed in his name (Gen 17:1-27). The covenant with
Moses and the people at Sinai established God as the suzerain
God of a newborn nation bound to God by covenant as they
were reminded of his historical acts of kindness and benevo-
lence towards them (Exod 19:1-9). The covenant with David
made God the patron of a dynasty charged with shepherding
the people (2 Sam 7:1-29). The prophets Jeremiah and Ezekiel
looked to the future to a new covenant, not written on stone for
the people in general but written on the heart of every individual (Jer 31:29-34; Ezek 18:2; 36:22-28). Jesus now speaks of his
blood which is to be poured out, the blood of the covenant. A
whole new relationship of God 'with the many' is being established. The blood of Jesus ratifies this (new) covenant just as the

blood of the sacrificial lambs at the first Passover was sprinkled on the doorposts, marking out the children of Israel as the first-born of God in contradistinction to the first-born of the Egyptians (Exod 12:7, 13), and at Sinai the sacrificial blood was sprinkled on the people to ratify the covenant whereby they became the chosen people of God: 'You will be my people and I will be your God' (Exod 24:1-8; cf Heb 9:19ff; 10:28ff). Zechariah would later speak of God setting the captives free from the waterless pit ' because of the blood of my covenant with you' (Zech 9:11).

The imminence of Jesus' death symbolised by his broken body and spilled blood seems to mark the end of his mission, of his coming to announce the arrival of the kingdom of God. His mission appears to have been thwarted, his project defeated, his task a failure. But all is far from lost. Immediately following the words and actions over the bread and cup in Mark and Matthew, and immediately before them in Luke, Jesus looks to the final triumph of the kingdom. The earthly table-fellowship may be over, but as he announces a fast he speaks the final words of hope in the face of his earthly failure and death. He will not drink wine until he will drink the new wine in the kingdom of God (Mk 14:25; Mt 26:29; Lk 22;18).

Earlier in the gospel, when he was challenged because the disciples of John and the disciples of the Pharisees were fasting but his disciples were not, Jesus responded that it would not be right for them to fast while the bridegroom was still with them, but the day would come when the bridegroom would be taken away, and on that day they would fast (Mk 2:19-21). Now the bridegroom is about to be taken away and it is the bridegroom himself who will fast. Speaking of a fast that will come to an end when he drinks new wine in the kingdom of God points forward to the eschatological, heavenly messianic banquet. Coming after the solemn predictions of Judas' betrayal and followed closely by the prediction of the denials by Peter and the flight of the disciples, all of which are fulfilled within the immediate context of the gospel itself, this prediction/prophecy gains a profile of credibility for its fulfilment, even though it points to a context beyond the bleak horizon of the gospel (Mk 14:18, 25, 30). Only God can bring that about. J. P. Meier states:

> The prophecy in Mk 14:25 is thus a final cry of hope from Jesus, expressing his trust in the God who will make his king-

dom come, despite Jesus' death. To the end, what is central to
Jesus' faith and thought is not Jesus himself but the final triumph of God as he comes to rule his rebellious creation and
people – in short, what is central is the kingdom of God.[29]

Fasting was done as an act of repentance, as an expression of
mourning, as an accompaniment for prayer of petition (often in
sackcloth and ashes), as a preparation for contact with the holy
or as a preparation for the Day of the Lord.

The reader may see Jesus here as fulfilling the role of the
obedient, faithful, servant suffering on behalf of the many and
praying all the time for sinners. If so, then the fasting can be seen
as an accompaniment to his prayer on behalf of the people, of
the many for whom his blood has been poured out (Mk 14:24), of
the many for whom his life is given in ransom (Mk 10:45), at this
critical moment (cf Is 53:12) as he places his own fate in the
hands of God. In his moment of failure and rejection, Jesus
stands in solidarity with human kind and places his hope in God.

The reference to the kingdom of God here at the end of his
ministry forms an inclusion with his initial call to 'repent for the
kingdom of God is close at hand'. It emphasises that it is an 'already but not yet' presence of the kingdom.

iii. Disciples Flight and Jesus' Prayer in Sorrow.

a. Jesus predicts the disciples' flight (& Peter's denials) Mk 14:26-31
The third 'unit' sets the scene of Jesus' distress and his appeals to
the sleeping disciples in Gethsemane between his prediction of
their abandoning him and their actual flight from the garden.
On the way to the garden Jesus predicts their flight (and Peter's
denials) and his prediction comes to pass as they leave the garden, Jesus in chains and the disciples in flight.

The gloom of isolation and imminent catastrophe engulfs the
scene and thickens until Jesus' death next day. Meanwhile he
will be betrayed by a table companion, deserted by his disciples,
denied by Peter, rejected by the Jewish authorities, executed by
the foreigners, cast out from the holy city and people, and finally
die alone.

'After they had sung the hymns' (*hymnêsantes*)[30] they set out

---

29. J. P. Meier, *op. cit.*, vol 2, 308.

30. 'Hymns' is probably a better translation than the usual 'having sung
a hymn', as it very likely refers to the Hallel Psalms 113 to 118 which
were sung on festal occasions.

for the Mount of Olives, a ridge stretching for about three miles
from north to south on the eastern side of the city. Heading for
the Mount of Olives, they had to cross the Kidron Valley. From
there one has a spectacular view of the city and Temple and it
was there that Jesus told the disciples about the forthcoming destruction of the Temple and repeatedly warned them to 'look
out' and 'watch'. It was there, too, that Jesus, according to Luke,
wept over the city (Lk 19:41-44). From there too he entered the
city in triumph as he approached from Bethany and Bethphage.
Zechariah's vision describes the Day of the Lord when God
plants his feet on the Mount of Olives and the eschatological battle and judgement will take place (Zech 14:4). Human crisis and
divine judgement are very much associated with the area they
traverse between the supper room and the Mount of Olives.

Jesus' crossing to the Mount of Olives re-echoes the story of
David. The reader remembers David's sense of abandonment
crossing this same valley when his son had betrayed him and
raised a rebellion against his authority. The reader now sees
Jesus and hears his words in similar circumstances. David fled[31]
from the city and made his way across the Kidron, when his son
Absalom rebelled against him. He arrived at the Mount of
Olives weeping and praying only to discover that he had been
betrayed also by his close personal adviser and friend Ahitophel
(who later took his own life, the only suicide in the Old
Testament apart from soldiers in battle not wishing to be taken
by the enemy) (2 Sam 15:13-31; 17:23).

Retracing this historic and tragic journey of David, the shepherd king, Jesus tells his disciples that they will all desert (him)/
fall away, 'for it is written, "I will strike the shepherd and the
sheep will be scattered".' This is a loose quotation from
Zechariah (Zech 13:7). The original text in Zechariah states:
'Strike the shepherd so that the sheep will be scattered.' Here in
Mark it is: 'I will strike the shepherd and (as a result) the sheep
will be scattered.' The scattering is a result of their failure in discipleship when they come under threat to their lives as the shepherd is struck down. 'You will fall away/lose faith/desert' is a
better translation of *skandalisthêsthe* than 'you will be scandalised'
because the English word means 'shocked, greatly surprised in a
negative way, seriously disappointed' but the Greek word *skan-*

---

31. The LXX and Mark use the same verb for David and Jesus and their
entourages leaving the city, *exerchesthai*.

dalon means 'a trap, a snare, a stumbling block that causes one to fall and be lost' as it was used of the seed that fell away and produced no harvest because of trials and persecutions (Mk 4:17). It was used of Peter himself in Matthew's gospel when he refused to accept Jesus' first prediction of his passion and death (Mt 16:23, cf Mk 8:33).

However, as in the passion predictions, there is a note of hope, a promise of resurrection. As Jesus went before them on the journey from Galilee to Jerusalem, full of foreboding, so too after his resurrection he will go before them, that is, he will, as a shepherd, lead the scattered sheep back to Galilee, and await them there, not only to the geographic location, their home place, but also to the place where they left eveything to follow him when the arrival of the kingdom was proclaimed, and mighty words and deeds accompanied its proclamation. Even there the heavy hand of the Jerusalem authorities had fallen but now Jesus has come to the centre of opposition and the final struggle is about to take place. After his vindication, his resurrection, he promises to lead them back to Galilee.

Jesus predicts the scattering of the sheep when the shepherd is struck down. Peter responds as on previous occasions in the gospel when he speaks either for the group, or for himself. Here again Jesus has to correct his well-meaning impetuosity or add a note of caution to his optimism (Mk 8:29, 32f; 9:5; 10:28; 11:21). His response here is rather ironic. 'Even if all fall away, I will never forsake you.' The grammar of the sentence emphasises Peter's self assurance which could be translated as, 'Not I, of all people!' The use of *ephê* rather than the more frequent *elegen* brings out the idea of a boastful pronouncement as though to illustrate the point that Jesus and the others *spoke* but Peter *announced* or *declared*. As the story unfolds it will be Peter who makes the most emphatic denial of Jesus, a denial that will be a major factor in the story whenever it is told. In fairness to Peter, however, it should be said that the others had already run away so the storyteller's spotlight had been removed from them.

The solemn response of Jesus in an 'amen I say to you' pronouncement, using *soi* and *su*, the singular pronoun 'you', points deliberately and exclusively to Peter: 'Amen I say to *you* that *you*, today, this very night before the cock crows twice will have denied me three times.' The double use of 'you' responds to the emphatic 'I' on Peter's lips as he dissociated himself from the predicted failure of the others: 'Though they lose faith (fall away), I shall not.' The triple time reference, "to-day, this very night, before the cock crows twice", emphasises how quickly and unexpectedly (from Peter's point of view) it will happen. Furthermore, the triple denial emphasises the deliberate nature of the denial. From putting himself forward as the leader of the followers he will emerge as the leader of the renegades! In John's gospel Jesus tells him: 'You cannot follow me now, but you will follow me later' just before he predicts his denials (Jn 13:36f), and in Jn 21 Peter is given three opportunities to undo his triple denials as he responds to Jesus' question, ' Do you love me' and he is told to 'feed my lambs, feed my sheep' and then told how when he grows old he will be bound and led to where he would rather not go (to martyrdom) (Jn 21:15-18). This Johannine emphasis, twenty to thirty years after Mark's account, shows how high a profile Peter's denials continued to have in the early church and how they may well have been used as a high profile example of denial, repentance and restoration for the *lapsi*, those who had fallen away during the persecutions of Nero or Domitian.[32] In this way Peter's denials became a great source of hope and reassurance to those who had fallen away during persecution and had subsequently come to regret their failure. Some time later Pliny the Younger wrote about the Christians being given three opportunities to affirm or deny whether they were Christians, a practice that was probably in use before Pliny's time in the reign of Trajan (c.110 AD).[33]

Peter responded very forcefully about his willingness to die with Jesus. And all of them (*pantes*) said the same. Ironically the scene is set for all of them (*pantes*) to flee the scene and for Peter to deny twice that he was a disciple and then to deny on oath that he ever knew him! However, all of them had drunk from the cup of Jesus' blood of the covenant, 'poured out for many', and ironically 'the many' for whom it was poured out included themselves.

b. Jesus in Gethsemane Mk 14:32-42
They come to the garden called Gethsemane, a name which

32. For a study of Peter's denials and their function and importance in the gospel as a whole see A. Borrell, *The Good News of Peter's Denial. A Narrative and Rhetorical Reading of Mark 14:54*, 66-72. Atlanta: Scholars,1998.
33. Pliny, *Epistles*, 10.96:2,3.

means 'the oil press', signifying a spot on the Mount of Olives opposite the Temple and city where the cultivation of oil has been well attested.[34] Central to the scene in Gethsemane is the prayer of Jesus, highlighted against the failure of the three 'special' disciples to 'keep watch' and the fear which caused all the disciples, those chosen 'to be with him' to 'flee from him'.[35] Within the larger intercalation, the alternating scenes between Jesus' watching and praying and the disciples' failure to keep watch and pray, function like a series of 'internal' intercalations enclosing scenes of prayer and scenes of failure within each other for the emphasis of contrast.

Jesus seeks comfort from Peter, James and John (Mk 14:33-34)
On arrival, Jesus removes himself from the body of disciples, instructing them to 'sit there while I pray.' He brings Peter, James and John further on with him. They were the same three to whom he gave special names on their appointment (Mk 3:16f), the three who accompanied him to the house of Jairus (Mk 5:37), to the mount of transfiguration (Mk 9:2) and together with Andrew, the ones to whom he spoke close to this very spot about the coming disaster on the city and Temple and the end of the world as we know it (Mk 13). As he now becomes (*erchesthai*) greatly distressed (*ekthambeisthai*) and troubled (*adêmonein*), he confides in them: 'My soul is sorrowful even unto death.' The use of *erchesthai*, 'began', here is not just a characteristic of style as throughout the gospel but seems to emphasise the moment of his embarking on the suffering of his passion and death. The verbs *ekthambeisthai* and *adêmonein* mean respectively 'a profound disarray, expressed physically before a terrifying event; a shuddering horror' and 'a basic awareness of being separated from others, a situation that results in anguish.'[36] The calm, determined, 'cerebral' quality of his predictions of his own suffering at various points so far in the story and his foretelling of the betrayal by Judas, the flight of the disciples and the denial by Peter, all under the rubric of God's great design, now gives way

---

34. R. E. Brown, *The Death of the Messiah*, 1:148f.
35. See the extensive treatment in R. E. Brown, *The Death of the Messiah*, Vol I,110-310, and also D. M. Stanley, *Jesus in Gethsemane*, New York: Paulist, 1980. See also the article by J. Murphy-O'Connor, 'What Really Happened at Gethsemane?' *Bible Review* 14/2 (1998) 28-39, 52.
36. R. E. Brown, *The Death of the Messiah*, Vol 1, 153.

to a 'gut reaction' in the face of impending death and the reaction of the heart in the need for companionship. The reader thinks of the prayer of the psalmist: 'My heart is in anguish within me; and the terrors of death have fallen upon me. Fear and trembling come upon me, and horror (LXX darkness) overwhelms me' (Ps 54 (55):5f).

Scholars have discussed what exactly 'unto death' means. It could mean sorrow at the onset of death, or sorrow so great that it could kill, or such sorrow that makes one wish to die. R. E. Brown seems closest to Mark's context when he assesses the various conjectures and draws the conclusion:

> In the context of being surrounded on all sides by enemies, Sirach 51:6 affirms, 'My soul has been close to death; my life has gone down to the brink of Sheol.' If Jesus is the weary prophet in Mk/Matt, in part it is because he foresees his disciples scandalised and scattered by his arrest and death, after they have betrayed and denied him. The very thought of this is enough to kill him, and he will ask God to be delivered from such a fate.[37]

He instructs the three disciples to 'remain here and watch'. When he instructed them in his discourse on the Mount of Olives he repeatedly told them to 'look out (*blepete*)' and finished the discourse with an emphatic: 'What I say to you, I say to all, "Watch!" (*grêgoreite*)' (Mk 13:35, 37). The parable of the doorkeeper, which he had used on that occasion to illustrate his point about 'watching', spoke of the various watches of the night, evening, midnight, cockcrow and morning. Now he urges these same three whom he had singled out to be with him on a number of special occasions, to 'watch', *grêgoreite, grêgorêsai* (Mk 14:35, 37). From the tone and distressed attitude of Jesus, so uncharacteristic of his previous predictions of his suffering, it is obvious that something is about to happen this night and at this critical moment Jesus renews his exhortation: 'Watch!' 'Watching' is not simply staying awake physically and being ready for danger through the various watches of this night, but also a command to maintain spiritual alertness, awareness of what is really taking place at a level beyond the immediately perceptible events.

---

37. *Ibid.*, 155f.

Jesus prays to the Father Mk 14: 35-36

Going on a little further he falls to the ground and prays that if it were possible the hour might pass him by. This 'indirect speech' of the narrator gives two of the essential elements of the 'direct speech' of the prayer that is to follow. 'If it be possible' sets the petition in the context of acceptance of God's design, even if it entails God's refusal of the petition. Using the term 'the hour' Jesus is using the same term that he used in connection with the great design of God for the ending of the world as we know it in Mk 13:32. Here it points to the place of the passion in the overall context of God's design for the people and the world. There follows the direct speech of Jesus' prayer. Using the familiar Aramaic and Hebrew address of a son to his father, *abba*, the only example of its use in the gospels (translated as 'Father', for the non Jewish reader), Jesus first acknowledges the omnipotence of the Father, 'all things are possible to you', then he follows on with the petition, 'remove this cup (*potêrion*) from me', and ends with a statement of acceptance of the Father's will, 'yet not as I will but as you will'. 'The cup (or chalice)' is a traditional image regularly used for 'the cup of suffering' or the outpouring of the wrath of God by way of punishment.[38]

The reader is reminded of the psalms of lament, where the just one pours out spontaneous sentiments of sorrow and distress to God. Jesus' lament is 'at once fearful and yet trusting God'.[39] D. Senior comments on the prayer:

> With stunning boldness Mark presents Jesus as engulfed in the prayer of lament. In the tradition of the just ones of Israel – anguished before death, tormented by the betrayal of friends, vulnerable to enemies – Jesus clings to the one thread that gives ultimate meaning to his existence, his faith in the God of Israel.[40]

F. J. Moloney comments in similar vein. Speaking of the psalms of lamentation he points out how they come from

> … someone in a situation of suffering, abandonment, hopelessness, and violated innocence. But through all the expressions of fear, suffering, and hopelessness and the questions

---

38. Is 51:17, 22; Jer 25:15f; 49:12; 51:7; Lam 4:21; 23:31f; Ezek 23:23; Hab 2:16; Ps 74 (75):8f. It is sometimes for good fortune, God's favour (Ps 23:5).

39. F. J. Moloney, *op. cit*, 290.

40. D. Senior, *op. cit.*, 70.

put to God, a profound trust is expressed in the ultimate victory of God over the source of evil ... The passion has begun,
and these words of lament and anxiety point forward to the
horror of the events that will follow. Jesus' sudden change of
attitude indicates the unrelenting nature of the suffering that
he is about to endure. However, it does not take away from
him the trust that – whatever may happen to him – God will
have the last word.[41]

The Father-Son relationship proclaimed in the opening verse of
the gospel, acknowledged by the Father at the baptism and
transfiguration and voiced by the demons when challenged and
vanquished, is now witnessed from the other side of the relationship. The Son acknowledges the Father from the depths of
human isolation and suffering: 'Abba, Father, all things are possible to you ... yet, not what I will but what you will.'

Jesus again seeks comfort from Peter, James and John Mk 14:37-38
Jesus comes to the three disciples he had singled out from the
group and brought forward to be near him on this occasion.
Having told them to 'watch', he finds them sleeping and challenges them. These are people who had specifically stated their
intention and assured him of their resolve and ability to be with
him in spite of anything that might happen. James and John had
assured him they could drink the cup he had to drink and be
baptised with the baptism with which he was to be baptised (Mk
10:38f). Peter had protested that even if all lost faith he would
not, and would be willing to die with him rather than disown
him (Mk 14:29-31). Addressing Peter, significantly not calling
him by his disciple's name Peter, but by his 'personal' name
Simon, Jesus says 'Could you not watch one hour?' In the parable of the doorkeeper he had told them about the necessity of
watching during all the hours of the night. Now he finds they
cannot watch even one hour. Again he issues the instruction:
'Watch and pray lest you enter into temptation.'

Watching and praying are very important in the face of the
peirasmos, the 'testing' that lay ahead. Jesus reminds them that
the *peirasmos*, in this case, the reaction of the hostile world under
Satan's influence about to break upon them, will pose a real
threat to their frail humanity, even in spite of their 'spiritual'
commitment to Jesus as his disciples. He further points out that

41. F. J. Moloney, *op. cit.*, 291f.

'the spirit is willing, but the flesh is weak' and already this is
being proved true in their failure to keep watch.

Jesus prays to the Father Mk 14:39
Jesus returns and continues praying, using the same word(s).

Jesus again seeks comfort from Peter, James and John Mk 14:40-42
Jesus again returns to the disciples and his sense of isolation is
further increased by finding the disciples still sleeping. The
'weakness of the flesh' is now highlighted by the statement that
'their eyes were heavy' and 'they did not know how to answer
him.' It is reminiscent of their reaction at the transfiguration
when Peter 'did not know what to say' (Mk 9:6). Jesus returns to
the sleeping disciples a third time, implying that in the meantime he had been praying for the third time. Three is a number of
completion. Three prayers and three failures to watch match
each other as complete demonstrations of Jesus' attitude and the
failure of the disciples. Peter will later deny Jesus three times,
again showing a completeness of attitude and action (Mk 14:30,
66-72). As Jesus tells them to 'sleep on and take their rest' he is
pointing out that their opportunity to 'watch and pray' with the
one who chose them 'to be with him'(and especially now at this
critical moment of the *peirasmos*) has passed. As Jesus moves towards his great moment of resolve when he says 'that the scriptures might be fulfilled', the disciples sink further into failure
until at the moment of Jesus' resolve 'they all left him and fled'
(Mk 14:50).
      Jesus is seen to take a definite initiative as the traitor and his
company approach. Far from cowering or running away Jesus
proclaims: 'The deal is done (*apechei*).[42] The hour has come.

---

42. *apechei* is almost impossible to translate at this point and scholars
have made many suggestions. In Greek the verb *apechein* usually has a
commercial or financial meaning, as in the receipt of payment or set-
tling of a debt. In this context it would refer to the payment of the traitor,
the making of the deal, which is how I translate it above. In this I am influenced mostly by R. E. Brown, *Death of the Messiah*, vol 2, appendix III,
1379-83. He summarises the many different approaches to a translation
and suggests as a translation: 'The money is paid.' Other approaches
have been influential, but are not very clear or convincing. The Vulgate
translates *apechei* as *sufficit*, 'it is enough', and this translation has been
widely used. But to what does it refer? Enough of Jesus' reprimand?
Enough watching and prayer? Enough talk of sorrow and the

Arise! Let us go!'[43] Jesus' final invitation to the disciples to accompany him, 'Arise, let us go,' will be too much for them as
they have not 'watched and prayed.' It is the hour, the opportunity for the apparent triumph of evil, of the power of Satan over
the Son of Man, the apparent frustration of the promise of the
arrival of the kingdom and the fulfilment of God's design. 'The
Son of Man is handed over (*paradidotai*) into the hands of sinners.' Jesus' first proclamation in the gospel, after the *handing
over* of John the Baptist was, 'the kingdom of God is close at
hand'. Now at the end of his ministry he proclaims: 'The one
handing me over is close at hand.'

a. The disciples' flight at Jesus' arrest Mk 14:43-53
Jesus' initial proclamation of the nearness of the kingdom was
followed throughout the first part of the gospel by a whole series of words and deeds introduced by *kai euthus*, 'and immediately', as though his proclamation set the inrush of the kingdom
in motion. Now his announcing of the nearness of his betrayer is
similarly followed by *kai euthus*, 'and immediately', emphasised
by the assertion that his words were fulfilled 'while he was still
speaking'. It was as though his 'Arise, let us go, behold the betrayer is at hand' had set the action in motion. The betrayer is
immediately identified as 'one of the Twelve', not however, any
longer described as a disciple 'with him (with Jesus)', but as one
who is now in very different company. 'With him there was a
crowd with swords, and clubs, sent by the chief priests and the
scribes and the elders', the very group of officials who challenged Jesus' authority and lost out in his counter question
about the Baptist's authority (Mk 11:27-33). Meanwhile he had
also outranked both the Pharisees and the Sadducees in their
own fields of expertise and drawn attention to the hypocrisy

---

peirasmos? The verb *apechei* can also mean 'it is far off' (or 'is it far off?').
In this sense Jesus' statement would read: 'Is it far off ? The hour has
come!' Some have suggested it is a mistranslation of the Aramaic *kaddu*
which means 'already'. Some mss like Codex Bezae and Old Latin mss
have variant readings.
43. This resolve of Jesus is presented in a dramatic fashion and high
christology in John's gospel where Jesus astounds the arresting party
with his question 'Whom do you seek?' and presents himself for arrest
with the 'I am' response to their seeking of 'Jesus of Nazareth'.
Underlying the very different accounts of Mark and John is the firm resolve of Jesus.

and greed of the scribes and other religious leaders. He aimed
the parable of the wicked tenants at the authority figures, and
now they are adding another victim to the list of rejected messengers! Now their response comes in terms of violent arrest
under cover of darkness, away from the crowd who supported
Jesus and saw through their lack of authority when confronted
by him.

Again the term 'betrayer', ho *paradidous,* is used for Judas as
the narrator relates how he arranged a sign, 'the one I shall kiss,'
for the arresting party to know whom to seize (ironically the
verb *kratein* is used, 'to take hold of by power or force.' It is the
verb so often used to describe Jesus' taking control over sickness
and demonic possession). Some commentators wonder why it
was necessary to point out Jesus since he was well known to the
crowds and authorities in the city and Temple area where he
preached and disputed openly in the sight of all and in the full
light of day. Maybe it was rather difficult to spring a surprise arrest on one of a group gathered in the darkness and in the shade
of the olive trees. Maybe 'kissing or embracing' Jesus brought
Judas close enough to take hold of him in the event of an attempted escape while the arresting party approached. John's
gospel speaks of a company of Roman soldiers coming with the
arresting party. If they had been drafted into the city for the feast
they may well need to have Jesus pointed out to them. Whatever
the reason, it afforded the betrayer the opportunity to write the
betrayer's kiss into the record of humanity's darkest moments, as
it became the sign to 'lay hold of him and lead him away safely'.
The 'kiss' is accompanied by the title 'rabbi', 'master', an address highlighting the heinous nature of the deed and illustrating the treachery and poignancyof the moment. It is quite possible that the greeting 'Rabbi' and a Mediterranean or Oriental
style kiss would have been a customary way for a disciple to
greet a teacher. The action and the word are said to take place
'immediately', *euthus.* 'And coming, immediately approaching
him, he says "Rabbi" and he kissed him'. Again the word 'immediately' signifies the inexorable unfolding of God's design.
The predictions/prophecies of Jesus throughout the gospel are
now being fulfilled.

As they laid hands on him and took charge of him (again the
verb *kratein* is used), their violent action provoked a violent reaction. The reaction on the part of 'one of the bystanders' must

have come from one of the disciples. John's gospel will later name the person as Peter and name the victim Malchus, a servant of the high priest. Mark, however, uses the action to make a point. The disciples were those chosen 'to be with him', but all this night so far they have failed in this regard. Now instead of being the ones 'with him' they are described as 'the bystanders' (*hoi parestêkotoi*). One of them, drawing his sword and striking the servant of the high priest, cut off his ear (or earlobe, since *ôtarion* is a diminutive of *ôtion*?).[44] (Did Mark not know his name, or did he protect his identity, and the identity of the striker, by not mentioning their names?)

In reply Jesus asked his captors if they had come to arrest him with swords and clubs as in the case of a robber, though he had been teaching in the Temple day after day and they never laid hands on him. The implication is clear. Their deed is foul and needs the cover of night. Jesus accepts his fate as a fulfilment of the scriptures: 'in order that the scriptures may be fulfilled.' Fulfilling the scriptures is fulfilling God's will. No specific scriptural passage is quoted or alluded to, but the widespread thrust of the ill treatment of God's servants, the just ones and the suffering servant spring to mind, together with the consistent understanding that in spite of the apparent evil in all that is happening, God has a grand design for all his people and the world.

As the arresting party laid hold of Jesus the disciples, instead of 'going with him' as he had asked moments before when he said: 'Arise, let us go, behold, my betrayer is close at hand', all left him and fled. The structure of the sentence emphasises the universality of the flight. 'And leaving him, they fled, all (of them)', *kai aphentes auton ephugon pantes*. Placing 'all' at the end, the sentence highlights the ' all' (*pantes*), recalling Jesus' prediction on the way to the garden that 'all' would fall away, and repeated in Peter's protests (Mk 14:27). Jesus' prophecy about striking the shepherd and the sheep being scattered is now fulfilled.

The fleeing youth
The final scene in the garden is as evocative as it is puzzling. Its meaning is clear, but who is the young man? At the beginning of the ministry the two pairs of brothers and Levi left everything,

44. See the article by B. T. Viviano, 'The High Priest's Servant's Ear: Mark 14:47,' *RB* (1989) 71-80.

their families and livelihoods, the nets, the boats, the men em-
ployed, the counting house, to follow Jesus. Now this young
man who is described as a fellow follower (of Jesus, with the disciples), *synêkolouthei*, is captured together with Jesus. Instead of
'following with Jesus' he follows with the disciples in their flight
as he leaves everything, even the clothes that covered his naked-
ness, to get away from him.

Scholars have puzzled over the possible identity of the
young man. Some have suggested it might be John, son of
Zebedee, James the brother of the Lord, Lazarus, John Mark,
Mark the evangelist. Some have suggested that his attire
showed he was disturbed in his sleep in a house nearby and
came to investigate the happenings in the garden. Others have
seen a baptismal reference with the person going naked into the
water to identify with the dying and rising of Christ. Others still
have drawn a comparison between the fleeing youth, really an
adolescent, *neaniskos* rather than *neanias*, leaving the linen cloth
behind and the young man in white at the tomb on Easter morning. Others see a connection with the *sindona*, the burial sheet.
Perhaps such speculation distracts from the main point, the
panic and poignancy of the scene as all that is left of Jesus' disciples as he is led away to death is a linen sheet in the hands of his
captors.[45] R. E. Brown, having given a comprehensive overview
of the various theories, concludes:

> This young man's attempt to follow Jesus into *peirasmos* is a
> miserable failure; for when seized as Jesus had been, he is so
> anxious to get away that he leaves in the hands of his captors
> the only clothes he wears and chooses the utter disgrace of
> fleeing naked – an even more desperate flight than that of the
> other disciples … In Mark 10:28 Peter described to Jesus a
> model of discipleship that Jesus praised: 'We have left all
> things and have followed you.' This young man has literally
> left all things to flee from Jesus.[46]

---

45. For some of the recent theories see the articles by M. J. Haren, 'The
Naked Young Man: A Historian's Hypothesis on Mark 14:51-52,' *Bib* 79
(1998) 525-31; H. M. Jackson, 'Why the Youth Shed His Cloak and Fled
Naked: The Meaning and Purpose of Mark 14:51-52,' *JBL* 116 (1997) 273-
89, and S. R. Johnson, 'The Identity and Significance of the *Neaniskos* in
Mark,' *Forum* 8 (1992) 123-39.
46. R. E. Brown, *Death of the Messiah*, vol I, 303.

The flight of the disciples not only leaves Jesus to face his terrible ordeal alone but it seems to signify the undoing of his mission and the wiping out of his standing as a person who drew disciples to himself. Greco-Roman society highly prized philosophers and holy men who drew a following. Jewish society inherited the tradition of the prophets and the Wisdom teachers with their schools of followers and the Rabbis drew followers in accordance with their reputations. The last word on the Baptist's life in the gospel described how his disciples had come to give him fitting burial. But in the case of Jesus, his known disciples, and even the unknown young man who was a 'fellow follower' with the disciples, have left him and fled.

Except for Peter, no more is heard of the disciples in the gospel of Mark, except the risen Jesus' message to them that he will go before them into Galilee and that they would see him there (Mk 16:7).

iv. Jewish Trial and Peter's Denials

a. Peter ' follows' Jesus at a distance Mk 14:54
The fourth 'unit', again an intercalation, places the Jewish trial of Jesus in the middle of the story of Peter's following him 'at a distance' to the high priest's house where he denied him three times.

'And they led Jesus to the high priest'. Mark does not give the name of the high priest anywhere in the gospel.[47] Jesus is now in the power of the forces that opposed him all along. They gather under cover of darkness. Mark describes those who gathered as 'all the chief priests, the presbyters and the scribes', a combination well known already for their hostility. They now have their opportunity.

Though we were told that all the disciples had left Jesus and fled in the garden, we now read that Peter 'followed him' but *makrothen*, 'at a long distance,' 'at quite a distance', or to use the English idiom, 'at a safe distance' as far as the courtyard of the high priest. The play on 'followed', the technical term for the allegiance of a disciple to his master, is not missed on the reader, and neither is the cautious, even cowardly, 'at a (safe) distance'. The disciple who is called to be 'with the master' now takes his

---

47. R. Pesch, *Das Markus Evangelium*, 2.425 suggests that this is because he was still reigning and his name was known as the gospel story was formed.

place with the servants of the enemy as he 'sits with them,' *synkathêmenos*, warming himself at the light of the fire.

b. Jesus' Jewish trial Mk14:55-65

Mark (like Matthew) conveys the idea that Jesus was tried by 'the whole Sanhedrin' during the night.[48] Mark and Luke do not give the name of the high priest but Matthew mentions Caiaphas as the high priest in question (Mt 26:57). It may well be the case historically that the term *synedrion* is loosely used and best understood here as an *ad hoc* 'assembly' rather than a formally convened meeting of the complete Sanhedrin. Mark is building up a picture of the quiet, even silent, dignity of Jesus in the face of the forces massed against him. In doing so he describes how in spite of 'the whole Sanhedrin', 'all the chief priests, elders and scribes', 'the whole cohort', 'the many false witnesses', Jesus still maintains his dignity, as he did in the garden when facing arrest.[49] The parallel account of the trial in Luke is set in the early morning. John, who is probably the most accurate historically, does not have a trial of Jesus before the Sanhedrin as such but an interrogation before the former high priest Annas, who then sends him bound to Caiaphas (Jn 18:12-24). The exact nature of the session appears to be more accurately remembered by John as a interrogation for the purpose of presenting a case to the official (Jewish? and) Roman court. Legally a trial should have been in the presence of the high priest Caiaphas, and it is very unlikely that the Sanhedrin, which must have contained many rigorously legal minded members, would have been formally convened in haste for a night session with all the appearances of a kangaroo court. Also the remark of Pilate, as reported by John 'Take him yourself and try him by your own

---

48. Some important studies of the trial of Jesus prior to the works of R. E. Brown and D. Senior, already mentioned, were: J. Blinzer, *The Trial of Jesus. The Jewish and Roman Proceedings Against Jesus Christ Described and Assessed from the Oldest Accounts*, Westminster, Md: Newman,1959; S. G. F. Brandon, *The Trial of Jesus of Nazareth*, London: Batsford,1968 and E. Bammel (ed), *The Trial of Jesus*, Studies in Biblical Theology, Second Series 13, London, SCM Press, 1970; J. R. Donahue, *Are You the Christ? The Trial Narrative in the Gospel of Mark*, Missoula: Scholars 1973; D. Juel, *Messiah and Temple: The Trial of Jesus in the Gospel of Mark*, Missoula: Scholars,1977.

49. Cf R. H. Gundry, *op. cit.*, 12.

law' (Jn 18:31) seems to point to there not having been an official court trial. R. E. Brown comments:

> John may be more accurate in describing on this night before Jesus died only an interrogation by the high priest that would quite plausibly be held at 'the court (= palace) of the high priest'.[50]

The night session was deeply embedded in the tradition(s) because of the double 'trial', that of Jesus and that of Peter, both of which took place simultaneously during the night. As Jesus is led before the assembly of chief priests, elders and scribes, Peter follows him into the high priest's courtyard and sits there with the guards warming himself at the fire. The two 'trials' follow. The 'trial' of Jesus is sandwiched between the two parts of the story of Peter in the courtyard. It is an intercalation but it is also a parallel account. Jesus holds his ground before the important people in spite of the lying witnesses. Peter loses his nerve before the unimportant maid servant and the bystanders and denies their true witness in relation to his discipleship and his association with Jesus.

The chief priests and all those assembled were seeking testimony against Jesus to put him to death but found none. The verb 'seek', *zêtein*, has been used several times already of the authorities in descriptions of their hostile activity or intention against Jesus. After the 'cleansing' of the Temple 'they sought how to destroy him' (Mk 11:18). After he told the parable of the wicked tenants and added the saying about the rejected stone becoming the corner stone, 'they sought to arrest him, but feared the crowd' (Mk 12:12). At the approach of the feast they were seeking a way to arrest him by stealth in order to kill him (Mk 14:1). On their behalf Judas sought an opportune way of handing him over (Mk 14:11). Now their 'seeking' continues in their attempt to find testimony against him in order to put him to death. They find none. Jesus' innocence, proclaimed by himself at the moment of his arrest, is vindicated in the initial investigation of the assembly. The narrator tells us that many bore false testimony, and their testimonies did not match. Some of the false testimony is given in direct speech.'Some of us heard him saying: "I will destroy this Temple made by hands and in three days I will build another, not made by hands"'(Mk 14:58).

Worse than an outright lie, which is easily contradicted, is a

---

50. R. E. Brown, *Death of the Messiah*, vol I, 404.

verisimilitude, something that has an aspect and appearance of
the truth but is presented with an untrue slant. Such is the case
with the statement about the Temple. Sticking strictly to Mark's
narrative, what Jesus said on the occasion of his action in the
Temple was, 'Does not scripture say: "My house shall be called a
house of prayer for all the peoples?" But you have made it into a
robber's den' (Mk 11:17). Jesus never spoke of destroying the
Temple or rebuilding it on that occasion. The statements about
destroying and rebuilding the Temple are heard on the lips of
false accusers and mocking enemies.[51] In the apocalyptic discourse when he speaks privately to the four disciples about the
coming destruction of the Temple he does not say he will destroy or rebuild it. Looking at the broader New Testament tradition one sees that in John's gospel Jesus does not say 'I will destroy this Temple and in three days build it up,' but rather:
'Destroy (i.e. if you, or anyone, destroy) this Temple and in
three days I will build it up' and the narrator adds that he was
speaking of the Temple of his body (Jn 2:19-22). Subtleties of
Jesus' position, lost, misunderstood or deliberately misrepre-
sented in transmission lent themselves to false accusation. But
even in this the testimony was conflicting. According to the
Torah two or three witnesses are required to gain a conviction.
Nobody is to be convicted on the testimony of one witness (Deut
17:6; 19:15). Furthermore the prescription in the Torah against

---

51. In St John's gospel, however, these statements are not heard on the
lips of opponents, but form the basis for a high christological statement,
or *logion*, on the lips of Jesus himself, and they serve the purpose of raising the issue onto another plane (Jn 2:19-22). Matthew uses another *logion*
in the context of the dispute about breaking the Sabbath. Having pointed
out that the Temple priests are blameless in 'breaking' the Sabbath by
carrying on their ministry, Jesus makes a profound christological statement in the *logion* 'something greater than the Temple is here', and then
goes on in true prophetic style to quote the text: 'What I want is mercy
not sacrifice', before making a second christological statement in the *logion*
'The Son of Man is master of the Sabbath' (Mt 12:5-8). The synoptics
thus portray Jesus breaking the mould and transcending the institutions and practices of Israel's past. In all the gospels his attitude to
Temple, Torah and Sabbath is of central significance and displays his
greatest claims to divine authority. The many variations on the statement about the Temple point to a widespread diffusion of the theme
which therefore must have sprung from historical reminiscence rather
than from the creation of a midrashic style commentator.

bearing false witness is being flagrantly violated (Exod 20:16; Deut 5:20).[52] Jesus' innocence should now be acknowledged, but the 'seeking' continues with the high priest's direct intervention. Given the ongoing hostility towards Jesus by the priestly group throughout the story so far one is most likely correct in assuming that his intervention is motivated by the desire to make Jesus incriminate himself, since all the testimony of others has so far failed to do so.

To the conflicting evidence Jesus made no reply and the high priest in the presence of the whole assembly asked him had he nothing to say. Dramatically, and intimidatingly, standing out in the middle, the high priest questions Jesus, saying, 'Have you no answer? What do these witness against you?' By law Jesus was not required to answer contradictory and transparently false witness. He was silent and did not answer.[53] The reader is reminded of the suffering servant of Deutero-Isaiah or the just one in the Psalms and the Book of Lamentations who offers no resistance, opens not his mouth and in whose mouth there are no rebukes, suffering blows and insults in silence. The Fourth Song of the Suffering Servant comes immediately to mind where the servant is silent like the lamb led to the slaughter, having been taken by force and by law, and with nobody to plead his cause (Isa 53:7). So too do the passages in the Psalms such as Ps 37 (38):13-15 which reads: 'But I am like the deaf, I do not hear, like the mute who cannot speak; I am like the one who, hearing nothing, gives no sharp answer in return. For I put my trust in you, YHWH, and leave you to answer for me, Lord my God.' Lamentations 3:28-30 speaks of the good man sitting in silence and offering his neck to the striker and enduring insults.[54] R. E. Brown says that, for Mark, Jesus is now resigned to his fate and knows that nothing he says will change the outcome of the proceedings. His silence is therefore a sign of his contempt for the hostile proceedings.[55] It is also in keeping with Jesus' regal bear-

---

52. Significantly the Decalogue prohibition on false witness was quoted earlier in Jesus' discussion with the rich young man (Mk 10:19).

53. The classical middle voice is rare in NT Greek. It was common 'as a technical legal term for response'. cf R. E. Brown, *Death of the Messiah*, Vol 1, 464.

54. The silence of Jesus is quoted in 1 Peter 2:21, 23 as an example to be followed by 'fellow sufferers', the persecuted Christians of Asia Minor to whom the letter was written.

55. R. E. Brown, *Death of the Messiah*, Vol 1, 464.

ing throughout the passion narrative. He had already, in Mark's account, refused to respond to Judas or to the one wielding the sword in his defence.

The central point of the passage now follows. The high priest puts a leading question to Jesus. 'Are you the Christ, the Son of the Blessed?' The high priest's term ' Son of the Blessed' is a circumlocution for 'Son of God' which avoids pronouncing the Holy Name, but the meaning is the same. The reader knows the truth of Jesus' identity from the opening verse of the gospel, from the voice at the baptism and transfiguration and from the witness of the demons. He is the Christ, the Son of God. Jesus is now forced into the situation of admitting that this is who he really is. Up until now he had been very careful to avoid messianic acclaim and enthusiasm. He ordered Peter and the disciples 'not to tell anybody' on the occasion of Peter's proclamation of faith in his being the Messiah (Mk 8:28-30). He ordered demons and humans to be silent after deeds that might be construed as messianic (Mk 1:44; 3:12; 5:43; 7:36; 8:26; 9:9). He had carefully prepared his approach to Jerusalem as a countersign to popular messianic expectations (Mk 11:1-11). He openly challenged the teaching of the scribes (and by implication the popular understanding) that the Messiah was 'merely' a Son of David and set the role in a whole new dimension of 'Lord'. On former occasions when his identity, authority and destiny were in question he referred to himself in terms of the Son of Man and so the reader already knows that the Son of Man not only has power/ authority on earth to forgive sins (Mk 2:10), and to declare himself master of the Sabbath (Mk 2:28), but that he is destined to suffer grievously and be put to death (Mk 8:31; 9:31; 10:33f), and that he will rise from the dead (Mk 8:31; 9:9, 31; 10:33f). Furthermore he has come not to be served but to serve and to give his life as a ransom for many (Mk 10:45) and at the end of the world those who are ashamed of him in this sinful and adulterous generation will find themselves embarrassed when the Son of Man will come in the clouds with great power and glory (Mk 8:38) as he sends his angels to gather the elect from the four winds, from the ends of the world to the ends of heaven (Mk 13:26f).

Now under the spotlight of the high priest's leading question, Jesus himself says what the reader has already been told in the gospel concerning his being Son of God and his future coming in glory as Son of Man. He responds with a statement of self revelation and identity 'I am'. The simple affirmation 'I am', *egô eimi*, is primarily a statement of self identification in this context but the reader cannot avoid the overtones of 'I am' as a phrase occurring in theophanies, a self designation of the divine, and a phrase used already by Jesus when he calmed the fear of the disciples as he came to them over the water (Mk 6:50). Now Jesus again returns to the theme of the Son of Man and proclaims that they will they will see the Son of Man, sitting at the right hand of the Power and that he will come with the clouds of heaven. In the persecution of the holy people by Antiochus IV, Epiphanes, of Syria, Daniel was promised that final authority would be given to 'one like a Son of Man' (Dan 7:13). Now that Jesus' passion has begun, the process is set in motion whereby he will be established as the glorified Son of Man, at the right hand of the Power, that is, enjoying all authority and from there he will return 'with the clouds of heaven'.

In response to Jesus' reply to his question the high priest circumvents due legal process in his action and in his words. By tearing his garments he declares Jesus' statement a blasphemy, and then says 'what further need have we of witnesses? You have heard the blasphemy!' On previous occasions they sought to trap him in his speech. They now seem to have succeeded. The understanding that nobody can incriminate himself, later incorporated in the Talmud,[56] may already have operated as a principle. If so it points further to the fact that this was not an official meeting of the Sanhedrin, but an assembly of powerful members of the Sanhedrin opposed to Jesus.

Tearing one's garments was a gesture indicating indescribable grief. There is a long history of the gesture in the Old Testament as a reaction on hearing the news of the death of a leader or a loved one. Jacob tore his clothes on hearing of the death of Joseph (Gen 37:34). Joshua tore his clothes and prostrated himself before the altar as he pleaded with God to spare the people from the Amorites (Jos 7:6). David did likewise on hearing of the deaths of Saul and Jonathan (2 Sam 1:11f). Elisha tore his clothes as he lamented the departure of Elijah (2 Kings 2:12). The practice was known in the broader Greco-Roman world. R. E.

56. *b. Sanhedrin*, 9b. It is however, difficult to know for certain how closely the actual procedures at the time of Jesus correspond to those later contained in the Talmud.

Brown quotes the examples of Licinius Regulus tearing his clothes in the Roman Senate when he was omitted from the list of selected members and of the emperor Augustus who tore his clothes on hearing of the defeat of Varus in Germany.[57]

The practice of tearing one's garments was long established as a response to blasphemy. The messengers of King Hezekiah, on hearing the blasphemous remarks of the commander of the Assyrian armies, tore their clothes. The Assyrian cup-bearer-in-chief stood on the city wall and taunted them in the hearing of the people of Jerusalem in their own Judean language that their God could not save them, their king or their city any more than the gods of the other subject peoples saved theirs. When the messengers returned to Hezekiah with their clothes torn the king responded by tearing his own (2 Kings 18:30, 37; 19:1). The law, later enshrined in the Mishnah, stating that the judges in a blasphemy trial should tear their clothes on hearing the blasphemy, may have been in force at the time of Jesus. If not, at least the general understanding of the gesture, which eventually was enshrined into law, was well established.

What garments did he tear? Was he wearing the formal ceremonial, liturgical robes of the high priest which were not supposed to be worn outside the Temple area, and were guarded by the Romans in the Antonia fortress and only released by them for solemn festivals? Did he usually wear them at Sanhedrin meetings? One can only speculate and, as already noted, one has to ask whether it was a formal meeting, and whether the Romans would have released the vestments for a hastily convened night meeting (though they may have already been released for the celebration of the feast). Whatever clothes he tore, the gesture was clear.

Then the high priest put the question to the assembly: 'What is your opinion?' 'They all condemned him as deserving death.' No examination of the meaning of blasphemy or how Jesus may have been guilty of it follows. There is no account of individual opinions given by the members or votes taken.

After a lengthy discourse on the various uses of blasphemy/blaspheming/blasphemer, R. E. Brown concludes that in Mark's gospel, from the beginning of his ministry when Jesus is accused of blasphemy because of his words pronouncing the forgiveness of sins (Mk 2:7), through to his trial, when he answered 'I am' to

---

57. R. E. Brown, *Death of the Messiah*, Vol 1, 517.

his being questioned about his being Christ/Messiah and Son of the Blessed, and his adding of the remark about the Son of Man sitting at the right hand of the power and coming on the clouds, the suspicion is that he is 'arrogantly claiming what belongs to God alone'.[58]

His condemnation is followed by physical abuse and mockery of his prophetic role. In fact one could apply the term 'blasphemy' to the abuse inflicted on him! Luke actually describes his treatment at the hands of the guards as blasphemy against him (Lk 22:65). The abuse which involved spitting at him and the mockery directed at his prophetic role, blindfolding him to test if he could identify his tormentors, are marks of utmost contempt. The temple guards (*hypêretai*) inflicted blows on him. The great irony of the scene is that in doing so they are in fact fulfilling his prophecy/prediction of his passion (Mk 10:33), and doing so in a context where another prophecy has been so recently fulfilled as his disciples fled and left him alone. Still another prophecy is being fulfilled, simultaneously with their mockery, in the triple denial of Peter, who has already taken his place, not with Jesus, as a disciple should, but *meta tôn hypêretôn*, 'with the guards', the companions of those inflicting blows on Jesus (Mk 14:54). One is reminded of the fate of the righteous one in the Book of Wisdom who is 'tested with insult and torture' and 'condemned to a shameful death' because he claims to have knowledge of God and to have God as his father (Wis Sol 2:12-20).

a. Peter denies knowing Jesus and being his disciple Mk 14:66-72
All four gospels agree that the first person to challenge Peter was a 'servant girl'.[59] This servant of the high priest, seeing Peter warming himself, looked at him and said: 'You, too, were with the Nazarene, Jesus.' This could be paraphrased: 'You too were a disciple of the Nazarene, Jesus.' It is most unlikely that she simply meant 'you were with him in the garden' as a young servant girl would never have been in that armed band at night on such an errand. He denied it saying, 'I do not know or understand what you are saying.' The verb, 'denied', *êrnêsato*, here is in the aorist tense, so a single denial is meant. Though some scholars comment on the inelegance or inaccuracy of the use of

59. See the article by N. J. McEleney, 'Peter's Denials – How Many? To Whom?', *CBQ* 52(1990) 467-72.

'*oute ... oute*' ('neither know nor understand') as negativing par-
ticles on two verbs which are in fact virtually synonymous, in
fact the immediacy of anxious repetitive speech comes through,
as Peter at first pretends not to know what she is saying or of
what she is accusing him. Psychologically and emotionally it
rings very true to life and the account follows through logically
as the pressure mounts on him, to straight denial and finally to
rejecting and cursing Jesus. After this first denial in which he refused to acknowledge that he was 'with Jesus' he went out into
the outer courtyard.[60] He thus removes himself to a distance
from the threat of further recognition, but does not leave the
property completely, still 'holding on' to something of his discipleship and his boast never to abandon Jesus. The servant girl
seeing him again started saying to the bystanders, 'This man is
(one) of them.' Again he denied it. The verb 'denied' this time is
in the imperfect tense, *êrneito*, and signifies repetition of the denial. He is now not only denying being 'with Jesus', that is, being
a disciple, but also denying his fellow disciples, 'that he is one of
them.' The third recognition comes a little later from the bystanders who say, 'Truly (*alêthôs*) you are (one) of them. You are
also a Galilean.' Matthew points out that he was identified as a
Galilean because of his speech (Mt 26:73). There is a great irony
in the fact that the bystanders recognise Peter as being 'truly' a
disciple in spite of his denials. The only other use of 'truly'
(*alêthôs*) will be in an even more ironic situation when the
centurion, 'seeing how he died', proclaims that Jesus is 'truly
(*alêthôs*) the Son of God.'

The recognition and challenge to Peter are more serious now.
It is no longer a relatively unimportant young maidservant who
recognises him, but a group, possibly made up of various elements. Also they are convinced of the accuracy of their recognition: 'Truly, *alêthôs*, you are one of them.' They can see, or rather,
hear that he is a Galilean. This piles the pressure on Peter who
now makes a much stronger denial: 'He began to curse and to
swear (an oath): "I do not know the man of whom you speak".'
Was he cursing Jesus or, the more likely possibility, calling
down a curse on himself if he was lying?

60. Some mss (Old Latin, Vulgate and Syriac Peshitta) have 'and a cock
crew' at this point. As the better mss such as Sinaiticus and Vaticanus
do not have it, it is likely that it was introduced at this point to harmonise with the other gospels, or to provide a first crowing, since only
the second is mentioned.

As so often throughout the gospel, the words and deeds of Jesus explode on the scene with the formula 'and immediately', so here, too, the prophecy of Jesus is immediately fulfilled as the cock crows. 'And immediately the cock crew for the second time, and Peter remembered the word Jesus had spoken to him: "Before the cock crows for the second time, you will have disowned me three times".'

As Peter remembers he is overcome with grief. Much ink has been spilled on Mark's description of his griefstricken reaction, expressed in the two words *epibalôn eklaien*. The verb *eklaien*, in the imperfect, describes a repeated or sustained 'lamentation' as one would mourn for the dead. But how should *epibalôn* be translated? It has been variously translated as 'having thrown himself down, having broken down, having thrown himself outside (rushed out), having thrown himself into (burst into tears), having cast his mind upon (Jesus' prediction) or his eyes upon (Jesus), having thrown some covering over his head, or having beaten himself, (struck his breast),' he lamented. I wonder if it was not a combination of confused gestures, a rushing out, a striking of the breast, clapping the hands to the head and raising them in the air, a combination regularly seen in frenzied grief. Matthew avoids the difficulty by simply saying, *kai exelthôn exô eklausen pikrôs*, 'and going out, he wept bitterly'.

The crowing of the cock reminds Peter of Jesus' prophetic statement: 'This very night, before the cock crows twice you will have denied me three times'(Mk 14:30) and provokes his repentance. The cock crew for the second time. The first crowing of the cock is at first light, the second at sunrise. Peter had denied him three times 'that very night', before the sun rose, just as Jesus had predicted.

v. The Roman Trial and the Call for Crucifixion

a. The Jewish authorities hand over Jesus to Pilate Mk15:1-5
The fifth 'unit' sets the choice of Barabbas the bandit and the rejection of Jesus, followed by the cry of the mob to crucify the King of the Jews, in the midst of Pilate's trial of Jesus, a trial which (as in the case of John's account) focused very much on his kingship.

Sunrise and a change of location from the house of the High Priest to the court of Pilate signal another major development in the story of Jesus' passion.[61] The Roman trial is composed of three short episodes, each highlighting the theme of Jesus' kingship or his royal, messianic status, depending on one's point of view, whether it reflects the secular-political view of the Romans or the religious-political view of the Jews. First Jesus is interrogated by Pilate about whether or not he is the King of the Jews (Mk 15:2-5). Then the hostile mob reject 'the King of the Jews' in favour of a revolutionary, Barabbas (Mk 15:6-15). When Pilate hands him over for crucifixion the soldiers mock the King of the Jews (Mk 15:16-20).

A brief statement mentions a meeting of the Sanhedrin from which Jesus is taken to Pilate. Was it because the law required a second hearing, on the following day, before passing judgement in capital cases?[62] Was this a second meeting in the morning or a resumptive reference back to the meeting during the night? It seems from Mk 14:64 that their decision had been taken the night before, 'they judged him'.[63] The Jewish leaders bound and led him away and now they 'hand him over' to Pilate. The sequence of events follows the third prediction of the passion: 'The Son of Man will be *handed over* to the chief priests and the scribes, and they will condemn him to death, and *hand him over* to the Gentiles …'(10:32). Right from the arrest of the Baptist, '*hand over*' has been the recurring phrase throughout the gospel predicting Jesus' passion.

Mark, however, does not state why they did not execute him themselves (by stoning?) but took him to Pilate.[64] Mark does not describe any real surprise on Pilate's part at being presented

---

61. For recent studies on Pontius Pilate see H. K. Bond, *Pontius Pilate in History and Interpretation*, Cambridge and New York: Cambridge University Press, 1998; and B. C. McGing, 'Pontius Pilate and the Sources,' *CBQ* 53 (1991) 416-38.

62. Technically, in the Jewish way of reckoning the day from sunset to sunset, it would have been the same day.

63. Whereas Mark states they 'judged' him at the night session, Matthew has him 'judged' at the morning session. John does not say he was judged during the night trial and he refers to no morning trial, and Luke has only a morning trial.

64. John, however, gives a reason, 'it is not permitted to us to put anyone to death'. Does this 'not permitted' refer to Roman or Mosaic Law? Is it a pointer to their inability to secure a legitimate death sentence on Jesus in Jewish law or to the fact that the Romans had removed the power of capital punishment from them some time before the Jewish War?

with Jesus for trial. Does this reflect the fact that the Romans were involved in the arrest as is implied by John in the reference to the 'cohort' of soldiers (Jn 18:12)? Mark does not show an agonising or dithering Pilate, just a business-like official who asks, in response to the call of the mob for his crucifixion, 'Why, what evil has he done?' and then without scruple in spite of his own implicit judgement of innocence, hands him over in spite of there being no case against him. Mark points out that he did so in order to placate the hostile crowd who, under pressure from the Jewish authorities, had rejected Jesus in favour of Barabbas. In this way Mark continues to emphasise the role of the Jewish authorities. The other gospels, also for apologetic and theological reasons, put even more emphasis on Pilate's predicament in order to show that he was placed in a no-win situation by pressure from the Jewish authorities and the crowd, and under threat of a report being sent to the emperor (Jn 19:12). From a theological point of view the rejection of Jesus and his claims by the legitimate Jewish authorities and their scholars/legal experts was of great religious significance, just as it was of great political significance for Jesus and his followers that Pilate considered him innocent of any political charges.

In the Roman trial in Mark there is no explicit reference to the religious charges, the statements about the Temple or the blasphemous claims about being the Christ, the Son of the Blessed One or the Son of Man who will return in glory. Pilate immediately addresses the matter as it would have concerned his authority as Roman governor.[65] 'Are you the King of the Jews?' he asked, though the term has nowhere been used in the gospel so far. 'King of the Jews' has a completely secular ring, whereas 'King of Israel', used later in mockery at the crucifixion (Mk

65. Here again, Mark reflects a tradition found in John. After the raising of Lazarus, when the Sanhedrin met, they were confronted with the question: 'What will we do, because this man does many signs. If we let him continue thus, everyone will believe in him?' (Jn 11:47f). It was then Caiaphas had moved from the 'religious' concern to a 'political' one, presenting the danger that the Romans would come and destroy the holy place and the nation (Jn 11:48). After the triumphal entry into the city the Pharisees lamented to each other, 'Look, there is nothing you can do about it. The world has gone after him,' (Jn 12:19). The Jews were primarlily concerned with the religious implications of Jesus' activity, but they realised that these matters were of interest to the Romans solely because of their possible political implications and repercussions.

15:32), is a religious, messianic designation, on the lips of Jews. Jesus' response: *su legeis*, 'It is you who say it', parallels his response to the high priest. It functions on two levels. It does not deny his kingship, though it is not a resounding affirmation like his response at the Jewish trial, possibly because the term has political overtones which he would rather avoid. It also says equivalently, 'Don't put words in my mouth to my legal detriment' or as a modern lawyer might say by way of objection: 'Don't lead the witness or the accused.' It implies that the question should not have been asked. However, the question and Jesus' response are central to the life and death of Jesus since his official death notice (*titulus*), displayed on the cross, will describe him, and his crime, in terms of his being 'King of the Jews.'[66] Pilate's failure to condemn him there and then is followed by a string of accusations by the Jewish authorities, again a parallel with the 'trial' before the high priest. As the Jewish authorities 'kept accusing him of many things' the reader is left to wonder if they used the 'religious' arguments or switched to political ones, accusing him of aspiring to political or revolutionary power. Another parallel to the Jewish trial follows as Jesus, to Pilate's amazement, again makes no reply and remains silent before his accusers and bearers of false witnesses. In this he is like the lamb dumb before the shearers, the suffering servant (Isa 53:7) and the just one abandoned by friends and surrounded by lying accusers (Ps 108/109:2-3). Throughout the litany of mockery that will surround him from here on until he expires on the cross, Jesus will remain silent until his final prayer of abandonment and the loud cry he utters as he dies (Mk 15:34, 37).

b. Crucify the King of the Jews ! Mk 15:6-11
Pilate is now not only non-condemnatory, but convinced of Jesus' innocence and aware of the motive of those who handed him over. He knows they handed him over through *phthonos*, jealousy breeding malicious spitefulness, a vice described in the Book of Wisdom as the devil's motivation for bringing death

---

66. The death notice may well be the historical bedrock beneath the tradition of the trial. cf N. A. Dahl, *The Crucified Messiah and Other Essays*, Minneapolis: Augsburg,1974, 10-36. R. E. Brown, *The Death of the Messiah*, 1:729-32, suggests the Roman question about Jesus' claim to royal status may well be the oldest stratum in the passion narrative; similarly, J. Painter, *Mark's Gospel*, 199.

into the world (Wis 2:24).[67] However, the pressure from the Jewish leaders which fails to convince Pilate is successful in turning the crowd against Jesus and in favour of Barabbas.

Probably the historical reality lying behind the Barabbas incident is more complex than the impression given by the account in the passion narratives. In Mark it serves to make the point that disciple, Jewish authority, Roman authority and hostile crowd/mob, all played a part in the 'handing over' of Jesus to death, thereby fulfilling the scriptures and the divine plan. The crowd in the synoptic tradition(s) shows no hostility to Jesus throughout the ministry. In fact the enthusiasm of the crowd is highlighted in response to Jesus' teaching and miracles, and on the occasion of his triumphal approach to the city. As in many other cases, the Johannine tradition throws another light on events, particularly in Jerusalem. There the crowd during the ministry when Jesus visited the city, was divided into those who were favourable or willing to listen and learn and those who were hostile to the point of wanting to arrest him (Jn 7:40-44) or stone him for blasphemy for his teaching in the Temple (Jn 10:31). He escaped with his life from the Temple and the disciples thought his return to Judea to the dying Lazarus would cost him, and them, their lives (Jn 11:8). After the raising of Lazarus an element of the crowd went to report the matter to the authorities (Jn 11:46). It is quite possible also that a more militant element, possibly Galileans with zealot tendencies, were disappointed with his non-militant approach, and saw him as undermining their influence with the broader crowd, a block on their revolutionary path. This combination of a Jerusalem crowd who played up to the Jewish authorities and some disgruntled Galilean zealot types would not take much persuasion to reject Jesus and request the release of Barabbas, a rebel with blood on his hands from a previous (unspecified) outbreak of rebellion. Whatever their motive or mixture of motives, the Jewish authorities were able to manipulate them for their purposes and Pilate was able to use them for his purpose, avoiding the explosive situation of a foreign governor executing a prominent native and risking a violent reaction.

All four gospels speak of the custom of freeing a prisoner at

67. See A. C. Hagedorn and J. H. Neyrey, '"It Was Out of Envy that They Handed Jesus Over" (Mark 15:10): The Anatomy of Envy and the Gospel of Mark', *JSNT* 69 (1998), 15-56.

Passover. Therefore the custom cannot be easily dismissed,
though it has come under severe scrutiny from historians. They
point out that outside the New Testament no other record of
such a custom at Passover has been found. However, similar
customs are recorded. It may have been an application of the
Jewish practice of buying the freedom of a prisoner on the occasion of Passover as a practical way to commemorate their liberation from the slavery of Egypt.[68] It could equally have been an
application to this specific time and place of the broader custom
of offering an amnesty on Roman festivals and special occasions
such as the emperor's birthday. If so it was probably one of
those half official local customs that are often used to bring
about a compromise with a nod and a wink, and probably not
officially recorded for posterity. D. Senior, drawing attention to
the discussion by R. Pesch, sums up the position very well:

> It is unlikely, however that such an unusual event would
> have been fabricated by the tradition. Release of a prisoner
> fits into the liberation motif of the Jewish Passover and may
> have been a concession on the part of the Roman administra-
> tion of Judea.[69]

Scholars also point out the extraordinary nature of the co-inci-
dence of the arrival of the crowd at the Praetorium just at the appropriate moment when Pilate is in a difficult position. It does
not seem so unlikely if one considers the possibility of a crowd
carefully 'stirred up' or 'rented' either to put pressure on Pilate
or to provide opposition to the Jewish authorities in Pilate's interest, or a crowd simply gathered out of curiosity as news of the
arrest spread through the festal crowd.

The presence of the hostile crowd in the scene highlights,
perhaps in a simple and dramatic way, the complexities of the
situation which Pilate manipulated in his own interest and
which the evangelists were able to exploit for their apologetic
and theological interests.[70] In a very real way Pilate was governed by those he was appointed to govern.

68. E. Bammel, 'The Trial before Pilate', in *Jesus and the Politics of His Day*, ed. E. Bammel and C. F. D. Moule. 427; reflecting the practice in *m. Pesah*, 8.6.
69. D. Senior, *op. cit.*, 110; R. Pesch, *Das Markusevangelium* II, 462.
70. John develops it in line with his theology throughout the gospel where Jesus has been repeatedly described as Son, Son of God and Son of Man. In his discourses, he had contrasted his paternity with that of his critics. He is now accused of blasphemy for calling himself God's

a. Pilate hands over Jesus to crucifixion! Mk 15:12-15

Whatever the exact historical details, the evangelists use the offer of an amnesty to great effect. Mark shifts the call for Jesus' execution away from Pilate, thus clearing Jesus and his contemporary and subsequent followers of any charge of sedition or seditious intentions, and also brings into play what was probably an important element in the remembered story of Jesus, the hostility of an element of the crowd. With the rejection by the crowd Jesus is left without any support. His entire movement seems now to have been wiped out. Mark places the blame squarely on the shoulders of the Jewish authorities who worked on the crowd.

Pilate uses the term 'King of the Jews' in introducing Jesus to the crowd as a possible candidate for release, and when they reject him he again uses the term in asking what he will do with him. He cunningly manipulates the situation to make it appear Jesus was rejected by his own, and so avoids a possible riot. (The leaders of the people had found it necessary to have Jesus arrested by stealth for a similar reason.) The predictions of the passion all spoke of the Son of Man 'being put to death' without referring to the exact manner in which it would take place. Now the word 'crucify' is introduced, and on the lips of the mob, who shout repeatedly: 'Crucify him!' Pilate hands over the innocent one for crucifixion.

A historical note:

The reader wonders how accurately the evangelists generally, and Mark in particular, portray the historical character of Pilate, since literary, theological and apologetic considerations abound in the narratives. Pilate was appointed Prefect (not Procurator) of Judaea in 26 AD, a position he held until he was removed, following complaints, in 37 AD.[71] His appointment may have owed a good deal to the recommendation of his friend Seianus, the regional Roman official, a known anti-Semite. Pilate himself also pursued policies which offended Jewish sensibilities. He

---

Son. He is put up beside Barabbas, a name which means in Aramaic, 'Son of the Father'. The reader naturally asks, 'who is his father and what does he stand for?' John's account is highly symbolic and theological, but the irony is equally striking in Mark.

71. A contemporary inscription in Caesarea, the seat of his administration, calls him Prefect.

wanted to place Roman standards with the image of the emperor
Tiberius in Jerusalem in spite of serious objections and only
stopped when he realised that people were ready to die rather
than have the Holy City so profaned. He took Corban money
(funds dedicated to Temple use) to build an aqueduct and
clubbed to death those who protested at his action.[72] Luke 13:1
speaks of his murder of Galileans while they were sacrificing in
Jerusalem. Eventually he was removed after his mishandling of
religiously motivated trouble between Jews and Samaritans.[73]
His fall may have been facilitated by the fact that he no longer
had a powerful ally in Seianus, whose removal from office in 31
AD had left him vulnerable in a changed, or changing, relationship with the authorities, and in particular with the emperor
himself in Rome. This fact is borne out in John's gospel by his
fear of a negative report about him reaching the emperor's ears
and losing his standing as *amicus Caesaris*, friend of Caesar.[74]
Philo of Alexandria, in *De Legatio ad Gaium*, an appeal to Gaius
(Caligula) against anti-Semitism, speaks of Pilate as 'naturally
inflexible, a blend of self-will and relentlessness' who governed
by bribery, insults, robberies, executions without trial and great
cruelty.[75] Allowing for exaggeration and even some fabrication
in the process of making his impassioned appeal, Philo still
paints a very unflattering portrait of Pilate and his methods of
government. The evangelists, living in the Roman Empire at difficult times, (and especially Mark, if he was in fact writing in
Rome, particularly around the time of the great Neronic persecution) would not want to be too outspoken about Pilate, since he
had been such a high ranking official, and so he was 'white-
washed' somewhat, shown to be vacillating rather than unjust,
basically favourable to Jesus, and played upon by the Jewish authorities and the mob.[76] For apologetic reasons it was highly desirable that he be shown not to have believed the charges against
Jesus, especially the political charge of claiming to be a rival
king.

72. Josephus, *Antiquities* 18.3.1; *Jewish war* 2.9.2-3.
73. The trouble arose at a Samaritan religious procession in 35 AD.
74. Tacitus, *Annals*, 6, 8. Tacitus states that anyone who was a close
friend of Seianus was a friend of Caesar (Tiberius).
75. Philo, *Legatio ad Gaium*, 301f.
76. See the portrait of Pilate in R. E. Brown, *Death of the Messiah*, Vol 1,
698-705.

vi. Mockery and Crucifixion of the King

a. Mockery of the King of the Jews by Gentiles Mk 15:16-20

The sixth 'unit' sets the crucifixion of the King of the Jews in the midst of the story of his mockery. It comes between the mockery of the King of the Jews by the Roman soldiers and the mockery of the Christ, the King of Israel, by Jewish opponents and passers by. Mockery is the backdrop to his unjust condemnation and execution. It will be the dominant note struck throughout Jesus' final hours. In the biblical tradition mocking the good man's hope is the ultimate weapon in the destruction of the victim.

After Jesus was *handed over* for execution, the Romans carried out the customary scourging, a preliminary to crucifixion, starting the flow of blood and weakening the victim so that the crucifixion would not drag on too long.[77] The physical abuse was accompanied by what the Bible portrays as the greatest personal abuse, mockery, which aims to destroy the person's self worth and identity and, in the religious context, to ridicule the person's faith and hope in the God who saves. The soldiers struck him on the head with a reed and spat on him. They used the opportunity to crown him with thorns and mock his kingship. In the third prediction of the passion (Mk 10:38) Jesus had foretold how he would be mocked and spit upon. Just as he was mocked at the high priest's house in relation to the charges brought against him there and to his revelation of his identity, so too here the mockery revolves around the charges and revelation of his identity as 'King of the Jews'.

The passion narratives all pick up on this theme of mockery which is so dominant in the psalms of lamentation. In his response to the mockery the true nature of Jesus' kingship is highlighted in the calm dignity he displays in the face of the mock coronation, robing, royal salute and acts of obeisance. He thus turns the trappings of earthly power and kingship back on themselves in the countersigns of a crown of thorns, a purple

---

77. The placing of the scourging and mockery of kingship in the middle of the Roman trial in John seems to be for literary and theological reasons. The central position in a chiasm highlights the theme of kingship which dominates all four gospel accounts. The synoptic account which places the scourging (and accompanying mockery) at the end of the Roman trial is more in keeping with the historical facts where scourging was a preliminary to crucifixion, carried out after the passing of the death sentence.

robe stained with blood, and a mocking salutation. The unjust torture of the one already declared innocent places Jesus at the epicentre of human suffering and the mockery makes him king among the suffering servants of God.

The crowning with thorns as depicted in art emphasises the suffering from the thorns piercing the skin and causing blood to flow, with accompanying discomfort and pain. However, this is not the emphasis of the gospel and in fact it misses the real point of the exercise. Mockery is the motive. Statues and pictures of gods, heroes and 'divinised' emperors showed them with a halo of radiating beams of light around their heads. The plaited large thorn bough imitated this 'radiating' image, a blatant mockery of kingship and divinity. It was accompanied by the purple cloak and reed in the hand, symbols of imperial dignity and office, and by the mock obsequiousness of the soldiers' salutation of the emperor. This is as ironic as it is significant. They led him into the Praetorium, and dressed him in royal purple, put a crown of thorns on him and called the cohort together to render him mock homage. The first readers of Mark's gospel would have been very familiar with the role of the military in making and unmaking emperors. The ultimate power rested with them especially since their murder of Caligula and their forcing the Senate to accept Claudius. Their power and influence had been very much in evidence ever afterwards in the unmaking and making of a series of emperors from the suicide of Nero, because of a military threat, to the accession of Vespasian in the year of the four emperors, all created by the military in 68-69 AD. Their king-making power is displayed here in the mock coronation and salutation of Jesus.

The reader knows that the divine source of all power is revealed through Jesus and the apparently all-powerful mocker is ultimately powerless. The irony is striking. The one who is in a position to mock a victim appears to be all-powerful in dealing with him. The two powers are here placed side by side, the worldly power represented by the might of Rome, apparently omnipotent, the other, the power of the kingdom proclaimed by Jesus, apparently impotent and defeated. The unfolding story will reverse them and just as the Roman military mocked the 'King of the Jews', their commander and representative, the centurion will be the first person to acknowledge the divine status of the one they have mocked.

The striking of his head places Jesus in the company of all those represented by the Songs of the Suffering Servant of (Deutero) Isaiah[78] and the persecuted righteous one of the Wisdom tradition whose enemies 'test him with insult and torture' and 'test what will happen at the end of his life' (Wis Sol 2:17-20). In the synoptics Jesus is stripped of his 'kingly' attire after the mock ceremony and led to crucifixion. (In John's gospel he goes to his death robed and crowned as a king.)

Jesus has now been *handed over* by a disciple, *handed over* by the Jewish 'court', *handed over* by the Roman court and is crucified. All shared in the guilt of his judicial execution. R. E. Brown puts it succinctly:

> For neither Jew nor Roman was it enough that Jesus die; his claims had to be derided. In a sequence where Judas hands Jesus over to the chief priests (14:10-11), and the chief priests hand Jesus over to Pilate (15:1), and Pilate hands Jesus over to be crucified (15:15), it becomes clear that disciple, Jewish leader, and Roman leader all have a share of guilt.[79]

b. The King of the Jews is crucified Mk 15:21-27

The change of location from the Praetorium to the place of crucifixion, Golgotha, marks the beginning of the final dramatic episode in Jesus' life. Mark's is the shortest of the accounts of crucifixion and it is deceptively simple.[80] It avoids concentrating on the physical cruelty involved. It is laden with allusions to Psalms 21 (22) and 68 (69), the prayers of lamentation on the lips of the suffering just one.

At the beginning of the gospel as everything moved so rapidly *kai euthus*, 'and immediately', became the repeated expression highlighting the inrush of the kingdom. On the way to Jerusalem the tempo had slowed to a walking pace. In the last week of Jesus' life the action was marked by day by day indications as

78. Isa 42:1-9; 49:1-6; 50:4-9; 52:13-53:12.
79. R. E.B rown, *A Crucified Christ in Holy Week,* 29.
80. For a study of crucifixion in the ancient world, see J. A. Fitzmyer, 'Crucifixion in Ancient Palestine, Qumran Literature, and the New Testament,' *CBQ* 40 (1979) 493-513 and M. Hengel, *Crucifixion in the Ancient World and the Folly of the Message of the Cross,* Philadelphia: Fortress, 1977. See also T. E. Schmidt, 'Mark 15:16-32: The Crucifixion Narrative and the Roman Triumphal Procession,' *NTS* 41 (1995) 1-18; and E. Bammel, 'Crucifixion as a Punishment in Palestine,' in E. Bammel (ed), *The Trial of Jesus,* 162-165.

the slower approach prepared for the final drama. Now on the
final day the action slows down to hour by hour timing. Just as
Jesus three times predicted his passion and three times prayed
in the garden for the cup to be taken away, and just as Peter
three times denied him, so now the triple formula appears again.
Mark makes a triple time reference to the crucifixion, pointing to
the third, sixth and ninth hours. He also divides the mockers of
the crucified Jesus into three groups.[81]

The repeated use of the historic present tense keeps the reader
immediately involved in the unfolding action. The first period,
culminating with the crucifixion at the third hour, focuses on
what the Romans did to Jesus, all described in the historic present which creates a vivid effect and involves the reader more
closely as though it were happening as one reads. They (the
Roman soldiers) lead him out to crucifixion, they compel Simon,
they bring him to Golgotha, they crucify him, they divide his
garments. Summing up their actions and pinpointing the hour,
Mark uses the aorist tense for the third reference to 'crucify' in
the pericope: 'It was the third hour when they crucified him.'
The second period running from the third to the sixth hour is a
period of mockery where the triple formula is seen in the mockery of the crucified by the passers-by, by the chief priests and
scribes, and by those crucified with him. The third period, from
the sixth to the ninth hour is a period of darkness which culmi-
nates in the final moments of Jesus' life.[82] 'The solemn marking
of the hours is perhaps intended to remind us that what is taking
place is in accordance with God's plan and is the fulfilment of
his purpose.'[83]

As they led him out to crucify him at Golgotha, the place
called the skull, they enlisted a passer-by, Simon of Cyrene, to
carry his cross. Cyrene is in North Africa and so Simon may
have been a pilgrim from the Diaspora for the Passover. Only
Mark among the evangelists identifies him by way of reference
to his sons Alexander and Rufus, both having Greco-Roman
rather than Semitic names. Nothing else is known of him. His

---

81. The use of the present tense and the triple rhythm probably point to
an underlying oral 'recital' of the events which have been expanded by
Mark with the reference to the offering of the drink.
82. The timing is at variance with that in the Johannine tradition (Jn
19:14).
83. M. D. Hooker, *op. cit.*, 373.

sons were obviously known, if only by name, to the readers of the gospel. There is a reference by way of a greeting in Rom 16:13 from Paul to a Rufus and his mother which *may* point to one of the sons, particularly if Mark's gospel was written in Rome. Willingly or not, Simon found himself in a role that identifies the true disciple, 'taking up his cross.'[84] As the cross of Jesus becomes his to carry he has also become, in the broader Christian tradition, a model of Christian service to those in need.[85] The description of him as 'coming from the country' has sometimes been used in arguments about whether he was coming from work in the fields, and therefore a pointer to the fact that it was not the day of the Passover Feast. The reference, however, may simply be a statement of the direction he was following. It may even be pointing out that 'coming from the country' meant he was a pilgrim approaching the city en route to the Passover Festival and was unaware of the commotion in the city surrounding the impending executions, and happened upon them suddenly. It may be the case that able-bodied men avoided these occasions lest they find themselves dragooned into a situation like Simon was, and so the information that he was coming from the country was an explanation of how he got involved.

At the scene of the crucifixion they (the soldiers) offered Jesus wine mixed with myrrh which he refused to take. This is the only compassionate action in the cruel scenario. As Mark tells it, though he curiously changes tense from the present to the perfect, it appears to be the action of the Roman soldiers. It may be a reminiscence in the tradition of an action usually done by compassionate women from Jerusalem, perhaps like those lamenting Jesus' treatment in Luke's account (Lk 23:27f). The tradition of offering a drink to kill the pain is mentioned in the Talmud, reflecting Prov 31:6f.[86] However, as it stands in Mark's account it appears to be the action of the soldiers. Refusing the drink emphasises Jesus' willingness to accept in full consciousness the suffering laid down for him by the will of, and in the de-

84. Luke adds, 'behind Jesus' (Lk 23:26), a further emphasis on the disciple's 'taking up his cross and following Jesus'.
85. The Johannine tradition does not mention Simon or his involvement. It emphasises Jesus' control and independence throughout the passion narrative. M. D. Hooker, *op. cit.*, 372, points out that John may also have been reacting against Gnostic assertions that it was Simon and not Jesus who was crucified.
86. *b Sanh* 43a., reflecting Prov 31:6-7.

sign of, the Father. Psalm 68 (69) comes to mind as one reads of his being offered wine mixed with myrrh. The personal effects such as clothing were seen as the property of the executioners. Ps 21 (22):18 comes to mind when lots are cast for his clothes. Ps 21 (22) will be quoted when he calls out 'My God, my God, why have you forsaken me?' These biblical allusions put Jesus' suffering in the context of the individual just person making lamentation in the psalms.

The charge is inscribed on the notice (*titulus*), 'The King of the Jews'. This brings to a climax a series of royal 'acclamations'. Bartimaeus, the crowd accompanying him to the city, the question of Pilate to Jesus, Pilate's questions to the crowd, all culminate now in Jesus' being raised up in the view of all with the title 'King of the Jews' above his head, pointing to the crime for which he is being crucified. It is an ironic statement of truth. Mark notes how the two crucified with Jesus were put one on his right and the other on his left. The sons of Zebedee had sought the positions at his right and left (Mk 10:37), not realising the nature of his kingdom and kingship! Jesus is now reckoned with the unrighteous, with two robbers/bandits.[87] When they had come to arrest him in the garden, Jesus had asked: 'Have you come out as against a robber/brigand with swords and clubs to arrest me?'(Mk 14:48). Significantly he now ends his life in the midst of brigands.

The reference to the actual crucifixion is brief, stark and to the point. It was probably not necessary to elaborate on it in any ancient document since it was widely practised, and therefore well known and feared as a form of execution in the ancient world. The Romans used it for slaves, serious criminals and those who rebelled against Roman rule. The victim was fixed naked to the cross to die slowly, possibly over a number of days, struggling for breath in a constant action of raising the body to

---

87. *Lêstai*, means robbers or bandits (Mk 15:27//Mt 27:38) with connotations of activity of a revolutionary nature; *kakourgoi*, 'evildoers' is used in Lk 23:33; John just says 'two others' (Jn 19:18). *Lêstai* was used of the buyers and sellers in the Temple in calling it a 'den of robbers', and when Jesus was arrested he asked: 'Have you come out as against a *lêstês*?' Some mss of Mark added verse 28, 'He was taken for a criminal,' quoting the fulfilment of Isa 53:12 but it is missing from the oldest and most reliable mss. It may have been prompted by Lk 22:37, which is quoted in a different context, the arrest, but indicates a similar association with evildoers.

breathe against the pressure of the ropes and / or nails keeping the body fixed to the cross. In addition there was the excruciating pain from the preliminary flogging and the crucifixion itself, and the torment from sun, thirst, insects and the taunts of whoever wished to express a mocking opinion. That nails were used to affix Jesus to the cross is known from the reference to the marks of the nails in Jn 20:25 (and by implication from the references to his hands and feet in Lk 24:39f). Several ancient writers commented on the horror of crucifixion. Josephus called it 'the most pitiable of deaths'[88] and Cicero the Roman philosopher and orator spoke of it as 'a most cruel and disgusting penalty' and 'the extreme and ultimate penalty for a slave.'[89] It was a form of execution designed not only to inflict physical pain, but also to humiliate and shame the victim and thus obliterate his memory and eliminate any possible following he may have gathered in life. This was a very important consideration in a society which put such emphasis on honour and shame, and particularly on honourable death as the final crowning of the honourable life of a teacher of wisdom, philosophy or religion. It is no wonder that Jesus' death was to prove, in the words of Paul to the Corinthians, 'a stumbling block to the Jews and foolishness to the Gentiles' (1 Cor 1:23). The crucifixion was usually carried out in a public place as a deterrent to other malefactors. The Aramaic name, Golgotha, is interpreted as 'the place of the skull', probably indicating the shape of a low lying mound of earth near the roadway approaching the city gates, a place of maximum exposure and most effective deterrent.[90]

a. Mockery of Christ, King of Israel, by Jews Mk 15:29-32

The passers-by mock him. Ironically the verb 'blaspheme' is used. Jesus had been accused of blasphemy. Now as he himself is 'blasphemed' the themes of his Jewish and Roman trials will be used against him in mockery. Mockery is one of the very dominant aspects of the suffering encountered by the just one in the psalms of lamentation. The gestures of making faces and

---

88. Josephus, *War*, 7.203.
89. Cicero, *In Verrem*, 2.5.64,66.
90. The history of Christian art has imaginatively portrayed the skull of Adam underneath the place of the cross, and portrayed the blood of Jesus flowing onto the skull of Adam through a fissure in the rock, symbolising the universality of salvation for all humankind.

wagging their heads recall the words of Ps 21 (22):7: 'All who see me mock at me, they make mouths at me, they wag their heads', and of Lam 2:15: 'People passing by the city look at you in scorn. They shake their heads and laugh at the ruins of Jerusalem.' The scoffing exclamation 'Aha!' recalls Ps 34 (35):21: 'They open wide their mouths against me; they say "Aha! Aha! Our eyes have seen it".' Similar sentiments are found in Ps (39) 40:15 and 69 (70):4.

The triple mockery, by passers-by, the chief priests and scribes and those crucified with him, is skilfully used to embrace the full theological canvas of the gospel story. The passers-by mock him in precisely the terms of the charge brought against him at the Jewish trial about threatening to destroy the Temple and rebuild it in three days, and they challenge him to save himself and come down from the cross. Ironically it is precisely in dying on the cross that he is establishing the Temple not made by hands, built on the rejected cornerstone. His teaching to those who would follow him as disciples had emphasised the fact that to save one's life one must lose it, and in losing one's life one saves it (Mk 8:35).

The chief priests and the scribes mocked him among themselves (probably at a safe and dignified distance from what was happening!), saying: 'He saved others, he cannot save himself!' Ironically their mockery is a testimony to the 'saving work' of Jesus during his ministry and how he fulfilled his claim that he had come to serve others rather than to be served himself, and eventually to give his life 'as a ransom for many'. Their mockery continued with: 'Let the Christ, the King of Israel come down from the cross now so that we can see and believe.' The echoes of Ps 21 (22) are heard also in the mocking comment about God coming to save him: 'He hoped in the Lord, let him deliver him; let him rescue him if he be his friend'(Ps 21 (22):9). Ironically their blasphemy is a proclamation of the truth of Jesus' kingship, and significantly it is articulated in the more 'religious' term, 'King of Israel,' rather than the more secular ' King of the Jews'.

To round off this 'cascade of abuse'[91] Mark refers back to the opening of this scene with the reference to those crucified with him and points out that even those sharing his terrible suffering and death mock him. In telling him to come down from the cross, they ask him to vacate the place where he is King of the

---

91. D. Senior, *op. cit.*, 117.

Jews, the King of Israel. Jesus is now isolated to the point of not even sharing the company and mutual fellow feeling of those executed with him. He will die alone and in agony with the mockery of enemies resounding in his ears.

Much of Jesus' teaching was about 'seeing' and 'believing'. The disciples were told that 'those outside' would see the parables as riddles 'so that seeing they would not see'. Jesus criticised the disciples for not seeing the significance of the multiplication of the loaves (Mk 8:18). The healing of the blind man in two stages and the healing of the blind Bartimaeus pointed to the deeper significance of seeing, in both cases a gift from the healer. Peter's faith at Caesarea was a 'partial seeing'. Jesus' teaching on 'seeing' is about the true nature of faith. The Pharisees demanded a sign just after they failed to read the sign in the multiplication of the loaves (Mk 8:11f). Here his enemies are demanding that 'seeing and believing' be facilitated on their own terms and that he come down from the cross so that they would see and believe. Matthew and Luke in their accounts of the temptations in the desert, proleptically presenting the temptations that would surface in his ministry, spoke of the 'religious sign', throwing himself from the pinnacle of the Temple so that the angels, in keeping with the promise of Psalm 90 (91), would protect him and by implication people would see and believe. Here, in the very real circumstances of the crucifixion, Jesus encounters that very temptation on the mocking lips of his enemies.

vii. Portents and Cries. The Death of Jesus

a. Darkness over the earth and the cry of Jesus Mk 15:33-36
In the seventh 'unit' the death of Jesus is set between the great cosmic sign (the darkened sun) accompanied by the cry of Jesus and the great sign in Israel (the torn veil of the Temple) accompanied by the cry/confession of the centurion.[92]

Mark now moves on to describe the apocalyptic darkness over the whole land/the whole earth, *eph' holên tên gên*, from the sixth to the ninth hour, that is from noon to 3 pm, when the sun is normally at its brightest. 'The reader is led up to the death of

---

92. See D. Ulansey, 'The Heavenly Veil Torn: Mark's Cosmic Inclusio,' *JBL* 110 (1991) 123-125.

Jesus through a foreboding tunnel of gloom.'[93] It is reminiscent of the prophecy of Amos about the Day of the Lord when the land will be visited by the judgement of God: 'It will mean darkness, not light' and on the day of punishment God 'will make the sun go down at noon and darken the earth in broad daylight' (Amos 5:18; 8:9). Jesus had spoken to the disciples in his apocalyptic discourse about the frightening portents that would herald the end time: 'In those days the sun will be darkened, and the moon will not give its light' (Mk 13:24, quoting Isa 13:10). Now the death of Jesus is heralded by such a sign. This darkness is more than a literary 'pathetic fallacy' or alignment of natural phenomena with a terrible event. It is more than the ancient belief in signs and portents heralding the deaths of great people and the approach of significant tragic events.[94] It is the harbinger of an eschatological event in the history of salvation. The reader is being made aware that the moment of God's definitive intervention into the human story has arrived.[95] The darkness 'covers the whole earth'. 'Covering the whole earth' is not just a 'geographic' reference, but a theological statement of the universal nature of the eschatological event taking place and of its significance for all nations.[96]

At the ninth hour Jesus pierces the eschatological darkness as he breaks his silence and screams (*eboêsen*) with a loud cry (*phônê megalê*). His lament: 'My God, my God, why have you forsaken me?' (Mk 15:34) is the opening verse of Psalm 21 (22) which has been echoing through the passion narrative so far (Mk 14:17; 15:24, 29, 30f) and it is here quoted in Jesus' mother tongue, Aramaic (*Eloi, Eloi, lama sabachthani*) and then translated into Greek for Mark's readers. Quoting the psalm, Jesus addresses his Father, not with the familiar *abba*, but as God, and in so doing is completely identified with all those who address God in lamentation from a situation of total isolation and apparent abandonment. It is a cry of faith, a prayer when all supports are

---

93. D. Senior, *op. cit.*, 122; See also V. Taylor, *op. cit.*, 593; R. E. Brown, *Death of the Messiah*, Vol 2, 1035f traces the allusions to the theme of light and darkness right through the Old Testament.
94. It was common belief that the deaths of great people were marked by signs and wonders. See R. Pesch, *op. cit.*, 2:493f and J. Gnilka, *op. cit.*, 2:321.
95. F. J. Moloney, *op. cit.*, 325.
96. R. E. Brown, *Death of the Messiah*, 2:1036.

taken away, an address to God when all that is left is naked faith in the face of torment and abandonment, when even God appears to have turned away. Though the psalm goes on to develop the themes of faith and hope in God's deliverance and thanksgiving for that deliverance, the sense of the quotation in Mark's account is that of the opening description of utter desolation of the one who calls out to God in the words, 'I cry by day and you give no reply, I cry by night and find no peace' (Ps 21 (22):2). The reader is left to hope that the succeeding sentiments of faith and hope in the psalm will find fulfilment in a response from God. Meanwhile Jesus, losing his life, drinking the cup of suffering to the full, in obedience to the Father (Mk 14:36; cf 10:38), has denied himself everything, even the sense of closeness to the Father as his intimate *abba* address in prayer has been replaced with the anguished cry to a 'distant' God. Paul describes Jesus' humility in taking on the human condition as an emptying of self in his obedience 'unto death, even death on a cross' (Phil 2:8), which Paul elsewhere describes as ' becoming a curse' (Gal 3:13) or 'being made sin' (2 Cor 5:21), both emphasising the total oneness of Jesus with the human situation of being alienated from God and under judgement of the Law. Donald Senior comments:

> The emphasis falls on the experience of torment and abandonment … In Mark's account Jesus dies in agony, a wordless scream on his lips … Jesus' trust in God will not be broken, but Mark allows the fierce assault of death to be felt. The lament of Jesus issues from the darkness leading up to the fateful ninth hour (15:33).[97]

However, as F. J. Moloney points out so succinctly, 'Jesus' focus is entirely upon God, however desperate his cry.'[98] As he cries out in abandonment some of the bystanders think he is calling Elijah and run to dip a sponge in sour wine, place it on a reed and offer it to him to drink, mockingly saying that they would wait to see if Elijah would come to rescue him. It was widely believed that Elijah would come to the aid of the righteous in their need and there are many accounts in rabbinic literature of such appearances of Elijah.[99]

97. D. Senior, *op. cit.*, 124.
98. F. J. Moloney, *op.cit.*, 327.
99. The expectation had it roots in 1 Kings 17:1-24 and was developed in rabbinic literature. F. J. Moloney, *op. cit.*, 327, n 270, lists several examples.

All four gospels speak of the offer of the drink, but in different ways. Luke portrays it as a deliberately mocking gesture, offering him cheap wine and saying: 'Save yourself if you are the king of the Jews' (Lk 23:36), a provocation which calls to mind Ps 68:22 (69:21) with its mocking of the just one with poison for food and vinegar for drink. In Jn 19:29 the drink of cheap wine is offered in response to Jesus' cry, 'I thirst'. In Mark and Matthew the drink is offered when Jesus calls out the first line of Ps 21 (22). The offer of the drink and the reference to Elijah are linked together in Mark and Matthew, though it is more likely the wine (*oxos*) was the cheap wine drunk by the soldiers (and in Jn 19:29 the drink seems to be offered by a soldier) whereas the comment about Elijah was more likely from a Jewish onlooker. Both reactions seem to have been fused together in the tradition. Matthew quotes the verse in Hebrew, *Eli, Eli* ... 'which scholars believe is more likely to have been original since it is more easily mistaken for a call to Elijah, than the Aramaic *Elôi, Elôi* ...'[100]

b. The death of Jesus Mk 15:37
A second loud cry from Jesus heralds his death. No words are reported this time. 'Jesus gave a loud cry and breathed his last.' D. Senior again expresses very eloquently the full impact of the text of Mark:

> Mark's description of the instant of death is raw and stunning ... The other evangelists all soften this moment, giving Jesus in death a greater sense of control as he once again prays Psalm 22 and hands over his spirit (Mt 27:50), or dies with the resignation of Psalm 31 on his lips (Lk 23:46) or with a sense of completion and deliberateness (Jn 19:30). But for Mark Jesus dies without such control; he screams and expires. The torments of the Just One have crossed the final boundary ... No New Testament text more boldly expresses the reality of Jesus' humanity or the manner of his dying.[101]

Jesus' refusal of the drink, his cry to God in the psalm of abandonment and his final great cry point to his conscious and active

---

100. It was widely believed that Elijah, who was taken up into heaven (2 Kings 2:11f) would come to inaugurate the time of the Messiah. But, as the reader knows, Mark has already described the coming of Elijah to prepare the way in the person of John the Baptist, and he too had been put to death!
101. D. Senior, *op. cit.*, 125f.

faith in God when all, even God, seemed to have abandoned him. R. H. Gundry points out how Jesus, issuing his final great cry, died 'in a burst of strength', not with a whimper or following the usual lapse into unconsciousness.[102]

a. The Temple veil torn and the cry of the centurion Mk15:38-39

As Jesus breathed his last (*exepneusen*), the veil of the Temple was torn in two from top to bottom.[103] For Mark, as for all the evangelists, the death of Jesus was intimately linked to the destruction of the Temple and the emergence of a new Temple. Mark consistently shows the Temple in negative light in his gospel. In chapter 11 the action of Jesus in the Temple, contained within an intercalation of the cursing and withering of the fig tree, sounds a loud prophetic-style condemnation of the Temple and a clear prediction of its demise. His words re-echo the threat of Jeremiah against the Temple when he called it a robbers' den and predicted it would share the destructive fate of Shiloh. They re-echo also the hopeful prophecy of Trito-Isaiah that it would change radically and become a house of prayer for all nations (Mk 11:17; Jer 7:8-15; Isa 56:7). At the conclusion of the parable of the wicked tenants Jesus spoke about the stone rejected by the builders and its destiny to be the cornerstone, understood in terms of the cornerstone of a new Temple (Mk 12:10). In his apocalyptic-eschatological discourse on the Mount of Olives he predicted that 'not a stone would be left upon a stone'(Mk 13:2). During his Jewish trial (Mk 14:58) the false witnesses accused him of threatening to destroy the Temple 'made with hands' and in three days to raise another 'not made with hands'. As he hung on the cross he was taunted by the passers-by with his reported sayings about the Temple (Mk 15:29). Now as he dies the first reported result is the very significant tearing of the veil of the Temple from top to bottom. There were two veils both described as *to katapetasma* (Exod 26:33,37; LXX) and the text does not specify which is meant.[104] One veil covered the outer entrance and door and so could be seen by all, even by Gentiles forbidden to

---

102. *Ibid.*, 13.

103. Scholars debate whether the veil mentioned is the veil dividing the outer and inner part of the Temple or the veil enclosing the Holy of Holies. Probably Mark is not thinking of the distinction, but in a general way of the veiling of God's presence.

104. Josephus similarly describes them, *Ant* 8:3.3.

enter the sanctuary. The other veil (without an accompanying door) covered the entrance to the Holy of Holies, the most sacred part of the Temple, where the high priest entered the Divine Presence once a year on the Day of Atonement, *Yom Kippur*, to make reparation for the sins of the people. It is the opinion of most scholars that this is the veil intended by Mark. However, symbolically, the tearing of either or both provides a powerful symbol of the judgement of God at the very core of the most holy centre of Israel.[105] Mark sees the tearing of the veil primarily in judgemental terms, but another, positive, dimension must also be remembered. The tearing of the veil signifies the opening up to all and sundry of the previously hidden presence of God and of the approach to the mercy seat.[106] 'A new Temple is built on the destroyed body of Jesus as privileged access to the old Temple comes to an end.'[107] The new temple will be a house of prayer for all nations (Isa 56:7) and its inauguration will be immediately seen in the response of the executioner who stood facing Jesus as he died. 'The centurion, on seeing how he died, said: "Truly this man was the Son of God".'[108]

Exactly how the centurion understood his own profession of faith at that moment can only be a matter of speculation. In a Roman's religious vocabulary to proclaim someone son of a God or of a divine being was the greatest accolade possible as, for example, when Augustus was proclaimed *Filius Divi Julii*. The centurion was here presented with a whole new religious scenario focused on the person of Jesus and 'on seeing how he died' professed his belief in him and what he stood for.

---

105. Matthew more or less shares Mark's negative view of Jerusalem and the Temple, but Luke has a very positive view throughout, and in this instance sees the tearing of the veil as an 'opening', the revelation to all nations of the inner sanctum with its mercy seat.
106. This is the primary emphasis of Luke who has a positive attitude to the Temple throughout the gospel (Lk 23:45).
107. F. J. Moloney, *op. cit.*, 330.
108. The Greek expression *huios theou* does not have the definite article and so has at times been translated as 'a son of God'. However, the term *huios theou* is used in the verse that contains it at the beginning of the gospel, without the article (Mk 1:1). The Semitic construct case does not use the article and a very direct translation from a Hebrew or Aramaic idiom in the earliest tradition would probably not have the article either. Furthermore, if the centurion spoke Latin, there is no definite article and *Filius Dei* would be translated exactly as *huios theou*.

Jesus' own people had taunted him with the challenge to come down from the cross so that they would *see and believe*. In this great twist of irony at the end of the gospel, the centurion, a pagan, representative of the greatest power in the world, whose cohort had mocked Jesus as King of the Jews with royal apparel and imperial salute, is moved to faith in him precisely in his not coming down from the cross but rather in *seeing how he died*. He is the first human being to acknowledge the true identity of Jesus. Unlike Matthew, who portrays the centurion's statement of faith as a reaction to the portents that accompanied Jesus' death, Mark emphasises the fact that the centurion was facing Jesus and 'on seeing how he died' he made his confession of faith.

The centurion's confession reflects the opening words of the gospel, the voice of the Father at the baptism and transfiguration, and the 'preternatural' awareness of Jesus' identity on the part of the demons. Now, a Gentile, an 'outsider', acknowledges the crucified one as the Son of God. The question hinted at often, 'Who can this be?' and pointedly put to the disciples at Caesarea Philippi in the double question: 'Who do people say that I am?' and 'Who do you say that I am?' has been answered. On that occasion at Caesarea Philippi Peter rejected any such ignominious death on the part of the Messiah when Jesus first predicted his passion and death. Now Jesus' true identity is acknowledged, precisely in response to such a death, and by 'an outsider'. The centurion now becomes, in the words of D. Senior,

> ... a sign of the community's future mission. But he also takes his place alongside other 'outsiders' who had been magnetised by Jesus' presence while the chosen disciples, the family of Jesus, and the leaders of Israel had remained dull and uncomprehending.[109]

His words form the climax of Mark's gospel, for they are the words used in the confession of Christian faith, and they are found in the mouth of a Gentile at the moment of Jesus' death.[110] The representative of the military might of Rome whose soldiers earlier mocked Jesus with the trappings of earthly kingship and imperial power now witnesses to the reversal of status and roles as earthly power gives way to the divine power shining through apparent human weakness, folly and failure.[111]

This is the high-point of the confessions of faith in Mark, an-

109. D. Senior, *op. cit.*, 131.
110. M. D. Hooker, *op. cit.*, 379.
111. See T. H. Kim, 'The Anarthous *hyios theou* in Mark 15:39 and the

swering the question articulated or implied throughout the gospel: 'Who can this be?' or ' Who do you say that I am?' The reader is challenged to share the faith of the centurion in this darkest moment in the story.

viii. The Watching Women. Deposition and Burial of Jesus

a. The women watching the crucifixion Mk 15:40-41
The eighth 'unit' sets the deposition and burial of Jesus in the midst of the description of the women from Galilee watching his crucifixion and burial.[112]

Mark mentions women from Galilee standing at a distance. Three terms, all associated with discipleship, are used to describe their relationship with Jesus: 'they *followed him*', 'they *ministered to him*', 'they came up *with him* to Jerusalem.' The names of some of the women are given. The names of Mary of Magdala and Salome are quite straightforward, but how is one to understand 'Mary of James the Younger and of Joses mother?' The Greek expression can be variously interpreted as 'Mary, wife of James the Younger and mother of Joses', or ' Mary, daughter of James the Younger and mother of Joses' or 'Mary, mother of James the Younger and of Joses.' It could also be regarded as a reference to two people, 'Mary the wife of James the Younger together with the mother of Joses' (which is the case in the variant reading), though it is less likely because of omitting the personal name of the second person (Mk 15:40f; cf Mt 27:55; Lk 23:49).[113] There were many other unnamed women in the group.

Roman Imperial Cult,' *Bib* 79 (1998) 221-41; J. Pobee, 'The Cry of the Centurion – a Cry of Defeat,' in E. Bammel (ed) *The Trial of Jesus*, 91-102; E. S. Johnson, 'Mark 15:39 and the So-Called Confession of the Roman Centurion,' *Bib* 81 (2000) 406-13, and T. W. Shiner, 'The Ambiguous Pronouncement of the Centurion and the Shrouding of Meaning in Mark,' *JSNT* 78 (2000) 3-22.
112. See K. E. Corley, 'Women and the Crucifixion and Burial of Jesus. "He Was Buried: On the Third Day He was Raised",' *Forum* 1 (1998) 181-225 and P. L. Danove, 'The Characterisation and Narrative Function of the Women at the Tomb (Mark 15:40-41;16:1-8),' *Bib* 77 (1996) 375-97.
113. Matthew mentions the mother of James and Joseph. Are these the James and Joses of Mark? Matthew does not mention Salome by name but refers to the mother of the sons of Zebedee. Is the Salome, mentioned by Mark, their mother? Did the evangelists mention by name only the people present at the crucifixion who would have been known to their readers (Mt 27:56)?

Commentators point to the fact that Mark seems to emphasise that they were watching from a distance (Mk 15:40). The same phrase is used of Peter 'following from a distance' to the courtyard of the high priest. In the case of Peter it was a cautious following, in a state of fear that was to result in the denial of his master and of his own discipleship and to end up in his running away in tears. Some commentators point to the fact that the women watched from a distance was a sign of their being fearful and cautious like Peter, and they see this fear as coming to a climax with their later running away from the tomb in fear. This is not necessarily the case. It is equally, if not more likely that they watch from a distance because they were kept at a distance from the scene of an execution. Their presence throughout the crucifixion, their observation of the deposition and disposal of the body and their coming to the tomb on the first day of the week are pointers to their intuitive tenacity, loyalty and generosity, and to the practical mindedness of women. The practical concern of these women followers about the humanitarian and ritual aspects of proper burial and mourning rites is in keeping with the other portrayals of women in the gospel as exemplified by the tenacity of the Syro-Phoenician woman, the determination of the woman with the issue of blood, the loyalty and intuition of the woman in Bethany and the generosity of the widow at the Temple. Their presence stands out in contrast to the murderous intent and injustice of the male establishment figures who brought about the condemnation, the cold cruel efficiency of the military in carrying out the crucifixion, the cowardly flight of the disciples and the falling to pieces of their leader Peter. The presence of the women, introduced with an adversative *de*, is a counterbalance to all that has taken place: 'But (*de*) there were also the women watching from a distance' (*êsan de kai gynaikes apo makrothen theôrousai*).

b. The deposition and burial Mk 15:41-46
It was already afternoon on the day of Preparation, the day before the Sabbath, when Jesus died and so in keeping with the custom of burying the dead on the day of death, (or at latest next day, an option ruled out in this case due to the Sabbath) it was necessary to obtain the body and bury it forthwith.[114] Though

---

114. The concern about burying the body before the Sabbath would not be so crucial if the day of crucifixion was in fact the actual Passover

the Romans were wont to leave the bodies of crucified criminals hanging on their crosses till they decayed, as a warning to other evildoers, they were known to respond to Jewish requests in line with the prescription of Deut 21:23 that the bodies of criminals should not be left overnight at the place of execution.[115]

When the Baptist was murdered, his disciples came and took the body away for proper burial. In the absence of his disciples, a stranger, Joseph of Arimathea,[116] comes to render this service to Jesus. Again a 'minor' character exhibits the qualities one would have expected in the disciples. He associates himself with the executed Jew. He is described by Mark as an influential member of the council (most likely the Sanhedrin) and a man 'seeking the kingdom of God.' Describing him in this way would probably point to his openness to Jesus and what he stood for, and his desire to do what was seen as one of the good works, to provide fitting burial for someone who had nobody to provide such a service. Matthew, however, describes him as a disciple (Mt 27:57), John describes him as a disciple, though a secret one, through fear of the Jews (Jn 19:38), and Luke points out how he had nothing to do with the plan and action of the Sanhedrin against Jesus (Lk 23:50f).

Joseph bought a linen cloth and having wrapped the body in it, laid it in a tomb cut from the rock. The description is one of a hurried burial. The tomb cut into the rock would be the tomb of a well-to-do person. Though Mark does not actually say it belonged to Joseph, it is a reasonable assumption. Matthew states that it was Joseph's own new tomb (Mt 27:59f). The piety and courage of a man of standing, the wrapping of the body in linen and the use of a tomb hewn from rock rendered honour to the corpse. A tomb hewn from the rock was a sign of an important

---

Feast and already a festal day with Sabbath style observance, nor would the buying of the linen sheet have been so easy. Though the scene of preparing the Last Supper (Mk 14:12-116) seems to suggest it was a Passover meal at the beginning of the Feast, this concern about the burial and its details about buying the sheet seem to coincide with the Johannine dating of the crucifixion on the day before the Passover, implying that the Passover Feast and Sabbath coincided next day. A very great deal of ink has been used in the discussion of this question.

15. Josephus, *War*, IV, 5.2.

16. Usually identified as Ramathaim, a village about twenty miles from Jerusalem.

and wealthy person.[117] The stone rolled to the mouth of the tomb protected the corpse from predatory beasts and preying birds, again protecting the corpse from the shame to which executed criminals were usually exposed.[118]

Seeking the body of a crucified rebel could put one in danger, or at least cause uncomfortable questions to be raised about association with the deceased, especially if the person asking for the body was not a relative. Joseph therefore showed courage (*tolmêsas*) in making the request (Mk 15:43) for those condemned in Jewish courts were not allowed honourable burial[119] and those crucified by the Romans were usually left to decay at the place of execution. Joseph's request could have been refused and the refusal could have been accompanied by hostile questioning. Pilate was amazed to hear that Jesus had died so quickly, as death by crucifixion could drag on for days. The centurion was questioned and confirmed the death. The emphasis on Pilate's amazement and his questioning of the centurion (the executioner) who gives explicit witness to the death may reflect an apologetic against rumours in Markan circles that Jesus had not actually died before he was taken down from the cross. The likelihood that Pilate's question and the centurion's response were included, and emphasised, for this apologetic reason in Mark's gospel is highlighted by the fact that these two verses (Mk 15:44,45) do not appear in Matthew and Luke. Matthew has his own apologetic, not refuting a rumour that Jesus was taken down from the cross before he was dead, but refuting a rumour about the dead body being removed from the tomb probably caused him to include the account of the sealing of the tomb and the placing of a guard to prevent the disciples taking the body and proclaiming that he was risen (Mt 27:62-66). In addition, for Mark Jesus' quick death very probably reduces the element of shame.

117. The sterward Shebna is condemned as a self promoting official with ideas of grandeur for carving himself such a tomb in Isa 22:15-19.
118. F. J. Moloney, *The Gospel of Mark*, 334, n 304 looks at the traditions of the burial and differences of opinion among scholars as to whether historically Jesus had an honourable burial, even though a hurried one, or the burial of a common criminal. Mark's position is that he was buried with honour and his tomb was well known. Cf R. H. Gundry, *op. cit.*, 13 who sets the burial in the ongoing glory-suffering equation of the gospel.
119. R. E. Brown, *The Death of the Messiah*, 2:1209-10.

a. The women watching the burial Mk 15:47

After the account of the burial Mark states pointedly that two of
the women, Mary of Magdala and Mary, mother of Joses,
watched where he had been buried and took note of the place
where he was laid. Matthew says Mary of Magdala and the
other Mary were sitting opposite the sepulchre, and Luke says
the women who had come from Galilee took note of the tomb
and the position of the body (Mk 15:47).

In the next sentence Mark names Mary of Magdala, Mary
mother of James, and Salome, and tells how they went to the
tomb as the sun was rising on the first day of the week. Mark's
intention, like that of Matthew and Luke, is very clear. The
women who saw him crucified were the same women who saw
him buried and discovered the empty tomb. Their witness to the
death, burial and resurrection is Mark's primary reason for referring to their presence at the crucifixion. The very close similarity of all three synoptic accounts seems very likely to point to
an ancient, well rehearsed 'apologia' for the resurrection, emphasising the fact that the same people had witnessed Jesus'
death, seen him placed in a clearly identifiable tomb and later
found that the tomb was empty. The story of these women and
their presence on Calvary/Golgotha focuses on them as witnesses to the truth of the underlying facts surrounding the
death, burial and resurrection which found expression in the
early kerygma learned by Paul and repeated in his First Letter to
the Corinthians: 'I handed on to you what I had received myself,
that Christ died for our sins according to the scriptures; that he
was buried; and that he was raised to life on the third day in accordance with the scriptures' (1 Cor15:3f).

ix. The Empty Tomb and the Terrified Women Mk 16:1-8

a. The women come to the tomb (16:1-2)

The ninth 'unit' sets the good news of the Risen Christ in the
context of the women's going to the tomb on the first morning of
the week.

As the Sabbath ended Mary of Magdala, Mary (mother, wife
or daughter?) of James, and Salome bought spices in order to
come and anoint the body of Jesus, as it had been hastily buried
without washing or anointing. Very early on the first day of the
week, they came to the tomb as the sun was rising. The first day
of the week is, in fact, in the Jewish manner of counting, three

days after or the third day after the crucifixion, the day foretold by Jesus as the day of the resurrection in the various passion predictions throughout the gospel (Mk 8:31; 9:31; 10:34).[120] The double time reference, 'very early, as the sun was rising' is a typically Markan idiom, but here the two time references are separated by the reference to approaching the tomb. The second reference 'as the sun was rising' in turn takes on a symbolic meaning as well as its temporal indication. The darkness which descended over the whole earth at the crucifixion was the last reference to light and darkness in the gospel and now that darkness is being lifted with the rising sun.

Some commentators point to the unlikelihood of anointing a body so long dead, when decomposition may already have set in. Matthew may have that in mind when he says they were going there to 'see the tomb' (Mt 28:1) and John says Mary Magdalene (mentioning her alone) 'came to the tomb' (Jn 20:1), both cases pointing to a visit 'to mourn', or 'to pay one's respects' at the first opportunity after the Sabbath. However, Luke reflects Mark's account as he says they went there 'taking the spices they had prepared' (Lk 24:1). Two factors may be of relevance. Anointing the body with aromatic spices was intended to counter in some measure the odour of putrefaction. Even if the women did not intend to actually anoint the body so long dead already, spices could be placed beside the body or somewhere within or beside the tomb as a means of supplying the missing rituals and showing due respect. Secondly, there was a belief at the time that the spirit hovered round the body for three days[121] so that for three days in some way the body remained intact and the fourth day saw the onset of putrefaction. This was evident in the case of the story of Lazarus, where interference with the tomb was seen as out of the question because it was the fourth day and the odour of putrefaction would be present (Jn 11:17, 39). Maybe within the first three days the women approaching the tomb considered Jesus' body as still 'suitable' for anointing. These two considerations, placing the spices near the body or in the tomb or anointing the body within the first three days, are worth noting if one sees a historical reminiscence rather than a conjecture about their purpose in coming to the tomb bringing

---

120. 'Three days' also reflects the theme of rebuilding of the destroyed temple, an allusion to Jesus as the new temple (14:58; 15:29).
121. St B., II, 544.

spices. In Mark's account the hasty burial and the women's consideration of bringing spices to anoint the body so long after death re-echo and re-emphasise the significance of the anointing by the woman in Bethany, which Jesus interpreted as 'anointing beforehand for my burial' (Mk 14:3-9).

b. The young man's news and commission Mk 16:3-7

The enormity of what they are about to discover is prepared for in their discussion about rolling back the stone from the mouth of the tomb. In asking *who* would roll back the stone they were not prepared for the fact that *God* had rolled it back already. The divine passive 'it had been rolled back' is a statement that God had rolled it back. The women's action of 'looking up and seeing' (*anablepsasai theôrousin*) is like a ritual action in the context of divine activity and presence. The awkward position of the description, ' for it was very large' (a description which one would think should come at the end of the previous verse) emphasises not only the fact that the stone was physically very large but also the enormity of God's work in reversing the irreversible character of death, symbolically represented by the stone at the mouth of the tomb. In the parallel account Matthew states that 'an angel of the Lord', that is, a divine agent, rolled it away. It is Matthew's equivalent of the divine passive, avoiding the predication of specific physical action to God and having to use the Divine Name in the process.

As they entered the tomb they saw a young man (*neaniskos*, youth) sitting at the right hand side dressed in a white garment.[122] Matthew speaks of 'an angel of the Lord', and it seems Mark similarly thinks of the young man as an angel, a messenger of God. As in all biblical accounts of 'divine encounters' or theophanies, the recipients of the 'vision' are terrified (*exethambêthêsan*)[123] and they are in turn reassured by the divine visitor

---

122. The angelic formula/announcement differs in the accounts, highlighting the individual approaches of the synoptics, but also, by contrast, emphasising the uniformity of the underlying tradition of the fact of the women's witness to the empty tomb.

123. This verb is used only by Mark in the New Testament. The prefix *ek/ex* has the force of emphasising a degree of 'emotion' which 'takes one out of oneself'. Here it has the meaning 'frightened out of one's wits'. In Mk 9:15 when the crowd see Jesus coming towards them after his descent from the mountain, they are 'stricken with awe' (NRSV). In Mk 14:33 when Jesus takes Peter, James and John aside in the garden he

with the words: 'Do not be alarmed!' (*mê ekthambeisthe*). Theirs is
a natural reaction for people already in mourning and grief and
now finding themselves in such extraordinary and unexpected
circumstances.

In a statement that has the ring of a liturgical formula or summary proclamation, the young man says: 'You seek Jesus of
Nazareth who was crucified. He is not here. He has been raised.
Look there is the place where they laid him.' From a grammatical
point of view, *êgerthê* can be translated as 'He has been raised' or
'He is risen'.[124] In this context the emphasis is on the activity of
God in response to the final cry of Jesus: 'My God, my God why
have you forsaken me!' God has not forsaken his Son. He has
been raised, that is, God has raised him. The mockers were saying they would believe if they 'saw' him come down from the
cross, and some were waiting 'to see' if Elijah would come to
take him down! Now, the women who were faithful to the last
'have looked up and seen' the action of God in removing the
stone are now invited to behold, to see, 'the place where they
laid him'.

The young man now commissions the women to go and say
to the disciples and Peter: 'He goes before you into Galilee.
There you will see him as he told you.' On the way to
Gethsemane Jesus had foretold them that, as it was written, they
would all desert him: 'I will strike the shepherd and the sheep
will be scattered. But after I am raised up I will go ahead of you
to Galilee' (Mk 14:28). Just as he 'went ahead of them' on the
way to Jerusalem so now he would 'go ahead of them' into
Galilee. 'Go ahead' in this context means ' lead' rather than simply 'precede'. M. D. Hooker puts it very clearly:

> Mark … is certainly saying something far more significant
> than that Jesus will arrive in Galilee before the disciples. This
> is no mere rendezvous but a call to the disciples to follow
> Jesus once again. On the way to Jerusalem, Jesus had gone

becomes 'distressed and agitated', 'He is taken out of himself' with distress (*êrxato ekthambeisthai kai adêmonein*).

124. The three passion predictions (Mk 831; 9:31; 10:34) use the verb
anistêmi, as does the warning at the end of the transfiguration scene not
to reveal what had happened until after Jesus was risen from the dead
(Mk 9:9). The promise to go ahead of them into Galilee after the resurrection in 14:28 uses the verb *egeirein* which is also the verb used by the
young man in the tomb. It is also the verb used in the healings when
Jesus 'raises' people or tells them to 'rise up' from their sickness.

ahead … and the disciples had seen him and followed. Now they are called to follow him, even though they cannot see him. What looks like an inconsistency in Mark may be a deliberate attempt on his part to underline that this is what discipleship means, now that Jesus has been raised from the dead.

The young man proclaimed the resurrection of Jesus and commissioned the women as witnesses to the disciples and Peter. Peter is mentioned separately and specifically, probably because of his denials and the renouncing of his discipleship. Maybe he had separated himself from the others in the aftermath of the traumatic and personally embarrassing events. Symbolically he had left the group of disciples. The others were still 'disciples who had fled in fear'. Peter had denied his discipleship, his having been 'one of them' and his ever having known Jesus.

Scholars speculate on the significance of a meeting in Galilee.[125] It was the native place of the disciples, the place where they were first called and left everything to follow Jesus. It was the area of their first mission and could again be the starting point for a whole new mission, to Jew and Gentile, since it was Galilee of the Gentiles, where Jew and Gentile lived in close proximity.

It probably also reflects the tradition of a meeting with the risen Jesus and a new commissioning in Galilee, as later reflected and developed both in the 'commissioning' scene on the mountain in Mt 28:16-20 and in the 'fishing' and 'breakfast' meeting in Jn 21:1-23 with its special emphasis on the 'restoration' and new commissioning of Peter. Just as Luke-Acts points to Jesus' telling the disciples to stay in Jerusalem until the fulfilment of the promise, so too there may well have been a tradition that he also told them to return to Galilee, as is implied here in Mark and also in Mt 28:16 which states: 'Now the eleven disciples went to Galilee to the mountain to which Jesus had directed them.' Both traditions find expression in the Jerusalem and Galilee 'appearance' stories respectively.

a. The women flee from the tomb (and tell nobody) Mk 16:8
The women went out and fled from the tomb. Trembling and bewilderment took hold of them and they said nothing to anyone

---

125. Some understand the meeting in Galilee as an eschatological meeting. This is not a generally accepted view.

for they were afraid (*ephobounto gar*). The silence and fear of the women are puzzling in the light of the broader New Testament traditions. It would be easy to see their fear as a 'holy awe' which overcame them initially and then gave way in the face of the good news they were sent to announce to the disciples and Peter. If Mk 16:8 followed immediately after Mk 16:6 without the intervention of Mk 16:7, with its solemn commission to bring the news of the resurrection to the disciples and Peter, together with the promise of Jesus to go before them into Galilee, a promise already indicated in Mk 14:28 on the way to Gethsemane, it could easily be taken to mean 'holy awe'. However, the inclusion of 16:7 with its solemn commission changes the meaning and Mark points to the fact that they did not carry out the commission and emphasises that they did not do so because of fear. There is widespread agreement among scholars that Mk 16:8 marks the end of the original gospel of Mark. It ends therefore with the failure of even the most loyal followers, the women who remained with him to the grave and beyond. They join the disciples in flight and fear and fail to carry out their commission.

From every point of view it is an ending as strange as it is un-expected. Even at the level of the grammar, ending a sentence or paragraph, not to mention ending a whole book, with *gar* ('for'), is strange. The story itself seems to have ended in mid-course, without a solution. The final prediction and promise of Jesus about a re-grouping and meeting in Galilee is left unfulfilled, just as the final commission of Jesus through the women to Peter and his disciples is disobeyed.

All appears lost. The disciples have fled. Peter has denied his master, denied being a disciple and denied ever having known him. Jesus himself has suffered a terrible death. The women re-mained faithful all through the nightmare of those recent nights and days, but now even his dead body, the final focus of their at-tention, is taken from them. The first terrible impact is the empti-ness of the tomb.[126] John's gospel captures a similar sentiment in

126. It is extraordinary how so much writing on the empty tomb misses the point that the loss of the body of a loved one can be an even greater trauma in the long run than the death itself. The proper disposition of a body and the tangible reality of a grave or urn are of huge emotional and psychological importance during the bereavement process leading to a healing and closure. The impact of the emptiness of the tomb is too easily overlooked.

the weeping of Mary Magdalene and her lamentation: 'They
have taken the Lord out of the tomb and we do not know where
they have laid him' (Jn 20:2). This is the final straw and they follow the disciples in flight and fear.

As the reader reels with the shock of the abrupt ending and
the apparent final collapse of Jesus' mission, the words of G. W.
Geyer come to mind: 'We can legitimately suppose that the author of Mark intends us not to feel satisfied with our reading but
instead would seek us to feel agitated, unsettled and confused.'[127] This is no mythological story, no Isis and Osiris,
Cybele and Attis mystery religion with a happy ending. Human
vulnerability and weakness are experienced and exposed. They
are exposed precisely in terms of fear which has been presented
as the opposite of faith throughout the narrative of Mark's
gospel. The reader can almost hear Jesus saying to the women
(and to the reader) at this point: 'Why are you frightened?
Where is your faith?'

The challenge for the reader at this point is to see that Mark's
narrative is complete but the Christian story is not. Though the
narrative does not tell us about the meeting of Jesus with Peter
and the disciples in Galilee with all its significance for their 'renewed' discipleship and universal mission, the Christian story
points to the fact that it took place and because it did we have
the 'disturbing' narrative of Mark which we can now read as
'the beginning of the good news of Jesus Christ, the Son of God.'
The reader can read and re-read the gospel of Mark and see how
the superscription that identifies Jesus as Christ and Son of God
'transforms the crucifixion from the shameful death of a common criminal into the awe-inspiring death of a divine being who
is God's appointed agent.'[128] From first to last the initiative belonged to God. The agent was sent by God, the kingdom was
God's project, and the vindication of Jesus and of the good news
he proclaimed, in the face of total human failure, belonged exclusively to God. The very fact that there is a gospel of Mark and
a Christian community for whom it is written is the proof.
Mark's story is but 'the beginning of the good news of Jesus
Christ, Son of God'.

---

127. G. W. Geyer, *op. cit.*, 66.
128. R. H. Gundry, *op. cit.*, 4.

A Historical Note

The earliest written witness to the resurrection is in Paul's First Letter to the Corinthians (1 Cor 15:3-8). It mentions the burial, but does not mention the empty tomb or the account of the women finding it. Paul's interest is in the reality of the risen Christ and his ongoing presence in the community. Some writers cast doubt on the story of the empty tomb because of this 'omission' on Paul's part. In so doing they overlook two vital factors. Paul's interest is not in the 'pre-paschal' or 'historical Jesus'. He has little or no interest in telling the story of Jesus and his associates prior to his resurrection and glorification, except for his reflection on the institution of the Eucharist which he does to correct abuses in Corinth (1 Cor 11:23-33). His interest is in the risen Christ, not in the empty tomb or the women's experience. Furthermore there is a sound legal and logical principle which states that absence of evidence is not evidence of absence. The fact that Paul does not mention something does not mean it did not happen. Secondly it should be kept in mind that if, as appears to be the case from Matthew's explicit account, there were rumours about disciples stealing the body (Mt 28:11-15), the story of the women's visit in the early hours before sunrise may have been kept quiet for a long time for apologetic reasons. Stories of followers going under cover of darkness to the tomb would serve to reinforce suspicions of their having stolen the body. This silence and the resulting lack of knowledge about the women's visit to the tomb may have also been a factor in prompting Mark to emphasise the fact that they told nobody.

A Lost Ending?

Such an abrupt conclusion, just two words in Greek, *ephobounto gar*, 'for they were afraid' (Mk 16:8) has prompted scholars to speculate on the possibility that the original ending was lost, through wear and tear of the end of a scroll or the loss of the final page of a codex. However, it is unlikely that such a loss would have gone uncorrected if it happened to the original copy before other copies were made. It is also most unlikely that it happened in exactly the same manner to a number of early copies so that the original ending did not survive in any one of them. Some writers have also speculated on the possibility of Mark's failure to finish the work through the intervention of death or some other obstacle. That is pure speculation. It seems most likely that the 'abrupt' ending of Mk 16:8 is original. The intended readership may well have been familiar with an earlier proclamation of the resurrection and are being given 'the beginning of the good news' in the pre-paschal ministry of Jesus in the gospel of Mark. A changed real readership has, however, caused later scribes to 'supply' endings from other gospel traditions.

A factor to be kept in mind is that the tradition of the resurrection, involving empty tomb and appearance accounts, may have been well known from earlier preaching and liturgical celebration. The 'longer ending' drawing on these earlier traditions was probably added at a later date to the gospel of Mark because of its apparently abrupt ending.

LATER ENDINGS

The Longer Ending. Mk 16:9-20 (text included in most Bibles)
For external and internal reasons the longer ending, Mk 16:9-20, is regarded as a later addition to the gospel (though it may represent a summary of more primitive traditions later developed in the other gospels). It is absent from most important manuscripts. Eusebius and Jerome state that is was wanting in most Greek manuscripts known to them. It is written in a different style, uses different vocabulary, has different theology/christology and is clearly trying to 'come to terms' in a new situation with the challenging ending of the original gospel, written at a different time and in different circumstances. It is clearly a 'summary' gleaned from the traditions developed in the other gospels and Acts. The intended readership may well have been familiar with an earlier proclamation of the resurrection and are being given 'the *beginning* of the good news' in the story of pre-paschal ministry of Jesus in the gospel of Mark.

This longer ending, though it is not from Mark, has been accepted by the main churches as part of the canon of scripture. At first reading it seems familiar to the reader because it reflects traditions familiar from the other gospels and Acts. However, it seems to be more a reflection of the traditions that were later developed in the other books, than a straightforward summarising of their contents. It radically changes the character of the gospel of Mark if it is seen as an integral part, but if seen as 'separate' from the main narrative, it serves as a linking of the Markan story into the overall canon and faith of the church.

Mary Magdalene Mk 16:9-11
The first appearance of the Risen Christ is reported as an appearance to Mary Magdalene and she brings news of the resurrection to the disciples who are mourning and weeping. They do not believe her. This broadly corresponds with the account in Jn 20:11-18. Mary Magdalene is described as in Lk 8:2 as one from whom seven demons had gone/been driven out. And Luke's report that the disciples did not believe her is also reflected here (Lk 24:11).

Two on the Road to the Country Mk 16:12-13
The next appearance reflects the tradition of the two disciples who encounter Jesus while walking on the road into the country. They returned to tell the others, but they did not believe them (unlike Lk 24:34f where their testimony is accepted and confirmed by the account of the appearance to Simon). This tradition is developed at length in Lk 24:13-35 in the account of the disciples on the road to Emmaus.

The Eleven. The Mission. The Accompanying Signs Mk 16:14-18
The reference to their being at table is reminiscent of the appearance in Lk 24:41f. Jesus reprimands them for their lack of faith and stubborness/hardness of heart which prevented them believing those who had seen him after he had been raised, a criticism close to the main critique of the disciples throughout Mark's gospel. (Some manuscripts have a further interpolation at this point, 'the Freer *logion*, treated below.) The command to go into the whole world and proclaim the good news to all creation reflects the universal mission in Mt 28:16-20 and Acts 1:8, and the importance of baptism is emphasised as in Mt 28:19. The signs, casting out demons and healing the sick, accompanying the mission, are those promised on their first mission in Mk 3:15; 6:7, 13. Speaking in strange tongues and picking up snakes are mentioned in Acts 2:4; 28:5f. Drinking poison without coming to harm is not found elsewhere in the New Testament. Unlike the rest of the gospel, the signs are not seen as an integral part of the mission revealing its deeper meaning, but as an accompanying display of divine power authenticating the mission. (As such they are at odds with Jesus' refusal to perform signs and wonders to authenticate his own mission.)

The Ascension. Mk 16:19
Mk 16:19 briefly refers to 'the Ascension' in a manner reminiscent of Acts 1:11. The Ascension is the high point of Luke's
gospel and the departure point for the story in Acts (Lk 24:50f;
Acts 1:9-11). Luke is fond of the title 'Lord' and of the kerygmat-
ic proclamation of Jesus' victory and exaltation. Both are in evidence here with the use of the formula 'the Lord Jesus' which reflects the glorification theme, 'sitting at the right hand of God',
drawn from Ps 109 (110) which was used by Jesus himself at his
Jewish trial: 'You will see the Son of Man seated at the right
hand of the Power' (Mk 14:62) and in his question about the
scribes' teaching about the Christ being the son of David (Mk
12:36) in which he quoted the psalm.

Conclusion. Universal Mission Mk 16:20
They went out and preached everywhere. 'Going out' signifies
going out to preach and carry on the mission. In the broader
New Testament scenario the disciples go out from Jerusalem
where the ascension took place in Luke and Acts and where
Jesus tells them they will be his witnesses in Jerusalem, Judea,
Samaria and to the ends of the earth (Acts 1:8). Its generalised
nature also reflects the commission in Mt 28:16-20, and the statement 'the Lord working with them, and confirming their message through the signs that accompanied them' reflects the
promise in Mt 28:20: 'Behold, I will be with you all days, even to
the end of the age.' It reflects also the prediction of Jesus in the
eschatological discourse in Mark that the gospel would be
preached to all nations (Mk 13:10).

The 'Freer Logion' at Mk 16:14
This *logion* or saying is inserted in the codex W, preserved in the
Freer Museum in Washington, from which it has acquired its
name. Jerome quotes the beginning of the *logion*. It is clearly an
attempt to soften the rebuke directed at the disciples in Mk
16:14, by way of explaining their hardness of heart and unbelief
in terms of the influence of superior demonic influence 'in this
age of lawlessness and unbelief' which is 'under Satan'.

The Shorter Ending. Mk :9-10 (text given in italics as it is not included in most Bibles)

They reported all these things briefly to Peter's companions. Afterwards, Jesus himself sent out through them, from east to west, the sacred and imperishable proclamation of salvation. Amen.

This shorter ending of two verses (Mk 16:9-10) is clearly a scribal attempt to conclude the gospel with a statement that the women did as they were told and announced the message to the disciples and Peter. This short ending, found in a few Greek manuscripts and versions is obviously the work of a scribe anxious to explain how the women were silent and did not speak to anyone, and still the disciples knew what they had experienced. The scribe attempts to explain the 'silence' as a discreet silence, telling only those who had a right to know, and telling them only the bare essentials, summed up in the term 'briefly' (*syntomôs*). Peter gets special mention, as in Mk 16:7. The universal mission 'from east to west' reflects the prediction of Jesus in Mk 13:10 and the appearance accounts which focus on universal mission (Mt 28:16-20; Acts 1:8), and the description 'sacred and imperishable proclamation of salvation' reflects the language of someone familiar with a more 'Hellenised' theological language which would be quite at home in a letter of Paul or in the Acts of the Apostles.

Appendices

1. THE WORLD OF MARK

There is widespread agreement among scholars that the early Christian document which we call *The Gospel of Mark* was written between the mid-sixties and early seventies of the first century. It therefore first saw the light of day in a very troubled world when Christian, Jew and Pagan all had reason to feel an apocalyptic sense of foreboding as the apparently secure foundations of empire and religion as they knew them were swept away.

Beginning with the great fire of Rome, which destroyed in whole or in part ten of the fourteen regions of the city, a series of crises involving persecution of Christians, political instability verging on empire-wide civil war, the Jewish revolt against Roman rule in Palestine resulting in the destruction of Jerusalem and the Temple, and the enslavement or dispersion of a huge number of the Jewish population, all followed in quick succession.

The fire of Rome began on 19 July in the year 64 and continued for nine days. The devastation of fire was followed by the ravages of plague. It far surpassed the earlier fires in Rome and was destined to leave a mark on history for many reasons. It had political repercussions for the Romans themselves, leading ultimately to the suicide of Nero and the ensuing political upheaval. As it did not destroy the Trans-Tiber (Trastevere) region, where there was a great colony of Jews and other foreigners, fingers could be pointed to possible foreign arsonists in a city where anti-semitism was long established and xenophobia was rife. This level of suspicion ultimately facilitated the savage persecution of the Christian community in the city as the emperor sought to divert the anger of the citizens from himself. A huge number died in the persecution, many betrayed other members, possibly family and friends, to save themselves, and the leading Jewish-Christian figures, Peter and Paul, were among those put to death.

Nero was out of Rome at the outbreak of the fire and came back on hearing the news. He issued instructions for the rebuilding of the city, and laid down strict safety standards, as Augustus had done before him. But he purchased a large tract of land of about a hundred and twenty acres between the Palatine and Esquiline hills at rock bottom price and proceeded to build the lavish Domus Aurea. When he moved into it he proclaimed, 'Now I can live like a human being.'[1] This extravagance happened at a time when Rome had come to loathe him and his methods and when the elimination of his opponents had filled the people with disgust and horror. Rumours began to circulate, all the more ominous because of the already existing hostility towards him. The disaffected populace spoke of his having started the fire to buy the land cheaply for the Domus Aurea and further his ambitious plan for a whole new city. It was even rumoured that he sang an ode on the burning of Troy as he watched the city burn.[2] Given his fondness for the theatre, music and all kinds of entertainment, his sense of the tragic and dramatic may well have occasioned such a response to the fire. After all, not long afterwards he went on a tour of the theatres of Greece in 67-68, neglecting public business and incurring enormous expenses, and on his return he was finally driven from office. Even his long standing advisors like Seneca were intolerable to him because of their advice and criticism, so he invited the philosopher to end his own life. He already had lost the steadying hand of his domineering and scheming mother when he had her despatched. The populace was angry. The Pisonian conspiracy, with its mixed aristocratic and military elements, posed a real threat to his life. Military disaffection was on the cards as the Praetorian Guards turned against him. The military, represented in the capital by the Pretorian Guard, had become the king makers since they murdered Caligula and forced the Senate to accept his uncle Claudius in his place. Now in the wake of a threat from the Praetorian Guard and the consequent condemnation by the Senate, matters came to a head forcing Nero to end his own life rather than submit to the military to be judiciously executed in the old fashioned military way which was execution by being cudgeled to death. He sensed he was under great threat and he was not underestimating the real danger to his life and rule. In this predicament he needed a scapegoat. He found one in the Christians and manipulated the popular prejudice against them. The persecution of Nero, however, was savage to the point of

---

1. Suetonius, *Lives, Nero*, xxxi.
2. *Ibid.*, xxxviii.

moving the hostile crowd to pity for the victims of one man's brutality.[3]

Subsequent comments on the persecution serve as an invaluable witness to the prejudice of society in general and of the civil authority in their regard. That society in general had such a very bad opinion of the Christians is obvious from Tacitus' account of the persecution unleashed by Nero. This account records the public opinion of the Christians in the sixties of the first century. It also records the opinion of Tacitus himself half a century or more later and must, indirectly at least, point to an unchanged public opinion in the early second century, since Tacitus hands on these judgements of society without question. He wrote:

> But neither human resources, nor imperial munificence, nor appeasement of the gods, eliminated sinister suspicions that the fire had been instigated. To suppress this rumour, Nero fabricated scapegoats – and punished with every refinement the notoriously depraved Christians (as they were called). Their originator, Christ, had been executed in Tiberius' reign by the governor of Judea, Pontius Pilate. But in spite of this temporary setback the deadly superstition had broken out afresh, not only in Judea (where the mischief had started), but even in Rome. All degraded and shameful practices collect and flourish in the Capital.
>
> First, Nero had self-acknowledged Christians arrested. Then, on their information, large numbers of others were condemned – not so much for incendiarism as for their anti-social tendencies. Their deaths were made farcical. Dressed in wild animals skins, they were torn to pieces by dogs, or crucified, or made into torches to be ignited after dark as substitutes for daylight. Nero provided his gardens for the spectacle and exhibited displays in the Circus, at which he mingled with the crowd – or stood in a chariot dressed as a charioteer. Despite their guilt as Christians, and the ruthless punishment it deserved, the victims were to be pitied. For it was felt that they were being sacrificed to one man's brutality rather than to the national interest.[4]

This prejudiced attitude of society resembles the attitude to other foreign peoples and religions. A religion that did not recognise the gods of the state and had no part in religious prac-

3. Tacitus, *Annals*, XIV,xliv.
4. *Ibid.*

tices other that its own left itself open to charges of superstition and anti-social behaviour. Such anti-Christian prejudice smacks very closely of a transfer of anti-Semitism to the Christians, of the type summed up in the remark of Tacitus that the Jews had hostile hatred against all others (*adversus omnes alios hostile odium*).[5] Referring to the Judean origin of the religion similarly reminds one of the contempt for things foreign which frequently showed itself in remarks like that of Juvenal that the mud of the Orontes was flowing into the Tiber.[6]

Suetonius offers a similar picture of anti-Christian prejudice. Tacitus was given to 'black and white' characterisation after the fashion of Sallust, but Suetonius also gives a similar picture in his remark that the Christians were a race of people with a new and evil superstition (*genus hominum superstitionis novae et maleficae*),[7] and this confirms the impression that Tacitus portrays of a prejudiced view on the part of society at large. They both accept and hand on this public opinion of the Christians. It continued into the early second century and was accepted by the imperial authorities when Trajan ruled that the very fact of being a Christian was in itself a crime without there being any evidence of other misbehaviour.[8] This ruling came in response to the letter from Pliny the Younger in Asia Minor when he was troubled by anonymous denunciations of Christians.[9] The bad reaction of society to the early church was therefore more widespread than Rome itself.

The Christian writer, Clement of Rome, writing to the church in Corinth in the mid-nineties of the first century, paints a similar picture to that of Tacitus in describing the numbers who died in the persecution. Tacitus was to write that a 'huge number', *multitudo ingens*, were put to death. Clement wrote in Greek and also said that a 'huge number', *poly plethos*, were put to death.

---

5. Tacitus, *Annals* II, lxxxv,5; *Histories* V,I; cf C. Thiaucevert, 'Ce que Tacit dit des Juifs au commencement du livre V des Histoires', *REJ* 19, 57-84; A. Hild, 'Les Juifs ä Rome devant l'opinion et dans la litterature', *REJ* 11, 174-186; E. M. Smallwood, *The Jews under Roman Rule*, 202; W. Wiefel, 'The Jewish Community in Ancient Rome and the Origins of Roman Christianity', in *The Romans Debate*, ed. K. P. Donfried, 100-119. cf Juvenal, *Satires*, I,iii, 60.
6. Juvenal, *Satires*, I, iii, 62.
7. Suetonius, *Lives, Nero*, xvi.
8. Pliny the Younger, *Ep.* X,96,97.
9. *Ibid.*

Clement wrote to the Corinthians in an attempt to stop the bitter factions that were tearing the church in the city apart. He spoke of the *zêlos*, the fanatical zeal, which had plagued the church in Rome and been responsible for the deaths of many, including those of Paul and Paul at the time of the Neronian persecution: 'by reason of jealousy and envy the greatest and most righteous pillars were persecuted and contended even unto death' (1 Clement 5:2).

Five emperors sat on the throne between the summer of 68 and the succession of Vespasian in 69. Nero commited suicide in 68 and was succeeded by Galba. The following year, 69, is often referred to as 'the year of the four emperors'. The changes in personnel at the pinnacle of power did not, however, signify a palace revolution, domestic *coup d'etat* or senatorial conspiracy. Each change signalled massive military activity throughout significant provinces of the empire, military intervention in Italy and in the capital and the threat of a return to the chaos of the civil wars that heralded the demise of the Republic and the birth of the Empire. When Nero reluctantly took his own life (rather, when he had his servant run him through with his sword) he did so to avoid the punishment decreed for him by the Senate at the instigation of the military, that he be clubbed to death. His downfall at the hands of the Praetorian Guard and the Senate was largely precipitated by the threat from Galba and the legions in Gaul and this in turn triggered action through the empire. The armies of the Upper and Lower Rhine, the Danube and the Levant all sprung into action, marching on the capital to enthrone their imperial candidates. The armies from the Rhine, joined in Northern Italy by those from Illyricum and Moesia, left a trail of destruction as they progressed towards Rome. The army from the Levant crossed Asia Minor as their candidate Vespasian hurried to Egypt to stop the supply of grain and starve the capital into accepting his candidature. Meanwhile Galba's short reign came to an unceremonious end when he was lynched in the Forum, and after a short spell in office the usurper Otho took his own life on hearing of the defeat of his own forces in northern Italy by the supporters of Vitellius. The forces of Vitellius and Vespasian finally reached Rome and their rival armies fought each other in the streets and marketplaces of the capital, a city still struggling in the aftermath of fire, plague, tyranny and imperial extravagance. Vitellius was lynched when the Danubian legions overpowered his forces and his cause was lost. A reign of terror followed until the new emperor Vespasian arrived in Rome in 70.

As these disastrous events were taking place in Rome and the advancing armies left a trail of destruction, the outbreak of hostilities between the Jews and Romans in Palestine began. It was a war that was to end in the ravages of the siege and the destruction of the holy city and Temple, the enslavement and dispersion of a vast multitude of Jews and an emerging division between those Jews who followed the way of Jesus and those who followed the emerging rabbinic Judaism of Jamnia (*Yavneh*).

Vespasian became emperor and his son Titus oversaw the destruction of Jerusalem and the Temple, a catastrophe described by Josephus:

> … the Temple Hill, enveloped in flames from top to bottom, appeared to be boiling up from its very roots; yet the sea of flame was nothing to the ocean of blood, or the companies of killers to the armies of the killed; nowhere could the ground be seen between the corpses, and the soldiers climbed over heaps of bodies as they chased the fugitives …[10]

Jews and Christians of Jewish and Gentile stock had lost their mother city, the origin, focus and referent of their religious lives and the powerful symbol of unity.

Meanwhile to calm the Roman mob with bread and circuses Vespasian began the building of the Flavian amphitheatre (later nicknamed the Colosseum after the colossal statue of Nero erected beside it) with the slave labour of the Jews taken captive by the XV legion. It was followed by the building of the Temple of Peace celebrating the defeat of the Jews and erection of the permanent triumphal Arch of Titus with its representations of the spoiling of the Temple and the capture of its sacred furnishings and vessels. The message of victory and conquest was written loud and clear in the architecture and monuments of the city.

When the whole empire reverberated to the sound of war and rumours of war as contending legions marched against each other and invested the capital; when emperors were made and unmade in quick succession by force of arms and the cities of Rome and Jerusalem experienced the ravages of fire and sword; when the Christians in Rome suffered unspeakable persecution under Nero and the Jews in Palestine suffered the horrors of war, siege, defeat, exile and enslavement; at some point during

10. Josephus, *Jewish Wars*, Bk VI, iv, v.

these terrible times, the gospel of Mark was written. It proclaimed a very different kingdom and a very different king as it
announced 'the beginning of *the good news* of Jesus Christ, Son of
God.'

2. WHO WROTE THE GOSPEL?

The gospel does not name its author, does not state where it was
written or who were the intended audience or readers.
Conclusions can be attempted from an examination of the text itself, and from what was stated about these questions in ancient
writings. However, the author places such an emphasis on suffering and persecution that it is reasonable to draw the conclusion that persecution, as a present or past experience, or the real
threat of it, was part and parcel of the experience of the situation
in which, or for which, the evangelist wrote. Betrayal and the
handing over of friends and family seem also to have been part
of that experience.

Traditionally the authorship of the second gospel is attributed to a person called Mark. Eusebius records the witness of
Papias who is reporting the witness of John the Elder that Mark
was the interpreter of Peter and wrote down his preaching.[11]
The anti-Marcionite prologue states that Mark was the interpreter of Peter and adds that he wrote 'in the regions of Italy'
and 'after Peter's death'. In addition it supplies the information
that he was 'stump-fingered', which smacks more of a historical
reminiscence than a literary criticism of his style. Justin Martyr
spoke of 'Peter's Memoirs' and may very well have been referring to the gospel of Mark, because he uses the peculiarly Markan
expression 'sons of thunder' for the sons of Zebedee.[12] Irenaeus
wrote that Mark was the disciple and interpreter of Peter who
transmitted the things preached by Peter, and he too adds that
he wrote after the deaths of Peter and Paul.[13] Clement of
Alexandria is quoted by Eusebius as saying that those who
heard Peter besought Mark to record his words, and adds that
Peter neither promoted nor tried to prevent the exercise.[14]
Eusebius, in another passage, quotes Clement as saying that

---

11. Eusebius, *Ecc Hist.*, III,39,15.
12. Justin Martyr, *Dialogue with Trypho*, 106, 3; cf Mk 3:17.
13. Irenaeus, *Adv. Haer.*, 3,1,1f.
14. Eusebius, *Ecc Hist.*, 6,14,6f.

Peter subsequently was moved by the Spirit to be pleased with the result and to ratify it for reading in the churches.[15] Clement also asserted that Peter was preaching to Roman Knights who besought Mark to undertake the task. Such a detail has an authentic ring at least. Origen states that Peter instructed Mark to undertake the task and refers to him as 'my son Mark' (cf. 1 Pet 5:13). Jerome speaks of him as the interpreter of Peter and adds that he was bishop of Alexandria.[16]

This tradition is impressive for several reasons. First of all, even if it one argues that the Papias' testimony is its mainstay, still no contending tradition emerged in antiquity either in east or west. Important communities prided themselves on their Apostolic Founders and it is unlikely that a 'secondary' figure like Mark would be a likely subject as pseudonym to lend authority to the work. In so far as emphasis on authority is concerned, Peter is there from the start but the account of his involvement moves from not impeding Mark, to instructing him to write and finally to ratifying and imposing the work, as is seen in the Fathers and early Christian literature.

The question, however, remains: 'Who was Mark?' Was this Mark the same John Mark described as an assistant of Paul in Acts 12:12 and 13:5, 13 and as an assistant of Peter in 1 Peter 5:13? Since Mark was a common name in Greco-Roman circles it is difficult to draw any definite conclusions regarding the exact identity of the Mark to whom the gospel is attributed. Pointing to a person of that name who is mentioned in the early Christian story and associated with leading figures like Peter and Paul does raise at least a very strong possibility that it is the same person, but it is not definite proof.

---

15. *Ibid.*, 2, 15, 2. Another testimony of Clement of Alexandria survives in the Latin *Adumb. in 1 Pet 5:13*.
16. Origen, quoted in Eusebius, *Ecc Hist.*, 25, 5, has Peter instructing Mark to write; Eusebius, *op.cit.*, 2,16, has Mark 'who was sent to Egypt' and Jerome, *Commentary on Matthew, Proemium*, 6, speaks of Mark as '*interpres apostoli Petri et Alexandrinae Ecclesiae primus episcopus*'. The combination of these two affirmations may well account for the belief of Chrysostom, *Homilies on Matthew*, 4, 1, that Mark wrote the gospel in Alexandria.

3. Where was the Gospel written?

a. The Traditional View: Rome

Though Mark is later associated with Alexandria, the association with Peter has traditionally been taken as a pointer to Rome as the place of the writing of the gospel at the request of the people (and the Knights).[17]

Rome as an important church, which the letter to the Romans shows clearly when Paul asserts, 'Your faith is spoken of all over the world,' through its reputation and communications could quite easily have its gospel spread and accepted in other communities (Rom 1:8). In addition to this, the internal evidence of the gospel shows a Latin context. The Greek of Mark's gospel has more Latinisms than any other gospel and this may very well point to a very Latinised readership/audience. Words such as *dênarion* (denarius) *kenturiôn* (centurion), *kênsos* (census), *kodrantês* (quadrans), *krabattos* (grabattus), *legiôn* (legion), *xestês* (sextarius), *spekoulatôr* (speculator), and composite words or phrases such as *hodon poiein* (*iter facere*), *hikanon poiein* (*satis facere*) are examples of the Latinisms in Mark's text.[18] Some of these occur elsewhere, but the number of them in this gospel, combined with the fact that *kenturiôn, xestês, spekoulatôr* and *hikanon poiein*, occur only in Mark makes a definite impact and strengthens the traditional case for accepting the Roman origin of the gospel. Furthermore, against the acceptance of an eastern venue, there is also the fact that the bronze *kodrantês* coin mentioned in 12:42 seems not to have been in use in the eastern part of the empire.[19] Though one may quibble with some of these Latinisms, the overall impression is difficult to deny.

The Latinisms would fit well into a context where Roman Knights were at least part of the intended readership/audience.

17. Though Mark is associated with Alexandria, the Peter-connection points to the non-Alexandrian origin of the work since there is no tradition of Peter in that city. Furthermore it has to be remembered that this Alexandrian tradition does not arise until late, when John Chrysostom asserted that the gospel was written in Egypt, a testimony that goes against the local tradition of Clement of Alexandria and Origen, which we saw above. It may have arisen from a misinterpretation of the statements of Eusebius and Jerome who mention, in the same sentence, Mark's being in Egypt and his writing the gospel.

18. cf respectively Mk 12:15; 15:39, 44f; 12:14; 12:42; 2:4; 5:9; 7:4; 6:27; 2:23; 15:15.

19. V.Taylor, *op. cit.*, 88.

Who were the Knights (Equites)? They were the second rank in the Roman nobility, after the Senators, who prided themselves on being at the top of the social order, and though a very small proportion of the population as a whole, they carried a weight of influence and prestige way beyond their numbers. The Knights were below the Senators and could be made by the emperor. Experts in business, commerce and industrial management, the emperors came more and more to rely on them for financial and managerial skills. Like the Senators, they had grown wealthier during the civil wars and now in the imperial times were living off that wealth.[20] Many of the centurions had been knights who renounced their rank on joining the military and on promotion again entered the aristocracy.[21] Many of the centurions of Italic and Gallia Narbonensis origin joined the ranks of the aristocracy on their return from service. Furthermore, the fact that the Latinisms are military, commercial and legal terms points to a 'better class' Roman audience into which the Knights would fit very well.

Rome was well represented in Palestine. Military and administrative personnel were there in plenty, and the whole history of the empire points to the cultural and religious influences such people brought back to Rome. Of specific interest are certain persons named in the New Testament as being impressed by, or even involved with, Jesus and his followers. There was the centurion whose servant was healed and whose extraordinary faith was proclaimed by Jesus to be greater than any in Israel, and the centurion who professed his faith in Jesus at the foot of the cross.[22] Then there was the centurion Cornelius, and his household, who received the Spirit in the presence of Peter (Acts 10:1-11:18). The recruitment of centurions in the Julio-Claudian period was from the legions which were still of Italic or Gallia Narbonensis origin. Many were chosen from among the Knights, who thereby renounced their status as Equites. On promotion many entered the ranks of the aristocracy. Given the closely knit nature of the Roman family, it is obvious that the faith of the head of the household was often the key to the con-

20. J. G. Gager ' Religion and Social Class in the Early Roman Empire', in *The Catacombs and the Colosseum*, ed. S.Benko and J. J. O'Rourke, Valley Forge, Pa: Judson, 1971, 99ff; M. Rostovtzeff, *Rome*, 146, 152, 175-177;
21. H. J. Rose, 'Centurio', *OCD*, 180; H. M. D. Parker, 'Legio', *OCD*, 492f.
22. Lk 7:10 / / Mt 8:10 and Mk15:39 / / Mt 27:54 / /Lk 23/:47.

THE GOSPEL OF MARK

version of the household and perhaps to their functioning as a believing household or primitive house church. The gaoler at Philippi, a very 'Roman' city, for example, was converted and brought Paul and Silas to his home to celebrate the conversion of the whole family to the faith. In response to his urgent question, 'What must I do to be saved?' they had told him to become a believer in the Lord Jesus and he would be saved together with his household (Acts 16:19-34). He may very well have been a Roman. Military or administrative personnel from any of the areas where the church was becoming established could equally have been converted and returned with a believing household to Rome. There was also the wife of Pilate who seems to have been impressed by Jesus (Mt 15:27:19) and Mark mentions the sons of Simon of Cyrene, Alexander and Rufus, as though they were well known, a point of significance whether they were Jews or Gentiles, if we accept that the gospel of Mark was written in Rome (Mt 27:19 and Mk 15:2). Thus, in addition to the regular Jewish contacts between the Roman synagogues and Jerusalem, there was a regular pagan contact between the pagan Roman and Italic scene and Jerusalem. It is reasonable to assume that a missionary activity could have begun through some such contacts from the earliest days of the church. Any of these people returning from service in Palestine, or any other area that had experienced Christian missionary activity, could have continued their practice as a believing household on returning to the capital, and thus started or augmented the tradition of Gentile Christianity in Rome centered on house churches. Though we do not have any more precise details, the tradition that Mark wrote at the instigation of the people and/or the Knights would well fit into this scenario of returning officers, former knights, or newly promoted into the aristocratic ranks and moving among the Knights at Rome. Eusebius' comment, taken from Clement of Alexandria, translated by S. P. Kealy reads:[23]

> Mark, the follower of Peter, while Peter was preaching publicly the gospel at Rome in the presence of some of Caesar's knights and was putting forward many testimonies concerning Christ, being requested by them that they may be able to commit to memory the things that were being spoken, wrote

---

23. S. P. Kealy, *Mark's Gospel, A History of its Interpretation*, New York: Paulist Press, 1982, 18.

from the things that were spoken by Peter, the gospel which is called 'according to Mark.

The fact that some of Jesus' teachings have been cast in non-semitic and non-biblical language, for example, the list of vices that comes out from within a man and the allegory added by way of explanation to the parable of the sower, together with the presentation of the prohibition on divorce which adds the clause that forbids the wife to divorce her husband, further reflect a 'pagan' audience/readership.[24] The divorce clause reflects accurately the situation of women seeking divorce in the context of a growing liberalisation and feminism in Rome.

Furthermore, as seen from the commentary, the gospel of Mark reflects many aspects of popular dramatic writing and performance. It is said that there was very little written in Greek in the first century that did not show evidence of the theatre.[25] Mark's gospel was written in a decade when several dramas were written in Rome. The theatrical genre specialised in the resolution of the protagonist's identity, already revealed to the audience/readership, who then observed the reaction of the other actors and their gradual coming to an understanding of that identity. This would resonate with the experience of Greek tragic theatre which was widely popular in Rome at the time of the writing of Mark's gospel.[26]

Further adding to the possible Roman dimension of the gospel is the appropriateness of the emphasis on suffering to the circumstances of the Christians in the city as we know them to have been in the sixties (Mk 8:34-8; 10:38f; 13:9-13), and the apocalyptic discourse may well reflect aspects of the Neronic persecution (Mk13:9-13, esp. 13:12f).

The presentation of the passion account in Mark can be seen in terms of a martyrology wherein the Roman power is focused on the emperor's representative, the centurion, whose cohort salute Jesus in mock imperial fashion until the typical martyrological motif of reversal of roles puts the representative of Roman imperial military might in the role of the powerless and sees him confess that the executed one whom he and his cohort

24. cf respectively Mk 7:20-23; 4:13-20; 10:12.
25. A. Stock, *Call to Discipleship, A Literary Study of Mark's Gospel*, Good News Studies I, Dublin, Veritas 1982, studies the literary-theatrical character of the gospel.
26. *Ibid.*, 27-30.

mocked is truly the Son of God (Mk 15:39). This would have
been a powerful haggadic story for a persecuted community, in
which they could see the cry of the centurion as a cry of defeat.[27]
It could equally be the gospel of the centurion and his family
from the class of knights who had come to faith in the one whom
they and/or their peers had encountered directly or indirectly
through their contacts with Palestine and other areas where the
church was being established.

b. Recent Views. Syria-Palestine as place of origin

The traditional view, outlined above, that the gospel was written
in Rome in the aftermath of the persecution of Nero, remained
more or less unchallenged until the middle of the twentieth century. There had been some earlier voices speaking in favour of a
venue closer to Syria-Palestine but they were a minority. The
Peter-connection, for example, gave rise to speculation that perhaps Antioch, where Peter had worked, could have been the
place of origin of the gospel. This was the view of J. V. Bartlet,
who considered it further confirmed by the fact that it was nearer
to the area of Papias' influence and would make the work easily
available to Matthew and Luke.[28]

    V. Taylor's celebrated commentary on Mark (1956) reflects
the widely held traditional position, but from then on many
leading Markan scholars have challenged the traditional con-
sensus. The general trend has been to see the gospel as having
been written somewhere in the Syria-Palestine area in the context of the Jewish War and the destruction of the Jerusalem and
the Temple. W.Marxen,[29] writing about the same time as V.
Taylor, suggests that Galilee was the likely situation, among a
Christian community who escaped the Jewish War. H. C. Kee
(1979)[30] suggests an apocalyptically minded community in

---

27. J. Pobee, 'The Cry of the Centurion – a Cry of Defeat', in E. Bammel,
The Trial of Jesus, Studies in Biblical Theology, Second Series, no 13,
Cambridge Studies in honour of C. F. D. Moule, London, SCM Press
Ltd, 1970.
28. J. V. Bartlet, *St Mark*, Century Bible, Edinburgh: T. C. and E. C. Jack
Ltd., 1922, 36f; cf Taylor, *The Gospel according to St Mark* (2nd ed 1972),
32 and n 6.
29. W. Marxen, *Der Evangelist Markus* (E.T. *Mark the Evangelist*,
Philadelphia Fortess, 1969)
30. H. C. Kee, *The Community of the New Age*, Philadelphia: Westminster,
1977.

southern Syria, G. Theissen (1989)[31] also thinks in terms of
southern Syria, near Palestine. J. Marcus (1992)[32] suggests one of
the Hellenist cities of Palestine. M. D. Hooker says: 'All we can
say with certainty, therefore, is that the gospel was composed
somewhere in the Roman Empire – a conclusion that scarcely
narrows the field at all.'[33] F. J. Moloney (2002) states that:

> The traditional location of Rome has much to offer, but the
> background of the fall of Jerusalem to Mark 13 suggests a
> location closer to these events ... I find it impossible to deter-
> mine an exact location, region or city ... I suspect that the
> traditional location of the birth of Mark in the city of Rome
> leaves too many questions unresolved. Thus I would agree
> with Morna Hooker: 'All we can say with certainty, there-
> fore, is that the gospel was composed somewhere in the
> Roman Empire – a conclusion that scarcely narrows the field
> at all!' I would, however, narrow the field to the extent that
> the place in the Roman Empire that produced the gospel of
> Mark must have been reasonably close to Jerusalem.[34]

However, Rome as the place of origin of the gospel still has its
supporters. J. R. Donahue and D. J. Harrington (2002) in *The
Gospel of Mark,* in the Sacra Pagina series, acknowledge the very
significant drift away from the traditional position but still 'opt
for a date around 70 CE and for an original audience among the
persecuted Christians at Rome.'[35] They go on to explain that
they propose 70 as a date for 'the final composition of the
gospel.' They also raise the very important issue of whether one
should regard the gospels as directed to one particular community or regard them as destined for circulation throughout the
Christian mission.[36]

The conclusion of this writer is that the gospel of Mark does
not reflect a single writing venture but a writing completed in

---

31. G. Theissen, *Lokalkolorit u. Zeitgeschichte in den Evangelien,* 1989. E.T.
The Gospels in Context, Minneapolis: Fortress,1991.
32. J. Marcus, 'The Jewish War and the Sitz im Leben of Mark', *JBL* 111
(1992) 441-62.
33. M. D. Hooker, *The Gospel According to St Mark*, 8.
34. F. J. Moloney, *The Gospel of Mark*, 14,15.
35. J. R. Donahue and D. J. Harrington, *The Gospel of Mark*, Collegeville:
The Liturgical Press, 46.
36. Ibid. They draw attention, inter alios, to R. Bauckham, *The Gospels for
all Christians. Rethinking the Gospel Audiences*, Grand Rapids: Eerdmans,
1998.

stages. Whereas Mark 13 is probably correctly seen as reflecting the reaction of the Christians in the Palestine-Syria area, it stands apart in its genre, language and outlook from the rest of the gospel. It is not specific enough in itself to determine whether it refers to the Caligula statue crisis, the lead up to the Jewish war, its early stages and dire forebodings or its final outcome in the destruction of the city and temple. It lacks, for example, the precision of the *vatinicia ex eventu* of Luke. It could therefore be an independent 'unit' formed before or after the composition of the rest of the gospel, and included in the final production. Furthermore, the lack of any precise knowledge about the Christian communities in the Syria and Palestine area leaves a lot open to speculation.

Apart from Mark 13 the body of the gospel could fit into any of the 'Romanised' cities of the empire and there is no need to look beyond the traditional venue.

Furthermore, there is no compelling reason to believe that the gospel was written in one place. Most of the apostolic figures and their associates were on the move from place to place. This may well explain a Roman and a Syro-Palestinian dimension to the gospel.

4. MARK AND THE OTHER GOSPELS

Mark's gospel plays its part in the development of the New Testament narrative of Jesus and the furthering of insight into Jesus' person, life, death and resurrection. Much ink has been spilled on the inter-relationship and direction of influences among the synoptic gospels of Matthew, Mark and Luke and on the relationship of Mark and John.

Augustine regarded Mark as a digest or summary of Matthew.[37] His influence was probably the main reason why this opinion of Mark continued until the nineteenth century. Two arguments against Mark's summarising Matthew spring to mind immediately. Firstly, the central prayer, the Our Father, and the major teaching about Christian living, the Sermon on the Mount, are absent. Absent also is any reference to the elaborate infancy narrative. Furthermore Mark's use of the Old Testament is very different to Matthew's many direct quotations with their specific references to fulfilment of scripture. Secondly, a later gospel summarising Matthew is unlikely to have changed

---

37. Augustine, *De consensu evangelistarum*, 1.2.4.

Matthew's relatively benign portrait of the disciples into the very critical portrait in Mark. Mark's vivid and colourful narrative does not look like a 'digest' of the much sparser narrative style of Matthew. All these indications seem to point clearly to the fact that Mark is not a summary of Matthew.

Both Mark's art and his relationship to Matthew and Luke are very differently assessed since the nineteenth century with the rise of historical criticism. Mark is now seen as very subtle and having the 'art to conceal his art' in his deceptively simple and vividly descriptive narrative. His relationship to Matthew and Luke is also assessed very differently. The generally accepted 'Two-Source' hypothesis maintains that Mark was written prior to Matthew and Luke and that they both used Mark as a source together with another source, made up almost exclusively of sayings of Jesus, which the scholars have called Q (from the German word *Quelle*, meaning 'source'). According to this theory the Q source accounts for the 335 verses which Matthew and Luke have in common and which are absent in Mark. Furthermore, where there is disagreement between Matthew and Luke in the material shared by all three, one of them usually agrees with Mark. But there are certain difficulties with the theory.

First of all, there are a number of 'minor agreements' where Matthew and Luke agree against Mark in the triple tradition and this makes it difficult to see how they both could have used Mark as a source and independently come up with the same divergences from that source. Furthermore, a number of stories common to Mark and Matthew show significant differences. The narrative section of Matthew's gospel is far more sparse than that of Mark, which is more vivid and colourful. If Matthew followed Mark then he very severely edited his Markan source. Has Mark enhanced an older narrative or series of stories in the tradition which Matthew also used in his gospel, or did Matthew severely edit Mark's more vivid narrative? A good example is the story of the cure of the paralytic in Capernaum when Jesus pronounced the forgiveness of sins and upset the scribes. Mark's account (Mk 2:1-12) gives the very striking detail of the stretcher-bearers climbing onto the roof and, having stripped away part of the roof, leaving the man down in front of Jesus on the stretcher. Matthew's account (Mt 9:1-8) omits the rather dramatic detail of the climbing onto the roof and leaving the man down in front of Jesus. Is it possible that Matthew, had he been following canoni-

cal Mark, would have omitted such a significant and colourful
detail? In the account of the storm on the lake, Matthew omits
the details in the reference to where Jesus was sleeping in the
boat ('in the stern, on a cushion') and has Jesus challenge the disciples' faithless fear before calming the storm, and he makes no
reference to the other boats (Mt 8:23-27). Furthermore he usually
eliminates secondary characters and details from Mark's narratives, reducing the characters in a scene to Jesus and the person
with whom he is in dialogue, as for example in the healing of
Peter's mother-in-law where, unlike Mark, there is no reference
to the presence of any of the disciples (Mt 8:14f). Has Matthew
severely edited Mark, as G. Bornkamm asserted in his very influential treatment of 'The Stilling of the Storm in Matthew'[38] or
have Matthew and Mark both drawn their narrative from a
more primitive tradition and edited it differently? In a recent article in the *Proceedings of the Irish Biblical Association*, Seamus
O'Connell argues the case very convincingly that 'it is more
helpful to maintain that canonical Mark is a related but parallel
development to canonical Matthew'. He sums up the situation:

> Usually it is Mark who lengthens the parallel passage in
> Matthew and not Matthew who shortens Mark. In fact it may
> be more helpful to consider Mark creating new narratives
> from a source related to canonical Matthew, rather than the
> current accepted stance of Matthew developing new struc-
> tures on the foundation of canonical Mark.
>
> Mark is a work written with tremendous self-awareness
> and identity. The relative brevity of the gospel would have
> enabled a rhetor or scribe with a developed memory to have
> an awareness of every word, phrase and section of the
> work.[39]

This calls for a certain reservation in accepting the two-source
theory in its simple classical form, particularly in the relationship of Matthew and Mark.

When compared with the other major gospel tradition, found
in St John's gospel, Mark clearly represents a gospel very heavily
focused on Galilee, the surrounding area and the journey to

---

38. G. Bornkamm, 'The Stilling of the Storm in Matthew' in G.
Bornkamm, G. Barth and H. J. Held, *Tradition and Interpretation in
Matthew*, Philadelphia; Westminster / London, SCM,1963.
39. S. O'Connell, 'Towards the First Gospel. Redactional Development
in the Gospel of Mark', *PIBA*, 26 (2003), 66-88, 73.

Jerusalem, with only one visit to the city, at the end of his life
and ministry. John, on the other hand, concentrates heavily
throughout on Jerusalem and the many visits of Jesus for the pilgrimage festivals. In spite of the very different outline, language, imagery and theology, there are many points of contact
between the traditions, as pointed out in the commentary.

5. SOME EXPLANATORY NOTES

a. The Tradition(s) of the Anointing
Two similar stories have survived in the New Testament which
reflect each other in detail, and in popular telling they are often
confused.[40] First of all there is the story told only by Luke of the
woman with a bad reputation who entered the house of Simon
the Pharisee in Galilee, wept at Jesus' feet and dried them with
her hair. She is not named. In response to the indignant reaction
of those at table, Jesus commended her love and faith and said
many sins were forgiven her because she had loved much.[41]
There is another story of a woman, who anointed Jesus with expensive ointment in Bethany shortly before his death and, in response to those who pointed out that it was a 'waste' of the expensive ointment which 'should have been sold and the money
given to the poor', he responded by interpreting her action as an
anointing for his burial.

There are differences in detail between the various accounts
of this anointing in Bethany (Mt 26:6-13; Mk 14:3-9; Jn 12:1-8).
Matthew and Mark do not name the woman, but say the anointing took place in the house of Simon the Leper. John names the
woman as Mary (of Bethany) but does not mention the name of
the householder (Simon the Leper). In fact, he never mentions
any leper in his gospel. Matthew and Mark describe how she

40. See the text and comparative tables in R. E. Brown, *The Gospel
According to John*, I, 449-454.
41. Lk 7:36-50; Later tradition identifies her as Mary Magdalene, probably because she is named, immediately after the story of the woman of
bad reputation, as one of the women who accompanied him, whom he
healed of ailments and in her case, from whom he had driven out seven
evil spirits (Lk 8:2). Since the time of Gregory the Great the sinful
woman of Lk 7 (whom Luke was charitable enough to leave unnamed),
Mary of Bethany and Mary of Magdala have been regarded – wrongly –
as the same person and honoured as one saint. Preaching, art, literature,
stage and cinema have perpetuated the unfounded destruction of her
reputation.

poured the precious ointment on his head, resembling a 'messianic/royal or priestly' anointing and how Jesus in turn interpreted the action in terms of preparation for his burial. Unlike the synoptic accounts which mention the anointing of Jesus' head, John emphasises the fact that Mary anointed his feet and wiped them with her hair. Anointing the feet was an action particularly associated with preparation for burial. This is very significant in a context where the authorities have already decided on his death and sought help to bring it about. In a prophetic gesture prompted by love and hospitality, this devoted disciple now prepares him for burial.

The variations on the story of the anointing in Bethany and similarities with the anointing in Galilee pose some questions. Is it just a coincidence that the householder in Galilee, where the sinful woman wept at Jesus' feet, was also called Simon (Lk 7:36-50) or was there a fusion of detail between two similar stories in the tradition? Matthew and Mark speak of anointing Jesus' head, John speaks of anointing his feet. Is this another fusion of details or is it not possible that both took place in one great act of anointing, with tradition seeing significance in different details? The three accounts of the Bethany anointing emphasise the costly nature of the ointment, the indignation of the disciples (Mt) or of 'some who were there' (Mk) and the reference to the poor. John's gospel focuses the indignation and the reference to the poor on the person of Judas and this affords the narrator the opening to identify Judas as the betrayer and the opportunity to comment further on his dishonesty in managing the common fund. Luke and John, though describing two different events, both describe how the woman in question dried Jesus' feet with her hair. This may in some way reflect a custom in the Greco-Roman world, as seen in Petronius' *Satyricon*, where a diner wiped excess oil or potable substances from the hands onto the hair of servants.[42]

The similarities in detail between these three accounts of the anointing in Bethany and the account of the repentant woman in Galilee have led to a certain confusion and overlapping in detail. A 'cross over' in details may well be evident in the fact that Luke, Matthew and Mark, but not John, mention that it was an alabaster jar. Significantly too, Luke mentions the anointing of the feet, both in the initial account itself and in Jesus' rebuff to

---

42. Petronius, *Satyricon*, 27.

his host when defending the woman from criticism and prejudiced judgement of her character (and motives?). Later tradition
identifies the woman in Galilee as Mary Magdalene, probably a
confusion arising from the fact that the woman in Bethany is
called Mary, and Mary Magdalene is named in a summary statement as one of the women from Galilee who were with Jesus
and whom he healed of ailments, specifying Mary Magdalene as
one from whom he had driven out evil spirits. The summary follows closely on the story of the sinful woman but does not follow from it (Lk 8:2). The unwarranted assumption that it does
has wrongly given rise to the belief that Mary Magdalene was a
person of immoral life. The statement that Jesus cast seven devils from her (Mk 16:9; Lk 8:2) could mean that she was mentally,
physically or emotionally sick, or 'possessed'. Since the time of
Gregory the Great the repentant sinner, Mary of Bethany and
Mary Magdalene have been regarded – incorrectly – as the same
person and celebrated as one saint.

2. Herod Family Affairs

Herod Antipas was son of Herod the Great, the king associated
with the murder of the children in Bethlehem,[43] in addition to
the murder of several members of his family and anyone he felt
to be a rival. Such was his reputation for killing his sons that it
was said of him that it was safer to be his pig than his son. He
had several marriages and the children from these various marriages, whom he did not murder when they appeared to become
a threat, became entangled in incestuous unions. The relationships are intricate and scholars have been puzzled to the point of
confusion, and error, in working them out.

Herod the Great had several wives. He first married Doris
and they had a son Antipater, whom he murdered. He also married Mariamne the Hasmonean and they had two sons, Alexander
and Aristobulus, both of whom he murdered. Aristobulus had a
daughter Herodias, the Herodias who schemed against the
Baptist. She was granddaughter of Herod the Great.

Herod married another Mariamne, called the Boethusian,
and they had a son Herod (sometimes mistakenly called Herod
Philip). He married Herodias, his own niece. They lived in Rome
as private individuals. It was there that Herod Antipas, son of
Herod the Great and yet another wife Malthake, visited them,

---

43. Mt 2:16-18.

seduced Herodias and subsequently married her, when he divorced his own wife, the daughter of King Aretas IV of the Nabateans.[44] Herodias had now divorced one uncle for another, his brother. She had a daughter Salome, the dancer in the story of the Baptist (though her personal name is not given by Mark).[45] According to Mark that was the marriage that provoked the wrath of the Baptist. Mark calls him Philip when in fact his name was Herod, and this has caused confusion. Herod the Great also married Cleopatra of Jerusalem and they had a son Philip. He married Salome, his grandniece.

This network of incestuous relationships in high places was the very stuff of prophetic condemnations. The prophet challenged Herod about the unlawful state of his marriage (Luke adds 'and about all the other crimes Herod had committed').[46] Directly or indirectly this reached the ears of Herodias and John was arrested, and subsequently beheaded. There are some difficulties in establishing the exact historical details. Josephus, for example, says that John was imprisoned in the fortress of Machaerus, south of the Dead Sea. Mark's account seems to imply that he was imprisoned in the neighbourhood of Galilee near the location of the banquet. A further historical difficulty arises from the fact that Mark calls Antipas' brother, Herodias' first husband, Philip, when in fact his name was Herod.

3. The Feasts of Passover and Unleavened Bread

Naming a feast creates an atmosphere for the reader, conjures up a mood and provides a religious and theological framework for presenting the claims of Jesus and his ministry. Celebrating the feasts enabled the participants to share in the history of God's dealings with the people, revive their religious memory, sharpen their focus and heighten expectation for God's saving action in the present and the future. The Hebrew name for a feast is *zikkârôn*, from the verb *zâkar*, to remember. 'Remember-

---

44. This divorce was seen as a terrible insult by king Aretas and the Nabateans and it led to political trouble and bloody conflict. It may account in part for the bad blood that gave rise to the difficulties that arose between the Jews and the Nabateans to which Paul fell victim when he had to flee from Damascus after they had taken over the city.
45. Some of the mss describe the dancer as 'his daughter' rather than 'her daughter'. In the light of the story as a whole the better reading is 'her daughter'.
46. Lk 19:20.

ing' in the context of the Sabbath or a feast is not just a recalling of the past, but a making present for every subsequent generation of the experience of those who originally partook in the saving event. Liturgy makes the participants contemporaries of the events they remember in their celebration.

Originally the Passover (*Pesah*) probably combined an older nomadic, pastoral feast celebrated with the slaying of a sheep or goat and a settled agricultural feast of the grain (barley) harvest. The Passover sacrifice has its origins in the nomadic times when the shepherd sacrificed an animal and sprinkled the blood on the tent pegs to ensure fertility for the flock and safety for the inhabitants. The sacrificial meal was then eaten with bitter herbs gathered in the desert, in the nomadic style of someone ready for a journey. The feast of Unleavened Bread had its origin in an agricultural celebration of the barley harvest when all the old leaven was got rid of, and a new beginning was embarked upon with bread made from the new grain. The consecration of the first-born began as a feast recognising the gift of life from the Deity, with the sacrifice of the first born of the animals and the consecration of the first born of the children. The first born was believed to embody the best qualities. These older pastoral and agricultural festivals were eventually combined and historicised into a festival celebrating the Passover, Exodus and Wandering which brought the people to Canaan. The slaying of the lamb recalled the escape from the plague of death visited on the first-born in Egypt. 'It is the sacrifice of the Lord's Passover, for he passed over the houses of the people of Israel in Egypt, when he slew the Egyptians but spared our houses' (Exod 12:27). The sprinkling of the blood of the lamb symbolised the gift of life, and the sealing or anointing of the Israelites as the first-born of God. The blood became a sign of life given and protected by God, an anointing, symbolising Israel's position as God's children. 'The blood will be a sign for you upon the houses where you are; and when I see the blood, I will pass over you, and no plague shall fall upon you to destroy you' (Exod 12:13). 'The blood is the life' (Deut 12:23). 'The life of the flesh is in the blood. This blood I myself have given you to perform the rite of atonement for your lives at the altar; for it is blood that atones for a life' (Lev 17:11). The doorposts and lintels were anointed with the blood of the lamb, using sprigs of hyssop. The unleavened bread recalled the haste in which they began their journey from

Egypt, not giving the bread time to rise, and God's providence in feeding the people in the desert until they received the gift of the manna, the bread from heaven. The unleavened bread also celebrated the new beginning unfolding at the escape from Egypt as they left the old leaven behind. In this process of historicisation, all the elements of the Passover meal were eventually interpreted in historical terms. The celebration was communal, not individual, and all Israel was united in the remembering of God's mighty deeds in forming a people.

Many major events in the history of the people were marked by the celebration of the Passover. When Joshua led them across the Jordan to the Promised Land they encamped at Gilgal and kept the Passover in the plains of Jericho. On that occasion the manna ceased and they ate the grain, a bringing together of the feasts of Passover and Unleavened Bread. When Josiah completed his far-reaching religious reform programme he celebrated the Passover and when the returned exiles worshipped for the first time in the newly constructed Temple, they too celebrated the Passover.[47]

The Passover in Jesus' time was celebrated as one of the three great pilgrimage feasts. A hundred thousand people crowded into the city on these occasions, Zealots and revolutionaries could easily enter in the shadow of such crowds. In the afternoon of the day before the Passover the paschal lambs were ritually slaughtered and offered to God in the Temple. The liturgical instructions for the Passover feast in Ex 11-13 cover three of its ceremonies, the Passover sacrifice, the feast of Unleavened Bread and the consecration of the first-born. The sacrificial meal was eaten, if not in the precincts of the Temple, at least within the boundaries of the city. The meal had three main components, the sacrificial meal itself, the Haggadah or Passover instruction, and the Hallel or songs of praise, usually the psalms. The intense religious atmosphere added to the general political awareness of the time and often resulted in revolutionary activity and heightened messianic expectation. It was a time for political activists and revolutionaries to play on that expectation and a time for the Roman authorities to take special precautions. It was a time when a Jewish king, a son of David, might appear.

The lambs were slaughtered on the eve of the Passover, the 14th Nissan and the Passover meal was celebrated that evening

---

47. Josh 5:10-12; 2 Kings 23:21-23 / / 2 Chron 35:1-18; Ezra 6:19-22.

as the new day, the 15th Nisan began at sunset. According to the synoptics Jesus was crucified on the 15th, the Feast of Passover and therefore his 'last supper' was a Passover meal. According to John he was crucified on the eve of the feast (the 14th), his death very significantly corresponding in time with the slaughter of the Paschal/Passover lambs. His 'last supper' according to John was not therefore the Passover meal, but a highly symbolic meal celebrated in the general context and atmosphere of the feast. Many volumes have been written to explain the difference in timing between the synoptics and John. No one theory has been universally accepted. The use of different calendars is one of the more common 'explanations'.

List of Abbreviations

ABD	Anchor Bible Dictionary, NY Doubleday, 1992
Ant	Josephus: *Antiquities of the Jews*
ATR	Anglican Theological Review
BA	The Biblical Archeologist
Bel	Josephus: *The Wars of the Jews*
Bib	Biblica
BVC	Bible et Vie Chrétienne
BZ	Biblische Zeitschrift
CBQ	Catholic Biblical Quarterly
CD	Damascus Document
CC	Corpus Christianorum
De Somn	Philo: *De Somniis*
De Agr	Philo: *De Agricultura*
ÉtB	Études Bibliques
HTR	Harvard Theological Review
IDB	*The Interpreter's Dictionary of the Bible*
JB	Jerusalem Bible
JBC	*Jerome Biblical Commentary*
JBL	Journal of Biblical Literature
JR	Journal of Religion
JSNT	Journal for the Study of the New Testament
JSOT	Journal for the Study of the Old Testament
JTS	Journal of Theological Studies
LumVie	Lumière et Vie
LXX	Septuagint
LSJ	*A Greek-English Lexicon* (ed. H. G. Liddel, R. Scott and H. S. Jones).
MT	Masoretic Text
NovT	Novum Testamentum
NRSV	New Revised Standard Version
NTA	New Testament Abstracts
NTS	New Testament Studies
OCD	Oxford Classical Dictionary
PG	Patrologia Graeca-Latina (Migne)
PIBA	Proceedings of the Irish Biblical Association.
PL	Patrologia Latina
1QH	Qumran Hymns (from cave I)
1QM	Qumran War Scroll (from cave I)
4QF	Qumran Florilegium (from cave 4)

4QT	Qumran Testimonia (from cave 4)
1QS	Qumran Manual of Discipline (from cave I)
1QSa	Qumran Manual of Discipline. Appendix
RB	Revue Biblique
REJ	Revue des Études Juives
SNT	Supplements to Novum Testamentum
StB	H. L. Strack and P. Billerbeck, *Kommentar zum Neuen Testamentum aus Talmud und Midrasch* (vols 1-5, Munich, Beck,1922-55)
TalBab	The Babylonian Talmud
TalJer	The Jerusalem Talmud
TDNT	*Theological Dictionary of the New Testament*, G. Kittel and G. Friedrick. Vols 1-10, Grand Rapids, Eerdmans, 1964-76.
TS	Theological Studies
ZNW	Zeitschrift für die neutestamentliche Wissenschaft

Rabbinic Literature Prefixes

m.	Mishnah
t.	Tosefta
j.	Jerusalem Talmud
b.	Babylonian Talmud

Bibliography

COMPREHENSIVE BIBLIOGRAPHIES

Humphrey, H. M., *Bibliography for the Gospel of Mark 1954-1980*, New York: Mellen, 1981.

Mills, W. E., *The Gospel of Mark*, Lewiston, New York: Mellen, 1994.

Moloney, F. J., *The Gospel of Mark: A Commentary*, Peabody, Mass: Hendrickson, 2002. Extensive Bibliography, 363-384.

Neirynck, F. et al., *The Gospel of Mark, A Cumulative Bibliography*, 1950-1990, Leuven: Leuven University Press / Peeters, 1992.

OVERVIEW OF STUDIES

Blevins, J., *The Messianic Secret in Markan Research, 1901-1976*, Washington D.C.: University Press of America,1981.

Bultmann, R., *History of the Synoptic Tradition*, New York: Harper & Row, 1963.

Catchpole, D. R., *The Trial of Jesus: A Study in the Gospels and Jewish Historiography from 1770 to the Present Day*, Leiden: Brill, 1971.

Frei, H. W., *The Eclipse of Biblical Narrative: A Study in Eighteenth and Nineteenth Century Hermeneutics*, New Haven: Yale University Press, 1974.

Kealy, S. P., *Mark's Gospel. A History of Its Interpretation from the Beginning until 1979*, New York: Paulist, 1982.

Matera, F. J., *What Are They Saying About Mark?* New York: Paulist, 1987.

Orton, D. E., (ed.), *The Composition of Mark's Gospel: Selected Studies from Novum Testamentum*, Leiden: Brill,1999.

Oyen, G. van., *De studie van de Marcusredactie in de twintigste Eeuw*, Leuven: Leuven University Press, 1993.

COMMENTARIES

English Language

Achtemeier, P. J., *Mark, Proclamation Commentary*, Philadelphia: Fortress, 1975.

Anderson, H., *The Gospel of Mark*, New Century Bible, London: Oliphants, 1976.

Branscomb, B. H., *The Gospel of Mark*, The Moffatt New Testament Commentary, London: Hodder and Stoughton, 1937.

Broadhead, E. K., *Mark, Readings: A New Biblical Commentary*, Sheffield, 2001.

Cranfield, C. E. B., *The Gospel according to St Mark*, Cambridge Greek New Testament Commentary, Cambridge, 1959, 4th ed. 1972.

Donahue, J. R. and D. J. Harrington, *The Gospel of Mark*, Sacra Pagina 2, The Liturgical Press, Michael Glazier, Collegeville, Minnesota, 2002.

Dowd, S., Reading *Mark: A Literary and Theological Commentary on the Second Gospel*, Reading the New Testament Series, Macon, 2000.

Evans, C. A., *Mark: 8:27-16:20*, World Biblical Commentary 34B, Nashville, 2001.

France, R. T., *The Gospel of Mark. A Commentary of the Greek Text*, New International Greek Testament Commentary, Grand Rapids, 2002.

Gould, E. P., *A Critical and Exegetical Commentary on the Gospel According to Mark*, ICC. 27, 3rd ed., New York, Scribner's, 1901

Guelich, R. A., *Mark 1-8:26*, World Biblical Commentary 34A, Dallas, 1989.

Gundry, R. H., *Mark. A Commentary on His Apology for the Cross*, Grand Rapids: Eerdmans, 1993.

Hare, D. R. A., *Mark*, Westminster Bible Companion, Louisville: Westminster, 1996.

Harrington, D. J., 'The Gospel According to Mark' in *New Jerome Biblical Commentary*, eds. R. E. Brown, J. A. Fitzmyer and R. E. Murphy, Englewood Cliffs, NJ: Prentice Hall, 1990, 596-629.

Harrington, W. J., *Mark*, New Testament Message 4., Dublin: Veritas, 1979, Wilmington, Del: MichaelGlazier, 1979, (Revised 1985).

Harrington, W. J., *Mark, Realistic Theologian. The Jesus of Mark*, The Columba Press, Dublin, 1996, 2002.

Hooker, M. D., *The Gospel According to St Mark*, Black's New Testament Commentary, Peabody, Mass: Hendrickson, 1991.

Hurtado, L., *Mark*, New International Bible Commentary 2, Peabody, Mass: Hendrickson, 1991.

Johnson, S., *A Commentary on the Gospel According to St Mark*, Black's/Harper's New Testament Commentary, 2nd ed., London, A&C Black, 1977.

Juel, D. H., *Mark,* Interpreting Biblical Texts, Nashville, Abingdon, 1999.

Lagrange, M. J., *The Gospel According to St Mark,* (trans. from French), London, Burns Oates and Washbourne, 1930.

Lane, W., *Commentary on the Gospel of Mark,* New International Commentary on the New Testament, Grand Rapids, Eerdmans, 1974.

La Verdiere, E., *The Beginning of the Gospel; Introducing the Gospel According to Mark,* 2 vols. Collegeville: The Liturgical Press, 1999.

Mann, C. S., *Mark,* Anchor Bible 27, Garden City, New York, Doubleday, 1986.

Marcus, J., *Mark 1-8. A New Translation with Introduction and Commentary,* Anchor Bible 27, New York, 2000.

Marxen, W., *Mark the Evangelist,* Nashville: Abingdon, 1969.

Moloney, F. J., *The Gospel of Mark: A Commentary,* Peabody, Mass: Hendrickson, 2002.

Moule, C. F. D., *The Gospel According to Mark,* Cambridge Bible Commentary on the New English Bible, Cambridge: Cambridge University Press, 1965.

Nineham, D. E., *Saint Mark,* Pelican Gospel Commentary, Harmondsworth, Penguin 1964.

Painter, J., *Mark's Gospel: Worlds in Conflict,* New Testament Readings, London: Routledge, 1997.

Perkins, P., 'Mark', *The New Interpreter's Bible* 8. Nashville, Abingdon, 1995, 507-733.

Schmidt, J., *The Gospel According to Mark,* The Regensburg New Testament, trans by K. Condon, Cork: Mercier Press, 1968.

Schweizer, E., *The Good News According to Mark,* Atlanta, John Knox, 1977, SPCK, London 1975.

Stock, A., *Call to Discipleship: A Literary Study of Mark's Gospel,* Good News Studies 1, Dublin: Veritas, 1982.

Stock, A., *The Method and Message of Mark,* Wilmington, DE: Michael Glazier, 1985

Swete, H. B., *The Gospel According to St Mark: The Greek Text with Introduction, Notes and Commentary,* 3rd, ed., London, Macmillan, 1966.

Taylor, V., *The Gospel According to St Mark,* 2nd ed., London: Macmillan, 1966.

Williamson, L., *Mark,* Interpretation, Atlanta:John Knox, 1983.

Witherington, B., *The Gospel of Mark, A Socio-Rhetorical Commentary,* Grand Rapids: Eerdmans, 2001.

French Language

Cuvillier, E., *L'évangile de Marc*, La Bible en face, Paris-Genève 2002.

Delorme, J., *Lecture de l'évangile selon Marc*, Cahiers Évangile 1-2 Paris, 1972.

Drewermann, E., *La parole et l'angoisse. Commentaire de l'Évangile de Marc*, (trad), Paris, 1995.

Focant, C., *L'Évangile selon Marc*, Commentaire biblique: NT 2, Paris, 2004.

Lagrange, M. J., *Évangile selon St Marc*, Études bibliques, Paris, Gabalda, 1929; 6th ed. Études Bibliques, Paris, 1942; Eng Trans London, 1930.

Lamarche, P., *Évangile de Marc*, ÉtB. 33, Paris,1996.

Légasse, S., *L'Évangile de Marc*, Lectio Divina, Commentaires 5, 2 vols, Paris, Cerf 1997; Italian Trans. ediz. Borla, Roma, 2000.

Loisy, A., *L'Évangile selon Marc*, Paris, 1912.

Radermakers, J., *La bonne nouvelle de Jésus selon saint Marc*, 2 vols, Bruxelles, 1974.

Standaert, B., *L'Évangile selon Marc*, Paris, Cerf, 1997.

Trocmé, E., *L'Évangile selon Saint Marc*, Commentaire du Nouveau Testament 2., Paris: Labor et Fides, 2000.

German Language

Eckey, W., *Das Markusevangelium. Orientierung am Weg Jesu. Ein Kommentar*, Neukirchen, 1998.

Ernst, J, *Das Evangelium nach Markus*, Regensburger Neues Testament, Regensburg: Pustet Verlag, 1981.

Ernst, J., *Markus: Ein theologisches Portrait*, Patmos Verlag, Düsseldorf, 1987.

Gnilka, J., *Das Evangelium nach Markus*. Evangelisch-katholischer Kommentar zum Neuen Testament 2, Zurich, Neukirchen-Vluyn: Benziger Verlag/Neukirchener Verlag 1998.

Grundmann, W., *Das Evangelium nach Markus*, Theologischer Handkommentar zum Neuen Testament 2, Berlin: Evangelische Verlagsanstalt, 1973.

Haenchen, E., *Der Weg Jesu, Eine Erklärung des Markus-Evangeliums und der kanonischen Parallelen*, Berlin: Walter de Gruyter, 2nd ed., 1968.

Kertledge, K., *Markusevangelium*, Die Neue Echter Bibel. NT 2, Wûrzburg; Echter, 1994.

Klostermann E., *Das Markusevangelium*, Handbuch zum Neuen Testament 3, Tübingen, 1971, 5th ed.,

Lohmeyer, Ernst, *Das Evangelium nach Markus*, Kritisch-exegetis-cher Kommentar 2, 17th ed, Göttingen: Vandenhoeck & Ruprecht, 1967.

Lührmann, D., *Das Markusevangelium*, Handbuch zum Neuen Testament 3, Tübingen: J. C. B. Mohr (Paul Siebeck), 1987.

Pesch, R., *Das Markusevangelium*, 2 vols, Herders theologischer Kommentar zum Neuen Testament, 2, Freiburg: Herder, 1976.

Schmithals, W., *Das Evangelium nach Markus*, Ôkumenischer Taschenbuchkommentar zum Neuen Testament, 2 vols., Gütersloh, 1986.

Wellhausen, J., *Das Evangelium Marci*, Berlin, 1909, 2nd ed

Italian Language

Stock, K. SJ., *Marco: Commento contestuale al secondo Vangelo*, Bibbia e Preghiera, 47, Roma: Edizioni ADP, 2003.

LITERARY AND REDACTIONAL CRITICAL STUDIES

Alter, R., *The Art of Biblical Narrative*, New York: Basic Books, 1981.

Andersen, J. and S. Moore, *Mark and Method*, Minneapolis: Fortress, 1992.

Best, E., *Mark–The Gospel as Story, Studies of the New Testament and its World*, Edinburgh: T and T Clark, 1983

Bilezikian, G., *The Liberated Gospel: A Comparison between the Gospel of Mark and Greek Tragedy*, Grand Rapids: Baker, 1977.

Bonneau, G., *Stratégies rédactionnelles et functions communautaires dans l'évangile de Marc*, Études bibliques, Paris, 2001.

Bornkamm, G., 'The Stilling of the Storm in Matthew' in G. Bornkamm, G. Barth and H. J. Held, *Tradition and Interpretation in Matthew*, Philadelphia; Westminster / London, SCM, 1963.

Borrell, A., *The Good News of Peter's Denial. A Narrative and Rhetorical Reading of Mark 14:54, 66-72*, trans S. Conlon, Univ. of South Florida International Studies in Formative Christianity and Judaism, Atlanta: Scholars Press, 1998.

Brodie, T. L., *The Crucial Bridge. The Elijah-Elisha Narrative as Interpretative Synthesis of Genesis-Kings and a Literary Model for the Gospels*, Collegeville: The Liturgical Press, 2000.

Bultmann, R., *History of the Synoptic Tradition*, trans John Marsh, Oxford: Basil Blackwell, 1968.

Camery-Hoggatt, J., *Irony in Mark's Gospel. Text and Subtext*, Cambridge and New York; Cambridge University Press, 1992.

Collins, A. Y., *Is Mark's Gospel a Life of Jesus? The Question of Genre*, Milwaukee, 1990.

Collins, A. Y., *The Beginning of the Gospel. Probings of Mark in Context*, Minneapolis: Fortress Press, 1992.

Cook, J. G., *The Structure and Persuasive Power of Mark. A Linguistic Approach*, Atlanta,Scholars, 1995.

Davidson, O., *The Narrative Jesus. A Semiotic reading of Mark's Gospel*, Aarhus:Aarhus University Press, 1993.

Dewey, J., 'Mark as interwoven tapestry: Forecasts and Echoes for a Listening Audience ,' *CBQ* 53 (1991), 221-36.

Dewey, J., *Markan Public Debate:Literary Technique, Concentric Structure, and Theology in Mark 2:1-3:6*, Society of Biblical Literature Dissertation Series 48, Chico: Scholars Press 1980.

Donahue, J. R., *The Gospel in Parable. Metaphor,Narrative and Theology in the Synoptic Gospels*, Philadelphia, Fortress, 1988.

Dormeyer, D., *Das Markusevangelium als Idealbiographie von Jesus Christus, dem Nazarener*, Stuttgarter biblische Beiträge, Stuttgart, 1999.

Dowd, S., *Reading Mark. A Literary and Theological Commentary on the Second Gospel*, Macon: Smith & Helwys, 2000.

Edwards, J. R., 'Markan Sandwiches: The Significance of Interpolations in Markan Narratives.' *Novum Testamentum* 31 (1989), 193-216.

Freund, E., *The Return of the Reader: Reader Response Criticism*. New Accents. London: Methuen, 1987.

Horsely, R. A., *Hearing the Whole Story: The Politics of Plot in Mark's Gospel*, Louisville: Westminster John Knox, 2001.

Iersel, B. M. F. van, *Reading Mark*, Collegeville, The Liturgical Press, 1988.

Juel, D. H., *A Master of Surprise. Mark Interpreted*. Minneapolis: Fortress, 1994.

Kermode, F., *The Genesis of Secrecy. On the Interpretation of Narrative*, Cambridge, Mass and London: Harvard University Press 1979.

Kingsbury, J. D., *Conflict in Mark*, Minneapolis: Fortress, 1989.

Maher, S. J. K., *An Investigation of the Gospel Genre with Special Reference to Mark's Prologue*, Unpublished Research Material, Pontifical Irish College, Rome.

MacDonald, D. R., *The Homeric Epics and the Gospel of Mark*,New Haven and London: Yale University Press, 2000.

Malbon, E. S., *In the Company of Jesus. Characters in Mark's Gospel*, Louisville: Westminster John Knox, 2000.

Malbon, E. S., *Narrative Space and Mythic Meaning in Mark*, San Francisco: Harper &Row, 1986.

Meagher, J. C., *Clumsy Construction in Mark's Gospel: A Critique of Form-and Redaktionsgeshichte*, New York and Toronto: Mellen, 1979.

Neirynck, F., *Duality in Mark: Contributions to the Study of the Markan Redaction*, Leuven: Leuven University Press,1972.

O'Connell, S., 'Towards the First Gospel. Redactional Development in the Gospel of Mark', *PIBA*, 26 (2003), 66-88.

Perrin,N., 'Historical Criticism, Literary Criticism, and Hermeneutics: The Interpretation of the Parables of Jesus and the Gospel of Mark Today,' *JR* 52 (1972) 361-75.

Pryke, E. J., *Redactional Style in the Markan Gospel: A Study of Syntax and Vocabulary as Guides to Redaction in Mark*, Cambridge, Cambridge University Press,1978.

Stock, A., *Call to Discipleship, A Literary Study of Mark's Gospel*, Good News Studies I, Dublin, Veritas 1982.

Rhoads, D., J. Dewey and D. Michie, *Mark as Story: An Introduction to the Narrative of the Gospel*, 2nd. ed. Minneapolis: Fortress, 1999.

Schneiders, S. M., *The Revelatory Text. Interpreting the New Testament as Sacred Scripture*, San Francisco:Harper, 1991.

Tolbert, M. A., *Sowing the Gospel: Mark's World in Literary-Historical Perspective*, Minneapolis: Fortress, 1989.

Witherington III, B., *The Gospel of Mark. A Socio-Rhetorical Commentary*, Grand Rapids, 2001.

GENERAL

Abrahams, I., 'The Greatest Commandment' in *Studies in Pharisaisam and the Gospels*, First Series, Cambridge: Cambridge University Press, 1917.

Achtemeier, P. J., 'Toward the isolation of pre-Markan miracle catenae' in *JBL* 89 (1970), 265-91.

Ahearne-Kroll, S. P., 'Who are My Mother and My Brothers? Family Relations and Family Language in the Gospel of Mark', *JR* (2001) 1-25.

Ambrozic, A. M., *The Hidden Kingdom: A Redaction-Critical Study of the References to the Kingdom of God in Mark's Gospel*, Washington DC: Catholic Biblical Association,1972.

Balabanski, V., *Eschatology in the Making: Mark, Matthew and the Didache*, SNTS Monograph Series 97, Cambridge, Cambridge University Press, 1997.

Bammel, E., ' The Trial before Pilate', in *Jesus and the Politics of His Day*, ed. E. Bammel and C. F. D. Moule.

Bammel, E., (ed.), *The Trial of Jesus*, Cambridge Studies in Honour of C. F. D. Moule, Studies in Biblical Theology, Second Series 13, SCM Press, London, 1970.

Bammel, E., 'Crucifixion as a Punishment in Palestine,' in E. Bammel (ed), *The Trial of Jesus*, 162-165.

Barrett, C. K., 'The background of Mark 10:45', *New Testament Essays in Memory of T. W. Manson*, ed. A. J. B. Higgins, Manchester: Manchester University Press, 1959.

Barton, C. S., 'Mark as Narrative. The Story of the Anointing Woman (Mk 14:3-9),' *ExpTim* 102 (1991) 230-34.

Bauckham, R., 'The Brothers and Sisters of Jesus: An Epiphanian Response', *CBQ* (1994) 686-7000.

Baudoz, J-F., *Les Miettes de la table. Étude synoptique et socio-religieuse de Mt 15:21-28 et Mc 7:24-30*, Paris: Gabalda, 1995.

Bayer, H. F., *Jesus' Predictions of Vindication and Resurrection*, Tübingen, J. C. B. Mohr (Paul Siebeck), 1986.

Beasley-Murray, G. R., *Jesus and the Last Days: The Interpretation of the Olivet Discourse*, Peabody: Hendrickson, 1993.

Beavis, M. A., 'From the Margin to the Way: A Feminist Reading of the Story of Bartimaeus', *Journal of Feminist Studies in Religion*, 14 (1998), 19-39

Best, E., 'The Role of the Disciples in Mark,' *New Testament Studies* 23 (1976-1977), 377-401.

Best, E., *Following Jesus. Discipleship in the Gospel of Mark*, Sheffield: JSOT Press, 1981.

Best, E., *Disciples and Discipleship: Studies in the Gospel According to Mark*, Edinburgh: T & T Clark,1986.

Best, E., *The Temptation and the Passion: the Markan Soteriology*, 2nd ed., Cambridge, Cambridge University Press,1990.

Betz, H. D., *Nachfolge und Nachahmung Jesu Christi im Neuen Testament*, Beiträge zur historischen Theologie 39, Tübingen: J. C. B. Mohr (Paul Siebeck),1967.

Black, C. C., *The Disciples according to Mark: Markan Redaction in Current Debate*, Journal for the Study of the New Testament: Supplement Series 27. Sheffield: Sheffield Academic Press, 1989.

Black, C. C., 'Was Mark a Roman Gospel?' *The Expository Times* 105 (1993-1994) 36-40.

Black, M., *An Aramaic Approach to the Gospels and Acts*, Oxford, 3rd ed., 1967.

Blackburn, B., *Theios Aner and the Markan Miracle Traditions*, Tübingen: J. C. B. Mohr (Paul Siebeck), 1991.

Blinzer, J., *The Trial of Jesus. The Jewish and Roman Proceedings Against Jesus Christ Described and Assessed from the Oldest Accounts*, Westminster, Md: Newman,1959.

Bond, H. K., *Pontius Pilate in History and Interpretation*, Cambridge and New York: Cambridge University Press, 1998.

Boobyer, G. H., *St Mark and the Transfiguration Story*, Edinburgh, 1942.

Booth, R. P., *Jesus and the Laws of Purity: Tradition History and Legal History in Mark 7*, JSNTSS 13. Sheffield: JSOT Press,1986.

Böttrich, C., 'Jesus und der Feigenbaum. Mk 11:12-14,20-25 in der Diskussion,' *NovT* 39 (1997) 328-59.

Boring, M. E, 'Mark 1:1-15 and the beginning of the Gospel', *Semeia* 52 (1990), 43-81.

Borrell, A., *The Good News of Peter's Denial. A Narrative and Rhetorical Reading of Mark 14:54, 66-72*, Atlanta: Scholars, 1998.

Boucher, M. I., *The Mysterious Parable. A Literary Study*, Washington DC: Catholic Biblical Association 1977.

Brandon, S., *The Trial of Jesus of Nazareth*, London: Paladin, 1968.

Broadhead, E. K., *Teaching with Authority. Miracles and Christology in the Gospel of Mark*, Sheffield: JSOT Press,1992.

Broadhead, E. K., *Prophet, Son, Messiah. Narrative Forms and Function in Mark 14-16*, Sheffield: JSOT Press,1994.

Broadhead, E. K., *Naming Jesus: Titular Christology in the Gospel of Mark*, JSNT: Supplement Series 175. Sheffield: Sheffield Academic Press, 1999.

Brown, R. E., *The Death of the Messiah: From Gethsemane to the Grave. A Commentary on the Passion Narratives in the Four Gospels*, New York, Doubleday, 1994.

Brown, R. E., *A Crucified Christ in Holy Week, Essays on the Four Gospel Passion Narratives*, Collegeville, Minn: The Liturgical Press, 1986.

Brown, R. E., *The Birth of the Messiah: A Commentary on the Infancy Narrative of Matthew and Luke*, New York: Doubleday 1977.

Casey, M., 'The Original Aramaic Form of Jesus' Interpretation of the Cup,' *JTS* 41 (1990) 1-12.

Casey, M., *Son of Man: The Interpretation and Influence of Daniel 7*, London: SPCK, 1979.

Charlesworth, J. H., (ed), *The Messiah: Developments in Earliest Judaism and Christianity*, The First Princeton Symposium on Judaism and Christian Origins, Minneapolis: Fortress, 1992.

Claudel, G., *La confession de Pierre, trajectoire d'une péricope évangelique*, Paris: Gabalda, 1988.

Collins, A. Y., 'Mark and His Readers: The Son of God Among Greeks and Romans', *HTR* 93(2000) 85-100.

Collins, A. Y., 'The Composition of the Passion Narrative in Mark,' *Sewanee Theological Review* 36 (1992) 57-77.

Collins, A. Y.,'The Genre of the Passion Narrative,' *Studia Theologica* 47 (1993) 3-28.

Collins, A. Y., *The Beginning of the Gospel: Probings of Mark in Context*, Minneapolis: Fortress 1992.

Collins, A. Y., 'The Signification of Mark 10:45 among Gentile Christians', *HTR* 90(1997) 371-82.

Collins, A. Y., 'The Apocalyptic Rhetoric of Mark 13 in Historical Context,' *Biblical Research* 41 (1996) 5-36.

Collins, F., *Divorce in the New Testament*, Collegeville: The Liturgical Press, 1992

Collins, J. J., *The Sceptre and the Star: The Messiahs of the Dead Sea Scrolls and Other Ancient Literature*, ABRL; New York: Doubleday, 1995

Collins, J. J., ' The Nature of Messianism in the Light of the Dead Sea Scrolls' in *The Dead Sea Scrolls in their Historical Context*, (eds, T. H. Lim, L. W. Hurtado, A. Graeme Auld, and Alison Jack); Edinburgh: T&T Clark, 2000. 199-219.

Collins, R. F., *Sexual Ethics and the New Testament: Behaviour and Belief*, New York: Crossroads, 2000.

Corley, K. E., 'Women and the Crucifixion and Burial of Jesus. "He Was Buried: On the Third Day He was Raised,"' *Forum* 1 (1998) 181-225.

Cotter, W. J., 'For it was not the Season for Figs,' *CBQ* 48 (1986), 62-66.

Crossan, J. D., *In Parables. The Challenge of the Historical Jesus*,New York: Harper & Row, 1973.

Cuvillier, E., *Le Concept de PARABOLE Dans le Second Évangile*, Paris: Gabalda,1993.

Dahl, N. A., *The Crucified Messiah and Other Essays*, Minneapolis: Augsburg,1974, 10-36.

Dahl, N. A., *Jesus in the Memory of the Early Church*, Minneapolis: Augsburg, 1976.

Danove, P. L., 'The Characterisation and Narrative Function of the Women at the Tomb (Mark 15:40-41;16:1-8),' *Bib* 77 (1996) 375-97.

Daube, D., *The New Testament and Rabbinic Judaism*, London: Athlone, 1956; Peabody: Hendrickson 1994.

Dawson, A., *Freedom as Liberating Power. A socio-political reading of the exousia texts in the Gospel of Mark*, Fribourg: Universitätsverlag, 2000.

Derrett, J. D. M., 'Eating Up the Houses of Widows: Jesus Comment on Lawyers.' *NovT* 14 (1972) 1-9.

Dibelius, M., *From Tradition to Gospel*, trans B. L. Woolf, Library of Theological Translations, Cambridge and London: James Clarke, 1971.

Dillon, R. J., 'As One Having Authority (Mk 1:22): The Controversial Distinction of Jesus' Teaching', *CBQ* 57 (1995), 92-113.

Dodd, C. H., *The Parables of the Kingdom*, London: Collins 1936; New York: Scribner's, 1965.

Donahue, J. R., *The Gospel in Parable. Metaphor, Narrative, and Theology in the Synoptic Gospels*, Minneapolis: Fortress, 1990.

Donahue, J. R., 'Jesus as the Parable of God in the Gospel of Mark', *Int* 32 (1978) 369-86.

Donahue, J. R., 'A Neglected Factor in the Theology of Mark', *JBL*, 101 (1982), 563-94.

Donahue, J. R., *Are You the Christ? The Trial Narrative in the Gospel of Mark*, Society of Biblical Literature Dissertation Series 10, Missoula, Society of Biblical Literature, 1973.

Donahue, J. R., *The Theology and Setting of Discipleship in the Gospel of Mark*, Milwaukee: Marquette University Press, 1983.

Donaldson, J., '"Called to Follow," A Twofold Experience of Discipleship', *Biblical Theology Bulletin* 5 (1975), 67-77.

Dormeyer, D., 'Mk 1:1-15 als Prolog des ersten Ideal-biographischen Evangeliums von Jesus Christus', *Biblical Interpretation* 5 (1997) 181-211.

Draper, J. A., 'Wandering radicalism or purposeful activity? Jesus and the sending of messengers in Mark 6:6-56', *Neotestamentica* 29 (1995) 183-202.

Drury, J., *The Parables in the Gospels*, New York: Crossroads, 1985.

Drury, J., 'The Sower, the Vineyard and the Place of Allegory in the Interpretation of Mark's Parables,' *JTS* 24 (1973) 367-79.

Duff, P. B., 'The March of the Divine Warrior and the Advent of the Graeco-Roman King. Mark's account of Jesus' Entry into Jerusalem', *JBL* 111 (1992), 55-71.

Dunn, J. G. D., *Jesus and the Spirit: A Study of the Religious and Charismatic Experience of Jesus and the First Christians As Reflected in the New Testament*, London: SCM Press, 1975.

Dyer, K. D., *The Prophecy on the Mount: Mark 13 and the Gathering of the New Community*, ITS 2, Bern: Peter Lang, 1998.

Eckstein, H-J., 'Markus 10:46-52 als Schlüsseltext des Markusevangeliums,' *ZNW* 87 (1996) 33-50.

Enste, S., *Kein Markustext in Qumran: Eine Unterschung der These: Qumran-Fragment 7Q5=Mk 6:52-53*, Göttingen: Vandenhoeck & Ruprecht, 1999.

Evans, C. A., 'Jesus and the "Cave of Robbers": Toward a Jewish Context for the Temple Action,' *Bulletin of Biblical Research* 3 (1993) 93-110.

Fischer, G., and M. Hasitschka, *The Call of the Disciple. The Bible on Following Christ*, New York: Paulist, 1999.

Fitzmyer, J. A.,' Crucifixion in Ancient Palestine, Qumran Literature, and the New Testament,' *CBQ* 40 (1979) 493-513.

Fleddermann, H. T., 'A Warning about the Scribes (Mark 12:37b-40),' *CBQ* 44 (1982) 52-67.

Focant, C., 'Le rapport à la loi dans l'évangile de Marc,' *RTL* 27 (1996), 281-308.

Freyne, S., *The Twelve: Disciples and Apostles. A Study in the Theology of the First Three Gospels*, London: Sheed and Ward, 1969.

Fuller, R. H., *Interpreting the Miracles*, London 1963

Furnish, V. P., *The Love Command in the New Testament*, Nashville: Abingdon, 1972.

Gager, J. G., 'Religion and Social Class in the Early Roman Empire,' in *The Catacombs and the Colosseum*, ed. S. Benko and J. J. O'Rourk, Valley Forge, Pa: Judson, 1971.

Gaston, L., *No Stone on Another: Studies in the significance of the Fall of Jerusalem in the Synoptic Gospels*, NovT Sup 23, Leiden: 1970.

Geddert, T. J., *Watchwords: Mark 13 in Markan Eschatology*, Sheffield: JSOT Press, 1989.

Genest, O., *Le Christ de la Passion: Perspective Structurale. Analyse de Marc 14:53-15:47 des parallèles bibliques et extra-bibliques*, Recherches 21 Théologie. Tournai/Montreal: Desclée/Bellarmin,1978.

Geyer, D. W., *Fear, Anomaly and Uncertainty in the Gospel of Mark*, ATLA Monograph Series, No 47, The Scarecrow Press Inc., Lanham, Maryland and London, 2002.

Gibson, J. B., 'The Rebuke of the Disciples in Mark 8:14-21.' *JSNT* (1986), 31-47.

Giblin, C. H., 'The "Things of God" in the Question Concerning Tribute to Caesar (Lk 20:25; Mk 12:17; Mt 22:21),' *CBQ* 33 (1971) 510-27.

Glasswell, M. E.,'The use of miracles in the Markan gospel', in *Miracles*, ed. C. F. D. Moule, London,1965, 51-62.

Grassi, J. A., *The Hidden Heroes of the Gospels: Female Counterparts of Jesus*, Collegeville: Liturgical Press, 1989.

Grassi, J. A., *Loaves and Fishes: The Gospel Feeding Narratives*, Collegeville: The Liturgical Press, 1991.

Gundry, R. H., *Mark. A Commentary on his Apology for the Cross*, Grand Rapids: Eerdmans, 1993, 2000.

Hagedorn, A. C. and J. H. Neyrey, '"It Was Out of Envy that They Handed Jesus Over" (Mark 15:10): The Anatomy of Envy and the Gospel of Mark ,' *JSNT* 69 (1998) 15-56.

Hare, D. R. A., *The Son of Man Tradition*, Minneapolis:Fortress Press,1990

Haren, M. J., 'The Naked Young Man: A Historian's Hypothesis on Mark 14:51-52,' *Bib* 79 (1998) 525-31.

Hay, D. M., *Glory at the Right Hand. Psalm 110 in Early Christianity*, SBLMS 18, Nashville: Abingdon, 1973.

Hedrick, C. W., 'On Moving Mountains. Mark 11:22b-23/Matt 21:21 and Parallels,' *Forum* 6 (1990) 219-37.

Heil, J. P., *Jesus Walking on the Sea. Meaning and Gospel Functions of Matt 14:22-33, Mark 6:45-52 and John 6:15b-21*, Rome: Biblical Institute Press, 1981

Heil, J. P., 'A Note on "Elijah with Moses" in Mark 9:4', *Bib* 80 (1999) 115.

Heil, J. P., *The Transfiguration of Jesus: Narrative Meaning and Function of Mark 9:2-8, Matt 17:1-8 and Luke 9:28-36*, Rome: Biblical Institute Press, 2000.

Hengel, M., *Studies in the Gospel of Mark*, London, SCM Press, 1985, 14-28.

Hengel, M., *Crucifixion in the Ancient World and the Folly of the Message of the Cross*, Philadelphia: Fortress, 1977.

Hooker, M. D., *Jesus and the Servant: The Influence of the Servant Concept of Deutero-Isaiah in the New Testament*, London: SPCK, 1959.

Hooker, M. D., *The Son of Man in Mark: A Study of the Background of the Term 'Son of Man' and Its Use in St Mark's Gospel*, London: SPCK, 1967.

Horsley, R. A. and J. H. Hanson, *Bandits, Prophets and Messiahs. Popular Movements at the Time of Jesus*, San Francisco: Harper and Row, 1985.

Hull, J. M., *Hellenistic Magic and the Synoptic Tradition*, London, 1974.

Hunter, Faith and Geoffrey, ' Which is Easier? (Mk 2:9)', *ExpT* 105 (1993).

Iwe, J. C., *Jesus in the Synagogue of Capernaum: The Pericope and its programmatic character for the Gospel of Mark, An Exegetical-Theological Study of Mk 1:21-28*, Rome: PUG, 1994.

Jackson, H. M., 'Why the Youth Shed His Cloak and Fled Naked: The Meaning and Purpose of Mark 14:51-52,' *JBL* 116 (1997) 273-89.

Jeremias, J., *Jerusalem in the Time of Jesus. An Investigation into Economic and Social Conditions during the New Testament Period*, London: SCM Press, 1969.

Jeremias, J., *The Eucharistic Words of Jesus*, London: SCM Press, 1966.

Jeremias, J., *The Parables of Jesus*, London: SCM Press, 1963. New York: Scribner's, 1963; revised edition, SCM Press, 1972.

Johnson, E. S., 'Mark 15:39 and the So-Called Confession of the Roman Centurion,' *Bib* 81 (2000) 406-13.

Johnson, S. R., 'The Identity and Significance of the *Neaniskos* in Mark,' *Forum* 8 (1992) 123-39.

Juel, D. H., *Messiah and Temple: The Trial of Jesus in the Gospel of Mark*, SBLDS 31, Missoula: Scholars 1973.

Kelber, W. (ed.), *The Passion in Mark: Studies on Mark 14-16*, Philadelphia, Fortress,1976.

Kelber. W., *The Kingdom in Mark: A New Place and a New Time*, Philadelphia: Fortress, 1974.

Kingsbury, J. D., *The Christology of Mark's Gospel*, Philadelphia, Fortress,1983.

Kinukawa, Hisako, *Women and Jesus in Mark: A Japanese Feminist Perspective*, Maryknoll, N.Y., Orbis 1994.

Kinukawa, Hisako, 'The Story of the Hemorrhaging Woman (Mark 5:25-34) read from a Japanese Feminist Context,' *Biblical Interpretation* 2 (1994) 283-93.

Lindars, B., *New Testament Apologetic,: The Doctrinal Significance of the Old Testament Quotations*, London: SCM Press, 1961.

Lindars, B., 'Salvation Proclaimed. VII. Mark 10:45: A Ransom for Many', *ExpT* 93 (1981-82), 292-95.

Lindars, B., *Jesus Son of Man: A Fresh Examination of the Son of Man Sayings in the Gospels*, London: SPCK,1983.

Loader, W. R. G., 'Christ at the Right Hand. Ps CX.1 in the New Testament', *NTS* 21 (1974-1975) 81-108.

Lohse, E., *History of the Suffering and Death of Jesus Christ*, Philadelphia: Fortress, 1967.

Main, E., 'Les Sadducéens et la resurrection des morts: comparaison entre Mc 12:18-27 et Luc 27-37,' *RB* 103 (1996) 411-32.

Malina, B. J., *The New Testament World. Insights from Cultural Anthropology*, Louisville, Ky: W / JKP 2001.

Malina, B. J., *The Social History of Jesus. The Kingdom of God in Mediterranean Perspective,* Min: Fortress, 2001.

Mallon, E. S., 'The Poor Widow in Mark and Her Poor Rich Readers,' *CBQ* 53 (1991) 589-604..

Manek, J., 'Fishers of Men.' *Novum Testamentum*, 2 (1957-58),138-41

Manson, T. W., *The Sayings of Jesus*, London, 1949,

Manson, T. W., *The Teaching of Jesus*, Cambridge: Cambridge University Press, 1967.

Marcus, J., ' The Jewish War and the Sitz im Leben of Mark,' *JBL* 111 (1992),446-48.

Marcus, J., *The Mystery of the Kingdom of God*, SBLDS 90, Atlanta: Scholars Press, 1986.

Matera, F. J., 'The Prologue of Mark's Gospel',in *JSNT* 34, 1988.

Matera, F. J., *Passion Narratives and Gospel Theologies: Interpreting the Synoptics Through Their Passion Stories*, Theological Inquiries, New York: Paulist Press, 1986.

McEleney, N. J., 'Peter's Denials – How Many? To Whom?' *CBQ* 52 (1990) 467-72.

McGing, B. C., 'Pontius Pilate and the Sources,' *CBQ* 53 (1991) 416-38.

McKinnis, R., 'An Analysis of Mark X 32-34', *NovT*, 18(1976), 81-100.

Meier, J. P., *A Marginal Jew: Rethinking the Historical Jesus*, 3 vols. New York: Doubleday, 1991, 1994, 2001.

Meier, J. P., 'The Brothers and Sisters of Jesus in Ecumenical Perspective', *CBQ* 54 (1992) 1-28.

Meier, J. P., 'The Debate on the Resurrection of the Dead: An Incident from the Ministry of the Historical Jesus?' *JSNT* 77 (2000) 3-24.

Milavec, A., 'The Identity of the " Son" and "the Others": Mark's Parable of the Wicked Husbandmen Reconsidered,' *BTB* 20 (1990) 30-37.

Mullins, M., *Called To Be Saints: Christian Living in First Century Rome*, Dublin: Veritas, 1991.

Mullins, M., *The Gospel of John, A Commentary*, Dublin: The Columba Press, 2003.

Murphy-O'Connor, J., 'Fishers of Fish, Fishers of Men', *BR* 15/3 (1999).

Murphy-O'Connor, J., 'What Really happened at the Transfiguration?', *Bible Review*, 3/3, (1987) 8-21.

Murphy-O'Connor, J., 'What Really Happened at Gethsemane?' *Bible Review* 14/2 (1998) 28-39, 52.

Murphy-O'Connor, J., 'Jesus and the Money Changers (Mark 11:15-17; John 2:13-17),' *RB* 107 (2000) 42-55.

Nickelsburg, G. W. E., *Resurrection, Immortality, and Eternal Life in Intertestamental Judaism*, Cambridge, Mass: Harvard University Press, 1972.

O'Connell, S., 'Towards the First Gospel', *PIBA*, 26 (2003), 66-87.

O'Connell, S., *Don't you care if we perish? Unpublished Notes*, Maynooth: St Patrick's College, 2004. Used by permission.

O'Neill, J. C., '"Good Master" and the 'Good' Sayings in the Teaching of Jesus', *Irish Biblical Studies* 15 (1993).

O'Rourke, J. J.,'Roman Law and the Early Church',in *The Catacombs and the Colosseum*, ed. S. Benko and J. J. O'Rourke, Valley Forge, Pa: Judson, 1971.

Ossom-Batsa, G., *The Institution of the Eucharist in the Gospel of Mark*, Bern-Frankfurt: Lang, 2001.

Osiek, C., *What are they saying about the social setting of the New Testament?* New York: Paulist 1992, 33f.

Parker, H. M. D., 'Legio', *OCD*, 492f.

Perkins, P., *Love Commands in the New Testament*, New York: Paulist, 1982

Perrin, N., 'The Christology of Mark,' *JR* 51 (1971) 173-87.

Perrin, N., 'The Creative Use of the Son of Man Traditions by Mark,' *USQR* 23 (1968), 357-65.

Perrin, N., *A Modern Pilgrimage in New Testament Christology*, Philadelphia: Fortress, 1974.

Quesnell, Q., *The Mind of Mark*, Rome: PIB, 1969.

Rhoads, D., 'Losing Life for Others: Mark's Standards of Judgement,' *Int* 47 (1993) 358-369.

Richardson, A., *The Miracle-Stories of the Gospels*, London 1941.

Riesenfeld, H., *The Gospel Tradition*, Philadelphia, Fortress Press, 1970.

Rohrbaugh, R., (ed), *The Social Sciences and New Testament Interpretation*, Peabody: Hendrickson, 1996.

Rose, H. J., 'Centurio', *OCD*, 180.

Sabbe, M., 'John 10 and its Relationship to the Synoptic Gospels', in *The Shepherd Discourse of John 10 and its Context*, ed. G. N. Stanton, SNTS, Monograph Series, Cambridge University Press, 1991.

Schams, C., *Jewish Scribes in the Second-Temple Period*, Sheffield: Academic Press 1998.

Schenk,W., *Der Passionsbericht nach Markus: Untersuchungen z.Überlieferungsgeschichte d. Passionstraditionen*, Gütersloh: Gerd Mohn, 1974.

Schnackenburg, R., *The Gospel According to Mark for Spiritual Reading*, London,: Sheed and Ward, 1971.

Schmidt, T. E., 'Mark 15:16-32: The Crucifixion Narrative and the Roman Triumphal Procession,' *NTS* 41 (1995) 1-18

Schrage, W., *The Ethics of the New Testament*, Edinburgh: T& T Clark, 1988.

Scott, B. B., *Jesus, Symbol-Maker for the Kingdom*, Philadelphia: Fortress,1981.

Seely, D., 'Rulership and Service in Mark 10:41-45,' *NovT* 35 (1993), 234-50.

Seely, D., 'Jesus' Temple Act,' *CBQ* 55 (1993) 263-83.

Selvidge, M. J., *Woman, Cult and Miracle Recital. A Redactional Critical Investgation on Mark 5:24-34*, Lewisburg,NJ: Bucknell University Press, 1990.

Senior, D., *The Passion of Jesus in the Gospel of Mark*, Wilmington, Delaware: Michael Glazier, 1984.

Sherwin-White, A. N., *Roman Society and Roman Law in the New Testament*, Oxford: Clarendon Press, 1963.

Shiner, T. W., 'The Ambiguous Pronouncement of the Centurion and the Shrouding of Meaning in Mark,' *JSNT* 78 (2000) 3-22.

Shiner, W. T., *Follow Me! Disciples in Markan Rhetoric*, SBLDS 145, Atlanta: Scholars,1995.

Sloyan, G. S., *Jesus on Trial. The Development of the Passion Narratives and Their Historical and Ecumenical Implications*, Philadelphia: Fortress, 1973.

Smith, D. B., 'The More Original Form of the Words of Institution,' *ZNW* 83 (1992) 166-86.

Snodgrass, K., 'Recent Research on the Parable of the Wicked Tenants: An Assessment,' *Bulletin of Biblical Research* 8 (1998) 187-215.

Such, W. A., *The Abomination of Desolation in the Gospel of Mark: Its Historical Reference in Mark 13:14 and Its Impact in the Gospel*, Lanham: University of America Press, 1999.

Sugirtharajah, R. S.,' The Widow's Mites Revalued,' *Exp Times* 103 (1991) 42-43.

Sweetland, D. M., *Our Journey with Jesus: Discipleship according to Mark*, Collegeville: The Liturgical Press, 1987.

Tannehill, R. C., 'The Disciples in Mark: The Function of a Narrative Role,' *JR* 57 (1977) 386-405.

Taylor, N. H., 'Palestinian Christianity and the Caligula Crisis', Part 1, *JSNT* 61 (1996) 101-24; Part 2, *JSNT* 62 (1996) 13-41.

Telford, W. R. (ed), *The Interpretation of Mark*, Edinburgh, T&T Clark, 1995, 289-306.

Thiaucevert ,C., 'ce que Tacit dit des Juifs au commencement du livre V des Histoires', *REJ* 19, 57-84.

Tolbert, M. A., 'Is it Lawful on the Sabbath to do Good or to do harm?: Mark's Ethics of Religious Practice.' *Perspectives in Religious Studies* 23 (1996) 199-214.

Tuckett, C. M., 'Mark's Concerns in the Parables Chapter (Mk 4:1-34),' 69 (1988) 1-26.

Twelftree, G. H., *Jesus the Miracle Worker. A Historical and Theological Study*, Downers Grove, Ill: Intervarsity, 1999.

Viviano, B. T., *The Kingdom of God in History*, Collegeville: The Liturgical Press, 1991.

Watts, R. E., *Isaiah's New Exodus and Mark*, Wissenschaftliche Untersuchungen zum Neuen Testament 2. Reihe 88, Tubingen: J. C. B. Mohr (Paul Siebeck), 1997.

Wehnam, D. and C. Blomberg, eds, *Gospel Perspectives 6: The Miracles of Jesus*, Sheffield, 1986.

Weren, W. J. C.,'The Use of Isaiah 5:1-7 in the Parable of the Tenants (Mark 12:1-12; Matthew 21:33-46),' *Bib* 79 (1998) 1-26.

White, K. D., 'The Parable of the Sower,' *JTS* 15 (1964) 300-307.

Wilson, W. R., *The Execution of Jesus. A Judicial, Literary and Historical Investigation*, New York: Scribners,1970.

Wink, W., *John the Baptist in the Gospel Tradition*, Cambridge: Cambridge University Press, 1969.

Wrede, W., *The Messianic Secret*, (E. T. by J. C. G. Greig of *Das Messiasgeheimni in den Evangeliens*, 1901); London: Clarke, 1971.

Wright, A. G., 'The Widow's Mites: Praise or Lament? A Matter of Context,' *CBQ* 44 (1982) 256-65.

General Index

Index of Modern Authors